Microsoft SQL Server™ 2005:
The Complete Reference

Jeffrey Shapiro

New York   Chicago   San Francisco
Lisbon   London   Madrid   Mexico City
Milan   New Delhi   San Juan
Seoul   Singapore   Sydney   Toronto

The *McGraw·Hill* Companies

Microsoft SQL Server™ 2005: The Complete Reference

1234567890 DOC DOC 019876

ISBN-13: 978-0-07-226152-3
ISBN-10:　　0-07-226152-8

Sponsoring Editor
　Wendy Rinaldi

Editorial Supervisor
　Patty Mon

Project Manager
　Vasundhara Sawhney

Acquisitions Coordinators
　Alex MacDonald
　Mandy Canales

Technical Editor
　Todd Meister

Copy Editor
　Robert Campbell

Proofreader
　Michael Toporek

Indexer
　Kevin Broccoli

Production Supervisor
　George Anderson

Composition
　International Typesetting
　and Composition

Illustration
　International Typesetting
　and Composition

Art Director, Cover
　Jeff Weeks

Cover Designer
　Pattie Lee

005.7585
5

This book is dedicated to the loving memories of my mother,
Elaine Shapiro, my grandparents Beno and Rose Frank,
and my great aunt, Phyllis Koppel.

About the Author

Jeffrey Shapiro, MCSE, MCTS, MCPD, is the author
of *SQL Server 2000: The Complete Reference* as well as
11 other technology books. He is currently working on
a variety of SQL Server business intelligence projects
for Fortune 100 companies in Orlando, Florida.

Contents at a Glance

Contents

Part II   Administering SQL Server 2005

Part III   Programming SQL Server 2005

Acknowledgments

I have often imagined what it must be like for a sailor, stranded alone on a small yacht in the middle of a giant, angry ocean. Besides the loneliness there is that ever present danger that something will go bump in the night, and your boat will go down with you in it, food for the sharks, or for some giant squid that's waiting with hungry tentacles.

This book was completed over a period of five and a half months that were spread out over 18 months thanks to Hurricanes Wilma and Katrina in the summer and fall of 2005, and often I felt like that desperate sailor trapped in my lab surrounded by eight SQL Server machines, which at times seemed more like the life-threatening tentacles of that giant calamari lurking beneath the waves, especially when they don't work when you are out of power.

Fortunately, just as the boat seemed to take on water the lifelines would get thrown out to me, and the one soul that gets to be promoted to admiral is my wife Kim. Without her support, I would not have made it into safe harbor.

As any seafaring person knows, there is always a beacon of light guiding the way. The lighthouse of my life is my son Kevin, who is always there to calm me down enough that I may see the rocks and get through troubled waters, with a smile you hear from ten thousand miles away—beats the foghorn any day.

McGraw-Hill has a very special editing team that has made this book possible. They are led by Editorial Director, Wendy Rinaldi, to whom I am indebted for the opportunity to do this book and be part of McGraw-Hill's vision for excellence in technical publications.

Introduction

You don't have to read this introduction, but you should. It will save you some browsing time because it lays out the road map for this book, and it will allow you to best determine which parts to tackle according to your needs or discipline, your experience level, and your knowledge of SQL Server 2005.

SQL Server 2005 (or just SQL Server) is Microsoft's database management system, data analysis product, and just plain data everything product. This book's aim is to provide as complete an independent reference as possible to the relational database components, and where permissible and warranted, we will delve into general database and computing references . . . to illustrate applications with or for SQL Server 2005.

We have a long road ahead, so I am going to kick off with some advice on how to get the most out of this book. First, you do not need to have any database, programming, or system administration experience to use this book, but it would help . . . a lot. If this were a classroom setting, I would require you to take Databases 101 or Programming 101 as a prerequisite, only because it would help you get the most out of this book, and because otherwise you would hold up the class. But I am going to make the assumption that you know about programming, object-oriented technology, database management systems, data and computer communications, IS/IT practice, and so on. And when you come across concepts that confuse or befuddle you, you should take time out and get up to speed before continuing, because that will help you avoid costly mistakes down the road. At times I will go back to basics, just so that we all have a common point of departure.

For example, you are not going to find whole chapters devoted to normalization, or object-oriented design, or programming primers. This is not a book about building database applications with SQL Server, although several chapters cover the elements of Transact-SQL, the language you use to program SQL Server. There is no material in here to teach you how to build database applications with Visual Basic, C#, or C++. Nor are you going to get any long-winded historical "data," such as where SQL Server 2005 came from, or where it might be heading. SQL Server 2005 is too complex and vast a product to choke this book with information covered in hundreds of brilliant books devoted to these special subjects.

A Book for All Teammates

The aim of this book is to be as complete a reference to SQL Server 2005 as possible. It is of benefit to database administrators, operators, developers, consultants, network administrators, marketing and communications people, financial controllers, business and enterprise analysts, decision support staff, data owners, data stewards, business owners, and more.

What's Inside

The book is divided into four parts, and each part consists of several chapters.

Part I: SQL Server 2005 System and Platform Architecture

This part opens with an overview of both the system and platform architectures of SQL Server 2005. Gone are the days when a Microsoft product ran on just one OS of Windows. There are now several platforms on which you can deploy the product, albeit they are all Windows operating systems. Chapter 1 discusses aspects of all versions of SQL Server, from the Enterprise Edition that runs on megaservers and that can scale to support huge databases and serve thousands of concurrent users, to the Windows Mobile Edition that can run on tiny mobile devices and appliances.

Chapter 1 is designed to get you familiar with SQL Server as quickly as possible. It also places the product at the core of Microsoft's .NET initiative. Chapter 2 discusses SQL Server database architecture, while Chapter 3 goes on to discuss the client/server and DBMS architectures respectively. Chapter 4 introduces the administrative interfaces and applications to SQL Server, such as SQL Server Management Studio.

Part II: Administering SQL Server 2005

This part deals exclusively with database administration. Building on the overview in Part I, this part is aimed particularly at database administrators and operators (DBAs), the teammates tasked with platform administration, such as backing up and restoring databases, keeping servers healthy, keeping servers and data secure, supporting users, configuring services, managing availability and performance, and so on. Chapter 5 kicks off the part with a critical overview of SQL Server security, while Chapter 6 covers everything a DBA needs to know about databases and tables. Chapter 7 deals with the critical subjects of disaster recovery. We will also discuss the backup/restore services in some detail in this chapter.

Chapter 8 provides an introduction to replication and is suitable for DBAs just starting in this area. The replication subject would fill several chapters or even a book in its own right. You will thus be able to "graduate" from this chapter to a more advanced, dedicated treatise on the subject, or at least make some headway with the documentation in Books Online. Chapter 8 also covers log shipping and the new database mirror functionality in SQL Server 2005. Chapter 9 is an extensive chapter on the subject of clustering.

Part III: Programming SQL Server 2005

Application development is covered extensively in Part III. We kick off with a general discussion of programming SQL Server 2005 using Transact-SQL (T-SQL). We also look at the new support for the .NET Framework's Common Language Runtime in SQL Server. This part also provides extensive coverage of advanced data processing features, such as stored procedures, triggers, SQL queries, data manipulation (or modification) language, and so on.

Part IV: Working with SQL Server 2005

The final chapters, 15, 16, 17 and 18, deal with SQL Server operations, in particular, support for XML. With XML now the de facto data exchange language of the Internet, SQL Server's support for XML is mind-blowing to say the least. Chapter 17 thus provides full coverage to this essential subject. Chapter 18 covers performance monitoring, tracing, and troubleshooting.

Work in Progress

It goes without saying that no book can contain every fact that needs to be known, every tip that needs to be tried, and every note that needs to be noted, especially about something as vast as SQL Server. There is a ton of information about SQL Server that cannot fit into a book of any size, even if it is called the "Complete Reference." I would appreciate your advice and criticisms. I can be reached at jeffrey.shapiro@modelise.com, and you can pick up where many of these chapters leave off at the Internet Web page I have dedicated to this book, at www.modelise.com/compref.

SQL Server 2005 System and Platform Architecture

Getting to Know SQL Server 2005

SQL Server 2005 is Microsoft's relational database management system (RDBMS). It builds on a legacy of accomplishments spanning more than a decade of SQL Server development and critical success, from SQL Server 6.0, 6.5, 7.0, and 2000. But it is more than that. It is the most widely used and most scalable data management system in the world, currently deployed in hundreds of thousands of companies where it is in service day in and day out, storing the records of the digital universe that now supports our very existence.

Despite the lofty capabilities of this product, and its reputation for being highly complex, one of the key—and ambitious—objectives of this book is to get *all* database administrators and developers, young and old, using SQL Server 2005. If within a few chapters you don't see your way to becoming permanently hitched to this product, then my mission has failed. This chapter has thus been designed to be a warm-up for the benefit of novice users, traditional desktop RDBMS users, and gurus working on the dependable SQL Server 2000, other platforms, or older versions.

NOTE *Throughout this book I will often use "SQL Server" and "SQL Server 2005" interchangeably. When referring to an earlier version of SQL Server prior to SQL Server 2005, I will include the version being referenced.*

A DBMS for Everyone . . . and Everything

SQL Server 2005 is for old and new companies, small and large. It is equally at home with huge teams of developers and database administrators (DBAs) as it is with lone rangers or the DBA++ who does it all. It does not matter whether you work for a small company with no more than a handful of workers or for a giant multinational with tens of thousands of employees; SQL Server 2005 is for everyone.

Most database developers and administrators are introduced to databases through the likes of Microsoft's Access, Visual FoxPro, the infamous Borland Database Engine (BDE), or the legendary dBase. (I, for one, came up through the ranks—I still have my first dBase application that I created back in 1987. The last time I looked at it, it had more GOTO clauses than off-ramps on the interstate between Miami and Nova Scotia.)

You have probably always connected SQL Server with big companies, a complex programming environment, geeks like me and my friends who talk in tongues few understand—and very expensive computer equipment. Those days are over, gone forever. Not only do you have a choice of several Windows platforms for SQL Server (from Windows XP to Windows Server 2003 Release 2 and beyond), but you can carry SQL Server around with you in your back pocket on any Windows Mobile appliance. Imagine SQL Server on a chip the size of quarter. Now imagine it in a data center that can house the USS Ronald Reagan.

But why would you want to move to SQL Server? There are still many situations or applications today that can be satisfactorily serviced with a relational database product like Access or FoxPro. For starters, SQL Server is still expensive and complex to use . . . or is it?

How Critical Is Your Data?

There are important distinctions you need to make between SQL Server and a product like Access or FoxPro, and these revolve around the following three concepts, seen or felt mainly from the data consumer's perspective:

- Concurrent access to data
- Integrity of data
- Availability of data

Each of these factors spawns collateral factors that either support or violate modern trends in computing and technology, business rules and needs, and database modeling. Let's explore these three terms and see how they justify your consideration of a product like SQL Server 2005.

Concurrent Access to Data

It is becoming rare these days for businesses to create databases for one pair of eyes only, or a single process. Concurrent access to data, the sharing of databases among many users and processes, is thus an important consideration, if not the most important, when you are designing and creating data-driven software or relational database applications.

If you start with a "tiny" concern of 1–50 people, the more people that need access to your data and the faster they need it, the sooner will concurrency support break down. Yes, products like Access and FoxPro can support dozens, even hundreds, of users, all accessing the database concurrently. However, the database engines that underpin desktop relational database products begin to fall apart when the number and frequency of "hits" on the database files escalates to levels beyond which the desktop engines can cope.

A traditional desktop database product, such as the Joint Engine Technology (Jet) database engine in Access, uses file/server functionality to share the database files. This means that every time a client requires access to data, it needs to connect to the local database engine, which opens the database files on the network server to haul data across the network. The client application must thus be capable of making calls to a database engine installed in the local machine's processing space, because all that is installed on the server is the database files (such as *data.mdb*).

Opening and working with a database in this fashion requires every client to have access to a local database engine on the local machine. Each database engine makes its connection to the database, locks tables, and excludes everyone else until the data is either abandoned at the client or updated to the database table. The lock may not be noticeable to anyone requiring casual access, but it may cause a disaster when a write becomes critical and every process hitting the database files needs service.

Having complex database engine code on every desktop or client is a cumbersome and expensive exercise. No matter the cost of the RDBMS software, there will be considerable costs at the client to continue to support the traditional file/server database solution. You will often read about total cost of ownership (TCO) in this book, directly and indirectly, but it behooves you to know that the cost of deploying file/server data engines to fat clients is greater than that of deploying client/server database engines using thin clients. Even with the initial cost of the SQL Server product (free if you just need the Express Edition), client/server solutions are far cheaper. You also need to factor in the cost of hardware obsolescence and the cost of developing for and supporting fat-client solutions.

When selling managed data services or managed network services to a company, I draw attention to cost of ownership by showing how going cheap on software and development invariably costs more in the long term. It can even threaten the business. Support costs add up when you have consultants trying to fix corrupt flat-file databases, or your users sit around idle with nothing to do because Access has been corrupted for the umpteenth time, or the database files were destroyed.

And when dozens of clients all access such data independently of one another, you end up with what I call "the highway hysteria" factor. You can have hundreds of drivers who all use the turnpike all day long, and there are no accidents, and everyone stays clear of each other, and everything is just "cool." But come rush hour, everyone hits the road as units of independent insanity. Not one driver can know or predict what the other is doing, or react in time to avert disaster. At every rush hour, you can be sure someone is going to get hurt.

Client/server database systems are used everyday by all of us on the Internet. While an increasing number of these servers are SQL Server solutions, your client software need never know what technology is being implemented on the back end. The local computing device or client software can be "thin," such as a Web browser—and the user interface or client process can run on any operating system, on any platform. If every machine on the Internet required a local database engine to access data on the Internet . . . the Internet would have been a bad idea.

In client/server databases, the database server's engine alone controls access to the data, performs the queries, manages the database and the requests of every client, and keeps the database server operating in the best possible way. There is no highway hysteria, because the server is in control of every read or write request for data and can take the necessary steps to avoid accidents. If the highway itself were in control of all the cars, we would not have deaths on the road.

Obviously many situations, and many users, are dependent on traditional file/server database solutions. You can even argue that you are doing fine on your old dBase files. But as soon as you start sharing your data with more people and processes more often, and as soon as access to that data becomes mission critical, you have arrived at the bridge you will need to cross to come over to a client/server database solution like SQL Server. Many of the chapters ahead will help you make the transition, easily and painlessly, without having to spend a lot of money.

***

NOTE *Not all client/server RDBMS products are cheap. Some are priced out of the range of nearly all small businesses, and buying development for them can cause you to auction off one of your kidneys. SQL Server is one of the cost-effective products on the market and one of the cheapest to buy applications for. In the past it would have been a mistake not to admit that the other products were more expensive because they were so much better. That is definitely history. SQL Server 2005 is the killer package of databases, and since it still has the best price in the industry, it's like buying an oceangoing yacht for the price of an average speed boat.*

Integrity of Data

Data integrity constraints have never been high on the list of priorities on desktop databases, probably because it is not very difficult to violate them. Sure you have your validation rules. Access even supports declarative referential integrity, which means the *constraints* are defined in the database schema. But as long as your solutions rely on the client applications for validation, you expose the database to unreliable data.

It is too easy to modify a front-end application, like Access, and bypass validation rules and logic. You can secure the databases, but have you ever needed to find the password for an Access MDB file? If not, you should try it sometime. Dozens of tools on the Internet will hack the password for you in under a minute. And you thought the database was safe.

A client/server database is much more committed to ensuring the validity of data, along with ensuring that what goes into the database is as plausible as possible. The bigger the databases become, and the more complex the data model, the more vulnerable the data. It is thus vital to use technology that has been specifically designed to absolutely enforce integrity rules where needed, especially where your life and the lives of others depends on it. Only a dedicated service component like the SQL Server database engine can be trusted to enforce the constraints. In addition to several well-established SQL Server integrity features inherited from the earlier versions, SQL Server 2005 supports the concept of *cascading integrity* discussed in Chapter 12.

Cascading integrity works like a dream and saves many hours of programming because you use it everywhere to ensure that no orphaned records exist in your precious "normalized" tables and that related values are all concurrently updated when they need to be. Here's a simple example in a delete scenario: Let's say you modularize a little more by splitting *ship-to* and *bill-to* into two separate tables, leaving yourself with three tables, the main one being the customer's details, such as the name of the company and the primary contact information.

Now what do you do when you need to delete the customer from the database? Well, to ensure referential integrity, you have to delete the customer's record—usually linked to related tables via foreign key elements—in each table individually. If you don't, you'll have either records that can no longer be referenced or data that cannot be deleted (or updated) because of referential integrity constraints on the data. This might require you, as it has up to now, to build a manual cascade using triggers, a process that is time-consuming to code and that will degrade performance.

The cascade feature supports the ANSI definition for supporting cascaded delete and update operations. In other words, it means that a delete or update can automatically be *cascaded* from the record in the referenced table to a record in a referred table without the need for special trigger code. In the past, your triggers would typically have included code to switch between taking no action on an UPDATE or cascading a delete operation on DELETE.

I will cover *cascading integrity constraints* in detail in Chapter 11, which is devoted to the subject of data integrity in SQL Server 2005.

Availability of Data

Not a second goes by in our lives in which data is not critical to us. I once saw a bumper sticker that read "stuff happens—know about it." It is becoming more difficult to get along in our wired world without constant access to databases for accurate data or analytical information.

A person is denied access to drugs because a pharmacy's database is offline; a telecommunications system drops a call because a table is corrupt; an order is placed with our competitors because a price cannot be met or a quantity cannot be fulfilled; the list could go on forever. Businesses, people, processes, life itself, all depend on the availability of data every day. While both *data access* and *data integrity* might themselves be judged components of *availability*, it has mostly to do with just being online, being there when you need it, responding in a reasonable time frame.

Availability is a very large and complex subject, fully tackled in Chapters 7–9. When you consider what would ensure that a system or a database remains available, you look at many factors. These include load balancing, distribution and replication, access to large memory resources, mirroring, capability to work with very large databases, symmetric multiprocessing (SMP), 64-bit computing, clustering, and so on. Let's now look at the key applications for SQL Server 2005.

Line-of-Business Applications

Client/server database technology is most widely used in line-of-business (LOB) applications . . . wherever and in whatever situation you require a data repository in which to store, retrieve, query, and analyze information. These situations might be customer relationship management (CRM), enterprise resource planning (ERP), marketing and sales support (from simple contact management to sophisticated list management), technical support (arguably a function of CRM), manufacturing, financial services, research, and so on.

LOB applications also are no longer about rows of characters. Any form of data should be stored and made retrievable from a database, including large graphics files, sound and visual material, documents, and so on.

We need 360-degree views of our worlds, and especially of our customers, and sophisticated database solutions give us that. Take CRM, for example: Information about a customer needs to be made available to everyone in the enterprise. And the data should be used to better serve the customers, meet their expectations, anticipate their needs, and be responsive to their demands. This not only means that you need to be able to store data in multiple forms, such as sound and documents, but that once data is stored, it continues to provide value for the space in the database it occupies.

The Distributed Network Application

Computing today is a networked and distributed phenomenon. Enterprise networks (intranets) and the Internet support millions of clients. Client/server is the dominant model employed, and thin-client/server computing is now the norm. While it seems we have come full circle, clients no longer need to be more than the weight of their user interface. With native HTTP support in SQL Server 2005, 100 percent of the data access functionality and data processing can reside at the server.

Our networked and highly distributed world demands that software product be built according to interoperable client/server component systems. In this regard, the relational database products of yesteryear, which dump a huge footprint of code and functionality on a user's desktop computer, are out of touch with reality, essentially obsolete. Later, you'll learn how to move your data from these bloated legacy applications to the SQL Server environment, using business object models, HTTP and SOAP endpoints (Web services and remote objects), and more.

SQL Server 2005 is also one of the core products of the Microsoft .NET Framework, a "phenomenon" once thought to be a passing "fad" that has now matured and is threatening to be the dominant programming model on the Internet.

The .NET Framework experts forecast business-to-business trade over the Internet to exceed $4 trillion by 2010. The Internet has changed the way business is transacted between individuals and enterprises. Continents and oceans no longer separate the silk or spice routes of the world. Distances between partners, buyers, and sellers are measured in hops between routers on the Internet and not by physical distance any more. Whether you call it e-business or e-commerce, the Internet brings the following key benefits:

- Faster time-to-market

- Increased revenues, decreased expenses, greater profit

- Customer satisfaction and loyalty

- Greater agility in delivery of custom-configured products and value-added services

- Competitive advantage

We are already past critical mass levels on the Internet with respect to e-commerce. Practically everything is already online. The .NET Framework was billed by Microsoft as its "comprehensive, integrated platform for building and deploying applications for the Business Internet . . . ." For all intents and purposes SQL Server 2005 is the epitome of the integrated platform imagined in the latter part of the last century.

Another important buzz-phrase to remember is *digital nervous system* or *Dns* (in lowercase so as not to confuse it with Domain Name System). A Dns is what you have when the convergence of technology brings businesses together, allows businesses to instantly respond to dramatic changes in supply and demand, and allows businesses to reach customers quicker and to connect people to information. The Dns has many components, and the RDBMS supplies the storage facility, access to its data, and the interpretation and analysis of that data in the Dns. Taking SQL Server 2005 out of the Dns, or .NET, would be akin to taking the brain out of the human body (and possibly the soul too, if you believe that knowledge survives death).

SQL Server 2005 and the .NET Framework parts now fully cater to the following:

- **Internet standards**   The SQL Server 2005 .NET Framework technologies support the pervasive standards for data and program message interchange, information exchange, data presentation, and data transportation, such as TCP, SOAP, HTML, and XML.

- **Software scale out and scale up**   SQL Server can start out in your back pocket and scale out to incredibly powerful multiprocessor megaserver systems. Many of the world's largest databases run on the 64-bit version of SQL Server 2005.

- **Reliability**   Downtime is minimized when systems can be scaled out or distributed. The service level is practically guaranteed because an increasing number of single points of failure are eliminated. Physical memory in a system is no longer an issue.

- **Interoperability**   The more you integrate heterogeneous systems from a collection of reliable vendors, the greater will be your ease of integrating these systems, hence the support for core .NET Framework functionality, such as the common language runtime (CLR).

- **Time-to-market**   Interoperation translates into direct savings of time and materials. Result: faster time-to-market. The deeper and tighter the integration and interoperation of systems, the faster and easier they will be to deliver.

- **Ease of deployment, administration, and management**   The Windows Server 2003 Release 2 (R2) platform fully supports SQL Server 2005 and makes it easier to deploy and administer huge SQL Server systems. The more complex your system becomes, the more important it is to be able to easily deploy and manage it. While there is a steep learning curve in Windows Server 2003 R2, you can drastically ease your SQL Server 2005 administrative burden converting to the platform.

- **Full exploitation of Windows Server 2003 scalability**   Windows Server 2003 comes jammed with technologies and services to meet the availability, service level, and change control demands of the most demanding multitiered, distributed applications.

So, What Is SQL Server 2005?

SQL Server 2005 is not a database application development environment in the sense that Microsoft Access or Visual FoxPro is. It is a vast collection of components and products that holistically combine, as a client/server system, to meet the data storage, retrieval, and analysis requirements of any entity or organization. It is equally at home in environments ranging from the largest companies and commercial Web sites posting millions of transactions per day to small companies and even individuals and specialized applications that require robust data storage and persistent service.

SQL Server 2005 comes in several new editions to accommodate the needs and budgets of a wide range of applications. A full discussion of the various editions of SQL Server 2005 is included in *Microsoft SQL Server 2005: A Beginner's Guide* (McGraw-Hill/Osborne, 2005) by Dusan Petkovic.

The following overview of the key SQL Server 2005 design themes and base architectures provides a little history, and a quick introduction to the product for newcomers graduating from desktop systems and users of the other SQL Server platforms eager to make the jump to hyperspace. The architectures are then fully discussed over the next few chapters in Part I.

Central Design Themes

Back when Microsoft delivered SQL Server 7.0, it became very apparent that SQL Server 6.5 and earlier would become legacy products, essentially pre–Internet Age applications. A trio of tenets became the central theme in SQL Server 7.0: The product had to be *Internet enabled*, be *highly scalable* (to compete with the midrange and mainframe systems), and deliver the *fastest time-to-market.* In its quest to be the best, Microsoft's SQL Server development team has become obsessed with these themes.

But the release of SQL Server 2000 has also revealed a component model that allows SQL Server to scale down and compete in the small systems and desktop arena, even the tiny Pocket PC running the Windows CE operating system. This capability had taken many people by surprise, but, as mentioned earlier, databases are not the domain of the large enterprise alone. Today, with SQL Server 2005, no one is really surprised with its powerhouse of features and functionality. Today, business demands everything. If SQL Server 2005 did not dish up the goods, it would simply not survive in the digital market place. SQL Server 2005 thus

- Is fully Internet-enabled
- Provides the fastest time-to-market
- Is the most highly scalable
- Is the most portable

So you can see that no matter your needs, SQL Server 2005 can meet them. In the past, you might have gone with a small relational database product because SQL Server was a "big-business" product that came with a big price tag. But it comes in a variety of editions to meet the needs and budget of small business. If you need a small database to underpin your killer application, then even the free Express Edition leads the way. This is why I call SQL Server 2005 the *DBMS for everyone* (later you will see why it lives up to the title *"DBMS for everything"*).

Overview of the Core Architectures

Experienced SQL Server users (with at least versions 7.0 and 2000 under their belts) can breeze through this overview because I have written it for newcomers with two objectives in mind. First, it should be regarded as an orientation to get you to a level that will give you a better grasp of the fuller discussions of the architecture coming later. Second, during this overview you will be looking at the central design themes introduced earlier in more depth, and this overview will help you appreciate the new power you now have. I also point out several new features you can zero in on if you intend to breeze through this section.

You will also notice that I discuss several key architectures of SQL Server, but this is not the whole story. SQL Server is composed of number of collateral technologies and architectures, many of them lengthy and complex subjects themselves, that you will learn about in later chapters. And these include the replication architecture, the I/O architecture, the query processing architecture, language support, and much more.

The Database Architecture

SQL Server's database architecture is the subject of the next chapter, so I will save the interesting (and complex) stuff until then. However, to get a good footing in SQL Server, you should understand the basic database structure as early as possible, and this is why I go direct to the database architecture in Chapter 2.

SQL Server is not a difficult product to comprehend, even though (and I agree) it is often considered the most complex server product in Microsoft's server offering. I have managed all of the Microsoft server products in busy production environments and data centers, and not one other server product presents the challenge and technological "high" that SQL Server does.

I consider this to be the case in large part due to the three levels at which an IT professional interacts with and services the product: the DBA level, the SQL Server developer level, and the client applications developer level (touched upon in Part III). This is the only server product in the Microsoft server lineup in which the system administrator of a high-end, mission-critical system requires a lot more on the job than to be certified in bells and whistles. He or she needs to have a solid grounding in relational database theory and more than a smattering of programming skills. Quite frankly, if you want to be the best DBA in the company, you need to know about the server platform, such as Windows Server 2003; its hardware needs, such as storage, memory, and processing requirements; networking (for replication, clustered servers, and so on); security; disaster recovery; administration; SQL and Transact-SQL; relational theory; object-oriented design (the basics) . . . and you should be proficient in at least one mainstream .NET computer language, such as C#.

The SQL Server 2005 relational database engine comprises a number of highly scalable and well-tested components for storing, manipulating, analyzing, and accessing data. With the number of systems in use in the world running into the multimillions and the number of certified DBAs well into the six figures, SQL Server 2005 is most certainly proven technology.

However, it is also a brilliantly elegant product. It is by no means as convoluted as it appears, which is not the case for many of its competitors. While you can deploy SQL Server in the most demanding and complex situations, it also has the lowest barrier to entry of all the database products on the market. This is due in part to its architecture, and in large part to the huge installed base, which is supported by many books such as this one, dozens of devotee Web sites, and user groups in just about every major city in the world.

The SQL Server 2005 database engine stores your data in tables. Each of the tables holds data that represents information of interest and value to your organization. This data consists of a collection of classes of information (called domains) that, when understood as a whole, represent a unique and complete record of data in the database. For example, a row holding a social security number is not itself a complete record, according to your model, without somehow being linked to the name of a person. That person's name can be in the same row of data, in a value representing the domain *last names*, or in another table in the same database. The two rows taken together represent the record of your data, even though its values are spread among different tables.

Collections of tables—and there can be thousands of them—are stored in a container object known as a SQL Server database. Each database also stores objects that pertain to each database and its tables, including stored procedures, triggers, and so on.

A collection of databases can be managed as a unit by a single instance of SQL Server. System-wide management features include functions such as backup/restore, logins and security, replication, and data transformation.

The DBMS or Administration Architecture

SQL Server ships with a rich and powerful set of administrative tools. These are the tools that DBAs use to manage databases, user access, backups and restores, and other administrative functions. Microsoft has published the full APIs to these tools, enabling independent software developers to provide turnkey solutions that use SQL Server as their storage database. A computer telephony application is an example of a turnkey application that would typically include many automated administrative features, so that actual hands-on administrative involvement on the part of end-user database owners would be minimized or obviated. The chapters in Part II cover all the DBA tools and then some.

The Application Development Architecture

If you are a database applications developer (the client developer or SQL Server developer), you have a wide choice of APIs and technologies to use in programming SQL Server. If you are building applications that depend on SQL Server databases for their data stores, or that need to obtain the functionality of the SQL Server database engine and its other components, you can use a number of interfaces and technologies.

If you are accustomed to developing to the Open Database Connectivity (ODBC) API, or have legacy code to maintain, you can code directly to it to work with SQL Server 2005. However, you can also get to ODBC functionality via the object-oriented (OO) APIs, such as ADO.NET and OLE DB. These APIs are discussed in Chapters 10 and 11.

All Microsoft's modern OO database APIs enable you to encapsulate or encase Transact-SQL (T-SQL) statements within your code. Also, T-SQL can be used to access the ODBC extensions, even from within ADO.NET methods, and from standard ODBC applications. You can also continue to program SQL Server from the legacy object model APIs that encapsulate ODBC, such as Remote Data Objects (RDO) and Data Access Objects (DAO). However, it would make sense, for many reasons, to use the more modern ADO.NET libraries for data access.

SQL Server application development is simplest and fastest using the ADO.NET components, which can be used in any application development environment that supports .NET technology. Naturally, the easiest environment and language a novice can start with is Visual Studio 2005 and Visual C# 2005 and Visual Basic 2005.

OLE DB is more complex and typically used in old fashioned C++ applications. While it is extremely powerful, it makes little sense to extend or support direct OLE DB functionality in new development against SQL Server 2005.

To talk to SQL Server—that is, to ask it to save data, change it, return it, process it—you need to know SQL (or more accurately, Transact-SQL; but more about this in a moment). SQL is the international standards–supported computer language of the relational database. It is represented by the American National Standards Institute (ANSI) as well as the International Organization for Standardization (ISO). Its official name is the International Standard Data Base Language SQL, 1992. It is often known as SQL-92 and commonly referred to as "Sequel."

All relational database products support a flavor of SQL that is infused with support for the individual product and its extensions. Microsoft calls its version of SQL for SQL Server

"Transact-SQL," T-SQL for short. SQL, the base language, is not a perfect language by any means; it has its share of inconsistencies and mistakes, and each product deals with them in certain ways that reflect the needs of the users. For example, SQL supports the concept of a *persistent storage module (SQL/PSM)*, which allows stored procedures and similar functions to be grouped together where they can share and reuse programmatic data.

NOTE   *I will use the more convenient T-SQL acronym most of the time.*

With SQL Server 2000, the members of the Transact-SQL development team felt there was so little demand for adding PSM to SQL Server that they felt their time would be better spent in other badly needed areas (user-defined functions is an example, see Chapter 10, *Programmability*). However, with SQL Server 2005, while Transact-SQL is still not completely compliant with SQL/PSM, it goes beyond the SQL/PSM standard in its new functionality, such as the system-defined aggregate, and a variety of new data manipulation and mathematical functions.

These constructs can be referenced in stored procedures to take advantage of the proximity of the code to data. The objective: cutting down on the number of network round trips from client to server.

However, while T-SQL is extremely powerful, even more flexibility and omni-accessibility to code and data can be obtained using any one of the .NET languages that SQL Server 2005 supports. The ability to use a language like C# to write procedural code against SQL Server is perhaps the most revolutionary enhancement of the product, if not the most compelling reason to adopt it.

Yes, in SQL Server 2005, you can write procedural code in Transact-SQL, C#, J#, Visual Basic (managed) and Visual C++ (managed). Managed COBOL is also available. Everything you write in Transact-SQL, stored procedures, user-defined functions (UDFs), and triggers, can be written in one of the aforementioned languages.

Later, in the Part III chapters, we will discuss when you would choose T-SQL over C#, and the converse. Consider, however, that a UDF that executes a complex mathematical operation would be better written in C# because T-SQL is interpreted, whereas C# is compiled. In addition, T-SQL is not integrated with the .NET Framework as C# is. So it's impossible for T-SQL triggers or stored procedures to access external resources such as files, event logs, the registry, Active Directory, Web services, and the plethora of .NET assemblies such as the complex math libraries or data manipulation classes those found in the .NET Framework's regular expression library.

If what we just discussed does not blow your mind, consider that SQL Server procedural code can also be written as extended stored procedures (XPs), using the Open Data Services API in SQL Server 2005. These special system stored procedures can call COM objects that are loaded into the SQL Server process. XPs are not as safe as .NET or T-SQL stored procedures, because the code is not subject to any SQL Server control. You can do a lot of damage with a badly written XP, in the areas of memory management and thread management. The power is there, it's how you use it that matters. More about the "Xtreme" stuff in Chapter 10.

T-SQL is compliant with the SQL-2003 standard. It thus fully complies with SQL-92 and SQL-99's Entry Level features and also supports a number of features from the Intermediate and Full Levels. T-SQL is further discussed in Part III, which deals exclusively with programming. The latest version of SQL is the SQL 2003 (also known as the SQL-200n) specification.

In 1999 and 2000 Microsoft promised a number of new features for SQL Server 2000 which had to be held over for SQL Server 2005. These included enhancement of the TOP clause, the PIVOT clause, and support for the *common table expression (CTE)*. These enhancements, and many more, are now available in SQL Server 2005 and are discussed in the chapters of *Part III, Programming SQL Server 2005.*

The Client/Server Architecture

As explained earlier, SQL Server is a client/server database system. At home in both two-tier and multitier environments, it is capable of servicing very small databases in limited storage areas or very large databases, also known as VLDBs, in huge storage silos. A huge number of users can be connected to SQL Server at the same time, all sending queries and instructions to the server, performing inserts, updates, deletes, queries, and just about anything you can imagine doing with a database. But you can also install and operate multiple instances of SQL Server on the same computer, or your users can be querying a database under the control of instance *x* on one server while inserting data into a database under the control of instance *y* on another server. But before we get carried away, let's also look at more modest implementations.

SQL Server, as a client/server system, can be easily implemented as a two-tiered system on a single machine. Both the SQL Server engine and the user interface are installed on the same computer, much as you would install and use Access or FoxPro applications. Front-end or user-interface database applications communicate with SQL Server via the Windows Interprocess Communications (IPC) facilities and the Shared Memory protocol (explained in Chapter 2 and Chapter 4) and not over a network.

This capability makes SQL Server 2005 ideal for single-user needs, but it is also ideal for thin-client/server environments in which all users operate in terminal sessions on the same server-class machine hosting SQL Server. When the product is installed on Windows Server 2003 in Application Server mode, your users would have access to applications that send requests to the database server engine via IPC facilities. This is a much more elegant, safer, and cheaper solution than giving every user a copy of Access (which must be licensed), or a custom application, and having every user tax the system with application-side processing overhead.

But what if you need to implement a high-end or demanding application on the local machine? A good example that does not involve human users at all, but that is one I am intimately familiar with, is computer telephony.

Computer telephony systems are not small or trivial applications. A computer telephony application often requires access to a locally installed database, mainly because network latency, even measured in milliseconds, is not an option when you have hundreds of callers on telephone lines, all waiting for service. Using file/server system architecture for a high-end application can lead to disaster.

A computer telephony system has several telephony cards in it that can answer calls on a number of channels (in some systems the number of calls all appearing at the same time can be as high as several hundred per server). A file/server database engine like Jet or the BDE (child of the old Paradox engine) cannot handle such a dramatic burst of read or write requests during peak hours, often sustained for long periods. Each request for data or write to the database is essentially a user connection to the database, the user being a process thread spun out of the computer telephony application to the database server. Some of the requests for data services can be as simple as checking an extension number, or the number of rings to wait before forwarding the call, whereas others can be very complex, for instance, recording a voice message, or accepting an incoming stream of fax data.

Internet applications are not unlike computer telephony applications from a load perspective. You might have one stock exchange server chugging along servicing a modest number of buys and sells over the Web. Then suddenly an issue goes "gold" and ten servers are not enough.

This is where SQL Server's capabilities as a key role player in a multitier or *n*-tier client/ server system come to the foreground. In high-traffic Internet environments, you have situations in which zero data processing can be performed at the client, which does nothing but present data in a browser. In such situations numerous "client" processes might come into play to connect to more than one instance of SQL Server for a variety of reasons.

Transactions can be handed to legacy services like the COM+ Component Services (formerly known as Microsoft Transaction Server, or MTS) and Microsoft Message Queuing Services (MSMQ) or the new SQL Server 2005 Service Broker technology (see Chapter 17) for a variety of reasons. Such technology is key, for example, in banking applications over the Internet. Take funds transfer: First you need assurance from the server that money debited from *account A* gets credited to *account B,* and that the execution and result (success/failure) of the transaction is properly communicated to the user even over an unreliable connection like the Internet.

SQL Server's client/server architecture does not support traditional mainframe-type load balancing for extremely high volume. Instead the work is shared between servers that hold data partitions. The servers cooperate to share the load as a server "federation," which is a SQL Server term that means, essentially, the same thing as a server farm that allows a client to connect to any of a number of servers for the same service. (You will learn about database federations again in Chapter 13, but they and the other new features aimed at availability deserve some introduction here.)

High Availability

SQL Server 2005 benefits from the host of new scalability and reliability features of the truly mission-critical facilities of the Windows Server 2003 platform, and the client/server architecture.

A new feature is *database mirroring,* in which transaction logs from a source server are replicated to a single destination server. If the source system dies, your applications can immediately reconnect to the database on the destination server. The recovery instance can detect failure of the primary system and within seconds accepts connections from clients. You don't need any special database mirroring technology or hardware to make this work, and you need no special shared storage technology or fancy hardware. I will cover database mirroring in more detail in Chapter 8.

SQL Server can scale up and scale out. On the scale-up side, one Enterprise Edition server can address up to 64GB of RAM and can take advantage of the 64-way SMP support built into its Windows Server 2003 host architecture. And for advanced fail-over in the scale-up model, SQL Server 2005 includes enhanced fail-over clustering, among eight nodes on the Windows Server 2003 platform.

NOTE *SQL Server clustering support has been extended to the collateral services as well, such as Analysis Services, Notification Services, and Replication.*

SQL Server 2005 also does software scale-out. It operates on a high-availability model known as *shared nothing federations.* A federation of servers share load by distributing hits across all available SQL servers that are members of the federation. Instead of sharing physical resources, the servers share nothing. This is also known as the shared-nothing approach to clustering. Instead of servers sharing physical resources, identical, distributed, and updatable copies of the databases reside on each server, in an architecture made possible by a technique known as *distributed partitioned views.* All SQL Server servers are active in a federation.

The 64-bit versions of SQL Server 2005 have been optimized for the Intel Itanium processor. It fully exploits advanced memory addressing capabilities such as buffer pools, caches, and sort heaps. These new features reduce the need to perform multiple I/O operations to bring data in and out of memory from disk.

The Windows Server 2003 x64 platform provides the high performance architecture for both 32-bit and 64-bit applications. The x64 architecture comprises 64-bit extensions to the industry-standard x86 instruction set, which means your 32-bit applications can run natively on x64 processors. However, 64-bit applications are executed in 64-bit mode. Native 64-bit applications allow greater access to memory, thus speeding up numeric calculations per clock cycle by an order of magnitude. So you have a system that can handle your legacy 32-bit applications while at the same time paving the way to native 64-bit computing.

The Database Engine

The Microsoft SQL Server 2005 database engine, controlled by the SQL Server service *sqlservr.exe,* manages the databases and all related files and mechanisms that its instance owns on the host server. It is also responsible for processing all the T-SQL statements sent to it by client applications and processes. It also controls the execution of SQL Server components (the objects) installed in the database, such as stored procedures, triggers, and the integrity mechanisms we will discuss in Chapter 12 .

The SQL Server Database Engine *is* the DBMS. It is the only engine on the server that creates and manages the databases, juggles concurrent connections, enforces security, processes queries, builds and applies indexes, and so on. The database engine, which we will refer to as the DBMS from here on, is the largest and most important SQL Server entity. It is discussed in depth in the next chapter.

The Collateral Services

This very powerful collection of server components (*collateral services* is my term) makes up the "surrounding technology" of the SQL Server 2005 database engine. The collection consists of the following components:

- **SQL Server Agent**   The job scheduler and operator manager.
- **Full-Text Search**   The indexer for keyword-based queries of text data in SQL Server databases.
- **Microsoft Distributed Transaction Coordinator**   The service for facilitating distributed transactions.

- **SQL Server Analysis Services (SSAS)**   The technologies used for online analytical processing (OLAP) and data mining.

- **SQL Server Integration Services (SSIS)**   The technologies used for extraction, transformation, and loading (ETL). It replaces the SQL Server 2000 Data Transformation Service.

- **SQL Server Notification Services (SSNS)**   The technologies used for developing and deploying applications that generate and send messages to SQL Server subscribers.

- **SQL Server Reporting Services (SSRS)**   The technologies used for developing and deploying reports.

- **Service Broker**   The technologies used for the interapplication messaging service that can be used by developers for loosely coupled applications.

- **Replication**   The technologies used for replicating data from one database server to another.

We are going to be bumping into all these technologies and services throughout this book; however, as mentioned in the introduction, extensive coverage of SSAS, SSIS, and SSRS is not possible.

SQL Server 2005 can also be installed in multiple instances, even on the same host. Each instance is controlled by its own set of services; however, the Distributed Transaction Coordinator (overview coming up) is shared among all the instances on the same host. You can also run different versions of SQL Server on the same server.

The Server components can be started and stopped in a number of ways:

- On startup of the operating system, as determined by the Service Control Manager (SCM)

- Via the services of the SQL Server Configuration Manager. The SQL Server Service Manager provides the same services as the SCM, dedicated to the SQL Server services

- From the command line or command prompt using the *net* commands

SQL Server Agent

The SQL Server Agent has been designed to make the job of the DBA a lot easier, lowering TCO and the administrative burden. It is essentially a service that is used to schedule maintenance routines and activities on a target server. It is also used to monitor DBMS activities and alert operators or the DBAs, to potential threats and problems. The SQL Server Agent service is accessed and managed in Server Management Studio—and fully investigated in Chapter 4.

The SQL Server Agent is divided into the following three services. This architecture has been similarly implemented in a number of Windows services, such as the Removable Storage Services:

- **Alerts**   These are the actions that need to be taken when a specific event occurs on the server. Errors are good examples of alerts that a DBA or operator needs to be made aware of. For example, errors generated by incorrect logins or security problems can be sent to a DBA via e-mail, paging, or beeper services; the Windows messenger service; or a telephone call. The alert mechanism can also be configured to run certain jobs.

- **Operators**   The Operators service lets you define operators using their domain accounts or e-mail IDs. These people are typically members of a "database administrators group" defined in the Active Directory domain. You can send messages to all operators using a single e-mail message that gets sent to a group.

- **Jobs**   The jobs are the collections of steps that get executed by the Agent service. Jobs are defined in the service and then scheduled for execution at a later time or in response to an alert or event. Jobs can comprise packages built for SQL Server Integration Services or SSIS (successor to DTS) and include maintenance plans for backing up databases and performance management.

In addition to the SQL Server Agent service, you can interface with SQL Server Agent from applications that use SQL Management Objects architecture (SQL-SMO), and from any SQL Server client application that is programmed to transmit T-SQL statements to the server engine.

Full-Text Search

Full-Text Search extends the SQL-92 definitions for standard character-based searching, which is based on a system of comparison operators (equal to, less than, and greater than) applied to character constants and character strings stored in the database.

The engine, first, supports a powerful indexing model, which is implemented as full-text catalogs and indexes that you define for a database. These are not stored as objects in a SQL Server database but rather as independent files. Second, the engine processes full-text queries and determines which entries in the index meet the full-text selection criteria obtained from user input. The criteria can be words or phrases, words that are within a certain proximity to each other, or the inflections on verbs and nouns.

The search algorithm works as follows: For each search criterion processed by the engine, the identity of a row that meets the criterion and its ranking value is returned to the DBMS, which then builds the result set to return to the client.

The full-text catalogs and indexes are stored in separate files on the server, which are administered by the search service. Coverage of Full-Text Search will be limited to the section Table Design Considerations for Searchable Databases covered in Chapter 6.

The Microsoft Distributed Transaction Coordinator

The Microsoft Distributed Transaction Coordinator (MSDTC or just DTC) is a service that lets you program applications that can work with data drawn from several different data sources in one transaction. It also coordinates the updating of data to different databases, even databases that are installed in remote servers. The DTC is a key component of Microsoft's maximum availability strategy in that it ensures that an UPDATE succeeds on all distributed servers or on none of the servers. We use the DTC when users update data in distributed partitioned views on a federation of SQL Servers.

You can easily enlist the services of DTC in your applications by calling remote stored procedures from your application that apply to all "enlisted" servers. The DTC service can be managed from Management Studio. DTC services are discussed in Chapter 16. DTC is an essential component of a Web services data-access infrastructure.

The Analysis Services

SQL Server was originally conceived as an online transaction processing (OLTP) system or DBMS, built around the need to store large amounts of records, operational data, or transaction data culled from the concurrent transactions of a larger number of human users and computer processes. It has excelled at this capability, and this is what makes it ideal not only for the data storage needs of large enterprises and public institutions but for those of small-to medium-sized businesses as well. (See Chapter 17 on concurrency and transactions.)

However, operational data and the storage and retrieval thereof are only a part of what companies need in a DBMS. The ability to query data, and generate any type of business intelligence or management report, is one of the cornerstones of a relational database application, hence the invention of a query language like SQL.

The ubiquitous SELECT statement allows us to obtain information from our data and allows us to drill into the data to obtain information that could assist with decisions, and with business rules and direction.

An example: The statement SELECT * FROM CUSTOMERS WHERE CREDIT EQUALS 'GREEN' lets a marketing team safely derive a new list from the customer base list to which additional product offerings can be made. Marketing people will have a measure of sales confidence using the list because they know that any new customers garnered from their marketing efforts will be able to pay for the goods and thus generate cash flow.

This example is very simple because SQL SELECT statements can be vastly more sophisticated, complex, and deep. The more advanced and sophisticated the query, the more demanding it is to make it against a huge database holding thousands, millions, even billions of items. Aggregate queries, for example, are extremely taxing on huge databases. Reports might typically take days to generate. For the most part, therefore, relational data and relational (normalized) tables do not make effective analytical data storage facilities, but the specialized warehousing facilities offered by the Analysis Services do.

Apart from the strain, a more scientific analysis of data is needed to support the decision-making processes of enterprises, fields of research and endeavor, and even the whims of individuals. Humans have the uncanny habit of going around in circles, always making the same mistakes, never breaking out of the cycle. And they do this with their companies. It takes a lot of effort to make changes . . . and we need to be convinced by hard facts.

SQL Server's analysis services were introduced to the product back in version 7.0. Known as OLAP, these features are used to support decision support systems (DSSs) that can, for example, help a company to position itself in new and emerging markets, and to use data to detect shifts in market perception, buying trends, consumer habits, opinion, corporate health, and much more.

OLAP data is organized into multidimensional structures known as CUBES, and the analysis data is stored in data structures known as data warehouses and data marts. OLAP services are supported by a number of SQL Server components that form the Analysis Services.

The Analysis Services and the transformation of data for analysis make up a highly complex subject that is obviously beyond the scope of this book. Preparing OLTP data for the Analysis Services is covered in Chapter 17. The Analysis Services architecture is a major and critical component of SQL Server's collateral services architecture and not of the core database engine, which is why it is described as a Relational Database Management and Analysis

System, and why I call it the "DBMS for everyone and everything." (For a comprehensive treatment of Analysis Services and Business Intelligence, see *Delivering Business Intelligence with Microsoft SQL Server 2005* [McGraw-Hill/Osborne, 2005] by Brian Larson.)

I hope you are ready to tackle the complex material that lies in the chapters ahead. I also know that you are keen to see SQL Server 2005 in action and to get a feel for what it is capable of. You will be seeing code in this book, most of it in Part III. The chapters remaining in Part I will help you understand how SQL Server works, how to assess your needs, and how to install and deploy the product.

Database Architecture

At the conceptual level, the facility for data storage in SQL Server 2005 is the *database*. SQL Server's databases are fully compliant with the ANSI SQL-2003 definition of a database . . . with some remarkable extensions you will learn about in this chapter and throughout this book.

The databases do not themselves store data. Rather, the data is stored in *tabulated* structures (hereafter called *tables*), and these tables are stored within the confines of the database file, in a number of sophisticated file structures we will investigate later in this chapter.

Contrary to the terminology used in many circles, the term *database* will not be used to refer to the system as a whole. A SQL Server database is just the barn where the grain stores or silos are kept. It encompasses the mechanisms of management and functionality. Instead I will refer to the "system" as the *database management system* or *DBMS*. The client/server architecture and the DBMS will be the central subject of Chapter 3.

This chapter will thus explore the database architecture of SQL Server on various levels, often in very abstract terms. We will dig deeper in other parts of the book where we need to clarify both development and administration techniques.

From a conceptual level, the database is the container for all tables, indexes, constraints; security, programmatic, and other objects and properties used by the DBMS to manage the data. SQL Server databases are viewed from both the logical perspective—by developers, clients and users, and server components—and the physical perspective—by database administrators, system administrators, and server "machinery."

The logical perspective is essentially the external view of the *database,* seen by users and software developers alike. The physical perspective encompasses the internal view of the database. The internal view is primarily the view of the database administrator or DBA. Figure 2-1 illustrates the three abstract SQL Server database levels and the "entities" that "appreciate" these perspectives.

Besides the physical parts of the database, such as its file groups, this chapter kicks off with an overview of the logical components of a SQL Server database, such as tables and indexes.

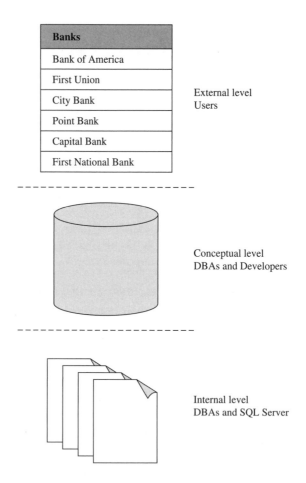

FIGURE 2-1
The three levels or views of a SQL Server database management system. The *internal level* contains the physical files of the database, the *conceptual level* is an abstraction of the physical files, and the *external level* is what your users interact with

Introduction to SQL Server Databases

The databases are split into two groups, *system* databases and *user* databases. The conceptual view of the databases is illustrated in Figure 2-2. The system databases include master, model, tempdb, msdb, and mssqlsystemresource (the new resource database).

The master database is used by SQL Server to keep an eye on the state of the system. It also records information about other databases in the system, disk space, usage, DBMS configuration, and so on. Master represents the system schema; and it is also often referred to as the *catalog,* which is database parlance, and not really a SQL Server term. Database objects, however, are not stored in master as was the case in earlier editions of SQL Server. system objects are stored in the new resource database mentioned earlier. Both master and the resource database are joined at the "hip," and the one cannot live without the other, as we will discuss shortly.

The model database is a database template. When you create a new database, the new database is a copy of model . . . actually, it is derived from it. If you need to create databases

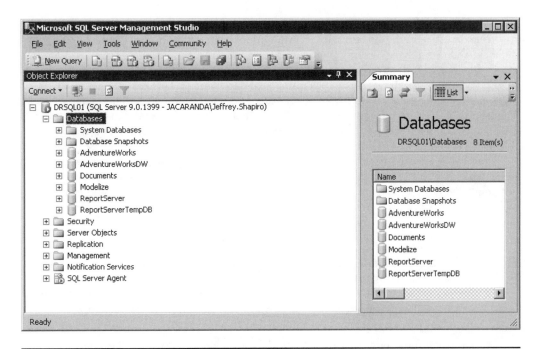

Figure 2-2 The *conceptual level* or *view* of SQL Server database, as seen from Microsoft SQL Server Management Studio

that are preconfigured with certain settings, you would create the settings in model, and all new databases would inherit the settings. The model database does not need to be installed in turnkey environments.

NOTE *You will learn about model and its application in later chapters, especially Chapter 6. It should be used to "bequeath" only, and most positively, the base properties that will form the foundation of all your databases, and not as a means of automatically configuring applications.*

Also derived from model is the tempdb database. This database stores all the temporary data that is needed by SQL Server during the lifetime of the SQL Server instance; in other words, until it is stopped and restarted. The data in tempdb is not saved, and the database and its tables are recreated when SQL Server is started.

Then there is the *msdb* database, which is used by the SQL Server Notification Services and the SQL Server Agent service, discussed in Chapter 4. SQL Server Agent is used for performing scheduled tasks such as database backup and data transformation.

The resource database does not show up in the Object Explorer (Databases node), and you can neither back it up nor restore it using SQL Server's backup mechanisms. The database is read-only and contains all of the fixed system objects that ship with SQL Server 2005. The objects in the resource database show up in every database you create and will appear in the schema of every database (see the discussions of sys schema in Chapters 4 and 6). The resource database is also discussed as part of a backup/restore strategy in Chapter 7.

The user databases are the databases created for and used by your applications. You can have one database in the system with a certain number of tables, or you can have many databases. One database, serving many needs and users, would be sufficient for most small line-of-business (LOB) applications needed by a small company. For the larger entities, you might have many databases, used by a number of departments and key management entities (KMEs). Only one instance of SQL Server is needed to manage all the databases. Thousands of users can connect to and be serviced on any number of databases, all under the auspices of one instance of the SQL Server engine. (You will learn much more about the role of the server in Chapter 3.)

The physical database files are nothing more than your typical file system files. In that the database can contain objects and properties—and the objects also contain properties— you might prefer to refer to the database file as, itself, an object. And you would be correct. SQL Server regards all the elements of and in its databases as objects; this goes for tables and indexes as well.

A database is split into two or more files as follows:

- **The primary data files,** which are named with the *.mdf* extension, keep tabs on the rest of the *user* files in the database. They are also used for data storage. You can use any extension on your primary data files (and the other files discussed next), but keeping the SQL Server standard extension will let you instantly recognize a data file when you see one.

- **The secondary data files** are also used for storage and are given the extension *.ndf.* There can be more than one *.ndf* file.

- **The log files** are where all the transaction log entries are stored. These transaction logs account for SQL Server's recoverability prowess, which I introduced in the preceding chapter. These log files are identified by the *.ldf* extension.

The files and their location can be viewed, in their physical abstraction, in Windows Explorer, as illustrated in Figure 2-3.

Tip *The database and log files are shown living together in one folder, which is not a good idea, especially if the disks are not redundant. Better to put the log files on their own hard disk (for better performance, too).*

Figure 2-4 illustrates the conceptual view of the internal environment from the Object Explorer in Management Studio.

Any number of instances of SQL Server 2005 can attach to a specific collection of databases. You can also detach from a collection of databases and reattach from another instance . . . even from another server. The only databases you cannot willy-nilly attach is Master and the earlier-discussed system databases. A Master database from one instance is incompatible with another instance of SQL Server. SQL Server can attach version 2000, 7.5, and earlier databases, and you can then perform online upgrades on them. Attaching and detaching are demonstrated in Disaster Recovery in Chapter 7.

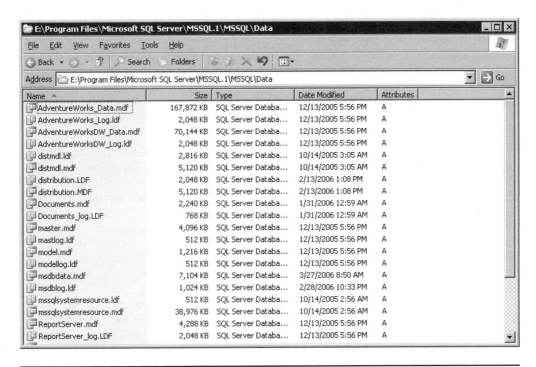

FIGURE 2-3   Database files as seen from Windows Explorer

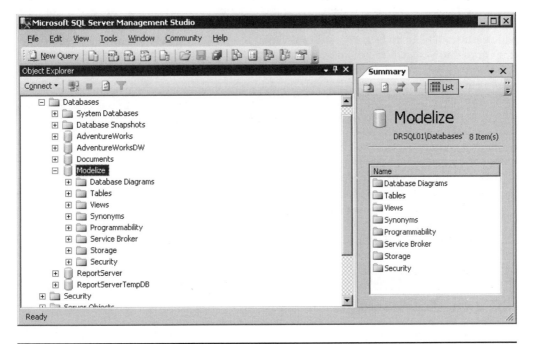

FIGURE 2-4   The objects inside a SQL Server database

The Logical Database Architecture

The window into the logical abstraction, the external level, of SQL Server 2005's OLTP database world uncovers an assortment of components. These objects and their properties are what you or your users work with, directly and indirectly, for the storage, manipulation, and retrieval requirements of your various applications.

Introduction to SQL Server Tables: The Conceptual Level

The unit or object of data storage in a SQL Server database is the *table*, which is the same thing as a *relation* in relational systems parlance. Each table contains data that relates to entities known, again, as objects. For example, a table in the accounts receivable database might contain debtors and their attributes, such as the names of the debtors, their account balances, terms, and credit periods.

Tables are similar to spreadsheets; they contain columns and rows (also known as tuples). The comparison to a spreadsheet, however, is a dangerous one because it can lead you down the wrong road to understanding how SQL Server works. Each column represents one attribute of the object, such as *name* or *customer number.* The rows represent the instances or quantity of the objects in the table.

Each row can be thought of as a record if it is not related to rows in any other table. For example, if you have ten rows in the *debtors* table, you actually have ten instances of debtors, or ten "records" of type debtor. (The instances can also be identical if there is no *unique* rule, primary key, or similar constraint in effect over the table . . . but more about that shortly.) The similarity to the spreadsheet's *page* or *worksheet* ends here, however, because the individual *"cells"* of the table are not accessed in the same way as cells of a spreadsheet.

The term *record* is correct database terminology, but you should take care not to confuse *records* and *rows,* because they are different things. The concept of a record extends beyond a single row in a table. In fact, a record is a combination of all the related rows of all tables in the entire database, which are linked by keys (discussed a little later in this chapter).

If you only have one table in the database, then of course each row can represent a complete and unique record. But if you break out the data into several tables, then your record spans to the other tables as well. I will refer to rows when our operations affect or act upon the individual rows in a table, such as the sorting of rows, a physical operation. But I will refer to records when referring to the actual data, such as when updating the value in a column. As you will also learn, deleting a row and deleting a record are two different things. Understanding the difference between a record and a row is a precondition to grasping the concept of referential integrity, which is covered in Chapter 12.

Creating Tables

There are two means of creating tables in SQL Server databases: interactively (through GUI tools such as SQL Server Management Studio) or directly with ANSI-compliant T-SQL syntax. The T-SQL code is a data definition language (DDL), and no matter which method you use, DDL is what gets sent to the server to create or alter the table. The following code is a simple clause that creates the "inventory" table:

```
CREATE TABLE Inventory (item char(120))
```

The code creates the table *inventory* and inserts one column called *item* of data type *char,* which is 120 characters in length. Creating the table interactively is illustrated in Figure 2-5.

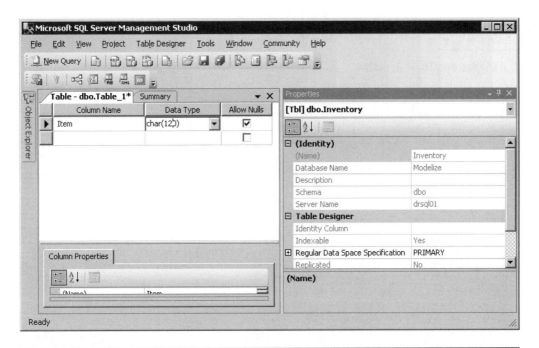

FIGURE 2-5   Creating a table using Management Studio

Naming Convention

Tables are named in code using dot notation representing a hierarchy comprising the database, the database schema that owns the table, and the table name. This is represented as follows: *databasename.schemaname.tablename*. The owner of the database, which is defaulted to the *dbo* schema if it is not specified, or a *user* with ownership rights and permission to create an object, is the only entity allowed to create or edit the objects within a database or a table.

NOTE *Owners, users, groups, and roles are discussed in depth in Chapter 5. You should not overly concern yourself with ownership at this point. Schemas are discussed in Chapters 6 and 7.*

Naming columns requires nothing more than common sense and conformance to the SQL Server convention, which specifies that the column name must be no more than 128 characters long. It can consist of letters; digits; or the symbols #, @, $, and _ (underscore).

TIP *Keep column names simple and if possible use PascalCase for column names (such as ColumnName or MyColumn). PascalCase makes your database model easier to understand and document.*

You also need to be careful not to use reserved words in your column names. A good example is the word "Group," which is a SQL keyword. You could use the term "Category" instead if the aim, for example, is to classify a collection of items. (See SQL Server Books Online, which lists SQL Server keywords.)

Data Types and Their Domains

As mentioned earlier, the objects in the database have properties, as do their child objects, and one of the properties of the column in the table is the data type. The data type defines the type of data that can be stored in the records of the column. In the preceding example, we specified that the *item* column supports the data type *char.*

The *domain* of a data type is an ANSI SQL term for specifying a set of allowable values in a column. In other words, it is all the allowable attributes that describe the data type, including its name and other properties, such as color and class. Domain is often thought to be synonymous with data type, but that is incorrect at the worst, confusing at the least. In a table identifying the records of used cars on a lot, one column of type varchar holds information pertaining to the color of each car. Color is not the data type; it is the domain (although you can create a custom data type called "car_color" with no problem). The domain can be used to specify a constraint on the column. For example, the inventory person is not allowed to use the term "off-white" but should rather use "cream."

Table in the appendix provides a list of the base data types supports by SQL Server tables.

Null

Data types can also hold the value NULL, which might seem confusing to you. While *null* is understood to be "nil" or "zero" or "no value" in some programming environments, SQL Server interprets the NULL value in a record to mean "unknown" or "missing." A blank space and zero are legal values in database records, but this is not the same thing as *null,* so you need to be very careful about passing these as parameters.

Using NULL requires special discussion, and it will be covered in Chapters 10 and 12. Also, in Chapters 15 and 16, I discuss NULL along with instructions on how to create tables and data types that either take or refuse NULL values. For now, when you create a table interactively, keep this option checked. In other words, allow NULL values in your records until you fully understand the implications of NULL usage and have properly modeled your database. You can always alter the table at a later date, but allowing a NULL is a convenient way to "play" with records that have missing values.

There are many circumstances where it seems impossible to accept anything other than NULL. On the well-known online auction site eBay, for example, the registration asks for several items that could be unknown or missing, such as gender. In many sections they use the item "unknown" as a possible value.

System Tables

You will notice when you create a new *user* database that a collection of system tables is also created by SQL Server and is associated with the user database. These tables are used by SQL Server to store configuration and various system data, such as indexes, relating to the user databases and applications (do not confuse these with the master database tables, but they can be considered as extensions to the catalog). You will have little need to work with the system tables in your database; however, SQL Server does not preclude you from referencing them in your applications, especially through stored procedures, or using the data in them for some special reason. System tables are further discussed in Chapter 6 and 7.

I mentioned earlier that you might also notice tables that are prefixed with the pound or number sign, such as *#temptable*. These are SQL Server temporary tables, which are stored in the tempdb database. They are used for storing temporary information. The server usually drops them when a user disconnects or they are no longer needed.

There are two types of temporary tables, *local* and *global*. The local temporary tables are application or user specific, and they are thus only visible to the connecting user. Global temporary tables, prefixed with two number signs, *##temptable*, are visible to all connections and are usually referenced by SQL Server and system-wide tasks.

The Table Data Type

SQL Server 2005 supports a special data type (a variable) that represents a table. Such a data type is similar to a temporary table that can be used to hold a result set for later application. Indexes and constraints (discussed shortly) can be applied to this *table* data type, but they have to be declared in the CREATE TABLE statement. The table data type is also discussed in Chapter 6, as is the common table expression or CTE (new to SQL Server 2005).

Views

Views are essentially virtual tables created with SQL code that can perform relational algebra on the data in a table or collection of tables.

NOTE *The term virtual is an ANSI SQL-92 term, but it is not a description I like (and I say so again later in this book). "Virtual" implies something that appears to be real but is not, such as virtual reality. "Views," on the other hand, are actual result sets, derived from base tables, and created using the SELECT statement, as demonstrated in Chapter 16.*

Views are very similar to Microsoft Access queries in that they are created using the query language and return data in tabular format. What makes a *view* a *view*, and not a *table*, is that the view's tabular structure is not stored in any database, nor is it persistent. Instead, a SELECT statement that retrieves the data for the view is stored in the database. In other words, *views* are for *viewing* only and in certain situations can update their source tables. Views are useful for a number of tasks:

- They can be used to hide rows in a table. In other words, a view might return only the collection of rows that pertain to a particular user or process.

- They can be used to hide columns in a table. A user, for example, can be restricted from viewing confidential information in the *customer* table, such as credit card information or credit status.

- They can be used in join constructions to collect columns from a number of tables into one object representing a single table. This practice is useful in the construction of a data source for reports, although there are pros and cons regarding the use of views to report.

- They can be used to perform operations on the data in tables, such as presenting the sum of all values in a specific column.

Creating a view is straightforward, although the SELECT statement of the entire view object can be as complex as a SELECT statement needs to be. Performance of views can also be enhanced using indexes on the views. The following code is an example of a simple view, and a simple SELECT statement. SELECT statements inside views can run to hundreds of lines of code.

```
CREATE VIEW inventory_view AS
SELECT item, quantity, value
FROM inventory_base
```

Views can also reference other views. In other words, you might return view "A" from the first CREATE statement and then create view "B" from the "A" view. The following code is such an example:

```
CREATE VIEW user_view AS
SELECT item, quantity
FROM inventory_view
```

Views are also a key feature used in SQL Server 2005 high-availability architecture. Using UNION views, data is partitioned across a number of SQL Server databases or instances of SQL Server running on separate servers. Partitioned views are the key component of SQL Server's scalability (scale-out) architecture. In terms of availability they provide a similar benefit, to the clustering of servers, without the possibility of shared hardware, such as the hard disk array, becoming the point of failure that crashes everything. The difference between clustering SQL Server and partitioned views is that all servers participating in the view are active. A cluster of SQL Servers might follow an active-passive architecture where one server in a two-node cluster remains inactive. You will learn about data partitioning and partitioned views in Chapter 9.

Data in views can also be manipulated using INSERT, UPDATE, and DELETE statements. Updates are "cascaded" down to the base tables, including all member tables that are referenced by the view.

Later, in Chapter 6, I look into the finer points of handling views, especially with respect to performance, joins, unions, and so on. I will also discuss indexed views, which, as I told you in the preceding chapter, force a view result-set to be stored in the database until the base table has to be altered.

Indexes and Keys

SQL Server indexes can be associated with tables and views to speed up the retrieval of rows, and to speed up updates and deletes. Indexes are very important in SQL Server, especially for complex databases. That's because, like all relational engines, SQL Server must first find a row in a table before the data can be presented or manipulated. By referencing an index, you are thus helping SQL Server find the row quicker. Indexes arrange the rows in the internal structures of the table, according to a peculiar logic or sorting algorithm.

A *key*, on the other hand, does not directly influence sorting, searching, and retrieval. A key ensures that a row in a table is unique. The debate on uniqueness has been raging since mankind emerged from a hole in the ground in the middle of nowhere. You cannot be lax about uniqueness in your database. Ask yourself how confused you would feel if you woke one day to find an identical person living in the same world as you. The same reasoning applies to the rows in a table. It might not seem a problem at first to add a duplicate row to a table, but what do you do when you need to delete one of those cloned rows? Exactly which row do you delete? How sure are you that you are deleting the right one?

You can create a key in a table on one or more columns. When you create a key on more than one column, you are allowing a value in a column to be unique by combining it with a value in another column. In other words, the key protects the uniqueness of the row if the combination of values in the unique one combines to give a unique key. An example: red + spanner and red + hammer gives you two unique tools that have identical values for the color column. If the unique key were specified on color alone, you would have more than a slight glitch.

The recognized name for the unique key on your primary table (you could call it a root table) is known as the *primary key*. You can also call it the candidate key, especially when it involves more than one column.

If you break out or modularize your tables into several related tables, you will need to connect them (so as to preserve the record) by creating a key in the foreign tables. This "table-hopping" key is called the foreign key, which is essentially the tie that binds the rows in the foreign table to the rows in the primary table, thus making them one record. The primary key/foreign key relationship is illustrated in Figure 2-6.

You can only have one primary key in a table, signified with the little key icon in the table designer. When you create the key, SQL Server automatically creates a clustered index in association with it. In Chapter 16, I have included examples of how searching on the primary key index helps speed up location of records.

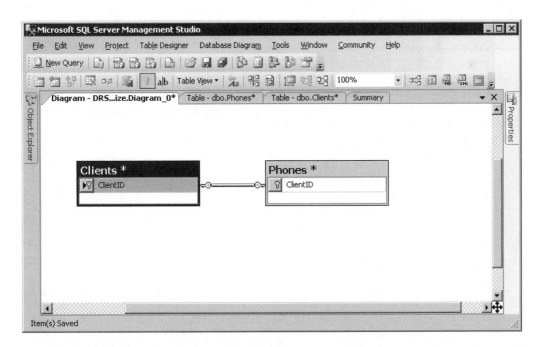

FIGURE 2-6   The primary key in *Clients* links the to the row in *Phones*. The rows thus combine to form a complete record. If you delete a row without cascading the delete to foreign tables, the rows in the foreign tables will no longer have a relationship with any other table as part of a record

Tables without indexes make SQL Server work harder. My son's room is like a database table without an index (and certainly without a key). Everything is lying around in no particular stack or order. He can never find what he is looking for. If the room were sorted, he would be able to locate the things he needs (although he swears he can find things faster in the chaos). I often call his room *the heap.* When you create a table or a view and do not impose any index on it, the rows are not stored according to any logic or system. Such a structure is also called a *heap* in SQL Server lingo.

Indexed keys can also be created when you define an index from the combinations of one or more columns in a table or view. Indexes and keys are persistent; that is, they are also objects and properties that are stored in a database. SQL Server thus maintains the sort order of rows—even when they are not being accessed. When you create an index, you can also specify that the data be stored in ascending or descending order.

NOTE *SQL Server 2005 keys have a 900-byte limit that caps the maximum size on an index key. SQL Server will permit the creation of an index key larger than the limit, but it will process the key with a warning or failure notice. Programmatic handling of indexes and key attributes is discussed at length in Chapter 12.*

Indexes can be created interactively using Management Studio, as illustrated in Figure 2-7, or in T-SQL code using the CREATE INDEX statement (see Chapter 12 for creating indexes interactively).

TIP *The creation and management of indexes is usually the responsibility of the DBA, so it will pay big dividends to become fully conversant in this subject.*

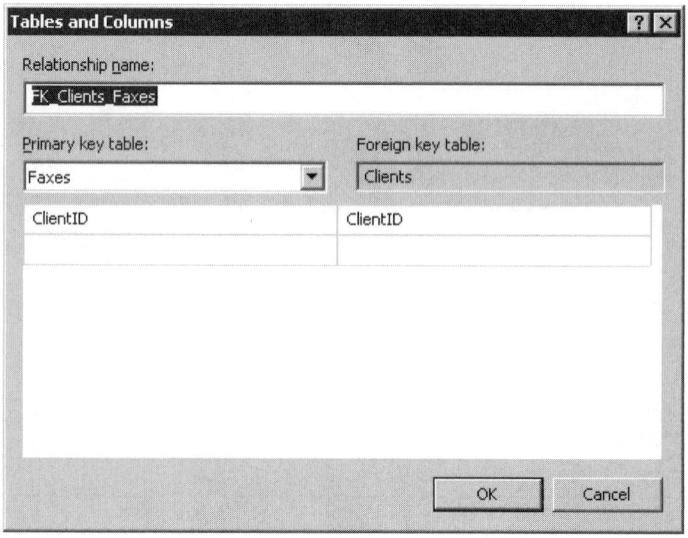

FIGURE 2-7
Creating an index using Management Studio

An index can also be created, as a substatement, inside the CREATE TABLE statement. (This is further discussed in Chapter 6, which discusses Data Definition Language.) The CREATE TABLE statement is illustrated as follows:

```
CREATE TABLE inventory
(item_id int PRIMARY KEY CLUSTERED)
```

You can create additional indexes for a table, targeted at certain columns. Multiple indexes require more resources, however, so you need to be conservative and limit new indexes to columns you know are frequently searched on. In other words, no two rows can have identical values for the index key. You can also specify a nonunique index, and that means you can have duplicate values for a particular indexed column in your table.

Another important attribute of the indexing architecture is that SQL Server indexes can be either *clustered* or *nonclustered.* The application of the two types of index is described as follows:

Clustered indexes store data in a table according to key values. The rows in the table are sorted in the order specified by the clustered index key. You can only create one clustered index per table, which is logical because you can only sort the rows according to one algorithm. When you impose an index on data, the data is *sorted,* which is the opposite of a *heap.*

Nonclustered indexes do not impose any sort logic on a collection of rows in a table, and the rows are essentially heaped. But the nonclustered index does maintain a pointer to rows in the table, which is in essence the key. The pointer starts out with the lowest row in the table. This pointer is also known as a row locator.

So, when you create an index you can specify that it be created according to certain requirements using the following parameters:

- **PRIMARY KEY**   Creates a primary key on the column or columns in the primary table.
- **UNIQUE**   Creates a unique index, not necessarily a key.
- **CLUSTERED**   Specifies the index should be clustered.
- **NONCLUSTERED**   Specifies the index should not be clustered.

You can also control how tightly packed a SQL Server index should be when you create one. The property that controls this is called the *fill factor,* and the higher the fill factor, the smaller the size of the index, which conserves the amount of disk reads. The *fill factor* default is usually 0 percent, as is illustrated in Figure 2-8. The more active a table (for instance, the more aggressive delete and insert activity it has), the lower should be the fill factor you set. This leaves space in the index for future keys.

Often complex queries that return a large number of rows in a view would benefit from indexing. Examples are views that are returned from complex aggregation routines and complex joins. Performance is greatly improved by defining indexes on such views. All indexes on views are dropped as soon as the views are dropped. For more information on placing indexes on views, see Chapter 6.

Large and complex databases and applications will require you to spend more effort designing adequate indexed solutions.

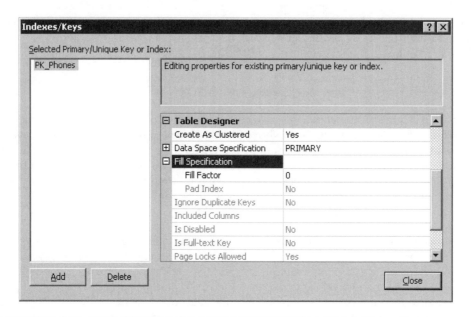

Figure 2-8   Specifying the fill factor of an index

Data Integrity Mechanisms

There are two classes of data integrity definitions that can ensure the "plausibility" of the data entered into SQL Server 2005 tables. (For a blow-by-blow account of integrity in SQL Server, see Chapter 12.)

First, you have data integrity definitions, which act upon the data values that are placed in the records stored within each column. These integrity definitions ensure that the data is of the right type, that they follow the value declarations encompassed in the domains of each data type, and that the data conforms to your own business or database rules and constraints. Data integrity definitions are thus local to an individual table and its records.

Second, you have referential integrity definitions that ensure that the relationships between tables are sound. *Referential integrity* ensures that data in a table refers only to data that actually exists in other tables. In other words, if you are going to refer to rows in other tables, you need to be certain that those rows exist. Referential integrity, as well as data integrity, is discussed at length in Chapter 12.

SQL Server provides four formal types of integrity machinery as follows:

- Constraints
- Rules
- Defaults
- Triggers

Constraints   *Constraints* are the mechanism of choice for ensuring data integrity. Constraints are essentially a system of rules that are applied to values that are inserted into a column. A constraint can be defined over the table or the column, or both. The column constraint applies only to the column, while the table constraint is declared independently of the column constraint and can encompass more than one column. This subject is further described in Chapter 12.

SQL Server 2005 supports five classes of constraints:

- NOT NULL
- CHECK
- UNIQUE
- PRIMARY KEY
- FOREIGN KEY

NOT NULL is the simplest constraint to implement; it prevents a column from accepting a NULL value. (As discussed earlier, NULL means that the record is deemed to be unknown or missing.)

A *CHECK* constraint enforces domain integrity by limiting what values can be inserted into the record. The CHECK evaluates a Boolean value; it determines if the value you are trying to insert meets the constraint (TRUE) or does not meet the constraint (FALSE). If a value "checks" out to be TRUE, it is rejected and cannot be applied to the row. Each column in a table can be protected with multiple CHECK constraints.

You can create CHECK constraints with the services of Management Studio (see Chapter 12). You can also specify a CHECK constraint in your T-SQL DDL code when you create a table. The following code is an example of a CHECK constraint (quantity) created in the T-SQL CREATE TABLE statement:

```
CREATE TABLE inventory
(item char(120), quantity int PRIMARY KEY, (quantity > 100))
```

A *UNIQUE* constraint enforces the uniqueness of the values in a column, or it can be used to check that no two rows are identical. As mentioned earlier, you can use a unique index to enforce uniqueness. However, the UNIQUE constraint is preferred; first; all you want to do is enforce uniqueness, because it requires a lot fewer resources than a primary key index. Indexes tax the system more than constraints do because constraints are evaluated when the column value is referenced, while indexes need to be updated every time you update the table.

The *PRIMARY KEY* constraint identifies the column with the values that uniquely identify the row in a table.

The *FOREIGN KEY* constraint applies to the relationship between tables and thus supports referential integrity. The integrity rule here ensures that the *candidate key* in the primary table refers to the *foreign key* in another table. This constraint prevents the problem of a row with a foreign key that has no corresponding candidate keys in the remote table.

The foreign key rule also ensures that you cannot delete a row that is linked to a foreign key (which would break the record). When you try to delete the row, the ON DELETE or ON UPDATE action can trigger one of two predefined events:

- **NO ACTION**   This will specify that the delete operation fails with an error.
- **CASCADE**   This will specify that the rows with the foreign keys that are related to the candidate keys are also deleted. This action is known as a *cascading delete*.

The ON UPDATE clause is used extensively to validate input; it is further discussed in Chapter 12.

Rules   *Rules* are similar to constraints and are the legacy integrity features of SQL Server. They have been kept in the product for compatibility with legacy code. CHECK constraints are more powerful than rules, and you should use CHECK constraints in all new code. (When you have designed a complex database with many tables, you'll thank heaven, or the SQL Server development team, for features such as cascading deletes.)

Rules are created externally to the CREATE TABLE statement and are thus objects that are bound to the column. This means that you can only have one rule bound to a column. Multiple CHECK constraints, on the other hand, can be applied to a column.

Defaults   *Defaults* are a form of "failsafe" value applied to a column so that no NULLs make it into the row. In other words, if your code creates a row and your user does not apply a certain value to a column, the default value is applied instead. Defaults can be generated out of the following constants:

- A constant value; for example, the value "0" for the column *quantity*
- A built-in or user-defined function that generates the value
- A mathematical expression that generates a value

Defaults are typically created using the DEFAULT keyword in the CREATE TABLE statement. They can also be applied using the system stored procedure sp_bindefault.

Triggers   *Triggers* are a valuable integrity tool that can be used alone or in conjunction with the integrity features we have just discussed. Triggers fire automatically when defined over UPDATE, INSERT, and DELETE statements issued in certain areas of your code, against target tables and views. A trigger is similar in purpose and function to an event that fires in software components, such as the *OnClick* events found in all software controls. Trigger creation is demonstrated in Chapter 13.

A trigger is defined with the FOR UPDATE, FOR INSERT, and FOR DELETE clauses to point the trigger at the correct actions. Triggers can be used in many different scenarios. They can be used in a similar fashion to IF . . . THEN . . . ELSE logic in most development languages. For example, you can define a trigger when the *quantity* value of a certain item in the *inventory* table reaches a certain level. You can then execute a number of routines that request replenishment or alert users or set applicable wheels in motion.

Triggers are essentially stored procedures that also contain T-SQL statements, and they can also be written in a .NET language for execution on the common language runtime (CLR). They can also be used to return a result set, or a dialog box when SELECT or COUNT statements are used within the trigger code. For example, let's say your order taker is about to make a sale that debits 50 units of *X items* to the *inventory* table. If there are fewer than 50 units of *X*, the trigger could query *inventory* and show the order taker just how many units he or she can debit from the table.

The FOR clause is used to dictate when the trigger fires. Triggers can be fired after your T-SQL code has executed or instead of the triggering action. Both AFTER and INSTEAD OF triggers are discussed in more detail in Chapter 13. I have demonstrated how to use these triggers to implement a server-side audit trail for any application.

Stored Procedures

A *stored procedure* is to SQL Server what a function call in a dynamic linked library (DLL) is to an application (although the user-defined functions are more like the functions of standard programming languages). It allows you to implement a collection of routines that can be accessed by any number of applications. Stored procedures are some of the most powerful features in all client/server database systems and can be used to enforce application logic and administer business or enterprise rules to all applications. Stored procedures are compiled T-SQL statements or CLR-executed methods that return data in one of five ways:

- They can provide parameters that can return data, such as an integer or a character, a cursor variable, and an error message.

- They can provide return codes (integers).

- They can provide result sets that are created from SELECT statements embedded in the stored procedure.

- They can reference external cursors (result sets) and stored procedures.

- On the CLR they can pretty much do anything.

(T-SQL stored procedures are compiled into so-called execution plans, which will be covered in the next chapter.) You, the SQL Server developer, create stored procedures that can then be called from any application. You can also create stored procedures for applications written by other parties. Stored procedures do not necessarily have to return data to the user either. They are executed on the server and can thus comprise logic that performs functionality without the knowledge or intervention of the user or referencing application. SQL Server is itself maintained by a collection of system stored procedures that cannot be accessed by users. Using stored procedures exclusively in certain applications means that absolutely all processing is performed on the server.

Your applications can execute stored procedures by merely issuing EXECUTE, EXEC, or CALL (ODBC) statements in the code. This is a similar practice to linking in or loading a DLL and issuing a call to a function. The difference is that a call to a function in a DLL results in the function being processed in the processing space of the calling application. All applications that have access to the DLL can call the function or procedure in the DLL.

Stored procedures are also very useful for applications that use SQL Server as a data storehouse. You would use them, for example, with the administrative software of a computer telephony application or an Internet application to perform automated system administration, without requiring manual intervention or human input in any way.

Your applications can also build stored procedures on the fly to meet certain requirements. These stored procedures can then be saved or stored in the tempdb. If they are stored in tempdb, they are later dropped when the application terminates or the user disconnects. If, however, your application needs frequent use of the stored procedure, it would be better to create the stored procedure once and then maintain it in the system for later use. We will discuss stored procedures at length in Chapter 14.

User-Defined Data Types

User-defined data types are made possible by extending the existing SQL Server 2005 base types with custom names and formats. To create a user-defined data type, you would call the stored procedure sp_addtype. The example in the following code creates a user-defined data type, *timeofdeath*, extended from the base data type datetime.

```
EXEC sp_addtype timeofdeath, datetime, 'NULL'
```

In this emergency room database, the user-defined timeofdeath data type records the time of death of patients. It can take values of NULL in the event the time of death is not recorded or the subject was dead on arrival. User-defined data types are discussed further in Chapter 11 when we deal with the CLR.

User-Defined Functions

SQL Server supports user-defined functions. These functions are built using T-SQL code, specifically the CREATE FUNCTION statement, and any .NET languages for functions created in managed code. The functions are used to return a value or a result code. They can return values as single scalars, such as integers, characters, and decimals. User-defined functions are useful for many application scenarios and can be used extensively in analytical and statistical applications.

SQL Server 2005 UDFs can also return the *table* data type. For example, a function can declare the internal table variable, insert rows into the table, and then return the table as the return value. You can also use a class of functions known as *inline* functions that can perform relational algebra on your tables, using the SELECT statement and returning the *table* variable.

User-defined functions can contain complex code comprising multiple SELECT statements. They are thus an ideal mechanism for returning tables where the complexity of the code precludes the generation of a view. Likewise, the user-defined function can also replace a stored procedure.

Properties

User-defined properties are known as *extended properties* and can be applied to all database objects. The architecture is thus OO in design (properties can publish information) and allows the database designer or developer to extend the collection of properties on database objects. The properties are essentially placeholders for information that can be used by applications.

The values of an extended property are of the sql_variant data type and can hold up to 7,500 bytes of data. The extended properties are created, managed, and deleted by the stored procedures sp_addextendedproperty, sp_updateextendedproperty, and sp_dropextendedproperty. The system function, fn_listextendedproperty, lets you read the value of an extended property.

Full-Text Indexes

SQL Server 2005 can create full-text indexes that are used for sophisticated searching of character string data. The full-text index stores information about certain words and their locations within their columns. This will allow you to create full-text queries and return either character string data or complete documents. You can search for instances of individual words or combinations of words.

The indexes are stored in catalogs, and each database you create can contain one or more full-text catalogs. The actual catalog and the indexes are not, however, stored in the database. They are stored externally as files and managed by the Microsoft Search service (see Chapter 3). Also, a full-text index can only be defined on a base table and not on the virtual objects, such as views and temporary tables.

The Physical Database Architecture

SQL Server 2005's physical architecture, its internal level, is highly complex. The architecture was extensively overhauled in version 8.0 (SQL Server 2000), and this version builds on those foundations. Earlier versions of SQL Server were very different on the inside, so if you are here from version 7.0, by-passing version 8.0 on the way over to 9.0, you need to listen up.

Pages and Extents

Pages and *extents* are to SQL Server what *cells* and *combs* are to a beehive. *Pages* contain the *rows*, which contain the data. Collections of pages make up *extents.* Extent collections are essentially what makes up your database. This next section explores pages and extents in more detail.

Pages

Looking at the internal level, we find that the fundamental base data storage object is the *page.* Each page is only 8KB in size, which means that a SQL Server 2005 database can store 128 pages in a megabyte.

Pages are managed and controlled in a similar fashion to other Windows OS objects. First, the page is identified with a globally unique identifier or object ID. Second, each page contains a 96-byte header that is used to store pertinent information about the page, including its type, available space, and so on. Table 2-1 lists the six types of pages that are used by the SQL Server 2005 database.

Page Type	Contents
Data	Pages that contain the data rows with all data, except text, ntext, image, nvarchar(max), varchar(max), varbinary(max), and xml data, when "text in row" is set to ON.
Index	All index entries.
Text/Image	The large object data types of text, ntext, image, nvarchar(max), varchar(max), varbinary(max), and xml data. Also contains the variable length columns when the data row exceeds 8KB of varchar, nvarchar, varbinary, and sql_variant.
Global Allocation Map (GAM), Shared Global Allocation Map (SGAM)	Indicates if extents are allocated.
Page Free Space	Information about page allocation and free space available on pages.
Index Allocation Map (IAM)	Information about extents used by a table or index per allocation unit.
Bulk Changed Map	Information about extents modified by bulk operations since the last BACKUP LOG statement per allocation unit.
Differential Changed Map	Information about extents that have changed since the last BACKUP DATABASE statement per allocation unit.

TABLE 2-1   Page Types Used by SQL Server Databases

Data pages store all the data in the rows except, as indicated, large amounts of data for the types text, ntext, image, nvarchar(max), varchar(max), varbinary(max), and xml. The "(max)" prefixed types and "xml" are new to SQL Server 2005. The aforementioned types are large extents of character and binary information, which are stored in separate pages (more about the large object data types later). The Text/Image data pages are also used for varchar, nvarchar, varbinary and sql_variant when the data row exceeds 8KB, as indicated in Table 2-1.

The layout of a data page is illustrated in Figure 2-9, which illustrates that the data is laid out serially on the pages in rows. The rows start from the top of the page, immediately after the header. Each page contains a region that stores the row offsets for the data pages. These row offsets are stored at the end of the data pages. The row offsets contain one entry for each row on the page. The row offsets also indicate how far the first byte of the row is from the start of the page. The row offsets are started at the end of the page—in other words, the first row offset is the last offset, stored at the end of the page. Each row on a page can hold up to 8,060 bytes of data. And the rows cannot span to other pages.

Extents

Extents are used to allocate space to tables and indexes. Each extent contains up to eight contiguous pages, which means that each extent is a maximum of 64KB in size. The database can thus maintain 16 extents per available MB of storage space.

There are two types of extents in SQL Server 2005, *uniform extents* and *mixed extents.* Uniform extents are the property or ownership of a single object. In other words, the object that owns the uniform extent also owns all eight pages in the extent. The mixed extent can be shared by up to eight objects. Each object is allocated a page. The object retains ownership of the page until its data requirement exceeds the limits of the page, after which it is assigned to a uniform extent.

Database Files and Filegroups

As discussed earlier, SQL Server databases are made up of a collection of three files: the primary data files, the secondary data files, and the log files. The data pages described previously are stored in these database files. Transaction logs are of course stored in the log files.

FIGURE 2-9
A SQL Server data page

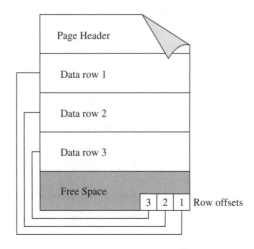

SQL Server gives these files the *.mdf, .ndf,* and *.ldf* extensions respectively but does not enforce these extensions for its own functionality. It is not recommended that you change them, however, especially if your backup mechanisms and scripts are associated with these file extensions.

When you create database files, either interactively with Management Studio or in T-SQL code, you can specify that the database files grow and shrink automatically (autoshrink). You need to specify a growth increment/decrement by which the file will grow or shrink as needed. This is illustrated in Figure 2-10. The file can also be allowed to grow until it has used all the space available to it on the system. You can also specify a maximum size for a database file.

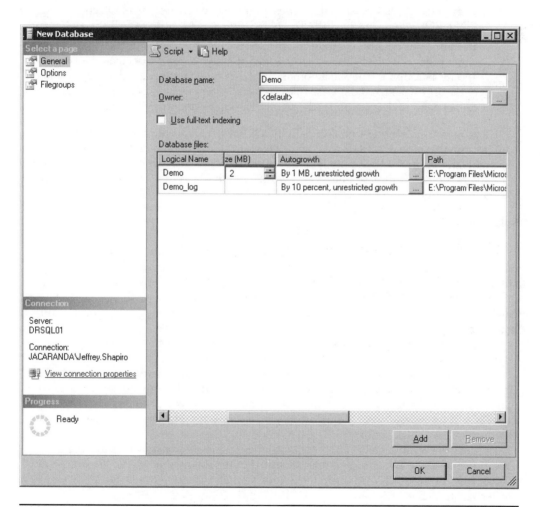

FIGURE 2-10   Configuring a database interactively

Filegroups   *Filegroups* are a useful management feature in SQL Server that let you assign database files to a group object. You can improve system performance by collecting files into groups and placing them onto specific disk drives and storage arrays. You can create filegroups for each disk drive and then assign the tables, indexes, or large object data types to these filegroups.

Log files cannot be part of a filegroup because they are maintained separately from data files. Also, you cannot assign files to more than one group. The following is a list of the three types of filegroups:

- **Primary**   The primary filegroup contains primary data. The system or built-in files are gathered up into the primary group.

- **User-defined**   The user-defined files groups can be created in T-SQL code using the FILEGROUP keyword in CREATE DATABASE and ALTER DATABASE statements.

- **Default**   The default filegroup is where all the files that have not been assigned to either primary or user-defined groups are kept. If you create a database and do not specify a group for it, it will automatically be assigned to the default group. Members of the db_owner fixed database role can manually move a file between groups. If you do not define a default group, the primary group assumes the role of default.

Filegroups are not an essential element in SQL Server 2005, but they can greatly ease the administrative burden. For example, you can create a backup regimen that backs up certain files or filegroups, instead of backing up the entire database. We will return to the filegroups in Chapters 6 and 7. Figure 2-11 illustrates working with filegroups interactively using the Management Studio.

Space Allocation and Reuse

SQL Server's database architecture has been designed to respond to frequent changes in the size and disposition of its databases. The net result of the wizardry in its internal mechanisms is a faster and more responsive system. This is especially important when you are working with very large databases (VLDBs), critical OLTP systems, or a large number of users. What goes on at the lower levels is not something a user can see (only feel), but both database developers and DBAs alike can benefit from knowledge of the architecture and how it operates.

At work under the "hood" is a data usage and space tracking system that appears to be relatively simple, which is its beauty. Coupled with the page-extent architecture, the system is able to easily monitor database allocation and space occupancy with little overhead. On close inspection of the pages, we find that the space allocation information is confined to only a few pages, which are densely packed. This means that you need less physical memory to hold the free space information, which translates into less use of virtual memory and thus less hard disk reads.

I alluded earlier to several types of allocation maps used by SQL Server to store the allocation of extents. Two are key to the recording of the extent allocations. These are the Global Allocation Maps (GAMs) and the Shared Global Allocation Maps (SGAMs), which are derived from the GAM bitmap.

The GAM records information that describes what extents have been allocated. Each GAM covers a whopping 64,000 extents, which translates into 4GB of data. The GAM, a bitmap,

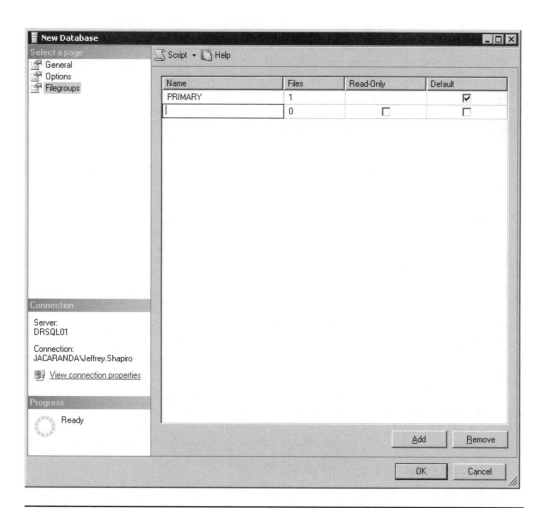

FIGURE 2-11   Configuring filegroups

provides one bit for each extent it covers. If a bit in the map is set to 0, it means that the extent related to the bit is being used. If the bit is set to 1, it means the extent is free.

The SGAM bitmaps provide information about which extents are being used as mixed extents. The reverse order of the bits is applied in the SGAM bitmap. If the GAM bit is set to 1, then the SGAM bit is set to 0. If the SGAM bit is 0, it means the extent is either free or not in use as a uniform or full mixed extent. In other words, it could be a mixed extent whose pages are currently in use. Table 2-2 further illustrates the bitmap information for current use of an extent.

Microsoft's use of bitmaps to manage usage is at once simple and ingenious because it allows for an elegant means of managing usage of databases using a tried-and-tested bitmapping technique. The algorithm is simple and thus virtually bulletproof. All the server is required to do is search the bitmaps for free extents and then change the state of

State of Extent	GAM Bit State	SGAM Bit State
Free, or not in use	1	0
Uniform extent, or a full mixed extent	0	0
Mixed extent with free pages	0	1

TABLE 2-2   The Bit States for Reporting the Current State of an Extent

the GAM bit and its alter ego, the SGAM bit. To free an extent, SQL Server ensures the GAM bit is set to 1 and the SGAM bit is set to 0.

Another use of bitmaps is demonstrated with the Page Free Space (PFS) pages that record whether an individual page has been allocated and how much free space is in the page. The bitmap records whether the page is empty, up to 50 percent full, up to 80 percent full, up to 95 percent full, or between 96 and 100 percent full. SQL Server uses this information when it needs to find free space for a row, or when it has to allocate a new page.

Closer inspection is required to fully appreciate the architecture at work here. Figure 2-12 provides a conceptual view of the data file and the order and sequence of pages in the data file. The sequence is not accidental. It allows SQL Server to search the data files because it always knows where to find the GAM page, which is page 2 in a zero-based collection (it is actually the third page in the data file; the file header at page 0 is the first page).

Space Used by Indexes   Indexes can consume a ton of space in databases. Index Allocation Map (IAM) bitmaps are used by SQL Server to keep track of the extents in databases that indexes use. Like GAMs and SGAMs, IAMs are stored in the respective databases that contain the objects in question. These IAM pages are allocated as needed and are stored at random in the file. SQL Server uses IAM pages to allocate extents to objects in the same fashion it allocates pages and extents to table data.

How Tables and Indexes Are Organized in SQL Server

The SQL Server table pages we described earlier are organized according to a system of linked or unlinked lists. When a clustered index is defined for a table or a view, the data rows are stored in the pages in the order based on the clustered index key. The data pages are linked by a doubly linked list, and the index is implemented as a B-tree index structure that provides a fast retrieval mechanism based on the clustered index key.

Data rows that are not stored in any order are called heaped tables and do not require their data pages to be sorted in any order either. And the data pages are not linked in a linked list. Rows in heaped tables are found by scanning the IAM pages that manage the

FIGURE 2-12
The order of pages
in the data file

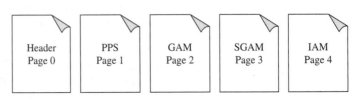

| Header | PPS | GAM | SGAM | IAM |
| Page 0 | Page 1 | Page 2 | Page 3 | Page 4 |

space allocated to a heap. SQL Server essentially scans the IAMs serially to find the extents holding pages for heap data. The table scan on a heap takes place as follows:

1. SQL Server reads the first IAM in the filegroup and scans all extents defined by the IAM.

2. SQL Server repeats the process for each IAM in the file.

3. SQL Server repeats the preceding steps for every file in the database or filegroup until the last IAM for the heap has been processed.

A single instance of SQL Server can support up to 249 nonclustered indexes on each table or indexed view. Nonclustered indexes also have a B-tree index structure similar to the one established for clustered indexes. However, nonclustered indexes have no control over the order of the data rows. In other words, the only time that data pages are sorted according to a system or order is when clustered indexes are established for the tables.

Every table, index, and indexed view is represented by a row inserted in the *sysindexes* table in its respective database. The row is uniquely identified by the combination of the object identifier (id) column and the index identifier (indid). The allocation of the tables, indexes, and indexed views is managed by a chain of IAM pages. A FirstIAM column in *sysindexes* points to the first IAM page in the chain of IAM pages managing the space allocated to the table, indexed view, or index.

Heaps are also allocated rows in the *sysindexes* table but have an index identifier of 0. When dealing with a heap, SQL Server uses the IAM pages to find the heap table pages in the data page collection because they are not linked.

Clustered indexes, tables, and views each have a representative row in *sysindexes* that has an index identifier or *indid* of 1. The *root* column points to the top of the clustered index B-tree to allow the server to use the index B-tree to locate data pages.

Nonclustered indexes, tables, and views also have rows in *sysindexes*. The values, however, of the indid range from 2 to 250. The root column thus points to the top of the nonclustered B-tree.

Tables that also have a text, ntext, or image column also have rows in *sysindexes* with an indid of 255. The FirstIAM column points to the chain of IAM pages that manage the text, ntext, image, nvarchar(max), varchar(max), varbinary(max), and xmlpages.

Transaction Logs

Transaction logs can be studied as components, at both the conceptual and internal levels of the database; from a physical perspective as well as a logical one. The subject is important enough to warrant introduction here under its own heading. Transaction logs are the footprints of SQL Server transactions. Not only can they trace transaction activity, but also they provide a near-perfect mechanism for recovery and redundancy of the data stored in tables. The transaction logs are capable of the following functions:

- They can be used to recover individual transactions. These are known as *rollbacks* in database server parlance. If a transaction's data is determined to be "questionable," the transaction that led to the insertion of the questionable data can be rolled back. The questionable data is removed from the database. The ROLLBACK statement is akin to the instant replay you see on television or in films.

- They can be used to recover incomplete transactions. Incomplete transactions may occur when SQL Server crashes in the middle of a transaction . . . which should never happen. The incomplete transaction is recovered when SQL Server restarts. When SQL Server restarts, it runs a recovery of each database. If certain transactions are found not to have completed (but they are sound in the log), they are rolled forward. At the same time, any transactions found to have caused questionable data are rolled back.

- They can be used to bring a database current from the last full or differential backup to the last transaction in the transaction log. It may, for example, happen that tables are damaged and you will need to restore a database from the last backup. The transaction log closes the "gap" between the last backup and the last transaction in the log. Any transactions that are not in the restored database are rolled forward and installed to the database.

The following list describes some of the operations stored in the transaction logs:

- The start and end of every transaction
- All INSERT, UPDATE, and DELETE transactions, including any transaction performed by system processes
- All extent allocations and deallocations
- The creation or termination of tables and indexes

Transaction Log Architecture

SQL Server transaction logs use a write-ahead log mechanism. This means that SQL Server ensures that no data updates are written to disk until they have been written to the log. The log record must in fact be written to disk before the data pages in the buffer are written to disk. In other words, SQL Server can ensure that a dirty page is not flushed before the log record associated with the dirty page is flushed (see the section "How Data Is Saved" in Chapter 3).

NOTE *Bulk insert and copy operations can cause a transaction log to fill up quickly. When you need to insert huge amounts of data for which you don't need transaction logs, nonlogged operations are supported. This is discussed in Chapters 16 and 17.*

Transaction logs are not tables but exist as separate files or collections of files in the database. The layout or structure of the data pages has no bearing on the log files. The log cache is also managed separately from the data cache. The log cache is, however, controlled by the database engine, but the code that is executed is not related to any data page functionality.

Log files are implemented over several files as needed. Like databases, they can be configured to "autogrow" as needed by the logging engine. This prevents you from running out of space in the transaction log (although truncation plays an important part here too). However, you will still need to make sure you do not run out of hard disk space. Chapters 7 and 8 also look at the truncation of transaction logs, which is an important subject for DBAs, because if stale log records are not deleted from the transaction log, your log files will just keep growing until your server runs out of hard disk space.

The Network Ahead

Let's take a break now from database architecture and look holistically at the roles played by the client and server components of SQL Server 2005. If you are new to client/server database systems, the paradigm shift from desktop applications, such as Microsoft Access and FoxPro, might seem steep. A number of areas will entail a learning curve. Understanding how to configure users in the database, server security and logins, roles, and so on can be a challenge. In Chapter 5, I go into the security aspect in a lot more depth. I have also included a deployment plan that offers step-by-step instructions on setting up your users for access.

As wonderful as SQL Server is, one of the drawbacks for newcomers is that it is so vast. It is not unusual to do everything right in the test or development environment, only to find users cannot connect when you roll out or deploy your production system. Chapter 8 will help you troubleshoot such situations. In the next chapter, I will put SQL Server's entrails under the spotlight again as we discuss the DBMS architecture.

RDBMS Architecture

This chapter investigates the core of the SQL Server 2005—the Database Management System (DBMS). You will be learning about its storage architecture and data input/output (I/O). I might add that the architecture and processes discussed in this chapter relate mostly to the SQL Server storage engine, while the architecture and processes discussed in Chapter 2 relate mostly to the relational engine.

For the most part, all SQL-driven database management systems operate on the same principles, just as all cars run on tires, gas, and a combustion engine. Some systems, however, work better than others do, and each DBMS is unique in how it makes use of memory, central processing unit (CPU), hard disks, and its query processing algorithms.

In this chapter, it will seem that I am straying into general relational database theory and architecture and moving away from SQL Server 2005. But the opposite is the case. If you are new to databases, C/S RDBMS systems, SQL, and SQL Server, you will greatly benefit from a general discussion on how a DBMS works in general and how SQL Server works in particular. You also need to investigate the claims that SQL Server 2005 leads the field in many transaction processing areas and is currently the most scalable product available; this chapter helps you meet that objective.

I believe you should first understand how a DBMS works—and then learn how SQL Server works in relation to general DBMS or transaction processing theory. It is thus a good idea to combine this chapter with a good book on the principles of relational database systems. Combining knowledge of the two will enable you to appreciate SQL Server better, understand how to make it work for you, and ultimately become a better DBA and SQL Server developer as you tackle the more complex "data" in the chapters that lie ahead.

If you are an experienced SQL Server or C/S DBMS engineer, you can skim the first part of this chapter. If you are new to SQL Server, however, I strongly recommend you understand how this DBMS works. Coupled with an understanding of the collateral components and resources, this understanding will help flatten the learning curve before you.

For the most part, you will be learning conceptually about SQL Server's internal environment: how data gets into the DBMS; how it gets stored, retrieved, and sent back out to the clients. We will not get into SQL Server 2005's CLR support in this chapter, but we do cover CLR specifics in Chapter 11. First let's get familiar with some of the important pieces before getting into deeper water. I will launch the discussion with a subject that all vendors make a lot of noise about: the Transaction Processing Performance Council's (TPC) transaction processing benchmarks.

The TPC Benchmarks

You should make a special effort to understand the TPC benchmark data that the important database vendors now publish. Microsoft published a number of benchmarks shortly after the release of the product indicating that SQL Server 2005 maintains the lead set by its predecessor SQL Server 2000 in DBMS systems with one of the lowest cost per transaction ratings on the market. What does this mean to you?

TPC benchmarks are to the DBMS what the MIPS ratings are to processors or CPUs or what horsepower is to a combustion engine. A DBMS needs to meet certain performance benchmarks before it can be considered worthwhile or competitive in both online transaction processing and decision support systems. The benchmarking is used to test algorithms, new versions of code, new hardware platforms, and so on. So DBMS vendors, including Microsoft, Informix, IBM, Oracle, Sybase, and others, use the benchmarks to test the veracity and reliability of their systems on certain platforms and in controlled testing environments. TPC benchmark tests are like Formula 1 events in motor racing. The manufacturers not only compete to prove superiority or market share, but they take what they learn at the races and incorporate the results into new products for consumers.

The nonprofit TPC—which can be found on the Internet at www.tpc.org—conducts the TPC benchmark tests. The TPC's purpose is to define the tests and disseminate objective performance data based on the benchmarks. The benchmarks have stringent test requirements and include a number of durability and reliability tests. The results of the tests are independently audited and published.

The two important benchmarks for SQL Server 2005 (and SQL Server version 2000) are the TPC-C benchmarks and the TPC-H benchmarks, respectively, for online transaction processing (OLTP) and decision support systems. They are described as follows:

- **TPC-C: OLTP**   TPC-C measures both performance and scalability of OLTP DBMS systems. TPC-C tests a wide range of database functionality such as selects, updates, and batch transactions. Most important, however, is that TPC-C measures *throughput* in business transactions per minute in a simulated order entry and distribution environment. The tests measure how many new orders are generated in a minute while the DBMS is executing four other transaction types, such as payments, status updates, shipping or deliveries, and inventory level updates. Throughput, in TPC terms, is a measure of maximum sustained system performance. The five transaction types have a certain predefined user response time requirement. The new order response time is set at five seconds. So, if your system generates a 500 tpmC number, it means that the system is generating 500 new orders per minute while fulfilling the other four requirements in the TPC-C workload. When you consider Internet applications or e-commerce solutions, you can see how the TPC-C benchmark becomes especially important.

- **TPC-H: DSS**   This benchmark, measured as TPC-H Composite Queries per Hour (QphH), simulates a decision support system containing large volumes of data that is synchronized with online production databases. The benchmark makes use of highly complex ad hoc queries designed to answer real-world questions. These include questions concerning pricing, promotions (such as target markets), supply and demand, profit and loss, and so on. It should come as no surprise, given the preceding tmpC rating, that SQL Server 2005 also leads the field in the TPC-H benchmarks.

TPC-C and TPC-H also produce price/performance numbers, the $/tpmC and $/QphH rates, respectively. These ratings are especially useful when determining cost for transaction or analysis performance. But the rating is not about the cost of the platform or computer, because that actually represents only a small part of the costing criteria in a DBMS. The rating takes into consideration the entire computing environment, including terminals, client computers, software, operating systems, the DBMS software, three-year maintenance plans, and so forth.

An example: How do you derive the $/tpmC for an OLTP system? Take the cost of the entire system and divide it by the tpmC benchmark. For example, if we take the cost of the entire system (say published at $5.3 million for a solution) and divide that by the tpmC, or 262,243, to arrive at the $/tpmC of $20.24. No doubt the highly scalable Windows Server platform (and HP server clusters would fill a small data center) is even more juicy than the actual tpmC number because an IBM RS/6000 with about 24 processors would cost you four times the $/tpmC for nowhere near a comparable tpmC.

It is also important to stress an interesting finding about scalability—and we will get into this further in Chapter 9—that the TPC benchmarks prove. When it comes to SMP scalability, less often means more, especially for DBMS systems. Linear SMP scalability is a jihad among DBAs, and many seem to think that midrange or UNIX systems with OS support for hundreds of processors is the answer to achieving DBMS scalability. Many also point out a so-called flaw in Windows Server 2003 that it still cannot support as many processors as its rival UNIX. The benchmarks thus prove SMP scalability to be a myth with respect to DBMS systems.

NOTE *The TPC monitors other benchmarks as well, such as the TPC-R rating, which measures the performance of standardized report generation. The benchmarks can be researched at www.tpc.org.*

An Overview of the DBMS Components

The SQL Server 2005 DBMS comprises a number of interconnected I/O architectures or modules. The following are key components of the database engine you should make a special effort to understand before attempting to program SQL Server 2005:

- **The relational database engine**   This component comprises several modules or collateral components that interact with each other on a common code base. With the storage engine and its modules, the relational database engine makes up the DBMS. The system also includes statement parsing and processing modules (for both SQL and XML), and the query processing system. The engine receives all communications from the client, passed to it as events from the Net-Libraries. The query containing T-SQL statements are first parsed, then preprocessed, and then compiled into execution plans, which are sent up against the data store, via the storage engine, for extraction. The extracted data is then built into the tabular data formation (the tabular data streams (TDS) protocol) that is sent back to the client through the Net-Libraries.

- **The storage engine**   This suite of components is responsible for the management of the database files and the management of the space within the files. While we include it as part of the DBMS, it is really at the center of SQL Server's database architecture, which is discussed in Chapter 2. The storage engine is also responsible for transaction logging and database recovery.

- **The transaction architecture**   Understanding the transaction architecture is key to understanding most of what makes up SQL Server 2005 and how you adapt the various features to your ends. There are essentially two transaction architectures that you will learn about in this book: a local transaction architecture responsible for the work that performs deletes, updates, inserts, and so on; and the distributed transactions architecture that involves or encompasses data from external sources. The latter is discussed in Chapter 16.

- **Concurrency control and transaction management**   Part of the transaction architecture, it deserves separate treatment. It is really a system of methods and algorithms that allow multiple users to exploit the databases under the management of an instance of the DBMS. Concurrency in SQL Server is handled by a pessimistic locking architecture built into the relational engine. The locking mechanism allows you to obtain locks on rows, pages, ranges of keys, indexes, tables, and whole databases. Besides the architecture discussed here, locking is also discussed extensively in Chapter 17.

The Relational Database Engine

You can look at the relational engine in two ways: you can study it at the core, or the relational kernel, or you can study it at a higher level with all its surrounding components that the kernel hands functionality off to. Studying the kernel at any lower level is beyond the scope of this book. A good analogy, however, is what we need to study in a steam locomotive engine, the pistons and drive shaft being the kernel, and the rest of the engine, comprising the coal burners, wheels, knobs, pulleys, levers (not to mention the engineer and the horn), representing a higher level. Let's look at the kernel in all its functional glory.

NOTE   *At the very core of the SQL Server relational engine, the kernel is the same code used for each version of SQL Server, from the Mobile Edition (which is embedded into your average Windows Mobile device) to the Enterprise Edition parked on the shared or clustered disks of a TerraServer. This is the reason you can write code for a handheld and execute it with very little modification on any other version of SQL Server 2005.*

At the kernel level, you have a highly optimized chunk of code that picks up inbound T-SQL statements from the Net-Libraries and optimizes it into native code for the most effective execution plan. (In many respects, the relational engine is like a compiler that preprocesses code into object code before compiling it into machine code. It is no different from the preprocessing algorithms used in many different kernels, aside from database systems.)

Memory Architecture

Sophisticated memory management architecture ensures that SQL Server 2005 gets all the memory it needs within limitations of the platform. Its memory management is conservative: the engine obtains memory as required and releases it as resources become free.

Two types of memory are used in the Windows Server 2003 operating systems: *physical* memory and *virtual* memory. The physical memory is the memory in the RAM chips installed on the system motherboards. Then you have virtual memory, which is a combination of all memory in the system and the architecture that makes it available to the OS. An important aspect of virtual memory is that it can include hard disk platter memory.

The advanced memory management facility on the Windows 2000 server platform (Address Windowing Extensions or AWE) enables SQL Server Enterprise Edition to work with a 32GB address space on 32-bit versions of the OS and SQL Server 2005, and up 64GB on 64-bit versions of the OS and SQL Server 2005. DBAs are still able to override the default and automated memory settings and specify fixed allocations (discussed in Chapter 4) should the application or environment require it. One area where this may be required is in the management of the memory pool, which is discussed shortly. The memory pool is where SQL Server stores its buffer cache of data pages.

On the Windows Server 2003 platform, 32-bit editions of both OS and SQL Server can access 2GB memory default, 3GB with the /3GB boot option parameter, and 4GB as a WOW (Windows on Windows) implementation (32-bit version of SQL Server 2005 running on a 64-bit OS). The 64-bit OS and SQL Server 2005 combinations provide access to 7TB (terabytes) on I64 architecture and 8TB on X64 architecture.

On most implementations SQL Server tries to maintain virtual memory on the server at between 4MB and 10MB less than physical memory. And the only way SQL Server can do this is by changing the size of its memory pool. When SQL Server loads up collateral processes, such as calls to remote stored procedures and OLE DB providers, or when other applications or other instances of SQL Server start, it will have to reduce the size of the memory pool to release memory it has acquired. You can set limits on just how much the memory pool can vary by setting values for *min server memory* and *max server memory,* which are exposed in the Management Studio (see Chapter 4).

Any new applications that start up on the server are instead allocated paged memory. Each instance of SQL Server 2005 is thus able to work with the memory on the system, to the mutual benefit of the other instances. (When using AWE on Windows 2000 Server, however, the system will require the assignment of static memory addresses.)

NOTE   *Chapter 4 discusses memory management.*

Page Files and the VMM

The *virtual memory manager (VMM)* manages all system memory and ensures that applications and the operating system have access to more memory than what is provided by the RAM chips installed in the modules on the motherboard. Memory chips are faster than virtual memory, a fact that is important for SQL Server.

The VMM has another important role: It guarantees that memory addresses used by multiple instances and applications do not "trespass" on each other. In the olden days of DOS, this problem created disasters. Memory management has evolved over the years, from the first versions of the Windows operating system to Windows Server 2003 Datacenter, which is one of the most sophisticated operating systems in existence. With each new version of the operating system, the virtual memory management has been improved, so the algorithms used by one Windows platform differ from the algorithms used in others. The memory management of SQL Server has also been vastly improved on Windows Server 2003. This means that for SQL Server 2005 to support instances on all 32-bit and 64-bit operating systems, the DMBS must use different caching algorithms.

The VMM has two major functions:

- The VMM manages a memory-mapped table that keeps track of the list of virtual addresses assigned to each process. An analogy might be a hotel in which all the guests are assigned to rooms and the concierge can consult a table to manage the guests, their check-in times, check-out times, dirty laundry, and so on. The VMM coordinates exactly where in the system the actual data mapped to the addresses resides. In other words, it acts as a translator service, mapping virtual memory to physical memory. This function is transparent to the applications, and they operate oblivious to the process that is providing them the illusion that they have access to physical memory.

- When processes use up all available RAM, the VMM moves the memory contents least accessed out to the hard disk. This is called paging.

Windows Server 2003 32-bit thus basically has access to at least a 4GB address space, although the space is virtual and can be made up of both RAM and hard disk space. Getting back to our hotel analogy, this is like having some important or high-rate guests residing in the main hotel building overlooking the ocean, while longer-term or low-rate guests occupy the annex overlooking the street. The total room count, however, is a sum of all the rooms in both buildings.

Although we talk about a 4GB address space, this space is actually relative to how the system uses memory. In actual fact, on Windows Server 2003, the default address space available to applications is only 2GB; in fact, it is even less than that, because the 2GB assignment is shared by all processes running in user mode. The other 2GB is reserved for kernel-mode execution.

So if you study Windows Server 2003 memory architecture, you see that the 4GB space is divided into an upper segment and a lower segment, both containing 2GB address spaces. The kernel-mode threads and processes are allocated the upper portion, while the lower space is reserved for both user-mode and kernel-mode processes. The upper portion also reserves certain lower regions of total address space, which is used for hardware mapping.

The lower portion is also maintained in paging pools comprising 4KB pages. There are a nonpaged pool and a paged pool. The pages in the paged pool are the pages that can get swapped out to disk. It is usually reserved for applications, which are the processes most likely to become idle. The nonpaged pool remains in physical RAM and supports the operating system functions and critical services. The size of each page is 4KB.

More about Paging

Paging is the process of moving data in and out of physical memory, a.k.a. RAM. When the RAM-based memory pool becomes full and the operating system is called on to deliver more memory, the VMM will kick idle data out of physical memory and relocate it to the hard disk in a structure called a *page file*.

The VMM manages the memory pool by assigning space in the pages that are identified as either *valid* or *invalid* pages. The valid pages are located in physical memory and become immediately available to an application when it needs it. You can think of them as being "online" to the application, like a line of credit. Invalid pages are "offline" and not available to any demanding application. The invalid pages are stored on disk.

Although idle applications and data are stored in the offline pages, the VMM maintains pointers to the addresses so that it can recover the data when it needs to. For example, when an application or data in the page file is referenced, the operating system needs to get it back to RAM as quickly as possible. At this point, a page fault is triggered, spawning a new thread to access the data in the page file. But for the recalled data to fit back into the active memory pool, idle data that has been hanging around gets bumped and sent offline to disk. Now you know why fast and reliable hard disks are recommended in data- and memory-intensive applications.

The VMM performs a series of housekeeping chores as part of the paging routines:

- It manages the data in the offline page file on a first-in, first-out basis. Data that has been on disk the longest is the first to make it back to physical memory when RAM frees up, unless something on the disk is explicitly needed. In other words, the VMM does not simply recall data idle on the hard disk to be idle in RAM. But the VMM continues to move data back and forth from RAM as long as RAM keeps freeing up and idle data needs to be paged out to the hard disk. The "hot" data the VMM keeps an eye on is known as the *working set.*

- The VMM performs what is known as *fetching* when it brings back data from the page file. In addition, the VMM also performs what is known as *page file clustering.* Page file clustering means that when the VMM fetches, it also brings back some of the surrounding data in the page file, on the premise that data immediately before and after the required data might be needed in the next instant as well. This technique thus tends to speed up data I/O from the page file.

- The VMM is smart enough to conclude that if there is no space in RAM to place returning data from the hard disk, the least needed data in RAM must be displaced and banished to the hard disk.

You can manage and control the parameters by which the VMM operates and factors such as the size of the page file; these are very important to understand.

Address Windowing Extensions

To support very large address spaces, such as 8GB on the 32-bit Windows Server 2003, the AWE have to be invoked. The AWE is to Windows Server 2003 what the old DOS extenders and EMS libraries were to the legacy PC-based operating systems and the early 16-bit versions of Windows (remember Pharlap?). The AWE is included in the 32-bit APIs that allow applications to address more than the 4GB that is addressable through the standard 32-bit API.

AWE lets applications acquire physical memory as nonpaged memory. It then dynamically maps the views of nonpaged memory to the 32-bit address space . . . you could call this *conjoined memory addressing.* A comprehensive, bit-by-bit investigation of AWE is beyond the scope of this book, because as a DBA or application developer, you can let Windows Server 2003 and SQL Server 2005 handle the additional addressing for you. All you have to do is enable the use of AWE.

TIP *You can unravel AWE in SQL Server 2005 Books Online.*

AWE is enabled for SQL Server 2005 applications using the system stored procedure sp_configure, which can take an *on* or *off* bit for enabling or disabling AWE, respectively. It has no effect on 64-bit systems.

The SQL Server Address Space

Each instance of SQL Server started up on your computer consumes an address space that is divided into a number of areas that hold the various modules of code that make up the DBMS. Each address space, for each instance, holds the following components:

- **The executable code**   This area of the address space includes the Open Data Services (ODS), the SQL Server engine code, and the SQL Server Net-Libraries. In addition, distributed queries can also independently load an OLE DB provider DLL into the address space, as will extended stored procedures and OLE Automation objects.

- **The memory pool**   This area of the address space is used for the data structures that use memory in an instance of SQL Server. The typical objects using the memory pool include the following:

  - **System-level data structures**   These are structures that hold global data for the instance, such as database descriptors and the lock table.

  - **The buffer cache**   This is the cache that holds the buffer pages into which data pages are read (discussed shortly).

  - **The procedure cache**   This is the cache that holds the execution plans for T-SQL queries that have been executed, or are in the process of being executed, in the instance. (See the section "SQL, Query Optimization, and Query Processing" later in this chapter.)

  - **The log caches**   These are the caches of buffer pages used to read and write the log pages. As discussed in Chapter 2, the log buffers and the associated log files are managed separately from the data buffers and the actual data files.

  - **The connection contexts**   The connection contexts maintain data representing each connection in the instance. The data includes state information and the parameter values for queries and stored procedures, cursor positions, and tables under reference.

- **The stack space**   The stack space is allocated by the operating system for threads that are started in SQL Server. The default stack size is 512KB.

The memory pool is a fluid structure, and SQL Server constantly adjusts the amounts of memory being allocated to various components to optimize performance. Every time a client connects, for example, SQL Server has to allocate memory to the new connection. And then it has to release it when the client disconnects. New and altered databases and all their objects are also constantly changing the allocation and usage of memory. The buffer cache, the procedure cache, and the log caches are also factors that influence how memory is used and released.

> **TIP** *The applications you create and how you code your queries can have a direct bearing on SQL Server performance. You want to keep the number of one-way and round-trips to the server as low as possible, but conversely you also have to keep the amount of data sent up and down as low as possible. I discuss this consideration in more detail in Chapters 15, 16, and 17.*

SQL Server, like all DBMS systems, strives to minimize disk thrashing by using the services of a buffer cache in memory. This buffer cache holds pages read from the database. According to the SQL Server development team, they have spent a lot of time making sure that SQL Server 2005 makes maximum use of the buffer cache and minimizes the disk I/O of database files. When the buffer runs out of memory, the operating system will start swapping pages out to the page file, using the processes described earlier. Naturally, the system will slow down, so it is important on mission-critical systems to add more "real" memory when the VMM goes into overtime. The bigger the buffer cache, the better SQL Server will respond. As you know, the Standard and Enterprise Editions of SQL Server can use all the memory you can install in a machine (minus the OS of course).

SQL Server I/O Architecture

The I/O architecture, which defines how data is read from and written to the databases, is the architecture underpinning all database management systems. It is also one of the key components of these products and one of the key architectures that sets them apart from one other. The system that has the fastest, leanest, and most innovative I/O architecture wins the transaction-load war and ultimately market share, as discussed earlier on the subject of TPC benchmarks.

SQL Server 2005 has lofty goals set for it. It is currently cleaning up. On the one hand, it must meet the needs of small businesses, while on the other, it competes with the heavyweights of the world. I believe Microsoft met the challenge, because SQL Server can scale from a single-user solution to an Internet deployment supporting thousands of users. Let's take a closer look at the I/O architecture that achieves this feat.

There are two locations from which an instance of SQL Server can read (and write) data: from memory and from the physical hard disk. It does not take much effort to imagine what would become of a hard disk if all the data required by clients was constantly read from the database—a barrage of continuous transactions might, literally, set the server on fire. So SQL Server, like all DBMS systems, stores a virtual copy of its most accessed data, and most recently accessed data, in memory. In other words, the read or write does not require the movement of physical parts.

When SQL Server starts and data is requested, it is loaded into virtual memory and occupies spaces allocated for it in the so-called buffer cache we discussed earlier. As you learned in Chapter 2, the data is stored in 8KB data pages on disk. The pages are made contiguous to form 64KB extents. Accordingly, the virtual data pages in the buffer cache are also 8KB in size.

Now, a *virtual read* (sometimes referred to as a "logical read," a term I have a problem with) occurs every time a client requests data that is stored in the buffer cache. If the data required is not in the buffer cache, SQL Server has to get the data from the hard disk, a *physical read*. Conversely, a *virtual write* takes places when data is updated or changed in memory. By *virtual write*, we mean that the data is updated in the cache as opposed to being updated on the disk. However, the data is not persistent, and if the electrical power that provides life to the cache is terminated, data loss ensues. From time to time, data must then be *physically written* to disk. But performance takes precedence over persistence, and the DBMS pushes the virtual management envelope by reading and writing to data more than once before it is saved to the disks.

The DBMS thus has to maintain a suitable buffer so that performance is maintained and the server is not forced to write and read excessively to and from the hard disk. However, the larger the buffer cache used by SQL Server, the less memory resources are made available to other applications. A point of diminishing returns arrives when the server saves on physical I/O but loses through the excessive paging that occurs to support other applications.

SQL Server pushes the so-called I/O envelope by using two Windows Server 2003 I/O features: *Scatter-Gather I/O* and *Asynchronous I/O*. Scatter-Gather I/O has often been cited as a killer feature of Windows Server 2003, but it was introduced to the operating system with Windows NT 4.0 SP2 many years ago. No doubt it was a target for enhancement in Windows Server 2003, and it is now built into the operating system. Essentially, this technology is responsible for moving data from disconnected areas of RAM to contiguous blocks of data on a hard disk. While you, the DBA or system administrator, do not have any control over the operating system's use of this technology, systems and software have to be specifically written to take advantage of it. SQL Server 2005 is one such system—actually, Scatter-Gather I/O was originally created for SQL Server.

NOTE *This is not exactly the same thing that the VMM does, because the shunting around of data by the VMM occurs without the cognizance of the application.*

The performance boost for SQL Server is more obvious when the DBMS reads data from the hard disk. For example: If SQL Server reads in a 64KB extent, it does not have to reserve a 64KB area in the buffer cache for the data. It can scatter the eight buffer pages directly into the buffer cache and later gather the eight pages by maintaining the cache addresses of the eight buffer pages.

Another I/O feature SQL Server makes heavy use of is *Asynchronous I/O*. If I/O were synchronous, every time SQL Server spawned a thread to read or write data, the entire system would have to wait for the I/O operation to complete before regaining control and moving on with the next process. But under *Asynchronous I/O*, SQL Server can carry on with other tasks while checking back periodically on the status of the I/O thread.

Using Asynchronous I/O functionality, SQL Server can spawn multiple concurrent I/O operations against files. You can throttle the maximum number of I/O operations by setting the *max async io* configuration option. The default is 32 threads of I/O execution for the 32-bit systems and 64 threads for the 64-bit systems. Only the most demanding of applications will require you to set more than the default. This is now a good point to launch into the subject of SQL Server's thread and task architecture.

SQL Server's Thread and Task Architecture

All DBMS products, like all major applications, are built on solid multithreading systems architecture. We don't need to discuss threading technology here at any deep level save to say that threading technology allows complex processes to make more effective use of the CPU. If you are new to software engineering practice or new to the concept of threading, you can find many books on the subject, and the subject is well covered in the MSDN library and in the Microsoft online knowledge base.

In the not-too-distant past, the only way we could execute processes in a system concurrently was to have multiple instances of applications running on the operating system. A multitasking kernel (the OS) was responsible for deciding which applications got preferential use of the CPU and when. This was how the early Windows operating systems worked. Later it became possible for an application to obtain a level of concurrent processor use within the application's address space by executing multiple process threads. Multithreading led to more reliable software because the operating system could properly manage the order and priority of thread execution.

It is important to understand that you cannot execute threads at exactly the same time on a single CPU, because threading is a synchronous technology. The operating system can, however, determine when to kill a thread or allow one thread to execute ahead of others (priority). On multiple-CPU systems, threads can run in a true concurrent state by being executed on parallel processors. In other words, if a computer has eight processors, it can concurrently execute eight threads.

An allied technology to threads is *fibers*. Fibers are similar to threads, but the application, rather than the operating system gets to control them. Fiber technology does not require the operating system's overhead of threading, which requires resources in both the user mode and the kernel mode of the OS. That said, fibers are not exactly separate from threads. They are derived from threads. A thread can spawn multiple fibers.

Fiber execution is an advanced technology. Many different activities go on in SQL Server at the same time, and all these processes compete for CPU time. At the core of the DBMS we find what appears to be functionality that is very similar to the part of the operating system that works with threads. This SQL Server kernel thus allows the system to work with both threads and fibers, without having to engage the kernel and user mode resources of the OS. And each instance of SQL Server maintains a pool of threads and fibers that are executed in this thread-fiber layer.

This is just one of the features that makes SQL Server as powerful as it is. You control the configuration of the pool via the *max worker threads* configuration option (see Chapter 4). You can also determine if your Enterprise Edition of SQL Server makes use only of threads or of threads and fibers. If you choose threads and fibers, the server is then placed into *fiber mode*. In fiber mode, SQL Server establishes one thread per CPU and then establishes one fiber per concurrent client connection. The number of fibers issued is based on what you set in the *max worker threads* configuration option (the default is 255).

When SQL Server receives a T-SQL statement over the wire, it issues a free thread or fiber (depending on the mode) from the thread stack to the inbound connection. If there are no free threads or fibers and the max worker threads value has not been reached, SQL Server will allocate a new thread or fiber. If the thread ceiling has been reached, SQL Server will have to find threads or fibers that are not being used and free them up.

While you may be tempted to set the *max worker threads* configuration higher than the default, you should note that a point will be reached at which SQL Server performance will begin to deteriorate. The reason is simple: Thread and fiber management and creation themselves consume resources, and a runaway thread scenario can bring an application to a standstill. In any event, most of the threads created spend a lot of time waiting around doing nothing, and they can safely be freed and reused without reallocation of resources—so you should never have a need to set the *max worker threads* value higher than the 255 default.

SQL Server Transaction Architecture

Every DBMS system needs to be a good OLTP system. This means that the integrity of the data must be ensured by the transactions that take place in the database whenever data is read, written, removed, or updated.

A *transaction* is a complete unit of work from the start of a query to the end of a query. A transaction cannot be broken or suspended, or resumed at some later date, without risking the integrity of the data, because it cannot lock up or command the exclusive service of the entire DBMS. Other transactions also need to do work in the DBMS (concurrency); that's the purpose of a DBMS or an OLTP system. A transaction cannot own the DBMS, exclusively holding or locking it until its work completes sometime in the unknown future.

Integrity is ensured by an *all or nothing* philosophy (atomicity). In other words, a transaction must complete without errors or not at all. A typical transaction is represented by the following code:

```
BEGIN TRANSACTION
      INSERT INTO CustDetails (CustID) VALUES ('15')
COMMIT TRANSACTION
```

A database table is assumed to be in a consistent or plausible state at the beginning of a transaction. The client signals the start of a transaction; this can be done explicitly by enclosing the transaction steps between, typically, the BEGIN TRANSACTION—COMMIT TRANSACTION statements. Transactions can also be started implicitly in SQL Server without BEGIN . . . COMMIT by merely sending a T-SQL query to the server, which places it into autocommit mode.

During the transaction, the DBMS takes whatever steps it needs to take in the execution of a query to maintain the integrity of the data under control of the transaction. At this point, the transaction "owns" the data it is currently working with, but at any point in the transaction the data may be in an inconsistent state. If multiple tables are being referenced or updated in the transaction, they naturally cannot all be updated at exactly the same time. During the course of the transaction, some rows may be updated and others not.

If an error thus occurs during the transaction, tables that have not yet been touched by the transaction will be left out of the loop. In the case of an error, a ROLLBACK TRANSACTION is required to restore all data affected in the transaction to its previous state. If no error occurs and the transaction completes successfully, the COMMIT TRANSACTION can be issued. After the issuance of a commit, all modifications become part of the database.

As discussed in Chapter 2, the transaction log provides us with the ability to roll back the database to a former state, even if the transactions were successful. The transaction logs record the sequence of events in a transaction from start to finish. The log contains sufficient information to either redo, or *roll forward*, a transaction or undo, or *roll back*, a transaction. The subject of recovery and the work performed by transaction logs is fully covered in Chapters 7 through 9.

Isolation, Concurrency, and Locking Architecture

Isolation and concurrency management is part and parcel of transaction management. All DBMS systems implement a system of isolation and concurrency mechanisms to ensure that multiple transactions, representing at least two and perhaps many thousands of users all working on the same database at the same time, are able to access the same data at—almost—the same time without crashing into each other. The isolation algorithms implemented by a DBMS, SQL Server included, also ensure that the transactions being instantiated by concurrent sessions in the DBMS do not interfere with one another.

Two concurrency specifications underpin the methods for ensuring concurrency: *pessimistic concurrency control* and *optimistic concurrency control*. They are defined as follows:

- **Pessimistic concurrency control** consists of a system of locking mechanisms that prevents more than one application from accessing the same data at the same time. The reason it is called *pessimistic concurrency control* is that it is deployed, usually, in high-transaction situations in which it is highly likely that many connections are going to contend for the same data in an uncontrolled state. Most transaction applications fall into this category. Shopping carts on the Web are a good example of a high-transaction environment in which the middle tier is required to open a huge number of connections to the same database and access the same rows of data for all the connections.

- **Optimistic concurrency control** involves situations in which connections or client applications do not lock the data they are accessing. The system simply checks the data, and if a contention arises, someone has to stand down from his or her transaction and start over. Optimistic control is possible in low-traffic or highly controlled environments.

Your applications or solutions will have to take into account the cost of locking database objects during transactions. Many high-stakes or mission-critical applications are controlled by a single scheduler that is perfectly aware of all the transaction threads it is establishing to a database server, such as a PBX system. Locking and unlocking are resource intensive, and the milliseconds that add up might cause serious problems for the application. A single scheduler needs to be aware of how and when contentions arise and deal with them using optimistic concurrency control algorithms.

On the other hand, most transaction processing DBMS environments will use locking mechanisms, especially when all sessions or connections are established by independent applications on the client, most likely initiated by human users who have no idea who else is in the databases they are working in.

Locks and Latches

SQL Server 2005 makes use of a sophisticated locking architecture to implement pessimistic concurrency control. Locking is essential in a system that can potentially have tens of thousands of users all working with the same pool of data. Locking is a means of enforcing or ensuring data integrity. It is a system of assurances that allow a process to safely work with data and to be assured that data is not going to be changed "behind its back," so to speak.

Locks are managed on a connection basis. In other words, a connection *AA* that requires a lock cannot use the lock created by connection *AB*, even if both connections were initiated by the same client application. Each connection must establish a lock created exclusively within the context of its connection. An exception can be found in the concept of bound connections, but I leave that subject for discussion in Chapter 16.

SQL Server also supports several types of locking modes. The modes include *shared, update, exclusive, intent,* and *schema.* Lock modes indicate the level of dependency the connection obtains on the locked object. SQL Server also controls how the lock modes relate to one another. You cannot, for example, obtain an exclusive lock on an object if shared locks are already acquired on the same object.

SQL Server threads or fibers place locks on databases, tables, rows, indexes, keys, key ranges, and pages. This approach is known as *locking granularity*. The locking granularity is dynamically determined by SQL Server (during formulation of the query plan discussed later) and needs no overt action on the part of the application or you, although this does not preclude the application from requesting a specific lock and lock mode. SQL Server determines exactly what locking level is needed for each T-SQL query it receives. One query may generate a row-level lock, while another may generate a lock that smacks down the entire database. The connections also respect the locks, no matter what the levels. In other words, if connection *AA* has a table lock on data, connection *AB* is prevented from establishing a row lock on the same table.

From time to time, SQL Server may decide to escalate a lock. For example, if a row-level lock consumes most of a table, the relational engine may escalate the lock to the whole table. The query processor usually determines the correct lock required by the query.

Locks are maintained only for the length of time needed to protect data at the level requested by the client. For example, share locks in SQL Server are held for a duration that depends on the transaction isolation level. The default transaction isolation level is READ COMMITTED, which corresponds to a share lock that persists as long as it takes to read the data. Scans also result in locks, but the duration of the lock in a scan is much shorter— essentially as long as it takes to scan the page and place a lock on the next page. Other locks are held for the duration of transactions, such as when a transaction isolation level is set to REPEATABLE READ or SERIALIZABLE READ (which are "clean" reads requiring noninterference by any other process).

Cursors are also protected from concurrency operations. A cursor may acquire a share-mode scroll lock to protect a fetch. Scroll locks are typically held until the end of a transaction. And updates also require locks on data, for the duration of the update transaction.

Like all modern DBMS systems, SQL Server includes mechanisms to prevent lock conflicts. If a connection attempts to acquire a lock on data that is already locked, the late connection is blocked from obtaining the lock and essentially waits until the first connection has completed the transaction. You will have to write your own "lock wait" handler in the client or stored procedure to decide how long your application's thread will wait for the opportunity to lock data. Applications obtain their locks on a first-come, first-served basis.

SQL Server also supports deadlock detection. The detection is proactive. In other words, an algorithm is employed to go out and ensure that threads are not frozen in a *lock deadlock*, which is a condition in a DBMS when two or more connections (mostly two) have blocked each other in a deadly embrace. If SQL Server detects such a condition, it will terminate one of the transaction threads, which will allow the remaining thread to continue (see "Deadlocking" in Chapters 16 and 17).

Latching and the Storage Engine

The storage engine manages another concurrency mechanism known as a *latch*. Latches occur when the relational engine asks the storage engine to return a row during the processing of a query. The storage engine latches the data page to ensure that no other process modifies the page during a transaction. For example, a latch will ensure that the page offset table entry pointing to the row does not get changed until the transaction has completed.

Reading and Writing the Data Pages

In previous versions of SQL Server, versions 6.5 and earlier, and other legacy DBMS products, the storage functionality and the relational functionality were part and parcel of a single unit. Since version 7.0 the two areas of functionality are encapsulated in separate engines: the storage engine and the relational engine. Both engines include a number of submodules responsible for the reading and writing of data. For the most part, you do not need to concern yourself with the core architecture; however, an understanding of how SQL Server accesses data will help you decide if you need to improve performance with additional or fewer indexes, or if you need to rewrite queries and so forth.

The role played by the storage engine was described in Chapter 2, but it works closely with the relational engine, across the OLE DB "bridge" that is the means by which the two components interface. This is illustrated in Figure 3-1. All read requests are generated by the relational engine, which makes use of specialized access algorithms (encapsulated in access objects) to read data in tables, with or without indexes or other objects.

Access methods are not part of any standard, such as SQL. The language is too abstract for that (although I will discuss Data Definition Language and the syntax for creating and working with indexes in Chapter 12). And access methods are proprietary; each vendor is free to do something special.

The relational engine determines the access method it needs to use to obtain data. These methods might involve local table scans, remote table scans, foreign tables scans, native files reads, index scans, keyed reads, and so on. The combination of these methods determines the general pattern of reads used by SQL Server. SQL Server can make use of a number of different access methods, including the Indexed Sequential Access Method (ISAM), which is used by desktop database systems such as Microsoft Access and Microsoft FoxPro. The database architecture discussed in Chapter 2 makes the reading of data as fast and efficient as possible.

How Data Is Saved

SQL Server works with a singly linked list that contains the addresses of free buffer pages. As soon as a data-reading thread requires a buffer page, it uses the first page in the free buffer list. We say that data pages are *dirty* when they contain data that has not been written to disk. Each buffer page contains a reference counter and an indicator that specifies

FIGURE 3-1
The relational engine and the storage engine are separate components of SQL Server 2005 (all editions)

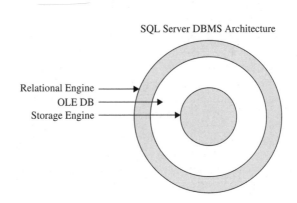

SQL Server DBMS Architecture

Relational Engine

OLE DB

Storage Engine

whether the data page contains dirty data. Every time a query references a buffer page, the reference counter is incremented.

Each instance of SQL Server maintains a lazywriter thread that has the honor of scanning through the buffer cache. Its first job upon system startup is checking the size of the free buffer list. If the free buffer list is below a certain preset point, which depends on the size of the cache, more free pages are added. The buffer pages are scanned frequently by the lazywriter thread, and at each scan the reference counter in the buffer page header is divided by 4. The remainder of the division is discarded. Finally when the reference counter is reduced to 0, the dirty page indicator is checked. If the indicator specifies that the page is dirty, the lazywriter schedules an event to save the data to disk. The writer event coincides with a free buffer page value that is predetermined internally.

The log files come into the picture because data in the buffer cache is first written to the transaction log as the transaction progresses. The purpose of writing to the log first is to allow SQL Server to roll back or roll forward the data before it is committed to the table. Then, in the event of a problem that causes suspect or no data to be written to the table on the physical disk, the commit or bad data can be rolled back. After the data is written to disk and the commit is sound, or if the data page did not contain dirty data, it is freed. Associations between the buffer pages and the physical data pages are removed. Finally the buffer page is returned to the free list. The size of the free buffer list is internally decided by SQL Server and cannot be configured by the DBA.

The writing of the transaction logs takes place outside of the regimen scheduled by the threads working on the buffer and data pages. The *commit* directive forces all pending log transactions to be written to disk.

SQL, Query Optimization, and Query Processing

It might seem a bit patronizing to call attention to the *query* word in Structured Query Language (SQL). It is crucial, though, that you as a PC database developer or administrator understand the special significance of the word in SQL Server, even in SQL Server Desktop Engine, which will replace Jet as the default Access database. Most Microsoft Access users, for example, never really construct or work with more than the most basic SQL statements, because most of the time they are working at a very high, often visual, level above the database and doing little else than storing data and navigating a grid. But for C/S databases in general and SQL Server in particular, everything you do starts and ends with the SQL query.

On the face of it, a *query* is a question or an enquiry into the data in the DBMS, but a SQL query goes a lot further than being just a question. A SQL query can be combined with Data Definition Language (DDL) and Data Manipulation Language (DML) to create and manipulate storage objects within a database; to add, delete, and transform data in the data storage objects; and to inquire into and analyze that data. And database management systems are managed and driven by humans using SQL.

Each database manufacturer supports the SQL standard. And to support custom and proprietary extensions in their products, they have each extended SQL in certain ways. To extend the SQL language to suit proprietary extensions in SQL Server, Microsoft invented the Transact-SQL extensions to the language. And now Transact-SQL, or rather T-SQL, is the de facto language you use to talk to SQL Server. If you have a background in standard SQL, adopting T-SQL will be easy. T-SQL is covered in Part III.

A good database client application should never place the burden of constructing SQL query statements on application users. I have been developing database applications for many years, and every client eventually requests features that enable users to sort, group, and interpret data. Even the smallest companies I have dealt with, three to four computers max, would tell me they need to know why they are doing better or worse this year than last, and that they need data that can shed light on the health of their businesses. And yet we experienced DBAs tend to think that data analysis is only for the Fortune 500.

How we allow our users to query and analyze data without having to learn SQL is a challenge. And if you think you can get away with giving them simple SQL to use for queries, then you can forget about the language of OLAP CUBES. When I first stumbled onto the multidimensional expression (MDX), I tripled my health insurance.

We tackle this tricky subject in later chapters, which cover the English Query. A good start on this road to user empowerment is to appreciate that SQL is really a very high-level language. It is the language that developers and administrators use to "talk" to a DBMS in a language and syntax that have been widely adopted, but at the developer or administrator level, and not the general user level. We will return to this thread in later chapters.

No DBMS, SQL Server included, uses (or can use) SQL as a procedural or instructional language. It is used to convey to the DBMS what a client requires; the server goes off and makes use of any optimal computer language it has been programmed to use to satisfy the request, after the SQL code has been translated.

At a lower level than SQL, the methods used to manipulate and analyze data are both algebraic and calculus in nature. In other words, the procedures to satisfy a query or directive on data are based on mathematical formulations. If we were required to study "raw" relational algebra or relational calculus, there would not be many of us DBAs and SQL developers around, but SQL Server is precisely programmed to deal with that. Consider the following expression:

```
TX WHERE EXISTS CREDITX
    (CREDITX < 5 AND
    T ( T#:TX, CREDIT:CREDITX, STATE:'NEW YORK'))
```

This is relational calculus, and the SQL version is

```
SELECT * FROM CUSTOMERS WHERE CreditRating < 5 AND State = 'NEW YORK'
```

For most of us, talking to a computer in such mathematical terms is difficult, to say the least. SQL, on the other hand, lets us talk to the computer in more comfortable terms. Hebrew is one of the best comparisons as a communications language. The old Hebrew comprises certain vowels and variations adopted by the ancient Rabbis who used the language to talk to God (whether God replied is another matter). Today, however, Hebrew is also available in a form without the vowels and variations of the Biblical code, which makes it a better lingua franca for the Jewish people of Israel, and yet a third variation of Hebrew, very different from the former, is used for handwriting.

The view from SQL on the underlying data is no different from the view from C# on machine code. You would only need to go down to assembler if you were writing code for the low levels of the operating system and talking directly to hardware. In the same way, a developer would not use the internal language of the database server unless he or she were programming logic into the engine, or creating a new engine.

To sum up, then, SQL offers a wide range of developers, administrators, and advanced analysts a means of conversing with a database management system. SQL is not ideal or enabled in any way to work directly on the data structures, storage systems, and mechanisms of a database.

But the computer still needs to translate our requirements into its own language, which is better optimized and suited to perform relational algebra and relational calculus at the lower level to carry out the queries. This field of study in databases is known as *query optimization.*

What Is Query Optimization?

If SQL's SELECT statement imposed constant procedures on the database engine, they would all operate in an identical fashion to obtain a result set. The net result would be inflexible architecture and the inability of the engine to take advantage of new technology, new processing power, and zillions of variables.

In the study of analytical problem solving, you learn that there is always more than one solution to a problem, and millions of possible outcomes, palatable or not. The methods used to query data address problems that can be solved in a variety of different ways.

The cliché "There are many ways to skin a cat" describes the problem that query optimization was obviously created to address. A result set can be derived through many different steps, and the optimizer's job is to evaluate each query to determine the quickest means of solving the query problem for the least cost. Cost analysis, performed by most database servers, and especially SQL server, is applied mainly in terms of file I/O (as opposed to I/O on rowsets), with memory and other resources being taken into account. The cost analysis is then combined with each step in the query, and an optimum *execution plan* is the result.

Of course, it is possible for a genius to knock out a theorem that proposes a solution an optimizer might deduce . . . after all, humans are responsible for the logic used by a computer to make such deductions in the first place. But a computer is able to solve such puzzles far quicker than humans, no matter their IQs. The computer, or its optimizer module, is suitably equipped to perform that optimization with a benefit of addressable memory that can tell it about the form that data is in (such as data types and structure), the number of records in a table, the number of distinct values, and so on. The optimizer is capable of taking into account all this data while it determines how best to carry out the whims of its users, expressed as SQL.

Optimization is thus a fundamental database server function that is required to empower a database server product to achieve acceptable performance and to continue to better this performance as it evolves. It is also needed because instructions received from humans in the form of SQL (and now XML) are too high above its native processing architecture to serve any performance function. And the more widely adopted SQL becomes, the more opportunity a database server has of becoming better at what it does at the low level. Humans don't care about how optimal a SQL statement is for a server, but they will notice if a query takes a few milliseconds longer to produce results, which can easily turn into seconds or minutes or hours the more complex the query and the fewer the resources available. In other words SQL Server has to care about optimization. Its life depends on it.

The Optimization Process

Every database server, every version of SQL Server, and every other DBMS system, such as those produced by Sybase and Oracle, are required to take the standard SQL request and convert it into the procedural language each product uniquely understands. How each product converts the SQL statement and what it then does with it are what make it unique. Algorithms, techniques, and guile are what are used to acquire market share and set the products apart from each other.

An UPDATE may cause triggers, functions, stored procedures, and integrity constraints to fire. These events thus kick off a chain reaction resulting in the opening of other result set comparisons and complex evaluations of collateral or linked data. A simple UPDATE could actually result in a hefty execution plan . . . a query domino effect, in a manner of speaking.

Although the optimizer is cost-based, it cannot be accurate all the time. What's more, a point of diminishing returns must come when the optimizer must realize that it cannot optimize any further, and that performance may even suffer on all further optimizations. So a certain amount of heuristic logic has to be built into a DBMS engine to allow it to determine when to draw the line . . . or decide when more is becoming less. SQL Server is no exception.

SQL Server invokes a number of essential steps that are required to optimize a query, but it is worthwhile to mention the three most important ones here:

- It must first transform the query into the low-level language of the engine. And it can do this by first parsing the SQL statement.

- It must then identify the possible procedures it can use to satisfy the query. Remember, the query can be manipulative, resultant, or both. This is essentially the optimization process.

- It must then generate query plans and choose the one that costs the least.

Let's look at the first steps taken by the SQL Server optimizer code:

The SELECT or any other SQL statement is a standard request format and does not influence procedures or invoke or define the functionality of the engine and its capability to extract or update data. It is merely a means of requesting and updating data and presenting it in a certain way. It does not tell the server how to go about getting that data, but the server understands what is required of it from the syntax and keywords of the SELECT statement. In other words, the SELECT statement is a "desire" or an end—not a means to obtain the end.

NOTE *I mentioned XML earlier, and it is important to see XML both as an extension to T-SQL and as an extended definition language for SQL Server. A powerful XML parser has been built into this product for the past several years.*

For the record, the SELECT statement is used to define only the following things:

- The format of the result set returned to the client. Usually the default format is sufficient for the client because it follows the schematic layout of the columns, but often "qualifiers" such as GROUP BY and ORDER BY clauses instruct the engine to present the data in alternative formats.

- The objects, mostly tables, that contain the data, or a part of the data, required by the client. The FROM clause is the subordinate component in a SELECT statement that identifies the source of the data. The FROM clause can specify more than one source.

- How tables and other source objects are connected for a combined result set. The JOIN clause is another subordinate clause that specifies the logical connection of the two or more data sources.

- Conditions or criteria that row data must meet to be included in the selection process. The subordinate clauses include the WHERE and HAVING statements.

Before the SQL statement—or the services requested by it—is passed to the query optimizer, it must first be validated by the statement parser, which is part of the greater relational engine, as opposed to the kernel we talked about earlier. The parser ensures that the SQL statement is syntactically correct and that it will be fully understood and productive. If the SQL code you sent is flawed, the parser will "throw" an exception and return a syntax error to the client application. (The error is sent out-of-band to the client; in other words, it is sent via a separate channel and not via the connection established by the client. SQL Server's error reporting mechanisms are explained more fully in Chapter 4.)

If the syntax "flies," the parser will break the statement into logical units. Such units include keywords, parameters or arguments, operators, and identifiers. The parser scans the text, inspecting delimiters, and determines what represents actual objects and what represents row values or variables. You can specify how SQL Server should evaluate what you send it. For example, you can change the character that represents a delimiter in a SQL Server statement. This can be done interactively through settings in Management Studio or in T-SQL code (in similar fashion to *define* statements in C or C++ code). We will deal with such advanced subjects in the programming chapters in Part III.

NOTE *Many a SQL Server expert will come to a situation that might require (or tempt) him or her to second-guess the optimizer and suggest a "hint" for consideration. While you might not be so bold, it is important to understand the factors that can influence performance.*

When all parsing is complete, the parser performs a grouping function, breaking down complex statements into smaller logical collections of routines and operations. In this fashion, using typical problem-solving techniques, the best query execution plan can be determined. In other words, the last function of the parser is to help the optimizer, which kicks in next, to see the "wood" for the "trees" in a complex request, thus contributing to the best execution plan. It is thus fitting that the format into which the original T-SQL statement is translated is called the *query tree*.

NOTE *A query tree is also known as a syntax tree or a sequence tree.*

The kernel finally compiles the query tree into a series of operations to perform against native rowsets stored in the databases. The kernel gains access to the databases via the services of the storage engine. The relational kernel and the storage kernel communicate via the OLE DB API using standard SQL SELECT statements that OLE DB can pass to the storage engine. (As you are aware, OLE DB is complex to code against—hence ADO and ADO.NET—but it is highly efficient and ideal for the interlocution of two kernels.) The following code represents a simple SELECT query issued by the relational engine to the storage engine:

```
SELECT CustID FROM CustDetails
```

Obviously, the execution plan here is a no-brainer for the kernel because the SELECT statement is of the simplest form. The plan here would thus consist of a simple SELECT statement. This is represented in the simple flow diagram illustrated in Figure 3-2.

The operations are defined against table or index objects or are both stored in the database. If no index objects are defined against the data, the execution plan is constructed only to perform the necessary table scan.

But what takes place when a SELECT statement rivaling Fermat's Last Theorem arrives over the wire? Here is something a little more complex, but still relatively simple:

```
USE MODERNIZE
SELECT OD.OrderID, OD.CustomerID, CUST.ContactName
 FROM dbo.Orders OD INNER JOIN
 dbo.Customers CUST ON OD.CustomerID = CUST.CustomerID
```

What you have here is a request for the return of two result sets from two tables that are joined to form a third result set. Although it is still not the most complex SELECT, the kernel breaks the statement into two execution steps, one for each table. It will call the OLE DB OPENROWSET method once for each table and then finally perform the necessary join of each rowset returned. When the relational kernel has finished working with the storage engine, it will format the result set to be sent to the client into the necessary tabular format and place that back onto the wire.

So what intervention, insight, or control do you have on the process I have just described? The good news for DBAs and developers is that SQL Server 2005 comes equipped with some marvelous tools to play with. Besides query hints, SQL Server Management Studio (see Chapter 4) will let you test a query for syntax, check out the execution plan, estimate execution plans, and so forth. It even lets you inspect the metrics derived in the optimization process, in calculations, and in steps taken to carry out the execution plan. I don't want to go into much detail about the SQL Query Analyzer here, because we use it a lot in the chapters in Part III. You will also later investigate and learn about the Index Tuning Wizard introduced in Chapter 12.

FIGURE 3-2
The steps taken by SQL Server to parse and optimize a T-SQL statement and create an execution plan

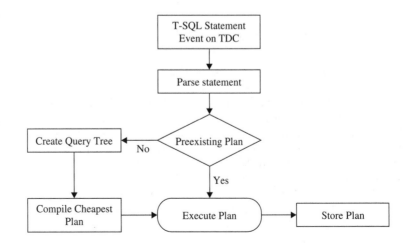

How the SQL Server query processor resolves indexes, views, partitioned views, stored procedures, and so on is discussed in the chapters that focus on these areas.

Caching and Reusing Execution Plans

Most SELECT statements are identical or may differ only in the values specified in the search expression. Consider the following SELECT statements:

```
SELECT * FROM CustOrds WHERE OrdValue < '400'
SELECT * FROM CustOrds WHERE OrdValue < '1000'
SELECT * FROM CustOrds WHERE OrdValue < ?
```

It is no doubt obvious that an intelligent optimizer will deduce that the preceding SELECT statements are likely to result in the same or very similar execution plans. It therefore would make no sense for SQL Server to recompile an execution plan if one has already been compiled for a previous user not too long ago.

SQL Server thus maintains a pool of memory, called the *procedure cache,* that it uses to store both execution plans and data buffers. I might add that the preceding examples are very simple, and if SQL Server determines that it would cost more to store such a plan than to recompile it, the plan will not be stored. The memory pool size varies and is different from system to system. It also changes according to state of the system. Any number of users can reuse SQL Server execution plans.

To further support a reuse policy, SQL Server also maintains a parameter data structure that is used to store the parameters sent in by each user. These structures are known as *execution contexts.* SQL Server places each user—actually each connection— executing a query into an execution context.

An execution plan that matches a user's query can be used instead of compiling a new execution plan. SQL Server needs only to obtain the parameter or variable value in the SQL statement and combine that with the already compiled execution plan. The result represents significant savings in time and resources, which translates into better response time by the end user.

At any time a statement is sent to the server, the server will first inspect the procedure cache to see if there is an existing execution plan that can satisfy the SQL statement.

NOTE *A number of factors can cause SQL Server to drop a plan. A change of data type is such a factor.*

The saving comes by obviating the need to build a new execution plan. It should thus be obvious that you can do a lot in your code to ensure that your SQL statements have a higher probability of being matched. Your goal as a DBA and systems programmer is to increase the chance that SQL Server will reuse complex plans that have already been compiled. The use of parameters in stored procedures and parameter markers in ADO, OLE DB, and ODBC applications goes a long way to ensuring this. No doubt this becomes more difficult when we start dealing with NULL values and three- and four-dimensional values, which will be discussed in Chapter 17.

The execution plan and context-matching algorithms have been enhanced in SQL Server 2005, and this greatly improves performance over versions 2000 and earlier. Like SQL Server 2000, SQL Server 2005 keeps the execution plan in the procedure cache until it is needed. Only old and unused plans are purged from the cache when space is needed and, obviously, when the system is restarted.

TIP *The DBCC FREEPROCCACHE is a directive you can use to purge the procedure cache and force SQL Server to recompile the procedure.*

The algorithm maintains an age counter that contains a replica of the query cost factor. This replica is incremented by the cost value in the age field each time the object is referenced by a connection. For example, let's say a query plan is given a cost factor of eight. Each time it is referenced, the value in the age counter doubles, becoming 16, 32, 64, and so forth. The lazywriter process, discussed earlier in this chapter, periodically scans the procedure cache and decrements each number in the age field by 1. Eventually, if the query plan is not being used, it is devalued to 0 and thereafter ignored. The plan will be kept in the cache until SQL Server needs memory, and any plans at 0 will be flushed.

There are other reasons to destroy the execution plans. They include the following:

- The schema is altered or objects, such as tables, are dropped or changed (the ALTER TABLE or ALTER VIEW statement is an example of such a change that will flush the cache).

- An index used by a plan is dropped.

- You explicitly issue a request to recompile (this is done by calling the sp_recompile stored procedure).

- Keys are being significantly changed. This could result from excessive transaction processing that fundamentally alters the table referenced by a query.

- Triggers, stored procedures, functions, and so forth are placed on tables referenced by your plan.

- Any function that causes the table to grow considerably will render an execution plan obsolete.

The subject of optimization and execution plans is exhaustive but essential when it comes to fine-tuning and optimization of both systems and applications, for DBMS systems in general and SQL Server in particular. In later chapters, you will build on the foundation you have gained in this chapter.

Inside Data Streams, Again

In the next chapter—in the section "Inside SQL Server Data Streams"—we will discuss the TDS, packet-moving mechanisms, that encapsulate data in a special transmission format that is sent to and from the server. TDS, however, is a constantly evolving protocol, and as SQL Server matures like the finest sauvignon, so will you have to deal with ensuring that legacy clients configured or developed for down-level TDS access can send and receive data to the server.

For the most part, down-level support requires no special intervention or labor on your part because SQL Server 2005, which is version 9.0 TDS, talks to TDS version 8.0 and lower versions. However, there are a few points that can trip you up.

The advanced data type support in TDS 9.0 can choke a TDS 4.2 client. TDS 4.2 was originally built for SQL Server 4.2, and the protocol was inherited by versions 6.0 and 6.5. It became obsolete with the great rewrite "event" of SQL Server in 1997 and 1998, which begot SQL Server 7.0 with its TDS 7.0 protocol. The TDS changed again with the advent of SQL Server 2000.

Specifically, TDS 4.2 clients do not support Unicode data types. When it happens that a TDS 4.2 client pulls Unicode data out of a version 8.0 table, the relational engine will have to convert the data to legacy character data before it can be sent onward to the client. What will happen is that Unicode data that has no ASCII equivalent, and there are more than 65,000 such characters, will draw a blank, literally, when it sends the data back. The result set data will then be full of holes back at the client.

NOTE *Unicode, or the Unicode Character System (UCS), is a two-byte (16-bit) system that represents all the languages of the world in a collection of 65,536 characters. ASCII is a 7- or 8-bit (1-byte) system that can only support 256 characters. Comparing TDS 4.2 and 9.0 is like comparing the vocabulary of a two-year-old with the vocabulary of an adult.*

TDS 4.2 clients do not support the version 7.0 and version 8.0 char, varchar, binary, and varbinary data types that are larger than 255 bytes, and SQL Server will thus truncate any values it needs to return to the client through TDS 4.2. As mentioned in Chapter 2, the preceding data types can now hold data up to 8,000 bytes.

TDS 7.0 clients also come up a little short against SQL Server 2005 and TDS 9.0. The sql_variant data type (discussed at length in Chapter 10 and Appendix) is not new to SQL Server 2005 but is essentially "Greek" to TDS 7.0. The relational engine will need to convert any data type of sql_variant to Unicode before transmission. TDS 4.2 clients need not apply.

What then is your strategy for ensuring that your clients can interpret and correctly present TDS 9.0 data? If you are new to SQL Server support and administration and are taking over a DBA function, you will need to know this.

First, as I will often repeat in this book, "thinner is better." The thinner the client, the less work you have to do later—as both a developer and a DBA—when new versions of SQL Server ship (roughly every five years). There is nothing worse for a DBA than to have to upgrade hundreds or thousands of fat clients that have more components than an early twentieth-century chronometer. And we'll debate client versus server processing again in Chapter 16, as well as *n*-tier deployment strategies in Chapter 17.

Second, when a client connects to SQL Server, its TDS packets are built according to the logic programmed into the data provider it is using. The data provider could be either the Microsoft OLE DB provider for SQL Server, or the ODBC driver, or the DB-Library DLL (which is currently in the sunset years of its life). So you need to ensure that your clients are calling the correct versions of these drivers or providers on their computers; otherwise, the TDS packets they will be sending will be targeted to earlier versions of SQL Server. This does not cause as many problems for data on the way in, because the server-side libraries will be able to understand the inbound packets. The problems arise, as discussed, when the packets are sent back to the client and data get transformed beyond recognition. A blob of thousands of bytes will just not make it to the other side, because SQL Server will see that you connected on TDS 4.2 and make the necessary adjustments.

Pulling the Relational Train

What I describe in this chapter is very sparse in comparison to what SQL Server does to execute the fastest queries and return data quickly to impatient clients. There are a number of collateral processes that take place, and I describe them in later chapters as necessary. You will also be introduced to techniques that can produce more efficient queries that result in faster responses from SQL Server 2005.

Connecting to and Administering the Database Engine

The responsibilities of the SQL Server database administrator (DBA) have changed a lot in recent years. As popular as this DBMS is now, its DBA of the not-too-distant past was not your typical data center resident guru. After all, it was not too long ago that a gigabyte of memory in a Windows server was as wild an idea as growing asparagus on Mars.

Prior to version 7.0, SQL Server was outclassed in many high-end services, such as mission-critical support for huge numbers of concurrent users, very large databases (VLDBs), and a service level supporting tens of thousands of transactions per minute. The mainframe and midrange DBAs had it all—and nothing could challenge their eminence. Or so they thought.

This chapter highlights the administrative functionality that ships with SQL Server 2005, as well as the APIs and architectures that provide all the necessary hooks that can be used to directly program its maintenance and administrative services.

The Server-Side Components

A very powerful collection of server components makes up the so-called "back end" of SQL Server 2005. The collection consists of the following components:

- **Database Engine**   Implemented in the MSSQLServer service
- **SQL Server Agent**   Implemented in the SQLServerAgent service
- **Full-Text Search**   Implemented as the SQL Server FullText Search
- **Microsoft Distributed Transaction Coordinator (MS DTC or just DTC)**   Implemented as the Distributed Transaction Coordinator service

The SQL Server FullText Search (formerly Microsoft Search) service is not available on any client or workstation operating system. SQL Server 2005, like its predecessors, can also be installed in multiple instances, even on the same host Windows Server 2003 computers. Each instance is controlled by its own set of services; however, the DTC (overview coming up) is shared among all the instances on the same host. You can also run different versions of

SQL Server on the same server. Working with multiple instances and different versions is not further covered in this book.

The Server components can be started and stopped in a number of ways:

- On startup of the operating system, determined by the Service Control Manager (SCM) and cluster resources on failover nodes.

- From the command line or command prompt using the *net* commands or directly executing the service executable.

Let's now look briefly at the four server components that, combined, make up the SQL Server 2005 DBMS.

The Database Engine

As we have discussed in the first three chapters, the Microsoft SQL Server 2005 database engine, MSSQLServer, manages the databases and all related files and mechanisms that its instance owns on the host server. It is also responsible for processing all the T-SQL statements sent to it by client applications and processes. It also controls the execution of SQL Server components (the objects) installed in the database, such as stored procedures, triggers, CLR-hosted stuff, and the various integrity mechanisms we will be discussing in forthcoming chapters.

The SQL Server Database Engine *is* the DBMS. It is the only engine on the server that creates and manages the databases, juggles concurrent connections, enforces security, processes queries, builds and applies indexes, and so on. The database engine, which we will refer to as the DBMS from here on, is the largest and most important SQL Server entity. The collateral services such as Analysis Services and the reporting components are beyond the scope of this book.

SQL Server Agent

SQL Server Agent has been designed to make the job of the DBA a lot easier, lowering TCO and the administrative burden. It is essentially a service that is used to schedule mainte-nance routines and activities on a target server. It is also used to monitor DBMS activities and alert operators or the DBAs, to potential threats and problems. The SQL Server Agent service is accessed and managed in Management Studio and is divided into the following three services. This architecture has been similarly implemented in a number of Windows services, such as the Removable Storage Services:

- **Alerts** These are the actions that need to be taken when a specific event occurs on the server. Errors are good examples of alerts that a DBA or operator needs to be made aware of. For example, errors generated by incorrect logins or security problems can be sent to a DBA via e-mail, paging or beeper services, the Windows messenger service, or a telephone call. The alert mechanism can also be configured to run certain jobs.

- **Operators** The Operators service lets you define operators using their domain accounts or e-mail IDs. These people are typically members of a "database adminis-trators group" defined in a Windows domain. You can send messages to all operators using a single e-mail message that gets sent to a group.

- **Jobs**   The jobs are the collections of steps that get executed by the Agent service. Jobs are defined in the service and then scheduled for execution at a later time or in response to an alert or event.

In addition to the Agent services in Management Studio, you can interface with the SQL Server Agent from applications that use SQL Server Management Objects architecture (SQL-SMO) and from any SQL Server client application that is programmed to transmit T-SQL statements to the server. We will investigate SQL Server Agent and its components later in this chapter.

Full-Text Search

Microsoft Full-Text Search extends the SQL-92 and SQL-2003 definitions for standard character-based searching, which is based on a system of comparison operators (equal to, less than, and greater than) applied to character constants and character strings stored in the database.

The engine, first, supports a powerful indexing model, which is implemented as full-text catalogs and indexes that you define for a database. These are not stored as objects in a SQL Server database but rather as independent files. Second, the engine processes full-text queries and determines which entries in the index meet the full-text selection criteria obtained from user input. The criteria can be words or phrases, words that are within a certain proximity to each other, or the inflections on verbs and nouns.

The search algorithm works as follows: for each search criterion processed by the engine, the identity of a row that meets the criterion and its ranking value is returned to the DBMS, which then builds the result set to return to the client.

The full-text catalogs and indexes are stored on the server in separate files, which are administered by the search service.

The Distributed Transaction Coordinator

The MS DTC is a service that lets you program applications that can work with data drawn from several different data sources in one transaction. It also coordinates the updating of data to different databases, even databases that are installed in remote servers. The DTC is a key component of Microsoft's maximum availability strategy in that it ensures that an UPDATE succeeds on all distributed servers or on none of the servers. We use the DTC when users update data in distributed partitioned views on a federation of SQL Servers.

You can easily enlist the services of DTC in your applications by calling remote stored procedures from your application that apply to all "enlisted" servers. The DTC service can be managed from Management Studio and the SQL Server Configuration Manager. We will return to the DTC in Chapter 9, as part of cluster installation.

SQL Server Logs and Activities

SQL Server logs a huge number of events and activities that you can use for troubleshooting and management from a variety of components. You use the Log File Viewer to display the log files. With the Log File Viewer open, you work within the Select Logs pane to select the logs you wish to display. We will discuss the Log File Viewer later in this chapter.

Connecting to SQL Server

Remember, in Chapter 1 I briefly discussed the client-side application development environments, APIs, and libraries you can use to write applications that connect to SQL Server. Now you will learn about the communications mechanisms and data streams that make it possible for any modern programming language and the management utilities to create applications that can connect to and exchange data with SQL Server.

Interprocess Communications

SQL Server 2005 communicates with its clients via interprocess communication (IPC) mechanisms. A facility of the Win32 API interprocess communications architecture, IPC allows separate or isolated processes to safely communicate with each other. IPC can be invoked between processes on the same host or between remotely placed hosts over a network, even one as large as the Internet. The process on one computer opens a connection to a process running on another computer, and data is transmitted and returned between the two processes. Such a facility makes it easy to communicate and interact with a SQL Server centrally and concurrently with many users.

SQL Server clients can connect to SQL Server, open connections, transmit data such as XML and T-SQL, and call functions and procedures (like .NET services and remote method invocation and other distributed processing architecture). IPC is an asynchronous facility and does not block the client from performing local duties, or even from opening up communications with other processes. If you wish to dig into IPC further, any good book that comprehensively covers the Win32 API will do.

There are two parts to an IPC: the *API* and the *protocol*. The API is the function set used to "speak" to and "listen" to the network IPC. When an IPC is between a client and server on the same host, the local *Named Pipes* or *shared memory* components are used for the IPC. If the processes are split across a network, the network IPC is used. SQL Server has facilities for a number of network IPC options. Now, let's look into SQL Server's so-called Net-Libraries, the staging ground for SQL Server IPC communications.

The Client and Server Net-Libraries

SQL Server makes use of a collection of libraries called Net-Libraries that provide the necessary communication between the client applications and SQL Server. The stack of services in which the Net-Libraries collection is located is illustrated in Figure 4-1, which shows the services listed in the Configuration Manager. Note that Banyan VINES, Multiprotocol, AppleTalk, and NWLink (IPX/SPX) are no longer supported. The Net-Libraries handle the task of calling the IPC APIs to send data from client to server and vice versa. The Net-Library essentially allows the service providers to hand off this task to a separate collection of functions.

The client applications you build or support make a call to one of a number of service providers—ADO.NET, ADO, OLE DB, ODBC, DB-Library, or the Embedded SQL API—which then exchanges data with one of the Net-Libraries supported by SQL Server 2005. Table 4-1 lists the supported Net-Libraries.

If SQL Server is installed on the local host (such as the free SQL Server Express or the SQL Server Developer's Edition), as illustrated in Figure 4-1, the client's shared memory Net-Library is used. If SQL Server is installed on a remote host, the client's network

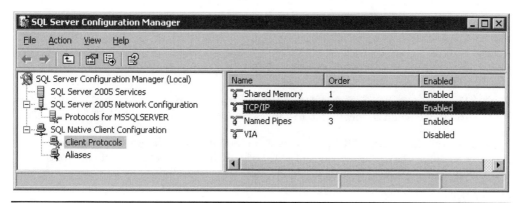

FIGURE 4-1   SQL Server Configuration Manager for managing protocols and SQL Server protocols

Net-Libraries are used to establish IPC communications over the network. The clients can use any of the Net-Libraries available to them.

The Net-Library sits at the top of the network stack, where it filters and routes data to the correct Net-Library dedicated to a protocol. It allows SQL Server to support multiple protocols, which is why it is called the Super Socket Net-Library. At the server end you will find the identical architecture, which allows for communications from the server to the client. In addition, the Primary Net-Library routes packets over legacy networks to any secondary Net-Library routers that may exist on the network. This lets SQL Server support legacy network APIs.

The Net-Library–IPC communications functionality is positioned far below both the client and server processes, and you will have little to do with them. For legacy applications that will connect to SQL Server 2005, you need only configure your applications to support the respective service provider used by your code. ADO.NET and ADO, for example, sit above OLE DB. As a DBA, you might have more to configure, especially if you are not using a Microsoft network. For example, the Primary Net-Library is also used to implement the Secure Sockets Layer (SSL) for encrypted communications between client and server.

Each instance of SQL Server can listen in on a collection of Net-Libraries, and you might find that when you installed SQL Server, you installed the default Net-Library on a network that does not support it. This is where the Client Network Utility comes into the picture.

Working with Net-Libraries

The SQL Server Configuration Manager is used to set up and configure the client and server Net-Libraries. When you install the server, both the client and server Net-Libraries are installed, as is the SQL Server configuration manager. If you're distributing client applications, you may need to ensure that the Microsoft Data Access Components (MDAC) you are supporting in your client are installed on the target computers.

If your applications support the .NET Framework and ADO.NET, then you need only ensure that a version of the .NET Framework that works with your apps is supported on your target computers. SQL Server installs all the Net-Libraries, but only one or two may actually be active. The client and server Net-Libraries can be enabled or disabled, as you need, for each instance of SQL Server and for every client, or proxy process. When you disable a Net-Library, or deactivate it, it remains on the system for later use.

On the client side, you will need to be involved in the following DBA work:

- Enabling or Disabling client Net-Libraries.
- Specifying the order in which client Net-Libraries are made available for all connections (except server aliases).
- Defining server aliases that define specific Net-Libraries and connection parameters to invoke when connecting to instances of SQL Server from version 7.0 and earlier.

The default instance of SQL Server listens on the same default, or preconfigured, network addresses as earlier versions of SQL Server. This allows clients that were once connected to earlier versions of the DBMS to maintain connectivity, albeit to a new version of the server. Table 4-1 shows the default network addresses that instances of SQL Server listen on.

What Table 4-1 also demonstrates is that when your client Net-Library connects to an instance of SQL Server 2005, it needs only the network name of the computer running the instance and the instance name. For example, when your application attempts to connect to SQL Server, *dbnetlib.dll* opens the connection to UDP port 1434 (the monitor) on the computer network name specified in the connection definition. The name need not be a UNC or NetBIOS name either, because the network name could be a TCP/IP address followed by the name of the SQL Server instance. Such hard coding is, however, not good practice or practical for software deployment. And if your network is unable to resolve the name, there is obviously a "pothole" in your network somewhere.

There are several possible causes for a connection failure related to the Net-Libraries over a network:

- The requested instance of SQL Server is not running. The host may be down, or the service may be stopped.
- The Net-Library being invoked on the client is not active on the server. (This is akin to trying to call someone who does not have telephone service.)
- The computer name cannot be resolved. (You could troubleshoot this by trying to attach to a TCP/IP address instead.)
- The SQL Server port 1433 is unavailable. This can happen if the network administrator prevents access to this port, or some other application is blocking the access. For example, over a wide area network, a firewall or a router may inadvertently filter out ports 1433 and 1434.

Net-Library	Default Instance Address	Named Instance Address
TCP/IP Sockets	TCP Port 1433	Chosen dynamically when the instance is started
Named Pipes	\\computername\pipe\sql\query	\\.\pipe\MSSQL$SQLNAME\sql\query

TABLE 4-1   Default Network Address that SQL Server 2005 Monitors

If the client and server are on the same machine, it is relatively easy to reference the default instance.

Inside SQL Server Data Streams

Now that you know how your clients open communications to SQL Server, the client/server communications architecture will become clearer when you find out what gets sent up and down the connection. Client and server make use of an application-level formatting protocol known as the Tabular Data Stream (TDS) to format data for transmission and reception. You might think of this protocol as the pattern-storing technology in your average Star Fleet transporter. Without the pattern protocol, we would not be able to reassemble a human or an object after transportation. TDS packets are encapsulated in the packets that are built by each protocol's Net-Library. The TCP/IP Sockets Net-Library, for example, encapsulates the TDS packets inside the TCP/IP packets or the TCP/IP protocol.

With support for XML, the contents of the TDS packets can be either a relational result set or an XML document. If you specify the FOR XML argument in your T-SQL code, the database engine will stream an XML document back to the application (this is also supported in OLE DB). If FOR XML is not specified, the database engine will send a result set back to the client application.

Without FOR XML, the TDS packet contains the rows of the result set, with each row tabulated to show one or more columns according to what you specify in the SELECT statement. XML is packaged in the TDS packet as one long stream of data, with each packet restricted to being no more than 4KB in size.

SQL Server's packet size can also be configured. The default is the same size as TDS packets. If SQL Server packets are configured smaller than TDS packets, the packets will be disassembled on the sending computer and packaged into smaller packages. The protocols on the client computer reassemble the inbound packets.

SQL Server 2005 Administrative Architecture

In the preceding chapter I provided an insight into the various database and database server architectures on which SQL Server is built. You learned that SQL Server is able to dynamically acquire and free resources as needed. We discussed its ability to automatically manage and self-administer the procedure cache, the buffer cache, the data pages, and so on. You also learned how it processes queries, parses SQL statements, compiles procedure plans, and more. However, with large OLTP or data mining environments, you may still need to monitor the system, institute change control rules, and ensure that your deployment meets the service level requirements you or your customers have set for the system.

SQL Server thus provides a collection of services that allow you to schedule the automatic execution of repetitive tasks, such as backing up data, replication, and running reports. These services also include the SQL Server Agent, which, as mentioned earlier, provides you with a graphical or interactive environment you can use to configure schedules and tasks to run at regular intervals or upon events that occur in SQL Server and in the operating system. You can also program SQL Server to automatically respond to errors and exception conditions, and to send e-mail or pages to operators and on-duty administrators.

Microsoft has also published the administration APIs it used to build the graphical tools that ship with the Developer, Standard, and Enterprise Editions. These APIs support all the administrative services of the server. You can thus code your own applications for end users or include administrative routines in your data-dependent applications. The APIs and programming models have been encapsulated into a management framework, the programming of which is beyond the scope of this book.

Transact-SQL and Stored Procedures for DBAs

In the past chapters, I talked a little bit about Transaction-SQL, or T-SQL. If you are new to SQL Server administration, you should prepare yourself do get your hands dirty with some SQL programming. T-SQL is the language used for all commands sent to SQL Server; however, the language also supports statements that direct administrative functions and work orders in SQL Server. SQL supports several language subdivisions, the most important being Data Definition Language (DDL), which is sometimes called schema definition language, and Data Manipulation Language (DML).

DDL covers the commands that create, alter, and drop database objects, such as tables, indexes, and views. DML is the subdivision of the language that returns the values that are to be found in the tables at any given time and provides the directives for altering or deleting those values. Statements such as SELECT, INSERT, and UPDATE are typical DML directives. T-SQL has extended these subdivisions with directives that SQL Server will understand. A good example is the DENY statement. There are other subdivisions, but we can talk about those in the chapters in Part II and in Appendix.

Stored procedures are also extensively used to manage the internals of SQL Server. A good example is sp_compile, which forces the relational engine to recompile a query plan, or the sp_configure stored procedure, which is used to configure SQL Server (see Appendix).

Higher-level components or management objects, such as the SQL-DMO library we discussed earlier, typically call the T-SQL DDL commands and stored procedures. In other words, the methods used in the high-level objects do not provide any native manipulation or definition code but rather call across town to a DDL definition or some system-level stored procedure.

Introducing SQL Server Tools

It goes without saying that you do not need to program a line of code to effectively administer SQL Server 2005; although you open yourself up to a lot more opportunity if you do. As one Microsoft SQL Server developer put it, "Ya gotta do what ya gotta do to keep your job." My assessment of where SQL Server is going as a product tells me you don't have much to worry about as long as you stay on top of things. Let's now turn to the install and go to tools you can use to administer SQL Server 2005.

SQL Server's GUI and command-line tools and utilities are listed as follows:

- **SQL Server Management Studio**   This is the principal administration suite used to administer SQL Server 2005. It allows you to carry out a number of administrative tasks such as adding servers and server groups; managing users and their rights and permissions; and managing databases, tables, indexes, and so on. Management Studio has query windows that can be used as a developer's test bench for designing and testing T-SQL queries, batches, scripts, and so on (stuff you previously did in Query Analyzer). You can run the studio from the command line by executing SQLWB.EXE. For serious SQL Server development, you will use Visual Studio 2005 because you can step through execution of the stored procedure in it. In addition you also now have **Profiler90.EXE**, which launches the profiler from the command line (see Chapter 18) and **DTA.EXE**, the command-line access to the Database Tuning Advisor (see Chapter 18).

- **Import/Export Wizard**   This tool can be started from within Management Studio from the context menus of the Databases and Tables nodes. This tool is actually a wizard that will take you through the steps required to import and export data from OLE DB and ODBC databases.

- **SQL Profiler**   If you need to capture Microsoft SQL Server events from a server, this is the tool to accomplish that task. You can also use the profiler to audit SQL Server 2005. The profiler and monitoring is covered extensively in Chapter 18.

- **SQL Server Configuration Manager**   This tool is also used to start, stop, or pause the SQL Server services on the server. (I introduced this utility earlier in the chapter). It manages the Net-Libraries that connect to SQL Server clients and servers.

- **Administrative wizards**   A healthy dose of administrative wizards can be accessed from the Management Studio. These include wizards to create backup jobs, indexes, stored procedures, and so on. We will be talking about them in various chapters.

- **Old command line utilities**   A number of command-line utilities ship with SQL Server 2005. These are installed by default into the *%drive%:\Program Files\ Microsoft SQL Server\MSSQL\Binn* folder and the *%drive%:\Program Files\ Microsoft SQL Server\90\Tools\Binn* folder. Among these are utilities that are backward compatible with SQL Server 2000. These are the BCP, ISQL, and OSQL executables. BCP is a tool used for bulk copying of data, while ISQL and OSQL are used to send T-SQL statements to the server from the command line. ISQL works with the OLE DB provider, and OSQL works with the ODBC provider.

- **SQLCMD**   The SQLCMD utility replaces and combines in one command-line environment the OSQL and ISQL programs that were available in the earlier versions of SQL Server. This executable lets you connect to any instance of SQL Server via the OLE DB library. Once connected, you can run any T-SQL script. SQLCMD is especially useful for connecting to a "dead" server via the Dedicated Administrative Connection. You do this by specifying the -A switch at the command prompt.

Let's now turn to an overview of the SQL Server Management Studio. The other graphical and command-line utilities are beyond the scope of this chapter, and I cover them in later chapters.

Getting Started with SQL Server Management Studio

At first glance, SQL Server Management Studio might seem intimidating. So it helps to get an overview of it before you start using it. If you have used SQL Server Management Studio for the Beta or early adopter versions of SQL Server 2005, I suggest you go through this section because there are many new properties to configure, especially with respect to the Windows operating system.

Our work with SQL Server Management Studio here is going to be limited to registering and exposing servers and exploring the various nodes and options. This will help you become familiar with this exhaustive suite of tools so that you know what to grab for when working on SQL Server concurrently with the tough discussions that lie in wait. We will cover starting up, connecting to servers, navigating the environment, and some basic configuration.

Incidentally, Management Studio connects seamlessly to version 8.0 databases, which is SQL Server 2000. You can register version 8.0 databases and access all database objects, such as tables, procs, triggers, views and so on. There is one area I strongly recommend you do not open on SQL Server 2000 with SQL Server Management Studio, and that is Data Transformation Services (DTS) the predecessor to SQL Server Integration Services (SSIS) that now ship with SQL Server 2005.

Management Studio will let you see a list of old DTS packages but it will not let you open a package for editing unless you download a bunch of DTS management parts from Microsoft. I don't intend to list them here or go into the subject in any depth because I am not the only one that has had grief with this process. I lost one package to corruption and decided that if I needed to work with DTS then the tool to use is the tool that was provided with SQL Server 2000 for the purpose, the very reliable SQL Server Enterprise Manager.

SQL Server Management Studio can be started from the Microsoft SQL Server menu under Programs. When its main window first appears and when you start it for the first time, you need to configure connection to a database engine before you can manage it.

Connecting to Servers

Management Studio manages the components and modules of each server as a hierarchy of services. In turn, each server is part of a collection of servers. Servers can be added to and removed from the server collection in Object Explorer as needed.

The idea behind managing a collection of servers or registering them with Management Studio is that you can simply attach to an instance of SQL Server from a single copy of Management Studio. This means you can manage hundreds of servers or instances from a single copy of Management Studio.

If you are working on a high-bandwidth network, you can hook up each server remotely from a local copy of Management Studio. However, if you are working on a low-bandwidth network, it might make more sense to log on to the server and run a local copy of the Studio on the remote server. Remote access is best via a RDP terminal session under Windows Server.

Getting Around Management Studio

As soon as you have connected to the server, you can drill down to the services you need to manage and configure. To disconnect from a server, you can right-click the connection and select the Disconnect menu item. Management Studio automatically disconnects from all servers when you close the MMC console.

NOTE *A thorough understanding of how to set up and customize the Management Studio is well worth acquiring. This book is not the forum for that, but there are several works on the market that cover the basics and Visual Studio.*

The program is divided into the following hierarchy of administrative sections:

- Servers
- Databases
- Security
- Server objects
- Replication
- Management
- Notification services
- The SQL Server Agent

The Management Studio is home to a substantial number of wizards. They can be easily accessed from the menus. You can also access the wizards from the Tools menu and in context menus as you drill down into the various folders representing your server's services.

Configuring the Server Instance

Each instance of SQL Server 2005 can be specifically configured, interactively, in the SQL Server Properties dialog box. None of the properties is set in stone, and you can return to them after this initial walkthrough, as needed. Rather than offer a full explanation in this chapter, we will return to each tab as it relates to a chapter subject in the remaining chapters, where necessary. To access the properties dialog box, you need to perform the following steps:

1. Select the server in the tree, right-click and select Properties. The registered SQL Server Properties dialog box loads to the General tab, as illustrated in Figure 4-2.

2. On the General tab, enter the general server options such as the authentication mode and general security settings.

3. The Memory tab is used for configuring the instance's management of memory. These options will vary depending on the server's role, environment, number of connections, and so forth.

4. The Processor tab lets you configure threads, fibers, the number of processors, and so forth. It also lets you manage the query plan threshold for parallel queries.

5. The Security tab, the subject of Chapter 5, lets you manage security. Of special importance is the capability to change the system account.

6. The Connections tab lets you change the number of concurrent connections.

7. The Database Settings tab lets you manage several DBMS-oriented options, such as triggers, data interpretation, and so on. The mail login name of the mail client can also be set from this tab. The Database Settings tab provides the facility to interactively set a number of default database settings. These include settings for the recovery models, the default log directory, and the default index fill factor.

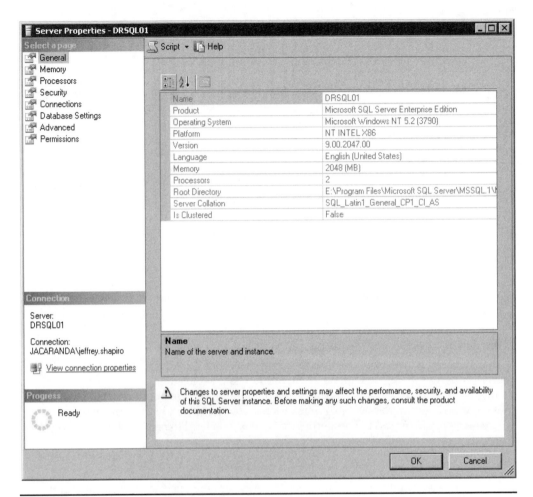

FIGURE 4-2   SQL Server Properties dialog box

Many of the variables or properties that drive each instance of SQL Server can be accessed via system stored procedures and a number of system functions. And, as discussed earlier, you can tune and lube your server via the management object models. Most experienced DBAs find it easier to work with SQL Server with tried and proven scripts they have developed over the years. Several command-line utilities are another option, especially if the command prompt is more familiar turf for you than "clicky" Windows icons.

SQL Server's Automated Administration Architecture

SQL Server 2005, like its predecessors, comes equipped with an impressive array of management interfaces and services. This chapter looks at several aspects of its automated administrative functionality:

- The ability to program SQL Server to perform administrative tasks automatically and to keep you, the DBA, informed
- The ability to troubleshoot SQL Server when temperatures start to rise, in the server room and under your collar
- The ability to monitor the performance of SQL Server

We will look at the automated administrative architecture and describe how to work with SQL Agent. Then we will explore SQL Mail and Database Mail for automating e-mail alerts for both legacy applications and new projects.

SQL Server 2005's administrative architecture provides a facility that allows the DBA to program the server to administer for itself the many repetitive actions and duties it needs to perform to ensure service level, availability, and optimum performance.

This is not only useful for you as the DBA, allowing you to spend more time doing things like index management, query performance optimization, and so on, but it is also an ideal mechanism for turnkey operations in which a DBA is typically not available. The ISV or integrator can install specialized scripts and upon deployment of a product can allow the SQL Server DBMS to self-administer its databases and other objects.

The automation capability is not only limited to features such as backup, index defragmentation, and so on, but you can program the server to automatically fire replication events and specialized scripts that are deployed to meet certain business rules and objectives.

SQL Server Agent

The chief component of the automated administrative capability is the SQL Server Agent (named Agent for brevity in this chapter). It is a separate binary layer that executes your administrative jobs and alerts. The Agent runs as a service named SQLServerAgent on Windows. You can also deploy it to the workstation.

Jobs

A *job* is the central and definitive administrative task managed by the Agent. Each job is a collection of one or more steps. Each step can be a T-SQL statement, an operating system command, an executable program, a replication agent, or some Visual Basic, Java, C# or batch command driven script. You can run the jobs once, or you can schedule them to repeat periodically. Using the many functions you have at your disposal, you can create some of the most advanced scripts that execute on SQL Server only if the server is in a specific state.

For example, using T-SQL you can assess processor activity, monitor it for a certain length of time, and then decide if the time is right to begin a backup, a defragmentation, or a distributed query, or else you can check if the boss is logged on and working so that you can go out and catch a cappuccino.

The Agent can run your jobs at the specified times, without the need for any human intervention. You can code the most complex procedures with error-checking logic and flow control and design them to allow SQL Server to address any condition it will likely encounter at any time. The effort you put into the Agent will pay big dividends and can make the difference between working at all hours or going home early.

SQL Server Agent is most useful for the scheduled running of various ETL, packages (which stands for Extract, Transform and Load). These SSIS packages, discussed earlier in this chapter, are themselves highly sophisticated programs. One common usage of ETL packages is to move data from various data repositories on the enterprise network, such as those that live in the likes of huge Teradata data warehouses, into the fact tables and dimensions of your SQL Server based data warehouses and data marts. Under SQL Server Analysis Services, SQL Server Agent can be used to schedule the ETL packages, purge and load CUBES and perform sophisticated functions used by the business intelligence community.

Events and Alerts

When SQL Server 2005 is installed, it records all its significant events in the Windows application log facility. Each entry in the log is called an *event*; you can define alerts that watch the event log and trigger the Agent to start a job when such an event is encountered. The Agent compares the events in the application log against the alerts you defined; if it encounters a match, a job can be fired.

SQL Server creates events for errors with a severity of 19 or higher. These events are also raised if a RAISERROR statement is executed using the WITH LOG clause, or the xp_logevent system stored procedure is executed. This allows T-SQL scripts, triggers, stored procedures, and applications to raise events that can be used to fire a job.

Operators

SQL Server Agent Operators are the e-mail and page addresses you define in SQL Server for use in alerts. You can define an alert that either e-mails or pages a specific person. Instances of SQL Server running on Windows Server 2005 can also use the Windows net send command to send a network message to a Windows user or group. There are numerous methods for detecting an alert and making sure someone gets your message—short of sending a note in a bottle.

Triggers

Triggers are used to enforce business logic and however, triggers can be integrated with automated administrative tasks by using either RAISERROR or xp_logevent to generate an event that fires an alert.

Using the SQL Server Agent

To automate administration, you need to perform the following activities:

- Establish which administrative responsibilities or server events occur regularly and can be administered programmatically.
- Define a set of jobs, alerts, and operators by using SQL Server Management Studio, T-SQL scripts, or SQL-SMO objects.
- Enable the SQL Server Agent service.

Jobs, alerts, and operators are the three main components of SQL Server's automatic administration services.

A *job* is a specified series of operations that you must define to be performed sequentially by the SQL Server Agent. You use jobs to define the administrative tasks to be executed. The jobs can be executed one or more times and can be monitored for success or failure each time a job is executed.

You can execute jobs as follows:

- On a local server or servers; or on multiple remote servers
- According to a schedule
- On the occurrence of one or more alerts

Alerts signal the designated operator that an event has occurred. An event can be any action or process that executes on the server. For example, it can be a job starting, like a backup, or system resources reaching a certain threshold, such as CPU pegged at 100 percent for a certain amount of time, suggesting that a resource is locked or has failed. You must first define the conditions under which an alert is generated. You also need to define which actions the alert will take. For example, you can program alerts to do the following:

- Notify one or more operators.
- Forward the event to another server.
- Execute a job.

An *operator* is the individual responsible for the maintenance of one or more instances of SQL Server. In a large data center or corporation, the operator responsibilities are assigned to many individuals. A large, busy data center with many servers might employ many individuals to share operator responsibilities. They watch the servers for alerts and fix small things. The operators usually escalate problems to DBAs that are usually off duty. Operators do not also have the skills necessary to fix database problems when they occur. In a small company, however, an operator might be the DBA, and possibly even the CTO. An operator is notified of alerts in one or more of the following ways:

- **E-mail**   Through e-mail you can define the alias of an operator or the alias for a group of individuals. When something acts up, all the aliases are notified at the same time. With Windows Server 2003 you can create a distribution group and send e-mail to it. All members of the group will then be notified.

- **Pager**   A message can be sent to a pager using a dial-up service. This would obviously require you to set up a modem and configure dial-up services to a host network. An e-mail can also be used to send a pager message.

- **Net send**   This facility is an ideal mechanism to write net send commands to the command console.

Defining Operators

The primary attributes that define an operator are name and contact information. You need to define operators before you define alerts. To notify an operator, you must set up one or more of the following in the following order:

- When sending e-mail, if you are using the legacy SQL Mail for any particular reason, you must configure a MAPI-1–compliant e-mail client. The SQL Server Agent demands a valid mail profile be set up in order to send e-mail. Examples of MAPI-1 clients include Microsoft Outlook. Your mail server can be any MAPI-compliant mail server, such as Sendmail (essentially obsolete) or the modern, highly sophisticated Exchange 2003 or Exchange 2007 Servers. You should, however, use the newer architecture in SQL Server 2005 encompassing Database Mail.

- When sending a page, you need third-party pager-to-e-mail software and/or hardware. Intel has such functionality in its original LANDesk product, acquired from its purchase of WinBeep, a beeper/pager utility that gets activated through Windows. You need such technology in place before you can start a vibration on anyone's belt.

- To use net send messages, you must be running on the Microsoft Windows Server 2003 or later operating system, and the Messenger Service must be running on the target computer you need to hit with a message. I find net send is the most ineffective method used to raise the attention of an operator. It unusually ends up alerting hackers that a net send facility on your server is worth breaking open.

Naming an Operator

Every operator must be given a name. The operator names must be unique, and they can be no longer than 128 characters. You also need to include the operator's contact information, which defines how you notify the operator. When using e-mail notification, the SQL Server Agent establishes its own mail session using the mail profile information supplied in the SQL Agent Properties dialog box.

When using pager notification, paging is typically implemented using an e-mail service (using a modem to direct-dial a network can be cumbersome, yet more certain of getting a page out). To set up pager notification, you must install software somewhere that can read mail and convert it to a pager message and send it to a pager network. The software can take one of several approaches, including forwarding the mail to a remote mail server at the pager provider's site. For this to happen, the pager provider must offer this service. In many cases the software you need is part of the local mail system. If it isn't, it is not hard to find, nor is it very difficult to create such a facility using Visual Basic 2005 or C#.

A variation on the first approach is to route the mail by way of the Internet to a mail server at the pager provider's site. The mail server processes the inbound mail and then dials the network using an attached modem. The associated software is proprietary to pager service providers. The software acts as a mail client that periodically processes its inbox either by interpreting all or part of the e-mail address information as a pager number, or by matching the e-mail name to a pager number in a translation table.

If all your operators share a pager provider, you can use SQL Server Management Studio to specify peculiar e-mail formatting that might be required by the pager-to-e-mail system. The special formatting can be a prefix or a suffix, as follows:

- A *Subject* line
- A *CC* line
- A *To* line

If you are using a low-end alphanumeric paging system such as a system that is limited to the transmission and reception of only 64 characters per page, you might have to shorten the message sent by excluding the error text from the pager notification. This may also be a limitation of a typical SMS message.

Designating a Fail-Safe Operator

A fail-safe operator can be designated if all notifications to designated operators fail. For example, let's say you define several operators for pager notifications and not one of them receives notification. The fail-safe operator is then notified when the following takes place:

- The operator(s) responsible for the alert cannot be paged. Reasons for this include incorrect pager addresses and off-duty operators.
- The SQL Server Agent cannot access system tables in the msdb database. The sysnotifications system table specifies the operator responsibilities for alerts.

The fail-safe operator is a safety feature, so you cannot delete the operator assigned to fail-safe duty without reassigning fail-safe duty to another operator or deleting the fail-safe assignment.

Configuring SQL Server's Mailing Engines

SQL Mail is the legacy facility that provides a mechanism for the reception of e-mail generated by SQL Server. Database Mail is the new SQL Server process for sending e-mail messages from the database engine. Using either, your database applications can send e-mail messages to users. The messages can contain query results, and can also include files from any resource on your network. Database Mail is designed for reliability, scalability, security, and supportability. SQL Mail has been provided for backwards compatibility, while Database Mail provides a more reliable, scalable and securable solution.

Database Mail provides background, or asynchronous, delivery to the platform. It is invoked When you call proc sp_send_dbmail to send a message. This prompts Database Mail to add a request to a Service Broker queue. The external e-mail component receives the request and delivers the e-mail. The proc is non-blocking, which provides scalability.

With Database Mail you can create multiple mailing profiles within a SQL Server instance. This allows you to specify the profile that Database Mail uses when you send a message, keeping the process database or application specific. The profile you create and also be email account specific.

Security and scalabilty is the big deal with Database Mail. Not only is it 64-bit compatible, but the Database Mail stored procedures are secure. Database Mail is disabled by default. The SQL Server Surface Area Configuration tool can be used to enable the Database mail stored procedure. You will also be prompted to enable Database Mail when you first attempt to set up a profile. To configure Database Mail, you must be a member of the DatabaseMailUserRole database role in the msdb database.

Database Mail enforces a configurable limit on the attachment file size. It can also maintain a list of prohibited file extensions preventing a developer from attach files with an extension that is on the list. The system is also audited and keeps messages and attachments that were sent in the msdb database. You can easily audit Database Mail usage and review the retained messages.

Messages can be created that provide you with the status of a job or a warning caused by an alert. The mailers can even include a result set, or data obtained by a collateral query. They let SQL Server send and receive e-mail but they must first be configured to establish and obtain a client connection with a mail server such as Microsoft Exchange. Let's first discuss SQL Mail.

SQL Mail

SQL Server makes use of two services to handle e-mail. MSSQLServer processes mail for all of the mail stored procedures. SQLServerAgent, however, does not use SQL Mail to send its e-mail. The Agent has its own mail capabilities, configured and operated separately from SQL Mail.

SQL Server Books Online refers to SQL Server Agent mail features as SQLAgentMail to distinguish it from the SQL Mail features provided by MSSQLServer. SQL Mail works by first establishing an extended MAPI connection with a mail host, while SQLAgentMail establishes an extended MAPI connection on its own. Both SQL Mail and SQLAgentMail can connect with Microsoft Exchange Server, or any Post Office Protocol 3 (POP3) server, even a UNIX POP3 server.

To get SQL Mail going you need a post office connection, a mail store (mailbox), a mail profile, and an Active Directory domain user account, which is used to log on to an instance of SQL Server. The SQL Mail facility comprises of a number of stored procedures, which are used by SQL Server to process its e-mail messages. These are then received in the defined SQL Mail account mailbox on the mail server or to reply to e-mail messages generated by the stored procedure *xp_sendmail*.

By using SQL Mail extended stored procedures, messages can be sent from either a trigger or a stored procedure. SQL Mail stored procedures can also manipulate data, process queries received by e-mail, and return a result set in a reply to an e-mail.

To process e-mail automatically, you must create a regularly scheduled job that uses the stored procedure, sp_processmail, which checks your SQL Mail mail profile and then checks your mailbox for e-mail. The sp_processmail procedure uses xp_sendmail to execute query requests contained in the text of the e-mail and then returns the result set to the original sender and any additional recipients that might be included in the communication.

SQLAgentMail

SQLAgentMail can use its own domain account and mail profile that is different from the one set up for SQL Mail. With SQL Server, you can configure SQLAgentMail e-mail messages to be sent when either of the following takes place:

- **An alert is triggered**   The alerts can be configured to send e-mail notification upon the occurrence of specific events. SQL Mail is not required. For example, an alert can be configured to notify an operator per e-mail of a particular database-related event that needs immediate attention.

- **A scheduled task event**   This fires when something like a database backup or a replication event succeeds or fails.

Your e-mail can be sent to a list of recipients, informing them of the status of scheduled jobs for possible user action. This is an ideal service if you want to make sure that a backup job is proceeding according to standard operational procedures. This facility is also useful for gathering up a regular log of events that can be later referenced. As mentioned earlier you can send a result set by e-mail to any list of recipients. That result set might be data generated from a call to a system stored procedure, such as sp_who. Mail can be generated on firing of a trigger designed to alert an operator or administrator. An example of such a trigger is the identification of a user or users that try to access a certain database. For example, a report on an unauthorized attempt to access and inventory database could trigger an e-mail sent by SQLAgentMail to the designated operators. A result set containing connection information can also be e-mailed in the alert.

Configuring and Using SQL Mail

SQL Mail must be configured to run in an e-mail profile created in the same domain account that is used to start an instance of SQL Server. Under the Management folder in SQL Server Management Studio, you will find an icon representing the SQL Mail Service, and you can determine from that if the service is running. You can also start SQL Mail automatically by clicking Autostart SQL Mail When SQL Server Starts on the General tab of the SQL Mail Configuration dialog box.

Configuring and Using Database Mail

The Database Mail Configuration Wizard is used to install or uninstall Database Mail, or to create and configure Database Mail accounts and profiles, and the related system parameters. The first screen you arrive at in the configuration lets you name and describe a profile. There is a button on this dialog box that lets you add SMTP accounts. The process is no different from configuring any SMTP mail client to communicate with an SMTP server.

Once you have created the profile and account, you will be able to determine if the profile is for public or private access. If the profile is for private use, you will need to specify the users or groups that have access to the profile. Finally, you will be able to specify the profile parameters that govern the mailing process. You will be able to set retry attempts, attachment specifics, file sizes, logging, and so on.

Maintenance Plans

Using various management utilities of SQL Server, such as Backup/Restore, combined with various scripts, procedures, schedules, and processes, you can set up so-called maintenance plans to automate a collection of management procedures in SQL Server. The maintenance plan feature lets you collect the activities into a package that is then executed using the components of SSIS. The SQL Server Agent is then enlisted to run the jobs and provide the necessary logging and alert system. SQL Server 2005 Integration Services must be installed on the instance of the server or server nodes in a cluster you are managing. SQL Server 2005 lets you create the following when you are creating maintenance plans:

- Workflows that combine a variety of maintenance procedures.
- Custom Transact-SQL scripts and various objects (including CLR-based objects introduced in Chapter 11).
- Conceptual hierarchy for maintenance plans, including error checking and switching.
- Plans that are editable in a graphical environment.
- Plan that can also be scheduled to run at different times.

Due to the various integrated services used by the maintenance plans, you need to log on to SQL Server using Windows Authentication. Maintenance plans are only supported using Windows Authentication. You also need to be a member of the sysadmin fixed server role to create and work with maintenance plans.

To create a maintenance plan, you can use the Maintenance Plan Wizard, or you can create a plan using the design palette. Maintenance plans can be used to create a workflow of the maintenance tasks required to make sure that your database performs well, is regularly backed up in case of system failure, and is checked for inconsistencies. Although the Maintenance Plan Wizard can be used for creating core maintenance plans, creating these plans manually gives you much more flexibility. In SQL Server 2005 Database Engine, maintenance plans create a job that performs these maintenance tasks automatically at scheduled intervals. You must be a member of the sysadmin role to create and manage maintenance tasks.

For basic or base maintenance plans you should start with the wizard. Later you can use the designer tools' enhanced workflow and expand the plan. Note that maintenance plans are only displayed if the user is connected using Windows Authentication. Object Explorer does not display maintenance plans if the user is connected using SQL Server Authentication. To understand how the maintenance plans work, turn to Chapter 7, where I create a maintenance plan for backing up a collection of databases.

The Network Ahead

If you are new to client/server database systems, the paradigm shift from desktop applications, such as Microsoft Access and FoxPro, might seem steep. A number of areas will entail a learning curve. Understanding how to configure users in the database, server security and logins, roles, and so on can be a challenge. In Chapter 5, I go into the security aspect in a lot more depth.

As wonderful as SQL Server is, one of the drawbacks for newcomers is that it is so vast. It is not unusual to do everything right in the test or development environment, only to find users cannot connect when you roll out or deploy your production system.

PART

II

Administering SQL Server 2005

Security

I have good reason to place security at the beginning of Part II. I have met many DBAs and developers who do not fully appreciate the security environment required in the implementation of SQL Server. There have been many horror stories: users running amok, unauthorized use of tools, external processes corrupting data, untrained administrators dropping databases and tables, theft, acts of God, self-mutating viruses, and so on. Here are two stories of many I have encountered in network and database administration.

I recently took over the administration of a database for a direct marketer. Now this person had been making millions selling mailing lists for almost 25 years but was not pleased with his "DBA." During the needs or requirements analysis I was taking before providing a quote for my services, I discovered a table called *CCN*. Lo and behold, what I stumbled on was a gold mine of about 75,000 credit card numbers, linked of course to the customers who had been buying the database owner's mailing lists.

I did a sort on the data and pulled about 25,000 current and active credit cards, so the database was valuable to a person of malevolent intent, to say the least. To the credit (no pun intended) of my moral virtue, I deleted the view, advised the owner of the risk, did a backup of the database and the system, and then locked down the machine. The table had been completely exposed; there was no proper domain or network security protecting the server, nor was a system administrator-password-protecting the DBMS. I told the owners that by the end of the week I would give them my proposal and a quote to take over administration of the asset.

The next day I was called; the current DBA had vanished, and the database server with all the credit card information had vanished with him. I had never been hired faster in my life. The server, incidentally, was never recovered, but the credit cards were never compromised.

The second story was more recent. A client I was consulting for (a Fortune 500 company, and one of the world's largest food distributors) suspended the credit of one of its yogurt ice-cream outlets, which threatened closure of the store because he was in a cash-flow crunch. But that did not deter the desperate ice-cream seller. He hired someone to hack into the company's databases and managed to keep himself supplied for several weeks until the credit manager found out.

My guess was that the storeowner hired someone to do the hacking, but security was so lax that breaking into the database was easier than selling frozen yogurt on a hot day in Miami. I was called in to look for evidence, but not before the hacker managed to feed several thousand hungry yogurt lovers. The hacker got away clean, having also deleted the delivery information; we had no evidence that the deliveries had actually been made to his location.

I can tell you many more stories, but you don't need a book to tell you that data security is one of the most important subjects in database administration. I find it odd it is not given more attention.

Many DBAs and developers are more concerned about data integrity than data security. I don't see why the validity or plausibility of data should be deemed more important than avoiding compromise of it. After all, how valid is valid data when you don't have it any longer or it has been seriously compromised? I am not underplaying data integrity, and you'll find the chapter that deals with it (see Chapter 12) just as vociferous. I just know many DBAs out there that will tell you about the mother of all triggers or stored procedures they wrote, and yet they still manage a system with no system administrator password. So rife is this problem that Microsoft made a special effort in the SQL Server 2000 days to force us to use a password for the SA. And in SQL Server 2005 security is even more sophisticated.

This chapter looks at data security in general and how SQL Server 2005 presents itself as a bastion of the data it keeps and of the services it provides. It is a complex chapter for a complex subject, and you should read it before creating any facilities for logging in and using the database. And DBAs who have been baptized by fire will find discussions of new security services, especially with respect to Window Server 2003, refreshing.

If you need to configure SQL Server 2005 for secure access as quickly as possible, go directly to the section "Creating and Configuring Database Roles" and thereafter "Creating and Configuring Users."

Data Security Primer

I find it necessary to actually define the difference between data integrity and data security. No one defines the difference better than database guru C.J. Date does: "Security means protecting the data against unauthorized users; integrity means protecting it against authorized users." With the data integrity definition out of the way, we can deal with the subject of data security, unencumbered by misconceptions.

Objects and Ownership

The meaning of *data security* comes into focus when you explore the concept and philosophy of ownership. If you have a background in network or general computer security, the concept of data ownership will be a lot clearer because objects and ownership are at the root of network and information technology security—especially on Windows operating systems and the NT file system (NTFS).

It also helps that your data "Gestalt" is formed around the concept of objects. In other words, everything that makes up your data environment comprises objects. As long as a user (human or otherwise) possesses a data object, the attributes of the objects fall under certain laws of ownership, and ownership is what makes us human (and a good reason why Communism has essentially failed).

Everything in a database management system is an object—from the service providers; to the Network-Libraries; to collections of stored procedures, functions, and more. The database is also an object. It has attributes, such as tables, that are objects. A table is also an object that contains attributes. The attributes of a table are the rows, or tuples, which are themselves objects with attributes.

If you keep going down the "object hierarchy," you will keep discovering objects, until you get down to the world of subatomic matter, which is also understood in terms of objects and ownership. We can think of the hierarchy as an object chain, an important concept in SQL Server security we will later discuss.

Data objects, as a collection, become information at a point when the combined objects and their collections, seen as the sum of their parts, yield facts. And information, suggesting a substance of value, is also an object of ownership. Ownership, no doubt, was the reason "databases" were created hundreds of years ago, when people needed a system determining ownership. They may have used caves, or clay pots, or holes in a tree as repositories, but databases they were, no more and no less.

Trust

Adopting the view that objects have owners, software engineers can enforce rules of ownership on objects much as banks protect money. You are not the owner of the object until you can prove you are, via identity. Sure, if you deposit money in a bank account, you are the de facto owner of it because you created the account and placed the money in it. You created the credit balance with the bank. But you do not get access to the money once it is placed in the custody of the bank unless you can prove to the bank clerk that you are the owner. Like the bank teller, the database needs to know that you are who you say you are.

This brings us to the concept of *trust*. If a system, such as a database, is able to validate your identity (you are who you say you are), you are allowed to interoperate or interact with the system under a certain level of trust. Each system rates its level of trust differently. Some systems, even people, trust a person fully (which you may argue is foolish). Other systems delegate levels of trust. The higher the trust relationship, the more rights of access you have.

Rights and Permissions

The more you are trusted, the more access you will get to objects and information (such as by being trusted with the delete permission). For example if you can be fully trusted, you are given access to information and functionality, both on a network and in a DBMS. The access is a *permission,* which is not a finite quantity; the rule is the need-to-know. You can be assigned certain *levels of permission* on a need-to-know basis. In a database, you might be *permitted* to read some data but not delete it. On a file system, you might have *permission* to read some files but not to delete them. The permissions model is illustrated in Figure 5-1.

Permissions are not the same thing as *rights*. We all have rights—given to us by God and country and our systems administrators. Often those rights (even the God-given ones) are withheld from us. If you have ever had cause, as I have, to argue for or claim your human rights, you will know that the difference between *rights* and *permissions* is as profound as night is from day.

The Windows Server 2003 security system distinguishes *rights* from *permissions.* The "right to log on locally" may be assigned to you. But having permission to log on locally is another matter altogether because permission to do so overrides the right. It is important as a DBA to distinguish between the two; it will make your life a lot easier when dealing with people who like to show muscle.

What kind of security soup does this all boil down to? To sum up, everything in a database, including the database, is an *object*. Objects have *owners,* and owners are usually

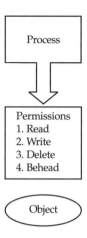

FIGURE 5-1
Permissions
protect the object

allowed to do whatever they want to the objects. But just because you think you have the *right* to do whatever you want, with what you own, that doesn't mean you can. Society in general, and database administrators in particular, have the final word on what's *permitted*. The rules of society do not permit you to beat up your children, just because you "own" them. And business and database rules might forbid you from deleting databases and data, whether you own them or not.

Change of Ownership, Schemas and Security

Change or transfer of object ownership is perfectly feasible in computer and software engineering. Transferring ownership of databases objects is as simple as transferring the ownership of a file, as you will soon see. However, keep in mind that ownership can usually only be *given* or *transferred*. It can only be *taken* in most cases by a system or database administrator, or a security principal (a user or computer account) with the highest level of trust and permission of a security system, such as a file system or DBMS.

Databases and their objects can now be managed under a namespace mechanism that is granted ownership of the database and all its objects in SQL Server. Users and roles are given access to schema namespaces so that they can manage a database and its objects without exclusive ownership of the objects, as was the case with SQL Server 2000.

If a user leaves town, you can simply transfer ownership of the schema to another user without affecting the database and its objects. Schemas are created in SQL Server Management Studio (SSMS) under the Security Page in Database Properties. Or they can be created and managed in T-SQL with the CREATE SCHEMA statement. Here is an example:

```
CREATE SCHEMA name AUTHORIZATION owner
```

You can also create and manage schemas interactively under the Security node of a database.

Authentication

You cannot just walk in off the street and lay claim to property that is in the *trust* of an authority, be it a bank, a network folder, or a database. You first have to prove you are the owner—not the same thing as proving identity.

Ownership can only be contested, however, after identity is verified—and this is called *authentication*. The simplest mechanism for proving identity to a network, proving that you are who you say you are, is by providing a user identification (user ID) and the password that goes with it. This combination of elements is often called the "ID-password pair." Once your identity can be proved, you are assigned a level of trust with which to go about your business, in the bank, on the network, in the database. But you are still prevented from accessing objects you have no permission to access.

Note *Windows Server 2003 provides several new mechanisms beyond the simple ID-password pair for proving identity. The operating system now has support for smart card readers, as well as for biometric devices that scan retinas, fingerprints, and voiceprints, and can verify signatures, hand geometry, and so on. These devices are underpinned by certificates that store electric signatures and personal identification numbers. Using certificate-driven security (encryption services, keys, and so on) requires a certificate authority (the server architecture that services a public key infrastructure, or PKI).*

Checking that the security principal has ownership of a certain object confirms or rejects ownership. Usually, if you create an object, you have full rights to it. But this rule cannot be stretched too far. Just because you created an object on the network, such as an important document or database information, that does not give you the right to delete it. In fact, some employee manuals go so far as to state that anything you create automatically belongs to the corporation and that you have to comply with policy with respect to deleting or altering what you created.

I was involved in a case recently when an employee managed to encrypt a database and refused to hand over the password when her employment was terminated. It took us half a morning to crack the password, and the company had the employee arrested for attempted destruction of property.

To better understand the technical issues of ownership and access control, it helps to discuss the business (and philosophical) aspects first.

Access Control

Understanding access control is paramount if you strive to be an effective system administrator, especially a DBA who is mandated to protect information assets of the company. For many enterprises today, information is all they own; it's certainly more valuable than what can be carried off on the back of a truck.

For the most part, the system administrator implements access control as directed by senior management, such as change control boards (CCBs) and security councils. For example, you'll get a request to allow an accounts payable clerk named Sally to access a certain database and to give her certain abilities in that database, such as the ability to update information. However, the levels of access control and access control management are the domain of the system administrator. In other words, you are expected to know how to implement the controls, and screwing up could cost you your job.

At all change control meetings I have attended over the years, I have seldom been told to "provide access to Sally but make sure she cannot write checks to herself." You are expected to make sure that Sally cannot write checks to herself, but you also need to ensure that she can manage accounts payable without hindrance. Remember, you are being held in the highest of trust and being paid well in return (I have heard more about CPAs embezzling from the company than about system administrators or DBAs doing so).

There's a lot of power in the hands of the DBA—a good reason why effective (and secure) security plans should be implemented and followed to the letter. But don't go anywhere; you will be getting a heads-up on that in this chapter whether you like it or not.

Access is not a technical requirement; rather, it derives from business policy and rules. So you need to put aside your technical cravings and consider some basic database access control management. (In a large company, though, you'll probably not need to make or manage access policy, just implement it.)

Levels of Security

You can divide access control policy into several classifications. I like to use what I learned in military intelligence, which classifies data according to its levels of sensitivity, using the labels *confidential, restricted, secret,* and *top secret.* Data that is sensitive, but not damaging, can be classified as *confidential.* Everyone in the enterprise is given access to this level. You are required to consider everything you learn about the business and its affairs as *confidential.* The drug testing procedures of a company could be considered confidential information.

The next level is *restricted,* which means that a subset of the members of the organization have access to information that could cause problems if the information became widely known. *Restricted* information could include short-term information, or information a company feels should be disseminated to a larger collection of its employees, such as the percentage increases for annual bonuses or product launch plans.

The definition of a *secret* has long caused aggressive debate. In a company, a secret is information shared by a very small number of employees (can you really share a secret with yourself?). For example, the discovery of a new formula might be considered secret, known perhaps only by the most senior executives and immediate product staff. Secret information is provided on a need-to-know basis. You are not given secret information unless you need it to perform your duties. And you need to be proven trustworthy first.

And finally we deal with the stuff of which spy novels are made, *top secret.* Information classified as *top secret* could be disastrous for a company if it were revealed. Such information could be corporate credit cards, bank accounts, digital signatures, cash assets, patent plans, blueprints, algorithms, information that could be used in the public trading of a corporation's shares, and so on.

I consider the passwords of employees as *top secret* information. If an employee becomes loose with his or her password, he or she should be disciplined under rules that deal with the unauthorized divulgence of *top secret* information. This is especially important when SQL Server is providing access on the basis of Windows/Active Directory authentication *alone.* Figure 5-2 provides a different "view" on the restriction levels—a pyramid whose pinnacle represents the smallest segment of people that have access to the information and whose base represent the largest segment of people that have access to the information.

How do you translate the level discussed here to databases? I consider any access to the data in the databases to be confidential, which means that everyone and anything that has access to the DBMS must meet requirements for access to confidential information. They need to be authenticated to the DBMS in some way that enforces the policy of the enterprise. This is achieved by having a user ID and a password, or some recognized means of obtaining trusted authentication and thus the trust of the DBMS.

FIGURE 5-2
The pinnacle
represents the
smallest segment
of people that have
access to the
information

Top Secret

Secret

Confidential

Restricted

While all data in the DBMS is considered *confidential,* certain areas of it could be considered more sensitive, upgraded to *restricted, confidential, secret,* and *top secret.* Looking at the table in Figure 5-3, we can easily identify certain columns as *restricted,* such as job descriptions (*JobDesc*); certain columns as *secret,* such as annual bonuses (*AnnBon*); and certain columns as *top secret,* such as drug tests (*DrugTest*).

The safest means of protecting the top secret information would be to make DrugTest a stand-alone table in the database and restrict access to it accordingly, but SQL Server 2005 provides sufficient mechanisms (views, stored procedure or select permissions, and the like) to ensure that the drug test results are adequately protected. You might balk at the idea of labeling your information like a CIA or MI5 agent, but you need to think along these lines if you don't want to end your career by "acts of omission." We'll get back to this later when we discuss the data security plan.

This brings us to another level in our discussion of access control: distinguishing between the protection of *information* by users or employees, and the protection of *data* by users or employees. I agree it borders on the integrity versus security issue; however, you will need to protect data used by members of trusted groups from accidental or even intentional damage. And often the lines of functionality will be blurred, because you will use the same constraints and restrictions to enforce both security policy and data integrity.

Pop Quiz: A breakdown in what at Los Alamos led to the risk of losing nuclear secrets, when two hard disks containing the data were found missing from the vault? Choose one of the following:

A.) Data integrity?

B.) Data security?

C.) Both of the above?

Point taken?

FIGURE 5-3
Columns classified
according to the
sensitivity of the
data

JobDesc (Restricted)	AnnBon (Secret)	DrugTest (Top Secret)

Windows Security 101

The NT File System (NTFS) protects objects by verifying that a security principal has access to an object. The file system also verifies what level of access has been granted to a security principal, such as *read, write, delete,* and *execute. Deny* is also an access level, although it prevents access to the object. So how does the file system know who you are without having to reauthenticate you every time you need access to an object? And how does it know what level of access your authentication carries? On Windows domains, this is achieved using *access tokens, security identifiers (SIDs),* and *access control lists (ACLs).*

Access Tokens and the Security Identifier (SID)

An *access token* is a "badge of trust," which acts as a proxy, assigned to you after you successfully authenticate to a Windows Server or Active Directory. The token is the means by which the security system grants you right of passage on the network or in and across the domain, although the passage and access to resources is carried out by the system on your behalf, by the token. A token's right of passage is not open-ended or unlimited. It can be revoked by a security system, or the administrator, and is revoked when you log out.

You can compare the token to an access badge for passage in a protected area. The holder of the badge or token is given the right of free passage around the offices of the enterprise. On a Windows domain, it gives you the right of passage around the network or to connect to the database management system, which is SQL Server, no doubt.

The access token is the "token" by which your continued trust is measured and monitored while you are connected to the network. It is not a guarantee of access to systems and services, but it is used to verify access or that a trust authority, such as the domain administrator, trusts you. As you know, it is not a guarantee that you have access to SQL Server. It is the means you have to assert your right to access.

Every access token holds the SID for a security principal, which is assigned to the access token after you log in successfully. The SID is a unique value of variable length that is used to identify a security principal to the security subsystem, and ultimately to a resource such as SQL Server. The security principal or user account is also known as a *trustee* to the Windows kernel. When referencing a user or a group for security purposes, Windows refers to the SID rather than the user or group name.

Every object has an associated ACL that stores the SID and the level of access a security principal might have on an object. Whenever you or the network administrator provides or denies access to an object, the SID's corresponding access level in the object's ACL is also updated. The access token-SID-ACL model is illustrated in Figure 5-4.

The permission list controls exactly what level of access you have to the file system object. SQL Server 2005 operates in a similar fashion; however, there are some differences we will discuss later in this chapter.

Figure 5-4
The access token-
SID-ACL model

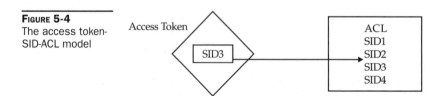

NOTE *Do not confuse the SID with the object identifier or OID. The OID is a means of enumerating objects and identifying objects with a globally unique identifier (GUID), thus guaranteeing their uniqueness.*

SIDs guarantee that an account—a security principal—and all its associated rights and permissions are unique. If you delete an account and then recreate it under the same name, you will find that all rights and permissions of the deleted account are removed. The old SID gets deleted with the original account. In this respect, if you delete an account, the login created in SQL Server will have to similarly be deleted because it will hold data related to the old SID. The old login will not work if you recreate the user account in Active Directory because the SIDs will be different.

When you create an account, the system also creates the SID and stores it in the security structures of Active Directory. The first part of the SID identifies the domain in which the SID was created. The second part is called the *relative ID* or RID and refers to the actual object created. The RID is thus relative to the domain.

When a user logs in to the computer or domain, the SID is retrieved from the Security Accounts Manager (SAM) database or Active Directory and placed in the user's access token. From the moment of login, the SID is used in the access token, a form of user impersonation, to identify the user in all security-related actions and interactions.

Windows Server 2003, and services such as SQL Server and Exchange, use the SID for the following purposes:

- To identify the object's owner
- To identify the object owner's group
- To identify the account in access-related activity

Special, well-known SIDs get created by the system during installation to identify built-in users and groups, such as the Administrator account and the Administrators security group. When a user logs in to the system as *guest*, the access token for that user will include the well-known SID for the guest group, which will restrict the user from doing damage or accessing objects that a user is not entitled to.

Trusted Access

Once a security principal, or an imposter, has gained access to a system, it becomes very difficult to get them out short of shutting down the system, denying access, or terminating their network connection. Authentication is thus a very critical area for operating system manufacturers, and they rightly invest a lot of money building software to adequately validate authentic users as quickly as possible, and to block access to villains.

No matter how clever are the authentication schemes used, if a person is able to obtain a valid user ID and password, and that person obtains an unfettered connection to the network login point, he or she will gain access to your system. (Biometrics prevents this, but more about that later.) It is then up to the security mechanisms on the network, access control, to keep the "perp" in check. Tools like auditing software and alerts can help, but often they raise the alarms too late.

The answer lies with Kerberos. Microsoft made a considerable investment, for Windows Server 2003, in the Kerberos protocol, which is an open standard that works on a system of tickets, based on the concept of shared secrets, and implemented using secret key cryptography. Sounds like spy novel stuff for us DBAs, but it is essential in the new world of digital nervous systems and distributed computing and data services. Here is a brief introduction to shared secrets.

Shared Secrets

The Kerberos protocol operates on the concept of a *shared secret*. The term "shared secret" refers to a secret known by a few entities (two or more). Take a gang of bank robbers about to rob a bank. You know the drill. One of the robbers is disguised as a guard, and all the other robbers are hiding in plain sight, as the bank's customers. They are all sharing a secret; they know the guard is not for real and they are about to hold up the tellers. No one else knows this. In other words the secret is known only by the people about to rob the bank; the tellers have no idea their day is about to be ruined. But if all the gang members are disguised so well that they look like regular customers, how do they tell each other apart from the real customers? In this regard, each member of the gang can identify another member by confirming that the other person knows the secret. I can't tell you what the secret is, because I am not a member of the gang . . . it could be a triple wink means "we have three seconds to get out" or something. Likewise, the shared secret in Kerberos is between Kerberos and the *security principal* (the human user or a device). The protocol guarantees that no other entity is able to learn the secret.

Here's another analogy from the Digital Age: Two people engage in a steamy cyberspace love affair and engage each other in a private chat room every night. They need to be sure that their communications can be trusted, that they are truly from the other party, and not a spy or an investigator masquerading as the other party, lurking in the chat room. So in order to be sure that the partners are genuine, they both agree, offline, that something in the messages between them will confirm that the message can be trusted.

However if someone is analyzing the correspondence and looking for repeating word arrangements, it will not take them long to discover the secret key. For example, you cannot comment on the weather, or grandma's cat, indefinitely before someone else catches on. On a network, using inspection software, it would take seconds to intercept a message and fool an authentication service into thinking that it is engaged in trusted communications.

So how do the two cyber-lovers devise a plan to be certain that their engagement is secure? The answer is to use secret key cryptography and encrypt the communications. They would both hold keys that can decrypt their messages. And the spy would not be able to read their steamy words. The key itself must naturally be kept secret.

For the plan to work, the secret key must be symmetric. This means that it must be capable of both encryption and decryption. In other words, as long as the two correspondents share a private secret key, they can encrypt their love letters at will and be sure that the other partner, and only the other partner, is able to decrypt it.

The practice of secret key cryptography is not new but goes back to before the Cold War days when insurgents perfected secret key techniques and cipher science. In fact, it is said that had not the allies seized the Enigma key from the Nazis and cracked the secret communications about their war plans, the swastika would be flying over a Germany that spans the world.

The implementation of Kerberos in Windows Server 2003 is fully compliant with the Internet Engineering Task Force's (IETF) Kerberos v5. This standard, which was originally developed by MIT, is supported by many operating systems, which means that the authentication services in the Windows Server 2003 domain can be trusted in other Kerberos networks (known as realms), such as networks running Mac OS, Novell NetWare, UNIX, AIX, IRIX, and so forth.

I have written a lot about the Kerberos protocol in Windows Server 2003; and I consider it largely beyond the scope of this book to explore it in actual deployment detail. However, there is one exception that has to do with the *Single Sign-on Initiative* (delegation) and the Kerberos ticket granting service; I will return to that point later in this chapter.

At this juncture, you need to grasp that the widespread security philosophy used in most IT environments is that once a security principal has gained access to the network or a system, it becomes a *trusted principal*. This means that it is granted a certain level of *trusted access*.

But trusted access, like the levels of security earlier discussed, can be controlled. If you manage a system that is very difficult to break into, or that employs highly sophisticated authentication technology, such as scanning the retina in your eye or the rings of your teeth, would it make sense to control access in the same fashion at every door within the enterprise? It all depends on the *secrets* you are holding and the respect you have for the information and data that belong to the enterprise and its shareholders.

So now we have another security pyramid, illustrated in Figure 5-5, that we can use to illustrate the issue. At the pinnacle is the highest level of trusted access, requiring the system to demand the utmost in trust from the user. And at the base is the lowest level of trusted access. At the pinnacle, you will use all the security tools in the book to make sure that trusted access stays trusted, not compromised.

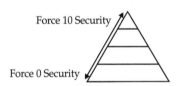

FIGURE 5-5
The base of the pyramid

Force 10 Security

Force 0 Security

Some systems, however, need facilities to allow even nontrusted access. SQL Server 2005 is one such system, and this brings us to an investigation of the *trusted-nontrusted access* mechanisms it deploys.

SQL Server Access

There are two ways, called "authentication modes," into a SQL Server 2005 party. If you have "connections," you can enter by special invitation. This special invitation requires that you know someone on the inside, usually the Boss, aka. the SA. To gain access, you need to go to the back door, where you will be asked for your login name and password. If you can match both, you can get in. This mechanism was once the primary way into SQL Server (at least for people who carried some firepower).

This first access mechanism was once known as standard mode (version 6.5 and earlier). It is "nontrusted" access. In other words, anyone that comes to the door is suspect and has to be authenticated on the spot; they do not have a referral but need to match a login name with a password. From SQL Server 7.0 and later, this access mechanism was downgraded to the least-preferred method of gaining access.

The second way to get into SQL Server is through a referral network, a system that supports the tenet that a friend of my friend is also my friend. To gain access via the referral system, you need to go to the front door and present a vouchsafe to secure your access. The "bouncer" will recognize the vouchsafe and let you in, or toss you out onto the street.

The vouchsafe in question is the access token assigned to you when you successfully logged in to the network. And advanced notice of it, using the security identifier, is stored in the SQL Server trusted login information. This second access mechanism is known as Windows Authentication (formerly Windows NT Authentication). If SQL Server does not recognize the vouchsafe, it has no (or incorrect) SID information, and you do not have a SQL Server login and password to offer as an alternative, you are politely declined entry.

There are more advanced or secure means of implementing trusted access that can be achieved by SQL Server, but for now you should understand the basics. There are thus only two ways to configure SQL Server 2005 access. The preferred method is via *Windows Authentication* (no back doors). The other, for nontrusted access, is called *Mixed Mode Authentication*. The latter lets you in via Windows Authentication or via SQL Server Authentication. Both methods are illustrated in Figure 5-6.

In the past there has been some debate concerning which method is more secure. Many DBAs felt that Windows Authentication, although defined as trusted access, was less secure. The weaknesses in Windows NT 4.0 security, via the services of NTLM, a challenge-response mechanism, were primarily responsible for this perception. There is good reason: Once you are authenticated to the network or domain, there is very little, aside from auditing, to retry or retest your trustworthiness. To many, the ability to just "slide" into SQL Server by virtue of being logged into the network using a login known by SQL Server is scary. And many NT networks are as secure as a child's shoelaces. The network administrator might have groups and permissions out the wazoo, only every ACL has the *Everyone* group with full access embedded in it for posterity.

On the other hand, how secure is SQL Server security? How secure is a lock if you have its key or the combination number . . . ? The subject of Windows Server 2003 domains is different story, however. Thanks to Kerberos and its system of tickets, the debate of trusted versus nontrusted security can finally rest in peace. To understand how it secures SQL Server 2005, you need to understand a little about Kerberos tickets.

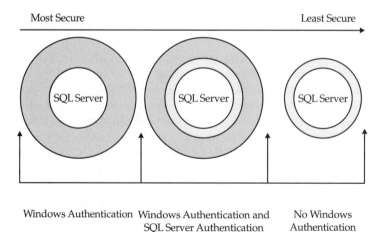

Figure 5-6   Different methods of authenticating to SQL Server

Changing Authentication Modes

You can set and change the authentication modes described here as follows:

1. Open SQL Server Management Studio (SSMS) as described in Chapter 4, in the section "Introducing SQL Server Tools," right-click the server name, and select Properties.

2. Next click the Security page. Under Server Authentication you can select the authentication mode you wish to use. Choose either Windows Authentication or Windows and SQL Server Authentication. Advice: choose Windows and SQL Server Authentication.

3. Click OK to save the setting. You will see a message box suggesting that the service should be restarted before the setting affects the server.

4. To restart the service right there in SSMS, simply right-click the server in Object Explorer and choose Restart. You will need to do this off peak or outside production hours if the server is already accessed by users.

Kerberos Tickets: The Keys to Trusted Access

With Kerberos, authentication is a done deal as long as the information between the parties can be decrypted, or as long as one party can prove that it is the real thing by being in possession of the decrypting key in the first place, like our cyber-lovers discussed earlier. Now, what if someone on the network steals the key, or manages to bug previous authentication sessions and somehow builds a key? Kerberos takes care of this problem because it assumes that someone will be nasty enough to try and hack in.

The Kerberos authentication process kicks into gear as soon as a user or service tries to gain access to a domain (or Keberos realm, to be more precise). At this stage of the authentication, Keberos assumes that the network is not secure and that it is possible for anybody to infiltrate the communication between the client and the server.

When Kerberos receives an authentication request from the Windows security services, it performs the following steps before any access to the network is permitted:

1. It looks the user up in a directory, in our case Active Directory, and retrieves the encryption/decryption key it shares with the user to decrypt the user's authentication message.

2. Next it looks at the information in the message. The first item it checks is the time field, which is the time on the clock of the user's workstation or machine from which the user attempted to log in. If the time on the sender's clock is out of sync by five minutes, Kerberos will reject the message (Kerberos can compensate for the different time zones, and daylight saving time). However, if the time is within the allowable offset of five minutes, Kerberos accepts the message. But wait, there is more.

3. Kerberos now checks to see if the time is identical or older than previous authenticators received from the partner. If the time stamp is not later than and not the same as previous authenticators, Kerberos allows the user to authenticate to the domain.

However, it is also important to know that the authentication is *mutual.* Kerberos will send back a message demonstrating that it was able to decrypt the user's message. This means that the partner server or device is able to verify that it, too, is not masquerading. This is something that NTLM, the legacy Windows authentication service, could never do. Kerberos sends back only select information, the most important being the time stamp that it obtained from the original authentication from the client. If that time stamp matches the client's information, then the client is sure that Kerberos and not some imposter decrypted the message.

Key Distribution

So authenticating to Kerberos works well for authentication to the domain, but what about accessing resources once the client has logged in? After all, the whole idea of logging in is to connect to SQL Server and to start working. So how is the connection to SQL Server trusted in the way described earlier? Remember, NTLM and Windows/Active Directory security services cannot vouch to SQL Server that, just because the client logged in okay, he or she is touched by an angel. To put it differently, "How trusted is trusted access?" On the old Windows NT 4.0 domain, I would have balked at the idea of "trusted access" because NT was as outmoded in a digital nervous system as a Model-T on Mars. SQL Server trusting a user on an NT network is like you or me trusting a used car salesperson, just because he or she is dressed well. But you can safely implement trusted access on Windows Server 2003, Active Directory because with a PKI in the picture or even just native Active Directory security you can distribute keys.

Essentially, Kerberos has the capability to forward a "letter of credit" for every client it can vouch for to the server. This letter of credit is a session key, which tells SQL Server "this guy's for real." In other words, it acts as a broker. This in fact is where the name Kerberos, the protocol, comes from. You may recall from Greek mythology that Kerberos (or Cerberos) was a three-headed dog that stood guard over the gates of Hades. Kerberos, the protocol, also has three heads: the client, the server, and a mediator or proxy. The proxy is known as the *Key Distribution Center (KDC)*—it doles out session keys that it fabricates when the client authenticates. In Windows Server 2003, the Key Distribution Center is installed on the Active Directory Domain Controller.

If you have not studied Kerberos extensively, the authentication process just described might sound too complex and bandwidth-intensive to be of use on a modern network. If decrypting the messages and checking time stamps has to be repeated between clients and servers all the time, and if the KDC has to keep sending all the network resources copies of every user's session key all the time, it would seem to be a tremendous drain on resources. Every server would have to store session keys from thousands of users. But this is not the case—what in fact takes place is ingenious, is simple, and has no impact on the network.

Session Tickets

Instead of following the logical option and sending the "letter of credit" to every server and every client at one time, the KDC sends two copies of the session key (one belonging to the server) to the client and then attends to other connections. The client thus holds the SQL Server host's copy of the key until it is ready to contact the server, usually within a few milliseconds. This process is illustrated in Figure 5-7.

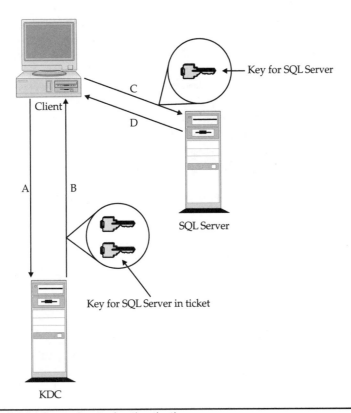

Key for SQL Server

Client

C

D

A

B

SQL Server

Key for SQL Server in ticket

KDC

FIGURE 5-7   Key distribution and mutual authentication

The KDC invents a session key whenever the client contacts it to access a SQL Server host (A). The KDC sends the session key to the client, and embedded in the session key is the session ticket (B). Embedded in the session ticket, which really belongs to the SQL Server host, is the host server's session key for the client.

As soon as the client receives the session communication from the KDC, it opens the ticket and extracts its copy of the session key. Both items are then stored in volatile memory. When the client is ready to contact SQL Server (C), it will send the server a packet that contains the ticket still encrypted with the server's secret key and the time authenticator encrypted with the session key.

If everything checks out, the SQL Server host grants access to the client (D) because the server knows that a trusted authority, the KDC, issued the credentials. After the connection is allowed, the Net-Libraries can do their thing and begin login to SQL Server; credentials can then be passed into the instance and teamed up with the SQL Server login. As soon as the client is done using the server, the server can get rid of the session key that the client was using to communicate with the server. The client will instead hold the session key and represent it to the server each time it needs to access it. But no other client can try to connect to SQL Server under the guise of a user that just disconnected or might still be using the system.

Session tickets can also be reused, and as a safeguard against ticket theft, the tickets come with expiration times. The time-to-live for a ticket is specified in the domain security policy, which is discussed later in this chapter in the section "The SQL Server Security Plan." Typical ticket life is usually about eight hours, the average login time. When the user logs out, the ticket cache is flushed and all session tickets and keys are discarded.

Kerberos, Trusts, and Login Delegation

Kerberos provides the technology that allows Windows Server 2003 domains to interoperate as bidirectional, transitive trusts, as long as the domains are part of a contiguous namespace (such as an Active Directory tree). Domains in separate domain trees or in separate forests can, however, share an *interdomain key,* and one KDC becomes the proxy for the other and vice versa. This makes for a secure environment that can safely allow a user in a foreign domain to connect to SQL Server.

Once an interdomain key has been established, the ticket granting service in each domain is registered as a security principal with the other domain's KDC, allowing it to issue ticket referrals. Clients in their own domains still need to contact their local KDCs for access to a foreign resource. The process is as follows:

1. The local KDC checks to see if the resource needed by the client resides in another domain.

2. If it does, it sends the client a referral ticket for the resource in the other domain.

3. The client then contacts the other domain's KDC and sends it the referral ticket. The remote KDC authenticates the user or begins a session ticket exchange to allow the client to connect to resources in the remote domain. The domain-to-domain trust model is illustrated in Figure 5-8.

What takes place on a Windows Server 2003 network is as follows: The client delegates authentication to a server by telling the KDC that the server is authorized to represent the client. In lay terms, that is like telling the KDC that the SQL Server machine you are authenticated to has power of attorney to deal with the second SQL Server machine. This is similar in process to the concept of the access token, another form of attorney, agency, proxy, or what Microsoft calls "impersonation"—an unfortunate word.

Delegation can be done as follows:

1. The client can obtain a ticket from the KDC for the referred server. Upon connection to the login server, the client must hand this ticket to the server. Such a ticket is called a *proxy ticket.* Difficulty arises in this scenario because the client needs advance knowledge of the other server, which becomes a management cost in both the client and server tiers.

2. The better option is to allow the client to issue the login server a ticket granting ticket (TGT), which can be set up upon initial presentation to the SQL Server login server, which can then use this TGT to obtain a ticket for the referred server, as needed. Such a ticket is also known as a *forwarded TGT.*

The forwarded tickets are managed in Kerberos policy in Active Directory. Kerberos policy is managed in the Default Domain Group Policy object and is something you need to

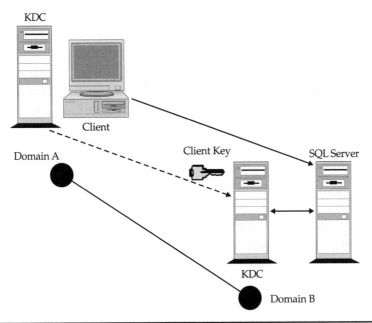

KDC

Client

Domain A

Client Key

SQL Server

KDC

Domain B

FIGURE 5-8   The domain-to-domain trust model under Kerberos

set up outside of SQL Server at your domain controller. You or your network administrator will need to manage the policy object in Active Directory, by a process you'll find described in Windows Server 2003 help or a good book on Windows Server 2003 security.

You will notice when you set up delegation that each ticket has a time-out period that can be defined in Active Directory. If a connection remains idle for too long, the ticket will expire and all subsequent attempts to execute a distributed query or a remote stored procedure will fail. The user will have to disconnect from the login server and reestablish the connection if your application keeps the connection open. This is an added security benefit, because most well-written applications should not keep connections open indefinitely. In distributed or *n*-tier scenarios, it is unlikely your client will be maintaining open-ended connectivity to the server.

Looking at the connection from the viewpoint of the secondary server, when SQL Server instance A connects to SQL Server instance B and executes a distributed query that references tables on instance B, then instance B has access to your login credentials. Instance B can then validate your individual permissions to access the data from the tables referenced.

On a Windows network, you have to specifically define a login on A to connect to B. The login is global and is used regardless of which user executes the distributed query on A. Instance B will not have any knowledge of the actual user executing the query, and you cannot define permissions specific to individual users connecting from A. You will have to define a global set of permissions for the login account used by A. The solution on Windows is also less secure. For example, you cannot audit what the specific users are doing in B.

Configuring Delegation

There are a number of things to consider before you can support delegation. The following checklist highlights the necessary components to manage or configure:

- **DNS**   You need to install a DNS server as the locator service for Kerberos. The DNS service that ships as part of Windows Server 2003 Server is the best DNS to use because it is tightly integrated with Active Directory and supports dynamic updates. If you already use another brand of DNS, note that the governing RFC (1510) specifies how DNS should resolve KDC hosts to IP addresses. In a Windows Server 2003 domain, the KDC is usually installed on the Active Directory server, the domain controller. They are not connected in terms of application process space and run as separate services. However, since the KDC is always installed on the DC, it is possible to resolve a KDC by looking up the host address of a domain controller. Client computers in a Kerberos realm need to send their messages to the IP address, and if the IP address of the KDC cannot be resolved, it generates an error message to the client indicating that the domain cannot be located.

- **Active Directory**   You will need to install Active Directory if your primary network is not a Windows Server 2003 network. It is also possible to install Windows Server 2003 servers in non–Windows Server 2003 domains or networks (such as Linux), and they can still participate in Kerberos authentication. You will need to ensure that they resolve to the correct host addresses, which might not be Active Directory domain controllers. The utility called *ksetup.exe* (in the Windows Server 2003 Resource Kit) is used to configure clients and servers to participate in Kerberos realms that are not Windows Server 2003 domains.

- **TCP/IP**   All computers participating in SQL Server delegation will need to be running TCP/IP, and you will need to ensure that TCP/IP is the Net-Library being used by all clients and servers.

- **Computer Account**   Your SQL Server computer should have an account in Active Directory. Find or create the account, open to the General tab of the server Properties dialog box, and ensure that the appropriate Delegation option is checked. This is illustrated in Figure 5-9.

- **Service Principal Name (SPN)**   A *service principal name* (SPN) identifies an instance of SQL Server as a security principal. The SPN is defined or set using the *setspn* utility, which can be found in the Windows Server 2003 Resource Kit. The SPN is typically created by a Windows Server 2003 domain administrator. The syntax to create the SPN is as follows:

```
setspn -A MSSQLSvc/Host:port serviceaccount
```

The SPN is assigned to the service account of the SQL Server instance on your primary server so that the instance, or rather the service account representing it, is attested as being authenticated, at the particular socket address. For example, to create an SPN for SQL Server, you need to run the following code at a command prompt:

```
setspn -A MSSQLSvc/mcsql00.cityhall.genesis.mcity.org:1433 micsql
```

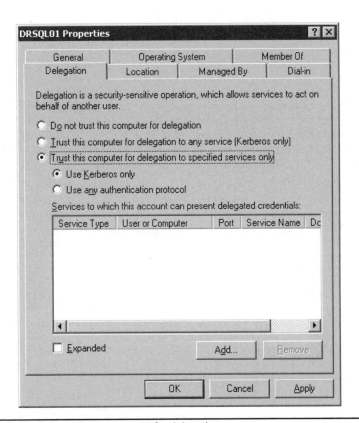

FIGURE 5-9   Configuring the computer account for delegation

- **User Account**   The account of the user (login) must be set up for delegation. Open to the Account tab on the user's Properties dialog box in Active Directory. Ensure that the appropriate Delegation option is checked. This is illustrated in Figure 5-10.

The preceding steps are all that is needed to enlist delegation, but there is obviously a lot more to Kerberos and delegation than what we discussed here, and it exceeds the scope of this book. Numerous books have been written that deal exclusively with Kerberos. However, Kerberos security is the de facto pervasive security mechanism that protects Windows Server 2003 domains and their server products, such as SQL Server 2005.

So given that Kerberos security provides a much higher level of trusted access than earlier, it actually makes sense to configure a server for Windows Authentication mode only.

Secure Sockets Layer

We touched upon TCP/IP in Chapter 4, in our discussion of the SQL Server Net-Libraries. You will likely need to implement SSL TLS (Secure Sockets Layer/Transport Layer Security) layer, especially with respect to network rollout, and *n-tier* database applications architecture, in a large rollout. *SSL/TLS* has been around in several Windows products for a while. It is a

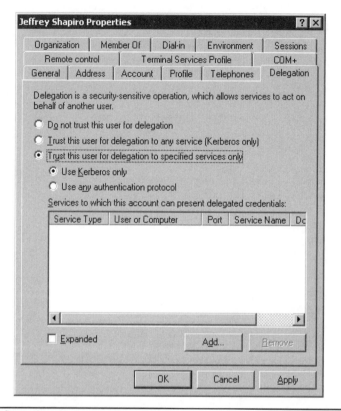

FIGURE 5-10   Configure the user account for delegation

widely supported protocol both on corporate networks and on the Internet. SSL/TLS is also supported in Internet Information Server (IIS) and Microsoft Exchange.

Windows Server 2003 uses SSL/TLS and X.509 certificates to authenticate smart card users for network and DBMS access and for data protection. SSL/TLS is used to secure a wide range of communications such as network traffic, IIS traffic (Web and FTP), e-mail, and client-DBMS transactions created in browsers or standard applications.

Microsoft Certificate Services

Two levels of public key cryptography from which SQL Server security can benefit are at work inside Windows Server 2003. One level is implicit and expressly built into the operating system. It is at work in Kerberos and IPsec, as described earlier, and does not require attention from you, other than some minor configuration management. (Microsoft Certificate Services also provides certificates to the Windows Server 2003 Encrypting File System [EFS].) The second level is explicit. It requires you to build a public key infrastructure to accommodate a pervasive use of public key cryptography to access highly sensitive data in SQL Server.

Public Key Infrastructure

A *public key infrastructure (PKI)* is a collection of services and components that work together to a common end, a secure computing environment. Such an environment will allow you to secure all database transactions, both on an intranet and over the Internet, to secure your Web sites and your company's Web-based online transactions, to deploy smart cards and biometrics for authentication, and more.

A PKI gives you the ability to support the following public key services:

- **Key Management**   The PKI issues new keys, reviews or revokes existing keys, and manages the trust levels between other vendors' key issuers.

- **Key Publishing**   The PKI provides a systematic means of publishing both valid and invalid keys. Keys can also be revoked if their security is compromised. PKI handles the revocation lists so that applications can determine if a key is no longer to be trusted (this is similar in practice to the bad credit card lists published by the banks for the benefit of merchants).

- **Key Usage**   The PKI provides an easy mechanism for applications and users to use keys. Key usage provides the best possible security for the enterprise.

Digital Certificates

As discussed earlier in this chapter, public keys are encapsulated in digital certificates. I can think of no better example of a digital certificate than your driver's license. The license number is the key. It is what gives you the right to get into a motor vehicle and use a public road. The driver's license is issued by the Department of Motor Vehicles (DMV). It is laminated so that it cannot be tampered with and is an object of trust that proves that you received the "key" from a trusted authority, which in this case is the DMV.

How do you validate a digital certificate? A *certificate authority (CA)*, which issues the key, is the equivalent of the DMV in the preceding analogy. The CA signs the certificate with its digital signature. You can validate the digital signature with the CA's public key. But who vouches for the CA? A *certificate hierarchy*, a system of vouchsafes that extends all the way up to the root CAs that have formed an association of authorities. Microsoft is a CA that can directly issue public keys, which are handled by the Microsoft Certificate Services.

A PKI is a collection of services and components that collectively create the infrastructure. A Microsoft PKI depends on Active Directory for the publishing of key information, and all certificates, revocation lists, and policy information is stored in the directory.

Managing a Microsoft PKI is not difficult and is even less time-consuming than managing logins, roles and users, databases, and database access. If you are managing SQL Server 2005 on a Windows Server 2003 network, many of your day-to-day activities already encompass the facilities of a PKI.

Trusted Access Versus Nontrusted Access

As you can see, you can lock down access to SQL Server to the "nth" degree. Why then does the support for Mixed Mode linger? For starters, backward compatibility with earlier versions of SQL Server is a good reason. Second, if you have a remote SQL Server 2005 system, on a secure WAN segment, or anywhere for that matter, and it sits in a nontrusted domain, or as a stand-alone server on a non-Windows network, there is no means of presenting client authentication in the network communication. In other words, the connection cannot raise a Security Support Provider Interface (SSPI) to the SQL Server. This means that the only way to gain access is to transmit the internal user ID and password pair to SQL Server for access.

SQL Server Security: The Internal Environment

Let's now put aside the access control story and work within the DBMS. Once users are inside SQL Server, their objectives are to access the databases (and in the case of administrators, the DBMS). Your objectives as the DBA are to ensure that they access only the data and objects they are allowed to access. You also have to ensure that users do not destroy data, through either mala fide or bona fide actions. The mechanisms you have to secure data, at the object level, are very similar to the security mechanisms out on the file system or in the operating system.

As mentioned earlier, a database is an object that itself consists of objects . . . in much the same way a cell contains protoplasm and cytoplasm. We refer to this hierarchy of objects as an object chain, as illustrated by Figure 5-11. All objects in the chain inherit ownership from the parent object when they are created on the connection that first created the parent. Subsequent connections that can create objects become the owners of the new objects.

What good are permissions if you don't have users to use them? Figure 5-12 examines the access "tree" that towers above the object and its permissions. At the root of the tree, we have the objects, and the connection to it is via the permissions we have discussed. Roles or users have to go through the permissions to access the objects, as you now know. User objects are split into two entities: They can be individual users derived from several sources, or they can be "roles," which are groups of individual user accounts. Users can also be given aliases, but we'll get to that information soon.

At the very top of the tree, you'll find an entity called the *login level*, or *logins*. The login level controls access to the system itself. Access to the database is given by connecting the user account at the lower level with the login at the "server" level. The login, as you know, is associated with either a SQL Server nontrusted login or a security principal (trusted), a domain user account given to an external trusted Windows domain account, or an external nontrusted user that is assigned an internal SQL Server user ID account and password. *Logins* are managed interactively in Management Studio. They can also be managed programmatically, as is specifically discussed in Appendix.

Users

SQL Server users can be described as follows:

- **Built-in users and system roles**   When you first create an instance of SQL Server 2005, when you install it from scratch, the first user ID created is the System Administrator, or SA. This is the first user given login access and exists for access before any form of domain or network security exists. This user is created at the big bang of SQL Server 2005, when the instance is created and it needs a "first cause," known for some time now as "SA." SA has access to all of SQL Server.

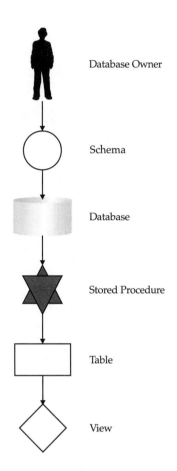

FIGURE 5-11
The object-
ownership chain

Database Owner

Schema

Database

Stored Procedure

Table

View

Several built-in system roles are also added (they are discussed shortly), and both domain and SQL Server users can use these roles. By the way, all members of your domain's BUILTIN\Administrators group and the server's local BUILTIN\Administrators group are members of the sysadmin system role, which gives any members of these groups trusted access at the same level as the SA.

- **Database users**   Database users are the database "connections" your logins access. If the user is nontrusted, the login will require an ID and password pair to match what is stored in the system's user tables. Database user security is managed on the Users node of a database tree in Management Studio. You can also fully manage database users programmatically, using T-SQL (and of course, triggers and stored procedures also play a part in server and database security). To be clear on the difference between logins and users: Logins allow you to connect to SQL Server per se; users allow you to connect to databases, objects, and the DBMS per se.

- **Guest user**   The *guest* user requires special mention. The guest user is predefined in SQL Server when you first install the instance. It is automatically given access to

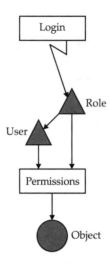

the master database, albeit with no permissions that it could use to hang itself. The purpose of the guest user account is to allow any login to connect to a database, if you explicitly allow this, without having to demand "name, rank, and serial number" at every connection. The guest account is useful for casual access to the database, to look up data without risking data, and so forth.

If you add the guest account to a database, SQL Server will check a login attempt, as usual, to see if a valid user name or alias is assigned. If not, it will check to see if the guest has access to the database. If the guest has access, the nonauthenticated user will be admitted as a guest of the database owner. Allowing guests into the database is totally at the discretion of the database owner or system administrator.

Roles

To me, a security group is to a user account what a shoelace is to a shoe. If you lose the shoelace, you will either lose the shoe or lose your balance. Every domain I currently manage is put together using the building blocks of security and distribution groups. No user under my care is ever excluded from a group—even if I only have one user on the domain, that individual gets to be a member of a group.

I was thus one of many Windows sysadmin/DBAs to be delighted to discover a similar concept established in SQL Server. Roles were added to SQL Server with version 7.0; they are very important to SQL Server 2005 management and count big time toward easing the cost of administration.

If you have worked with groups, then roles will not be too difficult to grasp. Collect the users that require the same services, access, and permissions for logins on databases and objects into a role. Then apply the object's permissions to the role. The role members are then granted (or denied) access by role membership and not on an individual user basis. Whenever you have a new user that requires access, you can simply add the user to the role for it to inherit the same level of access as everyone else in the role.

When working with Windows groups, when I need to remove a security account's access from a file or folder, I simply remove it from the group. Specifically denying a user access is not a common occurrence and is usually motivated by some ill intent on the part of the user. Denying access is also a costly management practice because you have to keep track of the actual account and the object that access has been denied to. And you also have to recall what level of access was denied on top of everything else.

With the exception of one role I will discuss, roles apply to database access and to the objects inside the database to which permissions must be set. Roles, like user groups in the OS, can be nested. So you can create a small role for a group of troublemakers and nest it inside a group of angels. If the troublemakers cause trouble, out they go without affecting the other kids. However, the best feature of a role, again like a user group, is that the user can be a member of more than one role, and that makes for some powerful access control and user management.

Roles are available as either predefined "house" roles or as user-defined roles. And they come in several flavors listed shortly. The term "user-defined" is really a misnomer because it is the DBA that will create these roles . . . or members of the *db_owner* or *db_security* predefined database roles discussed shortly.

The following lists the roles and the primary "roles" they play in the DBMS:

- Public role (built in)
- Server roles (built in)
- Database roles (built in)
- User-defined database application roles
- User-defined standard roles

Public Role

The public role is added to every database you create and is added to the system databases when you install SQL Server 2005. The public role works like the *Everyone* group in the OS environment with one exception: The *Everyone* group can be removed from objects to fully secure the system. The Everyone group to me is like the proverbial fly buzzing around your head. The Everyone group can be a real nuisance because every time you create a resource or establish a service, the Everyone group gets added. So I go to the parent and ensure that child objects do not inherit the Everyone group from it. Simple cutting the inheritance connection from the parent object, which forces you to add exactly the groups you need to the resource, does this, but with SQL Server it is not as simple as just going to the parent object and getting rid of "Everyone."

Removing Public is not so easy to do with SQL Server. For starters, access to Public is given as soon as you create the database. Second, every user that gets permission to access the database gets added to the public role. The saving grace of the public role is that it is not a weak link in the security environment of SQL Server as Everyone is to the operating system or network. Instead, it is a convenient way of providing quick default access to users of the database. If you are worried about security, you should know that while the users are added to Public, they are not automatically handed the keys to the vault. You have to go into Public and set access permissions for each object the role can access.

In addition Public is a convenient means of providing all database users with a common set of permissions they should all have.

Server Roles

Server roles are fixed roles, predefined or built into SQL Server 2005. The server role is the only role that is applied outside of the database objects. The server role is a useful container that allows its members to administer the server and perform role-wide tasks. There are a number of server roles in SQL Server 2005, as defined in Table 5-1.

Database Roles

Database roles are fixed roles that apply to the databases of an instance of SQL Server. There are nine fixed administrative database roles and one fixed user role in SQL Server 2005. The fixed user role is public, which we have already discussed. The administrative roles permit a wide range of database administrative chores, such as backing up and restoring, running DDL against the database, and database security. Table 5-2 lists the nine roles and their functions in a database.

All databases can have the fixed database roles listed in Table 5-2, but membership is restricted to a database. For example, a member of db_ddladmin on the database SHOES1 is not automatically a member of the same role in SHOES2. This is referred to as the *scope* of the role.

You cannot nest predefined roles, not even in a user-defined standard role. If you want to let a DBA do both backup administration and login management, the user will have to be added to both roles.

Application Roles

The first question I asked when I encountered roles for the first time was "What about applications?" Surely an application can be a "login" without having to create a special account for the operator of the client machine. For example, you are asked to create a time-entry application to track work hours. Does this mean every employee in the company must be added to a role, possibly to *Public*? Which groups would you want the network administrator to create? What about change control policy, and so on? The answer lies in the application role.

Fixed Server Role	Duties
Sysadmin	Has the run of the ship; performs everything.
Serveradmin	Configures the server; shuts down the server. Users in this role can run server-related administration tasks such as DBCC FREEPROCCACHE, RECONFIGURE, and so on.
Setupadmin	Manages linked servers and startup procedures.
Securityadmin	Manages logins and can read error logs. Users can add members to this role and so on.
Processadmin	Manages processes on a SQL Server instance.
dbcreator	Creates, alters, and restores databases.
diskadmin	Manager of the disk files.
bulkadmin	Has the right to run BULK INSERT.

TABLE 5-1   Fixed Server Roles

Fixed Database Role	Duties
db_owner	The big Kahuna: All activity in a database. This role essentially combines all the capabilities of the other database roles.
db_accessadmin	Adds and removes users and logins. This role allows its members to work with Windows users and groups.
db_datareader	Power to run SELECT on any user database. However, this role does not permit access to data editing functions.
db_datawriter	The converse of the preceding role. It has the power to run INSERT, DELETE, and UPDATE on any user database, but it does not permit the use of SELECT.
db_denydatareader	Can deny SELECT on any user database.
db_denydatawriter	Can prevent the change or deleting of data.
db_ddladmin	Can run DDL statements on a user database, but has no access to GRANT, REVOKE, or DENY (see Appendix).
db_securityadmin	Manages roles, membership, and permissions.
db_backupoperator	Performs backups, restores, DBCC, CHECKPOINT.

TABLE 5-2 Fixed Database Roles

This is how it works: When your application makes a connection to SQL Server, it calls the application role stored procedure *sp_setapprole* to request access. This SP takes two parameters in your statement, the name of the role and a password. The DBMS then works with the role in the context of a user on the database, and any permissions defined on objects in the database, in the application role, apply to the application. For example, if the application role only allows the application to select data, that's all the application will be allowed to do. You will not be able to write a routine that "gate crashes" a role to write data.

Application roles are user-defined and can be secured with passwords. And of course, there are a number of ways to encrypt the password, as discussed earlier. Also, no users are associated with application roles. In the time-entry example, you could create one application role that allows users to enter information, and another one for the HR managers that will allow their applications to access the information. You could also secure the application by requesting that a user provide the password required for advanced use of the application and pass the data to the SP password parameter for the application role. The application role is thus a very powerful tool, useful in a variety of client programming scenarios.

However, you should also understand that when an application makes use of application roles, any connection made to SQL Server in the context of a standard login is terminated. You have to close the connection to the application role and reconnect to the server if you require features or access in the context of a database user.

SQL Server also maintains any auditing you might have covering the *user*. So when you suspend user access and startup application access, auditing continues in the user context. In other words, SQL Server still knows who's pulling the strings.

The application role is also an excellent means of protecting data from being attacked using SQL Server tools and DBA "thorns" like Microsoft Access. The Query Analyzer tool, from the SQL Server 2000 arsenal, for example, is extremely powerful, can connect to SQL Server 2005, and in the wrong hands can destroy a database that is not adequately protected. And Access's grids do more than just run SELECT on data: one keypress and you can be in the table.

A downside of the application role, however, is that you have to hard-code a password into the client or force the user to provide one when attempting to connect to SQL Server. We are in the business of limiting the number of passwords, and the single sign-on benefit provided by Kerberos provides that very function thus, a second password might detract from that objective.

Standard Roles

Standard user-defined roles are containers you can create for a collection of users or groups from both trusted and nontrusted sources to provide access to a database. These roles are restricted to the database they were created in. The roles can also be used for nesting a number of roles. You can also use roles an alternative to groups from the Windows environment that you might not have access to or that may not yet exist. It will also be better to have the network administrator create the groups you need and add them to your roles.

Permissions

Microsoft introduced a new permissions system to SQL Server starting with version 7.0, its landmark product revision of the century and precursor to what we are now trying to drive. This system has been extended and further enhanced with SQL Server 2000 and 2005. It is based on the security model and the Windows NTFS permissions architecture, which we discussed earlier in this chapter. An "access control list" for a database object contains the names of users or groups of users that are granted access to an object, and the level of that access. A special "permission"—DENY—blocks a user or group (security principal) from accessing the object in a certain way.

Like its counterpart at the OS and NTFS levels, the user in SQL Server 2005 obtains the sum of permissions assigned to it at the individual and role levels (roles are discussed in a moment). In other words, if the user gets permission to select records in one role and in another role gets permission to insert and select records, the combined permissions are INSERT and SELECT. However, if another group on the same object denies SELECT, guess what?, the user is denied permission to SELECT, no matter that it is granted elsewhere. In Windows Server 2003 security, the object permissions work the same way. DENY is the most restrictive permission and overrides everything.

Inside the SQL Server DBMS, not all objects have permissions. Some objects by their nature or purpose cannot be shared or accessed, yet they all have some function to perform on data that is usually only called by its owner or an internal process. An example of such an object is an index on one end of the chain and the database at the other. No other users are allowed to access the objects until the owners authorize their access and set the access level.

A database object's access is provided through a system of permissions. At the very top of the object chain, the database itself does not immediately make itself available to users. Before users can access a database, the database owner must first explicitly grant access. This is achieved by allowing groups of users to have access to the database, and permissions can be configured interactively through Management Studio or via several programmatic options. Three types of permissions can be applied to SQL Server objects. These are as follows:

- Object permissions
- Statement permissions
- Implied permissions

Object Permissions

The following is a list of objects that have permissions. If a user can access an object, it means that access to the object must have a system of permissions that govern its access. The following list shows all schema-scoped system objects that are included with SQL Server 2005. "Securables" are system objects contained in the schemas named sys or INFORMATION_SCHEMA. These are the objects that fall into the access-permissions category.

- Aggregate function (CLR)
- CHECK constraint
- DEFAULT (constraint or stand-alone)
- FOREIGN KEY constraint
- PRIMARY KEY constraint
- SQL Stored Procedure
- Assembly (CLR) stored procedure
- SQL scalar-function
- Assembly (CLR) scalar-function
- Assembly (CLR) table-valued function
- Rule (old-style, stand-alone)
- Replication-filter procedure
- Synonym
- Service queue
- Assembly (CLR) trigger
- SQL DML trigger
- SQL inline table-valued function
- SQL table-valued function
- Table (user-defined)
- UNIQUE constraint
- View
- Extended stored procedure
- Internal table

Statement Permissions

Statement permissions control access to the T-SQL statements that create database objects or that cause SQL Server to perform specific database-centric activities (such as execute, update, create, select). While a database is an object, SQL Server 2005 classifies the permissions that apply to it as statement permissions. Statement permissions also apply to stored procedures, functions, tables, views, rules, and so on. These permissions are accessible in the Database Properties, Permissions dialog box in Management Studio.

You will seldom need to provide users with these statement permissions. But if your enterprise maintains a large SQL Server implementation and you have several DBAs assigned to specific tasks, they will require the appropriate permission in order to carry out their duties. You can't just give everyone access to SA anymore; that's a no-no in SQL Server 2005.

Implied Permissions

The third class of permissions is called *implied permissions*. These apply to a wide range of activities and can only be made available to, implicitly, members of the predefined roles in the DBMS or the database owners. Such permissions allow the use, for example in the ALTER TABLE statement, of an implied permission that is inherited by the database owner by virtue of ownership.

A database owner, for example, also does not require permission to delete a table, add data, create indexes, and so on because these permissions are implied (inherited) through ownership.

The system administrator gets the full deck of implied permissions, from installation through complete management to the final removal of an instance.

Checking Permissions

SQL Server 2005 put its Windows Authentication trust to the test when a user attempts to log in. At the time of login, a trusted connection is established if the so-called security principal, a user or a group, arrives armed with an access token and SID information. When you create a login for a client derived from a domain security principal, the login is created and the SID for the security account is fetched from Active Directory or the NT Security Accounts Manager (SAM). You can also create a trusted account without the domain because the SID *varbinary* variable can store a NULL or a GUID.

Each time a user connects over the trusted connection, its SID is compared to the SID on file in the SQL Server *sysxlogins* table (visit the *master* database). If the SID does not compare, the connection is rejected. Do you remember what was discussed earlier in this chapter about the SID? If you know what goes on in the world of Windows security, you'll remember that when you delete a user, computer, or group account, you also delete the SID. If you then create the exact same account, a new SID is generated because the old one was discarded when you nixed the earlier account.

The idea to use SIDs was born during the development of SQL Server 7.0, which replaced the old version 6.5 trusted mechanism that still uses access over Registry keys installed in the local host's Registry, and we all know how secure that is. SQL Server would check if the user had access to the Registry key, and if access was proved, login was granted. SQL Security Manager (may it rest in peace) was used to insert the usernames into the old *syslogins* table. I am reminding you of this legacy because upgrading to SQL Server 2005 can be scary if your objective is to inherit extensive databases and configuration information you may have on the old platform. Before you upgrade, you must make a special effort to clean up your legacy installations, and the one area to start with is your user account and login information.

SIDs are stored along with the user login information in the *sysusers* and *sysxlogins* tables and are used to pair the logins with the associated user accounts. Each user ID is then stored in the *sysobjects* table to determine ownership and in the *sysprotects* table to apply permissions to the objects (in similar fashion to the ACLs out in the NTFS). Yet another table, *systypes*, is used to determine ownership of any user-defined types.

Every time a user connects to SQL Server and is given access, its connection information is recorded in a snapshot structure called the *process status structure (PSS).* The PSS is not persistent but is lost when the connection ends. However, every connection is recorded in its own PSS, so an application or user making multiple connections to SQL Server will have multiple PSS snapshots. The PSS in fact is very similar to the access token that is associated with the user every time it requires access to file system objects, as well as to the Kerberos tickets that are required to provide access to servers and services on a Windows Server 2003 domain.

When a user attempts to access a database, the server checks the sysusers tables for any negative credit that may have been placed there, in the form of specific access denials placed on the database objects. These are unlikely to occur, because users generally obtain access via the *Public* role discussed above. If all checks out and the user has database access, the DBMS then scans the *sysmembers* table to check on the role memberships of the user. This allows the DBMS to check if the user is constrained from access or denied service by virtue of group or role membership.

Once a user's "persona" has been established by the server, object permissions are checked in the *syspermissions* table. Naturally the DENY permission information will be checked first; if it is present, the user will be blocked from accessing the respective resource on the level of access that has been denied. The combined access/denied scenario is cached to prevent system overhead every time the respective user attempts to access the same object.

SQL Server maintains a permissions cache that is kept up to date because permission status can change at any time. The permissions cache works like the procedure cache or the query plan cache. When permissions are changed, the DBMS increments a permissions counter that is compared against the value in the cache. If the value in the cache is lower than the counter value, the permissions are rescanned and the permissions cache is updated. There is a small overhead that is incurred at every permission rescan, but this is negligible because once a database model or design is settled, permissions are unlikely to be continually changed.

GUIDS for Nontrusted Users

SQL Server nontrusted users are assigned a 16-byte globally unique identifier in place of a SID (which will be absent when this user connects or when SQL Server is installed in an insecure environment). GUIDs are used in the same fashion as SIDs described previously are for trusted users. This allows the internal security architecture to remain the same for both trusted and nontrusted environments. In other words, all permissions-checking routines remain the same, no matter whether it is the SID or the GUID the security architecture revolves around.

Managing SQL Server Security

There are two directions you can come from to attack user access. First, you can go directly to the database you are managing and create users, and from there set up logins for the users, or you can set up logins as part of a DBMS-wide, or data center, security plan.

I prefer—actually enforce—the latter approach. Logins are created and managed by a member of the securityadmin or sysadmin roles, according to policy and mechanisms that go through a change control or management authority. I will tackle the subject of change control at the end of this chapter. Essentially, the change control board (CCB) is approached by a department head or application manager and requests user access to databases. Change control management approves the access and forwards the request to the DBAs for execution.

The routine I just described is identical to the one required in the external environment where the CCB (or its security manager) requests the network administrator to add, change, or delete user accounts and manage group and OU membership. This practice centralizes control and prevents breakdown in security requirements outlined in your plan. If you willy-nilly added logins at every turn or allowed anyone to create user accounts and logins on the fly, very soon you would have power user logins created for one database accessing others they should not access. Remember, logins are global and exist above all databases. So a login intended for one database can be used to access any other one (associated with a user, of course). I will discuss this issue further in the security plan to follow shortly.

The following sections first deal with surface area configuration, then we will get into the subject of creating *database roles*, then *logins*, and then *users*.

Surface Area Configuration

The more exposed a server or system, the less secure it is. Surface area reduction involves reducing the so-called "attack-surface" of a system by stopping or disabling unused components; thereby leaving it less exposed. Like the Windows Server 2003 platform it operates on, a number of features, services, and connections are disabled or stopped to prevent their access while a server is being introduced.

To perform surface area configuration use SQL Server Surface Area Configuration tool from the the Start menu, All Programs, Microsoft SQL Server 2005, Configuration Tools, and then click SQL Server Surface Area Configuration. The first page to appear is the SQL Server Surface Area Configuration start page.

On the start page, specify which server you want to configure. The default value is "localhost," but you can select a named server, and connect to it over the network.

After selecting the server to configure, you can launch tools to enable and disable features of the Database Engine, Analysis Services, and Reporting Services. Or you can enable or disable Windows services and remote connectivity. You can also use the Surface Area Configuration command line utility or SAC tool.

Using this tool you can import and export surface area settings making it easy to configure a number of servers off a template server. You simply export the configuration settings to a file and then use that file to apply the same settings to SQL Server 2005 components on other servers.

Creating and Configuring Database Roles

Database roles can be created programmatically or interactively using the Management
Studio. Roles are an internal environment security mechanism; in other words, they do not
have any relationship with an external object (like a Windows security principal) on which
their existence depends.

To create and manage a role, do the following:

1. Expand the database you are working in, expand Security and then Roles, and
   select the Database Roles node (under the root Roles node you have both Database
   Roles and Application Roles).

2. Next click New Database Role to add a role. The Database Role–New dialog box,
   shown in Figure 5-13, loads. Note that you can nest roles here, or add user members.
   Click OK and your role is created.

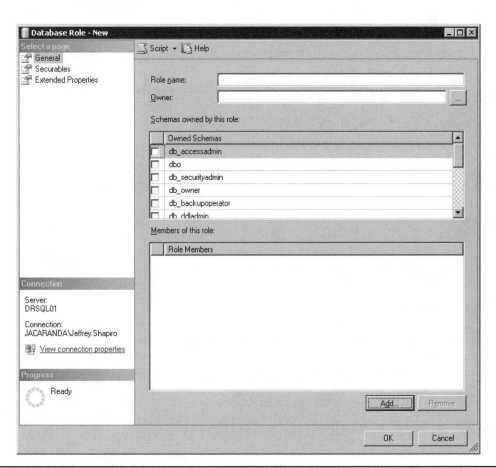

FIGURE 5-13   The Database Role—New dialog box

To define permissions for the role, follow these steps:

1. Select the role from the Details pane (or you can do this as part of the preceding Step 2), right-click, and select Properties.

2. From the Database Role Properties dialog box, click Permissions. The Permissions dialog box for the role will load (see the section "Permissions" earlier in this chapter).

Creating and Configuring Logins

Logins can be created programmatically or interactively using the Management Studio. Creating logins using T-SQL is discussed in Appendix. To create logins interactively in Management Studio, do the following:

1. Go directly to the Security node in Management Studio and expand the node. Right-click the node and select New Login from the context menu. The New Login dialog box, as shown in Figure 5-14, loads. Logins are created on the General page of the Login—New dialog box.

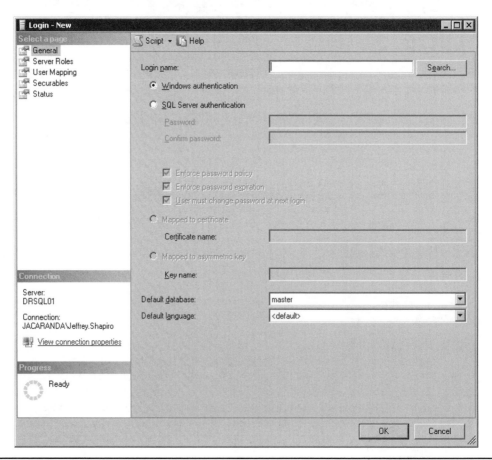

FIGURE 5-14   Login—New dialog box

2. Next, either enable Windows Authentication or, if you are supporting nontrusted access, enable the SQL Server Authentication options. If you are going to add users from security groups in the external environment to the login, the Name field accesses user accounts from the NT SAM or Active Directory. If you are creating a nontrusted login, you need to come up with a name and password for the login.

3. The last item you need to set on this page is the default database for the login. This default should usually be the database for which the login is being created; however, you can leave it at the default (*master*) or make the default database *pubs* or some other database that contains no data worth worrying about. Making *master* the default database is a risky proposition in my book, even though the login does not get immediate access to the data because it has to go through more checkpoints before it can reach into a table.

4. Now click the User Mapping. (You can bypass the Server Roles page because that is for DBA access, which we discussed in the earlier section on server roles.) The User Mapping page will let you select the databases to permit the login to access (still no access to data). You will also be able to select the database role for the login (if it has been created), but until you save this information and connect the role to a user account in a database, you still have no direct access to data.

You can drill further into permissions at this point, but I recommend you manage permissions through role creation and management in the respective database first. Unless you know your way around these pages like a blind fish in a cave, navigation here can be a little stressful.

NOTE *There are several items to notice about the logins and the User Mapping page. First, you can allow a login to access more than one database. Second, the login can be in more than one database role. Third, the database role is peculiar to the database that you select in the database list, on the User Mappings page.*

If you are adding a group of users from the domain environment, make sure the Windows Authentication section on the General page is checked.

Creating SQL Server Logins with T-SQL
The syntax in T-SQL to create a SQL Server login based on a Windows user account is as follows:

```
Create Login [domain\user] from Windows
```

The syntax in T-SQL to create a SQL Server login is as follows:

```
Create Login login_name with password='password'
```

The following options can also be included in your login creation scripts:

- **MUST_CHANGE**   Specifies that the user must change the password at the next login.
- **CHECK_EXPIRATION**   Specifies that SQL Server will check with Windows for the expiration policy affecting the login.
- **CHECK_POLICY**   Specifies that SQL Server defers to the Windows password policy over the login.

Creating and Configuring Users

To create database users from Management Studio, select the server in which the database resides and drill down to the database. To create users, do the following:

1. Go to the Users node in your target database. Right-click the node and select New User. The Database User—New dialog box loads, as illustrated in Figure 5-16.

2. Now select the login from the login pop-up Select Login dialog box. Both trusted and nontrusted logins are available to be used for the new user. You can make the User Name field the same as the login, or you can provide your own name, which then becomes an alias.

Next, select the schema and database role for the user. You can place the user into multiple roles (see the section "Creating and Configuring Database Roles" earlier in this chapter).

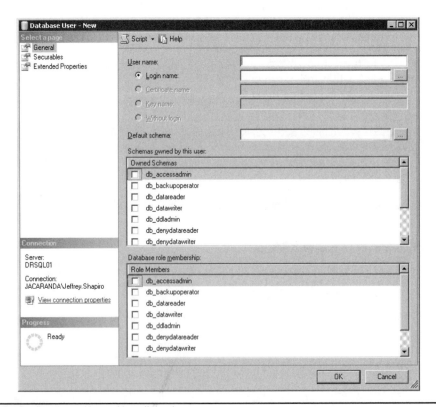

Figure 5-15 Database User—New dialog box

Deleting Logins and Users

As discussed earlier, logins and users are not joined at the hip. Deleting a login does not cause any loose ends with respect to a database user a login was using. Deleting users does not delete a login, nor does deleting a login delete a user. To delete a login or a user, do the following:

- To delete a login, expand the Security node under the SQL Server 2005 instance you are managing. In the Details pane select the login, right-click, and then select Delete.

- To delete a user, expand the User node in the database containing the user. Select the user in the Details pane, right-click, and then select Delete.

One thing to remember concerning the deleting of users: Users can own database objects, such as tables, views, and stored procedures. If you try to delete a user that owns objects that still exist in a database, the DBMS will prevent you from deleting the user.

There are several steps you can take to render a user "out of service" if it still owns objects in the database:

- Remove the permissions accessible to the user. Select the user, right-click, and select the Properties menu item. The User Properties dialog box will load. Click Permissions and clear or deny any permission defined for the user.

- Or, remove the user from any roles it has been placed in. Select the Properties option as described in the preceding step and then click the Properties button. The Database Role Properties dialog box will load. Remove the user from the role and then click OK.

- Or, using the stored procedure sp_changeobjectowner, you can transfer the ownership of the object to another user and then delete the user.

Securing Objects with GRANT, DENY and REVOKE

Three T-SQL DML statements can be used for code level configuration of permissions on objects. These are GRANT, DENY, and REVOKE. The systax for all three is as follows:

```
GRANT { ALL [ PRIVILEGES ] }
      | permission [ ( column [ ,...n ] ) ] [ ,...n ]
      [ ON [ class :: ] securable ] TO principal [ ,...n ]
      [ WITH GRANT OPTION ] [ AS principal ]
DENY { ALL [ PRIVILEGES ] }
      | permission [ ( column [ ,...n ] ) ] [ ,...n ]
      [ ON [ class :: ] securable ] TO principal [ ,...n ]
      [ CASCADE] [ AS principal ]
REVOKE [ GRANT OPTION FOR ]
      {
        [ ALL [ PRIVILEGES ] ]
        |
               permission [ ( column [ ,...n ] ) ] [ ,...n ]
      }
      [ ON [ class :: ] securable ]
      { TO | FROM } principal [ ,...n ]
      [ CASCADE] [ AS principal ]
```

These statements do not GRANT, DENY, or REVOKE all possible permissions on objects. Use the following list as a guideline:

- If the securable is a database, ALL means you can only reference BACKUP DATABASE, BACKUP LOG, CREATE DATABASE, CREATE DEFAULT, CREATE FUNCTION, CREATE PROCEDURE, CREATE RULE, CREATE TABLE, and CREATE VIEW.
- If the securable is a scalar function, then ALL means you can reference EXECUTE and REFERENCES.
- If the securable is a table-valued function, ALL means you can only reference DELETE, INSERT, REFERENCES, SELECT, and UPDATE.
- If the securable is a stored procedure, ALL means you can only reference DELETE, EXECUTE, INSERT, SELECT, and UPDATE.
- If the securable is a table, ALL means you can only reference DELETE, INSERT, REFERENCES, SELECT, and UPDATE.
- If the securable is a view, ALL means you can only reference DELETE, INSERT, REFERENCES, SELECT, and UPDATE.

The following list describes usage:

- **PRIVILEGES**   These are included for SQL-92 compliance, but it does change the behavior of ALL in the above list.
- **permission**   This argument refers to the name of a permission.
- **Column**   This argument specifies the name of a column in a table on which permissions are being revoked. The parentheses are required.
- **class**   This argument specifies the class of the securable on which the permission is being revoked. The scope qualifier :: is required.
- **securable**   This specifies the securable on which the permission is being revoked.
- **TO | FROM principal**   These arguments represent the name of the principal, the beneficiary. The principals from which permissions on a securable can be revoked vary, depending on the securable.
- **CASCADE**   This argument applies to DENY and REVOKE and indicates that the permission that is being denied or revoked is also denied or revoked from other principals to which it has been granted by this principal. When you use the CASCADE argument, you must also include the GRANT OPTION FOR argument.
- **AS principal**   This argument specifies a principal from which the principal executing this query derives its right to apply, deny, or revoke the permission.

See also Appendix for references to these statements.

Auditing

SQL Server 2005 provides a highly sophisticated auditing mechanism that allows you to perform auditing on two levels depending on the security plan requirements. I refer to the two levels as auditing according to data center security requirements and according to C2 security requirements. Now, your data center may require less of the C2 specification, and you should define your needs according to change control and data center security needs.

C2, however, applies only to stand-alone computers, so NSA certification will really only mean something to certain parties when SQL Server 2005 and Windows Server 2003 rate for the networked computer specifications (Red Book and Blue Book). Microsoft has gone above and beyond C2 with Windows Server 2003.

For what it's worth, C2 security is more than a just a rating because it tests things like the protection of objects and auditing. The audit trail facilities of SQL Server are highly advanced, and you can really push the event-logging envelope into outer space. I would almost go as far as saying that you can pretty much trace who passes wind in SQL Server 2005. Your auditing plans thus require careful consideration.

Auditing, like encryption, impacts performance. Every event is auditable, which means that the overhead to record the event accumulates and impacts server or DBMS performance. If you need to accommodate stringent auditing requirements, you might need to consider a second server to do nothing but audit all DBMS activity, or throw gobs of RAM and another processor or two at your base server.

You can audit using the SQL Profiler as discussed in Chapter 18. To configure login auditing right-click the server in SSMS, Object Explorer and select Properties. Go to the Security Page. Here you can choose both Login auditing and C2 audit tracing.

The SQL Server Security Plan

It should be clear to you now that SQL Server 2005 security is no simple matter. No matter how small or large your project might be, just blindly attacking logins, roles, permissions, users, and so on is a futile exercise that, while it seems easy enough in the beginning, can lead to certain chaos if not based on a solid security plan.

The architecture of SQL Server 2005 warrants that you divide the plan into two sections. One section deals with DBMS security, and the second section deals with data security. Splitting the plan according to the two priorities like this makes it easier to manage a complex security environment, to "divide and conquer," so to speak.

DBMS Security Plan

Locking down a DBMS is not an easy thing to do when you need to make sure that your authorized users do not have to walk the length of the Great Wall of China just to log in. Many applications typically require a user to first sign into the local area network and then again into the database. This means that you are forcing the user to remember two passwords. Such a scenario often leads to blank passwords or passwords that get exposed on sticky notes attached to monitors and so forth.

You will thus save yourself—the SQL Server security administrator—a lot of hardship by relying on the security mechanisms available to you in the external environment. The following items should be considered in the formulation of your own DBMS security strategy:

- Upgrade to Windows Server 2003
- Use Kerberos security and discontinue NTLM security
- Deploy IPsec and SSL in high-security environments

- Use middle-tier or proxy services
- Create SQL Server login groups
- Use group policy with organizational units
- Formulate server role assignment policy

Database Security Plan

Your database security plan requires you to identify all elements in the internal environment of the DBMS that can be mustered to protect data from theft and destruction. You will also need to formulate or recognize business needs that dictate that some data, or aspects of data, need to be made available only to workers that need it to perform their jobs.

Some aspects of data security can be achieved programmatically. Other aspects can be achieved by using the tools provided by Management Studio or using the administrative APIs, such as SQL-SMO. The following items must be considered in devising your database security plan:

- Formulate database DBA role assignment policy.
- Create user-defined database roles to protect database objects.
- Identify columns within a database that share similar security requirements.
- Identify logins that share similar security requirements.

In Review

The DBA has his or her hands full when it comes to the question of security. There are many areas to consider as we discussed in this extensive chapter. We do not only have to focus on the internal aspects of data security, such as who has access to what database objects, tables, views. and so on, but also what takes place in the outside world.

From this discussion, it is patently obvious the DBA assigned with security will require a good background in issues including network or distributed security, encryption, security protocols such as SSL and Kerberos, Access Control and Authentication theory, and so on. In addition, I believe it essential that the DBA have a good grounding in Active Directory; in the management of users, groups, and organizational units; in trusts; in delegation; and so on.

In my book, the good DBA will have migrated from general network security, trained in all aspects, including access control, group policy, and user and group management in Active Directory. The DBA who started a career in SQL Server should thus make a concerted effort to certify or train in network security. Connectivity and a working knowledge of networking is not as critical. For example, I believe it is more important to have a good understanding of delegation than to know how to configure a router or a subnet. Chapters 8 and 9, however, deal with a number of issues requiring more networking acumen, such as configuring replication and clustering.

Databases, Tables, and Indexes

SQL Server 2005 provides one of the most flexible database management systems around. And this flexibility does not come at a high price either. SQL Server databases can be small, large, very large, or gigantic. You can expand them, shrink them, infuse them with thousands of tables, copy them, move them, detach them, transform them, encrypt their objects, and so on. And you can have 32,767 databases for every instance of SQL Server, and, er, billions of tables.

A SQL Server database consists of numerous components and objects. I have discussed many of them in previous chapters—especially in Chapter 2—in which we studied the database architecture from several levels. This chapter guides you through creating databases and tables through several facilities provided as the data storage, data management, and data processing aspects of SQL Server databases. We will also look at table creation, working with the Table Designer features, and database diagrams.

SQL Server is famous for the way it handles two types of databases, OLTP databases and OLAP databases—Online Transaction Processing and Online Analytical Processing databases, respectively. The former architecture is used for managing data that is constantly changing, through INSERT, UPDATE, and DELETE statements. Data is retrieved (checked out) for editing and reporting via a variety of T-SQL SELECT queries.

The online part of the OLTP paradigm is to cater to multiple users as described in the architecture chapters in Part I. SQL Server transaction and concurrency models prevent users from bumping into each other.

OLTP databases can be very complex, especially if there are a large number of tables to process. However, a poorly designed OLTP database can create a severe bottleneck on the access and updating of OLTP data. Knowledge of database design is essential for SQL Server 2005 administration and development (obtained either through experience alone or by doing a Microsoft DBA certification course along with experience). It is not unusual to find SQL Server databases that contain over 600 tables, when only 15 or so would have been enough had the database been designed by a pro.

While this chapter does not get into database design per se, it will provide you with a foundation of knowledge for creating databases and tables and indexes.

The New SQL Server 2005 File System

SQL Server 2005 includes a number of features that improve performance, reliability, availability, capacity, and manageability of database files and filegroups over its predecessors. They are as follows:

- Page checksum and page-level restore combination
- Read-only filegroups on compressed drives
- Instant file initialization
- Database snapshots
- Row-level versioning
- Partitioning

Page Checksum Error 824 and Page-Level Restore

Error code 824 is detected if a checksum error occurs. This is produced by the page checksum feature, which helps increase data protection by giving you an early heads up on I/O errors that go unnoticed by the OS or any underlying hardware. Both data and the log files benefit from the feature when PAGE_VERIFY_CHECKSUM is enabled. (See the ALTER DATABASE statement later in this chapter.) The checksum can also be calculated and verified during BACKUP and RESTORE commands, which increases the reliability of database backups.

Why Do You Care about This?

The larger the database, the higher the chance of data loss going unnoticed. SQL Server will report the error, the operation that caused the error, the page in the database, and the file offset. If you see the error, there may be additional messages in the SQL Server error log or the system event, and they may provide more information about the error. If you get the error, then run DBCC CHECKDB immediately, before database integrity is risked (see Appendix).

If you unable to fix the problem with DBCC, then you may need to restore the affected pages by using online page-level restore (see Chapter 7) that is available in Enterprise Edition. Otherwise, a full restore with and application of transaction logs to save pending transactions may be in order.

Read-Only Filegroups on Compressed Drives

The read-only filegroup option is not new, and we will discuss it shortly. However, what is new is that you can now put these files on compressed drives. These will help you in your filegroup design by allowing flexibility in capacity planning and I/O.

Why Do You Care about This?

SQL Server 2005's support for read-only filegroups on compressed drives helps to improve capacity utilization, manageability, and I/O performance. Any secondary filegroup of a user database that is marked as read-only can be placed on compressed NTFS volumes. If the entire database is set to read-only, all filegroups can be placed on compressed volumes.

Instant File Initialization

SQL Server 2005 includes support for instant file initialization, a feature of the Windows Server 2003 and later operating systems. File pages are typically initialized by a process of writing zeros into the pages before the file gets used, a process that can negatively affect performance when databases are set to grow automatically. Instant file initialization can lessen the impact on server performance with large database files that are growing in size.

SQL Server uses instant initialization for data files and not for transaction logs. It can be used automatically by SQL Server as long as the SQL Server service account is given the Windows SE MANAGE VOLUME NAME privilege. Instant file initialization can occur both at database creation and for *tempdb* when a server is started up. It can also be applied when modifications are made to a database using ALTER DATABASE . . . MODIFY FILE statements (discussed later in this chapter).

Why Do You Care about This?

The zeroing process can have a negative affect on performance during modifications that trigger an autogrow. So when SQL Server 2005 is given the ability to use the instant file initialization feature, the zeroing out of data pages is skipped and the time to initialize a file for the creation of a very large database (VLDB) and *tempdb* is reduced.

Now if you decide to run SQL Server under the Network Service account (see Chapter 5), this permission defaults to OFF and you will need to enable it by the correct application of rights.

Database Snapshots

Database snapshots are a feature of the Enterprise Edition and are discussed in Chapter 7. However, if you plan to implement this feature, you should be aware of the effect it has on I/O performance and space requirements.

Why Do You Care about This?

Obviously storage space is taken by snapshots, but they are still better than full copies of the database because they use the sparse file technology provided only by NTFS, which is used to maintain efficiency.

There is one snapshot file for each data file in the source database. A page is copied to a snapshot file when it is updated in the source database. This mechanism is referred to as copy-on-write. The combinations of the pages in the snapshot and those that have not changed in the source database give a consistent view of the database at the time the snapshot was taken. Remember that if all pages in the source database are updated, the snapshot file can grow to a size similar to that of the source database file.

I/O performance can be negatively impacted when making a first-time update to a page on the source database because this leads to an extra write of the source page to the snapshot database. However, any subsequent changes to the copied page do not incur this extra write. Therefore, if a source database experiences only localized updates to certain pages, a snapshot database will have little effect on the I/O performance and storage efficiency. However, if there are many database snapshots of the same source database, a single modification to the source database can cause a ripple of several writes to each appropriate database snapshot. See Chapter 7 for more information on the snapshots.

Row-Level Versioning

As mentioned in Chapter 2, SQL Server 2005 includes a new technology called *row-level versioning,* which provides improved concurrent access, translating into higher throughput and performance. Row-level versioning is integrated with the following SQL Server 2005 features, discussed in Chapters 12 and 17:

- Snapshot isolation
- Multiple active result sets (MARS)
- Online index operations

Why Do You Care about This?

Besides the advantages just discussed, row-level versioning requires storage space on *tempdb* that affects the I/O performance of *tempdb* during reads and updates. This is caused by the additional I/O taken to maintain and retrieve old versions. Here's the issue in a nutshell: When a row in a table or index is updated, the old row gets copied to the version table that resides in *tempdb*. The row is stamped with the transaction sequence number of the transaction that performed the update, and the new record maintains a pointer to the old record in *tempdb*. However, the old record might still have a pointer to a yet older record, which in turn might point to an even older record. The result is a version chain that begins to impact transaction performance. See Chapters 13 and 17 for further guidance.

Data Partitioning

Data partitioning, mentioned in Chapter 2, is a feature that is available in SQL Server 2005 Enterprise Edition. As you may be aware, partitioning horizontally divides tables or indexes or both into smaller segments, or partitions. These can then be maintained and accessed independently from one other. This is a huge improvement over SQL Server 2000's partitioned views.

Why Do You Care about This?

Partitions must be assigned to filegroups, and thus the maintenance and performance gains of filegroups can be taken advantage of with a well-thought-out partition scheme. Designing for partitioning will impact your database and storage design, especially when setting up clusters and other high-availability solutions. See Chapter 9 for more information.

Understanding Filegroups

Databases and their contents, including tables, indexes, and various programmatic elements, are stored in files. These files are kept in filegroups. A filegroup is another form of container in SQL Server. To refresh your memory with respect to file location flexibility, you can store your data files in various locations and then use filegroups to manage them as a unit. For example, you could locate the primary file *papazulu.mdf* in the volume it was created on and then store the secondary data files (*papazulu1.mdf, papazulu2.mdf,* and *papazulu3.mdf*), if you need them, on a number of different drives (even locating each new file on its own hard disk). Then create a filegroup (called pzulugroup1) and assign all the papazulu secondary database files to this filegroup. When it comes to backup, you can then back up the filegroups instead of the three or four separate files. (The script to back up a filegroup is covered in Chapter 7.)

One of the best features of the filegroup, however, is the flexibility you get in managing your database objects. For example, if you have a huge table that is the constant target of queries and modifications, it would make sense to allocate it to a filegroup on a faster disk. Then most of the I/O for the database can be targeted to the faster disk.

Spreading database files around like this can help tremendously with performance because each file can be dedicated to its own hard disk. This might become a little expensive if you are using a RAID system for redundancy (RAID 5 will require at least three disks, of course). On the other hand, RAID configuration aside, if you are working with really large databases, your primary and secondary files might grow to sizes that bump up against the limits of your Windows Server file system file size. For more on RAID, see Chapter 9.

SQL Server fills all files in the filegroup on a proportional basis so that all files in the filegroup become full at the same time. When all the files in the filegroup are full, SQL Server will then expand all the files in the group one at a time on a round-robin scheduling basis if the database is set to grow automatically (discussed later in the section CREATE DATABASE).

There are four important rules to remember about filegroups; they may or may not count in your favor or figure in your database plan:

- A filegroup cannot be used by more than one database. You cannot take *papazulu* and assign it to the filegroup for the *tangocharlie* database. Likewise, files can only be members of one filegroup. The CREATE DATABASE and ALTER DATABASE statements have no facility for such multiallocation or designation, in any event.

- Transaction logs are not part of filegroups, although they can be located where the database plan takes them.

- The primary file is assigned to the primary filegroup, and the primary filegroup cannot be changed or altered.

- If you do not specify alternative filegroups for the secondary data files, all files are then placed into the primary filegroup. The disadvantage is that if the primary filegroup is filled up, then no further data can be stored in the catalog.

The Default Filegroup

As you discovered when you created your first database, it contains a primary filegroup, which becomes the default filegroup before any new filegroups are created, including any user-defined filegroups you specify. Later you can change the default filegroup using the ALTER DATABASE statement we will be discussing shortly.

The primary filegroup can fill up if autogrow for your database is turned off and the disks holding the primary group can run out of space. You can turn autogrow back on, but until you have worked out how to best reduce the size of the files, you may have no choice but to add a larger hard disk and then move the files onto this disk.

The reason for having a default filegroup is so that any object created without specifying a filegroup is assigned to the default filegroup. A problem may arise at a later date, however, in which you will not be able to add to the database because you are low on hard disk space and your primary default filegroup is full. You may then have to create a new filegroup and make the new group the default. In other words, you create a new filegroup so that new user-defined objects, such as tables and views, do not compete with the system objects and tables for data space.

Setting Filegroups Read-Only

SQL Server lets you mark a filegroup as read-only. This means that you cannot modify or add to the files in the filegroup in any way. Marking a filegroup read-only can come in handy. For example, your turnkey application can include data in the filegroup that cannot be removed, and you can store key configuration tables in the read-only file to prevent users from adding data to them (and this is the only filegroup you can then move to a compression-enabled disk).

Relational OLAP (ROLAP) and Hybrid OLAP (HOLAP) databases are also good candidates for read-only filegroups. By setting their filegroups read-only, you provide an additional safeguard against anyone writing to the databases. As you know, OLAP databases or warehouse data, once declared historical or temporal, should not be modified in any way that could render analysis questionable. In the event you need to add data and refresh a cube, you can easily change the file to read/write.

As mentioned earlier, you can place read-only filegroups, or an entire read-only database, on a compressed volume.

Filegroup Tips

When creating and working with your database, consider the following recommendations for your database files and filegroups:

- When creating your filegroups, create a secondary filegroup and make it the default filegroup. This will leave the primary filegroup dedicated to the system objects, free from interference from user-defined objects.

- Place the filegroups across as many physical disks (or logical disks for RAID sets) as you can so that you can spread the work across several disks. There is nothing worse than to have one disk in an array or cluster that is doing all the work, while the others sit idle.

- Try to locate tables that are used in complex and frequently accessed JOINs in separate filegroups that are then located on separate disks. You will see a marked performance improvement over a single-disk implementation because two or more disks are involved in the processing of the JOIN (in parallel) instead of one. Remember again that if you are using RAID, you will have to create several logical disks (each containing at least three disks for a RAID 5 configuration).

- Do not place transaction logs on the same physical disk as the filegroups, if you can help it. If the disk fails, you lose not only the database but also the transaction log. Recovery will thus be slow and painful, and if you are not doing frequent online backups, you could lose a lot of data.

- You can obtain a report on your filegroups at any time when you execute the system stored procedure sp_helpfilegroup. See Appendix for information about the result set returned from this proc.

Creating a SQL Server Database

Creating a database in SQL Server is as easy as cutting butter on hot corn. Many database solutions, however, call for specialized configurations that cater to VLDBs, replication, federations, and so on. So before you start creating away, there are a number of considerations to keep in mind with respect to the actual files:

- First, if you simply make the data files as large as possible (taking up most of the space on a disk), you need to be certain that the disk is going to be dedicated to the large database and nothing else. This practice can come back to haunt you in the future when database size priorities change and you can't do anything else on the disk until the database file size is reduced. Make the database file only as large as you truly expect it to grow.

- Second, allow the data files to grow automatically but place a ceiling on the file growth so that the files don't suck up every drop of storage juice on the server and explode. This practice allows you to monitor the files carefully and take appropriate actions (such as installing additional storage). Alternatively, as discussed, you can add more filegroups to secondary hard disks.

- If you do not want the database to grow beyond its initial size, set the maximum growth size to zero. This parameter prevents the file from growing beyond your initial settings, which is useful in turnkey situations, such as a voice mail system that gets shipped preconfigured to only store 100MB of voice messages. You can then sell additional storage quotas as needed.

- Watch for file fragmentation. Autogrowing files can become fragmented to a point where performance begins to degrade. Again, creating files on multiple disks helps keep the fragmentation in check.

There are several methods you can use to create a SQL Server database:

- T-SQL's CREATE DATABASE statement
- SQL Server Management Studio (New Database, Copy Database)
- The SQL-SMO object model
- SQL Server Integration Services (SSIS)

No matter the option that you use to create a database, SQL Server implements the creation of databases in two steps:

1. First, SQL Server initializes the new database using metadata derived from the model database to initialize the database and its metadata. To change defaults to suit the environment, you would need to alter the model database (such as by specifying collations other than the default).

2. Next, SQL Server fills the database with empty pages. The database, however, also stores the initial data that records how the space is to be used in the database.

If you created or altered objects in the model database, then these are exactly copied to all newly created databases. Whatever you add to *model*, such as tables, views, stored procedures, and data types, all are also included in all new databases. This is very convenient for turnkey systems or when you need to be creating new databases often, because it obviates the need to run a complex script every time you create a new database. In fact, after you've fine-tuned all the objects inside *model*, just executing CREATE DATABASE *database_name* would be sufficient and the database would be ready for users.

As highlighted in the CREATE DATABASE syntax coming up, the new database inherits the database option settings from the model database (unless you are using the FOR ATTACH switch that attaches an existing database).

For example, if the recovery model is set to FULL in *model*, the recovery model will be set to FULL in all the new databases you create. Any properties and options changed using the ALTER DATABASE statement on *model* are also used for new databases you create. If FOR ATTACH is specified on the CREATE DATABASE statement, the new database inherits the database option settings of the original database.

There are three types of files used to store a database (SQL Server does not enforce the file extensions shown here):

1. First, there is the primary file *(.mdf)*, which contains the startup information for the database. After the initial startup data, SQL Server uses the rest of the primary files to store user data. A SQL Server database cannot exist without its primary file.

2. When the primary fills to capacity, secondary files *(.ndf)* are used to hold the additional data. The secondary file is optional and may not be necessary if the primary is large enough or has enough hard disk accommodation to store all the data in the database. Secondary files can be installed to separate disks, or spread across multiple disks.

3. Finally, there are the transaction log files *(.ldf)*. These files hold the transactional information used to recover the database. You cannot operate a SQL Server database without a transaction log file, but you can specify more than one. The minimum size for a transaction log file is typically 1MB.

TIP *Back up the master database and the files for mssqlsystemresource whenever a new user database is created or altered.*

Let's explore the T-SQL CREATE DATABASE statement first, before looking into the interactive procedures using Management Studio. This will actually make it easier for you to understand what the GUI tools are doing.

CREATE DATABASE

For many DBAs, the T-SQL CREATE statement is convenient because it means that you can create a T-SQL script and run the script with a new database name whenever you need. Creating such scripts is obviously ideal for large requirements and typically suits a DBA or some process that needs to create databases regularly (such as turnkey systems where the script is run as part of system setup).

NOTE *You need to be a member of the sysadmin or dbcreator fixed server role or be given the appropriate permission to create and alter databases (see Chapter 5).*

Setting up databases for e-commerce hosting sites is a good example of where the T-SQL script is useful. When a new client needs a database, it becomes a matter of running the script against the target server and instance from one of the command-line utilities or a query window in Management Studio.

The simplest T-SQL CREATE DATABASE syntax is as follows:

```
CREATE DATABASE database_name
    [ ON
        [ PRIMARY ] [ <filespec> [ ,...n ]
        [ , <filegroup> [ ,...n ] ]
    [ LOG ON { <filespec> [ ,...n ] } ] ]
    [ COLLATE collation_name ]
    [ WITH <external_access_option> ]]
[;]
```

To attach a database,

```
CREATE DATABASE database_name
    ON <filespec> [ ,...n ]
    FOR { ATTACH [ WITH <service_broker_option> ]
        | ATTACH_REBUILD_LOG }
[;]
<filespec> ::=
{ (NAME = logical_file_name, FILENAME = 'os_file_name'
        [ , SIZE = size [ KB | MB | GB | TB ] ]
        [ , MAXSIZE = { max_size [ KB | MB | GB | TB ] | UNLIMITED } ]
        [ , FILEGROWTH = growth_increment [ KB | MB | GB | TB | % ] ]
) [ ,...n ]
 <filegroup> ::=
{FILEGROUP filegroup_name [ DEFAULT ]
    <filespec> [ ,...n ]}
<external_access_option> ::=
{
  DB_CHAINING { ON | OFF }
  | TRUSTWORTHY { ON | OFF }
}
<service_broker_option> ::=
{
    ENABLE_BROKER  | NEW_BROKER  | ERROR_BROKER_CONVERSATIONS
}
```

To create a database snapshot,

```
CREATE DATABASE database_snapshot_name
    ON
        (
        NAME = logical_file_name,
        FILENAME = 'os_file_name'
        ) [ ,...n ]
    AS SNAPSHOT OF source_database_name
[;]
```

These statements can be daunting and confusing, so let's go through simpler versions of them, making notes as we go along that will help us create a suitable database plan for our project.

Database Name

The database names must be unique within a server and conform to the rules for identifiers. The placeholder *database_name* can be a maximum of 128 characters. Typically SQL Server gives the log file the same name as the database name and provides the extension *.ldf*. You can specify your own log filename and path, a topic we will get to shortly. The following code, for example, creates a database named *papazulu* and assumes all the defaults derived from the model database:

```
CREATE DATABASE papazulu
```

In this case *papazulu.mdf* and *papazulu_log.ldf* are created in the default path and the files are entrusted with the default settings for file growth and permissions (the user that created the database is the owner). Conversely, the following code makes the databases go away as quickly as they came:

```
DROP DATABASE papazulu
```

Both the database and the log files are removed.

NOTE *The "user" that is allowed to create the database becomes the "legal" owner of the database, through a default schema. There may be circumstances, however, that dictate you need to change the owner (such as when the database is put into production). To change the owner, you can use the sp_changedbowner system stored procedure (see Appendix).*

ON

Now let's get a little more creative and install our database to a specific path. Naturally you need to be sure the path, server, and instance exist, or you could be trying to create into thin air. You also need to be sure you have domain permission and rights to create the remote database. *ON* is just a keyword that specifies that the disk files used to store the data portions of the database, the data files, are defined explicitly. It has nothing to do with making sure the database is switched on (which is what one newbie once asked me).

The ON keyword is followed by a comma-separated list represented by the *<filespec>* placeholder, which represents the items defining the data files for the primary filegroup (we will look into filegroups again later). The list of files in the primary filegroup can be followed by an optional, comma-separated list of <filegroup> items defining user filegroups and their files. The following code places the *papazulu* database on the C drive drive:

```
ON
(NAME = papazulu, FILENAME = 'C:\databases\papazulu.mdf',
 SIZE = 4,
 MAXSIZE = 10,
 FILEGROWTH = 1)
```

The *n* placeholder indicates that multiple files can be specified for the database.

If an object is created with an ON filegroup clause specifying a user-defined filegroup, then all the pages for the object are allocated from the specified filegroup. The pages for all user objects created without an ON filegroup clause, or with an ON DEFAULT clause, are allocated from the default filegroup. When a database is first created, the primary filegroup is the default filegroup. You can specify a user-defined filegroup as the default filegroup using ALTER DATABASE as discussed later in this chapter.

LOG ON

This *LOG ON* argument specifies that the disk files used to store the database log (log files) are explicitly defined. If you use LOG ON, SQL Server will expect you to provide the name and path to the log file. The keyword is also followed by a comma-separated list of <filespec> items defining the log files. If you do not specify LOG ON, then a single log file is automatically created with a system-generated name (the same as the database name) and a size that is 25 percent of the sum of the sizes of all the data files for the database. The following code specifies the path for the *papazulu* log file:

```
LOG ON
(Name = 'papazulus_log',
  FILENAME = 'D:\data\logfiles\papazulu_log.ldf',
  SIZE = 5MB,
  MAXSIZE = 25MB,
FILEGROWTH = 5MB)
```

FOR ATTACH

The *FOR ATTACH* is built into the CREATE DATABASE statement, but it allows you to attach a database that was detached earlier or from somewhere else. You should use the sp_attach_db system stored procedure instead of using CREATE DATABASE FOR ATTACH directly (see Appendix for usage). Use CREATE DATABASE FOR ATTACH only when you must specify more than 16 <filespec> items.

Naturally, this is easier in Management Studio but not always possible. You need to have the <filespec> entry to specify the first primary file. The only other <filespec> entries needed are those for any files that have a different path from when the database was first created or last attached. A <filespec> is needed for all files that need to be included in the attach process.

The statement is useful for some processes that require you to detach and attach in code. The database you attach, however, must have been created using the same code page and sort order as the SQL Server instance you are trying to attach it to.

You will also need to remove any replication objects installed to the database using the sp_removedbreplication system stored procedure if you plan to attach a database to a server other than the server from which the database was detached.

Collation Name

The *collation_name* placeholder specifies the default collation for the database. The collation name can be either a Windows collation name or a SQL collation name. If none is specified, the database is assigned the default collation of the SQL Server instance that you are creating the database on. (Collations are discussed in Chapter 10.)

PRIMARY

The *PRIMARY* keyword specifies that the associated <filespec> list defines the primary file. As you know, the primary filegroup contains all of the new database's system tables. It also contains all objects not assigned to any user-defined filegroups. The first <filespec> entry in the primary filegroup becomes the primary file, which is the file containing the logical start of the database and its system tables (in other words, all other files are secondary because the database can have only one primary file). If you do not specify the PRIMARY file, the first file listed in the CREATE DATABASE statement becomes the primary file.

NAME

NAME specifies the logical name for the file defined by the <filespec>. The NAME parameter is not required when FOR ATTACH is specified. The following line from the earlier example specifies the logical filename:

```
NAME = 'papazulu',
```

The name must be unique in the database and conform to the rules for identifiers. The name can be a character or Unicode constant, or a regular or delimited identifier.

FILENAME

The *FILENAME* specifies the file system filename for the file defined by the <filespec>. The placeholder *os_file_name* is the path and filename used by the operating system when it creates the physical file defined by the <filespec>. The path in *os_file_name* must specify a directory on an instance of SQL Server. Also, if you try to specify the *os_file_name* on a compressed file system, the statement will fail.

You can also install a file to a raw partition, which is a hard-disk partition that has not been formatted for any file system (such as FAT or NTFS). If you create the file on a raw partition, the *os_file_name* must specify only the hard-disk letter of an existing raw partition; no path information can be used. And you can only create one file on each raw partition. Files on raw partitions do not autogrow, so the MAXSIZE and FILEGROWTH parameters are not needed when you specify the *os_file_name* for a raw partition (I will go over raw partitions a little later in this chapter).

SIZE

The *SIZE* keyword specifies the size of the file defined in the <filespec>. When a size parameter is not supplied in the <filespec> for a primary file, SQL Server takes the size of the primary file in the model database. When a SIZE parameter is not specified in the <filespec> for a secondary or log file, SQL Server makes the file between 512KB and 1MB.

When you specify size, you can use the kilobyte (KB), megabyte (MB), gigabyte (GB), or terabyte (TB) suffixes. If you leave out the suffix, the default is MB. The number should not be fractional or include any decimal notation, such as 5.5MB. If you must create a database and a half or some similar fraction, move down to the next measurement. For example 5.5MB would be 5632KB. The minimum value for the *size* parameter is 512KB. The size specified for the primary file must be at least as large as the primary file of the model database.

MAXSIZE

The *MAXSIZE* option specifies the maximum size to which the file defined in the <filespec> can grow. The *max_size* parameter is specified as explained in the *size* parameter. When you specify size, you can use the kilobyte (KB), megabyte (MB), gigabyte (GB), or terabyte (TB) suffix. If you leave out the suffix, the default is MB. The number should not be fractional or include any decimal notation, such as 5,500MB. It is important to know in advance what the *max_size* will be because if it is not specified, the file will keep growing until the disk is full.

UNLIMITED

This is the converse of the maxsize parameter and specifies that the file defined in the <filespec> can grow until the disk is full.

FILEGROWTH

This argument specifies the growth increment of the file defined in the <filespec>. The *FILEGROWTH* setting for a file cannot exceed the MAXSIZE setting. What FILEGROWTH means is that every time space is needed, the file is expanded by the value defined here. As discussed earlier, you need to specify a whole number and no decimals. A value of zero (0) specifies no growth.

The FILEGROWTH value can be specified in MB, KB, GB, TB, or percent (%). If a number is specified without an MB, KB, or % suffix, SQL Server assumes a default in MB. When % is specified, the growth increment size is the specified percentage of the size of the file at the time the increment occurs. If FILEGROWTH is left out completely, the default value is 10 percent and the minimum value is 64KB. The size specified is rounded to the nearest 64KB.

NOTE *After the database has been created, or at any time for that matter, you can display a report on a database, or on all the databases for an instance of SQL Server, by executing the system stored procedure sp_helpdb. To get information about the space used in a database, use sp_ spaceused. You can also use sp_helpfile for a report of the files in a database. See Appendix for details about the results returned when you execute these system procs.*

Examples

The following script creates the *papazulu* database against the instance you are connected to. You do not need to specifically include USE MASTER at the start of the script, because SQL Server 2005 knows that anyway. Also, depending on the tool you are using, the use of GO might not be necessary (keep the code simple).

CAUTION *Do not create user objects, such as tables, views, stored procedures, or triggers, in the master database.*

```
CREATE DATABASE papazulu
ON
(NAME = papazulu,
    FILENAME = 'c:\program files\microsoft
      sql server\mssql.1\data\papazulu.mdf',
```

```
    SIZE = 10,
    MAXSIZE = 50,
    FILEGROWTH = 5 )
LOG ON
( NAME = 'papazulu_log',
    FILENAME = 'c:\program files\microsoft
     sql server\mssql.1\data\papazulu_log.ldf',
    SIZE = 5MB,
    MAXSIZE = 25MB,
    FILEGROWTH = 5MB )
```

ALTER DATABASE

The *ALTER DATABASE* statement is a little more complex than the CREATE statement. This code essentially adds or removes files and filegroups from the database. You can also use it to modify the attributes of files and filegroups, such as by changing the name or size of a file. ALTER DATABASE provides the capability to change the database name, filegroup names, and logical names of data files and log files.

The ALTER DATABASE syntax is as follows:

```
ALTER DATABASE database_name
{
    <add_or_modify_files>
  | <add_or_modify_filegroups>
  | <set_database_options>
  | MODIFY NAME = new_database_name
  | COLLATE collation_name
}[;]


<add_or_modify_files>::=
{
    ADD FILE <filespec> [ ,...n ]
        [ TO FILEGROUP { filegroup_name | DEFAULT } ]
  | ADD LOG FILE <filespec> [ ,...n ]
  | REMOVE FILE logical_file_name
  | MODIFY FILE <filespec>
}


<filespec>::=
(
    NAME = logical_file_name
    [ , NEWNAME = new_logical_name ]
    [ , FILENAME = 'os_file_name' ]
    [ , SIZE = size [ KB | MB | GB | TB ] ]
    [ , MAXSIZE = { max_size [ KB | MB | GB | TB ] | UNLIMITED } ]
    [ , FILEGROWTH = growth_increment [ KB | MB | GB | TB| % ] ]
    [ , OFFLINE ]
)
```

```
<add_or_modify_filegroups>::=
{
    | ADD FILEGROUP filegroup_name
    | REMOVE FILEGROUP filegroup_name
    | MODIFY FILEGROUP filegroup_name
        { <filegroup_updatability_option>
        | DEFAULT
        | NAME = new_filegroup_name
        }
}
<filegroup_updatability_option>::=
{
    { READONLY | READWRITE }
    | { READ_ONLY | READ_WRITE }
}
<set_database_options>::=
SET
{
    { <optionspec> [ ,...n ] [ WITH <termination> ] }
}

<optionspec>::=
{
    <db_state_option>
  | <db_user_access_option>
  | <db_update_option>
  | <external_access_option>
  | <cursor_option>
  | <auto_option>
  | <sql_option>
  | <recovery_option>
  | <database_mirroring_option>
  | <service_broker_option>
  | <date_correlation_optimization_option>
  | <parameterization_option>
}

<db_state_option> ::=
    { ONLINE | OFFLINE | EMERGENCY }

<db_user_access_option> ::=
    { SINGLE_USER | RESTRICTED_USER | MULTI_USER }

<db_update_option> ::=
    { READ_ONLY | READ_WRITE }

<external_access_option> ::=
{
    DB_CHAINING { ON | OFF }
  | TRUSTWORTHY { ON | OFF }
}
```

```
<cursor_option> ::=
{
    CURSOR_CLOSE_ON_COMMIT { ON | OFF }
  | CURSOR_DEFAULT { LOCAL | GLOBAL }
}

<auto_option> ::=
{
    AUTO_CLOSE { ON | OFF }
  | AUTO_CREATE_STATISTICS { ON | OFF }
  | AUTO_SHRINK { ON | OFF }
  | AUTO_UPDATE_STATISTICS { ON | OFF }
  | AUTO_UPDATE_STATISTICS_ASYNC { ON | OFF }
}

<sql_option> ::=
{
    ANSI_NULL_DEFAULT { ON | OFF }
  | ANSI_NULLS { ON | OFF }
  | ANSI_PADDING { ON | OFF }
  | ANSI_WARNINGS { ON | OFF }
  | ARITHABORT { ON | OFF }
  | CONCAT_NULL_YIELDS_NULL { ON | OFF }
  | NUMERIC_ROUNDABORT { ON | OFF }
  | QUOTED_IDENTIFIER { ON | OFF }
  | RECURSIVE_TRIGGERS { ON | OFF }
}


<recovery_option> ::=
{
    RECOVERY { FULL | BULK_LOGGED | SIMPLE }
  | TORN_PAGE_DETECTION { ON | OFF }
  | PAGE_VERIFY { CHECKSUM | TORN_PAGE_DETECTION | NONE }
}


<database_mirroring_option> ::=
{ <partner_option> | <witness_option> }
        <partner_option> ::=
    PARTNER { = 'partner_server'
            | FAILOVER
            | FORCE_SERVICE_ALLOW_DATA_LOSS
            | OFF
            | RESUME
            | SAFETY { FULL | OFF }
            | SUSPEND
            | TIMEOUT integer
          }
<witness_option> ::=
    WITNESS { = 'witness_server'
            | OFF
          }
```

```
<service_broker_option> ::=
{
    ENABLE_BROKER
  | DISABLE_BROKER
  | NEW_BROKER
  | ERROR_BROKER_CONVERSATIONS
}


<date_correlation_optimization_option> ::=
{
    DATE_CORRELATION_OPTIMIZATION { ON | OFF }
}


<parameterization_option> ::=
{
    PARAMETERIZATION { SIMPLE | FORCED }
}


<snapshot_option> ::=
{
    ALLOW_SNAPSHOT_ISOLATION {ON | OFF }
  | READ_COMMITTED_SNAPSHOT {ON | OFF }
}


<termination> ::=
{
    ROLLBACK AFTER integer [ SECONDS ]
  | ROLLBACK IMMEDIATE
  | NO_WAIT
}
```

Some of the arguments are explained in the text that follows.

Database
This is the name of the database *(database)* to be changed.

Add File
The ADD FILE argument specifies that a file is to be added to the database.

To Filegroup
The TO FILEGROUP argument specifies the filegroup, in the *filegroup_name,* to which to add the specified file.

Add Log File
The ADD LOG FILE argument specifies that a log file is to be added to the specified database.

Remove File

The REMOVE FILE argument removes the file description from the database system tables and deletes the physical file. The file cannot be removed unless empty.

Add Filegroup

The ADD FILEGROUP argument specifies that a filegroup is to be added. You also need to specify the name in the *filegroup_name* placeholder.

Remove Filegroup

The REMOVE FILEGROUP argument is specified to remove the filegroup from the database and delete all the files in the filegroup. The filegroup cannot be removed unless it is empty, not even from Enterprise Manager.

Modify File

The MODIFY FILE argument specifies the given file that should be modified, including the FILENAME, SIZE, FILEGROWTH, and MAXSIZE options. Only one of these properties can be changed at a time. NAME must be specified in the <filespec> to identify the file to be modified. If SIZE is specified, the new size must be larger than the current file size. FILENAME can be specified only for files in the *tempdb* database, and the new name does not take effect until Microsoft SQL Server is restarted.

To modify the logical name of a data file or log file, specify in NAME the logical filename to be renamed, and specify for NEWNAME the new logical name for the file.

For example, MODIFY FILE (NAME = *logical_file_name*, NEWNAME = *new_logical_name*...). For optimum performance during multiple modify-file operations, several ALTER DATABASE *database* MODIFY FILE statements can be run concurrently.

Compressed read-only filegroups prevent updates and save disk space because you can put the files on a volume that has data compression enabled. Perform DBCC CHECK on these files to make sure the files are not risking corruption. Remember, disk compression is also CPU intensive, so you need to think about this before you start moving all your read-only files to compressed volumes (remember, disks are getting cheaper by the nanosecond).

Modify Name

This argument allows you to rename the database. The new name is inserted in the = *new_dbname* placeholder.

Modify Filegroup

This argument lets you specify the filegroup to be modified. The information is required in *filegroup_name* { *filegroup_property* | NAME = *new_filegroup_name* }. If *filegroup_name* and NAME = *new_filegroup_name* are specified, these parameters change the filegroup name. See the discussion on filegroups earlier in this chapter.

With

The WITH <termination> argument specifies when to roll back incomplete transactions when the database is transitioned from one state to another. Only one termination clause can be specified, and it follows the SET clauses. ROLLBACK AFTER *integer* [SECONDS] | ROLLBACK IMMEDIATE specifies whether to roll back after the specified number of seconds or immediately. If the termination clause is omitted, transactions are allowed to commit or roll back on their own.

No Wait

The NO_WAIT argument specifies that if the requested database state or option change cannot complete immediately without waiting for transactions to commit or roll back on their own, the request will fail.

Collate

See the section in CREATE DATABASE discussed earlier.

Filespec

The <filespec> section controls the file properties where the NAME argument specifies the logical name for the file.

The *logical_file_name* is the name used by SQL Server when referencing the file. The name must be unique within the database and conform to the rules for identifiers. The name can be a character or Unicode constant, a regular identifier, or a delimited identifier (see Identifiers in the Chapter 10).

Filename

The FILENAME argument specifies an operating system filename. When used with MODIFY FILE, FILENAME can be specified only for files in the tempdb database. The new *tempdb* filename takes effect only after SQL Server is stopped and restarted.

The *os_file_name* refers to the path and filename used by the operating system for the file. The file must reside in the server in which SQL Server is installed. Data and log files should not be placed on compressed file systems.

If the file is on a raw partition, *os_file_name* must specify only the drive letter of an existing raw partition. Only one file can be placed on each raw partition. Files on raw partitions do not autogrow; therefore, the MAXSIZE and FILEGROWTH parameters are not needed when *os_file_name* specifies a raw partition.

Size

The SIZE argument specifies the file size. The placeholder *size* is the size of the file. The KB, MB, GB, and TB suffixes can be used to specify kilobytes, megabytes, gigabytes, or terabytes. The default is MB. Specify a whole number; do not include a decimal. The minimum value for *size* is 512KB, and the default if *size* is not specified is 1MB. When specified with ADD FILE, *size* is the initial size for the file. When specified with MODIFY FILE, *size* is the new size for the file and must be larger than the current file size.

Maxsize

The MAXSIZE parameter specifies the maximum file size, represented by the placeholder *max_size*. The KB, MB, GB, and TB suffixes can be used to specify kilobytes, megabytes, gigabytes, or terabytes. The default is MB. Specify a whole number; do not include a decimal. If *max_size* is not specified, the file size can increase until the disk is full.

Unlimited

This argument specifies that the file can increase in size until the disk is full.

Filegrowth

The FILEGROWTH argument specifies a file increase increment. The placeholder *growth_increment* is the amount of space added to the file each time new space is needed. A value of 0 indicates no increase. The value can be specified in MB, KB, GB, TB, or %. Specify a whole number; do not include a decimal. When % is specified, the increment size is the specified percentage of the file size at the time the increment occurs. If a number is specified without an MB, KB, or % suffix, the default is MB. The default value if FILEGROWTH is not specified is 10%, and the minimum value is 64KB. The size specified is rounded to the nearest 64KB.

The db_state_option

This <db_state_option> section controls the online state of the database; allowing you to place it online, offline or emergency.

    OFFLINE | ONLINE | EMERGENCY   Controls whether the database is offline or online.

The db_user_access_option

SINGLE_USER | RESTRICTED_USER | MULTI_USER   Controls which users may access the database. When SINGLE_USER is specified, only one user at a time can access the database. When RESTRICTED_USER is specified, only members of the *db_owner, dbcreator,* or *sysadmin* roles can use the database. MULTI_USER returns the database to its normal operating state.

The db_update_option

READ_ONLY | READ_WRITE   Specifies whether the database is in read-only mode. In read-only mode, users can read data from the database but not modify it. The database cannot be in use when READ_ONLY is specified. The master database is the exception, and only the system administrator can use *master* while READ_ONLY is set. READ_WRITE returns the database to read/write operations.

The Cursor_option

This section controls cursor options.

- **CURSOR_CLOSE_ON_COMMIT ON | OFF**   If ON is specified, any cursors open when a transaction is committed or rolled back are closed. If OFF is specified, such cursors remain open when a transaction is committed; rolling back a transaction closes any cursors except those defined as INSENSITIVE or STATIC.

- **CURSOR_DEFAULT LOCAL | GLOBAL**   Controls whether cursor scope defaults to LOCAL or GLOBAL.

The Auto_option

This section controls automatic options.

- **AUTO_CLOSE ON | OFF**   If ON is specified, the database is shut down cleanly and its resources are freed after the last user exits. If OFF is specified, the database remains open after the last user exits.

- **AUTO_CREATE_STATISTICS ON | OFF**   If ON is specified, any missing statistics needed by a query for optimization are automatically built during optimization.

- **AUTO_SHRINK ON | OFF**   If ON is specified, the database files are candidates for automatic periodic shrinking.

- **AUTO_UPDATE_STATISTICS ON | OFF**   If ON is specified, any out-of-date statistics required by a query for optimization are automatically built during optimization. If OFF is specified, statistics must be updated manually.

- **AUTO_UPDATE_STATISTICS_ASYNC ON | OFF**   If ON, queries that initiate an automatic update of out-of-date statistics will not wait for the statistics to be updated before compiling. Subsequent queries will use the updated statistics when they are available. If OFF, queries that initiate an automatic update of out-of-date statistics wait until the updated statistics can be used in the query optimization plan. Setting this option to ON has no effect unless **AUTO_UPDATE_STATISTICS** is set to ON.

The Sql_option

The sql_option section controls the ANSI compliance options.

- **ANSI_NULL_DEFAULT ON | OFF**   If ON is specified, CREATE TABLE follows SQL-92 rules to determine whether a column allows null values.

- **ANSI_NULLS ON | OFF**   If ON is specified, all comparisons to a null value evaluate to UNKNOWN. If OFF is specified, comparisons of non-Unicode values to a null value evaluate to TRUE if both values are NULL.

- **ANSI_PADDING ON | OFF**   If ON is specified, strings are padded to the same length before comparison or insert. If OFF is specified, strings are not padded.

- **ANSI_WARNINGS ON | OFF**   If ON is specified, errors or warnings are issued when conditions such as divide-by-zero occur.

- **ARITHABORT ON | OFF**   If ON is specified, a query is terminated when an overflow or divide-by-zero error occurs during query execution.

- **CONCAT_NULL_YIELDS_NULL ON | OFF**   If ON is specified, the result of a concatenation operation is NULL when either operand is NULL. If OFF is specified, the null value is treated as an empty character string. The default is OFF.

- **QUOTED_IDENTIFIER ON | OFF**   If ON is specified, double quotation marks can be used to enclose delimited identifiers.

- **NUMERIC_ROUNDABORT ON | OFF**   If ON is specified, an error is generated when loss of precision occurs in an expression.

- **RECURSIVE_TRIGGERS ON | OFF**   If ON is specified, recursive firing of triggers is allowed. RECURSIVE_TRIGGERS OFF, the default, prevents direct recursion only. To disable indirect recursion as well, set the nested triggers server option to 0 using sp_configure.

The recovery_option

This section controls database recovery options.

- **RECOVERY FULL | BULK_LOGGED | SIMPLE**   If FULL is specified, complete protection against media failure is provided. If a data file is damaged, media recovery can restore all committed transactions.

If BULK_LOGGED is specified, protection against media failure is combined with the best performance and least amount of log memory usage for certain large-scale or bulk operations. These operations include SELECT INTO, bulk load operations (BCP and BULK INSERT), CREATE INDEX, and text and image operations (WRITETEXT and UPDATETEXT).

Under the bulk-logged recovery model, logging for the entire class is minimal and cannot be controlled on an operation-by-operation basis.

If SIMPLE is specified, a simple backup strategy that uses minimal log space is provided. Log space can be automatically reused when no longer needed for server failure recovery.

NOTE *The simple recovery model is easier to manage than the other two models but at the expense of higher data loss exposure if a data file is damaged. All changes since the most recent database or differential database backup are lost and must be reentered manually. Check out recovery models in Chapter 7.*

The default recovery model is determined by the recovery model of the model database. To change the default for new databases, use ALTER DATABASE to set the recovery option of the model database.

- **TORN_PAGE_DETECTION ON | OFF**   If ON is specified, incomplete pages can be detected. The default is ON.

- **PAGE_VERIFY CHECKSUM | TORN_PAGE_DETECTION | NONE**   Discovers damaged database pages caused by disk I/O path errors. Disk I/O path errors can be the cause of database corruption problems and are generally caused by power failures or disk hardware failures that occur at the time the page is being written to disk.

The checksum is stored in page headers that already exist, and thus there is no extra storage cost associated with this feature. While you might see a slight performance loss during the calculation of the checksum, the benefit far outweighs the cost in additional CPU cycles to help preserve data integrity on valuable and large databases.

Creating a Database Using Management Studio

If you do not need to be scripting to create a database, then using Management Studio makes perfect sense. In addition to creating the database interactively, you can also manage or alter the database there. For example, you can manipulate the file sizes, filegroups, and so on. And you can attach and detach databases (which is a very convenient method of making copies of your database for distribution, provided you are sure the target is compatible).

To create a database interactively, do the following:

1. Connect to the specific server and SQL Server instance in which you want to create a new database. Expand the server node so that the node "Databases" is accessible. Select Databases and right-click. Now select New Database. The dialog box illustrated in Figure 6-1 loads.

2. On the General page, enter the database name of the database, enter the name of the primary data file, and specify the file path for both the database and transaction logs. The values for the properties follow the same recommendations discussed in the CREATE DATABASE section earlier.

3. On the Options page you can select various options and behaviors of the database, such as its recovery model and database state.

4. On the Filegroups page you can add more filegroups as needed or configure the primary filegroup.

After creating the new database and before you use it, you should back up *master*, which will now contain definitions and specifics related to the new database.

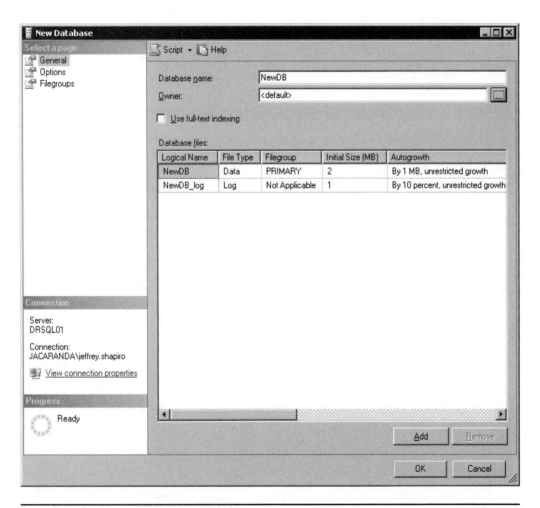

FIGURE 6-1 Creating a database interactively

Creating a Database Using the Copy Database Wizard

To create a database using the Copy Database Wizard, you need to do the following:

1. Open the target server in Object Explorer (in Solution Manager) and then expand down to the Databases node. Expand the Databases node and select a database. Right-click the database and select Tasks | Copy Database. The Copy Database Wizard appears. Click Next.

2. First choose the source server for the copy and authentication. This is shown in Figure 6-2. Click Next to arrive at the destination server option. Again you will be required to enter credentials to connect to the target server. Click Next.

3. The next screen prompts you for the transfer method. You can specify that the source database be first detached before the copy is done. This is obviously the faster of the options, but you must be able to log into the source and destination servers as the SSIS proxy account, as shown in Figure 6-3. The drawback is that the database cannot be in use. The slower option allows the database to stay online and uses the SQL Management Object API to perform the move.

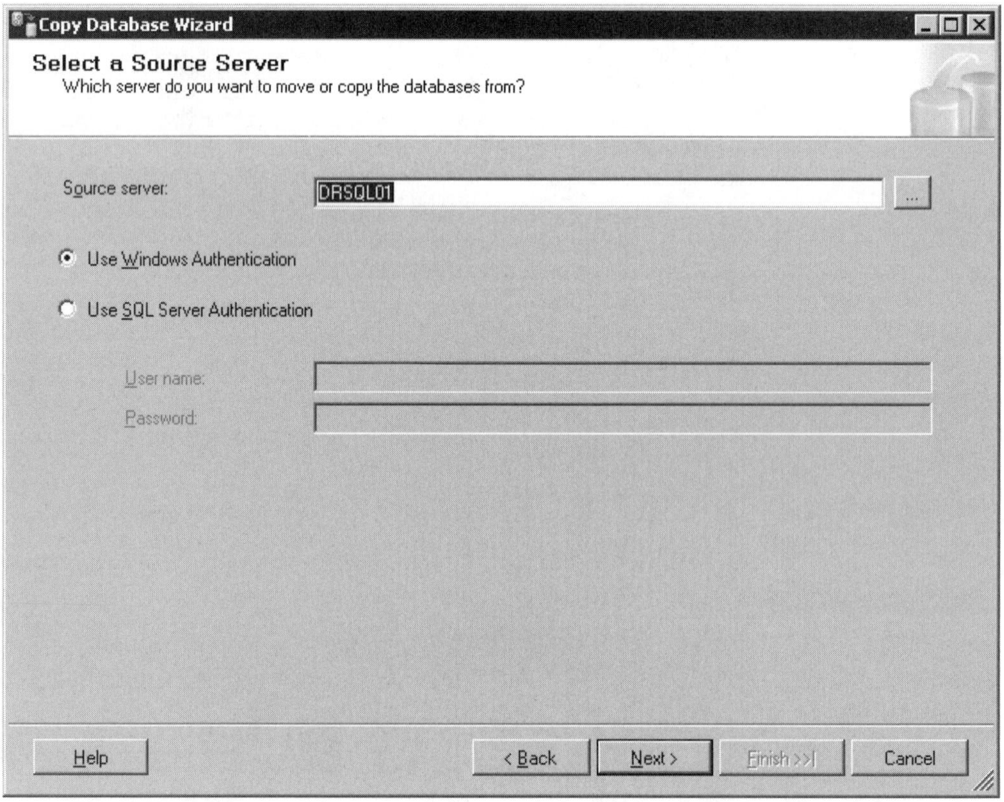

FIGURE 6-2   Choosing a source server for the copy

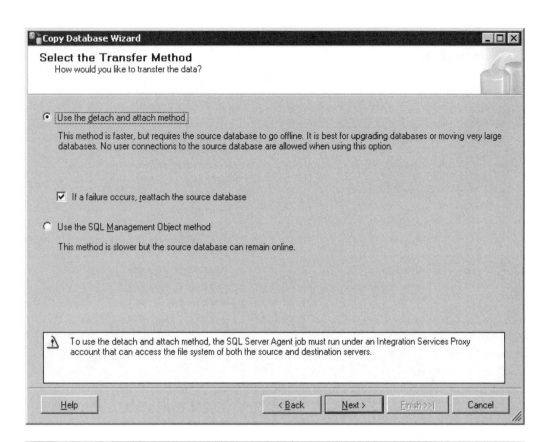

FIGURE 6-3   Choosing the transfer method

4. After choosing the transfer method, you will arrive at a screen that will ask you for the name of the database to either copy or move. This is shown in Figure 6-4. Make the choice and click Next.

5. The next couple of screens are straightforward. You get to configure the database files in a similar interface to the one shown in Figure 6-1. The remaining screens involve saving the job as a DTS package (as in SQL Server 2000). You can schedule the job to run at a later time or immediately.

There you have all the methods at your disposal to create a database. We will return to database performance in Chapters 16 and 17. Next we look to database internals, tables and indexes.

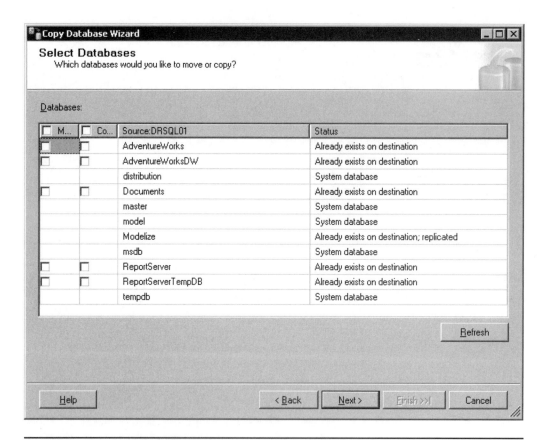

Figure 6-4   Choosing the database to copy

Tables

In the first part of this book, we discussed the architecture of SQL Server tables and how data is stored in them. Let's look at the tables in this chapter from a higher level, as objects we need to create and configure for our applications. A database can contain many tables, and the tables can contain many columns designed to hold different data types.

There are several ways that you can go about creating your tables, as described in the following list:

- Interactively in Management Studio, choosing the New Table option from the Tables node
- Interactively from within a database diagram when you right-click the canvas
- Through code; specifically, the CREATE TABLE and ALTER TABLE statements run in a query window
- Through SSIS
- Using the SQL-SMO object model

Each route represents a different mechanism for creating a table. In this section, we'll look at the CREATE TABLE and ALTER TABLE statements, along with the interactive design tools in Management Studio. The SQL-SMO object model is covered in Chapter 11. Using SSIS as a database creation tool is beyond the scope of this book.

Before you decide on the most convenient method of getting from point A to point B in table creation and configuration, let's first talk about database design. Modeling, architecture, design, and metadata creation are essential before we can build our databases and applications.

Granted, you will always be adding more tables, expanding existing ones, and changing the attributes of the tables (refactoring). Initially, however, you need to sketch out the basic design of the database and its tables before creating the objects in the database. You can use sophisticated modeling tools, such as ER-Win, Rational Rose, and Visio, or you can use the limited design tools you have in Management Studio (the more experience you gain in database design, the less tools you will need).

If you don't have any design tools handy, then a large whiteboard or a single large sheet of paper, pencils, and erasers will do. You could go from the whiteboard or paper to the design tool of your choice, or if you are strong at T-SQL, you could create what you need using the CREATE TABLE statement.

You should design the entire database or application from the get-go, and all the tables you'll need to get the job done at version one. Working tables piecemeal can be really taxing on the overall development project and is never recommended. You really need to see the entire logical model from a much higher level, rather than working on a table-by-table basis, and this is where modeling can be of use.

You will need to understand and formulate a plan around how the tables are going to be normalized, such as to what levels—3NF, 4NF, and so on; and you need to decide on the placing of primary and foreign keys, indexes, and data types. Constraints are not that important at this stage; I believe it's more important to get the logical design in place before worrying about the integrity of the data that's going into the tables. Integrity can come with the data integrity plan, which we discuss in Chapter 12.

So, on to table creation with the help of T-SQL.

CREATE TABLE

The CREATE TABLE statement may seem a little daunting if you have not seen or worked with it before. However, if working in source or script code is your thing, then you'll find CREATE TABLE (and ALTER TABLE) much more powerful and possibly a lot easier than working with the dialog boxes in Management Studio.

```
CREATE TABLE
    [ database_name . [ schema_name ] . | schema_name . ] table_name
        ( { <column_definition> | <computed_column_definition> }
        [ <table_constraint> ] [ ,...n ] )
    [ ON { partition_scheme_name ( partition_column_name ) | filegroup
        | "default" } ]
    [ { TEXTIMAGE_ON { filegroup | "default" } ]
[ ; ]
```

```
<column_definition> ::=
column_name <data_type>
    [ COLLATE collation_name ]
    [ NULL | NOT NULL ]
    [
        [ CONSTRAINT constraint_name ] DEFAULT constant_expression ]
      | [ IDENTITY [ ( seed ,increment ) ] [ NOT FOR REPLICATION ]
    ]
    [ ROWGUIDCOL ] [ <column_constraint> [ ...n ] ]

<data type> ::=
[ type_schema_name . ] type_name
    [ ( precision [ , scale ] | max |
        [ { CONTENT | DOCUMENT } ] xml_schema_collection ) ]

<column_constraint> ::=
[ CONSTRAINT constraint_name ]
{     { PRIMARY KEY | UNIQUE }
        [ CLUSTERED | NONCLUSTERED ]
        [
            WITH FILLFACTOR = fillfactor
          | WITH ( < index_option > [ , ...n ] )
        ]
        [ ON { partition_scheme_name ( partition_column_name )
          | filegroup | "default" } ]
  | [ FOREIGN KEY ]
        REFERENCES [ schema_name . ] referenced_table_name [ ( ref_column ) ]
        [ ON DELETE { NO ACTION | CASCADE | SET NULL | SET DEFAULT } ]
        [ ON UPDATE { NO ACTION | CASCADE | SET NULL | SET DEFAULT } ]
        [ NOT FOR REPLICATION ] | CHECK [ NOT FOR REPLICATION ] (
logical_expression )
}

<computed_column_definition> ::=
column_name AS computed_column_expression
[ PERSISTED [ NOT NULL ] ]
[
    [ CONSTRAINT constraint_name ]
    { PRIMARY KEY | UNIQUE }
        [ CLUSTERED | NONCLUSTERED ]
        [
            WITH FILLFACTOR = fillfactor
          | WITH ( <index_option> [ , ...n ] )
        ]
  | [ FOREIGN KEY ]
        REFERENCES referenced_table_name [ ( ref_column ) ]
        [ ON DELETE { NO ACTION | CASCADE } ]
        [ ON UPDATE { NO ACTION } ]
        [ NOT FOR REPLICATION ]
  | CHECK [ NOT FOR REPLICATION ] ( logical_expression )
    [ ON { partition_scheme_name ( partition_column_name )
        | filegroup | "default" } ]
]
```

```
< table_constraint > ::=
[ CONSTRAINT constraint_name ]
{
    { PRIMARY KEY | UNIQUE }
        [ CLUSTERED | NONCLUSTERED ]
                (column [ ASC | DESC ] [ ,...n ] )
        [
            WITH FILLFACTOR = fillfactor
            |WITH ( <index_option> [ , ...n ] )
        ]
        [ ON { partition_scheme_name (partition_column_name)
             | filegroup | "default" } ]
    | FOREIGN KEY
                ( column [ ,...n ] )
        REFERENCES referenced_table_name [ ( ref_column [ ,...n ] ) ]
        [ ON DELETE { NO ACTION | CASCADE | SET NULL | SET DEFAULT } ]
        [ ON UPDATE { NO ACTION | CASCADE | SET NULL | SET DEFAULT } ]
        [ NOT FOR REPLICATION ]
    | CHECK [ NOT FOR REPLICATION ] ( logical_expression )
}
<index_option> ::=
     PAD_INDEX = { ON | OFF }
  | FILLFACTOR = fillfactor
  | IGNORE_DUP_KEY = { ON | OFF }
  | STATISTICS_NORECOMPUTE = { ON | OFF }
  | ALLOW_ROW_LOCKS = { ON | OFF}
  | ALLOW_PAGE_LOCKS ={ ON | OFF} }
```

So let's go through the main arguments.

The database_name option

The *database_name* argument specifies the name of the database in which the table is created. If you omit the *database_name* in the script, SQL Server will install the table to the current table by default. You will obviously need a logon for the current connection and an associated user ID in the database specified here; and create table permissions are required.

The owner option

The *owner* is the name of the user ID that owns the new table; this must be an existing user ID in the database. If you do not specify an *owner*, SQL Server defaults to the user ID associated with the logon for the current connection in the database.

You can also transfer the ownership if you are a member of the sysadmin fixed server role or the db_owner or db_ddladmin fixed database roles. You can also create the table if all you have is create table rights, but you have to specify a user ID associated with the current logon. If you do not specify an owner but you are a member of the sysadmin fixed server role, the owner of the table will default to the dbo user.

The table_Name option

The *table_name* that you provide must conform to the rules for identifiers (see Chapter 16). The identifier must also be unique and fully qualified in dot notation. An example of a qualified unique identifier is *comptroller.account_pay* or *dbo.customers*.

The *table_name* can contain a maximum of 128 characters. Temporary table names must be prefixed with a single number sign (#), and they cannot exceed 116 characters. (See Chapter 16 for a discussion on the new table data type, which might suit your purpose better than temporary tables.)

The column_name option

The *column_name* represents the name of a column in the table. The column names must also conform to the rules for identifiers as discussed previously, and they must be unique in the table you are creating. The only time you do not need to specify a column name is when you create a column to hold *timestamp* data. SQL Server will just use "timestamp" for the column name if you leave it out.

The computed_column_expression option

The *computed_column_expression* refers to an expression defining the value of a computed column. A computed column is not physically created and stored in the table but is computed from an expression using other columns in the same table. You can create a computed column to hold a computing expression. For example, the expression "total AS subtotal * discount" returns a single value stored in this column.

The expression you use does not need to be a mathematical expression. It can also be another noncomputed column name, constant, function, variable, or any combination of these connected by one or more operators. The only exception is that the expression cannot be a subquery.

Computed columns can be used in select lists, WHERE clauses, ORDER BY clauses, or any other locations in which regular expressions can be used. The following exceptions, however, are important considerations:

- You cannot define a DEFAULT or a FOREIGN KEY constraint or a NOT NULL constraint definition over this so-called column. But the computed column can be used as a key column in an index or as part of any PRIMARY KEY or UNIQUE constraint. The proviso is that the computed column value must be defined by a deterministic expression and the data type of the result must be compatible with index columns.

  Using the nondeterministic function GETDATE(), for example, would not fly, because it changes with every invocation and thus cannot be indexed.

- You cannot reference a computed column from an INSERT or UPDATE statement. SQL Server may insert a NULL value into the column, and you can use the COLUMNPROPERTY function (AllowsNull property) to investigate the nullability of the computed columns. You can also call the ISNULL(*check_expression,* constant) function and if necessary change the value to a nonnull.

ON {*filegroup* | DEFAULT}

The ON {*filegroup* | DEFAULT} placeholder specifies a filegroup for the table (see the discussion on filegroups earlier in this chapter). If you do not specify ON, the table will be stored in the default filegroup.

The ON {*filegroup* | DEFAULT} can also be specified in a PRIMARY KEY or a UNIQUE constraint. If *filegroup* is specified, however, the index is stored in the named filegroup. If DEFAULT is specified, the index is stored in the default filegroup. If you omit the filegroup from a constraint definition, then the index will be stored in the same filegroup as the table.

When you specify DEFAULT here, you must delimit it, because it not a keyword. You can delimit it with double quotes (for example, ON "DEFAULT") or with square brackets (for example, ON [DEFAULT]).

Text Images in Filegroups

The TEXTIMAGE_ON { *filegroup* | DEFAULT } specification indicates that the text, ntext, image, xml, varchar(max), nvarchar(max), varbinary(max), and CLR user-defined type columns are stored on the specified filegroup defined in the preceding argument. However, TEXTIMAGE_ON is not allowed if there are no text, ntext, or image columns in the table. If you do not specify TEXTIMAGE_ON, the text, ntext, and image columns are stored in the same filegroup as the table.

TEXTIMAGE_ON is not allowed if there are no large value columns in the table. TEXTIMAGE_ON cannot be specified if <partition_scheme> is specified. If "default" is specified, or if TEXTIMAGE_ON is not specified at all, the large value columns are stored in the default filegroup. The storage of any large value column data specified in CREATE TABLE cannot be subsequently altered.

The data_type option

The *data_type* argument specifies the column data type. You can use any system- or user-defined data types. To add the user-defined data type, you can call the system stored procedure sp_addtype in the script, as long as you create it before trying to use it in a table definition.

The NULL/NOT NULL assignment for a user-defined data type can be overridden during the CREATE TABLE statement, but you cannot specify a length for a user-defined data type in the CREATE TABLE statement.

Default

The DEFAULT argument specifies the value that SQL Server will automatically insert in your column if you do not provide a value when using INSERT.

The constant_expression option

The *constant_expression* placeholder is used to specify a constant, a NULL value, or a system function used as the default value for the column.

Identity

The IDENTITY argument specifies that the respective column is an identity column. These are commonly used in conjunction with PRIMARY KEY constraints to serve as the unique row identifier for the table. The actual IDENTITY value or property can be of the data type tinyint, smallint, int, bigint, or the decimal(p,0), or numeric(p,0) columns. You must also specify both the seed and increment, or you can leave them out altogether, in which case the default of (1,1) will be used (*seed, increment*).

Seed

The seed is the value SQL Server uses for the very first row loaded into the table. If the seed is "1," the first row will be "1."

Increment

The increment specifies the incremental value added to the identity value for the preceding row. For example, if the last row ID was "2785" and the increment is "5," the next row's value will be "2790."

Not for Replication

The NOT FOR REPLICATION argument specifies that the IDENTITY property should not be enforced when a replication logon such as *sqlrepl* inserts data into the table. Replicated rows must retain the key values assigned in the publishing database, as demonstrated in the preceding chapter. The NOT FOR REPLICATION clause ensures that rows inserted by a replication process are not assigned new identity values. Rows inserted by other processes continue unaffected by this restriction. (You can also manage these values and values inserted by the publishers with CHECK constraints on the local table.)

Rowguidcol

This argument indicates that the new column is a row global uniqueidentifier column. There can be only one uniqueidentifier column per table and the ROWGUIDCOL property can be assigned only to a uniqueidentifier column. (Make sure not to install a ROWGUIDCOL on a database whose compatibility level is 65 or lower [version 6.5]. See Appendix or Books Online for system stored procedure sp_dbcmptlevel.)

It is important to understand that the ROWGUIDCOL property does not enforce uniqueness of the values stored in the column. It also does not behave like the identity column and automatically generate values for new rows inserted into the table. However, you can generate unique values for each column by either using the NEWID() function on INSERT statements or using the NEWID() function as the default for the column (NEWID() is discussed further in Chapter 16).

The collation_name option

The *collation_name* placeholder specifies the language collation for the column. (Collations are introduced in this chapter.) The collation name can be either a Windows collation name or a SQL collation name. Collations govern the management of text strings in the database, so this argument is applicable only for columns of the char, varchar, text, nchar, nvarchar, and ntext data types. If you do not specify the collation, the column will be assigned either the collation of the user-defined data type (if the column is of a user-defined data type) or the default collation of the database. The database collation is either specifically set or inherited from msdb.

The constraint_name option

The *constraint_name* argument is optional, but when you use it, you need to specify the constraint name, which must be unique to the database.

Null

The NULL | NOT NULL keywords are used to specify whether null values are allowed in the column. NULL is not really a constraint per se but can be specified in the same manner as NOT NULL.

Primary Key

The PRIMARY KEY argument is a constraint that enforces entity integrity for a given column or columns through a unique index.

Unique

The UNIQUE argument specifies the constraint that provides entity integrity for a given column or columns through a unique index. A table can have multiple UNIQUE constraints.

Index Clustering

Index clustering is specified through the CLUSTERED | NONCLUSTERED keywords used to indicate that a clustered or nonclustered index is created for the PRIMARY KEY or UNIQUE constraint. PRIMARY KEY constraints default to CLUSTERED, and UNIQUE constraints default to NONCLUSTERED.

You cannot specify CLUSTERED for more than one constraint in a CREATE TABLE statement, and you'll see that enforced, even by Management Studio. If you specify CLUSTERED for a UNIQUE constraint and also specify a PRIMARY KEY constraint, the PRIMARY KEY defaults to NONCLUSTERED.

Fillfactor

The argument [WITH FILLFACTOR = *fillfactor*] specifies how full SQL Server should make each index page when it creates it to store the index data. You can set the *fillfactor* values from 1 through 100, with a default of 0. A lower fill factor creates the index with more space available for new index entries without having to allocate new space.

Referential Integrity

Referential integrity is specified through the FOREIGN KEY . . . REFERENCES arguments. The FOREIGN KEY constraints can reference only columns that are PRIMARY KEY or UNIQUE constraints in the referenced table or columns referenced in a UNIQUE INDEX on the referenced table. This is done through the following arguments:

- The *ref_table* argument, which specifies the name of the table referenced by the FOREIGN KEY constraint.

- The (*ref_column*[,...*n*]) argument, which specifies a column or list of columns from the table referenced by the FOREIGN KEY constraint.

Cascading Referential Integrity

The ON DELETE {CASCADE | NO ACTION} and ON UPDATE {CASCADE | NO ACTION} arguments specify what action is taken on a row in the table created if a referential relationship with a row in a foreign table is established. The default is NO ACTION, which may not be wise (see Chapter 17). However, if CASCADE is specified and a row is deleted or updated in a parent table, then the row it references in the new table is also deleted or updated. If NO ACTION is specified, SQL Server raises an error and the delete or update actions on the rows in the parent table are rolled back. This is further discussed in Chapter 12.

Check

The CHECK argument refers to a constraint that enforces domain integrity by limiting the possible values that can be entered into a column or columns. The NOT FOR REPLICATION keywords are used to prevent the CHECK constraint from being enforced during the distribution process used by replication.

The *logical_expression* placeholder is a logical expression that returns TRUE or FALSE. The *column* placeholder is a column or list of columns, in parentheses, used in table constraints to indicate the columns used in the constraint definition.

The [ASC | DESC] placeholder specifies the order in which the column or columns participating in table constraints are sorted. The default is ASC. Finally, the *n* placeholder indicates that the preceding item can be repeated *n* number of times.

ALTER TABLE is almost identical to CREATE TABLE, so we will not go through the syntax for it, and besides, you can reference the entire syntax in Books Online.

Creating a table in Enterprise Manager is obviously a lot easier for a novice than going the T-SQL script route. As I mentioned earlier, however, by building a T-SQL script you afford yourself a thorough education on what it takes to build a database and put tables in it. In any event, most CREATE TABLE code only needs to be a few lines.

Creating a Table Using Management Studio

To create a table in Management Studio, you need to perform the following actions:

- Drill down to the database into which you need to add the new table, expand the database to reveal the Tables node. Right-click the Tables node and select New Table from the context menu. A table designing workspace will appear on the first tab of the workspace pane.

- Create and configure the columns as needed using the Column Properties pane. Note that the Table Designer menu becomes visible when you select New Table. If you chose to show the associated toolbar, it too will appear under the menu bar. The Table Designer lets you create and manage constraints, indexes, and so on. The integrity constraints, checks, and so on are fully discussed in Chapter 12.

The Table Designer essentially does what the T-SQL scripts do.

Working with Tables in Database Diagrams

Database diagrams are not something new. You can use the Database Diagrams workspace to add all the tables you need to relate for a complete record. The difference between the Database Diagrams tool and something like Rational Rose or Visio is that the tables are either added or created on the fly before they are related, while external tools are used to generate code or scripts or routines to run against SQL Server.

Nevertheless, you can start with the database diagram, as is described in the following two sections.

Database Diagrams

To create a diagram with or without tables, do as follows:

- Expand the database node for the database you are working with. Right-click the Database Diagrams node and select New Database Diagram from the context menu. The Add Table dialog box opens, from which you can "add" existing tables to the diagram work space. This dialog box is shown in Figure 6-5.

- You can also right-click anywhere in the New Diagram pane and select New Table from the context menu. The Choose Name dialog box loads. Enter the name and click OK. The new table is inserted into the database diagram, as illustrated in Figure 6-6. The features you have to work with here are identical to what is available from the Table Designer menus.

You can now work with the tables and add or delete from the database diagram as you need. The Database Diagram menus include a number of tools to use with diagrams.

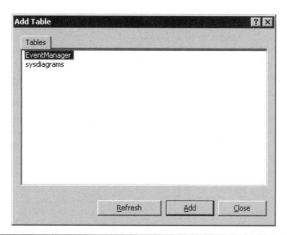

FIGURE 6-5   Adding tables to a Database Diagram workspace

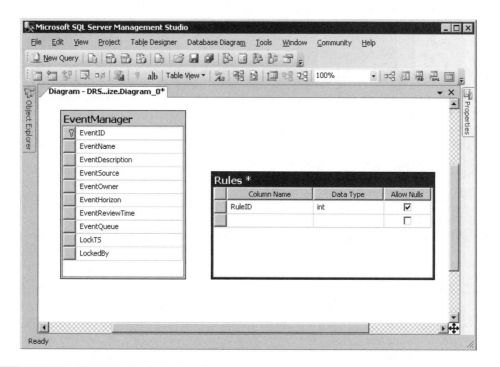

FIGURE 6-6   Working with the Database Diagram tool

For example, if you have too many tables to work with you can zoom into or out of the workspace by selecting the Zoom menu item.

NOTE *There are several options using Management Studio to generate SQL scripts to create databases and tables. As when using its predecessors, you can right-click any database, table, view, or object and choose to script the target to code as a CREATE or ALTER statement. There is also a button labeled Script on the New Database dialog box (see Figure 6-1) that lets you create scripts. You can then save the script to execute at any time.*

Moving Data, Log, and Full-Text Files

If you have never had a reason to move a SQL Server data, log, or full-text catalog to a new location, then you cannot call yourself a DBA. During the lifetime of a database or the SQL Server instance, there are a number of scenarios that may require you to relocate the database. The usual reason to move a database is that the disk on which the database resides runs out of space and you need to move the files to a bigger volume. Moving is made possible by specifying the new file location in the FILENAME clause of the ALTER DATABASE statement, as mentioned earlier. However, there are a few things to prepare before you make the move.

The simplest ways to move a database is are the backup/restore or detach/attach commands. These methods are also the only way to move database files to another instance of SQL Server or to another server. If you are moving the files to different disk locations on the same instance, you do not need to take the databases down. All it takes is the ALTER DATABASE statement.

Before you start, make sure you have the logical names of the database files you are going to move. You can get these names from the name column in the sys.master_files catalog view. Simply query the name column.

To move a data or log file, perform the following steps:

1. Execute the code ALTER DATABASE database_name SET OFFLINE. This will take the databases offline and allow you relocate them to their new home.

2. Once they are moved, you need to execute the following code: ALTER DATABASE database_name MODIFY FILE (NAME = logical_name, FILENAME = 'new_path\os_file_name'). This line rebinds the files to the instance.

3. Next run the code ALTER DATABASE database_name SET ONLINE. This brings the database back online for access.

4. You can then verify the file change by running the following query: SELECT name, physical_name AS CurrentLocation, state_desc FROM sys.master_files WHERE database_id = DB_ID(N'<database_name>');

To Relocate a File on Failed Hardware

If you have to move a file because of a disk or server crash, you can attach the files if they are intact, or relocate the file to a new location if you can run T-SQL against the server as follows:

1. Start the instance of SQL Server in master-only recovery mode by running the following command at the command prompt: `NET START MSSQLSERVER /f /T3608`.

2. If you are working against a named instance, then execute the following code: `NET START MSSQL$instancename /f /T3608`.

3. Next run sqlcmd commands or SQL Server Management Studio to run the following statement: `ALTER DATABASE database_name MODIFY FILE( NAME = logical_name , FILENAME = 'new_path\os_file_name' )`. The sqlcmd utility is discussed in Chapter 4.

4. Next, stop the instance of SQL Server and move the file or files to the new location.

5. Finally, start SQL Server using the NET START MSSQLSERVER command.

You can run these scripts against the active node of a SQL Server cluster.

Indexes

Why are indexes so important to database applications or database management systems? Well, that answer doesn't require much thought. An index helps you find data (row values) in a database quickly, without the system's having to step through every row in the table. Now, if you had a table with only five rows, for example, going to each row and looking at its value in a specific column, a table scan, is not a big deal. But what if the table contained a gazillion rows—not an unusual situation for the average Web site database, or my wife's contact file?

Imagine if the books we read were only a few paragraphs on a page. Would we still need an index at the back? Not at all. But we all know that most books contain a lot of pages, and without an index, it would be very difficult to find information rapidly without having to first scan through the entire book. I have indexed several books in a past life and the process is identical, from a logical or conceptual viewpoint, to the indexing of data in a table. You pinpoint exactly where in the book—the page number—a word or subject matter exists, and you list that word or subject matter in the index with the page number the reader can find it on. Professional indexers who practically index in their sleep can read through the printed pages at lightning speed and quickly build an index of information on all the pages.

Indexes are critical. This book has one. When I go to a bookstore, I hardly bother with the contents or the author's bio or what he or she has to say in the preface or introduction. I go directly to the index, look up an item I want information on, and hope I find it. If the item is indexed, I go to the page and read the information to establish whether the book is imparting knowledge on the subject matter I am interested in. If not, I put the book back on the shelf and move on.

Indexing tables is absolutely essential, but there was a time in the early days of the relational engine that indexing caused such a performance hit on databases that indexes were kept to a minimum. Indexes still incur overhead, and we'll look into that aspect shortly, but without them, looking for information in a table is a very loathsome exercise for the DBMS because it has to go through every row in the table to find the information requested by your query.

Indexes are database objects. A database index is a lot like a book index; it is a list of values in a table that contains the exact storage locations of the rows in the table that contain each value. Indexes can be created for a single column of values in a table or for a combination of columns. Indexes are usually implemented as B-trees. B-trees are sorted on the search key. If we create an index on *[company name]* and *[company number]*, the B-tree index can efficiently locate a value on either column.

When you build queries, as discussed in the chapters in Part III, they will execute faster and return data to the client if the correct indexes have been created for the data in question. It is obviously wrong to place an index on the company number when all queries are done on the company name. The index for the former value would never be used, and the queries on company name would have the DBMS looking for data like a late moviegoer looking for his or her seat in the dark.

Having said that, SQL Server might at times find that an index scenario has reached a point of diminishing returns (sorry about that pun), and that the indexing process is costing more in overhead than iterating through the table row by row. This is the point at which you need to reevaluate the indexing and either drop the indexes or rearchitect the table, which could mean rebuilding an index solution at the minimum or rethinking the current schema. More about this is a moment.

Indexes on Keys and Constraints

Some indexes are created automatically by SQL Server. For example, when you create a primary key for a table, you automatically get an index thrown in, free of charge. The same applies to a unique constraint.

The Cost of Indexes

I mentioned earlier that indexes do come at a cost. They do engage additional system resources and overhead for their upkeep and operation. For starters, indexes can become rather bulky, which means they can cause the size of the database file to swell. In addition, whenever you add, change, or delete data from a table, the index has to be updated and such maintenance consumes time and resources. Imagine what would happen if after this entire book was proofread and indexed and ready for the printers that I called up the copyeditor and asked her if I could delete a chapter and replace it with new information—the people at the National Hurricane Center would have a heart attack with the storm that would ensue. SQL Server, on the other hand, understands that its data changes all the time, and so it has built-in algorithms to ensure that index regeneration happens as efficiently as possible.

The life of the DBA would be so wonderful if SQL Server were capable of taking care of all the index details. Unfortunately, SQL Server sometimes requires your input in the creation and management of indexes. Indexes are different for every table. The data is different, and the table schemas differ from table to table. Each table might have different keys and constraints on them that impact the search and return performance. The subjects of index design and index tuning thus should not be ignored. We return to indexing in Chapters 12 and 18.

Performance, Optimization, and Tuning

You have to provide some thought to database design, relations, and the index creation process. In the olden days of exposed database engines—APIs that you had to write very low-level code for—index tuning, for example, was basically nothing more than creating and recreating indexes to find solutions that provided the best rate of return on the data you were querying. Today SQL Server comes equipped with the tools to make this job a lot easier.

The Microsoft SQL Server 2005 Database Engine Tuning Advisor and the SQL Server Profiler help you select and create an optimal database, collection of tables, sets of indexes, indexed views, and partitions without requiring an expert understanding of the structure of the database or the internals of Microsoft SQL Server.

The Database Engine Tuning Advisor, for example, analyzes the workload of one or more databases, reporting also on their physical implementation. Using batteries of tests comprising sets of T-SQL statements that execute against a database or databases, the Database Engine Tuning Advisor can recommend adding, removing, or modifying physical design structures in the databases.

For example the Database Engine Tuning Advisor can

- Propose a collection of indexes to implement. It does this using the query optimizer to analyze queries in a workload.

- Recommend aligned or nonaligned partitions for a database.

- Recommend indexed views for a database.

- Report on the effects of the proposed changes in indexes and queries.

- Consider alternatives in which you supply possible design choices in the form of hypothetical configurations for Database Engine Tuning Advisor to evaluate.

Chapter 18 is devoted to operations management of SQL Server 2005 implementation, and we cover the database and index in more detail in that chapter. However, let's first discuss here what good indexing practice comprises:

- Keep the number of update queries that either change or delete rows to a minimum. In other words try to change or delete as many rows as you can in as few queries as possible. This will ensure that index re-creation and maintenance overhead is kept to a minimum.

- Use nonclustered indexes on columns often queried. This practice lets you cover more columns with indexes without the cost of a clustered index. By the same token, you need to use the Tuning Adviser to see if an index on simple data is not more costly than a sequential table scan without an index, which is entirely feasible.

- Use clustered indexes on key columns. Also keep them for unique, identity, and nonnull columns, which typically benefit from clustered indexes.

- Evaluate your disk subsystems to help speed up data access and index creation. While SQL Server may have highly optimized index creating algorithms, the index creation and maintenance speeds depend on the hard disk technology employed. For starters, stick to hardware RAID technology, which is more efficient for database solutions than software RAID. Also use faster and more reliable hard disks in the RAID configurations.

- Get to know your data and investigate what costs and plans the query optimizer is consistently coming up with for your query and the indexes that have to live with it.

- Learn how to use the performance tools (see Chapter 18).

Besides these tips, you should take the time to fully understand the difference between clustered and nonclustered indexes. Also, if you have not read the architecture chapters in Part I, now is the time to do so because they provide you with insight into the underlying architecture of the databases and tables and how the data pages that comprise tables are structured and maintained. It helps to navigate the road when you know how it is paved.

In Review

This chapter exposes what it takes to create the two most important objects in SQL Server: the database and the table. SQL Server provides several options for creating these objects. You can create them using T-SQL script, or you can create them interactively, using wizards and the GUI tools that come built into Management Studio. We also introduced index creation.

I explored the T-SQL syntax needed to create databases and tables in code. While it might seem easier to create these objects graphically, there will come a time when you might only be able to create the objects by executing T-SQL code against the server. Most experienced DBA's find it easier, in the long run, to create and maintain the necessary scripts to create and alter tables and databases.

Temporary tables, the table variable, and common table expressions (CTEs) are discussed in Chapter 16.

SQL Server Disaster Recovery

Managing the disaster recovery (DR) plan for a data center is one of the most exciting roles in IT, if you like adventure, like bungee jumping or skydiving. I know this firsthand because I have been doing DR for some years now; you generally get the budget you ask for if the business's health absolutely depends on the servers you maintain (which is most of the time). In Miami, where I worked for some years, as soon as a hurricane watch goes into effect, the CEO hands the business to you. Now you're in charge and you had better have a good DR plan.

That said, disaster recovery is probably the DBA role (developers, you can skip this chapter if you are lucky enough to be part of a SQL Server team) that requires the toughest skin on an individual or the group. In businesses that can afford it, some DBAs do nothing else but manage DR and backup/restore. When disaster strikes, and it does, the future of the business, and everyone's job, is on the line. If you do things right and get the databases back online in record time, you are pretty much the darling of the company; if you fail, you'll be out the door in the time it takes to spell "rollback." Over the years that I have managed DR, I have seen several SQL Server databases go to the wall, and several Exchange installations go south too, and dozens of smaller database corruption issues, and so on. You have to expect it; you have to plan for it.

While we recovered every time and saved the day (except one situation I will relate to you later), the most important piece of advice I can give is that you can never be fully prepared for your day in hell, no matter how much you practice. Many things can go wrong in the heat of disaster. I once had to ask a CEO to leave the computer room because I thought he was going to get sick all over the servers.

This chapter will introduce you to some DR theory and how it applies to SQL Server 2005, especially with respect to backup and restore of SQL Server databases and their transaction logs. It will introduce you to the tools that ship with the product and the recovery features inherent in the system. It will also take you step-by-step through several backup and restore procedures, and describe techniques and practices to ensure database and transaction log availability.

For the most part, this chapter assumes you are supporting a high-end data center application, and that recovery and restore will be automated and highly sophisticated. However, with this chapter you will also learn how to use the power of SQL Server's integrated visual backup/restore features to manage smaller shops, in which you are required to perform daily backups, and to undertake manual recovery, such as by reentering lost transactions.

Establishing Baselines for Disaster Recovery

Establishing baselines is essential when it comes to assessing risk, managing disaster recovery, stopping loss, and so forth, no matter how big the database or how critical the application. When formulating a DR plan, no matter that you are starting from scratch or taking over from another DBA, it is critical to fully understand the business plan and the application's need for availability and service level. You thus need to establish the tolerance level for your enterprise or service to be without access to data and databases for a given time. In other words, how long do you have after a database goes offline, before the business begins to suffer serious harm? Many database or OLTP system clients do not understand their needs, so establishing a baseline is one of the most important exercises in a data center.

This might seem a frivolous activity, but it's not. You might think that all DR plans should aim to restore service immediately or at least very soon after failure. However, obtaining the dream of almost instant recovery requires a number of provisions. They include, in no intended order, trained DBAs, the right equipment, the right premises, the right demeanor, the right software, the right technology, and money. No doubt the last item is the most important one—a well-funded data center or contract makes life easy for everyone involved. In other words, establish the needs first and then see what you and SQL Server 2005 can do to rise to the challenge, while making sure you have the budget with which to fully implement the plan.

Baselines allow you to establish certain tolerance levels and then move out from there. For example, you might have service level agreements (SLAs) or quality of support requirements in place that will dictate requirements to you. A bank or an Internet ordering application will require a very different collection of DR ingredients than a casual order entry system.

Let's consider some baselines in terms of quality of support. First, you need to understand that no matter what technology or regimen you are using, you can only restore up to the point of your last complete backup and any available transactions that have been flushed from the transaction log file. The time from the last backup and the last duplication of the transaction log to the reception of a new transaction I refer to as *void time* or more precisely *void-backup time*. Some DBAs have called this the *transaction twilight zone*, the time just before a transaction is saved to the transaction log and saved from disaster.

I coined the term void time in the network administration realm to explain to users why the data or files they lost could not be restored to the last minute or second of their work. Void time is the useless time in which it is impossible, using conventional tape backup technology, to make a backup copy of a file. Backing up or duplicating data is a sequential process. The slowest technology, where the void time window is the widest, is tape backup. However, tape backup has the highest capacity for the least cost; the highest media safety, durability, storability, security, and so forth. The fast technology on the other end of the scale is a mirrored disk, but mirrored disks are expensive (if they are really large and fast) and have low security, storability, and safety attributes.

My aim in network administration is to narrow or close the void-time window as much as possible using whatever technology is available at the time. The higher the value of the work, the easier it is to justify the cost of fast backup technology. Conversely, the lower the value of the work, the harder it is to justify the cost.

This means that unless you are backing up every millisecond of the day, it is very difficult, in the event of a disaster, to restore to the last transaction or commit point saved to the log. As you learned in Chapters 3 and 4, SQL Server can back up the databases and logs to local tape devices or remote disk files all the time. It costs the DBMS some bandwidth— CPU and memory, but you need some powerful and expensive equipment to transfer data at terrific speeds to close the void-time window as much as possible. This integrated feature of SQL Server backup is known as *active backup* in the industry, and SQL Server has demonstrated record-breaking capabilities for concurrent or active backup during highly active OLTP states, in the order of hundreds of transactions per second (TPS). So you need to understand what is possible and if it works for you and the application owner.

I established a collection of backup baseline parameters to help me determine and then establish the database owner's backup and restoration needs, and I have been refining this theory over the years. The order of the items in the list of baselines determines what can be considered adequate in terms of the age of tape or file backed-up databases and transaction logs. It helps the database owners focus on a restore level because often they are not fully informed about what is possible or what it will cost. They just tell you that losing even one transaction is a disaster without understanding what it will take to ensure zero transaction loss and 100 percent availability—neither is possible, really, because it is very possible for a system to crash when data is still in volatile memory and has not been written to the hard disk, where it can be swept up to the backup device.

Once I have established the loss-tolerance level—the baseline—with the owner, I work out how to cater to it for an individual system or application—the service level need—and the cost. First let's establish the critical nature of our backup requirement, an exercise in pigeonholing. Consider the following list:

1. The backup is one month or more old. The database owner needs monthly and annual backup for archival purposes, analysis, or some legal requirement. Pretty standard stuff; probably backup of temporal data, a data warehouse, and so on.

2. The backup is between one and four weeks old. The database owner needs weekly backups for access to analysis data and possible rollback of the database to a certain point in time. Also pretty standard stuff . . . any inexpensive tape device will work.

3. The backup is between four and seven days old. This is the same as number 2, but the rollback period is days and not weeks.

4. The backup is between one and three days old. The database may have become corrupt and the database owner requires a restore of a recent backup. The lost data can be easily or cheaply recovered. This is not casual stuff any more. You require the establishment of a rotation scheme, backup windows, and schedules.

5. The backup is between 6–12 hours old. The lost data costs more to recover, but the database owner cannot afford to wait longer than a day, nor can he or she afford to return to a state older than 12 hours. The lost data of the past 12 hours can be manually recovered. We are getting onto delicate ground with this option. Backup/ restore management is now a daily chore requiring operator duties and daily log reports, typical data center jobs.

6. The backup is between two and five hours old. The database owner cannot afford to return to a database state older than five hours. The database must be brought current before the close of business. This involves data center operations, 24 × 7 attention of operators, access to DBAs via beepers and e-mail, and so on.

7. The backup has captured all transactions saved to the transaction log files in the past sixty minutes. The database owner cannot afford to lose more than an hour's worth of data. We now need highly sophisticated backup/restore operations, hourly backups, warm standby servers with log shipping (see Chapter 9), and so on.

8. The backup has captured the last transactions saved to the transaction log files. The database owner cannot afford to lose any transactions up to the point of system or database failure. There is usually little chance of manually getting back lost transactions. We now need full-blown active backup, with redundancy and fail-over architectures to ensure that all transactions can survive a disaster.

If you look at the list, you can safely say that levels 1–5 address very low transaction traffic situations and that any crash of a database or loss of the database server after the last backup will not cause the business serious harm. Such environments are typically order entry (not order taking) scenarios, and lost data can usually be recovered at low cost . . . manually reentered if need be.

Cost, of course, is relative. To lose a staff member for the day to rekey information is itself a costly exercise. Losing the day's data may mean little to one company, but a lot to another (my motto is "time lost is life lost"). If you feel you should be at a higher level, but you or the database owner can only afford a lower level, you may be courting disaster, risking a critical application on a shoestring budget—something to think about if you outsource to data centers or roll your own. If you are supporting a low transaction rate application, however, backing up databases overnight is usually not a problem, because no new data is entered to the database until the following business day. You are usually safe as long as you diligently perform backups.

From level 6 to level 8, you start to get into a gray area that requires careful attention to human and technology resources. At level 8, full or differential database backups will not capture the most recent transactions, because you'll need to be duplicating transaction logs at the same time the transactions are being flushed to the primary log. Some method of duplicating transaction logs to the last commit point is thus required. With online transaction processing systems, especially order-taking systems on the Internet, the loss of even one transaction can mean the loss of a customer. One lost customer can cause significant collateral damage.

SQL Server 2005 has the mechanisms to continue backing up data all the time it is in use, but as with any system, this can cause significant load on the server if you don't have sufficient bandwidth, both network and backup device capability. However, it is not so much the backing up or duplication or replication that takes time, but also the restoration of the lost server or the lost database, or hard disks and so on. When you get into a situation that dictates that you cannot afford to lose any transactions written to a transaction log, you might as well stop at level 6 with respect to tape backup and restore because you cannot achieve the higher levels with conventional tape backup practice (remember even a restore of the most recent backup still takes time to execute). Continuous or very aggressive conventional backups of both databases and transaction logs is not going to put you back in business seconds or minutes after meltdown.

In this regard, we might then revisit the list and classify levels 1–5 as archival or general availability backups. This means that you treat the backups as necessary only to restore a database to a certain point in time, after which time the data is not there or is bad. Levels 6–8 then require an alternative classification in terms of database access.

Levels 6–8 need to address three needs:

- **Requirement 1, Focus on availability**   The system must be back online as soon as possible so as not to lose any new transactions. For example, a customer on the Internet finds he or she cannot make a transaction or place an order and goes elsewhere if the situation persists longer than a few seconds. Money lost. At this level, you are already into automatic fail-over systems for service level.

- **Requirement 2, Focus on transaction recovery (disaster recovery)**   All transactions written to the log up to the disaster "event horizon" need to be recovered. In other words, being offline is not as critical as losing transactions.

- **Requirement 3, Equal attention to availability and transaction recovery**   We need both the availability level of requirement 1 and the disaster recovery functions of requirement 2, or the application or service will not fly. The risk of transaction loss is just too high, as is being offline.

If requirement 1 is the baseline you are dealing with, then you (the DBA) and the database owner (and you could be both) need to investigate redundancy options, such as warm server standbys, mirrors, replication, and fail-over clusters. Your options here fall under the industry terms and practices of *high availability*—the proactive arm of service level management.

Transaction loss due to media or data file failure is not usually an issue with requirement 1. The system goes offline, and at the point of failure no further transactions come in. You still have your database, and you still have your transaction logs. Hard-disk crashes are dealt with using RAID-level hardware, as discussed in Chapters 6 and 9, so having the most current database available when services come back up is not an issue. The issue is how quickly the actual system, the server and the hardware, returns to operational state.

If requirement 2 is the baseline you are dealing with, then you need to consider having highly available backups or duplicates of your data and transaction logs. In other words, as soon as a hard disk crashes or a database gets destroyed or a system gets destroyed, you would need to rapidly restore to the last transaction in the transaction log prior to the disaster. You would likely need both warm standbys and redundant hardware in addition to fully up-to-the-last-transaction duplicate copies of your databases and transaction logs. In requirement 2, the transaction log is the focus of your backup and duplication strategy, because only the transaction log and the safe backup or alternate duplication of it—its availability after a crash—can actually completely close the void-time window for highly valuable OLTP-based systems.

Requirement 2 dictates disaster recovery procedures, but it is perfectly clear that the dividing lines between availability and disaster recovery are blurry and endure considerable overlap. To clearly see the two IT disciplines, think of DR as a reactive process, an after-the-crash reactive activity (like restoring from tape), and availability as proactive activity (making sure that, when the system does crash, the application can continue). When you need the services of both requirements 1 and 2, you are really looking at requirement 3, which will dictate what you need to meet both levels—disaster recovery and availability are in full swing.

There are many situations in which a company or a client will not need a fail-over service or a mirrored or redundant server as urgently as some data centers can provide. The database users or customers might be inconvenienced, but if they cannot go elsewhere, there is no need to go into warp drive to get the service back up. In other words, losing the service a few times a year does not constitute bad customer support.

A good example: A few years ago I won a contract from a state department to set up an online database system servicing a call center. Part of the RFP (request for proposal) was an application that allowed parents dependent on child support to phone a voice-activated system to obtain account balances and information about the status of their child support payments from the database. Agents on the back end were updating information as well as servicing callers with special needs on rotary dial phones. The RFP called for a duplicate call center to be established on the other side of the country. In my presentation, I advised that a completely redundant call center and database application would cost almost three times what a single center would, given the cost of the additional standby staff. I advised that it was a complete waste of money. It was not critical that the database never be offline for a day, because no one was losing money, a life, or sleep over not gaining access.

I cited the number of times the existing system was "downed" for service for several hours and sometimes longer than a day, without anyone complaining. In this situation, it is more critical to have up-to-the-last-transaction restorability because callers were actually updating information on every call.

What SQL Server 2005 offers in terms of system availability, as well as scalability, is covered extensively in Chapter 9. We will also look at log shipping as well in the next chapter, along with database mirroring, a new feature in SQL Server 2005. The rest of this chapter is dedicated to all DBAs that have lost their logs; it covers database and transaction recovery.

Transaction Recovery

I have been careful not to interchange disaster recovery with transaction recovery, because the latter deals mainly with SQL Server's capability to automatically recover transactions and restore the state of a database after a system crash. It has nothing to do with restoring data and backed-up, or otherwise duplicated, transaction logs, a subject we will cover in this chapter.

Depending on how your backups are done and the nature of your backup technology, just starting up the disaster recovery process could take anywhere from ten minutes to several hours, spent reading the catalog, finding the right backups, and so on. In cases where backup media are off-site, you would need to take into consideration how long it takes after placing a call to the backup bank for the media to arrive at the data center. This could be anything from 30 minutes to 6 hours. And you may be charged for rush delivery.

Mission-critical disaster recovery, having backup media on-site, thus has to override the risk of data center destruction, fire, and theft. However, data center security has nothing to do with SQL Server 2005, so let's go direct to backup and restore options.

There is no question that you need a good tape backup environment with any server. For starters, you need to back up your system databases and schema catalogs as well, because that's where all system- or server-wide configurations, such as logins and maintenance plans, are stored. You also need to regularly back up your metadata repositories, data warehouses, and so on.

The most common form of backup is to a tape drive, and I will discuss the formats a little later in this chapter. The initial cost of a tape backup solution is really insignificant in relation to the benefit: the ability to back up and recover large amounts of data as quickly as possible. A good tape drive can run anywhere from $500 for good Quarter-Inch Cartridge (QIC) systems to $3,000–$4,000 for the high-speed, high-capacity Digital Linear Tape (DLT) systems.

A robotic library system can cost as much as $30,000 on the low end and six and seven figures on the high end.

Let's now consider two classes of restoration. I came up with this data while managing DR for a score of data centers in the food distribution business. If Burger King were out of fries or Long John Silver out of fish, I would always call to find out if my servers were still up, so I decided to come up with a formula to help me relax while away from the data center. This data also helped get the database owners and me rowing in the same direction.

The following list defines levels of database and transaction log restoration in terms of currency (was this the last transaction written to the log, or close to it?):

- **Zero loss (0)**   Transactions in the transaction log must be the last transactions taken before failure. In other words, you have zero tolerance for transaction loss (see Chapter 2 for information on transaction log management).

- **Ten minutes loss (10)**   Transactions received from real time back to ten minutes can be lost. It is thus acceptable to lose 10 minute's worth of transactions. The client process or order entry person can reenter the transactions.

- **Sixty minutes loss (60)**   Transactions received in the first hour can be lost. It is thus acceptable to lose one hour's worth of transactions.

- **Three hundred and sixty minutes loss (360)**   Transactions received in the last six hours can be lost.

The next list assumes you are at one of the preceding levels, but it defines how quickly you need the databases and transaction logs restored.

- **Zero wait (0)**   Transaction log restoration is required in real time (now). Let's call this the critical restoration level.

- **Ten minutes wait (10)**   Restore is required within ten minutes of losing the databases and transaction logs. Let's call this *emergency restore*. (By the way, loss could mean total loss as well as bad data.)

- **Sixty minutes wait (60)**   Restore is required within one hour of losing the databases and transaction logs. Let's call this *urgent restore*.

- **Three hundred and sixty minutes wait (360)**   Restore is required within six hours of losing the databases and transaction logs. Let's call this *important restore*.

All other restores that can occur later than six hours could be considered *casual restores* and are not factors for this exercise.

If we now look at both scales, we can establish a database and transaction log restoration rating in terms of an acuity index that considers the two scales: the highest level being 0/0 (zero loss for zero wait time to online status) and the lowest level being 360/360 (six hours to get back to online state, and restored data should be at the most six hours old at the time of disaster). It is no accident that the index sounds like a course in optometry. I felt it gave both the DBA and the database owner a "vision" of what was expected to be met on the service level agreement.

You can then present this index to a database owner, with the key of course, and then agree to the terms to meet the agreed-upon backup/restore acuity index. Figure 7-1 shows this in a visual hierarchy.

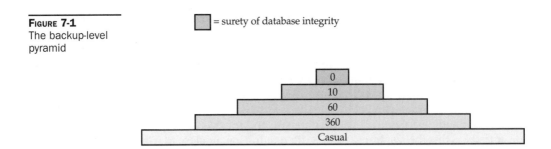

FIGURE 7-1
The backup-level
pyramid

The pyramid in Figure 7-1 illustrates that the faster the response to a transaction log or database restore, the higher the chance of restoring poor data. Each layer of the pyramid covers the critical level of the database or transaction log backup. This does not mean that critical transaction log restores are always going to be a risk, or that the restored transaction logs are flawed. However, it shows that databases or transaction logs backed up closest to the point of failure are more likely to be at risk compared to data that was backed up hours or days before the failure. If a hard disk crashes, the data on the backup tapes is probably sound, but if the crash is due to corrupt data or bad data (which might not cause system failure), the likelihood of bad transaction log data is going to be high closest to the point in time of the crash, and you'll need to consider restoring to a safe point in time (discussed later).

Another factor to consider is that often you'll find that the cleanest backup data is the furthest away from the point of restoration, or it is the most out-of-date. In other words, your soundest database or transaction log backup media may in fact be miles away, one hundred feet underground, in a vault.

In 1999, just prior to Y2K, I was maintaining backups of several SQL Server systems. But I was not required to check database consistency or database health. The database owner kept me out of the system except when I needed to monitor the backups or check on the schedules. One fine day the database went bad, really bad. A bunch of users somehow turned life in the easy lane upside down for the database owner. The DBA responsible for the integrity and consistency of the databases in question had me go back more than seven days to find backups that were healthy. By the time we found clean backups, the loss was running wild. The entire on-site backups for the week were corrupt (that was on a SQL Server 6.5 system, in case you were wondering). I started the restore process, and the DBA left to find a rope. Today's systems are much more resilient against such scenarios as long as you *actually* do the backups.

SQL Server 2005 Recovery Architecture

Before we can use the acuity index I discussed earlier and derive backup plans to meet an agreed-upon index, let's see what SQL Server 2005 is made of.

Past and present transaction log architecture in SQL Server allows the DBMS to recover to the last commit point written to the transaction log just before or at a system crash. As discussed in Chapter 2, the transaction log is a *write-ahead log*, so any committed transaction written to the transaction log (flushed from the main memory buffers of the DBMS) can be recovered upon system recovery and permanently committed to the database. Naturally this recovery process depends on the availability or consistent state of the transaction log after system recovery.

As soon as the system recovers, the DBMS rolls back all transactions that failed due to the collapse of the system, as is determined by built-in mechanisms that ensure the atomicity of the transactions. Client processes will thus be allowed to represent the transaction (I discuss how in later chapters that discuss distributed transactions, transactions in message queues, and so on). Transactions that survived the crash are committed to the database.

SQL Server 2005 introduces advanced recovery architecture to this DBMS platform in the form of recovery models. The recovery model centers on the transaction log as the object or mechanism of recovery, as mentioned earlier, that can restore to the last commit point written to the transaction log. The recovery model is really a transaction- and operation-logging mode (I am not sure why Microsoft calls it a model) that determines how much and what data is written to the transaction log and how it is used in recovery. The recovery model also determines how successful the transaction log will be in recovering the transactions between actual full and differential database file backups up to and including the last transaction written to the log.

There are three such recovery models in SQL Server 2005: *full, bulk-logged,* and *simple.* Table 7-1 discusses the attributes and benefits of each model.

Recovery models are set for a database as soon as the system is installed or a new database is created. The recovery model set for the *model* database is *full.* This does not mean that every time you create a database it will inherit the *full* setting installed for *model*

Recovery Model	Attributes	Benefits	Transaction Loss	Recovery
Full	Logs all transactions. Optimized for high-end OLTP systems.	Can recover to any point in time after database backup.	None, if the transaction log file is available.	To any point in time up to the last written transaction in the write-ahead log.
Bulk-logged	Optimized for bulk operations (BCP, BULK INSERT, and so on). Minimal log space is used.	Permits high-performance bulk operations with a recovery safety net.	None, if log is consistent and recovered or bulk copy is not the cause of the damage.	To the end of the last database and transaction log backup.
Simple	Optimized for low-end OLTP and database operations, and high-performance bulk operations.	Keeps log footprint small in bulk copy or insert operations because log is not normally backed up.	None, if log file installs consistent data to the database.	To the end of the last database backup.

TABLE 7-1 SQL Server 2005 Recovery Models

(see Chapter 2). New databases created in Management Studio are usually set for simple recovery. Changing the recovery model is done through the ALTER DATABASE statement using T-SQL as follows:

```
ALTER DATABASE <databasename>
SET RECOVERY [FULL | BULK_LOGGED | SIMPLE]
```

Do not use the angle brackets. For example:

```
ALTER DATABASE Modelize
SET RECOVERY FULL
```

To determine the recovery model set for your database, you can query the setting in the DATABASEPROPERTYEX property of the database as follows:

```
SELECT databasepropertyex('<databasename>', 'recovery')
```

You can also change the recovery model on the Options tab of your database's Properties dialog box. But don't go looking for radio buttons marked "recovery model" on the Options tab; you will not find them. To change the recovery option on the Options tab in your Database Properties dialog box (setting database options is fully discussed in Chapter 6), you need to select the recovery model from the Recovery model drop-down list, which is found on the Database Properties, Options tab in Figure 7-2. Other options, such as Log truncation, is set in the Backup Database options dialog box.

Understanding the Recovery Models

Let's now examine the so-called recovery models a little closer.

The *full recovery model* provides the greatest recoverability possibility for line-of-business OLTP operations. It is thus ideally suited to meet our 0/0 acuity index as discussed earlier. In other words, we get the fastest and safest or most complete restore and recoverability of data if the database operates under full recovery. The *full recovery model* also provides you with the greatest flexibility in terms of recovering a database to any point in time after the last full or differential backup.

The *bulk-logged recover model* was engineered for recovery under bulk-copy or BULK INSERT operations. The transaction log writing algorithms have been optimized for speed and log space reduction for operations such as CREATE INDEX and BULK COPY.

The *simple recovery model* is the easiest way to back up SQL Server databases because no transaction log backups are done and the transaction log is maintained in such a manner as to ensure the simplest recovery from server failure. After log truncation, log space is no longer needed for system recovery (after the transactions have been committed to the database) and the log space is reused.

Obviously you have a higher risk of data loss if a database is damaged or lost during normal business operations. However, most LOB applications do not need the more critical recovery models because backups are usually done during the night in any event. Also, a high-level backup/restore acuity index will not apply to "simple" data entry because the business will determine that to manually recover and reenter data costs far less than the technology to close the void-time backup window.

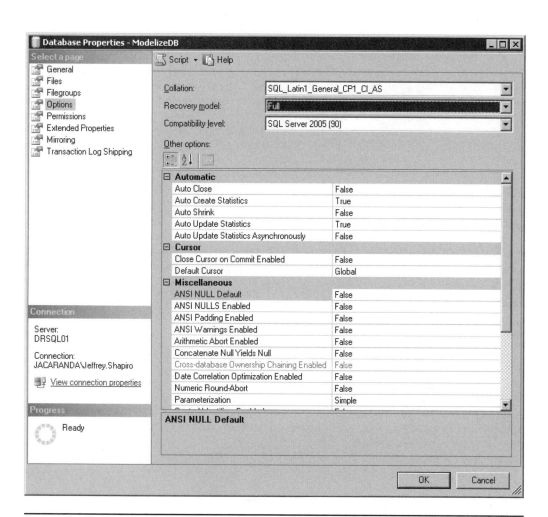

FIGURE 7-2   The Database Properties dialog box

SQL Server 2005 Backup and Restore Architecture

SQL Server 2005 contains a fully integrated backup/restore API that can be driven programmatically from T-SQL. Microsoft has also provided a built-in interactive user interface to the API in Management Studio that can get you up and backing up as soon as you start doing business or finish configuring (actually you never finish configuring, but you know what I mean).

The backup utility is fully functional and flexible enough to configure mission-critical backup/restore requirements or to meet the demands of an SLA demanding a 0/0 backup/restore acuity index. With the functionality you have now, you can plan an adequate and cost-effective backup/restore plan to deal with the possible disasters earlier discussed.

Using the internal backup facilities of SQL Server 2005 for backups is far better and cheaper than using an external, third-party backup solution. Even the smart new Backup program that ships with Windows Server 2003 will not be able to do the job. The reason is simple: the open files dilemma. When a database and its log files are in use, no external application will be able to back up the files, because they are essentially in use by the DBMS.

The only time you would be able to make an external backup of the database is when everybody is out of the database and the DBMS is shut down (all services have been stopped). There are third-party products that are able to back up open database files, but they are expensive and not as integrated as SQL Server's internal backup utilities. Products like NetBackup can back up online databases. They work well for one or a few servers, but they become very expensive and clunky when dealing with many servers and hundreds of databases. In short, SQL Server Backup provides as advanced an active backup solution as you'll need, possibly the most advanced in the DBMS industry.

SQL Server's backup allows you to back up databases while they are in use. Granted, you will see a drop in system performance, which you might choose to improve with more hardware, and faster tape drives, and some other techniques I will later discuss. Naturally, SQL Server will prevent any backups from going ahead while database alterations are taking place. Such activities include the following:

- Automatic or manual database size changing

- Object creation or deletion

- Index creation or deletion

- While performing nonlogged operations

If you start a backup and one of the preceding processes takes place, the process bows out with an error. If the process starts before the backup or restore, the backup or restore process bows out with an error.

That you can back up a database while it is in use means you have a lot more flexibility in your backup schedules and a lot more possibilities of performing backups on a continuous basis as opposed to off-peak times, or some ungodly hour in the middle of the night.

Types of Database Backups for SQL Server 2005

You have several backup options to consider with SQL Server 2005, depending on your DR plan and the baselines you have set for the data center. The following list categorizes these options:

- **Full database backup**   This operation just backs up the database files, which would include all the committed transactions. Before the data gets transferred to the tape, SQL Server makes sure data in the transaction log is committed to the database.

- **Transaction log backup**   This operation just backs up the transaction logs. However, the transaction log backup should be part of all database backup operations for full recovery.

- **Differential database backup**   This operation just backs up the portions of the database files that have changed since the last full backup, or since the last differential backup.

- **File/filegroup backups** This operation allows you to make the target of your backup a filegroup, rather than a database or a transaction log.
- **Snapshot backups** This operation allows you to take snapshot backups, which are very high-speed backups.

Table 7-2 lists the backup types in relation to the model options.

Full Database Backups

A full database backup backs up the entire database. The DBMS makes copies of all database objects, users, roles, tables, and so on. You can perform a full database backup using Management Studio, or you can program the backup facilities in the DBMS directory using T-SQL.

When the backup events fire, the DBMS flushes the data pages in memory to disk and then starts copying the data to the backup device assigned to the job. Any transactions that take place in the system after the backup starts are not backed up as part of the database backup. To back up the "late" transactions, you next need to back up the transaction logs. The latter "FYI" is important to remember, or you'll end up with missing data in your backups.

Transaction Log Backups

The only way you can restore to the last transaction before disaster is by backing up the transaction log, and the transactions in the log might not include any transactions that come in while the log is being backed up. In many respects, you can think of the transaction log as the incremental backup of the database, because in order to restore the entire worth of data (all transactions installed to the database and all transactions still in the transaction log that have not yet been installed to the database), you would first have to restore the full database and then restore the transaction log. Transaction logs are thus only useful with full and so-called bulk-logged data.

In large systems that have a huge amount of transactions underway, the transaction log at times may take longer to back up than the database. In very large systems, the transaction log has a tendency to grow to huge proportions, so you will need to balance your transaction log management requirements with your backup requirements, lest what you do for one countermands what you do for the other.

Model	Full Database	Database Differential	Log	File Differential	Snapshot
Simple	Required	Optional	Not allowed	Not allowed	N/A
Full	Required or file backups	Optional	Required	Optional	N/A
Bulk-Logged	Required or file backups	Optional	Required	Optional	N/A

TABLE 7-2   The backup types offered by SQL Server's online backup architecture

Transaction log backups are a must in the following situations:

- You cannot afford to lose any data between the last database backup and the point of failure.

- You want to return the database to a specific point in time, say ten minutes before meltdown. It is also possible to restore to a database state a day ago or even a week ago by restoring a database from an earlier backup set (see the section "Backing Up SQL Server" later in this chapter) and then restoring the transaction log recorded soon after that time.

- If the databases are constantly changing, your database backups will become outdated very quickly. Some applications work with a database of a relatively constant size but in which the data changes frequently. A good example is an air traffic information system where for any given day the number of flights for the day remains constant but the arrival and departure information is constantly changing.

- Backing up the transaction log forces some cleanup in the process because the operation truncates the inactive portion of the transaction log for you as part of the backup process.

Transaction Log Backups in Practice

First, the transaction log backup can only work when it is part of a full or bulk-logged recovery model (see the section "SQL Server 2005 Recovery Architecture" earlier in this chapter). Second, backing up a transaction log will only serve a purpose if it is part of an unbroken sequence of transaction log backups, which are made after every full or differential backup. If you lose a transaction log backup, if you miss it, or if your backup media get destroyed, you will have to start the backup set from scratch and start backing up the transaction logs all over again.

Truncation and the Transaction Log Backups

As discussed in Chapter 2, the DBMS truncates inactive portions of the transaction log. The inactive portion of the log is already committed to the database; therefore the "dead" portions of the log are no longer needed.

Truncation is something you define in your management of the DBMS and the database, and it is something you can do manually. However, the DBMS performs truncation automatically after a transaction log has been fully backed up, so any manual truncation would cause problems with the automatic truncation that occurs after backup.

NOTE *Understanding truncation log checkpoints is key to managing a backup/restore plan. Accordingly, please see Chapter 2 on transaction log architecture.*

When Not to Back Up Transaction Logs

The following rules apply to the backup of transaction logs:

- You should not back up a transaction log until a full or differential backup has successfully completed.

- If you have manually truncated the log just after performing the backup, you will have to back up the database again and then back up the transaction log.

Differential Database Backups

The SQL Server differential database backup only backs up the portions of a database file that have changed since the last database backup. It is important to understand that the meaning of the term "differential" is that the first differential backup has to compare the full backup to the database file, while subsequent differential backups are based on what has changed from the last differential backup.

You should also know that the differential backup is not a substitute for the transaction log backup. If you lost a system seconds after performing a differential backup, you will still have lost all transactions in the log that were not written to the database file on disk. Again, no matter how powerful your system, the latency between receiving the transaction and flushing it out to the transaction log on disk cannot be resolved by any backup technology (see "Establishing Baselines for Disaster Recovery" earlier in this chapter).

Differential backups should be used for backing up data in the middle of regular transaction processing time (and the full backup should take place off peak with longer intervals). On big systems receiving huge amounts of new data and data changes every day, a differential backup may seem like a full backup. In some situations a full backup might be very difficult to do on a huge database, even in the middle of the night.

Use the differential under the following circumstances:

- A small percentage of the full database changes every day.
- You need to perform more regular backups of your databases, possibly during regular hours with users logged in.

You might find that the transaction log backup is more suited to your needs for regular backups, especially during heavy or peak periods of online activity.

File/Filegroup Backups

A file or filegroup backup works just like a database backup, but your target object to be backed up is not the database, per se, but a file or collection of files that could reside anywhere on your network. (See "Filegroups" in Chapter 2.)

In this respect, backing up filegroups is similar to performing a SQL Server 2005 backup using an external backup program that has built-in open files capability. Such backup programs, such as NetBackup, also manage the backups of the transaction logs needed for the backups.

Why perform a filegroup backup? Depending on the technology used, there's one very good reason. File or filegroup backups and restores may be quicker to perform than regular backups. A very busy database, processing millions of transactions a day, may take forever to back up a database. This is not an uncommon problem in a busy data center, and database backups have often run into the next day, interfering with regular operations. If you have three filegroups, it might be quicker to back up a separate filegroup each day. In other words, you would have to back up each filegroup every third day. You would still have to back up your transaction logs on a daily basis in order to make a full restore to the point-in-time failure.

File or filegroup restores on a piecemeal basis are also possible. For example, if you lose a drive holding a filegroup, one of many drives holding your spread of database files, you can just restore the files or filegroups that went with the disk. Backing up and restoring files and filegroups is, however, tricky. You should practice on development databases or filegroups or do pilot filegroup backups on dummy databases. You must also be fully conversant with filegroup management because it can be easy to blunder both the filegroup management and the backups (see Chapter 2 for more information on filegroups).

Snapshot Backups

The idea of a snapshot backup is a simple one. Think: "smile, say cheese, and snap" and you've got the idea. But in order to take a "photographic" image of a database, the DBMS must allow a process to come in and take the snapshot. Essentially what the snapshot means is that the entire image of the database and the log files is (almost) instantly duplicated and then placed onto tape or another disk.

SQL Server 2005 supports snapshot backup and restore, but the snapshot hardware and software are usually provided by independent hardware and software vendors, such as NetBackup. SQL Server provides the necessary hooks in its backup/restore API, and it includes a virtual backup device, to allow a third party to come in and snap away, while it is fully operational.

The snapshot backups drastically reduce and practically eliminate the need for server resources to accomplish high-speed active backups. And as discussed earlier, this is very important for very large databases where availability is critical. The primary benefits of the snapshot backup are as follows:

- The snapshot backup can be created in seconds, with little or no impact on the server (depending on the hardware and software used).

- The snapshot can be restored just as fast, with little or no impact to the server (depending on the hardware and software used).

- You can back up to tape from another server without having to impact the production system.

- You can use the snapshot to very quickly create a copy of the production database for reporting, testing, or data transformation.

The snapshot backups function and provide the same features as the other type of backups discussed. And the transaction logs can be used with them just as they are with the standard full backup. Backup, restore, tracking, and cataloging takes place as if the backup were a standard backup.

Why then would you not use the snapshot backup and restore functionality all the time? The reason would be cost. The backup devices and software can be very expensive. But for very large databases or in mission-critical situations, the costs are discounted against the need to have 0/0 service level acuity, as discussed earlier.

Backup Devices

Three types of backup devices are defined by SQL Server 2005: disks, named pipes, and tape.

Disk Devices

The disk device is not a backup device in the same sense that a tape drive is. It is really a location, a file, on a hard disk or storage area network to place a backup file, which is the same object that gets stored on a tape cartridge. I am not sure why Microsoft called the backup file a disk device, but it is an unfortunate choice of nouns. (Windows Server 2003 Backup calls it a file. A file is a file in my book, so just don't go looking for any disk devices when you really need to be supplying the name of a file.)

You can back up to a file on any remote hard disk or other device (such as optical storage) on the network. All you have to do in the backup script or in Management Studio is define a UNC path to the drive of your choice. Naturally, SQL Server will need permission to access the destination through share points and the appropriate permissions.

Why would you want to back up to a remote disk, and plop a huge backup file on it? For starters, you might want to back up that file to an external backup library (discussed next) because SQL Server backup only works on locally addressed devices (they have to be physically attached to the server). Naturally you need your brain scanned if you back up to the same disk on which your database filegroup resides. If you lose the disk, you're history.

Tape Devices

Tape devices are the safest and fastest means of backing up SQL Server databases; however, there are few limitations.

The tape device you are using must be physically connected to the database server. This is a limitation that I think drives a number of DBAs back out to third-party vendors for their backup solutions because data centers typically prefer a centralized backup solution, using a robotic tape library. And if you scale out to multiple servers, every server will have to have a tape device. If you are using high-end devices like DSS or DLT, you could easily throw a few thousand dollars or more at each server. In such a scenario, if you still want to use SQL Server Backup, you will have to back up to the file "device" and then sweep that file up into an external tape drive. The only limitation I see with such a solution is that to restore the database, you first have to restore the file to the location you originally backed it up to (which will cost some time).

The backup functionality does not integrate with Windows Server 2003 Removable Storage, so you cannot program in operator alerts and other helpful bells and whistles like media management.

Later in the chapter, I will discuss backup bandwidth and suitable backup tape formats supported on Windows 2000 Server or Windows Server 2003.

Device Names

A backup device name is the "handle" SQL Server assigns to a logical or physical backup device. The device can either be a file on the disk, an actual tape drive, or some means of storing data. The device name is an alias or nickname that you can use to reference in your backup scripts. For example, the code

```
BACKUP DATABASE Customers TO DISK = 'C:\Backups\Modelize\FullBackup.Bak'
```

backs up the Customers database to the FullBackup file device, named Path\ FullBackup.

Backing Up SQL Server

There are several approaches to backing up SQL Server. First, you can use the Backup options in Management Studio. This is SQL Server's interactive option that can get you started doing database backups from ground zero. Second, there is the noninteractive attack on the DBMS API using T-SQL. Third, you can use the SQL-SMO object model, which publishes a backup object and a restore object that access the same API as with the T-SQL approach (see Chapter 11). Fourth, you can go with a third-party vendor, but this book is not the forum to discuss this option. If you're a whiz at T-SQL, then you may find the programmatic approach to be extremely powerful, and if you want to build your own backup application or user interface in Visual Basic (the .NET version) C++ or C#, then go the object model. But let's first deal with Backup in Management Studio because that is the easiest approach and the one most non-DBA database owners and many DBAs will use (and it is adequate in most circumstances).

Using Management Studio to Back Up SQL Server

The steps to take to create local simple backups of SQL Server databases or transaction logs are as follows (you can take a backup of a SQL Server database [ad hoc] at any time without a schedule):

1. Create a backup job. The backup job is managed by SQL Server Agent, which is discussed in Chapter 4.

2. Create a schedule to run the job. Both 1 and 2 here can be rolled into a SSIS package that gets activated as part of a maintenance plan (see Chapter 4).

Create the Backup Job

To create the backup, drill down to the database node under Databases on the DBMS instance to which your target databases are attached, right-click the node, select Tasks and then choose Back Up. The dialog box in Figure 7-3 loads. See the section "SQL Server Backup Bandwidth" later in this chapter to determine the resources needed to write the backup files out to a network disk.)

NOTE *Remember that you cannot use SQL Server Backup with a tape drive unit attached to a remote machine. You also need to leave at least 10MB free for the backup image (over and above your other needs, of course) on the hard disk where the SQL Server binaries are installed. If the DBMS cannot find free space, the backup will fail.*

Creating the backup job requires several steps. You need to determine if your backup job is going to be a full backup or a differential backup, whether to append to the media or overwrite existing media, and whether to run the job once only or schedule it to repeat at regular intervals.

If you are going to work to a full-differential rotation scheme, described later in this chapter, you'll need to create two jobs, one to run the full backup once a week, and one job to run the differential backups every day. Depending on your needs, you may have to create a third job to run transaction log and file or filegroup backups as well. You might find yourself very busy here, but the sooner you get cracking, the better.

On the General page, you need to set the following:

- **Database**   Choose your database in the drop-down list (this option is under the Source group).

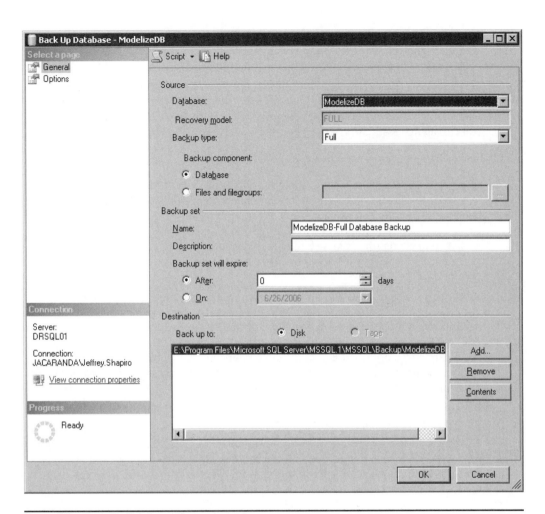

FIGURE 7-3   Back Up Database (General page)

- **Backup type**   Choose the type of backup you need to do—complete (full), differential, transaction log, or file or filegroup from the drop-down list. If the transaction log option is disabled, the database is probably in simple recovery mode (model), which does produce transaction log backups. The same limitation of simple recovery applies to file or filegroup backups. To obtain all four backup options, you need to set the recovery model on the target database to full (see "SQL Server 2005 Recovery Architecture" earlier in this chapter).

- **Name**   Provide a name for the backup; use anything you like or go with the default if that is convenient. This information gets written into the header section of the backup data. It will make it easier to find your backups in a disk or tape device when you need to restore.

- **Description** Provide a description of the backup job. This information is also written to the header of the backup data and is used to identify or manage your backups. It is not essential but makes backup life much easier.

- **Destination** Check the radio button that applies to the destination device for your backup. You have two choices: Tape or Disk (file). To add devices to the Backup To list, click the Add button (or click Remove to drop devices). If you click Add, the Select Backup Destination dialog box shown in Figure 7-4 loads.

On the Options page you need to set the following options:

- **Overwrite media** Check the radio option to either append to the media or overwrite the media. Overwriting the media obviously destroys all previous backups in the file. You can append a backup job to the media, which will let you choose previous backup days and times, but the disadvantage is that the media file will keep growing until the disk fills up. If you are backing up the directory to tape, you should overwrite the backup media because you can go back to previous days on tape.

- **Reliability** Depending on your needs, you might be better off using the appropriate DBCC command described in Appendix than the specified "Verify backup when finished" option. Verification can be somewhat resource intensive and will lengthen the time it takes to complete your backups. The same goes for the checksum check option; it is also resource intensive. You should enable reliability options to run in the middle of the night when the database is not needed or during times of low use.

- **Backup to a new media set** Check this option to specify a media set to be used or overwritten by Backup (See Figure 7-5).

- **New media set description** Check the Initialize and label media option to enable the fields "Media set name" and "Media set description" (see the section "SQL Server Backup by Design" later in this chapter, which discusses SQL Server 2005 media sets and families).

FIGURE 7-4
Select Backup
Destination

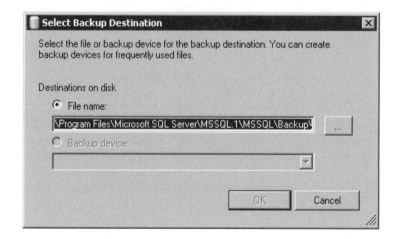

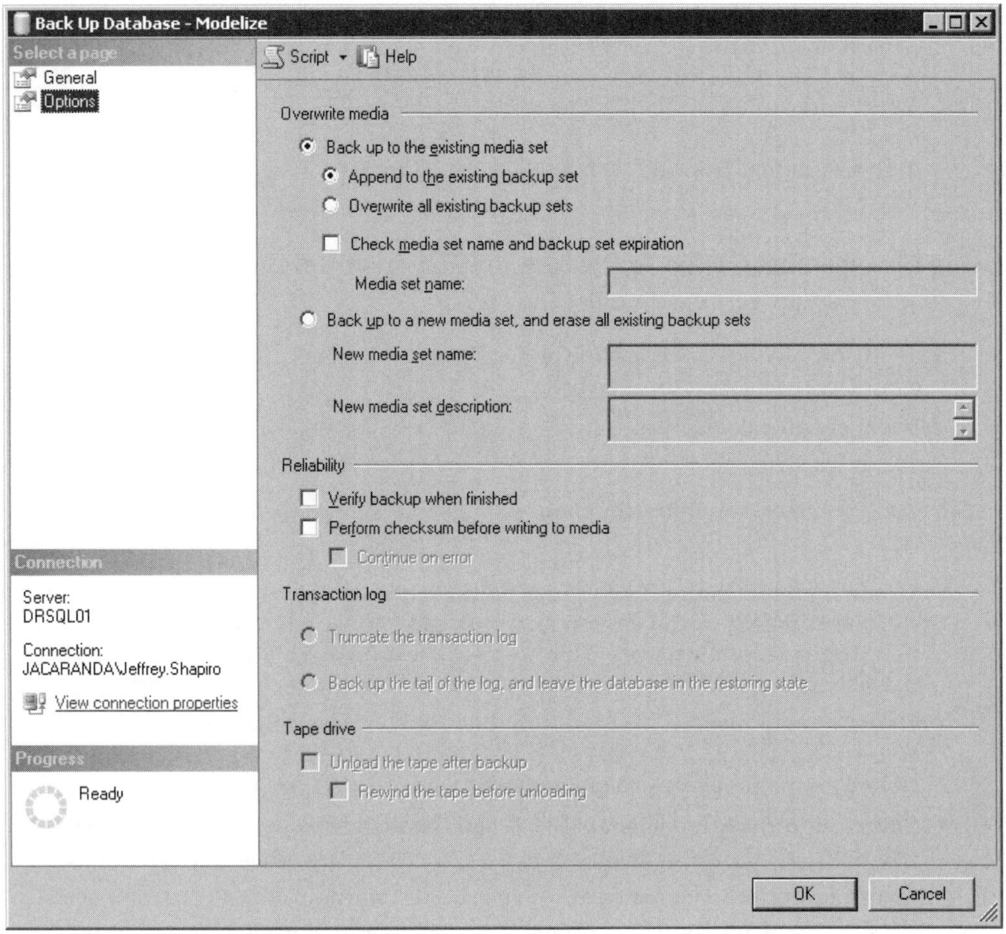

FIGURE 7-5   Back Up Database (Options page)

- **Tape drive**   Here you can specify the option that causes the tape to eject after the backup operation. This helps ensure that another process does not come around and overwrite the backup you just completed. You can also choose to rewind the tape. The option is disabled for obvious reasons if you are backing up to disk. (The "Transaction log" option is grayed out until a Transaction Log backup is performed.

At this point, if you click OK you will be scheduling the job to run immediately or without a schedule. You can go back to the General tab and select the Schedule option or continue with the default.

Backing Up the Transaction Log

On the General and Options pages, respectively, you need to set the following:

- **Backup**   Choose transaction log backup from the drop-down list (for Full recovery models).

- **Transaction log, Truncate**   Choose either to truncate the log or to back up the tail of the log.

Using Management Studio to Restore a SQL Server Database

To restore the backup, perform the following steps:

1. Drill down to the database node under Databases on the DBMS instance to which your target databases are attached.

2. Right-click the database, select Tasks, and choose Restore, Database, Files and Filegroups, or Transaction Log. The dialog box in Figure 7-6 loads.

To restore a database or transaction log, you need to perform the following on the General tab:

- **Destination for restore, To database**   Choose the database to restore in the drop-down list. The list can be written to, so you can provide a new name, essentially a new database, for the restore. This is a useful feature that allows you to restore a database to a new DBMS where it did not exist before.

- **Destination for restore, To a point in time**   If you choose this option, you will be able to select a time in the past to which to restore to. This is useful if you need to restore to a point where you know the database is a desired state.

- **Source for restore, From database**   If you choose this radio option, backup sets will show you the list of databases to restore from with a lot of useful information.

- **Source for restore, From device**   If you choose this radio option, then you need to select a backup file from the location on the hard disk, or from a tape drive, after which you will be able to see the list of databases to restore from with a lot of useful information.

To set additional restore options, click the Options item on the Restore database dialog box. The Options tab is illustrated in Figure 7-7.

Parameters on the Options tab are as follows:

- **Overwrite the existing database**   This option forces the restore to automatically overwrite the existing database.

- **Preserve the replication settings**   This option lets you preserve the replication settings that have been installed on the database.

- **Prompt before restoring each backup**   This option forces the restore operation to prompt you after each backup completes. You would use this option if all the restores were coming from one device or one cartridge and you wanted to cancel after the first full and the third differential restore. By having the prompt continue to pop up after each restore, you will be able to cancel before the fourth differential.

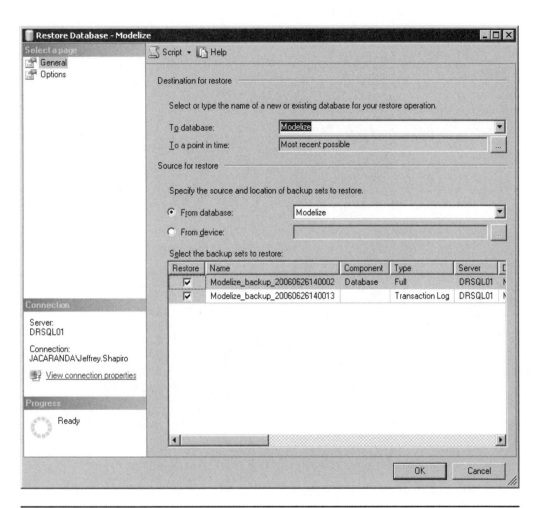

FIGURE 7-6   Database Restore

- **Restrict access to the restored database**   This option lets you restore the database but deny connections to it until a later time.

- **Restore the database files as**   The grid on the Options tab is related to this option, which lets you change the name and path of the restore target. You need to select the files in the left column (logical filename) and provide a new name and path in the right column (move to physical filename).

- **Recovery state, Leave database ready to use**   This option completes the entire restore process and processes the transaction log as part of the restore feature. This restore will require you to restore all your databases and applicable transaction logs as part of one process. After the restore is complete, the database and transaction log state is considered final and ready for use, and no additional transaction logs can be restored.

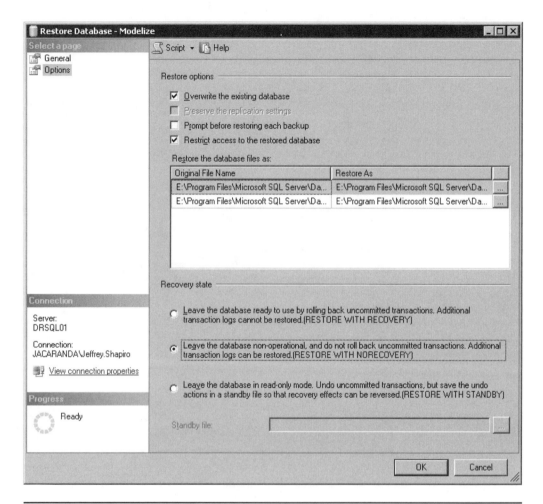

FIGURE 7-7   Restore Database Options

- **Recovery completion state, Leave database non-operational**   This option is the opposite of the preceding one. After the restore, the database is nonoperational and you can still restore additional transaction logs.

- **Recovery completion state, Leave database read-only mode**   This option allows you to restore the database, permit it to be operational but only for read-only access, and still be in a position to restore additional transaction logs. These options are important for log-shipping functionality and maintaining standby servers as discussed in Chapter 9.

NOTE   *A new feature of SQL Server 2005 lets the database become available as soon as a filegroup in a collection is restored. SQL Server will continue to allow access while restoring the remaining filegroups. If a filegroup needs to be accessed by a query, an error is returned noting that the database is offline.*

After you have provided all necessary parameters and you decided on the option, click OK to begin the restore. You will be notified by the DBMS whether the restore completed successfully or failed.

Using T-SQL Backup Scripts

The T-SQL BACKUP DATABASE and RESTORE DATABASE commands are very powerful and provide all the facilities you need to program extensive scripts that can completely replace the Backup/Restore facility provided by Management Studio, as just discussed. The syntax for the two commands is extensive, and you should reference them in SQL Server Books Online. The following code provides an example of a simple backup script and an example of a simple restore script:

```
-- Create a backup device for customers.
USE master
EXEC sp_addumpdevice 'disk', 'CustomersD',
   'c:\Program Files\Microsoft SQL Server\MSSQL\BACKUP\Customers.dat'
--Create a log backup device.
USE master
EXEC sp_addumpdevice 'disk', 'Customers_logD',
   'c:\Program Files\Microsoft SQL Server\MSSQL\BACKUP\Customers_log.dat'
-- Back up the full Customers database.
BACKUP DATABASE Customers TO CustomersD
-- Back up the Customers log.
BACKUP LOG Customers_log
   TO Customers_logD

RESTORE DATABASE Customers
   FROM CustomersD
   WITH NORECOVERY
```

It is well worth your while to become proficient in T-SQL backup scripts because once you are expert, backup and restore scripts can be easier to manage than the same process in Management Studio. The scripts can also be executed automatically by SQL Agent. In many facilities or data centers, you will be required to have T-SQL capability to code backup/restore scripts. The next section, which examines point-in-time restore, includes more advanced restore scripts as well.

Restoring a Database to a Point in Time

It is possible to restore your database to a certain point in time in the transaction log or to a named mark in the transaction log. Let's say a careless programmer does a database update and updates 10,000 rows of data instead of ten (trust me, it happens). You then need to restore the database to a point in time just before your lazy hacker hit the ENTER key and all Hades exploded.

To accomplish this task, you need to recover the database to the exact point in the transaction log before disaster struck. To do this, you need to examine the transaction log header information of each transaction log backup or the information in the *backupset* table stored in *msdb*. From these sources, you can easily and quickly find the backup set that contains the time to which you recover your database. All you then need to do is apply transaction log backups up to that point.

Before you start, remember that you cannot skip any transaction logs, because this would destroy the integrity of the data in the database. You also have to consider that there might be transactions that came in after the disaster. Sometimes the errors are discovered only after a huge number of good new transactions were committed to the database. Also, the transactions that you want to undo might compromise what appear to be good transactions that were accomplished on bad data. For example, computations, aggregations, row identification, defaults, and the like may no longer be viable after you remove or alter a huge bunch of records, and you will thus have to redo them. The process is as follows:

- First restore the last database backup but do not recover the database (this is the RESTORE WITH NO-RECOVERY in T-SQL code or the Leave database non-operational option in Management Studio).

- Next restore each transaction log backup in the same sequence in which they were created, recovering each database after each transaction log restore.

- Finally recover the database to the desired point in time within the final transaction log backup.

Point-in-Time Restore Using a T-SQL Script

To restore to a point in time using a T-SQL script, your script needs to code the following:

1. Execute a RESTORE DATABASE statement using the NORECOVERY option.

2. Execute a RESTORE LOG statement to restore each transaction log backup. The restore needs to specify the following:

   - The name of the database against which the transaction log will be applied.

   - The backup device holding the transaction log backup.

   - The RECOVERY and STOPAT information. This information is required in the point-in-time script; if it is missing or wrong, the restore will fail.

The following is an example of a point-in-time restore script of a database to its state as of 11:19 A.M. on October, 2005; it demonstrates the restore operation involving multiple logs and multiple backup devices:

```
RESTORE DATABASE Customers
    FROM CustomersD
    WITH NORECOVERY
GO
RESTORE LOG Customers_Log
    FROM Customers_LogD
    WITH RECOVERY, STOPAT = 'Oct 9, 2005 11:19 AM'
GO
```

SQL Server Backup Bandwidth

Bandwidth is an important consideration when backing up huge databases and extensive filegroups. For starters, forget about doing any significant backup over a WAN or Internet connection unless you have upward of a 1.5-megabit pipe to the source; but this will still not work for critical high-end OLTP systems. Anything less, unless it is a very small filegroup, will not provide a suitable facility for backing up a SQL Server database.

I routinely back up over a 10Mbit Ethernet network. Most data centers have a 100Mbit backbone, and putting your servers directly on that is key. But even a 100Mbit backbone is only as valuable as the speed of the server bus, network links, and hard disk I/O, along with the capabilities of the backup devices and so on.

The minimum rate of backup you could expect over a 10Mbit network is between 15MB and 45MB per minute, depending on the backup device. Local tape drives on fast computers using SCSI technology and high-end hardware can even achieve levels of around 200MB per minute, and even higher rates on RAID systems and extremely high-speed disk arrays.

What you then need to do is work out how large a database file or transaction log you are going to back up and then figure out how long it is going to take you to back up the data. If the data is mission-critical, you may want to back it up more often. Remember, data changes every minute of the day. Database applications can see as much as 20 percent of the data changing on the low end and as much as 80 percent changing on the high end.

I have provided a very simple formula for you to work out how long it will take to back up your databases and log files. Let's say we want to back up X amount to a certain device in Y time. Starting with the desired unknown Y, you would want to first figure out how much data you are going to try to back up on the local machine or over the network device. After you have calculated this, your equation will resemble:

```
Y = S / T
```

where Y = time, S = amount of data in megabytes, and T = transfer time of hardware (locally or over the network). The data transfer or backup rate of the LTO 3 is 576GB/hr, so multiply by 1,000 to get the rate per GB. The older DLT technology transfers at upward of 300MB per minute (hauling data off the local hard drives). Thus, your equation would be

```
Y = 2005 / 300
```

and two gigs would thus take just over six minutes to back up. Factor in another minute or more per 100MB for latency, cataloging, files in use, database updating, and so forth, and it would be safe to say that two gigs of data get backed up in less than ten minutes. Over the local area network, divide the transfer rate by a factor of ten, and the same two gigs takes over an hour to back up. Using LTO on the local network, you get transfer rate improvement by an order of magnitude.

SQL Server Backup by Design

I included this section to help you understand management schemes and regimens that need to be built to support service level requirements . . . starting with some basic backup/restore concepts.

Practicing Scratch and Save

SQL Server 2005 does not support the concept of *scratch and save* sets directly, but it provides the facility, and you can code this logic into your T-SQL scripts. This is something you have to design manually. Remember that it is not really up to SQL Server to enforce how you manage your backup strategy. The DBMS only gives you the tools to perform a backup and to restore data, and to manage your media according to a scheme you devise. It is worth mentioning what a *scratch and save set* is because you should understand the terms for more advanced, sophisticated database backup procedures.

A *save* set is a set of media in the media pool that cannot be overwritten for a certain period of time, and a *scratch* set is a set of media that is safe to overwrite. A backup set should be stored and cataloged in a save set for any period of time during which the media do not get used for backup. You can create your own database in SQL Server that provides rotation information into and out of scratch and save sets.

The idea behind the scratch and save approach is to protect data from being overwritten for predetermined periods, according to your backup plan. For example, a monthly save set is saved for a month, while a yearly set is saved for a year. Later when the "safe" period of time has expired, you can move the save set to the scratch set and target it for overwriting.

Once a set is moved out of the save status into the scratch status, you are tacitly allowing the data on it to be overwritten, essentially destroying it. A save set becomes a scratch set when you are sure, through proper media pool management, that other media in the pool contain both full and modified current and past files of your data, and it is safe to destroy the data on the scratch media.

Save and scratch sets enable you to ensure that your media can be safely recycled. If you do not manage your media according to a scratch and save routine or schedule, you make every set a save set, which means you never recycle the tapes. Recycling will risk tapes, because if they will be constantly used they will stretch and wear out a lot sooner.

Rotation Schemes

A *rotation scheme* is a plan or system you use to rotate the media in your backup sets. At the simplest level, a rotation scheme is a daily or weekly backup using one cartridge. This is not much of a DR scheme, because you would be writing over the media every day. So in order to determine the best rotation scheme, you need to consider what you are doing with the backups: Are you just archiving, doing version control, backing up a state, or managing a disaster recovery regimen?

From this description, you can deduce that the three main reasons for backups are archives, version control, and recovery. Data in an archival state, or required for analysis, need not be located on-site and is kept for record-keeping, reporting, and decision support; data in a version control period is stored off- and on-site for access to full weekly generations of the data, and to be used to restore the databases to certain points in time. Data in the recovery period is stored both on- and off-site and is either online or very near to the server.

Understanding Rotation Schemes

Let us now expand our rotation scheme. The first option would be to rotate the media every other day, so that you could be backing up to one tape while the alternate is in safekeeping somewhere. If the worst were to happen, a tape gets eaten by the device or something less common, you would still have a backup from the previous day. If the machine were stolen, you would be able to restore it. But rotating every other day is only useful in terms of total data loss. So you have a full backup of all your databases, every day. What about wear and tear?

A tape or a platter is a delicate device. Inserting and removing it every other day and writing to it over and over can put your data at risk. Tapes do stretch, and they get stuck in tape drives. Tapes should be saved according to the scratch and save discussion earlier in this chapter.

And then what about version control? Rotating with multiple media, say a week's worth, would ensure that you could roll back to previous states of a database or to points in time. We could refer to such a concept of versioning as a "generation system" of rotation (not sufficient for critical restore, however). In fact, one such standard generation scheme is widely used by the most seasoned of backup administrators to achieve both the ideals described—versioning and protecting media from wear and tear and loss. It is known as the GFS system, or Grandfather, Father, Son system.

Let's create a GFS scheme to run under SQL Server 2005 Backup. Most high-end backup software can create and manage a rotation scheme for you, but for now you will need a legal pad. So now let's put a label on one of our tapes or disks and call it Full, or First Backup, or Normal # 1—whatever designates a complete backup of the system and collection of files and folders.

The first backup of any system is always a full backup, and the reason is simple. Backup, and you, need a catalog or history of all the files in the backup list so that you can access every file for a restore and so that Backup can perform differential analysis on the media. Do your backups according to the procedures we discussed earlier. You should have had enough practice by now. And you are ready to go from a development or trial backup to a production rotation scheme.

As soon as you have made a full backup set, label the members as discussed and then perform a second full backup (or copy the first). On the first backup set, add the following information to the label:

- Full_First: January 2006
- Retention: G (which stands for Grandfather) or one year, dd-January-2006
- Serial number: Choose one, or write some SQL code to generate it

On the second set, add the following information to your labels:

- Full_First: Week1-January 2006
- Retention: F (which stands for Father) or one month, Week1-February-2006
- Serial number: Choose one, or write some SQL code to generate it

On the next day, you need to choose a second set of media, but this time only the files that have been changed will be backed up using the differential option. Let's say we are doing differential transaction log or database backups for example's sake.

On the differential set, add the following information to the label:

- I_First (or a day of the week): Mon, or First
- Retention: Seven days or every Monday
- Serial number: Choose one, or write some SQL code to generate it

On the next day, put in a new backup set and perform the next day's differential. This time, the label information is Tues or "Second." Then retain these media in a seven-day save set and store them in a safe place. On Wednesday, perform the third differential and on Thursday, perform the fourth differential. Let's now look at what we are achieving:

We have created a Grandfather set that we store for a year. If we started this system in January 2006, we will not reuse these tapes until January 2007; the retention period is one year; these are the oldest saved versions of the databases you will have.

The second copy set is the Father set of the scheme, and this set gets reused in four weeks' time. In other words: Every four weeks, the set can be overwritten. This does not mean that we only make a full backup once a month. On the contrary: Notice that we made one full set and four differential sets, so we are making a full backup once a week and four "diffs" Monday to Thursday. We only retain the weekly set for a month, meaning that at the end of each month you will have five full backup sets, one set for each week, retained for a month, and one set for each month, retained for a year.

What about the differential sets? These sets are the grandchildren of our rotation scheme. We save them for seven days and return them for scratching on the same day the following week. So what we back up on Monday gets written over next Monday, Tuesday gets written over on Tuesday, and so on. This also means that at any given time, your people can access the previous day's data, the previous week's data, the previous month's data, and the previous year's data. What we have created here is a traditional rotation scheme for performing safe and accessible backups of SQL Server databases, for low-end OLTP systems typical of most businesses.

There are variations on this theme, and you will need more than just seven of whatever media you are using if you apply the schemes to transaction log backups. For example, for the full GFS rotation, you would need the following for a single server that used one DLT tape drive:

- Daily backups (differential, rotated weekly): 4+
- Weekly Full (rotated monthly): 4+
- Monthly Full (rotated annually): 12+
- Total tapes: 20+

The best days for such a rotation scheme are Monday–Thursday (differential) and Friday (full). Even on big systems, you're unlikely to be doing a differential into the following day. And on Friday, you have the whole day and the weekend to do the full backup, at a time when the system is most idle. You could start after the last person leaves on a Friday and you would still have about 48 hours of backup time to play with; besides, the databases in most businesses are unlikely to be used over the weekends or holidays.

Creating a Backup Maintenance Plan

The Maintenance Plan feature lets you set up an end-to-end job process that will provide a backup job, predicated with various database verification routines, such as database integrity and index tuning, that can be appended with file clean-up and database backup verification.

To create a maintenance plan you can use the Maintenance Plan Wizard or drop plan components onto a Design "palette" as described in Chapter 4. The Wizard is easy to use and once a plan is created you can always go in and change the plan on the Design palette. To create a maintenance plan for backing up databases and transaction logs, do as follows:

1. Expand the Management node in SQL Server Management Studio, right-click on the Maintenance Plans node and select Maintenance Plan Wizard. The wizard starts and asks for a maintenance plan name. Provide a name that describes the databases and procedures you will perform. Click Next, the Select a Target Server dialog box loads. See Figure 7-8.

2. In this dialog box you can provide a description for the maintenance plan. Also choose the security information for the logged in user from Active Directory. You can also choose a SQL Server user account. Click Next.

3. You can now select a task from the predefined task list as shown in Figure 7-9. Choose items like "Back Up Database (Full)" and then click Next.

4. The Select Maintenance Task Order dialog box now loads. Here you can choose the priority or execution sequence of the various tasks on offer. After choosing the order of task execution, you can set various options.

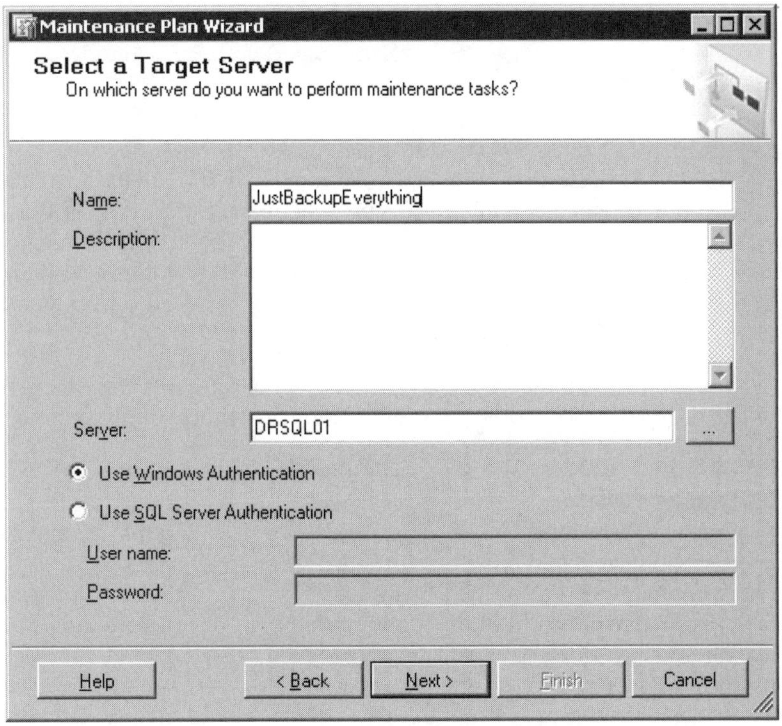

FIGURE 7-8
Selecting the target server for the maintenance plan

Figure 7-9
Select a
maintenance task

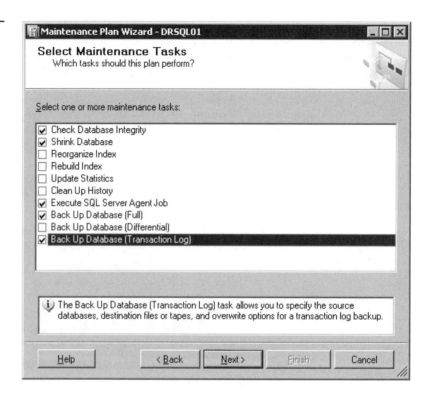

5. In the Databases drop-down list, choose the database to backup. You can choose all or just a selection of databases to include in the full backup process. From here on out, choosing the database type, schedules, and post operations is pretty straight forward. You will get a chance to define various SQL Server Agent actions combined with the alerts, notifications, and operators you set up under SQL Server Agent, as described in Chapter 4. Once you save the plan, you can find it as a leaf under Maintenance Plans.

The plan wizard makes it easy to create something fast and on the fly but it is not best for more advance scenarios and for extending or adding to existing plans. For this we must open up and work a plan interactively.

Sleeping at Night

The life of a DBA is filled with surprises. I have often had the strangest requests from users and seen some really interesting stuff. One scene I will never forget is the letter opener I found jammed into one of the DSS tape drives one morning, sticking out of the server by at least a foot. It appeared that the night operator was trying to remove a jammed cartridge and had no luck dislodging it. The morning log caused a lot of chuckles because the only problem in the report was "one of the servers has been impaled by a letter opener."

But one item on your list of things a DBA has to do that should be no surprise to you is recovering a database. As sure as the sun will rise in the morning, there will come a time when frantic executives come pouring into your office like Federal agents stalking America's most wanted. If you plan well and practice disaster recovery often, you should have no problem sleeping at night.

When I say "practice," I mean that you should set up development servers, wreck them, and then recover them. Trash your databases, the server binaries, and even the operating system and then restore the whole caboodle to the last transaction. Try all forms of backup and restore, and also delete transaction logs and so on.

Only then when the bits and bytes hit the fan will you be able to calmly say to the CEO or CFO "no problem, I will have you back in a jiffy." Woe upon the DBA who sits down at his or her smoking server spewing out the last sparks of a hosed disk array and saying "uh . . . now what."

In Review

This chapter deals with backup and restore for the most common forms of installation. In the next chapter, we will look at replication, log-shipping and various built-in and third-party mirroring.

Distributed Database Architecture

Database servers of the world unite. I hardly think that a zillion database machines are getting ready to take over the world and crush mankind. But no data store need be an island with SQL Server 2005 in the mix, because the system has all the necessary features that enable it to interconnect with other database servers (including non–SQL Server machines). These include other brands of database management systems, even Microsoft Access, cousin (now long distance) Sybase, and (ahem) Oracle and IBM. This chapter focuses on SQL Server's powerful replication, log shipping, and database mirroring features, which allow you to create a sophisticated distributed data network and non-clustered fail-over architecture. We will also look at one third-party solution to replicate your SQL Server data from one geographical location to another.

This chapter delves into what can be an extremely complex subject if not done with common sense. It will thus focus on what you need to know to get the skeletal replication, log shipping, or database mirror configuration in place as soon as possible, and how to best prepare your organization for such a topology. Once you have a basic understanding of what you are in for, and what SQL Server's distributed service consists of, you will have a leg up on getting ready to build a distribution network foundation on which to build more complex distributed services. But first, let's kick off with some theory.

Redundancy is considered an element of high availability, the subject of this and the next chapter. Redundancy provides some level of high availability without the cost of full-blown clustering. Redundancy in SQL Server can be achieved using stand-by servers, replication, log shipping, and database and disk mirroring techniques.

Replicated Databases

SQL Server's replication features make the platform one of the most powerful distributed database solutions on the planet today. Ever since the birth of data network, IT managers have had the need to distribute data around their enterprises and organizations. There are many reasons to distribute data among a collection of servers. You might have some special needs, but here is a collection that almost all DBAs can identify with:

- **Low to Medium Availability** Making data available whenever and wherever users and data consumers need it.

- **Redundancy**   Replication allows multiple sites to hold the same data. These sites may all work autonomously and access the servers closest to them on their network segments, but in mission-critical applications a redundant server holding the same information means that more than one copy of the database is accessible in the event of a disaster. This redundancy is useful when you have multiple sites spread across a wide geographical area and the users need to read the same data, especially for reporting applications. Replication is ideal for standby solutions, and as mentioned previously, low- to medium-availability scenarios. (Other choices for high availability in SQL Server 2005 include log shipping, database mirrors, and fail-over clustering, all of which are discussed in Chapter 9.)

- **Data migration**   Replication allows you to maintain multiple copies of the same data, which means that one server can cater to the OLTP read/write connections while another is configured for read-only or read-intensive applications. These might be data transformation services pulling data into staging tables for warehouses, or performing direct, "drill"-intensive work on the data, such as in online analytical processing (OLAP).

- **Autonomy/store forward**   Replication allows users, such as field agents and engineers, to work with copies of data while offline. Then when they reconnect, new data is propagated to other databases. Such a scenario could involve entering data into PDAs, mobile PCs, portable computers, and other data entry devices. When these devices are connected to the network, replication automatically makes sure the local data is replicated to the system.

- **Scale out**   Replication also allows you to scale out your data tier. In other words, data can be browsed in highly distributed applications, such as when data needs to be browsed from the Web from anywhere on the planet.

- **Data mining**   Replication allows you to increasingly aggregate read performance in analysis solutions.

- **Partitioning**   Replication also helps reduce conflicts based on multiple user data modifications and queries, because data can be distributed throughout the network and you can partition data according to the needs of different business units, departments, or users.

While availability and redundancy are your typical reasons for maintaining a distributed database network, several other factors require further discussion. Replication plays an important part in data mining and data warehousing operations. It is a useful tool that you can use to get data from point A to point B. Then when it is at point B it can be extracted, loaded into a staging database and prepared for transformation to an analysis database.

You can thus use replication to continuously update data marts and data warehouses. This is a far better solution to making periodic bulk extractions and inserts, which are resource intensive and potentially disruptive of day-to-day operations. In my book, it's better to have data replication taking place all the time than to spend evenings and weekends doing weekly extractions, loads, and scrubbing, or wasting time figuring out how to get huge amounts of batch transfers into the data warehouse before morning.

Understand that the replication services allow replicating data to be transformed. They do not enable the replication of the Analysis Services objects, such as dimensions or CUBEs.

They are used to help you set up a uniform data distribution network that moves data from OLTP (transaction) databases to data warehouses or data mart staging databases where data is scrubbed. These databases are used for drill- or query-intensive operations such as reporting, decision support, or analysis. SQL Server Integration Services (SSIS)—formerly Data Transformation Services (DTS)—can be used with replication services for an end-to-end data transformation and migration service. (SSIS is not part of the core database engine; it is thus not extensively covered in this book.)

The data used in decision support or OLAP services is predominantly read-only (used for queries and analysis). For analysis, database loading snapshot replication or transactional replication are often the types of replication used. But the idea is not to directly get data from the live OLTP system into the database. It makes more sense to replicate to an off-limits (read-only) database and then from there extract the data into the staging area, where you can treat it and scrub it before it is inserted into the data warehouse, where it will remain unchanged. For example, you might want to install surrogate keys into the database, and this is not something you want to do to an OLTP system that is a replication partner with other servers. SQL Server's snapshot replication technology allows the data and database objects to be copied and distributed exactly as they appear at a specific moment in time on the source server.

Replication is also an ideal solution that caters to the problem of data accessibility while you are disconnected from the main data sources. For example, you are disconnected when you are traveling or working at remote locations, in the car or at a home office that is not connected to the corporate data center all the time. Business users often need to use laptops or handheld computers when traveling, and they always need to access data, often on demand, such as in airports or hotel rooms. This is usually achieved by using a modem to dial into a corporate data center or connect to it via an intranet or the Internet connection, many of which now exist at most American airports.

When working online, you can use replication to receive data from the central server in the corporate data center when you connect to a WAN or LAN, or over the Internet. Then you can make changes to data immediately, or you can modify data offline and propagate the changes to the source databases and to other locations when you reconnect to the network.

Data modifications made at remote servers are performed asynchronously at the original server and then sent to other servers. Transactional replication (using the queued updating option we will later discuss) and merge replication are the types of replication most often used for mobile or disconnected users.

For example, let's say that my company has sales representatives in various regions who need to take current customer and order information with them and update it as they travel. The corporate office decides to publish data from the CUSTOMERS, ORDERS, and ORDER DETAILS tables stored in a central OLTP database and filter the data by the region where each sales representative works. The laptop or handheld computers used by the sales representatives will be the Subscribers to the data, and the sales representatives will be able to update the data as necessary when away from the office and offline. With replication, when the sales representatives reconnect to the network, they can synchronize their data changes with changes made at other locations.

Replicating is also useful over the Internet or the Web, which allows remote, disconnected, and anonymous users to access data when they need it and wherever they need it. For example, your Web site might allow users to browse items for sale, and you might have a large quantity of such hits to the main server. Using replication, you can make sure that data is available for read purposes on other servers. Since the browsing can take place at any server, it allows the site, using load-balancing technology, to handle more traffic.

Another use of replication and Web-based applications is to allow individual Subscribers to download or upload data changes with an application that uses an Internet browser, or by using a connection to the corporate network or share where the data resides. Obviously, you'll have collateral items on the IS list to cater to, such as integration with third-party firewalls or with ISA Server and IIS. You might also need to configure the file transfer protocol (FTP) to transfer the data over the Internet or HTTP and Web integration (a new feature for SQL Server 2005). One network solution you'll need to consider with replication services is the configuration of virtual private networks (VPNs) and virtual local area networks (VLANs).

Establishing Replication Requirements

I found that the best way to get into replication is to investigate your enterprise needs and then formulate a requirements document—a needs synthesis. Let's suppose your company has regional offices around the world. Some regional offices will only be reading the data, while other offices are responsible for keeping up-to-date information on the customers and orders in their particular regions.

Your regional office might only need to read the data and not make any changes. If that's the case, the central office can filter the data to create the appropriate partitions, which would be based on region information or some other criteria, and then publish that data to regional servers. The snapshot replication type or the transactional replication could be used to achieve your data distribution goals. It all depends on what you are trying to achieve.

Another example: A regional office or data center makes changes to the data and needs the autonomy of the data on its site. So the data can be filtered and replicated to that region. Then the regional office can make changes to its data as needed. When the changes need to be propagated to the central or corporate data center or other regional data centers, the remote data center can synchronize with the central data center such that the changes now made in the remote data center can propagated automatically to the central data center, which in turn can synchronize with other remote data centers. If the central data center needs to distribute the corporate data to other regional sales forces, it can republish the data to the necessary sites.

So you have several options for scheduling distribution of the data and modifying the data at the different remote data centers. If you maintain a continuous and reliable wide area network, multiple data centers can update the data and propagate the changes to the corporate offices immediately. The data is then propagated to other data centers within seconds (via the service of the immediate updating feature). In the case of a remote data center that is offline for a limited amount of time, data modifications can be stored in a queue until the connection is reestablished. This is called queued updating. So let's review the components of the replication service before we activate the components of our plan.

SQL Server 2005 Replication Services

SQL Server 2005's replication services are a set of technologies used for copying and distributing data and database objects from one database to another and then synchronizing between databases to ensure that the data in each database is consistent and durable.

NOTE *SQL Server 2005 can subscribe to a SQL Server 2000 publication, but not to a SQL Server 7.0 (version 7 of the database engine) publication. If you need to replicate from a version 7.0 database to a version 9.0 database, you need to get your data replicated to SQL Server 2000 first.*

Microsoft, obsessed with the publishing business, has built the replications services around a publishing industry metaphor to represent the components and processes in a "replication topology." The model is composed of the following components:

- **Publisher**   The Publisher is a SQL Server database that makes its data available to other databases that can receive from it. The Publisher can have more than one publication, and each publication can represent a logically related set of data. The publisher server is the source of the data to be replicated, but it is more than just a sender of data. It can also detect which data has changed during transactional replication, and it keeps track of all the publications it is responsible for.

- **Distributor**   The Distributor is a SQL Server database (possibly the same host as the publisher) that hosts the distribution database and stores history data, and/or transactions and metadata. The role of the Distributor varies, depending on which type of replication you implement. A remote Distributor is a SQL Server system that is maintained separate from the Publisher and is configured as a Distributor of replication. As mentioned, you can also have a server that is configured to be both a Publisher and a Distributor of replication data—a so-called local distributor.

- **Subscribers**   Subscribers are database servers that receive the replicated data. Subscribers subscribe to publications, and not to individual articles within a publication. They also subscribe only to the publications that they need, not all of the publications available on a Publisher, which means they get only the data they need to have, and not data from every database on the server. The Subscriber can also propagate data changes back to the Publisher or republish the data to other Subscribers. This depends on the replication option chosen, which allows the replication to be a two-way street.

- **Publications**   A publication is defined as a collection of one or more articles that originate from one database. This grouping of multiple articles makes it easier to specify a logically related set of data and database objects that you want to replicate as a unit.

- **Articles**   The article is not something you read in the *New York Times* magazine. It is a table of data, or a partition of data, or a database object that can be designated for replication. The article can be an entire table; a collection of columns (using the vertical filter) or certain rows (using the horizontal filter); a stored procedure or view definition; or the execution of a stored procedure, a view, an indexed view, or a user-defined function.

- **Subscriptions**   The subscription is a request for a copy of data or database objects to be replicated. A subscription defines what publication will be received, where it will be received, and when it will be received. Synchronization of the data distribution of a subscription can be requested either by the Publisher—in what is termed a push subscription—or by the Subscriber—in what is termed a pull subscription. A publication can support a concoction of both push and pull subscriptions.

There are also several replication "agency" processes that are responsible for copying and moving data between the Publisher and the Subscriber. These are the Snapshot Agent, Distribution Agent, Log Reader Agent, Queue Reader Agent, and Merge Agent. We'll get to these shortly.

Types of Replication

Three types of replications are available with SQL Server 2005: snapshot replication, transactional replication, and merge replication. SQL Server 2005 also permits a variation of the transactional replication allowing updatable subscriptions. Here the Publisher streams transactions to SQL Server Subscribers after they receive an initial snapshot of the published data. However, transactions that originate at the Subscriber are replicated back to the Publisher. Each replication option has its strengths and weaknesses; however, each is suitable only for a specific reason.

Snapshot Replication

Snapshot replication is the process of copying and distributing data and database objects in the exact state they appear in at a certain moment in time. Snapshot replication does not require continuous monitoring of changes because changes made to published data are not propagated to the Subscriber incrementally; rather, they are periodically replicated in a single effort. The subscribers are thus replicated to with every complete refresh of the dataset. They are not replicated to on a transaction-by-transaction basis.

Snapshot replication can take longer to propagate data modifications to Subscribers than the other forms of replication because the snapshot replication replicates an entire dataset at one point in time. Snapshots are typically replicated less frequently than other types of publications. Once a day in the evening is a good time to engage in snapshot replication. A data warehouse or a hot stand-by server is well suited to obtain snapshot replication data because the data does not need to be propagated to the replication database on the heel of every transaction. However, the dataset should be small because trying to replicate petabytes of data at one time might cause an entire city to cave in on itself as you suck up the entire neighborhood's Internet access getting data from A to B.

Options available with snapshot replication allow you to filter published data and allow Subscribers to make modifications to replicated data and propagate those changes to the Publisher and then to other Subscribers. This filtering mechanism thus lets you transform data as it is published. Snapshot replication is useful for

- Data that is mostly static (seldom changes), such as warehouse data replicating to a data mart

- Cases in which it is acceptable to have copies of data that are out of date for a certain period of time

- Small volumes of data

- Sites that are often disconnected, where high latency (the amount of time between when data is updated at one site and when it is updated at another) is acceptable

Transactional Replication

With *transactional replication,* an initial snapshot of data is propagated to Subscribers, so that the subscriber has what is called an initial load, something to start with. Then when data modifications are made at the Publisher, these individual transactions are immediately captured and replicated to the Subscriber.

Under transactional replication, SQL Server 2005 monitors INSERT, UPDATE, and DELETE statements, as well as changes to stored procedure executions and indexed views. It stores the transactions affecting replicated objects and then propagates those changes to Subscribers continuously or at scheduled intervals. Transaction boundaries are preserved. If, for example, 100 rows are updated in a transaction, either all 100 rows of the transaction are propagated or none of them are. When all changes are propagated, all Subscribers will have the same values as the Publisher.

Options available with transactional replication allow you to filter published data and allow users at the Subscriber to make modifications to replicated data and propagate those changes to the Publisher and to other Subscribers. You can also transform data as it is published.

Transactional replication is typically used when

- You want data modifications to be propagated to Subscribers, often within seconds of when they occur.

- You need transactions to be atomic (either all or none applied at the Subscriber).

- Subscribers are connected to the Publisher much of the time.

- Your application will not tolerate high latency for Subscribers receiving changes.

Merge Replication

Merge replication allows a collection of sites to work autonomously, online or offline. The data is then merged—with updates and insertions made at multiple sites replicated into a single, uniform result at a future time. The initial snapshot is applied to Subscribers as the initial load. Then SQL Server 2005 tracks the changes to the published data at the Publisher and at the Subscribers. The data is synchronized between servers at a predetermined or scheduled time or on demand using *rowguid* values (32-bit GUIDs) in an identity column that is added to each database table. Updates are then made independently (with no commit protocol) at more than one server. This means that the same data may be updated by the Publisher or by more than one Subscriber, and thus conflicts can occur when data modifications are merged.

If merge replication can introduce conflicting data, then why use it? You would use merge replication when

- Multiple subscribers need to update data at various times and the data has to be propagated to the Publisher and to other Subscribers.
- Subscribers need to receive data, make any changes offline, and then synchronize changes later with the Publisher and other Subscribers.
- The application latency requirement is either high or low.
- Site autonomy is critical.

Merge replication requires diligence on the part of the DBA. It includes default and custom choices for conflict resolution that you define when you configure a merge replication solution. So when a conflict occurs, a resolver is invoked by the Merge Agent to determine which data will be accepted and propagated to other data centers.

You have several options available to you when you configure merge replication. These include the following:

- Filtering published data horizontally and vertically (rows or columns), including join filters and dynamic filters
- The ability to use alternate synchronization partners
- The ability to optimize synchronization to improve merge performance
- The ability to validate replicated data to ensure synchronization
- The ability to use attachable subscription databases

Understanding the Replication Options

Options available with the types of replication allow you more replication solutions and greater flexibility and control in your applications. Replication options are

- Filtering published data
- Publishing database objects
- Publishing schema objects
- Updatable subscriptions
- Transforming published data
- Alternate synchronization partners

Table 8-1 presents the replication options and the replication types that support them.

Filtering Published Data

Filtering data during replication allows you to publish only the data or partitions of data that are needed by the Subscriber. You can filter data and thus create partitions that include only columns and/or only rows that you specify for replication.

With all types of replication, you can choose to copy and distribute complete tables, or you can filter your data horizontally or vertically with static filters. The merge replication is especially strong in filtering options, and you can use dynamic filters to customize the filter to correspond to a property of the Subscriber receiving the data.

Replication Option	Replication Type
Filtering Published Data	Snapshot, Transactional, Merge
Updatable Subscriptions (immediate queuing and updating)	Snapshot, Transactional
Updatable Subscriptions	Merge
Transforming Published Data	Snapshot, Transactional
Alternate Synchronization Partners	Merge, Transactional with Updatable Subscribers
Optimizing Synchronization	Merge

TABLE 8-1   Replication Options

When you filter data horizontally, you have the option of publishing only the data that is needed. You can also partition data to different sites and avoid conflicts that arise out of the situation where subscribers are viewing and updating different subsets of data. You can also manage publications in accordance with user needs or applications.

You also have the option of using user-defined functions in your static and dynamic filters, and you can even make use of customized functions. Merge replication also lets you use *join filters* and *dynamic filters.* The join filters enable you to extend filters created on one table to another. Let's say you are publishing customer data according to the state where the customer resides; you may want to extend that filter to the related orders and order details of the customers in a particular state. The dynamic filters, on the other hand, allow you to create a merge publication and then filter data from the publishing table. The filter value can be the user ID or a login retrieved through a T-SQL function.

Publishing Database Objects

You also have the option of publishing database objects, including views, indexed views, user-defined functions, stored procedure definitions, and the execution of stored procedures. You can include data and database objects in the same publication or in different publications. Publishing database objects is available with all types of replication—transactional, snapshot, and merger replication.

Publishing Schema Objects

You can also specify schema objects to be published. These might include such objects as declared referential integrity, primary key constraints, reference constraints, unique constraints, clustered indexes, nonclustered indexes, user triggers, extended properties, collations, and so on. You can also change destination table owner names and data formats to optimize for SQL Server 2005, SQL Server 2000, and non–SQL Server subscribers.

Updatable Subscriptions

An updatable subscription allows data at the Subscriber to be modified. Updatable subscriptions are possible with all three replication types, but the algorithms used differ from replication type to replication type. When using merge replication, data at the Subscriber is automatically updatable.

Specifically, the updatable subscription options available with snapshot replication and transactional replication allow you to make changes to replicated data at the Subscriber and propagate those changes to the Publisher and to other Subscribers. Such updatable subscription options include the ability to force immediate updating, queued updating, and immediate updating with queued updating as a fail-over.

Immediate updating also allows Subscribers to update data only if the Publisher will accept them immediately. This is a configuration option in the Publisher. If the changes are accepted at the Publisher, they are propagated to other Subscribers. The Subscriber must be continuously and reliably connected to the Publisher to make changes at the Subscriber, and such a reliable connection would be a dedicated and high-bandwidth WAN backbone.

Queued updating lets the subscribers modify data and store the modifications in a queue. The queue builds while the subscriber remains disconnected from the Publisher. When the Subscriber reconnects to the Publisher, the changes are propagated to the Publisher. If the Publisher accepts the changes, normal replication processes occur and the changes are propagated to other Subscribers from the Publisher. You can then store data modifications in a SQL Server 2005 queue or use Microsoft Message Queuing (MSMQ).

If you use immediate updating with the queued updating option, SQL Server lets you use immediate updating with the option of switching to queued updating if a connection cannot be maintained between the Publisher and the Subscribers. After switching to queued updating, reconnecting to the Publisher, and emptying the queue, you can switch back to immediate updating mode.

Transforming Published Data

A huge benefit of snapshot replication or transactional replication is the feature that lets you leverage the transformation mapping and scripting capabilities of SSIS. These can come into play big time when building a replication topology for almost any situation. Replication integrated with SSIS packages allows you to customize and distribute data according to the requirements of individual Subscribers. Your Subscriber, for example, might need to have different table names, different column names, or compatible data types.

By transforming the published data, you can filter data and simulate dynamic partitions of data so that data from one snapshot or transactional publication can be distributed to Subscribers that require different partitions of data. You also have the option of static partitions. These are created and filter separate publications for each Subscriber in accordance with the needs of each Subscriber.

Alternate Synchronization Partners

I alluded to the Alternate Synchronization Partners feature earlier. It allows Subscribers to merge publications to synchronize with servers other than the Publisher at which the subscription originated. This means that Subscribers can synchronize data even if the primary Publisher is unavailable; they essentially synchronize with alternate partners instead of the Publisher. This feature is also useful when mobile Subscribers connect to a faster or more reliable network connection that can give them access to an alternate Publisher, if the primary is inaccessible.

Getting Started with Replication

There are several ways to implement and monitor replication. There are many options, and each replication project's configuration will depend on the type of replication and the options you choose. Replication is composed of the following stages:

1. Configure a replication topology

2. Create a publication

3. Apply the initial snapshot

4. Create a push or pull subscription

5. Modify or transform the replicated data (if necessary)

6. Synchronize and propagate the data and schedule automatic synchronization

Rather than describing each and every step in dry, excruciating steps, let's get right down to configuring replication. We will first pull from an already-established publication partner; in the examples shown here, SQL Server 2005 subscribed to a publication on a SQL Server 2000 database. As mentioned in Chapter 4, replication can be configured interactively using SQL Server Management Studio, or with T-SQL scripts. Let's first configure replication with Management Studio before we talk about scripting.

Subscribing to a Publication

To subscribe to a publication (assuming a publication has been created), you need to take the following steps:

1. Open Management Studio and start the New Subscription Wizard. The fastest route to this Wizard is to drill down to the server that is going to become a subscriber and expose the Replication folder. Expand the folder to expose two subfolders, Local Publications, and Local Subscriptions. Right-click the Local Subscriptions folder and select New Subscriptions. Click Next to proceed.

2. The Publication step in the wizard now appears. You can select a Publisher, a SQL Server instance somewhere, from the combo-box, and then select the publication offered by the server. Select the publication, as illustrated in Figure 8-1, and click Next.

3. Your next choice is to select the distribution agent for your subscription. A distribution agent can be installed at the Publisher's host, or it can be any other machine running SQL Server. The default option, as shown in Figure 8-2, is to run the agent at the Publisher.

4. Next you get to choose any server on your network to receive the subscription; you are not restricted to the local host you may be at. As you can see from Figure 8-3, you can check any number of qualified servers. Choose a Subscription database from the Subscription Database column and click Next.

5. The next chore is to configure Replication Security. As shown in Figure 8-4 you can elect to choose default accounts or specific accounts (see Chapter 5). Click Next.

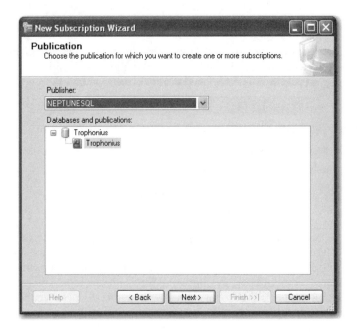

FIGURE 8-1 Selecting the publication

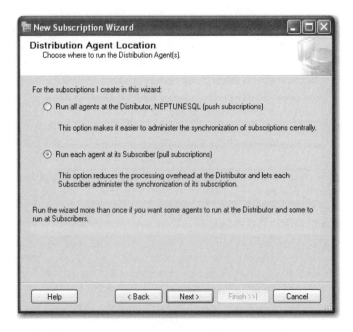

FIGURE 8-2 Running the agent

FIGURE 8-3 Choosing the subscription database

FIGURE 8-4 Configuring replication security

6. The Schedule step in the wizard now appears, as shown in Figure 8-5. Click the Agent Schedule drop-down to choose the replication schedule. You can choose to run the agent continuously or at certain times of the day that fit in with production schedules and maintenance windows. Click Next.

7. The next step, shown in Figure 8-6, allows you to determine when you want to initialize the subscription. At first synchronization of the data is the usual choice, but you may have other plans, and delaying the initialization after the first synchronization is an option. Choose your option and click Next.

8. The next step in the wizard prompts you to choose what runs after you click Finish. You have the option of delaying the creation of the subscription, and you can also generate a script. The two options are shown in the Figure 8-7. I mentioned at the beginning of this procedure that you can also run T-SQL against SQL Server to set up a replication plan. There was a reason that I said we should wait and configure the replication options first using Management Studio. Now you see can see why. The wizard lets you generate a script of everything we have configured interactively so far. This is a very useful option because you will see after you generate the script that it not something even the most experienced T-SQL programmer would want to do in code alone. The script is not exactly a piece of cake.

After you click Finish in the wizard, if you chose to create the subscription immediately, SQL Server will begin building the subscription. This process is shown in Figure 8-8. You can click on the Status column at any time to see a more detailed progress dialog.

FIGURE 8-5   Configuring the schedule

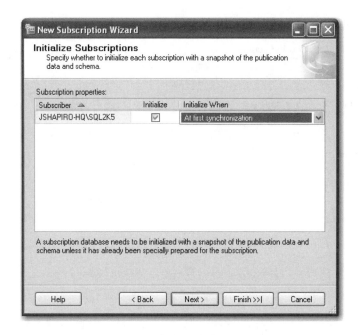

FIGURE 8-6 Initializing the subscription

FIGURE 8-7 Determining when to the create the subscription

FIGURE 8-8 Building the subscription

Configuring a Publisher

To configure a Publisher, you need to take the following steps:

1. Open Management Studio and start the New Publication Wizard. The fastest route to this Wizard is to drill down to the server that is going to become a Publisher and expose the Replication folder. Expand the folder to expose two subfolders, Local Publications and Local Subscriptions. Right-click the Local Publication folder and select New Publication. Click Next to proceed.

2. The Distributor step, as illustrated in Figure 8-9, loads. Notice here that the server you are setting up is configured as its own Distributor by default. Also notice, however, that you can select another server as a Distributor, but it must already be configured as such for selection here. We want to keep things this way using the default, so click Next.

3. The Specify Snapshot Folder dialog box, as illustrated in Figure 8-10, loads. Here again, accept the default and move on. You will then notice a warning about the share name used for the replication folder. By default, it is made accessible only to logins with local administrative rights. Let's not worry about that now, but remember that you may need to change this for remote services like pull agents at another time. Click OK to close the share warning, and then click Next.

FIGURE 8-9   Distributor setup options

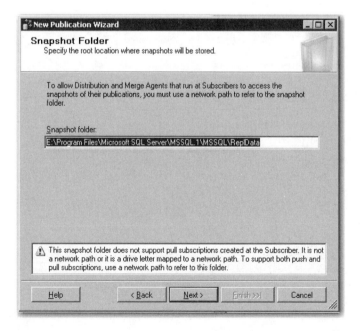

FIGURE 8-10   Snapshot folder

4. Accept the defaults chosen by the wizard, or you can go in and "tweak" the settings. Later, you can work with advanced settings and go over some of this stuff in more detail. Click Next and then click Finish.

Creating a Publication

Using transactional replication, you will now be able to set up replication that lets changes made at the Publisher we have just configured flow to Subscribers. But before that can happen, you first need to create a publication on the publisher. The publication allows our Subscribers to update their data from the Publisher in almost real time. Transactions will be set to replicate as soon as they commit in the publication, or they can be propagated to the subscribers at regular intervals. In other words, the publication will be configured to allow the subscribers to update either via Immediate Updates or Queued Updates.

To do this, we need to perform a series of steps using the Create Publication Wizard as follows:

1. Connect to your server as described earlier and expose the Replication folder. Right-click the Publications folder and select New Publication. Notice that SQL Server takes you direct to the database list because the server has already been configured for publications. The Publication Database loads. Select the database for the publication, as shown in Figure 8-11, and then click Next.

2. The Select Publication Type dialog box, as illustrated in Figure 8-12, loads. In that we are looking to replication transaction from one OLTP database to another, choose Transactional publication and then click Next.

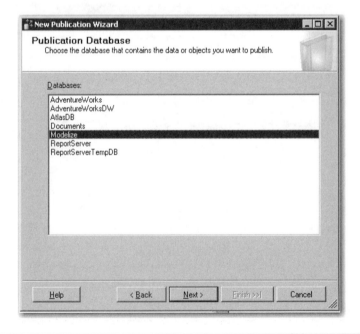

FIGURE 8-11   Choosing the Publication folder

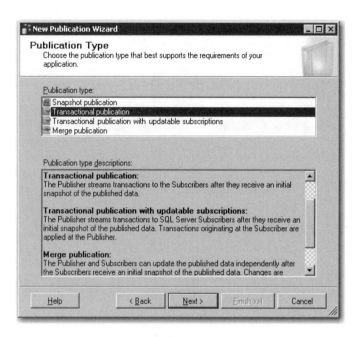

FIGURE 8-12   Choosing Publication type

3. The Articles dialog box, as illustrated in Figure 8-13, loads. In the tree check all the objects that you want to replicate. As illustrated, you can choose tables, stored procedures, and user-defined functions. (Any tables that do not contain primary keys are ignored for publication.) Click Next.

4. The Articles Issues now loads and lets you take note of any replication issues that you need to deal with. Click Next to go directly to the Filter Table Rows step. The step shown in Figure 8-14 appears. Add filters as needed. These are simply T-SQL statements you can apply to the data transfer process as shown in Figure 8-15.

5. The remaining steps are identical to ones in the subscription process we discussed earlier (see Figures 8-5 to 8-7). First the Schedule step in the wizard appears. You can choose to run the agent continuously or at certain times of the day that fit in with production schedules and maintenance windows. Click Next.

6. The next step lets you configure Replication Security. You can elect to choose default accounts, or specific accounts. Click Next.

7. The final step in the wizard prompts you to choose what runs after you click Finish. You have the option of delaying the creation of the publication, and as before, you can also generate a script.

That's pretty much all it takes to set up and configure a basic transactional replication scenario. Before you go off and replicate the world, consider the following advice on replication planning and deployment.

FIGURE 8-13   Choosing the Articles

FIGURE 8-14   Filtering Table Rows

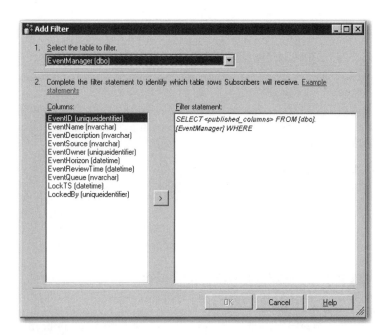

FIGURE 8-15   Application of Filters

Designing a Replication Topology

When your databases are widely dispersed over the Internet or across an extensive corporate WAN, supporting widely dispersed data centers, and you must replicate data, you have to define a replication topology to support the interconnection of servers and replication and synchronized updating of the data that resides on them. Not only must the topology take into consideration how the servers communicate, but it must cater to the synchronization that has to occur between copies so that data remains consistent and durable across the enterprise.

Designing a replication topology will help you, among other things, determine how long it takes for changes to get from a publisher to a subscriber, how updates are propagated, and the order in which updated information arrives at a subscriber. There are several steps you must take when designing a replication topology:

- You will need to select the physical replication model. This can be any one of the following models: a central publisher, a central publisher with remote distributor, a publishing subscriber, or a central subscriber.

- You will have to determine where to locate the snapshot files (which are used to create the first loads to the receiving databases). You will also need to determine how the publishers and subscribers will initially synchronize their data.

- You will need to decide if the distributor will be local or remote. You will also need to decide if the distribution database will be shared. More than one publisher can share a distributor, with each one using its own distribution database on the publisher. They can also share a distribution database, so you have lot to synthesize.

- There are many different types of replication options to use. You have had a tiny taste of a few in this chapter, and you will need to decide what options are going to be best for your solution.

- You will also need to determine whether the replication will kick off at the publisher—in what is typically called push subscription—or at the subscriber through (you guessed it) a pull subscription.

On a WAN, managing many subscribers and publishers can be a complex situation and requires the dedication of DBAs devoted to the replication process. Many data paths might exist between the servers, and your job will be to ensure that the data remains synchronized and the solution works to have subscribers obtain the correct versions of the data. Fortunately, replication technology has come a long way from the day data was updated in the morning and then overwritten again with yesterday's information in the afternoon.

Understanding the Physical Replication Models

The physical replication model is your blueprint for how you will allow data to be distributed across the enterprise or the Internet. Understanding the physical model means understanding how to configure the servers for replication services. If you are new to replication, and many people are, the following sections provide a point of departure, a proverbial leg up, so to speak.

The advice that you cannot be too careful about planning for replication deployment might seem like a gross understatement, but when you have a highly complex replication model, I cannot stress how important it is to properly plan the whole effort. Remember, you have to plan to maximize data consistency, minimize demands on network resources, and implement sound technical services that will prevent a disaster down the road. Many Internet or Web applications today consist of demanding replication needs, and if there is one factor that is a business killer, it is finding out after the fact that there is a flaw in the design of your replication topology, the models used, and so on. The following list of considerations should be noted before you begin to make any purchases or decisions that may prove expensive to undo later:

- Decide how and where replicated data needs to be updated, and by whom.

- Decide how your data distribution needs will be affected by issues of consistency, autonomy, and latency.

- Draw up a blueprint or architecture map illustrating your replication environment. Include your business users, your technical infrastructure, your network and security, and the characteristics of your data.

- Evaluate the types of replication you can use and the replication options that will work for your solution.

- Evaluate the replication topology options and the effect they will have on the types or type of replication you may be considering.

Let's now turn to standby servers.

Standby Servers

A *standby server* is a redundant server that you maintain and bring online if the main production server crashes and burns. The idle server contains a copy of the databases on the primary server and is deployed when the primary server becomes unavailable through scheduled maintenance or a crash. The standby server is useful if the primary is power-cycled once a week, or according to some schedule that takes it offline for a few hours or longer.

The standby server will allow your users to continue working oblivious to the fact that the primary server is unavailable. When the primary server becomes available again, any changes to the standby server's copies of databases must be restored back to the primary server. If you do not restore the databases, the data will be lost. When users start using the primary server again, its databases should be backed up and restored on the standby server.

There are three phases to implementing a standby server:

- **Phase I**   Creating the database and ongoing transaction log backups on the primary server

- **Phase II**   Setting up and maintaining the standby server by backing up the databases on the primary server and restoring them on the standby server

- **Phase III**   Bringing the standby server online if the primary server fails

All your user processes must log in to the standby server and restart any tasks they were performing when the primary server became unavailable. The user processes are not switched automatically to the standby server, and transactions are not maintained between the primary server and the standby server. If the primary server is taken off the network or renamed manually, and the standby server is renamed, the standby server will have a network name and address different from the server the users were using previously.

You must also periodically apply transaction log backups from the databases on the primary server to the standby server. This will ensure that the standby remains synchronized with the primary server and that the databases are the same. The more restores you do, the more in sync will be the two servers.

A standby server configuration is not the same thing as the virtual server configuration used in SQL Server 2005 fail-over clustering discussed earlier. A standby server contains a second copy of the SQL Server databases, and no shared cluster array is necessary. In a virtual server/cluster setup there is only one copy of the databases, stored on the shared cluster disk, available to any node that becomes active.

Creating the Backups on the Primary Server

When you set up the secondary standby server, you must create a full database backup of each database to be duplicated and then attach them to the standby servers. Frequently apply transaction log restores to the standby databases to keep them current with the main server. The frequency of transaction log backups created on the primary server will of course depend on the volume of transaction changes of the production server database, and you should follow the same guidelines discussed in Chapter 9.

When restoring a copy of *master* from a production server to a standby server, you cannot back up the transaction log of *master*. Only a database backup and restore of *master* is possible.

Setting Up and Maintaining the Standby Server

To set up and maintain a standby server, do as follows: Restore the database backups from the primary server onto the standby server in standby mode, specifying an undo file (one undo file per database). Standby mode is either specified in T-SQL backup/restore code or can be set interactively using the read only/undo file option on the Options tab on the Restore Database dialog box in Management Studio.

When a database or transaction log is restored in standby mode, recovery needs to roll back any uncommitted transactions so that the database can be left in a logically consistent state and used, if necessary, for read-only purposes. Pages in the database affected by the uncommitted, rolled-back transactions are modified. This will undo the changes originally performed by the uncommitted transactions. The undo file is used to save the contents of these pages before recovery modifies them; this prevents the changes performed by the uncommitted transactions from being lost. Before a subsequent transaction log backup is next applied to the database, the uncommitted transactions that were previously rolled back by recovery must be reapplied first. The saved changes in the undo file are reapplied to the database, and then the next transaction log is applied.

Be certain that there is enough disk space for the undo file to grow so that it can contain all the distinct pages from the database that were modified by rolling back uncommitted transactions. You must also apply each subsequent transaction log, created on the primary server, to the databases on the standby server. Remember to apply each transaction log in standby mode, specifying the same undo file used when previously restoring the database.

In standby mode, the database is available for read-only operations, such as database queries that do not attempt to modify the database. This allows the database to be used for decision-support queries or DBCC checks as necessary.

Bringing the Standby Server Online

When a primary server crashes, all the databases on the standby server are unlikely to be in complete synchronization. Some transaction log backups created on the primary server may not have been applied to the standby server yet. Also, it is likely that some changes to the databases on the primary server will have occurred since the transaction logs on those databases were last backed up, especially in high-volume systems. Before the users try to connect to the standby copies, you should try to synchronize the primary databases with the standby copies and bring the standby server online in the following manner:

1. Apply any transaction log backups created on the primary server that have not yet been applied to the standby server in sequence, assuming you have access to the primary server.

2. Create a backup of the active transaction log on the primary server, and apply the backup to the database on the standby server. The backup of the active transaction log when applied to the standby server allows users to work with an exact copy of the primary database as it was immediately prior to failure (although any noncommitted transactions will have been permanently lost [see Chapter 9]).

3. If the primary server is undamaged, which is usually the case when planned maintenance or upgrades occur, you can back up the active transaction log with NORECOVERY. This will leave the database in the restoring state and allow you

to update the primary server with transaction log backups from the secondary server. Then you can switch back to the primary server without creating a complete database backup of the secondary server.

4. Recover the databases on the standby server. This action recovers the databases without creating an undo file, and it makes the database available for users to modify. A standby server can contain backups of databases from several instances of SQL Server. For example, you could have a bunch of servers, each running a mission-critical database system. Rather than five separate standby servers, you could have one standby server. The database backups from the five primary systems can be loaded onto the single backup system, reducing the number of resources required and saving you money. It is unlikely that more than one primary system would fail at the same time. Additionally, the standby server can be of a higher specification than the primary servers to cover the remote chance that more than one primary system is unavailable at a given time.

The preceding procedure is very simple to implement. However, such a manual process can be very tedious. It also does not work well, if at all, for WAN-based solutions where you need to send transaction logs to the standby server across the WAN on a continuous basis, lest the transaction logs swell to a size that makes them impossible to manually transfer across a network. You can use a disk- or byte-level data replication utility, as described in the next chapter, or bring log shipping, mirroring, or both to the rescue. Let's look into both options.

Log Shipping

Log shipping is probably the easiest of the "follow the log file" fail-over scenarios discussed in this chapter that we will describe, obviating the need to constantly restore transaction logs to a standby server, as just discussed. Thus, the source and target databases are always in constant synchronization. This approach not only allows you to have a backup server, but it provides a way to offload query processing from the main computer (the source server) to read-only destination servers, one of the key motivators behind replication, but without the overhead and the possible intrusion (or rowguids) into the tables.

Introduced in SQL Server 2000, *log shipping* lets you configure a primary SQL Server instance to automatically send a copy of its transaction log backups to one or more secondary databases on separate secondary servers somewhere else. The target server is configured to receive the logs and apply them to the target databases. For additional protection a third monitor server instance can be installed to "watch" the process, record history and status, and raise alerts.

The source or active database must use the full or bulk-logged recovery model. Log shipping is not supported in databases configured with the simple recovery model. Also, as you will soon see, the destination servers must first be initialized with a full copy of the database to be log-shipped (just as they were in the standby server option earlier). You cannot start a log shipping scenario (or any other fail-over solution) with nothing on the target. Log shipping does not build databases, tables, triggers, stored procedures, or functions on the target servers. It is simply a procedure for getting transactions from a source server to a destination server, automatically, and with a number of data integrity options.

How It Works

Let's consider a company with five servers: ServerA, ServerB, ServerC, ServerD, and ServerE. ServerA is the source server, the server on which log backups are performed and made available for copy. Server C, ServerD, and ServerE contain the destination databases on which the log backups from ServerA are restored. Keeping these servers in synchronization with ServerA is ServerB, the monitor server on which the enterprise-level monitoring of log shipping occurs. Each destination or source server is maintained by only one monitor server.

To delve deeper into log shipping configuration, we see that it is a three-stage process. Logs are produced on your production servers and can then be shipped to multiple target servers, and the process is automated using the following sequence:

1. **Backups**   Transaction logs are backed up to the primary server. The backup process is part of a maintenance plan with a schedule that regularly produces transaction log backups.

2. **Copies**   The transaction log is automatically copied to the log shipping partner server, the server that is the beneficiary of the transaction logs.

3. **Restore**   The target server restores the log backups to its own instance.

If you plan to log ship to multiple targets, then Steps 2 and 3 are repeated for each target server instance.

In the log shipping scenario all configuration and administration of the log process is configured with SQL Server Management Studio. Management Studio can define an appropriate delay between the time ServerB backs up the log backup and the time Servers C, D, and E must restore the log backup. If more time elapses than you defined, ServerA will generate an alert using SQL Server Agent. This alert can aid in troubleshooting the reason the destination server has failed to restore the backups.

In a critical OLTP redundancy architecture, we do not use the monitor server as the source server, because it maintains critical information regarding the entire log shipping system. This means that the monitor server should be regularly backed up at the OS level, even cloned, so that its loss will not kill the entire log shipping setup. Also, if you maintain a monitor server independently of the source server, you will be assured of better performance and reliability for the monitoring process. Also, monitoring adds unnecessary overhead, which you don't need on your OLTP environment. Also, as a source server supporting a production workload, it is the most likely to fail, which would disrupt the monitoring. Finally, most high-availability environments that employ log shipping do so from one failover cluster (discussed in Chapter 9) to another, and a cluster node is not a good idea for the setup of a monitor server.

The secondary servers, which I prefer to refer to as "targets" in a log shipping configuration, are the servers where you want to keep a warm standby copy of your primary OLTP databases. Target servers can contain backup copies of databases from several different source or primary servers. For example, a department could have five servers, each running a mission-critical database system, and each server will have a partner target somewhere as long as its failure would be disaster for the company.

Rather than having five separate standby servers, a single standby server could be used. The backups from the five source systems could be loaded onto the single backup system.

This would reduce the number of servers needed, saving money in the initial layout and keeping cost of ownership in check. It is unlikely that all primary systems would fail at the same time. This scenario is perfectly feasible; however, you need to make sure the standby can carry the load of multiple primary databases, so it should be a "bigger" server in all aspects (memory, CPU, disk space, and so on). Otherwise, you would need to fall back to the source server as soon as possible.

Configuring Log Shipping Manually

SQL Server 2005 lets you perform manual log shipping from earlier-edition servers all the way back to a SQL Server version 7.0 Service Pack 2 (SP2) transaction log. It will do this if the pending upgrade option is enabled on the computer running the earlier versions of SQL Server.

To enable this option, simply execute the following code on the target server:

```
EXEC sp_dboption 'database name', 'pending upgrade', 'true'
```

When you are restoring the database after log shipping, you can recover only with the NORECOVERY option. Remember, however, that you cannot use SQL Server replication between SQL Server 7.0 and SQL Server 2005 systems. So if you need a widely distributed redundant SQL Server infrastructure with a variety of fail-over options, you need to upgrade to SQL Server 2005.

Configuring Log Shipping with Management Studio

To configure log shipping in Management Studio, you open the Database Properties dialog box and configure the options available. To configure servers for log shipping, perform the following steps:

1. Create a share on the primary database server at the data or transaction log folder above or at the point to which your logs are backed up. For example, at the e:\Program Files\SQL Server\..data\backup\tlogs\ path, you could create the \\logshipping\tlogs share. If you are going to log-ship off a SQL Server cluster, you will need to create a file share resource on the cluster, but you will first need to ensure that a cluster disk is available for SQL Server, as shown in Figure 8-16. Creating the share is shown in Figure 8-17 (see "SQL Server 2005 Server Clustering" in Chapter 9).

2. In the Database Properties dialog box check the first option, "Enable this as a primary database in a log shipping configuration." Next click the Backup Settings button. The dialog box in Figure 8-18 loads. Add a path to the transaction log backup folders on the primary server. Configure both the backup procedures and the schedule. (See Chapters 5 and 7 for more information on setting up backups and schedules.) The primary server instance runs the backup job and backs up the transaction log, as it would any local backup. The primary server places the log backup into a primary log-backup share, which it then sends to the secondary backup folder. In this figure, the backup folder is on a shared directory—the backup share we created on a cluster.

3. You now need to connect to a secondary server. Click the Add button on the main page for log shipping. The Secondary Database Settings page loads, as shown in

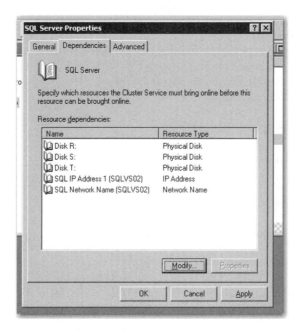

FIGURE 8-16   Allocating a disk resource

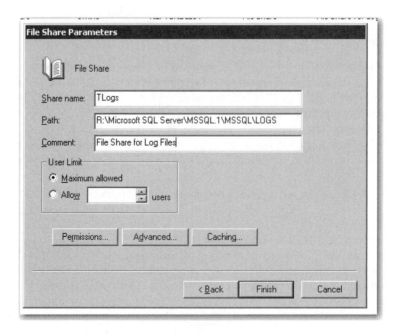

FIGURE 8-17   Creating the share on the primary server

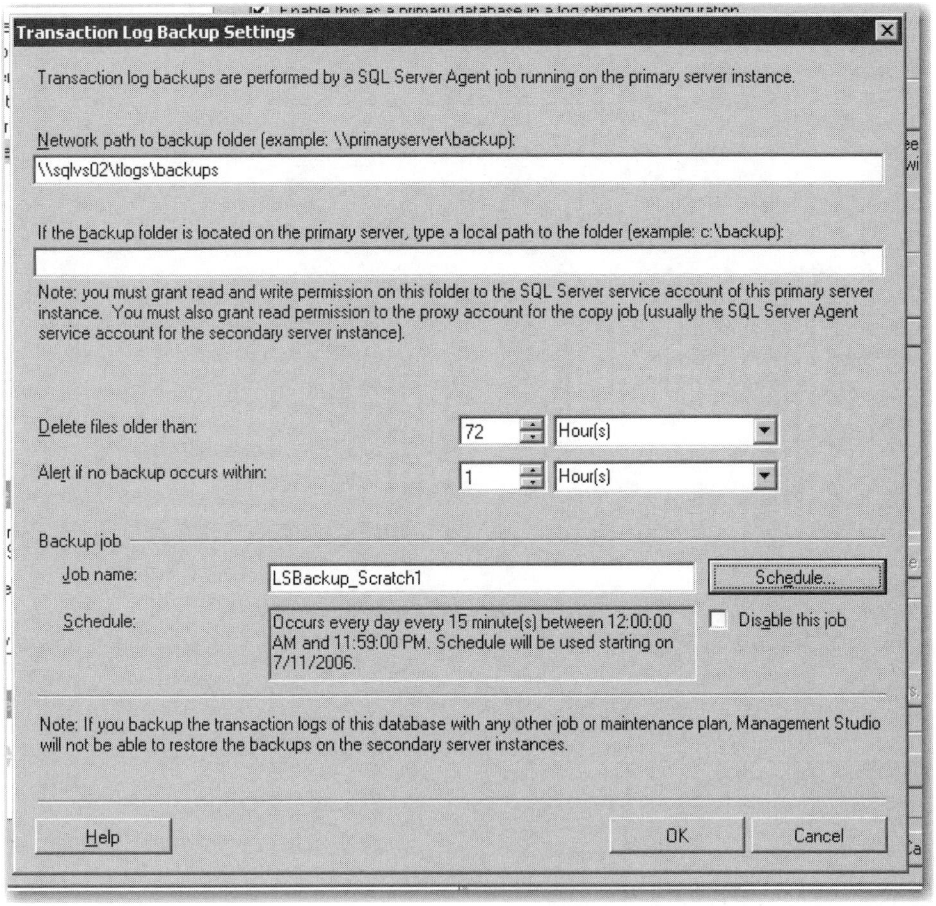

FIGURE 8-18   Backup settings

Figure 8-19. Click the Connect button. The familiar Connect to Server dialog box loads and prompts you for login credentials. On the first tab you have three options for creating the secondary databases. You can have Management Studio generate a full backup of the database and restore it to the secondary server; or you can restore an existing backup (a good option if you need to access a remote server that already has a full backup of the database on it). Given the second option, Management Studio can create the database on the secondary server, if it does not exist, or restore into an already existing copy of the database. Or the third option can be chosen, which will honor an already manually initialized database on the secondary server.

4. If you chose the first option, you can click the Restore Options button to specify folders for both data and log files. Or you can let Management Studio go with the default. If the primary and secondary servers are set up identically, then let Management Studio go with the default. Next click the Copy Files tab, as shown in Figure 8-20, and

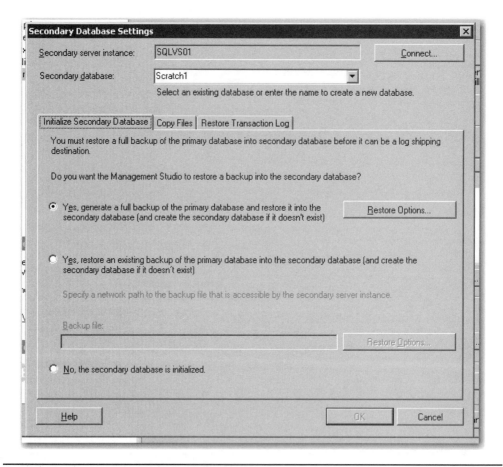

FIGURE 8-19   The Secondary Database Initialization tab

enter a path for the destination. Go with the default setting for the copy job and its schedules.

5. Click the Restore Transaction Log tab, as shown in Figure 8-21. Here you can choose the recovery mode (you would typically choose No Recovery Mode in order to have the database available). Also change the restore maintenance settings to suit your needs and provide a name for the restore job. I would advise that you simply go with the defaults until you have are comfortable configuring log shipping. Click OK to save the configuration. At this point the jobs are created (see the next section, "SQL Server Agent Log Shipping Jobs").

6. You now have an option to use another instance of SQL Server to monitor the log shipping process, or you can choose not to monitor.

In the Select Databases dialog box, select the These Databases check box, and then select the database to log-ship. If you select more than one database, log shipping will not work

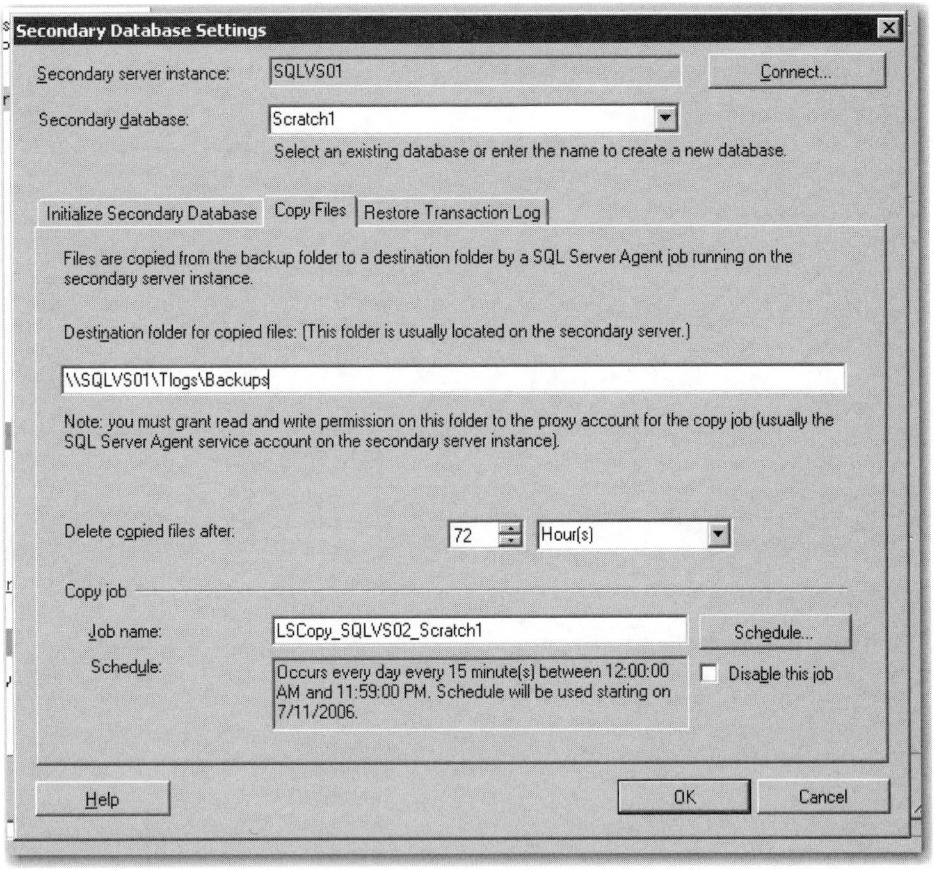

Secondary Database Settings   ☒

Secondary server instance: `SQLVS01`   Connect...

Secondary database: `Scratch1`   ▼

Select an existing database or enter the name to create a new database.

Initialize Secondary Database | **Copy Files** | Restore Transaction Log |

Files are copied from the backup folder to a destination folder by a SQL Server Agent job running on the secondary server instance.

Destination folder for copied files: (This folder is usually located on the secondary server.)

`\\SQLVS01\Tlogs\Backups`

Note: you must grant read and write permission on this folder to the proxy account for the copy job (usually the SQL Server Agent service account on the secondary server instance).

Delete copied files after: `72` ⬍ `Hour(s)` ▼

Copy job

Job name: `LSCopy_SQLVS02_Scratch1`   Schedule...

Schedule: Occurs every day every 15 minute(s) between 12:00:00 AM and 11:59:00 PM. Schedule will be used starting on 7/11/2006.   ☐ Disable this job

Help   OK   Cancel

FIGURE 8-20   The Copy Files tab

and the log shipping option will not be available. You are not allowed to select a database that is already configured for log shipping.

Select the "Ship the transaction logs to other SQL Servers (Log Shipping)" check box. Continue through the wizard, specifying the rest of the database maintenance options, until you get to the Specify the Log Shipping Destinations dialog box. Click Add to add a destination database. In order for this option to be available, you must have selected to use log shipping earlier in the wizard.

The secondary database must be initialized by restoring a full backup of the primary database. The restore can be completed using either the NORECOVERY or STANDBY option. This can be done manually or through SQL Server Management Studio.

A log shipping configuration does not automatically fail over from the primary server to the secondary server. If the primary database becomes unavailable, any of the secondary databases can be brought online manually.

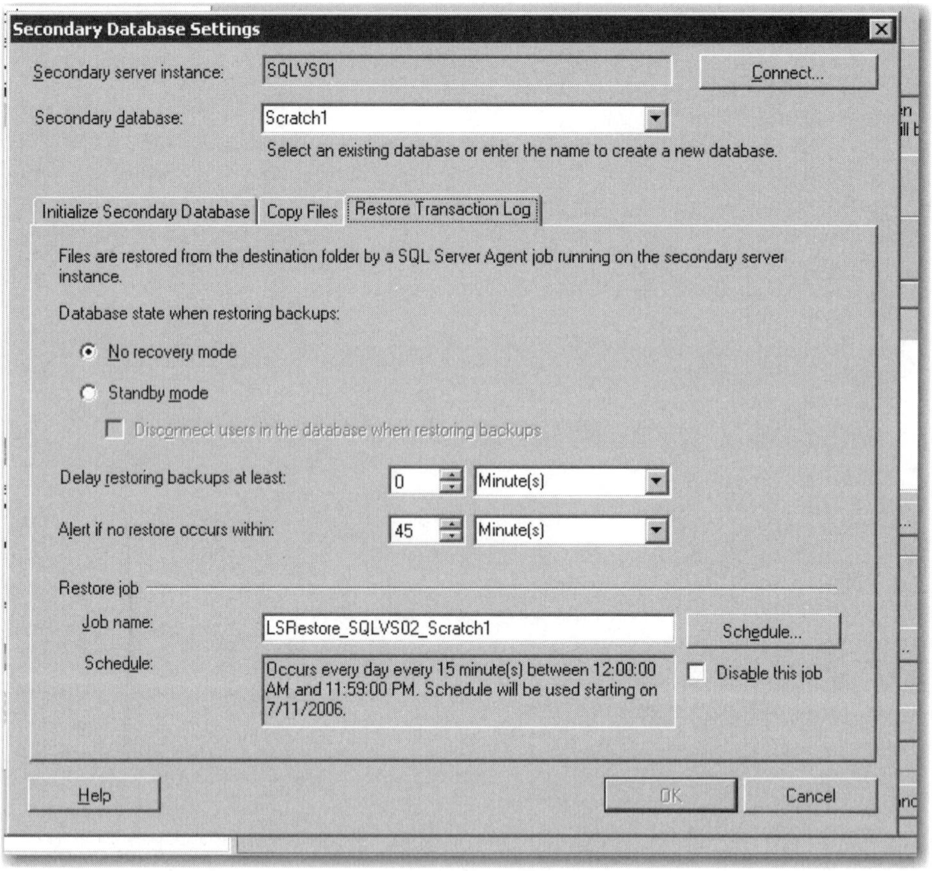

FIGURE 8-21   The Restore Transaction Log tab

The primary and secondary servers can be on the same computer; however, in this case, SQL Server fail-over clustering may provide better results (see Chapter 9 on the subject of fail-over clusters).

It may take a lot of effort to bring a secondary server online if you are recovering a large database and the production system has failed. To avoid the bottleneck, it is important that the configuration log ship and each transaction log be backed up as soon as it is created.

If, however, you need to assess the damage to a database on the primary server, say an accidental truncation of a table, you can delay applying transaction log backups to the secondary server. The delay gives you a chance to decide the best course of action, which may involve failing over to the secondary server or stopping log shipping until the crisis on the primary has been resolved. With a secondary server you also have the ability to recover a bad "call" on the primary server. For example, you can select data accidentally deleted on the primary server and reinsert it into the primary from the secondary, as long as you were able to stop the rolling forward of the log shipped data on the secondary in time to respond.

SQL Server Agent Log Shipping Jobs

Looking at your newly created log shipping configuration, you will see that SQL Server Agent has been assigned a number of jobs to maintain. These are as follows:

- **Backup Job**   This is the job that backs up the logs. The job is created on the source or primary server for each database to be log-shipped. This job executes the actual backup process, and stores backup history to the source and monitor servers. As demonstrated in the preceding chapter and Chapter 4, it can also be configured to perform maintenance work, such as deleting old backup files and history information. This job runs every two minutes by default, but you can change this.

- **Copy Job**   Copies the logs to the destination server. The copy job is created on the target or secondary server during the setup. The job retrieves the backup files from the source server to the destination on the target server (hence the need for an accessible share). It also pulls log history and gets the files over to the monitor server. You can customize the job schedule to suit the backup and maintenance plan on the source server.

- **Restore Job**   Performs the log restore on the target server. The restore job is automatically created on the target server instance for each log shipping configuration. The job also logs history on the local server and the monitor server, and it deletes old files and old history information. The SQL Server job category "Log Shipping Restore" is created on the secondary server instance when log shipping is enabled.

- **Alert Job**   Reports problems or events that arise in the process. If you decide to use a monitor server, then an alert job will be created on the monitor server instance. Both primary and secondary servers send history and status data to the monitor server. This alert job is shared by both the source and target servers, so any change you make to this job will affect all servers using the monitor server. If you do not use a monitor server, alert jobs are created locally on the source server instance and each target server instance. The alert job on the primary server instance raises errors when backup operations have not completed successfully within a specified threshold. The alert job on the secondary server instance raises errors when local copy and restore operations have not completed successfully within a specified threshold.

In the course of setup, you will be able to control how often the log backups are taken, how and when they are copied to each target, and how often the target servers apply the logs to their databases. So as not to have transaction logs growing out of control on the target servers, you should have the transactions copied to the targets and applied as often as a reasonable schedule will allow. Your network and bandwidth between the servers will obviously be a factor to consider.

On a given secondary server instance, the restore job can be scheduled as frequently as the copy job, or the restore job can delayed. Scheduling these jobs with the same frequency keeps the secondary database as closely aligned with the primary database as possible to create a warm standby database.

In contrast, delaying restore jobs, perhaps by several hours, can be useful in the event of a serious user error, such as a dropped table or inappropriately deleted table row. If the time of the error is known, you can move that secondary database forward to a time soon before the error. Then you can export the lost data and import it back into the primary database.

Mirroring

An alternative or complement (depending on the depth of your faith) to replication and log shipping for standby servers is database *mirroring*, which is new to SQL Server. It is available to SQL Server Standard and Enterprise Editions and works for databases configured for the full-recovery model (see Chapters 4, 6, and 7).

The model is straightforward. You simply mirror a database to another server, which acts as a "warm" standby. If the primary server fails, you can redirect your clients to the warm standby, where an identical copy of the database they just lost their connection to is available. The feature is a simple alternative to replication (which, as you learned earlier, can alter a database in ways that will not work for you), as well as to both fail-over clustering (especially over widely dispersed geographical locations) and log shipping. Database mirroring is also faster than replication or log shipping, which requires more effort to bring a fail-over online, and even more effort to fail back. In a mirror there is very little latency between the committal of a transaction on the source server and the target mirror. Thus a client can be quickly restored by connecting to the standby or fail-over server.

Database mirroring is not a new concept. In the example we will discuss here, one server is based in Florida and the mirror partner is based in California. Incidentally, the mirror functionality that now ships in SQL Server 2005 was added with the release of Service Pack 1 (SP1). As promised, we will also look at a third-party solution, Double-Take from Double-Take Software, Inc. However, the built-in option in SQL Server is free.

The mirror can be set up either synchronized or unsynchronized. When the mirror is synchronized, the solution supports rapid fail-over, which ensures that the last transaction to be committed or rolled back is synchronized with the target server. In other words, you will not experience data loss from committed transactions that get lost in the latency during a fail-over. If you do not synchronize, there is a possibility of data loss, which is proportional to the distance and network conditions between the source and target servers.

All your database servers are able to participate in multiple, concurrent database mirroring sessions, albeit only once per mirrored database. You can even configure a server to act exclusively as a partner or as a witness in all of its database mirroring sessions. A server instance can also act as a partner in some sessions and as a witness in other sessions. In this regard, mirror architecture is pretty flexible.

How SQL Server Mirroring Works

Two servers, the principal server and the mirror server, are set up as partners that share a mirroring session, each with its own role. The source server is known as the principal role, and the destination (stand-by) server is known as the mirror role.

Another way to look the roles is using the active-passive paradigm; in the mirror scenario we can have (at any given time) an active mirror and a passive mirror. This may be an easier concept to understand than referring to a principal mirror and a mirror role. Thus in a production environment, the principal or active mirror is the production database.

The actual mirror process is very simple. Unlike replication, which works at a logical level, replicating rows in each table, database mirroring actually sends every transaction from the active mirror to the passive mirror. The transactions are sent as log records, which the passive mirror simply applies to its copy of the database as if it initiated the transaction.

Synchronization implies that the passive mirror does not commit the transaction until it knows for sure the active mirror committed the transaction. The alternative is that the passive mirror gets the transaction and applies it without knowing the disposition of the transaction on the active mirror. The latter approach is faster because synchronization requires additional network traffic, I/O, and synchronous communication. However, asynchronous application of the transactions leaves the door open to the chance the mirrors will not be identical.

Fail-Over

Fail-over in the database mirror solution is a process known as "role switching." In other words, the roles of the mirror partner servers can be simply switched. The active mirror becomes the passive mirror (when it dies or is forced into that role), and the passive mirror takes over as the primary or principal server.

You can switch (or fail-back) the roles at any time after the former principal server is back online (and has its databases back online in a consistent state with the partner).

There are three possible roles in the database mirror solution:

- **Automatic fail-over**   Can be achieved with the high-safety mode setting and the presence of a witness server (discussed next).
- **Manual fail-over**   Can be achieved with the high-safety mode setting. The partners must be connected to each other, and the database must already be synchronized.
- **Forced fail-over**   Can be achieved with both high-performance mode and high-safety mode without automatic fail-over. The surviving server can seize the role of active mirror.

Witness Server

Okay, so let's go with the synchronous process. Not so fast. There is something else I did not yet tell you. The synchronous solution requires a third server instance, known as a "witness" server. This so-called witness server supports the fail-over process by verifying that the active server is up and functioning normally. So, just as in the log shipping options where you install a monitor server, here you need a witness server.

The passive server is also connected to the witness and seizes the passive role only if, while it is connected to the witness, the active server goes down. This may appear to be an elegant solution; however, it is not a cheap one. You now need to have three SQL Server instances up and running for a synchronous solution to work. And if the active mirror is an Enterprise Edition server, then the others in the "pod" need to be Enterprise Edition as well. In fact, you may be better off with a highly sophisticated mirror technology that replicates every byte on a volume (a solution we will also explore later in this chapter).

The Mirror Session

A database mirroring process, known as a mirroring session, begins as soon as the mirror database is ready and the server instances have been configured. The members of the mirror session all monitor the mirroring process and the state of the mirroring relationship between them.

Once the mirror starts, the target or recipient server will check the log sequence number (LSN) of the transaction log on the source servers and will begin to pull all subsequent transactions down to its instance. The source server immediately dispatches the transaction logs needed by the target, starting with the transaction after the last transaction sent to the server, if any. A queue is maintained between the partners so that unsent transactions that accumulated can be processed. Once the log is received, the target server writes it to disk before applying the transactions to the target database.

All the time during the mirroring session the source database remains available to clients. Upon each and every transaction made on the source server, it is sent directly to the recipient server. What transpires on the target or mirror server is a process that is identical to the log restore process described in Chapter 7, only the mirror process does the work automatically. The target server essentially repeats exactly what the source is doing with the transaction log. It rolls the database forward in the identical fashion, and it shrinks or truncates the transaction logs in the identical fashion. You basically have identical servers, one or more live and one or more ready to assume the role at any point in time.

If synchronization (or the so-called high-safety mode) is used, the source database confirms the new transactions as soon as the recipient has notified it the transactions have been saved to the target disk. Mirror synchronization is then achieved. If the target server for some reason cannot apply the transactions, the mirror server will pause the session and put the database into the SUSPENDED state. You can restart the session only when the failure has been resolved.

Creating a Mirror

You can use either Management Studio or a T-SQL script to configure database mirroring. Just like the script shown in the log shipping example earlier, a mirror script can be very time-consuming. If you use Management Studio, the interactive process automatically configures safety settings based on the mode you choose. Scripting is a little harder because you need to explicitly configure the safety of the transaction processing.

If the SAFETY option is set to FULL, the database mirroring operation is synchronous, after the initial synchronizing phase. If a witness is set in high-safety mode, the session supports automatic fail-over. If the SAFETY option is set to OFF, the database mirroring operation is asynchronous. The session runs in high-performance mode, and the WITNESS option should also be OFF.

Before a mirroring session can begin, the database owner or system administrator must create the mirror database, set up endpoints and logins, and in some cases, create and set up certificates. For a simple mirror configuration follow the tasks described here:

1. In the Database Properties dialog box (shown in Figure 8-22) click Configure Security. This action opens the Database Mirroring Security Wizard. This wizard will configure mirroring security on the principal mirror server, the target server in the mirror set, and the monitoring or witness server instance (if used). The first screen (after the initial information screen) lets you choose to configure the security on the witness server. Choose Yes and click Next.

2. The next option is a final confirmation (mainly for the Witness server). Accept the defaults shown in Figure 8-23 and click Next to advance.

3. The Principal Server Instance screen now loads, as shown in Figure 8-24. If you are configuring a database on the local server, the server instance option will be grayed out, as shown in Figure 8-24. You also need to provide a port number for the mirror communications to listen on. Here the default is 5022. The port you choose should be noted if you intend to mirror across a network (such as the Internet) that is

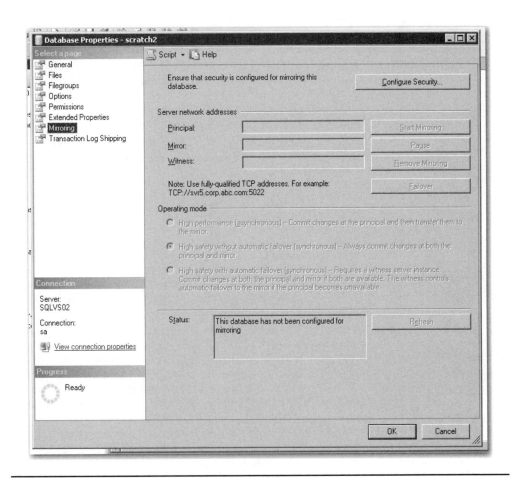

FIGURE 8-22 Database Properties, Database Mirroring page

routed and protected with firewalls. Also choose to encrypt the data stream by checking the "Encrypt data sent through this endpoint" option. The endpoint name defaults to "Mirroring," which you can change if you wish. Click Next to continue configuration.

4. The identical dialog box as shown in Figure 8-24 loads, only this time you need to choose and log in to the Mirror server instance. Note that SQL Server 2005 understands the Mirror server to be the remote instance that will receive the mirror stream for the source server, the principal server. Log in, choose the same port and encryption settings as in the preceding screen, and click Next to configure the Witness server. It too will have the same settings as the principal and mirror servers in terms of ports, names, and encryption. Click Next.

5. You are now ready to configure service accounts for the mirror partner servers. If you are using the same service accounts for all mirror partners and the Witness

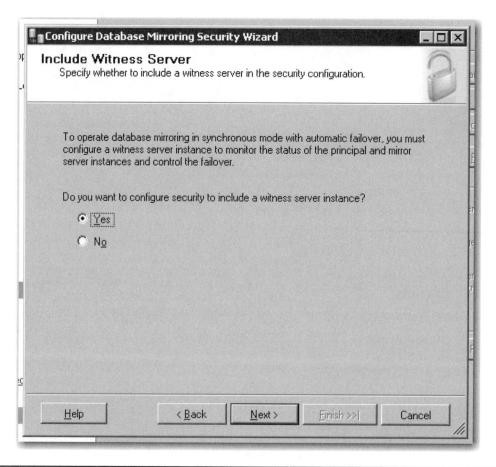

FIGURE 8-23   Confirming the architecture

server, you can simply leave the text boxes here blank, advance to the next screen, and click Finish. Once you click Finish, you will be given the option to start the mirror process. If databases are ready for mirror send and mirror receive, then simply click the Start Mirroring button. Otherwise, choose the alternative button to delay the mirror start. Before mirroring can start, a full copy of the source database must exist on the target server. This can be achieved by doing a full recovery backup and restore of the principal database to the remote server.

As mentioned earlier, you need to "seed" a mirror by at least taking a full database backup on the source or principal server. This means doing a backup of both the database and the transaction log and restoring both to the target server. It is critical to do this even if the remote database has already been attached and may be working as a production database. The quickest way to achieve the mirror partner database is to detach any target database that may conflict with the restore and then restore it as a new database.

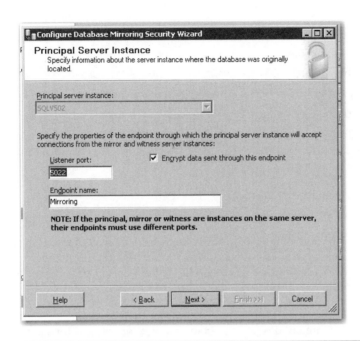

FIGURE 8-24   Configuring the Principal Server

If you install into an existing, attached database, you need to restore using the WITH NORECOVERY option. If, while you are seeding the mirror server, the principal server generates even more log backups, then these need to be applied as well, also using the WITH NORECOVERY option. Only after you apply the latest log backup can you start mirroring.

Resolving Mirror Errors

A host of network, operating system, or SQL Server issues can cause a database mirroring session to fail or not even get started. No matter at what stage your mirroring session, you need to be constantly vigilant for errors so that you can react in time to prevent a simple error from resulting in a complete stoppage of the mirror session.

There are two classes of error to consider in a mirroring session. The first, a "hard" error, occurs when a component anywhere in the system fails and renders database mirroring unable to continue. It will then report that a error has occurred. These components will report errors independent of mirroring, but mirroring will detect them and react accordingly. "Soft" errors occur when the mirroring subsystem detects that an error has occurred. Depending on how you set up to fail over, manually or automatically, if the database session is running in a high-safety mode with automatic fail-over and it is deemed synchronized, an automatic fail-over occurs.

Here are hard error causes that can interrupt the mirroring session:

- Bad network cable
- Bad network card
- Changes or failure in network topology (such as routers)
- Network services, such as DNS and Active Directory
- Firewalls devices and their configuration
- Endpoint configuration
- Network security
- Hard disk or server failure
- Operating system failure

SQL Server 2005 and its mirroring subsystems have no way of monitoring any of the preceding components or others. On a complex and mission-critical implementation you should not hesitate to configure a Microsoft Operations Server package for the SQL Server mirroring session.

Mirror Time-Out

So-called soft errors are not directly detectable by SQL Server, and thus if a soft error occurs, it could potentially cause the mirror session to wait indefinitely for a response. Thus database mirroring will time out a session if session "pings" are not responded to during fixed intervals.

As long as pings are sent and received according to the time-out settings, the mirror session will be deemed to be open and occurring. If a ping is not responded to, then the server will wait until the time-out before suspending the session. Once a ping is successfully received, the algorithm on the server instance resets its time-out counter on that connection.

Be aware that even if the target server is alive and replicating, it may still time out because of a bottleneck or an intermediate problem on the network. In this case the time-out value for a session may be too short for the normal responsiveness of either partner. This would produce a false failure. You thus need to factor this into your topology, especially over WAN communications.

Under the asynchronous nonmonitored session, the default time-out value is 10 seconds and cannot be changed. If you use synchronous or high safety with automatic fail-over, you can change the time-out period to suit the environment. You can change the time-out by using the ALTER DATABASE <database> SET PARTNER TIMEOUT <integer> statement (see Chapter 10).

Fail-Over

Failing over mirror partners is achieved in a process known as *role switching*. It is not unlike the role switching and seizing that you perform with an Active Directory role. To fail over from the principal server to the secondary, the secondary server takes over the principal role and brings its copy of the database online as the new principal database. If the former principal server is able to continue in the mirror relationship, it can become the new mirror database. You can fail the servers back to their original roles as needed. Role switching is actually the easy part of the mirroring paradigm. The hard part is redirecting the clients to the correct server instance, a subject we will tackle later in this section.

To provide automatic fail-over for a mirror solution, the session must have been configured under the high-safety mode, with a third, witness server monitoring the session. Before the fail-over can occur, the databases on both sides must be synchronized. The witness server must also be connected to the target server that will assume the principal role. The witness server verifies that the partners are up and functioning.

Manually failing over the server also requires high-safety mode. The partners must also be connected to each other, and their databases must already be synchronized. You can also force the fail-over under high-performance mode, but there is the risk of losing data as a result. You would force fail-over when the principal server has failed and is no longer connected to the mirror.

Restoring Connection to the Fail-Over Server

Failing over servers, no matter the technology—replication, mirrored servers, log shipping, or otherwise—requires work at the client or middle tier in terms of how connections to the principal or production database are achieved. Connection strings typically supply the name of the server instance where login can be achieved. A second name, known as the fail-over partner name, can be provided if the first connection attempt fails. The connection string must also supply a database name. This is necessary to enable fail-over attempts by the data access provider. Some other considerations to keep in mind follow.

Network Attribute

The connection string should contain the Network attribute to specify the network protocol. This ensures that the specified network protocol persists between connections to different partners. The best protocol for connecting to a mirrored database is TCP/IP. To ensure that the client requests TCP/IP for every connection to the partners, a connection string supplies the following attribute:

```
Network=dbmssocn;
```

See Chapter 5 for configuring the client protocol stack.

Server Attribute

The connection string must contain a Server attribute that supplies the initial partner name, which should identify the current principal server instance. The simplest way to identify the server instance is by specifying its name, <server_name>[\<SQL_Server_instance_name>]. For example,

```
Server=Partner_A Server=Partner_A\Instance_2;
```

However, when the system name is used, the client must perform a DNS lookup to obtain the IP address of the server and a SQL Server Browser query to obtain the port number of the server on which the partner resides. Those lookups and queries can be bypassed by specifying the IP address and port number of the partner in the Server attribute, rather than specifying the server name. This is recommended to minimize the possibility of external delays while connecting to that partner. A SQL Server Browser query is necessary if the connection string specifies the named instance name and not the port.

To specify the IP address and port, the Server attribute takes the following form, Server=<ip_address>,<port>, for example,

```
Server=123.34.45.56,4724;
```

The IP address can be IP Version 4 (IPv4) or IP Version 6 (IPv6).

Database Attribute

In addition, the connection string must specify the Database attribute to supply the name of the mirrored database. If the database is unavailable when the client attempts to connect, an exception is raised.

For example, to expressly connect to the AdventureWorks database on the principal server Partner_A, a client uses the following connection string:

```
" Server=Partner_A; Database=AdventureWorks "
```

Bundling the protocol prefix with the Server attribute (Server=tcp:<servername>) is incompatible with the Network attribute, and specifying the protocol in both places will likely result in an error. Therefore, we recommend that a connection string specify the protocol using the Network attribute and specify only the server name in the Server attribute ("Network=dbmssocn; Server=<servername>").

Failover Partner Attribute

In addition to the initial partner name, the client can also specify a fail-over partner name, which should identify the current mirror server instance. The fail-over partner is specified by the Failover Partner attribute. The simplest way to identify the server instance is by its system name, <server_name>[\<SQL_Server_instance_name>].

Alternatively, the IP address and port number can be supplied in the Failover Partner attribute. If the initial connection attempt fails during the first connection to the database, the attempt to connect to the fail-over partner will be freed from relying on DNS and SQL Server Browser. Once a connection is established, the fail-over partner name will be overwritten with the failed-over partner name, so if a fail-over occurs, the redirected connections will require DNS and SQL Server Browser. When only the initial partner name is provided, application developers do not need to take any action or write any code except about how to reconnect.

SQL Native Client verifies that it connects to a principal server instance but not whether this instance is the partner of server instance specified in the initial partner name of the connection string.

In Review

In this chapter we looked at replication in theory and introduced the three replication types available to SQL Server solutions: snapshot replication, transactional replication, and merge replication. We also investigated two additional forms of redundant and fail-over database solutions, log shipping and database mirroring.

Microsoft has gone to great lengths to build a database management system that is ideal for distributed database solutions and wide-area deployment on networks like the Internet. While its replication architecture is not new or revolutionary, it goes without saying that without replication, log shipping, and mirroring, none of the other features we discuss later in the book would be worth exploring for Internet applications. It is very unlikely today that anyone deploying SQL Server on the Internet or on a WAN would not be configuring for replication and fail-over, especially if the business is in the hurricane corridor in the southeast, tornado alley in the midwest, or the earthquake environs out in the west. Out of all the subjects a SQL Server DBA might have to master, none other might be as challenging and rewarding as setting up a distributed fully redundant network. To complete the fail-over scenario, let's now look at clustering.

CHAPTER

SQL Server 2005 High Availability

There are a number of dimensions that you need to keep in mind when considering investment and rollout of large or very busy systems: First, every system has its point of failure (POF). In the last chapter, we examined those points. It dealt with issues affecting storage, processors, memory—as well as the bottlenecks that can materialize at those points.

Second, performance and availability come at a price. Ergo, POF has meaning in monetary terms as well . . . the point at which the budget goes supernova. There is a point at which the cost consumes available funding and consumes all generated revenue from sales or investors.

Third, linear scalability, especially of processors, is a myth. There is a point at which throwing more processors at a system no longer has any advantage and may even begin to degrade performance. This is the point at which vertical scalability tapers off and horizontal scalability takes over, becoming not only desirable but also more reliable and less risky.

Fourth, there is no such thing as 100 percent availability of any single system. If there is one thing more certain to a good DBA or system administrator than death, taxes, and a headhunter around the next corner, it is that there will come a time when your server goes up in smoke. How you plan for that event is what's important. Some people run away from fires; others run for a bag of marshmallows. This brings us to a fifth dimension—manageability.

The more complex and delicate a system is to manage, the higher the cost of management and the higher the risk of system failure or loss. We have discussed a number of graphical tools in recent chapters, so we will not tackle more here, save for the interfaces for installing onto clusters, creating federations and partitions, and so on.

In this chapter, the largest for the most complex operational responsibility, we'll examine some availability theory, service level (SL), and availability and scalability solutions specific to SQL Server 2005. We will then wrap up the chapter with a step-by-step cluster exercise, as well as a recovering from a complete and utter disaster.

NOTE *One gigabyte (GB) = 1,024 megabytes (MB); one terabyte (TB) = 1,024 GB; one petabyte (PB) = 1,024 TB; one exabyte (EB) = 1,024 PB.*

Availability Management

Understanding availability management is an essential requirement for IS/IT in almost all companies today. Availability management practice involves the following efforts:

- **Problem detection**   This need requires IT to be constantly monitoring systems for advance warnings of system failure. You use whatever tools you can obtain to monitor systems and focus on all the possible points of failure. For example: You will need to monitor storage, networks, memory, processors, and power.

- **Performance monitoring**   The role supports service level by assuring that systems are able to service the business and keep systems operating at threshold points considered safely below bottleneck and failure levels.

- **Scaling up or out to meet demand**   This level keeps the business running by guaranteeing availability of critical systems in acceptable response times; that users are serviced quickly.

- **Redundancy**   Redundancy is the service-level practice of providing secondary offline and online (warm) replicas or mirrors of primary systems that can take over from a primary system (fail-over) with minimal (not longer than a few minutes) disruption of service to database users.

- **Administration**   The administration role ensures 24 × 7 operations and administrative housekeeping. The administrative role manages SL budget, hires and fires, maintains and reports on service-level achievement, and reports to management or the CEO.

Problem Detection

The problem detector (or detective) is the role that is usually carried out by the DBA-analyst who knows what to look for on a high-end, busy, or mission-critical DBMS environment. You need to know everything there is about the technology, the SQL Server platform, and the SQL Server availability and performance capabilities. For example, You need to know which databases are doing what, where they are placed, use of storage services, level of maintenance, and so on. You also need to be able to collect data from SQL Server, interpret it, and forecast needs. You need to know exactly when you need to expand storage needs. There is no reason in any type of situation to have users unable to use the database because the hard disks are full, or because memory is at the max, and so on.

I know that problem detection is a lot like tornado chasing (and a data center on a bad day with poor DR models in place can make the film *Twister* look like a Winnie-the-Pooh movie). But you need to get into the mode of chasing tornadoes before they happen because you can spend all of your time listening to the earth and looking up at the sky, and then whack! It comes when you least expect it and where you least expect it. Suddenly your 100-ton IBM NetFinity is flying out the window and there's no way to get it back. Might as well take a rope and a chair and lock your office door from the inside. According to research from the likes of Forrester, close to 40 percent of the IT management resources are spent on problem detection. With large SQL Server sites, some DBAs should be spending 110 percent of their time on problem detection and working with the tools and techniques described in the last chapter.

NOTE *There are several other SL-related areas that IT spends time on and that impact availability. These include change management and change control, software distribution, and systems management. Change management, or change control, is catered to by Active Directory and is beyond the scope of this book.*

The money spent on SQL Server DR gurus is money well spent. Often, a guru will restore a database that, had it stayed offline a few hours longer, would have taken the company off the Internet. So it goes without saying that you will save a lot of money and effort if you can obtain DBAs that are also qualified to monitor for performance and problems, and not just excel at recovery. Key to meeting the objective of ensuring SL and high availability is the acquisition of SL tools and technology. This is where Windows Server 2003 Server excels above many other platforms. While clustering and load balancing are included in Advanced Server and Datacenter Server, the performance and system monitoring tools and disaster recovery tools are available to all versions of the OS no matter where you install the DBMS.

Performance Management

Performance management aims to identify poor performance in areas such as networking, access times, transfer rates, and restore or recovery performance; it will point to problems that can be fixed before they turn into disasters. You need to be extremely diligent, and the extent of the management needs to be end-to-end because often a failure is caused by failures in another part of the system that you did notice. For example, if you get a massive flurry of transactions to a hard disk that does not let up until the hard disk crashes, is the hard disk at fault, or should you have been making plans to balance the load, or expand the disk array?

Scale-Up and Scale-Out Availability

In this area, you want to make sure that users do not find that they cannot connect to the database or that a Web page refresh takes forever because the database was choking, or that the server approaches meltdown because it is running out of memory, processor bandwidth, hard-disk space, or the like.

Availability, for the most part, is a post-operative factor. In other words, availability management covers redundancy, mirrored or duplexed systems, fail-overs, and so forth. Note that fail-over is emphasized because the term itself denotes taking over from a system that has failed.

Clustering of systems or load balancing, on the other hand, is also as much a disaster prevention measure as it is a performance-level maintenance practice. Using performance management, you would take systems to a performance point that is nearing threshold or maximum level; depending on your needs and guts, you may decide the failsafe level is 70 percent of system resources for each facility (I start topping when the gas meter shows a quarter tank).

At meltdown, your equipment should switch additional requests for service to other resources. A fail-over database server picks up the users and processes that were on a system that has just failed, and it is supposed to allow the workload to continue uninterrupted on the fail-over systems, although the users will have to reconnect.

But a fail-over is not only a server event. Other examples of fail-overs are mirrored disks, RAID-5 storage sets, and redundant controllers.

Understanding Scale-Up

How do you grow a system? The first thing that comes to the mind of most system administrators is to throw additional CPU bandwidth at the machine. In other words, if you are using a 3.00 GHz CPU and need more power, then add a bigger CPU. If the hardware, the motherboard, can take additional processors or support multiple processor cards that can be inserted into slots, then by all means add additional CPUs. After all, if the machine is performing poorly at, say, 300 MHz, bump it up another processor for an effective processor bandwidth of 600 MHz. Right? Wrong.

Unfortunately, no system (I don't care what operating system or hardware brand) improves linearly with the processors you add to it. In other words, if you double the number of processors, you would expect the throughput to double. This is called linear scale-up. You can also look at it another way. If you double the number of processors, you would expect response time to be cut in half (linear speed-up). But continuing linear scale-up cannot be sustained in practice because we live in a world governed by the laws of gravity, friction, inertia, and so on. One such law you would do well to understand is Amdahl's Law of Scalability.

In 1967, Gene Amdahl stated that the potential speedup to be obtained by applying multiple CPUs will be bounded by the program's "inherently sequential" computations. In other words, there are always going to be some segments in the program that have no alternative but to execute serially. Examples are reading input parameters, characters entered into the system by the serial machine known as a human being, or writing output to files. The time to execute such processes cannot be eliminated, even if it is possible to execute them in an infinitely small amount of time. In that sense, the upper bound on performance improvement is independent of the number of CPUs that can be applied.

In other words, the end result of the process cannot be achieved by any parallel computation. An example from the data processing world is the standard SQL query that can only derive a result set from the result set of a subquery. Obviously the two queries cannot happen in parallel. All we can do is ensure that the inner query happens as fast as possible on one processor while the outer query waits milliseconds behind it for the inner result set to compute.

In computer science or engineering terms, we can only squeeze out every drop of performance and bandwidth from our systems by increasing the percent of the processing that can be parallelized. This can be expressed in the following equation:

$$T_{N \, = \, T1(p)} \mid N \, + \, T_{1(1 \, - \, p)}$$

T_N is the computing time using N CPUs. T_1 is the computing time using 1 CPU, and p is the percent of the processors that can be parallelized. The linear speed-up limit as the number of processors (N) reaches infinity is $1 \, / \, 1 - p$. As p will always be below 100 percent, we will never be able to achieve perfect or constant scalability.

Despite the laws of physics that come to bear on our computer system, constant scale-up linearity of a system is also an impossible objective because a computer system is not the sum of its processor cycles. Just as the human brain cannot exist without the heart and nervous system, a computer system too comprises system buses, hard disks, speed of random access memory, the I/O capabilities of the operating system, and so on. These are all elements that we identified earlier as possible sources of bottlenecks in a system.

Database operations apply pressure to all areas of a computer system: the nature of the applications; the construction of queries; the condition (such as fragmentation) of files, of indexes, of filegroups; the use of hard disks; and the list can go on. This is the reason that it makes no sense to regard MIPS as any meaningful measure of relative database system performance. To sum it all up, there is substantially more to transaction processing than just the processor. Hence the advent of TPC testing, as discussed in Chapter 4, which even takes into account cost of systems, client access, and maintenance.

Arguing that one platform or product is better than another is also an exercise in futility because no one has achieved linear processor scalability. It is thus a myth and will be for a long time to come. Vendors such as IBM and Sun might spend millions trying to achieve the ultimate, but I consider it safe to say that 99.99 percent of businesses in the world do not have the budget or access to the technology that these vendors do for their public relations exercises.

Scaling Up: The Shared Memory Model and SMP

But now let's assume that your system has more than enough memory, that your hard disks are working perfectly, that your code is highly optimized, that no significant bottleneck can be identified on the system buses, and that only the processor is the bottleneck. You still need to improve system performance by increasing the number of threads and fibers executing concurrently, in parallel, and the smartest way to cater to the need is to add additional CPUs, as many as the system can take without impacting the collateral areas such as memory and hard-disk bandwidth.

This is known as symmetric multiprocessing, or SMP. You get vertical growth of the system's processing capability by adding more processors. The growth may at first continue in a straight line going up, but there will be a point that the various factors discussed earlier begin to pull the processing bandwidth or capacity down and the line starts to curve.

We call such an SMP system a shared memory system, one based on the shared memory model. Regardless of the number of CPUs in the system, there is only one contiguous memory space shared by all processors. The system runs a single copy of the operating system with the application executing oblivious to the additional processors. The DBMS software operates no differently on a single CPU; it just gets a lot more done because more tasks can be executed in parallel.

Shared memory SMP systems vary from operating system to operating system. In the server market, all vendors use the same or very similar processing architectures. We will not get into the differences between CISC and RISC and so on, because that discussion has little to offer in a book on SQL Server and the Microsoft operating systems.

Some operating systems scale better in the SMP arena than others; however, as mentioned earlier, the ability to add more processors or grow huge SMP systems, such as 96 CPUs, is not the only factor to consider, for these reasons:

- First in many cases is cost (boiled down to the $tpmC for want of a scale that has an expense factor). Once you begin to scale past eight processors, cost begins to escalate rapidly. Non-Intel platforms are known to rocket into the millions of dollars when the number of processors begins to climb into the high double-digits. A $12 million 64+ CPU system is beyond the budget of most companies. On the other hand, when compared to a legacy mid-range or mainframe system, 12 big ones might not be a lot of money.

- As SMP scales, so do the collateral systems components. A large SMP system will likely consume large amounts of memory. Storage is also another critical area. On a large SMP system, you will need huge arrays of hard disks, and the number of disks will explode as you configure for redundancy. Remember that RAID 5 requires three or more disks. Other areas that add to the costs include cooling systems, fans, duplexed controllers, redundant components, and so on.

- The parallelism achieved in multiple CPUs does not necessarily mean that all threads have equal and concurrent access to the shared resources. In fact, when you start going past the 12-CPU level, serialization in the accessing of resources can incur severe bottlenecks. In other words, you might have 32 CPUs going, but if all 32 threads operating in parallel need access to the same rows in a table, 31 of the threads have to watch their manners. All it takes is one transaction to lock the table for some time, and you have $11,999,000 of equipment standing idle for a few seconds. I am one CTO that would hate to have to explain what those seconds cost.

- Management becomes more costly. The more components you have in an SMP system, the higher the management and monitoring cost. With large arrays, multiple controllers and scores of CPUs, and miles more cabling come additional chances for bottlenecks.

- The single point of failure risk increases. Probably the most important factor detracting from a large SMP system is that the system is only as strong as its weakest link. If that breaks, whatever it might be, the system crashes and all 96 CPUs shut down . . . and a $12 million system goes south. Sure, you can fail over to another 96-CPU system; just throw another $12 million at the project.

However, probably the most unattractive aspect of the high-SMP systems and the shared memory model is that you get very little more for your money and effort. If large-SMP systems showed performance and processing power greater than any other system by an order of magnitude, there might be a case for them, but they don't. What model thus works best for SQL Server?

There is obviously a need to scale up a Windows Server 2003 and SQL Server 2005 system. Windows Server 2003 scales very well, far beyond the "sweet" point for a system. On a database management system, high transaction bandwidth or an extensive drill-down for analysis purposes works better when the application is able to spawn multiple concurrent threads across several CPUs. Parallelism has been engineered not only into the operating system but also into SQL Server.

The linear curve would show how you get a significant increase in performance for a given price when you go from one CPU to four CPUs, from four to eight, and from eight onward. For the most part, most of your money is spent in adding the additional CPUs. Hard disks, memory, controllers, and PCI buses—the same components the entire industry uses—are relatively inexpensive on a quad system. Even going to eight processors is relatively easy, and companies like HP are routinely building such systems. Going beyond eight is when things start to go awry—prices begin to rise sharply and returns begin to diminish.

For Windows Server 2003 and SQL Server 2005, we thus find that practical gains for the very high-end systems cap out at eight processors. Beyond that, it starts to make more sense to scale out, as discussed later in this chapter.

Scaling Up and Availability

When planning for high availability, you cannot simply grow a single machine and then place all your money in that one vertical system. All it takes is for a single point of failure to become a failure, and no matter how much the system costs, it is dead in the water. All mission-critical, 24 × 7, operations require some form of redundancy model that can ensure that, if a system goes, the enterprise does not come to a grinding halt.

There are several means of providing redundancy. The more effective the redundancy (the faster the fail-over capability), the higher the cost and the more complex the solution. On the budget scale, the cheapest fail-over system is an idle instance of SQL Server running on the same computer as the active one. The problem with this is that a hardware crash can take out the idle instance as well. Nevertheless, I will go into idle instance configuration later in this chapter.

Catering to hardware redundancy, the next cheapest fail-over is to have a warm standby server. The standby is a secondary server that will take over the connections for the primary if it fails. But there are some problems with such a scenario that make this model less than desirable in a mission-critical, 24 × 7 operation that cannot afford more than a few minutes offline.

Our next option, then, is to move to the shared-disk system model, which is catered to by the Microsoft Cluster Service (MSCS) that is available to the operating system of Windows Server 2003. The Cluster Service requires a single shareable disk array to be shared by at least two servers on Windows Server 2003 platforms; although it is possible to make a single-node virtual server with Windows Server 2003. All databases and log files that each instance of SQL Server requires are stored on the shared disk array. The array is usually a RAID-5 or RAID-10 storage unit. The two servers are connected together and communicate via a high-speed interconnect, known as the heartbeat.

The Cluster Service is an active/passive cluster, which means that one server stands idle and lets the active server take all the hits, at the hardware level (more about active/active later). The passive server waits until a fail-over event occurs from the Cluster Service and then takes over as the active server. The takeover event is known as the fail-over. The fail-over is automatic and does not require any operator intervention; however, it is not entirely seamless: clients will have to reconnect but service can be restored in under a minute in most situations. The databases are shared between the nodes on the shared storage unit, so there is no need to restore databases and transaction logs, a process that takes up considerable time.

I will not go too deeply into the actual Cluster Service here, but some background on how the Cluster Service works is a good idea.

SQL Server 2005 Scale-Up/Scale-Out

The SQL Server 2005 database engine is a fourth-generation robust server that can manage terabyte-sized databases accessed by thousands of users concurrently. Additionally, when running at its default settings, SQL Server 2005 has features such as dynamic self-tuning that let it work effectively on laptops and desktops without burdening users with administrative tasks. SQL Server 2005 on a hand-held device extends the SQL Server 2005 programming model to mobile Windows devices and is easily integrated into SQL Server 2005 environments.

SQL Server 2005 works with Windows Server 2003 fail-over clustering to support immediate fail-over to a backup server in continuous operation. SQL Server 2005 also introduces advances log shipping introduced with SQL Server 2005, which allows you to maintain a warm standby server in environments with lower availability requirements.

Scale-Out vs. Scale-Up with Microsoft SQL Server

DBAs tend to think "scale-up" before "scale-out" when database servers begin to show signs of stress. When server response time starts to degrade because of increased workload or larger databases, the usual reaction to the performance issue is to add bigger, faster, and more expensive hardware.

Hardware vendors currently double performance of their devices every 18 to 24 months, so it may seem that throwing hardware at the load problem is a solution, but there is point of diminishing return. There are also many associated problems with constant hardware upgrades. First, hardware does have its limitations. Given that hardware performance doubles every two years and you have the money to upgrade your hardware every two years, what do you do when you max out your new system after only 12 months? Do you just suffer with poor performance for the next year? That is probably not an option, especially after that expensive upgrade.

Even though hardware vendors are making eight-processor systems for the Intel platform, with gobs of RAM, as well as fiber-meshed, SAN-connected computers, the problem of scalability still exists. Sooner or later, you will have to wait for your hardware vendor of choice to release the next version of super-hardware to catch up with your desired performance counters. It gets more complicated: when a system reaches a certain point, further scaling up becomes so expensive that the cost is not worth the reward. Even beyond the hardware and compatibility issues, you'll probably encounter problems with software accessing the new hardware when you're trying to scale up past a certain point.

Scaling out, however, still requires you to add servers. But instead of bigger hardware you are simply adding more systems, which are pretty cheap, and getting cheaper. Scaling out solves the scale-up scenario for database servers. Here, the design is not share-everything architecture; it is share-nothing architecture. Essentially, share-nothing architecture means that each computer system of the cluster operates independently. Each system in the cluster maintains separate resources (CPU, memory, and disk storage that other systems cannot directly access).

Federated Database Servers

SQL Server 2005 improves on the support for updatable, distributed partitioned views. These views can be used to partition subsets of the rows in a table across a set of instances of SQL Server, while having each instance of SQL Server operate as if it had a full copy of the original table. These partitioned views can be used to spread the processing of one table across multiple instances of SQL Server, each on a separate server. By partitioning all or many of the tables in a database, you can use this feature to spread the database processing of a single Web site across multiple servers running SQL Server 2005. The servers do not form a cluster, because each server is administered separately from the others. Collections of such autonomous servers are called *federations of servers*. Federations of servers running SQL Server 2005 are capable of supporting the growth needs of the largest Web sites or enterprise database systems that exist today.

To improve the performance and scalability of federated servers, SQL Server 2005 supports high-speed system area networks such as GigaNet. (Distributed database architecture is the subject of Chapter 8.)

The Handling of Very Large Databases

SQL Server 2005 has high-speed optimizations that support very large database environments. SQL Server 2005 can effectively support terabyte-sized databases.

The T-SQL BACKUP and RESTORE statements are optimized to read through a database serially and write in parallel to multiple backup devices. Sites can also reduce the amount of data to be backed up by performing differential backups that back up only the data changed after the last backup, or by backing up individual files or file-groups. In SQL Server 2005, the time required to run a differential backup has been improved, making it proportional to the amount of data modified since the last backup.

Multiple bulk copy operations can be performed concurrently against a single table to speed data entry. The database console command utility statements are implemented with reduced locking requirements and support for parallel operations on computers with multiple processors, greatly improving their speed.

Operations that create multiple indexes on a table can create them concurrently.

Intra-Query Parallelism

When running on servers with multiple multiprocessors, or CPUs, SQL Server 2005 can build parallel execution plans that split the processing of a SQL statement into several parts. Each part can be run on a different CPU, and the complete result set can be built more quickly than if the different parts were executed serially.

Understanding the Microsoft Cluster Models

Microsoft technology offers several cluster models that are available to support SQL Server. They are as follows:

- **Model A**   High availability and static load balancing
- **Model B**   Hot spare solution with maximum availability
- **Model C**   Partial server cluster solution
- **Model D**   Virtual server only with no fail-over
- **Model E**   Hybrid solutions using the best of the previous models

Model A: High-Availability Solution and Static Load Balancing

Clustering SQL Server provides the ability to recover from resource failure immediately and provide seamless connectivity to your clients and client applications. The resources that can put your data tier in the dark upon failure can be physical, such as hardware, or logical such as a service failure. When resource failure is identified, the failed resource and any resources that are dependent on the failed resource are moved from the failed node.

Clustering is not limited to one fail-over server. Windows Server 2003 cluster support up to eight nodes. The clustering configurations can be a two-node cluster, such as one active server and one standby server waiting for something to fail on the active server, to as cluster solution as critical as eight nodes running their own services. As soon as a resource fails on one node, the next preferred node will be able to seize ownership of the resources and take over from the failed node, the so-called fail-over process. This is about as far as we need to go describing the actual clustering process on Windows Server 2003, as the Cluster Service itself is beyond the scope of this book.

Designing the SQL Server Cluster

Good planning is a vital ingredient of a SQL Server cluster (all clusters for that matter). But you need to have a clear understanding of what your solution needs and the applications that it supports is paramount. Let's discuss the particulars and some different configurations.

Documenting the Dependencies

You should first start with the physical disk as the first resource SQL Server depends on. Without physical disks in the system on which to install SQL Server, you cannot read any data and begin service. When a SQL Server virtual server fails over, you need to make sure that the first resource that is claimed by the new node is the disk; all clusters come into this world on a hard disk. The next resource in the order of priorities for continuing connectivity is the public network; next comes the network name (which depends on the network); and so on.

To make life easier for yourself, you should sketch or chart the resources and the sequence of the fail-overs. This will help you see what depends on what and what it needs to exist. Failing over the SQL Server virtual server before the network fails over does not make much sense.

Understanding SQL Server Active/Passive Configurations

Active/passive configurations require at least two nodes. One node does all the work. In other words, it processes all connections and serves data while the other node waits; it's the active partner. The passive node is actually a hot standby server. When a resource fails on the active node, the passive node gains ownership of all dependent resources and become the active partner.

An active/passive cluster configuration ensures that there will be minimal or zero performance degradation due to the failure on the node. As this also doubles the hardware costs (two identical servers), it is not always the most economical option.

A/A Configurations and Multiple Instances

An active/active SQL Server cluster configuration means that each participating node in the cluster is serving requests, but not as part of the same SQL Server instance. Active/active clusters may appear as if multiple servers are sharing the load of responding to client requests from multiple sources. This, however, is what load-balanced clusters do. An active/active SQL Server actually means that "multiple instances" of SQL Server are running on the nodes of the cluster; not that two nodes of the cluster are active over a single instance of the Master and the other system databases.

N+1 Configurations

N+1 configurations can the best of both worlds for clustering requirements. In an N+1 configuration the term N+1 refers to N nodes with an additional (+1) node running as a standby. This means in a failure scenario the (+1) virtual server takes ownership of the failed resource and any other dependent resource(s). This also means that you can receive more resource productivity out of your hardware and still have a hot standby node to be a dedicated resource in the event of resource failure. The cost is relative; if the application earns $50K a week, then you not only can afford this configuration, you require it.

In an N+1 configuration of four nodes, three of the nodes would be serving requests actively and one would be a hot standby partner that any node can fail to. Using N+1 configuration is more cost-effective that a traditional active/passive configuration because it is not a one-to-one active-to-passive ratio. You can support multiple instances of SQL Server, and in the event of a single node failure, performance would not be adversely affected. N+ 1 configuration also address the cost factor. Because an N+1 configuration has a standby node, it is more expensive, but it also doesn't have the one-to-one, active-to-passive, or functionally working–to–waiting for a failure ratio that active / passive configurations have. This makes it more cost effective than active/passive configurations. This also means that you must have at least three nodes for a true N+1 configuration.

In active/passive configurations all the instances of SQL Server are all owned by the same server. One node of the cluster owns all resources all the time. When resource failure occurs, all resources are transferred to the other node. In active/active configurations there are at least as many installed SQL Server instances as there are servers participating in the cluster, and so all of the clustered nodes are actively working and using their available resources. What are those resources?

For the default instance you will need

- A clustered host server (node)
- A SQL Server network name (this will be the Virtual SQL Server name using the Network Name resource)
- A SQL Server network IP address (it is not recommended that you use the public network for the heartbeat)
- Physical disk resources for the data and log files (best practice is to have these on separate disks to maximize performance)
- The SQL Server Service
- The SQL Server Agent Service
- The SQL Full Text Search Service

For any named instance you will need

- A clustered host server
- A SQL Server network name (this will be an instance name of SQL Server as "virtualservername\instance name")
- A SQL Server network IP address.

- Physical disk resources for the data and log files (best practice is to have these on separate disks to maximize performance)
- The SQL Server Service
- The SQL Server Agent Service
- The SQL Full Text Search Service

With multiple instance configurations each instance of SQL Server acts independently of the other. Each instance needs its own distinct set of resources. These instances only "interact" if and when multiple instances of SQL Server are owned by the same node. There are concepts to be understood and taken into consideration. The primary consideration is performance planning. Multiple instances require their own resources, and that takes careful planning and coordination. This involves all dependent resources, which are discussed in the next sections.

Standby Services: Advantages and Disadvantages

There are definite advantages and disadvantages to clustering standby services. Some are obvious, and some are not. Some of the items that we will review can be an advantage or a disadvantage, depending on the perspective (IT staff vs. Accounting) from which you are viewing these items.

High availability is the single most important factor when weighing advantages and disadvantages of clustering for an administrator. While most DBAs think performance is at the top of the list, performance problems cannot be easily addressed without considering a cluster. Using standby services, that is, services and resources that are not actively being used and are waiting for failure to occur, is most often a decision based on the availability of funding. Your business' high-availability goals can be achieved through a clustering solution that does not have standby services.

Multiple instance or active/active clustering is the most predominant form for a solution like this. The performance of your application(s) from the database perspective is where the decision to use or not use standby services is made. If standby services are not used and a multiple instance architecture is used, there are no available unused resources in the event of failure. The failed burden of the load is dispersed across the rest of the node(s) of the cluster. In our instance all resources for multiple installations of SQL Server are now owned and managed by a single server.

What if the load is too much for a single server to bear? The application may time out, report errors to end users, fail to serve requests, even crash the server completely. That is when my worst two enemies show up, data corruption and unpredictable results. Is your application still truly highly available? In the event of a disaster, can one server truly hold the entire load? The costs for hardware, software licensing, and a paid administrator are not small. Have you ever calculated the cost of one hour of downtime? Twelve hours? Twenty-four hours? In some scenarios, more than a few minutes and the company is facing a real loss, and the challenge of finding a new administrator.

Advantages of standby services are abundant. Most notable is the ability to be redundant. Resilience to recover from resource failure. In the event of failure of a single node, there will be no performance degradation because a twin of the failed system is available to serve requests at a moment's notice. Another advantage to standby services is the ability to continually provide services and stay up to date with Windows and security updates.

Load Balancing

Load balancing is a challenging feat in environments where the difficulties of managing multiple instances threaten the uptime of a server. With standby services each node of a cluster can own the resource pools as the opposite node(s) are brought up to date and rebooted if necessary. This configuration results in a greater amount of total uptime for connected clients and processes.

This model offers a high-availability solution and an acceptable level of performance when only one node is online. However, you can also attain a high performance level when both nodes are kept online, meaning they are both serving clients. The model has been designed to allow for maximum utilization of hardware resources.

In this model, you can create a virtual server on each node, which makes its own set of resources available to the network. A virtual server can be detected as the usual server and accessed by clients as any other server. Capacity is configured for each node to allow the resources on each node to run at optimum performance. You would aim, however, to configure the resources in such a way as to ensure that if one node went south, the other node would be able to temporarily take on the burden of running the resources from the other, potentially catering to a huge surge in connections and access to resources. Usually all the client services remain available during the fail-over; only performance suffers because one server is now performing the job of two.

This model is useful for the high availability needs of file-sharing and print-spooling services. For example, two file and print shares are established as separate groups, one on each server. If one goes to hell, the other inherits the estate and takes on the file-sharing and print-spooling jobs of the deceased server. When you configure the fail-over policy, you will usually ensure that the temporarily relocated group is set to prefer its original server. In other words, when the failed server rises from the grave, the displaced group returns to the control of its preferred server. Operations resume again at normal performance. Client will notice only a minor interruption. This model can be summarized as follows:

- **Availability**   High
- **Suggested fail-over policies**   Assign a preferred server to each group
- **Suggested fail-back parameters**   Allow fail-back for all groups to the preferred server

Business Scenarios

Using Model A you can solve two problems that typically occur in a large computing environment:

- First, a problem will occur when a single server is running multiple large applications, which can cause a degradation in performance. To solve the problem, you would cluster a second server with the first. Applications are split across the servers, both active service clients.

- Second, the problem of availability arises when the two servers are not connected. But by placing them in a cluster, you assure greater availability of both applications for the client.

Consider a corporate intranet that relies on a database server supporting two large database applications. The databases are used by hundreds of users who repeatedly connect to the database from sunrise to sundown. During peak connect times, however, the server cannot keep up with the demand on performance.

A solution would be to install a second server, form a cluster, and balance the load. We now have two servers, and each one is running and supports a database application. When one server goes down, we would be back to our original problem, but only for as long as it takes to bring the server back online. Once the failed server is recovered, we fail back and restore the load-balanced operations.

Another scenario might involve a retail business that relies on two separate servers. For example, one of them supports Internet Web services, and the other provides a database for inventory, ordering information, financials, and accounting. Both are critical to the business because without the Web access, customers cannot browse the catalog and place the orders. And without access to the database accounting applications, the orders cannot be completed and the staff cannot access inventory or make shipping arrangements.

One solution to ensure the availability of all services would be to join the computers into a cluster. This is a similar solution to the one formerly discussed, but with a few differences. First we would create a cluster that contains two groups, one on each node. The one group contains all resources that we need to run the Web-service applications, such as IP addresses and pooled business logic. The other group contains all of the resources for the database application, including the database itself.

In the fail-over policies of each group would specify that both groups can run on either node, thereby assuring their availability should one of the nodes fail.

Model B: The "Hot Spare"

Under this model we obtain maximum availability and performance, but we will have an investment in hardware and software that is mostly idle. The hot spare is therefore a redundant server. No load balancing is put in place here, and all applications and services serve the client on the hot active server, called the *primary node.* The secondary node is a dedicated "hot spare," which must always be kept ready to be used whenever a fail-over occurs. If the primary node fails, the "hot spare" node will immediately detect the failure and pick up all operations from the primary. To continue to service clients at a rate of performance that is close or equal to that of the primary node, it must be configured almost identically to the primary. For all intents and purposes the two servers, primary and secondary, are like peas in a pod.

This model is ideal for critical database and Web server applications and resources. We can use this model to provide a "hot spare" database node for all servers dedicated to supporting Web access to our databases, such as those servers running Internet Information Services. The expense of doubling the hardware is justified by the protection of clients' access to the data. If one of your servers fails, a secondary server takes over and allows clients to continue to obtain access to the data. Such configurations place the databases on a shared cluster. In other words the primary and secondary servers allow access to the same databases. This model provides the following benefits:

- **Availability**   Very high, redundant service.
- **Suggested fail-over policies**   Usually we would configure identical twin servers if the budget allowed it and we would not need a preferred server to fail back from in the event of a disaster. If money is an issue and you are forced to make one server Arnold Schwarzenegger and the other Danny DeVito, then the Arnold becomes the preferred server for any of the groups. When one node has greater capacity than the other, setting the group fail-over policies to prefer the more powerful server ensures performance remains as high as possible.
- **Suggested fail-back parameters**   As just discussed, if the secondary node has identical capacity to the primary node, you can prevent fail-back for all of the groups. But if the secondary node has less capacity than the primary node, you should set the policy for immediate fail-back or for fail-back at a specified off-peak hour.

Model C: The Partial Cluster

This model caters to the applications that cannot fail over on the same servers from which resource groups are set to fail over. First we need to configure applications that will not fail over when the server goes down. The applications can be installed on the server or servers that form part of the cluster, but they cannot use the shared disk array on the shared bus. These applications have the usual availability; if the server goes down, the application goes down too. Such applications would not be considered critical; otherwise, they would have to access the shared disk array and be installed on both servers.

A database application that might not be too critical to exclude from the fail-over could be the accounting database that only gets updated by a front-line system once a day. Accounting staff might lose access to the application for an hour or two, which might be acceptable if they spend part of their day munching on corn chips.

When the server failure occurs, the applications that are not configured with fail-over policies are unavailable and they will remain unavailable until the node on which they are installed is restored. They will most likely have to be restarted manually or, as services, set to automatically start them when the operating system starts. The applications you configured with fail-over policies fail over as usual, or according to those policies you set for them. This model provides the following benefits:

- **Availability**   High for applications configured for fail-over; normal for others
- **Suggested fail-over policies**   Variable
- **Suggested fail-back parameters**   Variable

Model D: Virtual Server Only with No Fail-Over

Here we would use the virtual server concept with applications on a single-node server cluster. In other words, this cluster model makes no use of fail-over. You could also call it the cluster that wasn't. It is merely a means of organizing the resources on a server for administrative convenience and for the convenience of your clients. So what's the big deal? Well, the main deal is that both administrators and clients can readily see descriptively named virtual servers on the network rather than navigating a list of actual servers to find the shares they need. There are also other advantages as follows:

- The Cluster Service automatically restarts the various groups of applications and their dependent resources after the server is restored after a crash. Applications that do not have mechanisms for automatic restart can benefit from the Cluster Service's automatic restart features.

- It is also possible to cluster the node with a second node at a future time, and the resource groups are already in place. All you need to do is configure fail-over policies for the groups and leave the virtual servers ready to operate. Often a full-blown fail-over cluster is reduced to a partial cluster because the primary or secondary node goes down hard and requires a few days or longer to repair.

This model lets you locate all your organization's file resources on a single server, establishing separate groups for each department. Then when clients from one department need to connect to the appropriate share-point, they can find the share as easily as they would find an actual computer.

- **Availability**   Normal
- **Suggested fail-over policies**   Not applicable
- **Suggested fail-back parameters**   Not applicable

Model E: The Hybrid Solution

As the model name suggests, Model E is a hybrid of the former models just discussed. By using the hybrid solution model, you can incorporate advantages of the previous models and combine them in one cluster. By providing sufficient capacity, you can configure several types of fail-over scenarios to coexist on the same two nodes. All fail-over activity occurs as normal, according to the policies you set up.

For administrative convenience, two file-and-print shares in a cluster (which do not require fail-over ability) are grouped logically by department and configured as virtual servers. An application that cannot fail over resides on one of the clusters and operates as normal without any fail-over protection.

- **Availability**   High or very high for resources set to fail over with other resources not configured to fail over.
- **Suggested fail-over policy**   Variable

Limitations of Server Clusters

Microsoft has published the following important limitations of Windows Server 2003 clusters:

- **Remote storage**   These should not be installed on a shared SCSI bus used by the cluster, and you should not configure remote storage devices as cluster resources.

- **Disk configuration**   External disks cannot be configured as dynamic disks or spanned volumes (volume sets) if they are to be used as cluster resources. The disks to be used for cluster storage must be configured as basic disks and must be formatted using the NTFS file system. They can be configured in hardware RAID configurations in a shared cluster array cabinet or storage unit. Windows Server 2003 does not support the use of dynamic disks or the features of dynamic disks, such as spanned volumes (volume sets), for cluster storage. You also cannot change an existing cluster disk, such as the quorum disk, to a dynamic disk.

- **File System**   The Encrypting File System, Remote Storage, mounted volumes, or parse points are not supported on cluster storage configurations.

- **RAID**   You cannot enable a write cache on an internal SCSI RAID controller, nor would you want to for a database application, because the data in the cache will be lost during fail-over. An example of an internal controller is a Peripheral Component Interconnect (PCI) card inside the node. You should enable a write cache on an external RAID controller. An external RAID controller is usually inside the disk cabinet, and the data in the cache will fail over. You cannot use software RAID. You can use hardware RAID to protect the data on your cluster disk as mentioned earlier.

- **Network configuration**   The Cluster Service only supports TCP/IP, and a single IP address is configured in it. All network interfaces used on all nodes in a server cluster must be on the same network. The cluster nodes must have at least one subnet in common.

- **Terminal Services**   You can use Terminal Services for remote administration on a server cluster node, but you cannot use Terminal Services for an application server on a server cluster node. If you require load balancing or high availability in a Terminal Service/Application Server environment you will have to acquire separate technology from Citrix Systems, Inc., the Microsoft Terminal Service partner.

SQL Server 2005 Server Clustering

Now that you have had a crash course in clustering, it is time to look at a SQL Server cluster that is a group of Window Server 2003 servers—nodes—that are grouped together and appear as a single system to clients. As for the Windows Server 2003 operating system, the base operating system must be either Windows Server 2003 Enterprise or Datacenter Server. The clustering also appears to administrators as a single system, rather than separate computers, no matter what server they are actively managing.

Besides the SQL Server binaries, a server cluster runs two separate groups of software to support cluster-aware applications. There is the group that runs the cluster, called the clustering software, and the group used to administer the cluster, which is the administrative software.

Clustering Software

The clustering software allows the nodes to communicate with each other over a high-speed interconnect network that runs between the nodes, which is also known as the "heartbeat" connection. The network between the nodes is a dedicated high-speed network that is in no way connected to the local area network. It is specifically dedicated to the messages that travel between the nodes. The messages that travel across the interconnect network trigger the transfer of resources upon a fail-over event, such as the shutdown of a service on one end of the disaster scale and the crash of the entire server on the other end.

The Cluster Service also includes software called the Resource Monitor. The Resource Monitor manages the communication between the Cluster Service and application resources. The Cluster Service runs under the control of the Service Control Manager on each node in the cluster. Its role is to control the activity, the intercommunications between the nodes, and the failure procedures.

The Cluster Service takes control of disaster on two fronts. First, if SQL Server on the active node fails, this signals the Cluster Service to try to restart SQL Server. If the SQL Server cannot restart or the failure is more severe, the Cluster Service will fail over to one of remaining nodes in the cluster and force the new node to become the primary server, or the active node.

The Administrative Software

As an operating system administrator, you use the cluster management software to configure, control, monitor, and maintain the cluster nodes. Windows Server 2003 includes the Cluster Administrator software for cluster administration. The software is installed when you add the Cluster Server components to the node. The Cluster Service can also be administered from the command line using the cluster command.

Understanding and knowing how to work with the Cluster Service in Windows Server 2003 is not necessarily something the DBA needs to do. But administration of Windows Server 2003 is a prerequisite course for Microsoft DBA certification and includes cluster administration.

When configuring clustering, you cluster resources into functional units, called *groups*. The groups are then assigned to individual nodes. If a node freaks out, the Cluster Service will transfer the groups that were being hosted by the dead node to the other nodes in the cluster. This is essentially the definition of fail-over. There a reverse process known as fail-back. When fail-back takes place, the failed node becomes active again. The groups that were failed over to other nodes are then transferred back to the primary node.

SQL Server 2005 Enterprise Edition and SQL Server 2005 fail-over clustering provide high-availability support. As described earlier in the discussion on fail-over or cluster models you can configure a SQL Server cluster to fail-over to a secondary node if the primary fails. This lets you minimize system downtime, and thus provide high server availability.

There are specific installation steps and configurations that must be followed to use fail-over clustering:

- First you need to specify multiple IP addresses for each virtual server that you create. SQL Server 2005 lets you to use the available network IP subnets, which provides alternate ways to connect to the server if one subnet fails. This also results in increased network scalability. On a single network adapter, for example, a network failure can disrupt operations because clients will not be able to connect to their databases. But with multiple network cards in the server, each network can be sitting on a different IP subnet. Thus, if one subnet fails, another can continue to function and provide service to the clients. Even if a router fails, MSCS can continue to function, and all IP addresses will still work. But if the network card on the local computer fails, well then, you have a problem. It is also common practice to place a redundant network card in the server and have it on standby in the event the primary card fails.

- Next you need to administer a fail-over cluster from any node in the clustered SQL Server configuration. To set up the Cluster Service, you must be working from the node in control of the cluster disk resource. This computer is often referred to the node that owns the disk resource, a shared array of SCSI disks, usually in RAID-5 configuration.

- You must also allow one virtual server to fail over to any other node on the fail-over cluster configuration. And you must be able to add or remove nodes from the fail-over cluster configuration using the setup program.

- The setup program will allow you to reinstall or rebuild a virtual server on any node in the fail-over cluster without affecting the other nodes.

- To perform full-text queries by using Microsoft Search service with fail-over, clustering also needs to be specifically configured.

Fail-over clustering also supports multiple instances. You will find that multiple instance support makes it easier to build, install, and configure virtual servers in a fail-over cluster. Your applications can easily connect to each instance on a single server just as they connect to instances of SQL Server running on multiple computers with no fancy clustering in place.

With multiple instance support, you can isolate work environments. For example, you can isolate development systems and testing systems from production systems or volatile application environments. You can also provide a different system administrator for each instance of SQL Server residing on the same server.

Modeling the Multinode Cluster

Before you install a SQL Server 2005 fail-over cluster, you must select the hardware and the operating system on which SQL Server 2005 will run. You must also configure Microsoft Cluster Service (MSCS), and review network, security, and considerations for other software that will run on your fail-over cluster. Before you begin the fail-over cluster installation process, review the items that follow.

Verify Your Hardware Solution

Your hardware must be listed on the Microsoft Windows Catalog and Hardware Compatibility list. The hardware system must appear under the category of a cluster solution.

NOTE *Individual cluster components added together do not constitute an approved system for fail-over clustering. Only systems purchased as a cluster solution and listed in the cluster group are approved. When checking the Microsoft Windows Server Catalog and Windows Hardware Compatibility List, specify "cluster" as the category. All other categories are for OEM use. For more information, see the Microsoft support policy for server clusters, the Hardware Compatibility List, and the Windows Server Catalog.*

Special hardware compatibility testing is necessary when implementing a fail-over server cluster on a storage area network (SAN). The entire hardware solution must be in the Cluster/Multi-cluster Device category of the Microsoft Windows Catalog and Hardware Compatibility List. For more information, see the Microsoft Knowledge Base for hardware compatibility and support for multiple clusters attached to the same SAN device.

If the cluster solution includes geographically dispersed cluster nodes, additional items like network latency and shared disk support must be verified. The entire solution must be on the Geographic Cluster Hardware Compatibility List. For more information, see the Microsoft Knowledge Base article "Windows Clustering and Geographically Separate Sites."

SAN configurations are also supported on Windows Server 2003. The Microsoft Windows Catalog and Hardware Compatibility List category "Cluster/Multi-cluster Device" lists the set of SAN-capable storage devices that have been tested and are supported as SAN storage units with multiple MSCS clusters attached. By matching the devices on this list with the complete cluster configurations defined in the Microsoft Windows Catalog and Hardware Compatibility List cluster category, it is possible to deploy a set of Windows servers and clusters on a SAN fabric with shared storage devices in a way that is supported by Microsoft.

Consider quorum disk resource sharing. In a server cluster, the quorum disk contains a master copy of the server cluster configuration and is also used as a tie-breaker if all network communication fails between cluster nodes. Depending on the type of server cluster you implement, the quorum disk may or may not be a physical disk on the shared cluster disk array. Although it is best to reserve an entire cluster disk for use as the quorum disk, resources other than the quorum resource may be permitted to access the quorum disk.

However, making the quorum resource share the same disk with other resources forces you to choose between two undesirable alternatives. Either you must configure the resource so that its failure does not affect the group, or you must allow the group to be affected by the other resource's failures. In the first case, you lose fail-over support for the resource; in the second, the quorum resource fails over along with the rest of the group that contains both the quorum resource and the failed resource. As a result, the entire cluster is offline for as long as it takes the group to fail over.

Verify Your Operating System Settings

Make sure that your operating system is installed properly and designed to support fail-over clustering.

Enable Windows Cryptographic Service Provider (CSP) on Windows Server 2003. If the CSP service is stopped or disabled on any cluster node, SQL Server Setup will fail with a Windows Logo Requirement dialog.

Enable the Task Scheduler service on all operating systems. If the Task Scheduler is stopped or disabled, SQL Server Setup will fail with Error 1058. For more information, see "How to: Enable Windows Task Scheduler Service in SQL Server Books Online."

SQL Server 2005 supports mount points; the clustered installations of SQL Server are limited to the number of available drive letters. Assuming that you use only one drive letter for the operating system, and all other drive letters are available as normal cluster drives or cluster drives hosting mount points, you will be limited to a maximum of 25 instances of SQL Server per server.

A mounted volume, or mount point, allows you to use a single drive letter to refer to many disks or volumes. If you have a drive letter, D:, that refers to a regular disk or volume, you can connect or "mount" additional disks or volumes as directories under drive letter D: without the additional disks or volumes requiring drive letters of their own.

Special Mount Point Considerations for SQL Server 2005 Fail-Over Clustering

The base drive, the one with the drive letter, cannot be shared among virtual servers. This is a normal restriction for virtual servers, but is not a restriction on stand-alone, multiinstance servers.

Take extra care when setting up your virtual server to ensure that both the base drive and the mounted disks or volumes are all listed as resources in the resource group. SQL Server Setup will not take care of this automatically, nor will SQL Server check for this during CREATE/ALTER DATABASE.

Ensure that the mounted disks or volumes are mounted under the correct lettered base drive.

Configure Microsoft Cluster Server

The Microsoft Cluster Server must be configured on at least one node of the cluster. MSCS is only supported if it is installed on a hardware configuration that has been tested for compatibility with the MSCS software. You will know soon enough if you can cluster your systems, as the cluster setup process does this check for you.

The MSCS must also be able to verify that the virtual server is running by using the IsAlive thread. This requires connecting to the server using a trusted connection. You must ensure that the account that runs the Cluster Service is configured as an administrator on all nodes in the cluster, and that the BUILTIN\Administrators group has permission to log in to SQL Server. These permissions are set by default, so these settings will change only if you change permissions on the cluster nodes.

If the BUILTIN\Administrators account is removed, ensure that the account that the Cluster Service is running under can log in to SQL Server for the IsAlive check. If it cannot, the IsAlive check will fail. The MSCS Cluster Service account must have sysadmin rights to SQL Server. These are configured automatically by the SQL Server setup process.

Other Software Considerations

Before installing SQL Server 2005 on a fail-over cluster, install and configure the Microsoft Distributed Transaction Coordinator (MS DTC). SQL Server 2005 requires MS DTC in the cluster for distributed queries and two-phase commit transactions, as well as for some replication functionality.

After you install the operating system and configure the base cluster, install and cluster the MSDTC as a cluster resource in its own group. This help ensure availability between multiple clustered applications (such as Microsoft Exchange, which also depends on the MS DTC resource).

Disk drive letters for the cluster-capable disks must be the same on all nodes to which the service can fail over. Ensure that all cluster nodes are configured identically, including COM+, disk drive letters, and users in the administrators group.

Verify that you have cleared the system logs in all nodes and viewed the system logs again. Ensure that the logs are free of any error messages before continuing.

If you install SQL Server 2005 into a Windows Server 2003 cluster group with multiple disk drives and choose to place your data on one of the drives, the SQL Server resource will be set to be dependent only on that drive. To put data or logs on another disk or use additional disk resources, you must first add a dependency to the SQL Server resource for the additional disk.

Network Considerations

To ensure that all clients can find your virtual server name, your MSCS solution should include use of a WINS server for NetBIOS resolution. WINS of course is not necessary if your clients are fully Active Directory and DNS integrated.

Verify that you have disabled NetBIOS for all private network cards before beginning SQL Server Setup.

The network name and IP address of your SQL server should not be used for any other purpose, such as file sharing. If you want to create a file share resource, use a different, unique network name and IP address for the resource.

SQL Server 2005 supports both named pipes and TCP/IP sockets over TCP/IP within a cluster. However, it is strongly recommended that you use TCP/IP sockets in a clustered configuration.

To create a fail-over cluster, you must be a local administrator with the "Log on as a service" permission, and to act as part of the operating system on all nodes of the virtual server. SQL Server fail-over clustering is not supported on domain controllers.

CAUTION *Before using fail-over clustering, you should consider that the fail-over clustering resources, including the IP addresses and network names, must be used only when you are running an instance of SQL Server 2005. You must not use the services for other purposes, such as file sharing (which should be done on a separate file server cluster).*

To create a SQL Server 2005 fail-over cluster, your first step is to create and configure the virtual servers on which the fail-over cluster will run. The virtual servers are created during SQL Server setup and are not provided by Microsoft Windows Server 2003.

The virtual server you will set up will include the following factors:

- You must have a combination of one or more disks in a Microsoft Cluster Service (MSCS) cluster group. Each MSCS cluster group must contain at least one virtual SQL Server server.

- There must be a network name for each virtual server. This network name is the virtual server name.

- There must be one or more IP addresses that are used to connect to each virtual server.

- There must be one instance of SQL Server 2005, including a SQL Server resource, a SQL Server Agent resource, and a full-text resource.

NOTE *If an administrator removes an the instance of SQL Server 2005 on a virtual server, then the virtual server, including all IP addresses and the network name, will also be removed from the cluster group.*

A fail-over cluster can be installed on one or more Windows Server 2003 Enterprise Server machines or the Windows Server 2003 Datacenter Server servers that are participating nodes of the cluster. A SQL Server virtual server, however, always appears on the network as a single Windows Server 2003 server.

Naming a Virtual Server

SQL Server 2005 relies on the existence of certain registry keys and service names within the fail-over cluster to allow operations to continue correctly after a fail-over. This means that the name you provide for the instance of SQL Server 2005, which includes the default instance, must be unique across all nodes in the fail-over cluster, as well as across all virtual servers within the fail-over cluster. In other words, if all instances failed over to a single server, their service names and registry keys would conflict. If INSTANCE1 is a named instance on virtual server VIRTSRVR1, there cannot be a named instance INSTANCE1 on any node in the fail-over cluster, either as part of a fail-over cluster configuration or as a stand-alone installation.

You must also use the VIRTUAL_SERVER\Instance-name string to connect to a clustered instance of SQL Server 2005 running on a virtual server. You cannot access the instance of SQL Server 2005 by using the computer name that the clustered instance happens to reside on at any given time. You should also understand that SQL Server 2005 does not listen on the IP address of the local servers. It listens only on the clustered IP addresses created during the setup of a virtual server for SQL Server 2005.

If you are using the Windows Server 2003 Address Windowing Extensions (AWE) API to take advantage of memory greater than 3 gigabytes (GB), then you need to make certain that the maximum available memory you configure on one instance of SQL Server will still be available after you fail over to another node. This is important because if the fail-over node has less physical memory than the original node, the new instances of SQL Server may fail to start or may start with less memory than they had on the original node. In any event, you should give each server in the cluster the same amount of physical RAM. Also ensure that the summed value of the *max server memory* settings for all instances are less than the lowest amount of physical RAM available on any of the virtual servers in the fail-over cluster.

If you need to configure or make available a cluster server configuration in a replication scenario, it is recommended that you use an MSCS cluster file share as your snapshot folder when configuring a Distributor on a fail-over cluster. When, for example, the server fails, the distribution database will be available and replication will continue to be configured at the Distributor.

Another thing: When you create publications, you need to specify the MSCS cluster file share for the additional storage of snapshot files or as the location from which Subscribers apply the snapshot. This will ensure that the snapshot files are made available to all nodes of the cluster and to all Subscribers that must access it.

If you want to use encryption with a fail-over cluster, you must install the server certificate with the fully qualified DNS name of the virtual server on all nodes in the fail-over cluster. For example, if you have a two-node cluster, with nodes named mcsql.cityhall.genesis.mcity .org and mcsq2.cityhall.genesis.mcity.org and a virtual SQL server "Virtsql," you need to get a certificate for "virtsql.cityhall.genesis.mcity.org" and install the certificate on both nodes. You can then check the Force Protocol Encryption check box on the Server Network Utility to configure your fail-over cluster for encryption.

It is also vital that you not remove the BUILTIN\Administrators account from SQL Server. The IsAlive thread runs under the context of the Cluster Service account, and not the SQL Server service account. The Cluster Service must be part of the administrator group on each node of the cluster. If you remove the BUILTIN\Administrators account, the IsAlive thread will no longer be able to create a trusted connection, and you will lose access to the virtual server.

Creating a Fail-Over Cluster

The following steps will let you create a fail-over cluster using the SQL Server setup program:

1. Have ready all the information you need to create your virtual server. Items must include cluster disk resources, IP addresses, network name, and the nodes available for fail-over. The cluster disks that you intend to use for fail-over clustering should thus all be in a single cluster group and owned by the node from which the setup program is run. You must configure your cluster disk array before you run the setup program, and this is done through Cluster Administrator. You will need one MSCS group for each virtual server you want to set up.

2. Start the setup program to begin your installation. After you have entered all the required information, the setup program will install the new instance of SQL Server on the local disk of each computer in the cluster. It then installs the system databases on the cluster disk or array. The binaries are installed in exactly the same path on each cluster node, so you must ensure that each node has a local drive letter in common with all the other nodes in the cluster.

3. If any resource (including SQL Server) fails for any reason, the services (SQL Server, the SQL Server Agent, Full-Text Search, and all services in the fail-over cluster group) fail over to any available nodes defined in the virtual server.

4. You install one instance of SQL Server 2005, creating a new virtual server and all resources.

Before you create a SQL Server 2005 fail-over cluster, you must configure Microsoft Cluster Service (MSCS) and use Cluster Administrator to create at least one cluster disk resource. Note the location of the cluster drive in the Cluster Administrator before you run SQL Server Setup because you need this information to create a new fail-over cluster. The following summarizes creating the cluster:

1. Run Setup and when you get to the Computer Name dialog box, click Virtual Server and enter a virtual server name. If Setup detects that you are running MSCS, it will default to Virtual Server. You must have configured your shared SCSI disks first. Click Next. The User Information dialog box loads.

2. On the User Information dialog box, enter the user name and company. Click Next. The Software License Agreement dialog box loads. Enter your license information. The Failover Clustering dialog box loads.

3. On the Failover Clustering dialog box, enter one IP address for each network configured for client access. That is, enter one IP address for each network on which the virtual server will be available to clients on a public (or mixed) network. Select the network for which you want to enter an IP address, and then enter the IP address. Click Add.

4. The IP address and the subnet are displayed. The subnet is supplied by MSCS. Continue to enter IP addresses for each installed network until you have populated all desired networks with an IP address. Click Next. The Cluster Disk Selection dialog box loads.

5. On the Cluster Disk Selection screen, select the cluster disk group where the data files will be placed by default and click Next. The Cluster Management dialog box loads.

6. On the Cluster Management dialog box, review the cluster definition provided by SQL Server 2005. By default, all available nodes are selected. Remove any nodes that will not be part of the cluster definition for the virtual server you are creating. Click Next. The Remote Information dialog box loads.

7. On the Remote Information dialog box, enter login credentials for the remote cluster node. The login credentials must have administrator privileges on the remote node(s) of the cluster. Click Next. The Instance Name dialog box loads.

8. On the Instance Name dialog box, choose a default instance or specify a named instance. To specify a named instance, clear the Default check box, and then enter the name for the named instance. Click Next. The Setup Type dialog box loads. (You cannot name an instance DEFAULT or MSSQLSERVER.)

9. On the Setup Type dialog box, select the type of installation to install. The Setup program automatically defaults to the first available cluster disk resource from the group you previously selected.

If you need to specify a different clustered drive resource, however, under Data Files, click Browse and then specify a path on a clustered drive resource. You will be required to select a clustered drive resource that is owned by the node on which you are running the setup program. The drive also must be a member of the cluster group you previously selected. Click Next. The Services Accounts dialog box loads.

On the Services Accounts dialog box, select the service account that you want to run in the fail-over cluster. Click Next. The Authentication Mode dialog box loads. From here on installation continues.

Step-by-Step Clustering SQL Server

Preparation for SQL Server 2005 clustered installation should starts with the operating system of the individual nodes. First make sure all security patches are up to date. This is easy to do if you are using R2 or later of the Windows Server 2003 operating system. Run the Microsoft Baseline Security Analyzer (MBSA) penetration tests. Also check if antivirus software is installed and configured properly, and not scanning the folders that will be holding your databases, both user and system. You should strive to lay a strong foundation from the operating system before the installation CD is even inserted.

Also, make sure that the minimum system requirements are met. Verify the requirements and that you meet them. If the OS is not a fresh install, then download the latest service packs and hotfixes and security patches from the Microsoft SQL Server Web site (www .microsoft.com/sql). You can also check if the Active Directory administrators have software updates locally and if they are online to serve you.

Next, you should have all of your necessary clustered installation resources information ready ahead of time. Here is a basic list of what you will need before you begin:

- Appropriate cluster hardware that has been certified by Microsoft.

- Windows Server 2003, Enterprise Edition, with its latest updates, installed properly as a cluster (clustering is not possible on the Standard Edition).

- Windows Server 2003 Cluster Service, properly installed and configured.

  The Windows Server 2003 Cluster Service needs to have been thoroughly tested to ensure that it is working correctly and that the Cluster Service account has been properly created. This means ensuring that the domain [user] account that you will be using for the SQL Server services has been added to the local administrators groups of all participating servers and is not a member of Domain Admins.

- That you (the installer) are a local administrator on all participating nodes of the cluster.

- A copy of the SQL Server installation CDs.

- A name you can assign to the SQL Server cluster. This is the virtual name that clients will use to access SQL Server. This name must consist only of letters or numbers, no special characters. You can default to the name of the cluster, but that is not always a practical solution.

- An IP address you can assign to the SQL Server cluster. This IP address will be assigned to the virtual server that clients will use to connect to SQL Server.

Make sure to use Microsoft Distributed Transaction Coordinator (MS DTC). SQL Server 2005 requires Microsoft Distributed Transaction Coordinator (MS DTC) on Microsoft Windows Server 2003 and Microsoft Windows Server 2003 operating systems. MS DTC is required in the cluster for distributed queries and two-phase commit transactions, as well as for some replication functionality. After you install the operating system and configure your cluster, you must configure MS DTC to work in a cluster by using the Cluster Administrator.

Using Cluster Administrator, go to New Resource, and create the MS DTC resource. Assign the MS DTC resource its own unique resource group.

Install Only One MS DTC Resource. When MS DTC is running in clustered mode, you create only one MS DTC resource on the entire cluster. Any process running on any node in the cluster can use MS DTC. These processes simply call the MS DTC Proxy, and the MS DTC Proxy automatically forwards MS DTC calls to the MS DTC transaction manager, which controls the entire cluster.

If the node running the MS DTC transaction manager fails, the MS DTC transaction manager is automatically restarted on another node in the cluster. The newly restarted MS DTC transaction manager reads the MS DTC log file on the shared cluster disk to determine the outcome of pending and recently completed transactions. Resource managers reconnect to the MS DTC transaction manager and perform recovery to determine the outcome of pending transactions. Applications reconnect to MS DTC so that they can initiate new transactions.

For example, suppose that the MS DTC transaction manager is active on system B. The application program and resource manager on system A call the MS DTC proxy. The MS DTC proxy on system A forwards all MS DTC calls to the MS DTC transaction manager on system B.

If system B fails, the MS DTC transaction manager on system A will take over. It will read the entire MS DTC log file on the shared cluster disk, perform recovery, and then serve as the transaction manager for the entire cluster.

The MS DTC transaction manager, MS DTC Proxy, and Component Services administrative tools are installed on each node of the Windows server cluster. The cluster uses the Microsoft Cluster Service (MSCS) as part of the setup of the Windows server cluster.

To install SQL Server onto the cluster, do as follows:

1. Click Setup on the SQL Server CD or DVD. The Welcome dialog box loads, select Next.

2. Enter the name of the virtual server. This is the name of the server client applications connect to. It is the name used in the connection strings and tools like Management Studio will use this name to open the instance of the server for management. This is illustrated in Figure 9-1. Click Next.

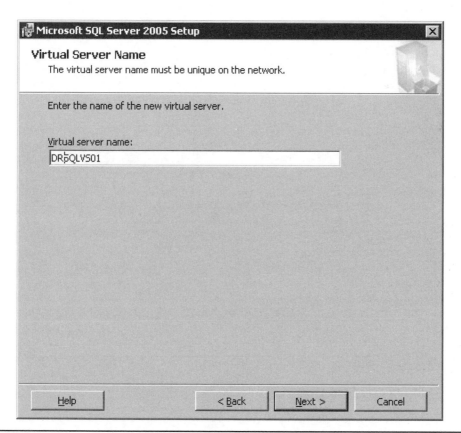

FIGURE 9-1   Setting the Virtual Server name

3. Next enter user information if it is not automatically selected; click Next.

4. You will be presented with the request to acknowledge the end user licensing agreement. Select Yes and continue with the installation.

5. The first cluster information is IP address used by the virtual SQL server. Under "Network to Use," select the public network connection your clients are going to connect to (via DNS). This is network connection that is connected to the LAN for client access (remember this is not the heartbeat). See Figure 9-2.

6. It is possible to add additional virtual IP addresses for multiple-instance clustering, but this is not necessary to configure the default installation or active/passive, single-instance installations of SQL Server on a cluster. Click Next to continue.

7. Next you need to tell SQL Server setup which logical disk of the shared disk array to place the logical database files. Please be sure that you do not select the Quorum drive. Here you are actually telling the SQL Server Setup Wizard where to install the SQL Server system database files. You also tell the SQL Server Setup Wizard that

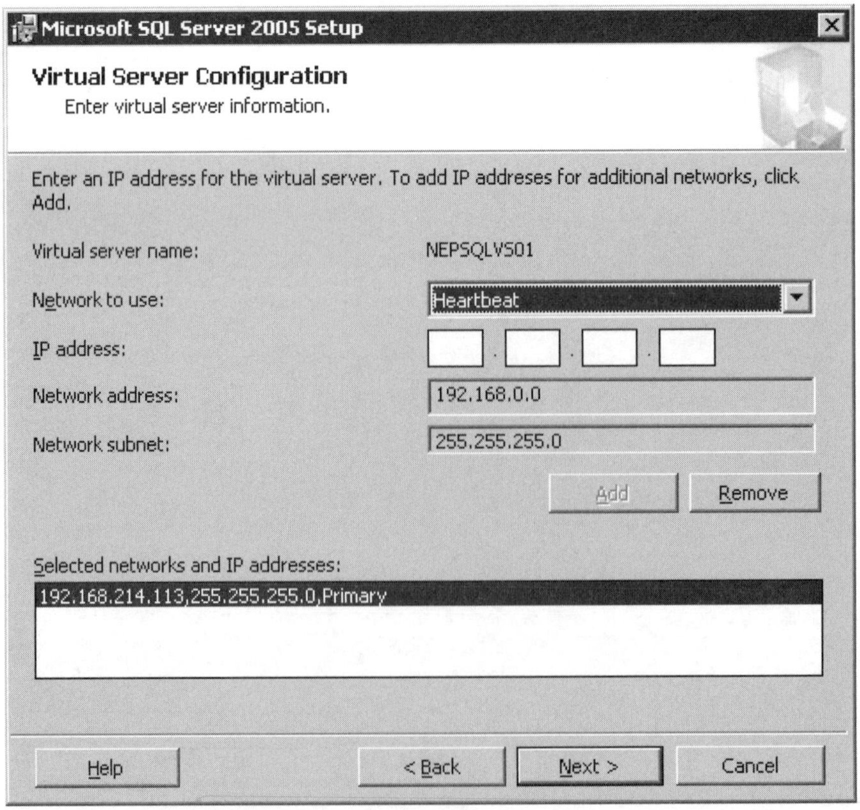

FIGURE 9-2   The IP address for the virtual server

the disk resource selected should become part of the SQL Server clustering resources. Thus if resource failure occurs, the disk resource used by SQL Server for system databases will fail over as one resource group with the rest of the dependent resources. Go ahead and select the appropriate drive and then click Next.

8. You now need to define which of the available nodes of the Windows cluster set should be used for SQL Server fail-over in the event of resource failure. Figure 9-3 illustrates this. Once complete, click Next.

9. In order to install SQL Server on the secondary node from the primary node, a remote SQL Server 2005 installation is performed. In order for a remote installation to work, the wizard must log in to the secondary node as an administrator.

    This dialog box tells the SQL Server setup wizard the name of the instance of SQL Server that you are currently installing. The figures represent a default instance of SQL Server on the cluster, and this will be a "default" installation. A named instance is only required if you intend to run more than one instance of SQL Server on the cluster, creating a multiple instance installation leading to active/active clustering and N+1 configurations.

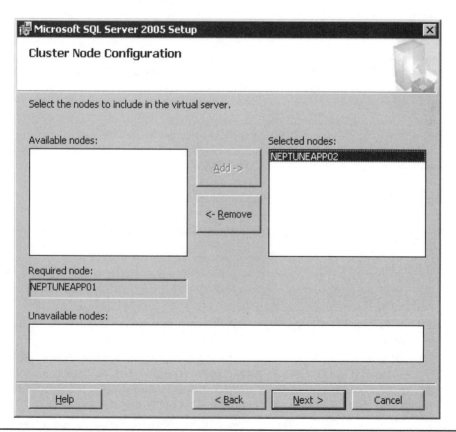

FIGURE 9-3   Specifying the available node

10. Now you will have arrived at what looks like the setup screen for SQL Server 2005. Take note of the "Destination Folder" locations. These should not have to be changed. If the destination folder for your SQL Server data files is not the logical drive on the shared storage disk array that you specified earlier during setup, there is a problem. The SQL Server 2005 "Program Files" need to be installed on the local disk of each node, not on the logical drive on the shared array. Verify this is correct for your setup and click Next.

11. Now installation proceeds much as it does on standard installs. Select which components you want to install. The default options are usually sufficient.

To finalize the installation, enter the SQL Server 2005 service account information, as is necessary for any SQL Server 2005 installation. Choose the appropriate authentication mode for your situation, the appropriate SQL Collation, the appropriate network libraries (usually TCP/IP) licensing mode, and you're done.

The SQL Server 2005 installation can finally commence. The messages displayed will change, giving you a watered-down explanation of what is going on behind the scenes. This process will take a fair amount of time to complete. Although you will not be prompted to do so, once the install is complete it is highly advisable that you reboot all nodes of the cluster. First, reboot the primary node (the node you have just run the SQL Server Installation Wizard on.

Make sure it comes up successfully. Next reboot the secondary node(s), and then be sure they come up successfully. Once you have a successful installation of SQL Server 2005 on the cluster, it's time to install the most recent SQL Server 2005 service pack. Even if you did not reboot the nodes of the cluster you will be prompted to reboot them before you can install the service pack.

There are some additional items that can be extremely helpful when running this installation. This includes copying the installation media to the local hard drive and running them from there instead of the CD-ROM drive. It is also helpful to copy the most updated service packs, hot fixes, and security patches to the local disk drive for installation.

Node Sense: Cluster Advice You Must Follow

Several products interact with Microsoft SQL Server 2005 fail-over clustering. To ensure that your fail-over cluster functions properly, you must understand these interactions.

- *Avoid sharing the SQL Server network name or IP address.* No additional resources should attempt to share the existing SQL Server network name or IP address. Any new resources added to the cluster group must have a separate and unique network names and IP addresses, if required.

- *Avoid file shares.* Using file shares on SQL Server data drives is not recommended, as it could hurt SQL Server behavior and diminish performance.

- *Avoid dependencies on SQL Server and the SQL Server Agent.* Adding dependencies on SQL Server and the SQL Server Agent is not recommended, as it could hurt SQL Server behavior. If a dependency must be made, it should be on the SQL Server Agent, and the SQL Server Agent should be set not to affect the group.

- *Use the Domain Name Service or Windows Internet Name Service.* A Domain Name Service (DNS) server or Windows Internet Name Service (WINS) server must be running in the environment where your SQL Server virtual server will be installed. SQL Server Setup requires Dynamic Domain Name Service (DDNS) registration of the SQL Server IP interface virtual reference. If the dynamic registration cannot be completed, Setup will fail and the installation will be rolled back. If no dynamic registration is available, you must have preregistered your server in DNS.

In Review

This chapter deals with the high-availability features now available in SQL Server 2005. We discussed the various scale-up and scale-out options and investigated the myth of linear scale-up and how adding more and more processors to a system has a point of diminishing return, both in terms of price and performance.

We also investigated the various clustering models possible using the cluster services of either Windows Server 2003 Enterprise Server or Datacenter Server. Creating virtual SQL Server servers and setting up the cluster server has been getting easier with each version of SQL Server since SQL Server 7.0.

If you do not need a cluster solution, or have budget constraints, you can configure standby (warm) servers that can be configured to replace the primary server if it goes down. Availability is not as immediate and there will also be delays and additional work involved in backing up databases and transaction logs and applying them to the standby server. The standby server will also have to be kept in read-only or standby mode so that the data cannot be modified, rendering it out of sync with the primary server.

This chapter caps our sojourn into the life of the SQL Server database administrator and his or her typical duties. The next parts deal with programming.

PART II

PART III

Programming SQL Server 2005

Transact-SQL Primer

No pocketful of chapters makes a treatise on Transact-SQL or T-SQL, the SQLese of the SQL Server 2005 DBMS. The subject is so extensive it can easily fill a 10,000-page book, and there are several such tomes available (well, not exactly 10,000 pages), not to mention the venerable SQL Server Books Online. But you have to start somewhere. This chapter is both a primer to the language and an introduction to the new T-SQL features and enhancements supported by SQL Server 2005. To test many of the examples in this chapter, I suggest installing the old favorite demo database, Northwind, from Microsoft.

This chapter is a concise overview of T-SQL's building blocks. It was tackled with newcomers to SQL Server in mind, as well as battleaxes needing either a refresher or a leg up on the new elements of the language. Also, this chapter should be considered as a "briefing" or, better, an introduction to the extensive reference to T-SQL in SQL Server Books Online and the advanced features discussed in later chapters.

No matter what API or environment you use, communication between client and server is via T-SQL. Knowing and using T-SQL is independent of the type of software you are running on the clients, be they fat, thin, thick, or rich. T-SQL is also the language you use to manage the DBMS, which is discussed in later chapters.

General office applications—line-of-business applications, report generators, SQL Server Management Studio, and so on—do not require a deep knowledge of T-SQL, because the code is usually embedded in the application. However, some applications need to support an end-user ability to query SQL Server databases, for instance, to find all accounts 30 days past due. This usually requires a user to know some menial T-SQL query syntax, but you usually allow your end user to visually construct a SQL query, which creates a statement under-the-hood and on-the-fly, so to speak.

SQL Server tools, such as the SQL Server Management Studio and the OSQL tool, require a deep knowledge of T-SQL because they accept direct T-SQL syntax for transmission to the server. The server returns results direct by to these tools, usually in the form of a result set or as tabulated data displayed in a grid or text window. As you learned in the earlier chapters SQL Server Management Studio is the essential tool for building T-SQL statements.

Application developers programming access to SQL Server data need a thorough understanding of T-SQL. They need to know as much as possible about the language, which requires comprehensive study and a lot of practice (beyond the scope of this book). This chapter covers the basics, such as syntax style, operators, and data types. Later chapters cover the more complex subject matter: stored procedure programming, triggers, user-defined functions, and so on.

T-SQL knowledge is essential in Internet applications or services. Even if you are going to latch onto XML, T-SQL is essentially still the facilitator for XML, especially when it comes to returning result set data as XML documents or inserting XML data into SQL Server databases as XML documents. T-SQL statements or queries can also be transmitted to SQL Server using URLs. However, most of the discussion in the next seven chapters relates to native use of T-SQL.

T-SQL: Basic Concepts

T-SQL is a procedural language with all the gravy and relish you might be accustomed to having in a language. Architecturally speaking, it can be compared to database programming languages like Clipper and DBase because it comes with all the basic elements of a programming language: variables, flow-control structures, logic evaluation, function and procedure call capability, and so on. (Yes, even GOTO lives on here.) That's the "Transact" or "T" part of the language. However, T-SQL is neither compiled like C nor interpreted like a p-code language. Rather, it is parsed like a just-in-time script language, and its intent and logic is converted into a native "sublanguage" that stokes the SQL Server engines.

The SQL in T-SQL supports SQL-92 through SQL-2003 DDL and DML that allow a wide range of database programmers who are up to speed on SQL to obtain a broad range of database server functionality, and then some. If you have never studied T-SQL before reading this book, but you know SQL, then you are certainly not a long way from being able to create applications that access SQL Server. Many database programmers coming over from the Access, FoxPro, Delphi, PowerBuilder, and JDBC worlds, for instance, are usually up to speed with SQL, and so getting up to speed with SQL Server is very easy. And because SQL is so widely used, I have left the SQL-native facilities like SELECT, UPDATE, INSERT, and JOIN for discussion in later chapters, where it is assumed you already know how to program in SQL.

T-SQL also provides access to DBMS mechanisms such as stored procedures and triggers. These are not defined by the SQL standard (which is the base language for all SQL extended DBMS interfaces), although some attempt at adding stored procedure–like facilities in SQL has been proposed in recent years. But hold your horses, we'll be getting the extended stuff like stored procedures in later chapters.

T-SQL Constants

T-SQL constants are literal or scalar values that represent a data type. The following constants are supported by the language (the data types are discussed later in this chapter):

- Character strings
- Unicode strings
- Binary constants
- Bit constants

- Datetime constants
- Integer constants
- Decimal constants
- Float and real constants
- Money constants
- Unique identifier constants

Character String Constants

Character string constants are surrounded by single quotation marks and can include alphanumeric characters (a–z, A–Z, and 0–9) and the additional characters, such as exclamation point (!), at sign (@), and pound sign (#). The bounding quotation marks are the default delimiter recognized by SQL Server. Setting the QUOTED_IDENTIFIER option for a connection to OFF can, however, change this, if using single quotation marks causes problems in your development environment, where strings are usually bounded by single quote marks, as in Visual Basic 2005 (VB), or by double quotes, as in C#.

The OLE DB drivers automatically set the QUOTED_IDENTIFIER to ON upon connection, and often an apostrophe can trash an application because SQL Server raises hell when it sees the apostrophe and thinks it's an identifier. In this case, the "official" solution is to add an extra quote so that you send something like 'St. Elmo's Fire' to the server as "St. Elmo's Fire".

Asking your end users to do that, however, is a cockamamie solution, to say the least, because it is unacceptable for your data entry people to have to remember to type an apostrophe twice. If you have this problem, and you most likely do, you can use a function like REPLACE(), which is a VB function (and there are equivalent functions in all languages), to add the second quote mark under the "sheets." You could also use a data-bound "text" control (which I am not fond of) to make the necessary adjustments automatically.

Also, if the QUOTED_IDENTIFIER option has been set OFF for a connection, character strings can also be enclosed in double quotation marks, but the OLE DB provider and ODBC driver automatically use SET QUOTED_IDENTIFIER ON when they connect to SQL Server. The use of single quotation marks is, however, recommended.

If a character string enclosed in single quotation marks contains an embedded quotation mark, represent the embedded single quotation mark with two single quotation marks. This is not necessary in strings embedded in double quotation marks.

Collations and code pages are also important considerations when it comes to strings. The character string constants are assigned the default collation of the current database attached to in the connection. However, you can use the COLLATE clause (discussed a little later in this chapter) to specify a different collation. The character strings you enter at the client usually conform to the code page of the computer. They are translated to the database code page, if necessary, upon transmission to the server.

Empty strings are represented as two single quotation marks with nothing in between. However, if you are working in database compatibility mode 6.x, an empty string is treated as a single space. The SQL Server Unicode strings support the concept of enhanced collations.

Unicode String Constants

The Unicode strings have a format very similar to character strings, but they are preceded by what we call the N identifier. The N stands for National Language in the SQL standard. Usage requires that the N prefix be uppercase. In the following example, "Jeffrey" is the character constant, but in order to provide a Unicode constant, I would have to provide N'Jeffrey'.

Unicode constants are interpreted as Unicode data. They are not evaluated using a code page, but they do have a collation, which primarily controls comparisons and case sensitivity. When you use the Unicode constant, you are assigned the default collation of the database you are connected to. But you can change this with the COLLATE clause to specify a collation. (See "Nchar and Nvarchar" later in this chapter.) The SQL Server Unicode strings support the concept of enhanced collations supported by SQL Server 2005.

TIP *Consider replacing all char, varchar, and text data types with their Unicode equivalents. This will help you avoid code page conversion issues.*

Binary Constants

The binary constants are identified with the suffix 0x (an empty binary string) and are strings composed of hexadecimal numbers. They are not enclosed in quotation marks.

Bit Constants

The number zero or one represents a bit constant. These do not get enclosed in quotation marks. If you use a number larger than 1, SQL Server converts it to 1.

Datetime Constants

You can use the datetime constants as character date values, in specific formats. They are enclosed in single quotation marks as follows:

```
'October 9, 1959'
'9 October, 1959'
'591009'
'10/09/59'
```

I have discussed the formats for the datetime constants later in this chapter.

Integer Constants

The integer constants are represented by strings of numbers and must be whole numbers. They do not get enclosed in quotation marks like strings and cannot contain decimal points. Integer constants are illustrated as follows:

```
2006
6
```

Decimal Constants

The decimal constants are represented by strings of numbers that are not enclosed in quotation marks but can contain a decimal point. The following examples represent decimal constants:

```
146.987
5.1
```

Float and Real Constants

The float and real constants are represented using scientific notation (see "SQL Server Data Types" later in this chapter). They are not enclosed in single quotes and appear as follows:

```
101.5E5
2E+100
```

Money Constants

The money constants are represented as strings of numbers. They can be whole numbers, or they can include the optional decimal point. You can also use a currency symbol as a prefix. They are not enclosed in quotation marks. Examples of money constants are as follows:

```
1200.08
$500.00
R35.05
```

Uniqueidentifier Constants

The uniqueidentifier is a string that represents the globally unique identifier (GUID), pronounced "gwid" or often as "goo ID." These constants can be specified in either character or binary string notation. The following example represents the same GUID:

```
'82B7A80F-0BD5-4343-879D-C6DDDCF4CF16'
0xFE4B4D38D5539C45852DD4FB4C687E47
```

You can use either notation, but the character string requires single quotes, as demonstrated here.

Signing Constants

To sign a numeric constant, merely apply the + or – unary operator to it. The default sign is positive if the operator is not applied. The following examples are signed:

```
+$500.00
-2001
```

T-SQL Expressions

An *expression* is a syntactical element or clause composed of identifiers, operators, and values that can evaluate to obtain a result. Like a sentence consisting of subject, verb, object to convey an action, the expression must be logically complete before it can compute. In other words, the elements of an expression must "add up." In the general programming environments, an expression will always evaluate to a single result. However, Transact-SQL expressions are evaluated individually for each row in the result set. In other words, a single expression may have a different value in each row of the result set, but each row has only one value for the expression.

The following T-SQL elements are expressions:

- A function, such as DB_ID(), is an expression because it computes to return a value that represents a database ID.

- A constant is an expression because it alone represents a value.

- A variable is an expression for the same reason a constant is.

- A column name is an expression because it too represents or evaluates a value.

- A subquery is an expression because it computes or evaluates a result.

- Mathematical operations are expressions; for example, $1 + 1 = 2$ or total $* 6 / 100$.

- CASE, NULLIF, and COALESCE are expressions (discussed a little later in this chapter).

The preceding list items are known as *simple expressions*. When you combine two or more simple expressions with operators, you get a *complex expression*. A good example of complex expression is your average SELECT statement. For example, SELECT * FROM CITY is a complex or compound expression because the statement can return the name of a city for each row in the table.

It is possible to combine expressions using an operator, but only if the expressions have data types that are supported by the operator. In addition, the following rules also apply:

- A data type that has a lower precedence can be implicitly converted to the data type with the higher data type precedence.

- Using the CAST function, you are able to explicitly convert the data type with the lower precedence to the data type with the higher precedence. Alternatively, you should be able to use CAST to convert the source data type to an intermediate data type, and then convert the intermediate data type to the data type with the higher precedence.

If you are unable to perform either an implicit or explicit conversion, then you cannot combine the two expressions to form a compound expression.

Expression Results

In addition to the preceding rules, the following also applies to SQL Server expressions:

- When you create a simple expression comprising a single variable, a constant, a scalar function, or a column name, the data type, the collation, the precision and scale, and the value of the expression are the data type, collation, precision, scale, and value of the referenced element.

- When you combine two expressions with comparison or logical operators, the resulting data type is Boolean and the value is one of TRUE, FALSE, or UNKNOWN. (See "Comparison Operators" in the next section).

- When you combine two expressions with arithmetic, bitwise, or string operators, the operator determines the resulting data type.

- When you create compound expressions, comprising many operators, the data type, collation, precision, and value of the resulting expression are determined by combining the component expressions, two at a time, until a final result is reached. The sequence in which the expressions are combined is defined by the precedence of the operators in the expression.

T-SQL Operators

T-SQL supports several operators that can be used to specify actions that are performed on one or more expressions. The following is a list of the operators that are supported in SQL Server 2005:

- Arithmetic operators

- Assignment operators

- Bitwise operators

- Comparison operators

- Logical operators

- String concatenation operator

- Unary operators

The Arithmetic Operators

These operators are used to perform mathematical operations on two expressions of any numeric data type. Table 10-1 lists the arithmetic operators. As indicated in the table, the + and – operators can also be used with the date data types discussed later in this chapter.

Operator	Purpose
Add (+)	Used to add two numbers. Also adds a number of days to a date.
Subtract (-)	Used to subtract two numbers. Also subtracts days from a date.
Multiply (*)	Used to multiply two numbers.
Divide (/)	Used to divide one number by another number.
Modulo (%)	Used to obtain the remainder of one number divided by another.

TABLE 10-1 Arithmetic Operators

The Assignment Operator

As in most programming languages, there is a single assignment operator. In T-SQL it is the equal sign. (This is unfortunate for experts in other languages where the equal sign is used to equate one expression [comparison] with another, as it is in Java which uses the colon-equal [:=] for assignment). In the following example, a simple use of the T-SQL demonstrates assigning a numeric value to a variable:

```
DECLARE @RecordCounter INT
SET @RecordCounter = 1
```

You can also use the assignment operator to assign a string to provide a name for a column heading when you display a result set. The equal sign is also a T-SQL comparison operator.

Bitwise Operators

T-SQL provides bitwise operators that you can use within T-SQL statements to manipulate the bits between two expressions of any integer or binary string-based data types (except *image*). Also, operands cannot both be of the binary string data type. Table 10-2 lists the bitwise operators and their purposes. It also lists the Bitwise NOT (~) operator, which applies to one operand. (See also the unary operators discussed later in this section.)

Table 10-3 lists the supported operand data types.

Operator	Description	Purpose
&	Bitwise AND	Bitwise logical AND operation between two integers.
|	Bitwise OR	Bitwise logical OR between two integers as translated to binary expressions.
^	Bitwise Exclusive OR	Bitwise exclusive OR between two integers as translated to binary expressions.

TABLE 10-2   Bitwise Operators

Left Operand	Right Operand
binary	int, smallint, or tinyint
bit	int, smallint, tinyint, or bit
int	int, smallint, tinyint, binary, or varbinary
smallint	int, smallint, tinyint, binary, or varbinary
tinyint	int, smallint, tinyint, binary, or varbinary
varbinary	int, smallint, or tinyint

TABLE 10-3   Operand Data Types

Comparison Operators

The comparison operators test equality between two expressions and are often used in WHERE clauses to test for a column value. They can be used on all expressions except expressions of the text and image data types. Table 10-4 lists the comparison operators in SQL Server and their functions.

The result of a comparison expression is that the data type of the return value is a Boolean of TRUE, FALSE, or UNKNOWN. It is also important to take into consideration that when SET ANSI_NULLS is ON, an operator between two NULL expressions returns UNKNOWN. If you switch SET ANSI_NULLS to OFF, the equal operator will return TRUE if it is between two NULLS.

You can also use the AND keyword to combine multiple comparison expressions like the following:

```
WHEN UnitsInStock >= 5 AND UnitsInStock <= 15 THEN 'Average Mover'
```

NOTE *You should also be aware that comparisons may be affected by the collations you are using.*

Logical Operators

The logical operators test for the truth of some expression. Like comparison operators, they also return a Boolean data type with a value of TRUE or FALSE. These operators, listed in

Comparison Operator	Description	Purpose
=	Equals	Used to test for equality
>	Greater	Used to test if one expression is greater than another
<	Less	Used to test if one expression is less than another
>=	Greater or equal	Used to test if one expression is greater than or equal to another
<=	Less or equal	Used to test if one expression is less than or equal to another
<>	Not equal	Used to test if one expression is NOT equal to another
!=	Not equal	Used to test if one expression is NOT equal to another (non–SQL-92 or later)
!<	Not less	Used to test if one expression is NOT less than another (non–SQL-92 or later)
!>	Not greater	Used to test if one expression is NOT greater than another (non– SQL-92 or later)

TABLE 10-4 Comparison Operators

Operator	Purpose
ALL	TRUE if all of a set of comparisons are TRUE.
AND	TRUE if both Boolean expressions are TRUE.
ANY	TRUE if any one of a set of comparisons are TRUE.
BETWEEN	TRUE if the operand is within a range.
EXISTS	TRUE if a subquery contains any rows.
IN	TRUE if the operand is equal to one of a list of expressions.
LIKE	TRUE if the operand matches a pattern.
NOT	Reverses the value of any other Boolean expression.
OR	TRUE if either Boolean expression is TRUE.
SOME	TRUE if some of a set of comparisons are TRUE.

TABLE 10-5   Logical Operators

Table 10-5, are used extensively in queries and are most common in WHERE clauses. For example, the statement

```
SELECT * FROM Customers WHERE LastName LIKE 'Shapiro%'
```

returns rows where the entire value (the operator tests the whole value) looks like "Shapiro."

String Concatenation Operator

The string concatenation operator is the addition sign (+), which is used to concatenate one substring to another to create a third derivative string. In other words, the expression 'the small bro' + 'wn fox' stores the value "the small brown fox." However, be aware that concatenation behavior can vary from database level to database level.

A version 6.5 (the database versions are referenced as 65, 70, 80, or 90) database treats an empty constant as a single blank character. For example, if you run 'the small bro' + " + 'wn fox' on a 65 database, you'll end up with the following being stored: "the small bro wn fox." (See also the string manipulation functions discussed later in this chapter and also the discussion of collation precedence.)

Unary Operators

The unary operators perform an operation on only one expression of any numeric data type. Table 10-6 lists the unary operators (see the bitwise operators discussed earlier in this section).

Operator Precedence

As in all modern programming languages, T-SQL operators are governed according to rules of precedence. An operator of a higher level is evaluated before an operator of a lower level. In compound expressions, the operator precedence determines the order of operations.

Operator	Description	Purpose
+	Positive	The numeric value is positive.
-	Negative	The numeric value is negative.
~	Bitwise NOT	Bitwise logical NOT for one integer as translated to binary expressions. Can be also be used on data types of type integer.

TABLE 10-6   Unary Operators

The order of execution or computation can significantly influence the result. The following list is in order of precedence, from highest (+) to lowest (=).

- + (Positive), – (Negative), ~ (Bitwise NOT)
- (Multiply), / (Divide), % (Modulo)
- + (Add), + (Concatenate), – (Subtract)
- =, >, <, >=, <=, <>, !=, !>, !< (Comparison operators)
- ^ (Bitwise Exclusive OR), & (Bitwise AND), | (Bitwise OR)
- NOT
- AND
- ALL, ANY, BETWEEN, IN, LIKE, OR, SOME
- = (Assignment)

Operators used in an expression that have the same operator precedence level are evaluated according to their position in the expression from left to right. For example, in the expression used in the SET statement of this example, the subtraction operator is evaluated before the addition operator.

```
SET @TheNumber = 3 - 3 + 9
```

You can also use parentheses to override the defined precedence of the operators in an expression. The expression within the parentheses is evaluated first to obtain a single value. You can then use the value outside of the parentheses.

```
5 * (3 + 2)
```

is the same as

```
5 * 5
```

In expressions that contain expressions in parentheses (nesting), the deepest expression is evaluated first.

Data Type Precedence

Often it becomes necessary to convert a constant or variable of one data type to another, and you would use the CONVERT() function described later in this chapter to do this. However, when you combine two data types with an operator, a *data type precedence rule* decides which data type gets converted to the data type of the other.

The data type precedence rule dictates that if an implicit conversion is supported (you do not require the use of the conversion function), the data type that has the lower precedence is converted to the data type with the higher precedence. Table 10-7 lists the base data types in order of precedence; the first entry in the table has the highest order, and the last entry has the lowest order. Naturally, when both data types combined by the operator are of the same precedence, no precedence ruling is required.

Data Type Order of Precedence	Type of Data
User-Defined Data Type (UDT) (highest)	User defined
xml	xml
sql_variant	sql_variant
datetime	datetime
smalldatetime	datetime
float	approximation
real	approximation
decimal	exact number
money	exact number
smallmoney	exact number
bigint	exact number
int	exact number
smallint	exact number
tinyint	exact number
bit	exact number
ntext	unicode
text	unicode
image	unicode
timestamp	unicode
uniqueidentifier	uniqueidentifier
nvarchar	unicode
nchar	unicode
varchar	unicode
char	unicode
varbinary	binary
binary	binary

TABLE 10-7   Base Data Types in Order of Preference

SQL Server Data Types

The following section explains the data types. This discussion is not in any order of preference or precedence, as discussed previously.

Integer Types (Exact Numerics)

The following list presents integers in order of precedence:

- **bigint** Integer, a whole number, data from –2^63 (–9223372036854775808) through 2^63–1 (9223372036854775807). The storage size is 8 bytes. Use bigint for large numbers that exceed the range of int. This integer costs more in terms of storage footprint. Your functions will return this data type only if the argument passed is a bigint data type. The smaller integer types are not automatically converted to bigint.

- **int** Integer, a whole number, data from –2^31 (–2,147,483,648) through 2^31 – 1 (2,147,483,647). The storage size is 4 bytes. This integer should suffice for most needs and remains the primary integer type in use on SQL Server.

- **smallint** Integer data from –2^15 (–32,768) through 2^15 – 1 (32,767). The storage size is 2 bytes.

- **tinyint** Integer data from 0–255. The storage size is 1 byte.

- **bit** This is an integer data type that takes 1, 0, or NULL. You can create columns of type bit, but they cannot be indexed. Also, if there are 8 or less bit columns in a table, the columns are stored as 1 byte by SQL Server, and if there are from 9 through 16 bit columns, they are stored as 2 bytes, and so on. This is a SQL Server conservation feature at work.

Decimal and Numeric Types (Exact Numerics)

The *decimal[(p[, s])]* and *numeric[(p[, s])]* types are data types with fixed precision and scale (p = precision and s = scale), as listed in Table 10-8. When maximum precision is used, the valid values are from –10^38 –1 through 10^38–1.

The precision (p) specifies the maximum total number of decimal digits that can be stored, both to the left and to the right of the decimal point. The precision must be a value from 1 through the maximum precision. The maximum precision is 38. The scale (s) specifies the maximum number of decimal digits that can be stored to the right of the decimal point. Scale must be a value from 0 through *p*. The default scale is 0; therefore, 0 <= *s* <= *p*. The maximum storage sizes vary according to the precision.

TABLE 10-8 Decimal and Numeric types

Precision	Storage Footprint in bytes
1–9	5
10–19	9
20–28	13
29–38	17

Money and Smallmoney (Exact Numerics)

The monetary data types are used for representing monetary or currency values as follows:

- **Money**   Values from –2^63 (–922,337,203,685,477.5808) through 2^63 – 1 (+922,337, 203,685,477.5807). This type has accuracy to one ten-thousandth of a monetary unit. The storage footprint is 8 bytes.

- **Smallmoney**   Values from –214,748.3648 through +214,748.3647. This type has accuracy to one ten-thousandth of a monetary unit. The storage footprint is 4 bytes.

Float and Real (Approximate Numerics)

These data types are the approximate number data types you use with floating-point numeric data. Floating-point data is approximate, and not all values in the data type range can be precisely represented.

The *float [(n)]*: This is for floating-point number data from –1.79E + 308 through 1.79E + 308. The *n* parameter is the number of bits used to store the mantissa of the *float* number in scientific notation. This dictates the precision and storage size. The *n* parameter must be a value in the range 1–53. The float[(*n*)] data type conforms to the SQL-92 standard for all values of *n* in the range 1–53. Table 10-9 represents values for *n* and the corresponding precision and memory costs.

The *real* is a floating-point number data type that ranges from –3.40E + 38 through 3.40E + 38. The footprint of *real* is 4 bytes.

Datetime and Smalldatetime

The date and time data types represent dates and times from January 1, 1753, through December 31, 9999, to an accuracy of one three-hundredth of a second (equivalent to 3.33 milliseconds or 0.00333 seconds). These values are rounded to increments of .000, .003, or .007 seconds. The footprint for *datetime* is two four-byte integers. The first four bytes store the number of days before or after the *base date,* January 1, 1900. The base date is the system reference date (values for *datetime* earlier than January 1, 1753, are not permitted). The remaining four bytes store the time of day, represented as the number of milliseconds after midnight.

The *smalldatetime* type from January 1, 1900, through June 6, 2079, has accuracy to the minute. With *smalldatetime,* values with 29.998 seconds or lower are rounded down to the nearest minute. Values with 29.999 seconds or higher are rounded up to the nearest minute.

The *smalldatetime* data type stores dates and times of day with less precision than *datetime.* SQL Server stores *smalldatetime* values as two two-byte integers, as opposed to two four-byte values in *datetime.* The first two bytes store the number of days after January 1, 1900. The remaining two bytes store the number of minutes since midnight.

TABLE 10-9   Float and Real

Value for *n*	Precision	Footprint in bytes
1–24	7 digits	4 bytes
25–53	15 digits	8 bytes

Char and Varchar

These are fixed-length (char) or variable-length (varchar) character data types.

- **char[(n)]** Fixed-length non-Unicode character data with a length of n bytes, where n must be a value from 1 through 8,000. Storage size is n bytes. The SQL-92 synonym for "char" is "character."

- **varchar[(n) | MAX]** Variable-length non-Unicode character data with a length of n bytes, where n must be a value from 1 through 8,000. Storage size is the actual length in bytes of the data entered, not n bytes. The data entered can be 0 characters in length. The SQL-2003 synonyms for varchar are char varying or character varying. MAX indicates that the maximum storage size is $2^{31}-1$ bytes. The storage size is the actual length of data entered plus two bytes.

When n is not specified in a data definition or variable declaration statement, the default length is 1. When n is not specified with the CAST function, the default length is 30. Objects using char or varchar are assigned the default collation of the database, unless a specific collation is assigned using the COLLATE clause. The collation controls the code page used to store the character data.

Sites supporting multiple languages should consider using the Unicode nchar or nvarchar data type to minimize character conversion issues. If you use char or varchar,

- Use char when the data values in a column are expected to be consistently close to the same size.

- Use varchar when the data values in a column are expected to vary considerably in size.

- Use varchar(max) when the data values in a column vary considerably, and the size might exceed 8,000 bytes.

When n is not specified in a data definition or variable declaration statement, the default length is 1. When n is not specified when using the CAST and CONVERT functions, the default length is 30.

In cases where you need to support multiple languages, you should use the Unicode nchar or nvarchar data types to minimize character conversion issues. However, if you use char or varchar and if SET ANSI_PADDING is OFF, when either CREATE TABLE or ALTER TABLE is executed, a char column that is defined as NULL is handled as varchar.

When collation code pages use double-byte characters, the storage size is still n bytes. Also, with character strings, the storage size of n bytes can be less than n characters.

Variable Usage   Variables of these types are used to store non-Unicode characters. The first data type is a fixed char variable that is padded with spaces to the length specified in n. The second data type stores data of variable length and is not padded. You can use either variable for storing strings that do not exceed 8,000 characters. These structures will also truncate the strings if they exceed the number of characters declared in n.

If you use SET ANSI_PADDING OFF in the CREATE TABLE or ALTER TABLE statement, then a char column defined as NULL will be handled as a varchar. If the collation code page uses double-byte characters, the storage size will still be n bytes. Depending on the character string, the actual or final storage size of n bytes can still be less than n characters.

Nchar and Nvarchar

Nchar and nvarchar represent Unicode character data types that are either fixed-length (nchar) or variable-length (nvarchar). They make use of the UNICODE UCS-2 character set.

- **nchar(*n*)**   This is a fixed-length Unicode character data type comprising *n* characters. The characters in *n* must be a value in the range 1–4,000. The storage size of the string is two times *n* bytes. SQL-92 or higher has synonyms for these types; nchar is national char or national character. Best practice suggests using nchar when the data entries in a column are expected to be constantly in the same size range.

- **nvarchar(*n* | MAX)**   This is a variable-length Unicode character data type comprising *n* characters. The string represented by *n* must be a value in the range 1–4,000. "MAX" indicates that the maximum storage size is $2^{31}-1$ bytes. The storage size of the string, in bytes, is two times the number of characters entered, and you are not required to actually enter characters. The SQL-2003 synonyms for nvarchar are national char varying and national character varying. Best practice suggests using the nvarchar type when the sizes of the data entries in a column are expected to vary considerably.

If you do not specify *n* in a data definition or a variable declaration statement, then the length defaults to 1. It defaults to 30 when you use *n* but do not use the CAST function. When you use nchar or nvarchar without specifying a collation in the COLLATE clause, the default database collation is used. Also the SET ANSI_PADDING OFF has no effect on these data types; SET ANSI_PADDING is always ON.

Binary and Varbinary

These are binary data types that can be either fixed-length, which is a binary value, or variable-length, which is represented by the varbinary data type.

- **binary [(*n*)]**   A fixed-length binary data type of *n* bytes. The value for *n* must be from 1 through 8,000. The storage size is *n* + 4 bytes. You would use binary when column data size remains constant.

- **varbinary [(*n* | MAX)]**   This is the variable-length binary data type consisting of *n* bytes. The value for *n* must be a value from 1 through 8,000; however, the storage size is the actual length of the data entered + 4 bytes, not the value for *n* bytes. MAX indicates that the maximum storage size is $2^{31}-1$ bytes. The varbinary type can cater to a 0-byte length. The SQL-2003 synonym for varbinary is binary varying; you use this data type to hold values that vary in size.

NOTE *If you do not specify n in a data definition or variable declaration statement, the default length is 1. When n is not specified with the CAST function, however, the default length of the data type is 30.*

Ntext, Text, and Image

These are fixed and variable-length data types for storing large non-Unicode and Unicode character and binary data. Unicode data uses the UNICODE UCS-2 character set. These types are being phased out and will be removed from future versions of SQL Server.

The ntext type is variable-length Unicode data with a maximum length of $2^{30}-1$ (1,073,741,823) characters. The storage size, in bytes, is twice the number of characters entered. The SQL-2003 synonym for ntext is national text.

The text type is variable-length non-Unicode data in the code page of the server and with a maximum length of $2^{31}-1$ (2,147,483,647) characters. When the server code page uses double-byte characters, the storage is still 2,147,483,647 bytes. The storage size may be less than 2,147,483,647 bytes.

The image type is variable-length binary data from 0 through $2^{31}-1$ (2,147,483,647) bytes.

Cursor

The *cursor* is a data type for variables or stored procedure OUTPUT parameters that contain a reference to a cursor. Any variables created with the cursor data type are nullable. You should also take note that the cursor data type cannot be used for a column in a CREATE TABLE statement.

The operations that can reference variables and parameters having a cursor data type are

- DECLARE @*local_variable* and SET @*local_variable*
- OPEN, FETCH, CLOSE, and DEALLOCATE
- Stored procedure output parameters
- The CURSOR_STATUS() function
- The sp_cursor_list, sp_describe_cursor, sp_describe_cursor_tables, and sp_describe_cursor_columns system stored procedures

Sql_Variant

The sql_variant is a SQL Server data type that stores the values of all standard SQL Server data types, except the data types containing large objects (LOBs), such as "MAX" text and image types, and the data types timestamp and sql_variant (itself). This type may be used in columns, parameters, and variables, as well as in return values of user-defined functions. The following rules apply to this data type:

- A column of type sql_variant may contain the values of several different data types. For example, a column defined as sql_variant can hold int, binary, and char values.
- A sql_variant data type must first be cast to its base data type value before participating in operations such as addition and subtraction. You may also assign it a default value. This data may also hold NULL as its underlying value. NULL values, however, will not have an associated base type, but that will change when you replace the NULL with data.
- You can use the sql_variant in columns that have been defined as UNIQUE, primary, or foreign keys. However, the total length of the data values composing the key of a given row should not be greater than the maximum length of an index, which is currently 900 bytes.
- Your table can have as many sql_variant columns as it needs.
- You cannot use it in the CONTAINSTABLE and FREETEXTTABLE statements.

- ODBC does not support sql_variant because it has no facility to cater to the notion of a variant data type. You should check out the specifics of the limitations in the SQL Server documentation. For example, queries of sql_variant columns are returned as binary data when using the Microsoft OLE DB Provider for ODBC.

- Precedence of sql_variant values goes according to the rules of precedence for the base data types they represent. For example, when you compare two values of sql_variant and the base data types are in different data type families (say int and bigint), the value whose data type family is higher in the precedence hierarchy is considered the higher of the two values.

- The precedence rule discussed previously applies to conversion as well. In other words, when sql_variant values of different base data types are compared, the value of the base data type that is lower in the hierarchy chart is implicitly converted to the other data type before comparison is made.

Table

The table data type (introduced in SQL Server 2005) can be used to store a result set for later processing. Its primary use is for temporary storage of a set. Use DECLARE @*local_variable* to declare variables of type table. The syntax for the table type is as follows:

```
TABLE ({ column_definition | table_constraint} [ ,...n ] )
column_definition:
column_name scalar_data_type
[ COLLATE collation_definition ]
[ [ DEFAULT constant_expression ] | IDENTITY [ ( seed , increment ) ] ]
[ ROWGUIDCOL ]
[ column_constraint ] [ ...n ]
    { [ NULL | NOT NULL ]
    | [ PRIMARY KEY | UNIQUE ]
    | CHECK ( logical_expression )
    }
table_constraint:
{ { PRIMARY KEY | UNIQUE } ( column_name [ ,...n ] )
| CHECK ( search_condition )
}
```

The parameters being passed to create a variable of type table make up the same subset of information used to create a persistent table object in CREATE TABLE. The table declaration includes column definitions, names, data types, and constraints. Note that the only constraint types allowed are PRIMARY KEY, UNIQUE KEY, and NULL.

Functions and variables can be declared to be of type table, and the variables can be used in functions, stored procedures, and batches. A table variable also behaves like a local variable. It has a well-defined scope, which is the function, stored procedure, or batch in which it is declared.

Within its scope, a table variable may be used like a regular table. It may be applied anywhere a table or table-expression is used in SELECT, INSERT, UPDATE, and DELETE statements.

Collations also need to be taken into consideration when creating this variable. (see Chapter 4). The type is also not suitable for use with INSERT INTO and SELECT INTO, and you cannot assign one table variable to another. Bear in mind that because the table type is not a persistent table in the database per se, it is unaffected by any transaction rollbacks.

Timestamp

This data type exposes automatically generated binary numbers that are guaranteed to be unique within a database. Timestamp is used typically as a mechanism for version-stamping table rows. The storage footprint is eight bytes.

The Transact-SQL timestamp data type is not the same as the timestamp data type defined in the SQL-92 standard. The SQL-92 timestamp data type is equivalent to the Transact-SQL datetime data type.

SQL Server 2005 introduces a rowversion synonym for the timestamp data type. Use rowversion instead of timestamp wherever possible in DDL statements. This practice will ease the migration to a future release of SQL Server in which rowversion is expected to be introduced as a new data type.

In a CREATE TABLE or ALTER TABLE statement, you do not have to supply a column name for the timestamp data type. For example, the statement

```
CREATE TABLE MyTable (PriKey int PRIMARY KEY, timestamp)
```

is devoid of a column name, so SQL Server will generate a column name of timestamp. The rowversion data type synonym does not follow this behavior. You must supply a column name when you use the rowversion synonym.

Naturally a table can have only one timestamp column. The value in the timestamp column is updated every time a row containing a timestamp column is inserted or updated. This property makes a timestamp column a poor candidate for keys, especially primary keys. Any update made to the row changes the timestamp value, thereby changing the key value. If the column is in a primary key, the old key value is no longer valid, and foreign keys referencing the old value are no longer valid. If the table is referenced in a dynamic cursor, all updates change the positions of the rows in the cursor. If the column is in an index key, all updates to the data row also generate updates of the index.

A nonnullable timestamp column is semantically equivalent to a binary(8) column. A nullable timestamp column is semantically equivalent to a varbinary(8) column.

Uniqueidentifier

This data type represents the globally unique identifier (GUID). A column or local variable of uniqueidentifier data type can be initialized to a value in two ways:

- Using the NEWID function.
- Converting from a string constant in the following form (*xxxxxxxx-xxxx-xxxx- xxxx-xxxxxxxxxxxx*, in which each *x* is a hexadecimal digit in the range 0–9 or a–f). For example, 6F9619FF-8B86-D011-B42D-00C04FC964FF is a valid uniqueidentifier value.

The comparison operators can be used with uniqueidentifier values. However, ordering is not implemented by comparing the bit patterns of the two values. The only operations that are allowed against a uniqueidentifier value are comparisons (=, <>, <, >, <=, >=) and checking for NULL (IS NULL and IS NOT NULL). No other arithmetic operators are allowed. All column constraints and properties except IDENTITY are allowed on the uniqueidentifier data type. (See Chapters 13 and 14 for examples and tips using uniqueidentifier.)

XML

XML is a data type that lets you store XML data in a column, or a variable of xml type. The stored representation of xml data type instances cannot exceed 2 gigabytes (GB) in size. The T-SQL syntax is as follows:

```
xml ( [ CONTENT | DOCUMENT ] xml_schema_collection )
```

The CONTENT variable, the default, restricts the xml instance to be a well-formed XML fragment. The XML data can contain multiple zero or more elements at the top level. Text nodes are also allowed at the top level.

The DOCUMENT variable restricts the XML instance to be a well-formed XML document. The XML data must have one and only one root element. Text nodes are not allowed at the top level. The xml_schema_collection represents the name of an XML schema collection. To create a typed xml column or variable, you can optionally specify the XML schema collection name.

Here is an example:

```
DECLARE @y xml (Sales.IndividualSurveySchemaCollection)
SET @y =  (SELECT TOP 1 Demographics FROM Sales.Individual);
SELECT @y;
```

Collation Precedence

The character string data types, char, varchar, text, nchar, nvarchar, and ntext are also governed by collation precedence rules. These rules determine the following:

- The collation of the final result, the returned character string expression.

- The collation used by collation-sensitive operators that use character string arguments but do not return character strings. Operators such as LIKE and IN are examples.

Data Type Synonyms

SQL Server 2005 provides data type synonym support for SQL-92 compatibility. Table 10-10 lists the SQL-92 types and the SQL Server 2005 synonyms.

These data type synonyms can be used in place of the corresponding base data type names in data definition language (DDL) statements, such as CREATE TABLE, CREATE PROCEDURE, or DECLARE @variable. The synonym has no use after the object is created because SQL Server references the base data type and has no notion of the high-level label.

This behavior also applies to metadata operations, such as sp_help and other system stored procedures, the information schema views, or the various data access API metadata operations that report the data types of table or result set columns.

SQL-92	SQL Server 2005
Binary varying	Varbinary
char varying	Varchar
Character	Char
Character	char(1)
Character(*n*)	char(*n*)
Character varying(*n*)	varchar(*n*)
Dec	decimal
Double precision	float
float[(*n*)] for *n* = 1–7	real
float[(*n*)] for *n* = 8–15	float
Integer	int
National character(*n*)	nchar(*n*)
National char(*n*)	nchar(*n*)
National character varying(*n*)	nvarchar(*n*)
National char varying(*n*)	nvarchar(*n*)
National text	ntext
Rowversion	timestamp

TABLE 10-10 Data Type Synonyms

The data type synonyms are expressed only in T-SQL statements. There is no support for them in the graphical administration utilities, such as SQL Server Management Studio. The following code demonstrates the creation of a table specifying national character varying:

```
CREATE TABLE CustDetails (PKey int PRIMARY KEY, A_Varcharcolumn national
character varying(10))
```

The column *A_Varcharcolumn* is actually assigned an nvarchar(10) data type. It is referenced in the catalog as an nvarchar(10) column, not according to the synonym supplied on creation of the object. In other words, metadata does not represent it as a national character varying(10) column.

T-SQL Variables

One of the first big surprises to befall an experienced Visual Basic or C# programmer is that T-SQL variables must be explicitly declared in a T-SQL module before they can be used. This is a requirement of T-SQL that makes it similar to a .NET language, Delphi, or Java when dealing with private or local variables that are not exposed to the other modules.

T-SQL variables are declared using the DECLARE statement. T-SQL identifies the actual variable with the at sign (@) character as follows:

```
DECLARE @VariableName VariableType
```

Note in this syntax that you cannot declare and use the variable without declaring the variable data type. For example,

```
DECLARE @aString char(10)
DECLARE @bString varchar(20)
```

This code declares two variables, the first a char string 10 characters long and the second a varchar 20 characters long. In Chapter 2, I listed the built-in data types.

T-SQL Functions

Past versions of SQL Server included numerous constructions and elements that were provided to obtain certain programming results and values, process the various data types, and implement various operations and conditions in the DBMS. These were persistent and were created to obviate the need to repeatedly recode such constructions. These elements, and many new ones, have now been brought together in a unified function collection in SQL Server 2005.

NOTE *Several administrative functions are included in the SQL Server function arsenal; see Chapter Appendix.*

Although they are built into SQL Server, they can be referenced from the outside—in T-SQL statements passed through the APIs and using profilers and query tools, like SQL Server Management Studio and the OSQL utility. Functions in SQL Server 2005 also replace the so-called "global variables" that were preceded by the double at (like @@CONNECTION).

SQL Server functions are true to the definition of "function" in that they can take a number of input values and return scalar values or result sets to the calling process. They can also take a blank value to return a specific predefined or predetermined value. For example, used with the SELECT statement, the function DB_NAME() returns a value that represents the current database you are connected to. And the function GETDATE() returns the current date and time. And NEWID() takes "nothing" as an argument and returns a system-generated GUID.

SQL Server 2005 also lets you create your own user-defined functions. But before we get to the user-defined functions, let's first investigate the myriad built-in functions, many of which you will want to start using the moment you put this book down.

Determinism of Functions

SQL Server functions can be *deterministic* or *nondeterministic*. This means that either they always return the same result any time they are called with a specific set of input values, which means the function is deterministic, or they return different results each time they are called with a specific set of input values, which means they are nondeterministic. This is known as the *determinism* of the function.

For example, a function like DATEADD is deterministic because it always returns the same result for any given set of argument values for the parameters passed to it. GETDATE, on the other hand, is not deterministic. It is always invoked with the same argument, but the return value, the current date and time, changes with each call of the function.

Function determinism was introduced in SQL Server 2000, and thus nondeterministic functions are constrained by the following usage rules:

- You cannot create an index on a computed column if the *computed_column_expression* references any nondeterministic functions.

- You cannot create a clustered index on a view if the view also references nondeterministic functions.

Built-in Function Determinism

SQL Server's built-in functions are either deterministic or nondeterministic according to how the function is implemented. You have no access to change the determinism. The aggregate and string built-in functions are deterministic; however, CHARINDEX and PATINDEX are not, as are all of the configuration, cursor, metadata, security, and system statistical functions. See BOL for a list of functions that are always deterministic.

String Manipulation Functions

T-SQL provides a rich collection of string manipulation and sting management functions. Many of these functions have equivalent functionality in generic programming languages such as VB, C++, and Delphi.

ASCII(*character*)

The ASCII(*character*) function returns the ASCII code value of type int of the leftmost character of the character expression evaluated. For example, the expression

```
SELECT ASCII('d')
```

returns "100." The expression can be of type char or varchar.

CHAR(*integer*)

The CHAR(*integer*) function is used to return the ASCII character of its integer code assignment. For example, the expression

```
SELECT CHAR(100)
```

returns "d," which is the converse of the ASCII() function. Remember, the ASCII codes run from 0 to 255, and thus a null value is returned if you are outside this range. You will obviously not be able to return a code for noninteger values. For example, CHAR(13) is the carriage return code and has no displayable value. On the other hand, you can use the CHAR() function to insert control characters into character strings. For example, the expression

```
SELECT CHAR(100)+CHAR(9)+CHAR(68)
```

returns the values d and D separated by a tab. The most common control characters used are Tab (CHAR(9)), line feed (CHAR(10)), and carriage return (CHAR(13)).

CHARINDEX(*expression1, expression2, startlocation*)

This function can be used to determine the starting position of the specified phrase in the character string. It is useful for searching textual data. The syntax for this function is CHARINDEX(*expression1, expression2, startlocation*). The arguments taken are as follows:

- **expression1 (expression1)**   Represents the expression that contains the sequence of characters to be found.

- **expression2 (expression2)**   Represents the actual string of characters to be evaluated.

- **startlocation**   Represents the starting position in ex2 from which to begin searching for ex1. If the start location is a negative number or zero, then the search begins at the beginning of ex2. In my testing of this function, omitting the start location after a comma delimiter causes an error. If you exclude the delimiter, the function computes.

For example, the expression

```
SELECT CHARINDEX('small', 'the very small brown fox', 0)
```

returns the value 10. Using this function, you can easily search for the starting point of a string in a particular record in your table. For example, the expression

```
USE NORTHWIND
SELECT CHARINDEX('Connection', CompanyName)
  FROM Customers WHERE CustomerID = 'EASTC'
```

returns the value 9. This type of expression is valuable when you need to get into a value and extract a subexpression. For example, in my record numbers for call center systems I tag an agent ID onto an order number and save the entire record as a record number. If a manager needs to check which agent worked the record, the system can extract the agent ID by first locating the starting point in the record where the agent ID begins and then run the GETCHAR() function on the rest of the record. This saves having to create another table or column that references the record number entity with the agent ID entity.

It should be noted that if either expression1 or expression2 is of a Unicode data type, the nvarchar and nchar types respectively, and the other is not, the other is converted to Unicode. In other words, if ex1 is Unicode and ex2 is not, then ex2 is converted to Unicode.

Also, if either expression1 or expression2 is NULL, the CHARINDEX() function returns NULL if the database compatibility level you have set is 70. If the database compatibility level is 65 or earlier, the CHARINDEX() function returns NULL only when both expression1 and expression2 are NULL.

DATALENGTH(*variable expression*)

This "function" deserves a place in a list of string manipulation functions. It is similar to LEN() referenced later in this section but returns the declared length of a variable or field. For example, the expression

```
USE NORTHWIND
 SELECT DATALENGTH(Phone)
 FROM CUSTOMERS WHERE CustomerID = 'EASTC'
```

returns the integer value of "28," while LEN() returns "14," the actual length of the string in the variable or field.

DIFFERENCE(*expression1, expression2*)

This function is used to determine the difference between the SOUNDEX algorithm values of two char or varchar strings represented in expression1 and expression2 (see SOUNDEX() later in this section). The return value is an integer on a scale of 0 to 4. The lowest value of "0" indicates the highest difference between the two strings. The highest value of "4" indicates that the two strings "sound" very similar. For example, the expression

```
PRINT DIFFERENCE ('foo', 'bar')
```

returns a value of "2," indicating the two strings do not sound the same but are similar in construction. Upon changing "bar" to "boo," the difference value increases to 3.

LEFT(*string, startindex*)

This function returns a character string that starts at a specified number of characters from the left of the varchar variable. In can be used in conjunction with the CHARINDEX() function to return the value of a string at the specified index. For example, the expression

```
USE NORTHWIND
SELECT LEFT(CompanyName, 5)
 FROM CUSTOMERS WHERE CustomerID = 'EASTC'
```

returns the varchar value "Easte." If you need to simply evaluate the string, just substitute the column name used in "expression" for a string; for example, LEFT('codered,' 4) returns "code."

The expression can be of character or binary data, a constant, a variable, or a column. It must also be of a data type that can be implicitly convertible to varchar. Use the CAST function to explicitly convert the string to varchar before you evaluate it.

LEN(*string*)

This function returns the number of characters, not the number of bytes, of the given string expression, excluding trailing blanks. For example, the expression

```
USE NORTHWIND
 SELECT LEN(Phone)
 FROM CUSTOMERS WHERE CustomerID = 'EASTC'
```

returns the integer value of "14," which will help us clean up the telephone number column in the *Customer* table of the Northwind database (see also DATALENGTH()).

LOWER(*string*)

This function converts all uppercase characters of character or binary data in the expression argument to lowercase and then returns the new expression. For example, the expression

```
USE NORTHWIND
SELECT LOWER(CompanyName)
 FROM CUSTOMERS WHERE CustomerID = 'EASTC'
```

returns the value "eastern connection." The string in *expression* can be a constant, a variable, or a column as shown in the example. The expression string must also be of a type that can be implicitly converted to varchar. Use CAST to explicitly convert the character. See also UPPER() later in this section.

LTRIM(*string*)

This function returns a character expression after first removing leading blanks. For example, the expression

```
PRINT ('                    my bunny lies over the hillside')
```

returns the value "   my bunny lies over the hillside", with spaces, but the expression

```
PRINT LTRIM('                    so bring back my bunny to me')
```

returns the value "so bring back my bunny to me," sans the spaces. The expression must be an expression of character or binary data. It can be a constant, a variable, or a column, but it must of a data type that is implicitly convertible to varchar. Otherwise, use CAST to convert the expression to varchar.

NCHAR(*integer*)

This function returns the Unicode character with the given integer code, as defined by the Unicode standard. For example, the statement

```
PRINT NCHAR(167)
```

returns the character "§." The value must be a positive number in the range 0–65535. If you specify a value outside this range, NULL is returned.

QUOTENAME(*string, quote character*)

This function returns a Unicode string with the delimiters surrounding the string. For example, the statement

```
SELECT QUOTENAME('PHONES','"')
```

returns the value "PHONES." And the statement

```
PRINT QUOTENAME('PHONES','[')
```

returns the value [PHONES]. The ', ", [,], {, and } are valid quote characters.

REPLACE(*'expression1', 'expression2', 'expression3'*)

This function finds all occurrences of the second string in the first string and then replaces it with the string in the third expression. For example, the statement

```
PRINT REPLACE('fog', 'g', 'o')
```

results in "fog" being changed to "foo."

This function can be used with both character and binary data.

REPLICATE(*character, integer*)

This function repeats a character expression for a specified number of times. It is useful for padding if you replicate a space instead of a character. For example, the statement

```
PRINT REPLICATE('0', 2)
```

returns the value '00'. The int expression must be a positive whole number. If it is negative, a null string is returned.

REVERSE(*string*)

This function returns the reverse of a character expression. For example, the statement

```
SELECT REVERSE('evol')
```

returns the value "love."

RIGHT(*string, integer*)

This function returns the part of a character string starting a specified number of characters from the right. For example, the statement

```
SELECT RIGHT('evol', 1 )
```

returns the value "l."

RTRIM(*string expression*)

This function is the converse of LTRIM. It snips all trailing blanks from the expression passed in the argument placeholder. For example, the statement

```
SELECT RTRIM('LOVE                    ')
```

returns the value "LOVE."

SOUNDEX(*string expression*)

This function returns the four-character code of the SOUNDEX algorithm that is used evaluate the similarity of two strings (see the DIFFERENCE() function discussed earlier). For example, the statement

```
SELECT SOUNDEX('WASH')
```

returns the value "W200."

The SOUNDEX() function converts an alpha string to a four-character code to find similar-sounding words or names. You can then use this value and compare it to another SOUNDEX() using the DIFFERENCE() function. The first character of the SOUNDEX code is the first character of the argument, and the second through fourth characters of the code are numbers. Vowels in the argument are ignored unless they are the first letter of the string. String functions can be nested.

SPACE(*value*)

This function returns a string of repeated spaces *x* number of times as indicated by the integer passed in the argument. For example, the statement

```
SELECT 'Y' + SPACE(1)+ '=' + SPACE(1) + '1'
```

returns the expression "Y = 1." If you are adding spaces to Unicode data, use the REPLICATE() function instead of SPACE().

STR(*float expression, length, decimal*)

This function returns character data converted from numeric data. For example, the statement

```
SELECT STR(42393.78, 8, 1)
```

returns the value "42393.8." The float expression must be an expression of an approximate numeric (float) data type with a decimal point. The length argument is the total length of the returned value including the decimal point, sign, digits, and spaces. The default is 10. The decimal argument is the number is the number of places to the right of the decimal point, rounded off as in the preceding example.

If you supply the values for *length* and *decimal* parameters to the STR() function, they must be positive. The specified length you provide should be greater than or equal to the part of the number before the decimal point plus any number sign you provide. A short float expression is right-aligned in the specified length, while the long float expression is truncated to the specified number of decimal places. For example, STR(12, 10) yields the result of 12, which is right-aligned in the result set. However, STR(1223, 2) truncates the result set to **.

STUFF(*string expression, start, length, ch expression*)

This function deletes a specified length of characters in a string and "stuffs" another set of characters at a specified starting point. You can use it to delete the characters in the middle of a string and replace them with new characters. For example, the statement

```
SELECT STUFF(PHONE,10, 1, '-')
   FROM CUSTOMERS
```

returns all telephone numbers from the PHONE column in the CUSTOMERS table with the space removed at the tenth character and the dash inserted instead. The value is changed from "(800) 555.1212" to "(800) 555-1212".

SUBSTRING(*string expression, start, length*)

This function returns part of a character, binary, text, or image expression. For example, the statement

```
SELECT SUBSTRING('(33428-5857)',2,5)
```

returns the value "33428" representing the first five digits of the nine-digit ZIP code.

The argument in the *string expression* can be a character string, a binary string, text, an image, a column, or an expression that includes a column (but not an expression that includes aggregate functions). The *start* parameter is an integer that specifies where the substring begins, while the *length* parameter takes an integer that specifies the length of the substring (the number of characters or bytes to return). (See Books Online for more information on using this function with the other data types.)

UNICODE(*unicode expression*)

This function returns the integer value, as defined by the Unicode standard, for the first character of the input expression. For example, the statement

```
SELECT UNICODE('§')
```

returns the value "167" as integer (see also NCHAR()).

UPPER(*character expression*)

This function returns a character expression with the lowercase characters converted to uppercase. For example, the statement

```
SELECT UPPER('noodle')
```

returns the value "NOODLE" (see also LOWER()) earlier in this section.

Mathematical Functions

The T-SQL mathematical functions are scalar functions that compute the values passed as arguments and then return a numeric value. All the functions are deterministic—in other words, they always return the same value for any given value passed as an argument—with the exception of the RAND() function, which returns a random value. The RAND() function, however, becomes deterministic when you use the same seed value as an argument.

In addition (no pun intended), the trigonometric functions, such as LOG, LOG10, EXP, SQUARE, and SQRT, cast the input value to a float before computing and then return the value as a float. Table 10-11 lists the mathematical functions and provides brief explanations of how to use them. For a complete reference to these functions consult SQL Server Books Online.

Aggregate Functions

The aggregate functions are used to perform a calculation on a set of values and then return a single value to the caller. Typically these values ignore NULL, but COUNT does not because technically NULL is a value. Aggregate functions are often used with the GROUP BY clause in a SELECT statement.

The aggregate functions are deterministic and thus return the same value when they are called with a given set of input values. These functions can only be used in the following situations:

- The select list of a SELECT statement—in a subquery or an outer query
- In a COMPUTE or COMPUTE BY clause
- In a HAVING clause

The Transact-SQL programming language provides these aggregate functions, listed in Table 10-12.

Function	Application
ABS(numeric)	Returns the absolute, positive value of the argument.
ACOS(float)	Returns the angle, in radians, whose cosine is the given argument.
ASIN(float)	Returns the angle, in radians, whose sine is the given **float** expression (also called arcsine).
ATAN(float)	Returns the angle in radians whose tangent is the given **float** expression (also called arctangent).
ATN2(float, float)	Returns the angle, in radians, whose tangent is between the two given **float** expressions (also called arctangent).
CEILING(numeric)	Returns the smallest integer greater than, or equal to, the given numeric expression.
COS(float)	A mathematic function that returns the trigonometric cosine of the given angle (in radians) in the given expression.
COT(float)	A mathematic function that returns the trigonometric cotangent of the specified angle (in radians) in the given **float** expression.
DEGREES(numeric)	Given an angle in radians, returns the corresponding angle in degrees.
EXP(float)	Returns the exponential value of the given **float** expression.
FLOOR(numeric)	Returns the largest integer less than or equal to the given numeric expression.
LOG(float)	Returns the natural logarithm of the given **float** expression.
LOG10(float)	Returns the base-10 logarithm of the given **float** expression.
PI()	Returns the constant value of PI.
POWER(numeric)	Returns the value of the given expression to the specified power.
RADIANS(numeric)	Returns radians when a numeric expression, in degrees, is entered.
RAND([seed])	Returns a random **float** value from 0 through 1.
ROUND(numeric, len)	Returns a numeric expression, rounded to the specified length or precision.
SIGN(numeric)	Returns the positive (+1), zero (0), or negative (-1) sign of the given expression.
SIN(float)	Returns the trigonometric sine of the given angle (in radians) in an approximate numeric (**float**) expression.
SQRT(float)	Returns the square root of the given expression.
SQUARE(float)	Returns the square of the given expression.
TAN(float)	Returns the tangent of the input expression.

TABLE 10-11   Mathematical Functions

Function	Application
AVG	Returns the average of the values in a group. Null values are ignored.
CHECKSUM	Returns the checksum value computed over a row of a table, or over a list of expressions. CHECKSUM is use for building hash indexes.
CHECKSUM_AGG	Returns the checksum of the values in a group. Null values are ignored.
COUNT	Returns the number of items in a group. COUNT always returns an int data type.
COUNT_BIG	COUNT_BIG always returns a bigint data type value. The only difference between COUNT and COUNT BIG is their return values.
GROUPING	This is an aggregate function that causes an additional column to be output with a value of 1 when the row is added by either the CUBE or ROLLUP operator, or 0 when the row is not the result of CUBE or ROLLUP. Grouping is allowed only in the select list associated with a GROUP BY clause that contains either the CUBE or ROLLUP operator.
MAX	Returns the maximum value in the expression.
MIN	Returns the minimum value in the expression.
SUM	Returns the sum of all the values, or only the DISTINCT values, in the expression. SUM can be used with numeric columns only. Null values are ignored.
STDEV	Returns the statistical standard deviation of all values in the specified expression.
STDEVP	Returns the statistical standard deviation for the population for all values in the specified expression.
VAR	Returns the statistical variance of all values in the specified expression.
VARP	Returns the statistical variance for the population for all values in the specified expression.

TABLE 10-12   Aggregate Functions

Date and Time Functions

These scalar functions perform an operation on a date and time input value and return a string, numeric, or date and time value. Table 10-13 lists the date and time functions and the information they return.

Text and Image Functions

These are scalar, nondeterministic functions that can perform an operation on a text or image argument. The following functions are supported in T-SQL:

- PATINDEX()
- TEXTPTR()
- TEXTVALID()

Function	Application
DATEADD()	Returns a new datetime value based on adding an interval to the specified date (see Table 16-11).
DATEDIFF()	Returns the number of date and time boundaries crossed between two specified dates.
DATENAME()	Returns a character string representing the specified datepart of the specified date.
DATEPART()	Returns an integer representing the specified datepart of the specified date.
DAY()	Returns an integer representing the day datepart of the specified date.
GETDATE()	Returns the current system date and time in the standard internal format for **datetime** values.
GETUTCDATE()	Returns the **datetime** value representing the current UTC time (Universal Time Coordinate or Greenwich Mean Time). The current UTC time is derived from the current local time and the time zone setting in the operating system of the computer on which SQL Server is running.
MONTH()	Returns an integer that represents the month part of a specified date.
YEAR()	Returns an integer that represents the year part of a specified date.

Interval	Value	Range
Year	Yy, yy	1753-9999
Quarter	Qq, q	1–4
Month	Mm, m	1–12
Dayofyear	Dd, y	1–366
Day	Dd, d	1–31
Week	Wk, ww	1–53
Weekday	dw	1–7
Hour	hh	0–23
Minute	Mi, n	0–59
Second	ss	0–59
Millisecond	ms	0–999

TABLE 10-13   Date and Time Functions

PATINDEX(%pattern%, expression)

This function returns the starting position of the first occurrence of a pattern in the specified expression. It returns zeros if the pattern is not found. The function works on all valid text and character data types. For example, the expression

```
SELECT PATINDEX('%.%', Phone)
  FROM CUSTOMERS
```

returns 11 records that contain a period in the string. Nine of these are reported to be in position three, which indicates that an IP address has been inserted into the *Phone* column. Records that do not qualify are returned as a zero value on the returned result set. In the preceding example, I used a single character as an example, but your pattern could be any combination of characters and spaces that form the pattern. In other words, the pattern is a literal string.

You can also use wildcard characters, but you must remember to insert the % character at the beginning and end of the pattern to be evaluated (except when searching for first or last characters). You can also use PATINDEX() in a WHERE clause. For example, the following statement

```
WHERE (SELECT PATINDEX('%Shapiro%', LastName)
  FROM CUSTOMERS)
```

returns all customers with a last name of Shapiro in the *CUSTOMERS* table.

TEXTPTR(*column*)

This function returns the text-pointer value that corresponds to a text, ntext, or image column in varbinary format. The retrieved text pointer value can then be used in READTEXT, WRITETEXT, and UPDATE statements. For example, the statement

```
DECLARE @pointer varbinary(16)
SELECT @ pointer = TEXTPTR(image)
FROM articles a, publications p
WHERE a.pubdate = p.pubdate
   AND p.runtitle = 'Daily News'
```

returns the image data you can then use in the client application.

For tables with in-row text, TEXTPTR returns a handle for the text to be processed. You can obtain a valid text pointer even if the text value is null. If the table does not have in-row text, and if a text, ntext, or image column has not been initialized by an UPDATE statement, TEXTPTR returns a null pointer.

TEXTVALID()

The TEXTVALID() function is used to check whether a text pointer exists. You cannot use UPDATETEXT, WRITETEXT, or READTEXT without a valid text pointer. Chapter 17 provides an example of the TEXTVALID() function.

Conversion Functions

SQL Server 2005 supports two conversion functions, CONVERT() and CAST(), that let you convert a variable or column of one type to another. Use of these functions is called *explicit casting* or *conversion* because SQL Server 2005 supports automatic conversion on several data types. In other words, the conversion functions can be used if you have no choice but to manually convert, or your application demands it for some reason.

CAST() does not do anything more than CONVERT(), but it is provided for compatibility with the SQL-92 standard. This discussion thus focuses on CONVERT(), and I will make mention of features that CAST() does not support. The syntax for this function is CONVERT(*data_type*, *variable*, *style*). The arguments are required as follows:

- **Data_type**   This is the target of the conversion, for example to convert a money value to a character value data type for use in the construction of a financial report, perhaps an invoice.

- **Variable**   This is the variable to convert to or the object of the conversion.

- **Style**   This is the optional variable when the target data type can take one or more style changes.

You can use either of the functions in SELECT statements, and in the WHERE clause, and anywhere else you provide an expression. The following example converts a column from 30 to 25 characters:

```
SELECT CONVERT(nchar(30), StockName)
```

The data type argument you use in CONVERT() can be any valid data type supported by SQL Server. If you use a data type that takes a length argument (nchar, nvarchar, char, varchar, binary, or varbinary), then you can pass its length in the parentheses that enclose the data type length.

You can also use the CONVERT() function to obtain a variety of special data formats. For example, the style argument (not supported by CAST()) is used to specify a particular date format required when you convert datetime and smalldatetime variables to character types. Table 10-14 lists the style values and the date formats returned.

The following example illustrates the differences between CAST() in the first SELECT statement and CONVERT() in the second SELECT statement. The result set is the same for both queries:

CAST():

```
USE NORTHWIND
 SELECT CAST(regiondescription AS char(2)), regionid
 FROM region
```

CONVERT():

```
SELECT CONVERT(char(2), regiondescription), regionid
FROM region
```

The result set is the same for both queries:

```
Ea  1
We  2
No  3
So  4
```

In the preceding example, we converted the region description column from 50 to 2 characters. A better example would be to convert a first name column to one character and compile a report listing of first name initials and full last names. CONVERT() is also useful when using LIKE in the WHERE clause.

Value sans Century	Value con Century	Date Format
1	101	mm/dd/yy
2	102	yy.mm.dd
3	103	dd/mm/yy
4	104	dd.mm.yy
5	105	dd-mm-yy
6	106	Dd mon yy
7	107	Mon dd, yy
8	108	Hh:mm:ss
9	109	Mon dd yyyy hh:mi:ss:mmm AM or PM
10	110	mm-dd-yy
11	111	Yy/mm/dd
12	112	Yymmdd
13	113	Dd mm yyy hh:mm:ss:mmm(24)
14	114	Hh:mi:ss:mmm(24)
20	120	Yyyy-mm-dd hh:mm:ss(24)
21	121	Yyy-mm-dd hh:mi:ss:mmm(24)

TABLE 10-14   Values for Datetime

As mentioned earlier, SQL Server automatically converts certain data types. If, for example, you compare a char expression and a datetime expression, or a smallint expression and an int expression, or char expressions of different lengths, SQL Server will convert them automatically. This is called an implicit conversion.

Expect the following behavior from the conversion functions:

- SQL Server reports an error when you attempt a conversion that is not possible. For example, trying to converting a char with letters to an integer will create an exception.

- If you do not specify a length when converting, SQL Server will supply a length of 30 characters by default.

- SQL Server will reject all values it cannot recognize as dates (including dates earlier than January 1, 1753) when you try to convert from datetime or smalldatetime. You can only convert datetime to smalldatetime when the date is in the proper date range (from January 1, 1900, through June 6, 2079). The time value will be rounded to the nearest minute.

- Converting to a bit will change any nonzero value to 1.

- When you convert to money or smallmoney, any integers in the conversion expression are assumed to be monetary units. For example, let's say you pass an integer value of 5 in the expression; SQL Server will convert it to the money equivalent of five dollars—expressed as U.S. dollars if us_english is the default language.

- All money value numbers to the right of the decimal in floating-point values are rounded to four decimal places by default. Expressions of data types char or varchar that are being converted to an integer data type must consist only of digits and an optional plus or minus sign (+ or –). The leading blanks are ignored. Any expressions of data types char or varchar converted to money can also include an optional decimal point and leading currency sign.

- You can include optional exponential notation (e or E, followed by an optional + or – sign, and then a number) in data types char or varchar that are being converted to float or real.

- When you pass character strings for conversion to a data type of a different size, any values too long for the new data type are truncated, and SQL Server displays an asterisk (*). This is the default display in both the OSQL utility and Management Studio. Any numeric expression that is too long for the new data type to display is truncated.

- You can also explicitly convert any text data to char or varchar, and image data to binary or varbinary. As discussed earlier, these data types are limited to 8,000 characters, and so you are limited to the maximum length of the character and binary data types; that is, 8,000 characters. When you explicitly convert ntext data to nchar or nvarchar, the output is confined to the maximum length of 4,000 characters. Remember that when you do not specify the length, the converted value has a default length of 30 characters. Implicit conversion is not supported with these functions.

- When you convert between data types in which the target data type has fewer decimal places than the source data type, the resulting value is truncated. For example, the result of CAST(10.3496 AS money) is $10.3496.

Style

The number you supply as the *style* argument is used to determine how the datetime data will be displayed. For starters, the year can be displayed in either two or four digits. By default, SQL Server supplies a two-digit year, which may be a problem in certain transactions. For example, the statement

```
SELECT CONVERT(char(50), GETDATE(), 101)
```

returns the date 07/06/2005, while the statement

```
SELECT CONVERT(char(50), GETDATE(), 1)
```

returns the date 07/06/00. Table 10-14 provides the values for the style argument.

T-SQL Flow-Control

The T-SQL language supports basic flow-control logic that will allow you to perform program flow and branching according to certain conditions you provide the switching routines. The routines allow you to test one thing or another in simple either/or constructions, or test for multiple values in an easy-to-use CASE facility. The T-SQL flow-control options are as follows:

- If . . . Else
- CASE
- While
- Continue/Break
- GOTO/Return

If . . . Else

This branching or condition-switching statement will execute an isolated block of code in a routine according to a qualifying condition. If the condition qualifies, the code in the *If* block is executed. If it does not qualify, the program moves to the block of code in the *Else* section of the routine. The block of code in the *Else* section can contain something of substance or very little.

The syntax of this statement is as follows:

```
IF condition
 Begin
   {do something here}
 End
Else
 Begin
   {do something here}
 End
```

This syntax is a little like Pascal; however, notice that no "end ifs" are required, but you should enclose your code in the Begin . . . End blocks. I say "should" because you can get away with omitting the Begin . . . End blocks in simple code segments. However, the Begin . . . End is essential when you need to make sure that all lines in the code segment are processed.

CASE

The CASE statement works the same as the CASE statements you find in all modern programming languages such as Visual Basic, or Delphi or Java. The T-SQL CASE statement can compare a variable or a field against several variables or fields. You could technically do this with multiple If . . . Else blocks, but that would be ugly to say the least, and you have no way to escape such a construction after a condition finds a match or tests true.

T-SQL CASE statements test a variable to be true by using the WHEN . . . THEN clause. For example, "WHEN the banana is yellow" THEN "eat it." After the WHEN tests true, the THEN condition is applied and execution flow continues through the CASE block. For example, the statement

```
SELECT ProductName AS 'Products', 'Popularity'=
CASE
  WHEN UnitsInStock <= 5 THEN 'Fast Mover'
```

```
    WHEN UnitsInStock > 5 AND UnitsInStock <= 15 THEN 'Average Mover'
    WHEN UnitsInStock > 15 AND UnitsInStock <= 1000 THEN 'Slow Mover'
END
FROM Products
```

returns the following table:

```
Chai                           Slow Mover
Chang                          Slow Mover
Aniseed Syrup                  Average Mover
Chef Anton's Cajun Seasoning   Slow Mover
Chef Anton's Gumbo Mix         Fast Mover
Grandma's Boysenberry Spread   Slow Mover
Uncle Bob's Organic Dried P..  Average Mover
Northwoods Cranberry Sauce     Average Mover
Mishi Kobe Niku                Slow Mover
...
```

Obviously the preceding statement might make more sense if the query also checked restock dates and other factors because an item could be considered a slow mover an hour after a new shipment arrived. However, it adequately illustrates a simple CASE usage.

You can do a lot with CASE, such as assign the obtained value in a case statement and then pass that out to a stored procedure or another construction. For example, consider the following statement:

```
DECLARE @Discount real
DECLARE @CouponCode char(5)
SET @CouponCode = 'CDKIG'
SET @Discount =
CASE @CouponCode
   WHEN 'CXDFR' THEN 10
   WHEN 'CDKIG' THEN 7.5
   WHEN 'CKIDK' THEN 8
END
PRINT @Discount
```

I use the discount variable obtained at the end of the CASE and apply it to an item for which the customer has a discount coupon I can identify with a coupon code. In this case, the discount is 7.5 percent. The variable @CouponCode could change from item to item. This can be wrapped up in a trigger, as demonstrated in the next chapter, allowing the server to appropriately apply the discount.

WHILE

The WHILE loop is a flow-control statement that executes a single statement or block of code between BEGIN and END keywords. For example, the following is a simple WHILE statement that increments a value:

```
DECLARE @Count smallint
SET @Count = 0
WHILE @Count < 10
   SET @Count = @Count + 1
```

To repeatedly execute more than just a single line of code, enclose the code between the BEGIN and END blocks, as demonstrated in If . . . Else. We will revisit WHILE in later chapters to demonstrate some advanced T-SQL features, such as triggers, cursors, and stored procedures.

Continue or Break

Use CONTINUE and BREAK to change or stop the execution of the WHILE loop. The CONTINUE keyword restarts a WHILE loop, and the BREAK terminates the innermost loop it is in.

GOTO and RETURN

These two flow-control statements let you jump out of your current segment and move to another location in the procedure, similar to the GOTO in VB or DBase. GOTO moves to a line identified by a label followed by a colon (*ArrivedHere*:). RETURN ends a procedure unconditionally and can optionally return a result.

The GOTO command is confined to a control-of-flow statement, statement blocks, or procedures, but it cannot go to a label outside of the current process. However, the GOTO branch can alter the flow and reroute it to a label defined before or after GOTO. The following example emulates a WHILE loop, and the RETURN is used to break out of the loop when a certain value is reached:

```
DECLARE @Counter int
SET @Counter = 0
Counter:
    SET @Counter = @Counter + 1
      GOTO CheckResult

CheckResult:
 IF @Counter = 10
  BEGIN
   PRINT 'You have reached '+ CAST(@Counter AS CHAR)
   RETURN
  END
 Else
  Goto Counter
```

WAITFOR

The WAITFOR statement suspends procedure execution until a certain time or time interval has passed. The following example prints the time exactly as prescribed in the argument, but notice the conversion and trimming that is needed to return the system time in a simple time format of 00:00 hours:

```
BEGIN
WAITFOR TIME '18:20'
  PRINT 'THE TIME IS '+ LEFT(CONVERT(CHAR(20), GETDATE(), 14), 5)
END

THE TIME IS 18:20
```

RAISERROR

RAISERROR is a facility supported by SQL Server 2005 as a flow-control feature, which is why I tacked it onto this section. However, you will use this facility in many places, such as triggers, stored procedures, transaction processing, and so on.

The syntax for RAISERROR is as follows:

```
RAISERROR ( { msg_id | msg_str } { , severity , state }
[ , argument [ ,...n ] ] )
[ WITH option [ ,...n ] ]
```

However, the simplest syntax to observe at this point for client information is simply RAISERROR(*Message, Severity, State*). Thus the syntax for a simple message to the user would be RAISERROR('This is a non-severe error', 1, 1). More about RAISERROR later.

TRY...CATCH

The new Try...Catch support in T_SQL now implements a error handling process for Transact-SQL similar to the exception handling in .NET Framework (such as in Visual Basic, C#, and C++). You can enclose your Transact-SQL statements in a TRY block and if an error occurs within the TRY block, control is passed to another group of statements enclosed in the CATCH block. The following syntax is the standard TRY...CATCH construct for T-SQL:

```
BEGIN TRY
     { sql_statement | statement_block }
END TRY
BEGIN CATCH
     { sql_statement | statement_block }
END CATCH
[ ; ]


Here is an example:
BEGIN TRY
  -- Test the impossible divide-by-zero to force an exception.
     SELECT 1/0;
END TRY
BEGIN CATCH
     EXECUTE MyErrorHandler
END CATCH;
```

Identifiers

The names that you give to databases and database objects when you create them are called *identifiers*. You don't have to supply an identifier with the same fanfare and excitement that you went through when your parents named you, but identifiers and how you use them are important.

Most of the time you need to supply an identifier at the instant you create, or define, an object. In some cases SQL Server does this for you. A good example of an object that automatically gets its own identifier from SQL Server is the *default* constraint object. In the next chapter I talk about referencing this identifier in your code.

The following code:

```
CREATE TABLE CoffeeTable (KeyCol INT PRIMARY KEY, Wood NVARCHAR(8))
SELECT Wood FROM CoffeeTable . . . .
```

is an example of naming the table and then referencing it by the identifier in the same stroke.

Often it becomes necessary to delimit identifiers with open/close square brackets ([]) when the identifiers do not conform to the rules for well-formed identifiers in T-SQL. For example, the table ImportedCoffee is fine, but *Imported Coffee* needs to be delimited.

It also makes good business sense as a T-SQL programmer to help the optimizer reuse execution plans and connecting identifiers as a SQL Server database namespace is important. In the following code examples both styles are accepted by SQL Server, but the latter is preferred:

```
--one way
USE Northwind
SELECT CustomerID FROM Customers
--better way
SELECT CustomerID FROM Northwind.dbo.Customers
```

As discussed earlier, the at sign (@) at the beginning of an expression is an identifier reserved for SQL Server use, as are the pound (#) sign, the dollar ($) sign, and the underscore (_). You cannot use pound as a subsequent character, but @, $, and underscore will fly.

Moving On

This chapter covers much of the "bits and pieces" you need to code in T-SQL. With what we discussed you'll be able to get cracking and, within a few chapters, come up with some smart queries. You might not be ready to code the query that calculates the age of the universe, so a good "complete reference" to T-SQL or SQL is a good idea. This chapter, the ones that follow, and the goodies you will find in Appendix go a long way to providing that reference.

While we dealt with a lot of the basic ingredients, we also touched on some new data type and functions, which I will refer to in the chapters ahead. So, let's move on to stored procedures and triggers and put some of the stuff we learned in this chapter to work.

Understanding the SQL Server Common Language Runtime

This chapter describes the .NET Framework and its Common Language Runtime (CLR) and how SQL Server 2005 now integrates this environment into its processing engine. The incorporation of a version of the CLR directly into SQL Server (in-process) has catapulted the product into the future, years ahead of itself. To fully understand how it works, this chapter looks at the various aspects of this runtime environment, because it is important to us going in from the ground up to create functions, stored procedures, triggers, data structures (such as arrays) and .NET SQL Server integrated applications, components, and other services.

With this concise coverage of the.NET Framework's runtime, you will be able to design and code applications with the runtime in mind, especially in the area of memory management, which represents the biggest change in the way we write any SQL Server–based applications. Knowing about the runtime is also especially important for programming with the correct security model, exception handling, referencing the correct assemblies to target namespaces, debugging assemblies, and otherwise managing assemblies (deployment and maintenance). All of these subjects make programming the SQL Server CLR far more complex than standard T-SQL.

This chapter examines the following key components of the Framework:

- **The Common Type System (CTS)**   The system that provides the type architecture of the Framework and type safety.

- **The Common Language Specification (CLS)**   The specification all .NET language adopters and compiler makers adhere to so that their languages can be seamlessly integrated into the .NET Framework.

- **The Common Language Runtime (CLR)**   The runtime and managed execution environment in which all .NET managed applications are allowed to process.

We will then break down the Common Language Runtime into several components to be discussed as follows:

- **Managed execution**   This section discusses what managed execution means, as well as how it differs from other execution environments such as VBRUN, SmallTalk's runtime, and the Java Virtual Machine (JVM). It also introduces the garbage collector.

- **The runtime environment**   This section discusses how the CLR works with metadata and Microsoft Intermediate Language (MSIL) to execute code. It also investigates the just-in-time (JIT) compilation architecture. We also briefly look at application domains and what they mean for your deployment requirements. And we also touch on the subject of attributes—a facility for allowing programmers to have more control over the execution and management of their code in the runtime environment.

- **Assemblies**   This section goes into assemblies in some depth and examines how .NET applications, class libraries, and components are packaged.

- **CLR and security**   This section introduces the security architecture of the CLR and how it affects your code and ability to deploy.

Even if you have not had any experience writing and compiling a .NET application outside the SQL Server engine, this chapter will give you the necessary information to hit the ground running—writing, compiling, and executing any stored procedure, function, trigger, or user-defined data type (UDT).

Getting to Know the Framework's Runtime

A Common Language Runtime, managed execution, and automatic memory management running compiled code are now the new order of the day for SQL Server 2005. I agree that programming to the CLR is a major paradigm shift for SQL programmers—especially the notion of a garbage collector doing memory housekeeeping. The .NET Framework does a lot of the work for you. The architecture that forms the foundation for managed execution is known as the Common Type System, or the CTS.

The Common Type System

The Common Type System is the formal definition of how all types in the .NET Framework are constructed, how all types are declared and used, and how they are managed. The CTS also lays the ground rules for protecting the integrity of executing code. Generally we talk about an *object model* in object-oriented programming, but the Common Type System is more than just an object model.

The CTS also specifies how types—classes—are referenced, and how applications and class libraries are packaged for execution on the CLR. The CTS describes class declaration, inheritance, referencing, and type management, not so much as SQL Server idioms but rather as .NET Framework idioms. In other words, all .NET development environments must walk the same walk and talk the same talk, if they hope to be tightly integrated with the platform.

In particular the Common Type System provides the following foundations for the .NET Framework:

- It provides an object-oriented model that is supported by all programming languages that have adopted the .NET Framework. In this regard it is responsible for the Common Language Specification, and how it is implemented by .NET adherents. This means you can use even COBOL to program objects for SQL Server.

- It establishes the foundations and reference framework for cross-language integration, interoperation, type safety, security, and high-performance code execution.

- It defines rules that languages must follow, which helps ensure that objects written in different languages can interact with each other.

You could also consider the subject of assemblies and namespaces, to be discussed later in this chapter, but let's look at the CTS object model to get our bearings and gain some perspective.

Later in this chapter you will come across references to the root of the object model, *Object,* and how it functions as the so-called "ultimate" object of the Framework. Figure 11-1 illustrates the model.

The Common Language Specification

Language interoperability is considered to be one of the Holy Grails of software development—and the .NET Framework has risen to the challenge admirably. By writing "CLS-compliant code," you assure that the classes you construct in one language can be used as is by other

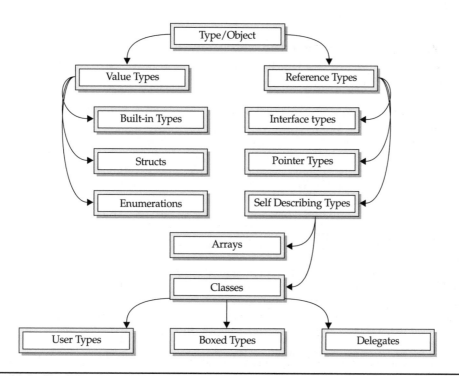

Figure 11-1   The CTS type model, which is the basis for the object model and hierarchy

languages and their respective IDEs and development tools. Imagine that—you can now create components that can be used by any language or development tool without complex COM and ActiveX interfaces and registration details, and upload them into the SQL Server CLR. To achieve the magic, the CLS requires that class and component providers only expose to consumers the features that are common to all the .NET languages.

The CLS is really a subset of the Common Type System (CTS), as I mentioned earlier. In other words, all the rules specified by the Common Type System in the runtime environment, like type safety, drive how the CLS governs compliance at the code construction and compilation levels. The CTS lays down the rules to protect the integrity of code by ensuring *type safety*. When the CTS was being created, the code constructs that risked type safety were excluded from the CLS. Thus your code is always checked for type safety. As long as you produce CLS-compliant code, it will be verified by the CTS.

The old cliché that rules can be broken is likely to be echoed in various far-flung shops. But when you program against the specs in the CLS, you ensure language interoperability for your intended audience and then some. CLS compliance ensures that third parties can rely on your code, and you obtain the assurance that the facilities you want exposed are available across the entire spectrum of developers.

Table 11-1 provides an abridged list of software development features that must meet CLS compliance rules. The table summarizes the features that are in the CLS and indicates whether the feature applies to both developers and compilers (All) or only compilers.

NOTE *For more comprehensive details, see the specification for the Common Language Infrastructure in the Microsoft .NET Framework SDK.*

The CLS includes the language constructs that are needed by all developers, of all .NET languages. That may seem like a tall order, but the specification it is not very big or complex such that a .NET language will find it very difficult to support. After all, many of the languages at the source-code level are as different from each other as fish are from birds. Just take a look at Smalltalk and compare it to Pascal, or compare C# or the managed extensions of C++ to Visual Basic.

Visual Basic does things in its own peculiar way. Thus, writing Visual Basic 2005 code to achieve one end may actually produce some strange nuances when packaged and then accessed in the C# side of the house. A good example is the big difference between the way properties are implemented in Visual Basic and how they implemented in C# (see the section "Understanding Assemblies" later in this chapter). Keep in mind that the CLR for SQL Server executes a fully functional subset of assemblies, so many of the issues you will have on standard CLR will not impact SQL Server.

Here are some of the immediate benefits of the CLR in general:

- Classes that were produced in one language can be inherited by classes used in other languages.

- Objects instantiated from the classes of a sender written in one language can be passed to the methods of receive objects whose classes were created in other languages. The receiving objects receive your arguments and process them as if they were written in the same language as the receiver.

Feature	Applies to	What Must Be CLS Compliant
General	All	Visibility and exposure; types that are exposed must be compliant, but global static fields and methods are not
Naming	All	Characters and casing keywords (compilers must prevent clashing so you need to understand the use of escape characters); names and signatures must be unique.
Types	All	Primitives (boxed types are not compliant), visibility, interface methods, closure, and constructor invocation (typed references are not compliant)
Type members	All	Overloading, uniqueness, and conversion
Methods	All	Accessibility and calling conventions
Properties	All	Accessor metadata, accessor accessibility, modification, naming, and parameters.
Events	All	Event methods and metadata, accessor accessibility, modification, naming, and parameters
Pointers	All	Pointers are not compliant
Interfaces	All	Signatures and modification
Reference types (objects)	All	Construction and invocation
Class types	All	Inheritance (all classes must inherit) from at least one compliant class
Arrays	All	Elements, dimensions, and bounds
Enumerations	All	Underlying types, the Flags attribute, and field members
Exceptions	All	Must derive from the base System.Exception class
Customer attributes	All	Value encoding
Metadata	Compilers	Compliance marking

TABLE 11-1   Abridged Version of the CLS

- Exception handling, tracing, and profiling are language agnostic. In other words, you can debug across languages, and even across processes. Exceptions can be raised in an object from one language and understood by an object created in another language.

Language interop helps maximize code reuse, which is one of the founding principles of all object-oriented languages, and something we shout out loud. The interoperability is achieved by the provision of metadata in executables and class assemblies that describe the makeup of assemblies, and the intermediate stage code that is understood across the entire Framework.

> **NOTE** *Components that adhere to the CLS rules and use only the features included in the CLS may be labeled as CLS-compliant components.*

Although the members of most types defined in the .NET Framework class library are CLS-compliant, some may have one or more members that are not CLS-compliant. These members are provided to enable support for non-CLS-compliant features, such as function pointers. C#, for example, can be used to access these so-called unsafe features while the architects of Visual Basic have decided to stay clear of unsafe code. The noncompliant types and members are identified as such in the reference documentation. More information about them can be found in the .NET Framework Reference. In all cases, however, a CLS-compliant alternative to a non-CLS compliant construct is available.

The Common Language Runtime

Your SQL Server applications, class libraries, and components live in two realities. The design-time reality is where you write source code, create classes and objects, design applications, and debug and compile your code. The runtime reality is an external environment, and for .NET applications, this external runtime environment is the Common Language Runtime, better known as the CLR (commonly referred to as just the runtime environment, or RTE, by the .NET architects), which typically runs on the operating system. In this book we are concerned about how the CLR operates within the operating environment of SQL Server. Figure 11-2 demonstrates the relationship of the CLR with the operating system and its various layers.

The code you write to target the CLR is called managed code. This means that the execution of the code in the runtime environment is *managed* by the CLR. What exactly the CLR *manages* is discussed shortly.

When I started programming in Java and Visual Basic in the mid-nineties, I was perplexed by the need to pay so much attention to the runtime environment. It took an effort to gather up all the runtime elements and make sure they were properly installed just to run the simplest application. I was always shocked to have to build a CD just to ship an application that could fit on a quarter of the space of a floppy disk.

As a Delphi programmer I did not need to concern myself with the need to ensure that a runtime layer on the target operating system would be able to support my application.

FIGURE 11-2
The CLR and its relationship to SQL Server

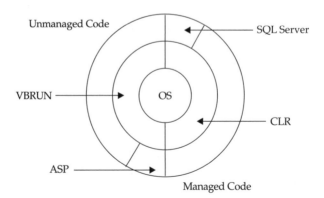

But then the big Delphi applications produced executables and Dynamic linked libraries (DLL) files that became rather bloated.

When I moved to VB and Java, I found it disturbing that a tiny executable of no more than 100K needed many megabytes of supporting libraries just to run. In the early days of Java making sure I had the support of the correct VM was a painful chore. Since I was only writing Windows applications, I learned to rather program against the Java components of Internet Explorer, to be sure that my Visual J++ apps would work. Testing for IE's JVM was actually the easiest way to deploy VJ++ apps back in 1997 or 1998.

After a few years, however, it became clear that the target operating systems my clients were running already had the supporting runtime environment I needed. This was more the case with the JVM than for VBRUN, mind you, because just about everyone already had the latest versions of Internet Explorer on their machines. In the new millennium, as long as your operating systems are well patched and service packs are kept up to date by your IT staff, worrying about the runtime for classic apps is a thing of the past. This is how it is with SQL Server. You don't need to worry about any supporting engine components, as we will soon see.

Microsoft Intermediate Language

When you compile your SQL Server code, it is changed to an intermediate code that the CLR understands and all other .NET development environments understand. All .NET languages compile code to this IL, which is known as Microsoft Intermediate Language, better known as MSIL or just IL for convenience in various places in this book. The idea of compiling to an IL is not new. As you know, two popular languages compile to an intermediate language (or level): Java and Smalltalk.

There are many advantages to IL (and several disadvantages we will discuss shortly). For starters, on the pro side, compilation is much quicker because your code does not have to be converted to machine code. Another of the major advantages of IL is that the development environments of the other .NET languages can consume components and class libraries from the other languages because at the IL level all .NET code is the same.

NOTE *MSIL represents a major paradigm shift in the compilation of code for the Windows platform. Gone are the days when vendors touted compiler speeds, robustness of linkers, and so on. Today thanks to Java and .NET, most of the code we write is first compiled to IL, and we don't have to do anything else as programmers to compile our code to the machine code level.*

Cross-language debugging and profiling is also possible, and so is cross-platform debugging as long as the CLR is the code management authority end to end. Exceptions caused by code that was originally written in Visual Basic can be handled by a C# application, and vice versa. Specifically, IL provides the following benefits:

- It provides cross-language integration. This includes cross-language inheritance, which means that you can create a new class by deriving it from a base class written in another language.

- It facilitates automatic memory management, which is fondly known as garbage collection. Garbage collection manages object lifetimes, rendering reference counting obsolete.

- It provides for self-describing objects, which means that complex APIs, like those requiring Interface Definition Language (IDL) for COM components, are now unnecessary.

- It provides for the ability to compile code once and then run it on any CPU and operating system that supports the runtime.

Figure 11-3 shows what happens to your code from the time your write and compile it in Visual Studio to execution.

Metadata

Once you have built an application, a class library, or a component and compiled it, the IL code produced is packaged up with its metadata in an *assembly*. The assemblies will have either an *exe* or a *.dll* extension, depending on whether they are executables or class libraries.

But the code cannot be executed just yet, because before the CLR can compile it to machine code, it first needs to decide how to work with the assembly. The metadata in the IL directs how all the objects in your code are laid out; what gets loaded; how it is stored; which methods get called; and contains a whole slew of data on operations, control-flow, exception handling, and so on.

The metadata also describes the classes used, the signatures of methods, and the referencing required at runtime (which is what gives you such powerful stuff as reflection and delegation, with its **AddressOf** operator). It also describes the assembly by exposing the following information about the IL code in the assembly:

- The identity of the assembly (name, version, public key, culture context, and so on)

- Dependencies, or what other assemblies this assembly depends on

- Security permissions, which are set by an administrator

- Visibility of the type

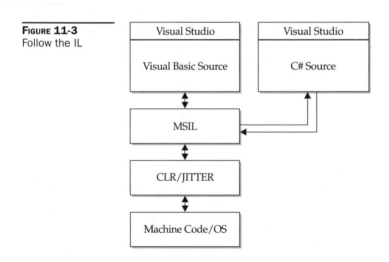

FIGURE 11-3
Follow the IL

- The parent of the type, or what it inherits from
- Type membership (methods, fields, properties, events, and so on)
- Attributes, which are additional elements used on types and their members at runtime.

All this data is expressed in the metadata and essentially allows the assembly contents to be self-describing to the CLR. Self-describing code makes all the hassles of registration, type libraries, and Interface Definition Language (IDL), as discussed, a thing of the past. But metadata does much more.

Self-describing files do not need to be identified or registered with the operating system. By packaging metadata within the executable file itself, the identification is a self-describing ability on the part of the assembly. You can also trust a self-describing assembly more implicitly than you can a file that publicizes itself in the registry, because registry entries date rapidly and their integrity can be easily compromised. Registry entries and their implementation counterparts (the DLLs and executables installed on the system) also can become easily separated.

If you intend your classes to be totally language agnostic, they need to conform to the CLS and not include elements not supported by all CLS languages. Because so many CLS languages are here now, and because many more CLS languages are on their way, you might want to further study the CLS in the .NET SDK.

Executable Code

Assemblies do not have *carte blanche* run of the CLR. Code is not always passed directly to the just-in-time (JIT) compiler. First, the IL code may undergo a thorough inspection if deemed necessary by the platform administrator. The code is given a verification test that is carried out according to the wishes of the network administrator, who might have specified that all .NET code on the machine must be executed according to a certain security policy. The IL code is also checked to make sure nothing malicious has been included. How the checking is carried out is beyond the scope of this book, but we will look at various security settings a little later in the chapter.

The code is also checked to determine whether it is type safe, that the code does not try to access memory locations it is restricted from accessing, and that references reference what they are supposed to reference. Objects have to meet stringent safety checks to ensure that objects are properly isolated from one another and do not access each other's data. In short, if the verification process discovers that the IL code is not what it claims to be, it is terminated and security exceptions are thrown.

Managed Execution

The .NET JIT compiler has been engineered to conserve both memory and resources while performing its duties. It is able, through the code inspection process and self-learning, to figure out what code needs to be compiled immediately and what code can be compiled later, or when it is needed. This is what we mean by JIT compilation—the code is compiled as soon as we need it.

Applications and services thus may appear to be slow to start up the first time, because subsequent execution obviates the need to pass the code through the "JIT'er" again. You can also force compilation or precompile code if necessary. But for the most part, or at least until you have a substantial .NET project underway, you will not need to concern yourself about cranking up the JIT compiler, or keep it idling.

During execution, the CLR manages the execution processes that allocate resources and services to the executable code. Such services include memory management, security services, cross-language interop, debugging support, and deployment and versioning.

Managed execution also entails a lot more than reading IL, verification, JIT, and so on. It also describes what the CLR does once it has loaded and executed an application. Three sophisticated operations of the CLR worth noting are *side-by-side execution,* isolating applications and services into *application domains,* and *garbage collection.*

Side-by-Side Execution

The autonomous, independent, self-describing, unique, versioned nature of an assembly allows you to execute multiple versions of the same assembly simultaneously. This is a phenomenon known as side-by-side execution. This is not something that has never been done before. It is, moreover, something that could never be done easily, and it could not be done with just any application.

Side-by-side execution has brought about the end of DLL hell, because you no longer have to maintain backward compatibility of libraries and components when new applications and assemblies are installed on a machine. Instead, applications that depend on yesterday's version of Smee's component will not break because a new application was installed with today's version of Smee's component. And when you need to junk the various versions of Smee's component when they are no longer being used, you can hit DELETE. However, you will need to explicitly reregister a DLL in SQL Server every time you make changes to the code and then re-register the component you are going to call, such as a function, a stored procedure, a trigger.

Side-by-side execution is possible because an executable assembly expresses a dependence on a particular assembly (the old Smee component). So as long as the old component is still around, any application that needs it still works. However, versioning on .NET is a little more intelligent than simple version numbers and assemblies that can be gone in a SHIFT-DELETE. Version policy can specifically force an application to upgrade to the new version of Smee's component.

NOTE *Just because you can run applications and assemblies side by side on the same computer, and even in the same process, it doesn't mean that conflicts won't crop up. You need good application design and proven patterns of software development to ensure that code is safe and reentrant.*

Automatic Memory Management

A boon for developers coding to .NET is the automatic memory management that it provides. This has been in achieved using a sophisticated memory-management algorithm called a garbage collector (GC).

Let's set the scene with an analogy. If you are a single person, you know what drag it is to schlep the garbage out in the morning. If you are not single, you may also know what a drag it is to be asked to schlep the garbage out in the morning. And if you have kids, you know what it is like to argue with them and still have to take the garbage out yourself.

See yourself in that picture? Programming and managing memory without a GC can be a drag. Now imagine that every morning, the garbage bag simply dissolves and you no longer have to worry about it. This is what the GC does for you. It *eliminates* the chores of managing memory in programming.

When you no longer need the object and nix the reference variable, when you assign the reference variable to another object, or when something just happens to cut the reference variable from the object, the object gets lost (it has *gone out of scope*). This means that you no longer have a way of referencing the object to reuse it.

In VB 6.0 and earlier days, objects that went out of scope, got lost, or simply were not needed anymore had to be explicitly disposed of (remember *Terminate events* [VB], *Destroy or Free* [Delphi], or *DeleteRef* [C++]). The problem in manual memory management is that when you have a lot of objects, you sometimes forget to dispose of them, you lose track of how many were created, and so on. So some of these objects never get cleaned up and you slowly start to "leak out memory." The .NET GC does not let this happen, because these "lost" objects are removed and the memory they occupied is freed.

This, of course, could mean that you can write a heck of a lot of code without having to worry about memory management. However, we need to say "yes, but" and add a big disclaimer: You *can* write a lot of code and never have to worry about freeing objects. And you will see that in the examples provided in this book. But the concept of not having to worry about memory management ever again is simply untrue—untrue for the .NET languages and untrue for Java.

To demonstrate, let's say you create an application with GC that is opening up sockets all over the Internet and about ten threads are running, each in its own little "slice" on the system, activating objects and basically being very, very busy. The algorithms in the application that work the threads need to create objects, work with them, and then dump them (for whatever reason, they cannot be reused by the thread). In this case, chances are that you are going to run out of memory just as quickly as you would in the unmanaged world because the GC cannot clean up after your threads as quickly as you need.

You might think that you could just call *Finalize* after each object is done with. But, sorry folks, GC algorithms do not work that way. You see, the finalization of objects in the GC world of managed execution is *nondeterministic,* which means that you cannot predict exactly when an object will be cleaned out. Objects aren't removed chronologically, so those that died earlier than others may end up getting removed out of order. GCs do not just stop and rush over to do your bidding. Like kids, they don't come running immediately when the garbage bag is near bursting.

There is something else you need to think about. Garbage collection can itself be a bottleneck. The boon of not having to set objects free has this trade-off: The GC is under the control of the CLR, and when the collector stops to take out the garbage, your threads have to mark time. This means that not only do you have garbage stinking up the place, but your threads get put on hold while the GC's dumpster pulls up at your back door. So now you no longer have memory leaks to worry about, but you might have "time leaks" instead.

Before you tear up this book and decide to go into shrimp farming, know this: The CLR allows you some management over the GC. A collection of GC classes and methods are at your disposal. This does not mean that you can force collection or make the cleanup *deterministic,* but it does mean that you can design your applications and algorithms in such a way that you have some degree of control over resource cleanup.

Here is something else to consider. Just because managed code is garbage-collected does not mean you can ignore application design and common sense. If you are coding applications that lose or nix objects, the GC is not going to work for you. In fact, you *should* return this book to the store (don't tear it up, though) and go into shrimp farming. Your patterns and design should be using the objects you create until the application or service shuts down. And objects that have to be removed should be kept to a minimum.

Despite our warnings, the GC is actually very fast. The time you might lose to collection is measured in milliseconds in the life of the average application on a fast machine. In addition, the GC can be deployed on multiprocessor machines, allowing its threads to be allocated to one processor while yours run on the other. And because the GC is such an important part of the CLR, you can bet that Microsoft will often send it back to the work-shop for tune-ups, oil changes, tire-rotation, and so on.

Understanding Assemblies

While namespaces can be understood as a logical grouping or encapsulation of classes, the assembly is a "physical" container for at least one built (compiled) executable or class file or module or some other resource, like an icon. If the assembly is a class library, then the class or classes it harbors are referenced by the fully qualified namespace (FQNS) name described in the preceding section. If the assembly is an executable file, an application, you reference it by the name of the physical file, which needs an entry point to allow the operating system initiate its execution.

NOTE *Assembly names and namespace names should not be confused. The two names, while often similar and sometimes identical, have very little to do with each other.*

At the physical level an assembly is many things, and the organization of its contents—Microsoft Intermediate Language code (MSIL) and metadata—is quite complex. While you don't need to know the ins and outs of the contents of the assembly, you need to fully understand what an assembly is and how to build it, name it, distribute it, and manage it in order to be effective in your development efforts. This section will help you achieve that so that you can navigate your software development results and the chapters of this book more easily. You will understand assemblies better if we separate them into the four types of units that the Visual Basic compiler can produce them as

- **Console executable**   This assembly is the standard, GUI-less, console Window that we have been compiling to so far in this chapter. Console assemblies have the *.exe* extension. OS entry into the executable is through *Main*. Console executable code is not supported in SQL Server.

- **Windows executable**   This assembly is the standard .NET Windows executable file. The assemblies are also given the *.exe* extension. OS entry into the executable is through *WinMain*. Windows executable code is not supported in SQL Server.

- **Class library**   This assembly is your standard .NET class library, which can be dynamically linked. These assemblies are given the *.dll* extension. They can contain one class or many. OS entry into the library is via *DLLMain*.

- **Class module**   This assembly is your standard class module, which is used as a container for compiled classes that still need to be linked into a project or as part of a formal class library before it can be used. These assemblies are given the *.netmodule* extension. No entry into this file is required because entry is via the *DLLMain* of the assembly it is linked to.

SQL Server's use of the CLR needs only to work with class library and class modules that have been specifically tailored to SQL Server. SQL Server obviously does not need to run Windows GUI application or console applications. It can be considered good .NET programming practice to name an assembly such that it describes the purpose and provides a hint of the types inside it and the purposes of these classes. The *System.dll* file that ships with the Framework is a good example. However, also naming the assembly "System" tends to blur the distinction between the assembly name and the namespace name (such as *System.Data,* which refers to both the namespace and the assembly name). I think it's better to give your assembly a name that does not "clash" with the root namespace name.

Before we discuss the four types of output files further and how they are produced, let's take a closer look at how assemblies are located by the runtime, the actual makeup of an assembly, and the roles they play in .NET Framework software development.

Locating Assemblies, Anytime

Most of time, the assemblies you create—executable applications, functionality, or resources—reside in a folder you create with an installation routine or utility. The default location when you are building assemblies is the project folder for Visual Studio.

The assemblies can be stored in the root folder of your application, or in subfolders. You have a lot of flexibility in where you house your assemblies and how you get them to their folders.

The other location for your assemblies is the Global Assembly Cache, or GAC (pronunciation rhymes with *wack*). Assemblies placed into the GAC must be shared and given strong names (described later in this section), so these assemblies would typically be used by more than one application or user, even concurrently. The concept of "registering" with the GAC is similar to registering with the registry, just not as fragile a process or as hard to maintain. For SQL Server you might create a folder for assemblies inside the SQL Server folder hierarchy under Program Files.

There are ways of overriding the default methods for locating assemblies. You can also redirect the path to an assembly. Assemblies can also interoperate with the COM and COM+ world and are accessible from unmanaged clients, something you would not typically do for SQL Server assemblies.

Microsoft suggests keeping assemblies private and thus out of the GAC if they do not need to be shared, which is a good practice for SQL Server CLR code.

What's in an Assembly

In the early days of developing for the Microsoft operating systems (usually one of the early shades of Windows), the compilers produced a file that was compliant with two standards, the Microsoft Portable Executable (PE) format and the Microsoft Common Object File Format (COFF). The two standards were created to enable the operating system to load and execute your applications, or link in the DLLs.

The formats specified how the compiled files were laid out, so that the OS found what it expected to find when it executed or loaded your files. The .NET assemblies adopt the PE/COFF combination to enable the runtime to process your files in the same fashion as the standard executable files you compile, and this is true on SQL Server CLR as well.

TIP *You can't ignore this section if are in charge of deploying, packaging, or installing assemblies to SQL Server.*

Metadata

Assemblies carry metadata so that they can describe themselves to the runtime environment (the CLR). The metadata describes code and class data, and other information like security. .NET assemblies are not compiled to machine code, like their native brethren, but rather to MSIL.

Metadata provides us with a simpler programming model than what we have been accustomed for so many decades. We no longer need to work with complex and finicky Interface Definition Files (IDL), dozens of cryptic header files that are so tedious and time-consuming to prepare, and external dependencies for code and components alike. This is why a .NET assembly is a no brainer to run on SQL Server.

When a .NET (PE) file is executed or loaded, the CLR scans the assembly for the metadata manifest that will allow it to interpret, process, JIT-compile (down to machine code) and then run the file. The metadata is not only for the benefit of the CLR but it identifies the assembly—allowing it to describe itself—to the SQL Server .NET environment or Framework, even across process boundaries.

Figure 11-4 illustrates how the contents of the PE/COFF assembly are assembled, hence the terms assembly—which is not a new term to computer language boffins. While it is convenient to keep calling the *.exe* files the compiler can produce executables, they are not really executable without the presence of the Common Language Runtime on the computer, an issue that is likely to disappear within a few years. Remember how the issue of having the Java Virtual Machine became a non-issue.

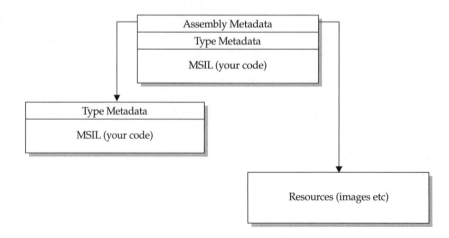

FIGURE 11-4   An assembly comprises several layers

More about Metadata

When you build or compile your file into the PE format, metadata is inserted into one portion of the file while your code is compiled down to MSIL and inserted into another portion of the file. Everything in the file is described by the metadata that is packed into the assembly, including inheritance, class code, class members, access restrictions, and so on.

When you execute an application and a class is referenced, the CLR loads the metadata of the respective assembly and then studies this payload to learn everything it has to know to successfully accommodate the assembly, its resources, and the requests of the contents.

The metadata describes the following:

- **Description of the assembly**   This metadata describes the identity of the assembly, such as name, version, culture, public key, and so on. It also holds references to types that are exported, the assembly's dependencies, and security permissions.

- **Description of the assembly's types**   This metadata describes the types in the assembly. The description includes the name, the visibility of the class, the base class, and any interfaces implemented. It also describes class members, such as methods, data fields, properties, events, and type composition or nesting.

- **Description of Attributes**   This metadata describes the additional descriptive modifiers that alter types and their members.

The metadata just described provides a sophisticated mechanism for allowing assemblies to describe themselves to the CLR. In other words the metadata includes everything the CLR needs to know about a module and its execution and interaction with other modules in the CLR. Since the assemblies do not require explicit registration to the operating system, application reliability is increased exponentially.

The metadata also facilitates language interoperability and allows component code to be accessed equally by any CLS-compliant language. You can inherit from classes written in other languages by virtue of the BCL, which is mostly written in C#.

The PE file is divided into a section for metadata and a section for the MSIL code. The metadata section references the MSIL sections via a collection of tables and heap structures, which point to tokens that are embedded in the MSIL code.

This also means that you cannot change the contents of the assemblies or "fix" the MSIL code without the assembly metadata knowing about it. This provides a consistent means of checking up on the integrity of the assembly contents—that it has not been compromised.

The metadata token is a four-byte number that identifies what the token references in the MSIL—a method, a field, and so on.

The Nature of the Assembly

In additional to the logical types of assembly described earlier, assemblies can be either static or dynamic and private or shared:

- **Static assembly**   This assembly is the .NET PE file you create whenever you compile and build a class library or some type of application. The namespaces we discussed earlier are typically partitioned across such assemblies. They can be in one assembly or partitioned across multiple assemblies.

- **Dynamic assembly**   This assembly is a memory-resident module that gets loaded at runtime to provide specific runtime services. A good example of dynamic assemblies is the *Reflection* class collection, which allow you to reference and access runtime type information.

- **Private assembly** This assembly is a static assembly that can only be accessed by a specific application. This assembly is visibly only to the application or other assemblies in its private folder or subfolder.

- **Shared assembly** This assembly is given a unique or strong name and public key data so that it can be uniquely identified by the CLR. It can be used by any application. A dynamic assembly can also be shared.

Let's now take a closer look at the contents of an assembly—and among other things its IL code. The quickest way to do that (besides reading this book) is to run the IL disassembler application that ships with the .NET Framework Software Development Kit (SDK). The file is called ILDASM. Double-click the application and the application will load.

Go to File | Open and aim the application at any assembly you might already have created. Let's first check out the assembly manifest so that we know what we are looking at.

The Assembly Manifest

The manifest is the critical requirement of the assembly because it contains the assembly metadata. However, you can compile an assembly to MSIL without a manifest, to produce a netmodule (see the section on module assemblies later in this chapter). Assembly manifests can be stored in single-file assemblies or in multifile assemblies in stand-alone files.

The assembly manifest's metadata satisfies the CLR's version requirements and security identity requirements, the scope of the assembly, and resolution of resources and types.

The assembly manifest provides the following metadata:

- Metadata that identifies the assembly, which includes the name, version number, culture (language and culture), public key, digital signature, and so on

- Metadata that identifies all the files that compose the assembly, as a single file or as many files that form a logical unit

- Metadata that provides for the resolution of the assembly's types, their declarations, and implementations

- Metadata that resolves dependencies (other assemblies on which this one depends)

- Metadata that allows the assembly to describe itself to the runtime environment

The manifest code in the assembly is exposed as follows:

```
.module SQLcr.dll
// MVID: {8A49956F-353C-4C11-9F7E-6C46EF6AF2FD}
.imagebase 0x11000000
.subsystem 0x00000002
.file alignment 512
.corflags 0x00000001
// Image base: 0x03680000
.namespace SQLcr.Ch11{
  .class /*02000002*/ private auto ansi sealed Welcome
  extends [mscorlib/* 23000001 */]System.Object/* 01000001 */
```

```
{
  .custom /*0C000001:0A000003*/ instance void [Microsoft.VisualBasic/* 23000002
*/]Microsoft.VisualBasic.Globals/* 01000003 *//StandardModuleAttribute/* 01000004
*/::.ctor() /* 0A000003 */ = ( 01 00 00 00 )


  .method /*06000001*/ public static void Main() cil managed
    // SIG: 00 00 01
    {
    // Method begins at RVA 0x2050
    // Code size       20 (0x14)
    .maxstack  8


  .language '{3A12D0B8-C26C-11D0-B442-00A0244A1DD2}',
  '{994B45C4-E6E9-11D2-903F-00C04FA302A1}', '{00000000-0000-0000-0000-
   00000000000}'
```

The Role of the Assembly

So now you have seen what goes into the assembly and what the manifest achieves. But what does the assembly do for you? Without getting lost in the minutiae of the Framework, let's investigate the essential roles of an assembly. An assembly is

- A type boundary
- A reference scope boundary
- A unit of deployment
- A unit of execution
- A version boundary
- A security boundary

Assemblies as Type Boundaries

On the file system the assembly looks like any other dynamic link library and, as discussed earlier, usually goes by the .dll extension, although it can also be a cabinet file (with the .cab extension).

First of all, you can build a class and make its source code available to any application. But you would mostly do that for your own use, and maybe for your development team members. However, I don't suggest you provide "raw" classes to your team members either, because with access to the actual source code there's no telling what problems can be introduced. You would only supply the raw source files if your user specifically requested or needed it, as do readers of this book, or your customers have opted to buy the source code of your components (usually as a safeguard against your going out of business).

The best examples of assemblies, as mentioned earlier, are the ones that contain the base class libraries that essentially encompass the .NET Framework. As mentioned earlier, SQL Server uses a subset of these. To compile a class to IL and package it up into an assembly is very straightforward. You simply build the class and specify to the compiler which assembly you want to put it in and under what namespace.

Classes (or types as they are known when they have been reduced to IL) are separated by the assembly in which they reside, which is why the assembly is known as a type boundary. In other words, two types can be placed onto the same namespace, but they can exist in individual assemblies. The problem arises when you try to reference the type in the IDE because you can only Import to one fully qualified namespace. The IDE, by the way, will not let you reference the second class twice but will report to you that you have already made the reference.

Assemblies as Reference Scope Boundaries

The manifest metadata specifies the level of exposure a type and its resources have outside the assembly, the dependencies of the assembly (other assemblies on which it depends), and how types are resolved and resource requests satisfied.

If the assembly depends on other assemblies that are statically linked to it, then their names and metadata are included in the manifest. Data such as the referenced assembly's name, version, and so on are stored in the manifest.

The reference scopes of the types in the assembly are also listed in the manifest. The types can be accessed outside the assembly, which is the process that lets you reference them by their FQNS, or they can be given friend access, which means that they are hidden from the outside world—only accessible to the types within the same assembly in which the friend resides.

Assemblies as Units of Deployment

When you execute an application, the application assembly calls into any other assemblies that it depends on. These assemblies are either visible to the application assembly, .exe file, in the same folder or in subfolders, or they are visible in the runtime environment because they have been installed in the GAC.

Assemblies installed in the GAC are shared, which exposes them to other assemblies that may need access to their internals. You might also ship utility classes, culture and localization classes, components, and so on, and these can be installed in the applications installation folder or also installed into the GAC. These assemblies let you build very thin application assemblies and allow you to keep successive deployments small, where you just need to change out the assembly that is outdated.

Also, versioning in .NET lets you or your users install new versions of your assemblies, without breaking the assemblies from previous installation and so breaking applications that have already been installed on the system.

Assemblies as Units of Execution

The CLR lets all shared assemblies execute side by side or be accessed side by side. What that means is that as long as you create a shared assembly, with a strong identity and a unique version number, and you register it into the GAC, the CLR will be able to execute the assembly alongside another assembly. The DLL conflicts of the past are thus abolished under the CLR because only the version number and unique public key data allow the CLR to distinguish between the assemblies.

You will also likely avoid the problem of a new assembly overwriting an older one, thereby "breaking" the previous installation.

The CLR also has no problem referencing any dependent assemblies because all the information it needs to be sure it is executing or linking in the correct files is each assembly's manifest. This is known as side-by-side execution. The only difference between the two assemblies is the version numbers of each.

Assemblies as Version Boundaries

The assembly is the smallest versionable unit in the CLR, which means that the types and other resources it encapsulates are versioned with the assembly as a unit. A class cannot stand alone and be accessed outside of the assembly architecture because there is no way to reference it. The class or type can be either part of the application assembly or stand alone in its own assembly, which provides the version data for it.

The version number is encapsulated in the assembly manifest, as shown earlier. The CLR uses the version number and the assembly's public key data to find the exact assembly it needs to execute and any assemblies that may be dependent on the specific version.

In addition the CLR provides the infrastructure to allow you to enforce specific version rules.

Assemblies as Security Boundaries

The assembly is a security unit that facilitates access control to the data, type functionality, and resources it encapsulates. As a class provider, the CLR allows you to control access to your assembly's objects by allowing you to specify a collection of permissions on an assembly. The client process—rich clients, thin clients, Web forms, or otherwise—must have the permission you specify in order to access the object in the assembly.

This level of security is known as *code access security.* When an assembly is accessed, the CLR very quickly determines the level of code access allowed on the assembly. If you have authorization, you get code; if not, you're history. The idea of controlling code access is fairly new and in line with the model of distributed functionality that is becoming so widespread. Code access security also employs a *role-based security* model, which specifies to the CLR what a client is allowed to do with the code it can access.

The security identifier of an assembly is its *strong name,* which is discussed in the next section.

Besides client access to assemblies, system resources also require protection from assemblies. The SQL Server CLR security secures access to system resources by comparing credentials and proxies of credentials to the Windows file system's security architecture.

Strong Names

Assemblies can be given strong names, which will guarantee their uniqueness and provide security attributes. The strong name is made up of the assembly's standard name (such as *codetimes.sqlserver.system*), its version number, culture, public key data, and digital signature. The strong name is generated from all this data, which is stored in the assembly manifest. If the CLR were to encounter two assemblies with the same strong name, it would know that the two files are 100 percent identical.

Strong names are issued by Visual Studio and by development tools that ship with the .NET SDK. The idea behind strong names is to mainly protect the version lineage of an assembly, because the guaranteed uniqueness ensures that no one else can substitute their assembly for yours, which otherwise would be a major security loophole. In other words, a strong name will ensure that no other assembly, possibly packed with a hostile payload, can masquerade as your assembly.

The strong name also protects your consumers and allows them to use the types and resources of your assemblies with the knowledge that your assemblies have not been tampered with. This is a built-in integrity check that will allow consumers to trust your code. Combined with supporting certificates, this offers you the ultimate security system for the protection of enterprise and distributed code.

The .NET Security Model

A number of mechanisms are in place to secure resources and assemblies from unauthorized users, hostile code, and viruses. Here are the three basic security levels:

- **ASP.NET Web application security**   This mechanism provides the means for controlling access to a Web or Internet site through authentication. Credentials are compared against the file system or against an XML file that contains lists of authorized users, authorized roles, and HTTP verbs.

- **Code access security**   This mechanism uses permissions to control assembly access to resources and operations. By setting permissions, you can protect the system from malicious code while at the same time allowing bona fide code to run safely. This form of *evidence-based security* is managed by administrators.

- **Role-based security**   This mechanism provides access to assemblies based on what it, as the impersonator of the user, is allowed to do. This is determined by user identity, role membership (like the roles you have in SQL Server 2005), or both.

As a SQL Server CLR developer, you need to consider security on a number of levels. You need to determine how your code will run in the target environment, how it will resist attack, and how you can handle security exceptions that are raised when your code is blocked.

NOTE *We don't condone writing assemblies for malicious or hostile use, but nevertheless there are developers out there with less than amicable intent who will be reviewing the .NET security model to figure out how they can get assemblies onto the .NET runtime.*

TIP *You can protect your assemblies from invasion through the technique of strong naming or digital signing. If your assemblies are going to find their way into the public domain, it is recommended that you both sign and strongly name them. A strong name is a unique name that is generated from the contents of an assembly, such as version numbers, simple names, digital signatures, culture information, and so on.*

You should fully investigate both strong-naming techniques and digital signing of the assembly—which is achieved through public key encryption technology via the services of a Public Key Infrastructure (PKI)—because most Chief Technical Officers (CTOs) are going to demand it, and because it is for your own protection.

Working with the SQL Server Base Class Library

The .NET Framework provides a number of classes, interfaces, and value types tailored to SQL Server that allow you to build functionality and develop solid applications and services. The remainder of this chapter will be devoted to a brief description of the class library hierarchy that is accessible from your development environment.

To facilitate interoperability, the .NET classes and types are compliant with the CLS. Any language compiler that targets the CLR can thus use them. However, as mentioned earlier all compilers do not equally support the class libraries.

The .NET Framework classes provide an extensive array of functionality related to basic I/O, threading, networking, security, data access, forms, Web services, and so on. You can use the classes and data types to build sophisticated applications and services, and components or controls that can be simply plugged into any .NET-compliant environment. Later chapters throughout this book delve into advanced use of the class libraries for stored procedures, triggers, functions, and the like.

You can derive from the .NET classes or extend functionality where permitted, or else you can implement an interface directly in your code from a runtime-based class that implements an interface.

The .NET Framework types are named using dot notation that denotes a hierarchy or a namespace. This is not unlike the naming notation used by Java, or the namespaces notation used by the Internet Domain Name System or the Active Directory namespace. For example, the *System.Data.ADO* namespace refers to the hierarchy of classes that represent the functionality of the ActiveX Data Object technology (as well as CLR database objects for SQL Server 2005). In order to gain access to the ADO in .NET, you would need to reference *System.Data.ADO* to directly reference the actual ADO class, which is the last name in the namespace "chain" of classes. If you were to reference *system.data,* you would not only reference ADO but also all other classes on the *system.data* namespace. If you do not need any other data class in your application, you would be wasting a lot of resources compiling in the other resources on the data namespace, such as the SQL types.

The dot notation syntax has no effect on the visibility and access characteristics of classes and their members. It also has no influence on inheritance or binding or the interfaces available. In fact, the namespaces can also be partitioned across assemblies, and a single assembly may contain multiple class namespaces.

It really doesn't take long to understand the nuances of the CLR and its various components. In fact, most of the developers on your team writing code targeting the CLR need never really worry about the CLR at all. Instead, you can elect one or two people to be CLR "diligent."

CLR specifics—especially the GC, application domains, and security—need to be hashed out in the design and modeling stage. Provide specific support for exception handling (by delegating the duty of adding security exceptions to your custom exception classes), and not only will projects come in ahead of schedule, but you can take Fridays off to go sailing or horseback riding.

Getting Started with the CLR

As mentioned in Chapter 5, the CLR is disabled on SQL Server 2005 for security reasons. You will need to explicitly enable it using the sp_configure stored procedure as follows:

```
sp_configure 'show advanced options', 1
GO
RECONFIGURE
GO
Sp_configure 'clr enabled', 1
GO
RECONFIGURE
GO
```

You are now ready to create some .NET components to run on the SQL Server CLR.

Creating CLR Database Objects

So now that you know how the CLR works and that SQL Server has its own in-process version of it for code execution, what exactly can you do? The following list describes the database objects that run on the SQL Server CLR:

- Stored Procedures
- User-Defined Functions (UDF)
- Triggers
- Aggregates
- User-Defined Type

As mentioned earlier, the functionality to create and deploy these objects is exposed in an assembly called system.data.dll, which is part of the .NET Framework. This assembly can be found in the Global Assembly Cache (GAC) as well as in the .NET Framework directory. When you create the class for any of the above listed objects you will need to reference the *system.data.dll* (version 2.0 of the Framework) assembly, which contains the following namespaces:

- System.Data
- System.Data.Sql
- Microsoft.SqlServer.Server
- System.Data.SqlTypes

The following code demonstrates a simple trigger on a table, that notifies an administrator that the table has been modified by someone:

```
using System;
using System.Data;
using System.Data.Sql;
using Microsoft.SqlServer.Server;
```

```
using System.Data.SqlClient;
using System.Data.SqlTypes;
using System.Xml;
using System.Text.RegularExpressions;

public class CLRTriggers
{
   public static void ChangedTableTrigger()
   {
       SqlTriggerContext triggContext = SqlContext.TriggerContext;
       switch(triggContext.TriggerAction)
       {
           case TriggerAction.ChangedTable:
               SqlContext.Pipe.Send("Table changed:");
               SqlContext.Pipe.Send(triggContext.EventData.Value);
               break;
           default:
               SqlContext.Pipe.Send("The table was changed:");
               SqlContext.Pipe.Send(triggContext.EventData.Value);
               break;
       }
   }
}
```

Once you have created a component to run on the CLR you can either deploy the project using Visual Studio 2005, or manually copy the assembly to the target server and then load it using T-SQL code in Management Studio as follows:

```
CREATE ASSEMBLY CLRTriggers
FROM '\\SOMEWHERE\MYCODE\CLRTriggers.dll'
```

The following code installs the assembly for the trigger

```
CREATE TRIGGER ChangedTableTrigger
ON CRM.Logins
FOR ALTER_TABLE
AS
EXTERNAL NAME NormalData.CLRTriggers.ChangedTableTrigger
```

If you need to nix the assembly you can either run the following T-SQL code

```
DROP ASSEMBLY CLRTriggers
```

or drill down to the \\MYSQLSERVE\\Databases\MYDB\Programmability\Assemblies right-click the assembly and select Delete.

That's all there is to creating a CLR database object for SQL Server 2005. The complexity will be in your code, not in the act of installing the assembly and registering the object.

Going Further

Further discussion of the CLR database objects is beyond the scope of this book, save for a short discussion on CLR stored procedures and functions in Chapter 14. See the Microsoft *SQL Server 2005 Developer's Guide* by Michael and Denielle Otey, Osborne/McGraw-Hill, 2005, for a more advanced discussion of objects such as UDTs and aggregates.

Data Integrity

Perhaps no other topic of discussion in database development, modeling, and management circles draws more attention, and often heated debate, than that of data integrity. It is astonishing that, despite the distance we have come in understanding, practice, and technology, so many database gurus (Celko, Codd, Date, Riordan, et al.) vary so widely in their respective philosophies. As a result, administrators and developers often handle integrity modeling and thus integrity programming by the seat of their pants. Even SQL Server Books Online defines data integrity in its glossary in a way more confused than a bat in broad daylight.

This book is certainly not the forum for a discussion of data integrity, and this is about as far as I want to venture in discussing relational database theory. But without exploring some concepts and accepting the only feasible definition of data integrity, you will not benefit from all the tools and new features that SQL Server 2005 supports with respect to data integrity modeling and programming.

Data integrity *definitely* is not a practice, a discipline, that ensures that data stored in a database is correct, *only that is it believable or plausible.* There is no way between this life and the hereafter that SQL Server 2005, or any other RDBMS, can guarantee that data in a database is correct. Get *correct* out of your vocab now. SQL Server 2005 has no way of knowing and thus ensuring that my area code is not 209 but rather 299, or that my last name is Shapiro and not Schapiro. I have even heard of a girl named Jeffrey. You need to start thinking, modeling, and programming SQL Server in terms of data plausibility, not in terms of data being right or wrong.

Only if you accept this definition will you be able to use the tools and techniques supported by SQL Server 2005 to ensure the integrity of your data, and thus its value as an asset to your enterprise. And after you start focusing on *integrity* in scalar terms and not *correctness* in absolute terms, you will have a lot more faith in the data in your database, and you will be able to afford it the trust and respect it deserves. After all, data that is not plausible or believable is a liability.

As I discussed in Chapter 1, human error caused my wife extreme grief when, after changing medical insurance companies, she was denied coverage for some time because the last name of her doctor, instead of Shapiro, was entered in the spouse's last name field. To my wife, the data integrity issue thus became a life-threatening one. To the medical insurance company, the issue almost exploded into a liability problem.

What would or could cause a last name, or surname, to be incorrect?

1. The wife goes by her maiden name.
2. A spouse mistakenly provides a pseudonym.
3. The couple just got divorced but agreed to maintain the coverage.
4. A child is covered by a stepfather but still goes by the last name of his or her biological father.
5. The first name is entered into the last name field.
6. The last name is typed incorrectly (Shapiro becomes Ahaoeuei with just a few slips of the finger).
7. The handwriting on the application form is poor, or the last name is omitted and the data entry person makes a wrong assumption.

This list could go on and on. And I am sure you could come up with dozens of scenarios that would also create questionable data, not only in last name values but also in many other places. Numbers, for example, present incredible opportunities to enter problematic data into a database.

But is this a question of *integrity*? If we accept that we program the DBMS to ensure that the data is as believable as possible, then it is. If we try to ensure that the data is correct, then it is not. Any value may in fact be correct when it is assumed to be wrong, and it may in fact be wrong when it is assumed to be correct. The only thing you can do to *help* ensure that data is believable is to help ensure that it was believable when it was entered into the database.

The best I can think of doing at the data tier to help ensure that a value, such as the spouse's last name, is believable is to force the client to go back and check the data before it can be entered, or to compare the data against known values. It is possible to even refer the record back to the client and request it to be entered by another user, possibly a supervisor who would take the fact checking to the next level. Asking Web surfers to fill in application forms over the Internet is a good idea because it cuts out the middle data entry person, the paper trail, and delay. And it puts the onus of ensuring the data plausibility on the client, who is more likely to ensure that his or her information can be relied upon.

I recently watched a horrifying story on CNN about an American pharmacist who gave a child a fatal overdose of a drug contrary to what had been correctly prescribed by the pediatrician. The excuse was human error, failure of the supervisor to double-check prescriptions, filling hundreds of prescriptions a day. Why, in heaven's name, in this day and age, are pharmacists still using typewriters and word processors to provide instructions about dosage and administration of dangerous drugs? A database should have been used to check that the dosage did not exceed safely levels for the drug prescribed. No computer program checked the dosage, and so a mother sent her child to bed and he never woke up. Now, whenever we buy drugs, we check the label and wonder "can we trust our lives to this data?"

Obviously, the subject of human error is beyond the scope of this book, other than to discuss what possible means we might have of preventing humans from entering questionable data into a database. Joe Celko touched on the subject in his marvelous book, *Joe Celko's Data & Databases: Concepts in Practice* (New York: Morgan Kaufmann, 1999). In a section titled "Models Versus Reality," he talks about *errors in models,* describing Type I and Type II error levels.

A Type I error is accepting as false something that is true, and a Type II error is accepting as true something that it false.

I agree without equivocation that the subject of errors in models is very important for database people to understand. Generations of people have been wiped out because of this problem. Sub-Saharan Africa, where I spent my childhood, is going to be wiped out because of AIDS. This could have been prevented, but the population there still believes, by and large, that AIDS is not sexually transmitted and that the publicity is just "Western propaganda." The fraud is in fact self-perpetuating or self-fulfilling, because millions of Africans still have unprotected sex.

Yes, we can use fancy programming tricks and system features such as triggers and stored procedures to lessen the likelihood of implausible data; we can even build more advanced *human* integrity checking into the client applications. How can we avoid problems like the one just described and still program SQL Server 2005 as wisely as possible? To arrive at a possible solution, let's first explore the integrity assurance features and functions of SQL Server 2005. After this discussion, we can redress the last name integrity issue and offer my medical insurance company some ideas before they get sued.

Understanding SQL Server Data Integrity

When it comes to the subject of data integrity, we are dealing with a whole new barrel of pickles, one that SQL Server 2005 can adequately tackle under the guidance of the SQL Server developer and DBA . . . who now fully understands that he or she is modeling to ensure that data is plausible, not that it is correct. But there is still one more subject to discuss here before you can model your SQL Server 2005 database: *business rules.*

Data Integrity and Business Rules

A check constraint or trigger can easily be used to prevent a customer from spending more than $500 on credit. You might agree that any number above $500 is considered risky, but another customer might not. To apply this reasoning to the real world, for example, an airline booking system may be programmed to resist assigning seats to frequent-flier passengers who try to redeem miles toward a ticket, because the *rules* dictate that a seat should first be assigned to a *cash* customer, as opposed to a *liability* customer. All airlines maintain seat assignment rules when it comes to frequent fliers; although they vary widely in their rules.

Another rule, at a lower level than the one just described, would be that all rows for a given table must be unique. This rule is one of the core tenets of the Date relational model (C.J. Date). According to Chris Date, one of the world's foremost database experts, the relational model should not allow for any NULLs or duplicates whatsoever. In fact, Date is outspokenly against NULLs and declares that they should never have been introduced into relational theory.

The Date rule declares that entity values (column values in a row) should never be NULL (unknown or missing). SQL Server 2005 lets you decide whether to abide by the Date rule or code to your own business rules, which may in certain circumstances allow both duplicate rows in a table and even NULL values.

Ensuring integrity is very much part of the relational database modeling, whether it is expressed in terms akin to calculus and algebra or according to Boolean logic or some other form of analysis. But data integrity, or the extent to which you manage it, as alluded to earlier, is also up to you. And this brings to us the subject of rules, specifically business rules.

Business rules are a hot topic in the new millennium. Yet they are really the abstract declaration of the data integrity requirements demanded by business owners and enterprise and data analysts. The "frequent fliers get last choice" rule discussed earlier is exactly the type of business rule about which we are talking.

We can look at this another way. We can say that the data integrity constraint logic is the formal definition of a business rule applied to corporate data. After all, you can scream about business rules and data integrity until the cows come home, but that will do nothing to a database that knows only unfettered character-based data, has more duplicates than bottle tops, and can do little about enforcing integrity (see Chapter 3). You will find, as we move from operational data support to analytical and temporal data support (discussed in Part III) in SQL Server 2005, that the formulation of business rules becomes more of a requirement than a luxury. Analytical data comes from operational data, so the more lax your integrity control in the OLTP system, the more effort you will have to expend when you need to get analysis data scrubbed before it can be copied to the data warehouse. Values like N/A, TBA, or "unknown" lessen the value in the data mine, and the information extraction becomes extremely time-consuming and expensive.

Figure 12-1 represents this discussion in conceptual terms. At the highest level—that is, the conceptual level—the enterprise and data analysts formulate rules with the business owners. This is also the requirements formulating level. In the middle is the modeling level that translates the business rules into database integrity requirements by database analysts and even DBAs. And at the lowest level is the development model that implements the integrity requirement as constraints, checks, and procedures in SQL Server 2005, implemented by DBAs and SQL Server developers.

Figure 12-1
Modeling the database for integrity and adherence to business rules

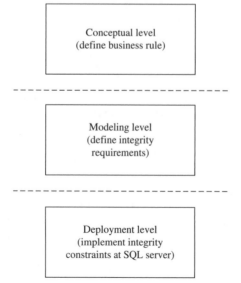

Conceptual level
(define business rule)

Modeling level
(define integrity requirements)

Deployment level
(implement integrity constraints at SQL server)

Now that our philosophical (and emotional) banks are charged, we can look at the level you are probably most interested in: implementing the integrity requirements. To do so, we must classify integrity into several governing sections as follows:

- Database and table integrity
- Referential integrity
- Entity integrity
- Type integrity
- Domain integrity
- Transition integrity
- Transaction integrity

Database and Table Integrity

Database and table constraint mechanisms are the broadest form of integrity control because they relate to the relationships between entities, multiple columns in a table, and multiple tables in a database. A good example of a database integrity violation is allowing a customer with bad credit to buy more goods and to put the order on account, or even allowing payment to be made by anything other than cash, letter of credit, or a credit card. The following pseudocode would thus enforce the rules of database integrity for the given example:

```
FOR Customers.Orders
IF Customer_Credit.Credit < 10
BEGIN
  RAISERROR 1.Message ('Customer must pay with cash or credit card')
  GOTO Cash
END
ELSE
BEGIN
  RAISERROR 2.Message('Customer is cleared for credit')
  GOTO Account
END
```

Another table-level constraint against integrity violation is the case of the orphaned row. If we delete an entity related to one or more entities through primary-foreign key relationships, we are deemed (to use a legal expression) to have violated rules of *referential integrity.* Referential integrity rules should be adhered to in every database deployment, which is why we devote a separate section to this topic.

Referential Integrity

By deleting a member row that is referenced by other entities or rows, we in fact leave the remaining undeleted entities orphaned and the record in tatters. In fact, the database is now in a poor state because no easy means now exists of identifying or finding the orphaned entities and removing the entire record. And if you have data in a database that can never be accessed or relied upon, the entire database becomes questionable.

I liken referential integrity violations to the habit some people have of not finishing an apple. If you cut the apple, take out a wedge, or only eat half of it, the remaining fruit darkens and quickly goes bad. So it is when you delete a row and violate referential integrity: over time the database goes bad also. As mentioned in the chapters in Part I, if you regard all the rows in linked tables as combining to represent a complete record, deleting a row in one table and leaving the related rows intact is akin to taking a bite out of an apple and then leaving it to go brown and rot.

On the other hand, referential integrity violation can also be said to have occurred when an entity references a nonexistent entity in the database. Referential integrity requires that there be no references to nonexistent values and that if a key value changes, all references to it change consistently throughout the database.

In the past, referential integrity would be maintained using triggers and many lines of code; we called this approach *procedural referential integrity (PRI)*. Most modern DBMS products now support *declarative referential integrity (DRI)*, which is essentially the opposite of procedural referential integrity. DRI makes use of built-in mechanisms to ensure or maintain referential integrity, while PRI is the responsibility of the database modeler or developer.

The declarative referential integrity constraints are enforced as follows:

- The integrity criteria are defined in the various database objects' definitions, such as foreign key (FK) existence.

- Checks, defaults, and rules trap the violations.

- SQL Server automatically enforces the integrity rules.

Procedural referential integrity constraints are enforced as follows:

- The integrity criteria are defined and enforced in your T-SQL code.

- The constraints are implemented in triggers and stored procedures (see Chapters 13 and 14), or the T-SQL code in other manual constraints.

Entity Integrity

Entity constraints, also known as *relational constraints,* define rules that govern rows and columns in tables and the tables as units. Uniqueness is one of the primary entity integrity rules to ensure. Of course, you can maintain a database that enforces no uniqueness whatsoever, but that would certainly render a table devoid of any integrity. For example, you can create and populate a table of orders and insert duplicate orders into the table willy-nilly. Your reasoning might be that, since customers can make duplicate orders, these duplicate orders should be stored without any constraints.

But is there such a thing as a duplicate order? Only in error, I believe, and a constraint should be designed to catch such an error. Each order is placed at a certain time and date. No order can be entered twice at exactly the same time. The description, quantity, price, and discount of an item might be duplicated, but the time the entry was made cannot. Besides, each order is a new transaction that differs from another transaction only in the time it was entered and the order number assigned to it. It is in fact unique.

CAUTION   *Although highly unlikely, it is possible for two users to enter the same record or data at exactly the same time. An identity column and table locks would prevent the two rows from competing on the question of their uniqueness.*

The tools we use to constrain entities are the primary keys (on identified columns), which can impose primary indexes, UNIQUE constraints, IDENTITY properties, and so forth. Table constraints are checked before any data can be allowed into the table. If the data violates the constraint rule—for instance, if it contains a duplicate row or a duplicate value on which we have installed a primary index—it is rejected.

Entity integrity is enforced using primary keys and unique indexes.

Type Integrity

Type constraint discussions generally cover domains, although data types and data domains are two separate concepts, and that is gospel. I have thus added domain constraints to the list, and we discuss domain integrity next. A type constraint enforces rules that govern correct use of the data type of a given value. Ensuring the consistent use of a date data type, for example, is a form of type constraint. Dates, decimals, currency, and the like are data types recorded in several formats that govern precision, but the data will become impossible to work with if such scalar values are not constrained to just one of the several formats required by your rules.

Assigning NULL values is another form of type constraint, even though we talk about NULL with respect to database and entity constraints. By allowing NULL values in a tuple (field), you are explicitly allowing the storage of *missing* or *unknown* values. If you disavow NULL values, you must either supply a value through some formula or supply a default value for the variable.

A NULL value, for that matter, is an oxymoron in a manner of speaking. You might ask yourself how a NULL value can be a *value* and replace something that is missing or unknown. It is, however, a convenient means of allowing a row to be inserted into the database even if it contains missing or unknown values. If your rules allow NULLs to be a temporary expedient, in they go. If not, out they go.

The rules of integrity should guide your use of the NULL. Ask yourself if your data is reliable if it is made up of missing or unknown values. If not knowing middle initials will not break your data, then the NULL represents a convenient placeholder until the initial becomes available. Inserting a default value would not be feasible, because you would be inserting a Type II error that could spell disaster: accepting as true something that may be false.

In this regard, you might consider NULL values to be a violation of database integrity as well. My rule allows NULL if it does not violate the integrity of my data or adversely affect the analytical value of the data. If it does, I must install a default value and code the logic, based on the business rule, that obtains the default. If you do not have the data for a value for a given row, you should instead assign a default value or obtain a value through an alternate formula. There is a lot of debate surrounding NULL. Nevertheless, SQL Server 2005 permits you the flexibility of either allowing or disallowing NULL values according to your needs . . . or ignorance.

Type constraints are defined in code and in the definitions of the data types, such as specifying NULL (allowed) or NOT NULL (disallowed). Integrity is ensured with automatic checks and procedural code.

NOTE   *A type constraint is a column-level constraint.*

Domain Integrity

Data domains are the logical grouping of values. For example, in my *items* table I have a color column that can take only one of five *colors.* Notice the emphasis on *only* because that is the focus of my domain constraints. The domain rule for the item dictates that it can only be red, blue, mustard, lime, or black. You might argue that mustard and lime belong to the domain *flavors,* and if you do, you have grasped the concept of a data domain, and you have joined the debate.

I tend not to agree that domain constraints govern data types; that is the work of type constraints. However, the check and constraint mechanisms might be the same for both, and many domain constraints have been cast along data type lines. For example, it is very convenient to constrain a numeric value by the type of integer. Domains can represent collections of data types, which is what leads to the incorrect definition that domains are data types, period. While domains are in fact data types, the definition of a domain should refer to a logical collection or grouping of data values and entities, not data types. As long as you understand the difference, you'll be okay.

Besides checks, you can use stored procedures and triggers to ensure domain integrity. For example, a stored procedure can populate a list or table at the client with allowable values from which to choose.

NOTE   *A domain constraint is also a column-level constraint.*

Transition Integrity

One of my clients has a simple rule that was more important to the IS managers than anything in the database: "Call center agents are only allowed to take an order and receive payment." The agent is not allowed access to any functions in the client application that debits items from inventory or causes a picker in the warehouse to go pack the items to send to shipping. Only a second-level stock manager is allowed to do that. My client manages its stock levels like a squirrel manages its acorns. Only stock managers can produce the pick and shipping data that will translate the order into a shippable collection of items. That was the business rule; I did not question it, I only implemented it.

Rules such as these are translated into what we call *transition constraints.* These constraints ensure that the status of records changes according to predetermined rules. Inventory levels and accounting databases need to adhere to strict transition constraints. For example, you should never credit to one table without debiting from another. Inventory cannot be debited if shipping is not credited.

There are several levels on which you can define or specify transition states. In most order-taking databases, these can be defined as follows:

1. Order entered.
2. Order taken, money taken, or credit approved.
3. Item back-ordered.
4. Items picked and packed.
5. Order canceled or paused.

6. Items shipped.

7. Obligation completed.

This list relates to the various transitions in a database. For example, an order changes from entered to taken only when either credit is approved or the items have been paid for. In other words, if transition integrity is maintained or enforced on the database, then an order entered can only be considered a de facto liability (the company owes the client the items) if money has changed hands or the customer is in good credit standing. A check on cash or credit will allow the order to go from a state of *entered* to a state of *taken*. Some companies do not consider an obligation completed until the order is on the road to the client. Only then do they actually debit the credit card.

Items also move through various states. For example, an *AllowBackorders* constraint can enforce a rule that either allows or disallows part of an order from being back-ordered. For example, a customer might request that the order should not ship until a part in the shipment is available for immediate delivery.

The aforementioned client also has another very important business rule. The items cannot be shipped and the software cannot produce the shipping label unless the shipping department has called the client and obtained a verbal agreement to accept the order. If the client agrees, only at that instant will the credit card be run or a debit applied to the account.

My client advised me the main reason for this rule is that about 95 percent of the shipments rejected by customers come from customers paying on credit accounts or credit cards. The customer changes his or her mind after placing the order and then refuses the delivery. My client then has to eat the loss on the shipping costs (often UPS Red or FedEx delivery) because the shipper has fulfilled.

Transaction Integrity

A *transaction* in the sense described here is a collection of operations on data that must be completed according to business rules as a unit, or the transaction is completely canceled. In this regard the transaction constraint is similar to the formal transaction monitoring in which SQL Server engages automatically and thus displays elements of atomicity (see Chapter 16). Transaction integrity in the preceding discussion is more a procedural integrity mechanism (something you usually have to code a solution for) that ensures that all of the components that are required for a complete transaction are entered and satisfy all of the preceding integrity rules before the transaction is committed.

Such transactions can, however, be applied over long periods, depending on the business needs and rules. Transactions can also happen over a short period, and several states can make up several transactions. For example, an order might be broken up into several transactions, one for each state an order is in.

Planning Integrity

In Chapter 6 we tackled the CREATE TABLE statement, but the primary objective of the methods discussed and the code demonstrated was to create tables, not to demonstrate the installing of integrity mechanisms. In this chapter, we go a step further and code the formal or declarative integrity constraint definitions into the CREATE TABLE and ALTER TABLE statements.

SQL Server provides the following built-in integrity or constraint mechanisms:

- The capability to provide default values and thereby avoid NULL
- The capability to code check constraint expressions that evaluate the values in the SQL statement to determine if they are allowed to be saved to the column
- The capability to code referential integrity constraints (cross-referencing foreign key columns)
- The capability to declare primary and unique keys that ensure uniqueness in a column or through the combination of columns
- The capability to use triggers as a form of constraint, which can also provide a trans- or intra-database integrity checking facility. Triggers are covered in the next chapter.

When you first create a table, you are in fact laying down the first integrity constraints in your database because you create columns that have different data types for different data. For example, you would not store a noncharacter value in a character data type, and you would not try to store a character in an integer data type.

When you design a database, one of the basic rules to follow is to use common sense. If you are storing integer data, then store it in integer columns; date-to-date columns; character-to-character columns; and so forth. Naturally you will come to situations that will require you to decide between variations of a data type (small integers, integers, or big integers), or to make decisions that rely on the precision and scale of data, such as values of type real or float, currency, and so on. Other times, your choice of data type will be related to storage requirements, system resources, and so forth. An example would be deciding to switch to the bigint data type because of the need to store very large numbers. But you would not incur the storage overhead of a big integer (bigint) if you were storing nothing larger than 99.

The format of the data being stored is also a consideration, because modern database systems do not store only characters and numerals any more. They also store binary information, images, objects, bitmaps, large amounts of text, and so forth. And SQL Server 2005 also allows us to build our own *user-defined* data types, which are discussed in Chapter 15.

The Integrity Plan

The integrity plan is one of the most important sections of your overall database definition, model, or architecture. You can use the flow diagram in Figure 12-2 to build your integrity plan.

Gather Business Rules

This section of the integrity plan identifies business rules that will impact the database model and architecture. These rules, as discussed earlier, differ from the integrity issues that are built in to the relational model from the get-go, such as referential integrity.

Sit down with the people responsible for establishing the business rules, or provide the facilities in your model and code for later easy incorporation of constraints to cater to the business rules.

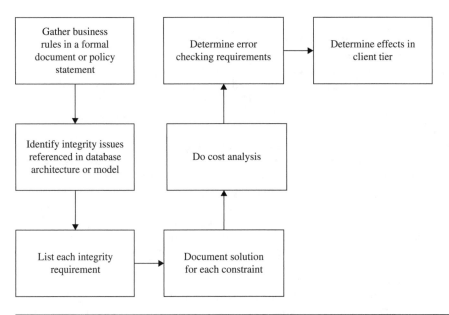

FIGURE 12-2   Creating an integrity plan

Identify Key Integrity Issues to Cover

These issues will be referenced in the architecture or will become patently part of it. For example, you might want to list attributes of the data that have legal implications if they render the data questionable. It is also important to plan for the prospect of warehousing the data, and constraining data in the operational databases with analysis in mind will make it easier to transform the data at a later stage.

List Each Integrity Requirement

This step is closely related to the preceding step, and they can be combined. Here you should list the precise integrity needs of the databases and tables right down to the values required.

You could list each table and link it to a list of integrity constraints required on its internals. For example, you will specify referential integrity requirements with linked tables, the primary key column, type constraints, and so on.

Document the Solution for Each Constraint

This section covers how you propose to deal with each integrity requirement. For example, do you plan to create unique constraints directly in T-SQL code or interactively in Management Studio (or possibly through the DMO object library)? Here you would also determine which integrity mechanism would be most suited for the task. For example, would a check constraint work or would you have to code a trigger?

Also document and establish procedures for maintaining and revising the constraints. If constraints are implemented in code, then you need to maintain source, version control, and so forth. You will also need to manage access, permissions to the constraint objects, and so on.

Do Cost Analysis

There is a cost attached to every constraint. The costs are both direct, in terms of their consumption of SQL Server resources and usefulness, and indirect, in terms of the costs of programming, maintenance, documentation, and so on. For example, using a stored procedure to check integrity is more expensive in all terms than using a trigger (besides, there are situations that only a trigger caters to). Using a trigger, on the other hand, is more expensive than using a built-in cascade. And, defaults or constraint objects are more expensive than check constraints and so on.

When performing cost analysis of constraints, you should also consider adherence to standards as a factor. For example, you should use built-in constraints because they are based on ANSI compliance and also conform to relational database rules.

Triggers, on the other hand, can be used to meet ANSI recommendations, but since triggers are entirely procedural, they cannot be considered ANSI-compliant. SQL Server can check code for errors, but it is not able to check trigger code for standards compliance. In fact, even if trigger code is syntactically correct, it might still nuke your data beyond recovery.

Determine Error Checking Requirements

When integrity is violated or a constraint traps problem data, SQL Server will report errors. You need to determine how best to check these errors and establish procedure for using the error logs to trap faults in design and development, data entry, or business-rule integration. In short, error checking and tracking can be used to reduce errors down the road.

Determine Effects and Requirements in the Client Tier

As discussed in Chapter 11, we don't want to build a client tier that collapses every time we make changes in the data tier, which is why we move the data processing to the data tier and code just about everything in triggers, UDFs, stored procedures, and functions.

If you plan well and manage the database model and architecture properly, the constraints in the data tier should have little impact on the clients. However, you will have a lot to think about if you need to maintain legacy client code that still maintains a lot of client-side data processing and logic.

It is also possible to code constraint or integrity checking in the client tier without adversely affecting development costs and management. For example, it is more useful in terms of server resource conservation to check for format or type and domain integrity violations before the data gets transmitted to the server. A mask over the telephone number in a client application, even a Web browser, will obviate the need for SQL Server to bounce back with an integrity violation that incurs an additional round trip (see the section "Check Constraints" later in this chapter).

Configuring and Programming Integrity

If we examine the T-SQL CREATE TABLE or ALTER TABLE statement in the previous chapters or in Books Online, we can see that these statements accept several arguments for setting up built-in or system (declarative) integrity constraints using default values, check constraints, foreign keys, primary keys, unique keys, and so on.

Default Values

The default value is used in a column that may or may not forbid NULL values. For example, a column of type integer might take a 0 as the default, while a character-based column might take "unknown" as a default value—or even something like "pending."

NOTE *A default value is not really a constraint per se because it does not restrict you from entering a certain value; it only kicks in when you do not provide a value.*

Default values do not just happen automatically when you insert new rows in a table. As demonstrated in the Chapter 16, you must explicitly tell SQL Server to apply the default value when performing a row insert. SQL Server can also create the row in the INSERT statement and apply all the default values for the row (in which case you would not specify columns in the INSERT statement). This is achieved using the DEFAULT VALUES clause in your INSERT statement.

The following code demonstrates the provisioning of a default value in the CREATE TABLE statement:

```
CREATE TABLE Items
(Amount int DEFAULT 0, Description varchar(50), Notes text NULL)
```

You are not limited in terms of T-SQL code as to how you can concoct a default value, as long as the default value does not violate the data type. For example, you can use system-supplied values, such as those that are returned from built-in functions, to provide a default value. The following code automatically provides information on the user who inserted the row:

```
CREATE TABLE NewOrders
(custID INT NOT NULL PRIMARY KEY,
 custName VARCHAR(30) NOT NULL DEFAULT 'new customer',
 createdBy varchar(50) DEFAULT User)
```

However, changing the default value is another matter altogether when you need to do things in T-SQL code, because you can't easily reference the default name, at least not according to SQL-92 or Microsoft specifications. The CREATE TABLE statement also provides no facility for providing a custom name that would be easy to reference in a script. SQL Server, on the other hand, provides a name for the default property, but it too cannot be referenced easily from front-end applications or T-SQL scripts.

So you cannot willy-nilly change the default when the MIS walks in and asks you to do so. You have to first delete it and then recreate it. Deleting the default can be achieved using the following ALTER TABLE statement:

```
ALTER TABLE [dbo].[NewOrders]
  DROP CONSTRAINT [DF__defs__Items__48CFD27E]
```

The constraint name in the preceding code was provided automatically by SQL Server, so you can see how difficult it is to reference it. This code works, but I had to open a query window in Management Studio to look it up and then script it out to a new query window.

This is a real pain. A better method is to look up the default name in the system tables. After looking for the information in the system tables and tinkering around with QA for an hour, I arrived at the following code to delete the default programmatically:

```
USE MASTER
DECLARE @dfltname varchar(100), @cmd varchar(1000)
SET @dfltname =
  (SELECT name FROM sysobjects sysobs
   JOIN sysconstraints scons ON sysobs.id = scons.constid
      WHERE object_name(sysobs.parent_obj)= 'NewOrders'
      AND sysobs.xtype = 'D' AND scons.colid =
   (SELECT colid FROM syscolumns where ID = object_id('dbo.defs')
    AND name = 'custName'))

SET @cmd = 'ALTER TABLE NewOrders DROP CONSTRAINT ' + @dfltname
EXEC(@cmd)
```

This is by no means an easy statement to comprehend, especially if you are new to T-SQL, so you might want to come back to it after you have gone through the next couple of chapters, which discuss SELECT, JOIN, aliases, EXEC, and stored procedures. In Chapter 14, I put the code in a stored procedure so that it's two parameters away from me when I need it.

As an alternative, you can create a default object (or several objects), install a default value as the object's property, and then bind and unbind the object to the column as needed. There are, however, a number of problems associated with default objects:

- They are not ANSI-compliant. The default objects have been dragged up through the ages from the romance between Microsoft and Sybase.

- The code to create the default object (CREATE DEFAULT) and the ensuing execution of system stored procedures sp_bindefault and sp_unbindefault is tedious.

- They are not true SQL DDL and as such are not as efficient as ANSI default constraints.

- You will be limited in the expression you use to provide a default value. As demonstrated earlier, a T-SQL ANSI default value can be derived from a sophisticated query/calculation providing a unique value each time the default in invoked. The makes the ANSI default more powerful by an order of magnitude.

- Managing defaults can drive you nuts. If you need to drop a column that has a default object fused to it, you first need to unbind the default from the column. You cannot simply delete the default either, because it might be bound to other columns.

As I am sure you are aware, you can create and manage tables from Management Studio, which essentially provides you with an interactive and visual "hookup" to integrity application for databases and tables.

You can create the default in Management Studio by opening the table in the Design Table console and entering a default value in the default value for the column selected. You can easily change the defaults in this manner. Adding or changing a default value in the

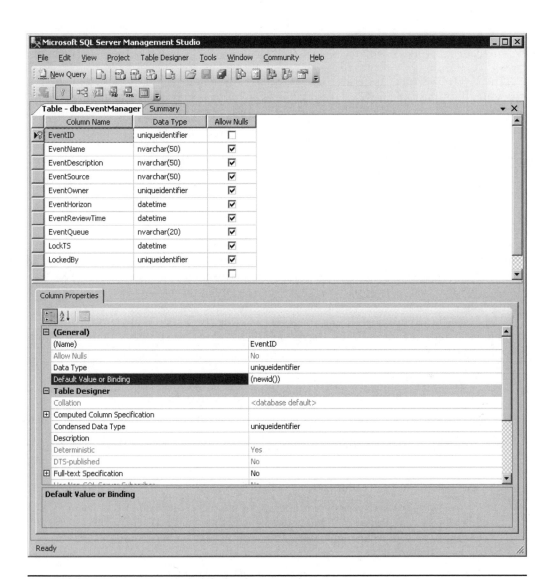

FIGURE 12-3   Adding or changing a default value on a column

console is illustrated in Figure 12-3. To add or change a default interactively, take the following steps:

1. Drill down to the database in question and expand the tree to access the table node. Expand the table node.

2. Select the table, and expand it further to expose the tree of columns. Right-click the target column and choose Modify. The properties of the column in edit mode opens in the details pane and gives you access to the column properties (see Figure 12-3).

3. Select the value and enter the value in Default Value or Binding option (under General). Close the dialog box to save the new settings.

The SMO object model provides similar access to the default property, but you will encounter the same difficulty in accessing the default objects in code. The following points about default constraints should be taken into account:

- The default mechanism is only activated on the INSERT statement.
- You can obviously only have one default to a column; there is no way of specifying a member of a default collection.
- The default cannot be used on identity columns or on timestamp columns.

Check Constraints

The *check* constraint is useful because a single constraint definition can be applied to more than one column. You can also define as many check constraints as you need. For example, if you want to ensure that data for a telephone number is inserted or updated as (XXX) XXX-XXXX, you can create a check to prevent a value of any other form from being committed to the database.

The first action to take in defining checks is to list the check requirements and definitions in your integrity plan as described earlier. A check constraints list might contain the following items:

- Telephone and fax numbers must be formatted (XXX) XXX-XXXX
- Social Security numbers must be formatted XXX-XX-XXXX
- Invalid states for UPS ground are Hawaii and Alaska

You can attach a check constraint in a database diagram (see Chapter 11) or the table designer as follows:

1. Select Modify on a column as described for Figure 12-3.
2. Go to the toolbar and select the Manage Check Constraints button (the last one). Note the three buttons at the far right of the toolbox on this console: These relate to the application of indexing, integrity, and constraints. Each button represents a different dialog box.
3. The Check Constraints dialog box loads, illustrated in Figure 12-4.
4. Click Add to create a new check constraint. Enter the check code in the constraint expression window. (You cannot check the expression syntax in this dialog box, and you will not be able to close the dialog, and thus save the check expression, if the code is incorrect. You might consider building the code in a query window first and testing it as T-SQL script, which for many architects, including me, is much slicker than fiddling in dialog boxes.) If the expression works, click the Save button on the toolbar and close the table designer.

The following code applies the preceding check constraints:

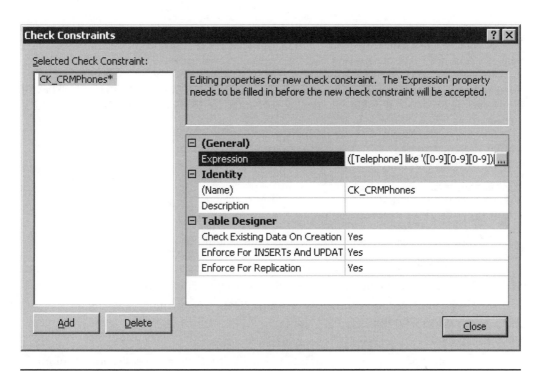

FIGURE 12-4   Adding a check constraint interactively in Management Studio

```
ALTER TABLE Customers
ADD CONSTRAINT phones CHECK (phone_no
LIKE '(XXX) XXX-XXXX')
```

and

```
ALTER TABLE Users
ADD CONSTRAINT socials CHECK (SSN
LIKE 'XXX-XX-XXXX')
```

and

```
ALTER TABLE Orders
ADD CONSTRAINT CK_states CHECK
(State <> 'Hawaii')
```

If you were just setting out to create the preceding Orders table, you might script in the constraint at the same time. The following creates the Orders table and then applies the constraint at the table level:

```
CREATE TABLE Orders
    (State varchar(40) NOT NULL,
     Shipper varchar(40) NOT NULL,
     CONSTRAINT CK_states CHECK (State NOT IN ('Hawaii', 'Alaska')))
```

The T-SQL syntax is rich, and so you can code for sophisticated expressions for the preceding checks and the other constraint objects. The preceding code added another U.S. state to check for in the constraint CK_states demonstrated earlier. The code obviates the need to add a second check for Alaska to keep it out of the UPS ground column in my table. Instead I used a comma-separated list and the expression tells SQL Server that *either* Hawaii *or* Alaska are *not* allowed in the column. I repeated the list technique in the ALTER TABLE statement as follows:

```
ALTER TABLE Orders
  drop constraint CK_states
go
ALTER TABLE Orders
ADD CONSTRAINT CK_states CHECK
  (State NOT IN ('Hawaii', 'Alaska'))
```

The following rules governing check constraints should be kept in mind:

- They only fire on INSERT and UPDATE actions.
- They can reference more than one column in a table, in the check expression.
- They cannot be used on identity columns, timestamp columns, and unique identifier columns.
- The check expressions cannot contain subqueries.
- You can attach as many constraints as you like to a column or collection of columns.
- You do not necessarily have to include the keyword CONSTRAINT in your code, but I would do so for clarity.
- You do not need to provide a name for the constraint. Knowing SQL Server's affinity for inventing names that look and sound like ancient Greek, however, I prefer to use a naming convention that makes it easier to read the code and document our team's solutions.

Otherwise, enjoy them.

TIP *Check constraints enforce domain integrity and I recommend you install them whenever necessary to keep garbage out of the database and ensure the integrity of the database. Using check constraints without regard for the client environment is a bad idea, especially in Internet applications where people connect through their Web browsers, because all manner of badly formatted strings, formats, and contradictory values will come flying at SQL Server, causing it to balk and flame the client, which causes network roundtrips and a degradation of resources. You should use client or middle-tier constraint mechanisms to avoid this, such as masked edit fields, allowable values lists, and so on wherever you can, leaving SQL Server as the last line of defense.*

Foreign Keys

If you examine the T-SQL CREATE TABLE and ALTER TABLE syntax, you will see that you can create the foreign key (FK) constraints to enforce and ensure referential integrity and cascading updates when you create the table. Also note that they can be created and managed when you alter tables and their columns.

When you create the keys, remember the following rules:

- The foreign key must reference a primary key or a unique key in the partner tables.

- Foreign keys do not automatically create indexes.

- Permissions apply, so you need to ensure that users have SELECT and DRI permissions enabled on the tables (this is discussed in detail in Chapter 16, with code examples).

The following code adds a foreign key constraint to the ShipTo table in my Customers database, which I called "FK_ShipTo_CustDetails," and the constraint references the *CustDetails* table:

```
ALTER TABLE [dbo].[ShipTo] ADD CONSTRAINT [FK_ShipTo_CustDetails] FOREIGN KEY
    ([CustID]) REFERENCES [CustDetails] ([CustID])
    ON DELETE CASCADE  ON UPDATE CASCADE
```

In this code, when I update or delete the row in the *CustDetails* table, the constraint ensures the ShipTo table's corresponding row is likewise deleted (referential integrity) or updated. To create the constraint in Management Studio, do the following:

1. Select Modify and then click the Relationships button on the toolbar. The Relationships dialog box loads, as shown in Figure 12-5.

2. Select the corresponding columns that represent the primary and foreign keys.

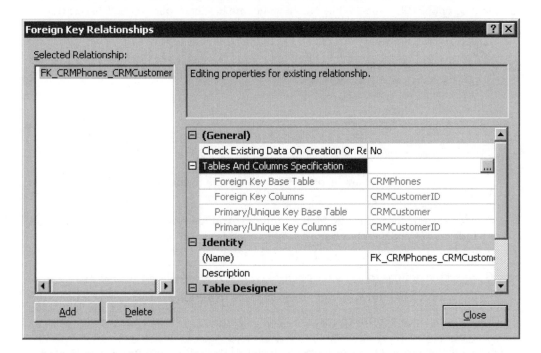

FIGURE 12-5 Adding a foreign key constraint

3. Select the options such as the cascades, deletes, and updates.

4. Change the name of the constraint, if you need to, and then close the dialog box to commit the changes to the table.

Primary and Foreign Keys

As discussed earlier, entity integrity ensures that rows in a table are unique. The tools to use to enforce uniqueness are the primary key constraints (PK), the unique key constraints (UK), and the identity property (discussed in Chapter 10). The primary and unique keys are also referenced in referential integrity constraints.

The primary key was discussed in Chapter 3 and again in Chapter 10, so I will not go over it again here.

If you examine the CREATE TABLE and ALTER TABLE syntax, you will see that you can create the primary key when you create the table and that it can be created and managed when you alter the table and its columns.

When working with the ALTER TABLE statement, you need to remember that you can only have one primary key in a table. In other words, there can only be one column that is the beneficiary of a primary key.

While you can modify the primary key interactively with the graphical tools, such as Management Studio, you have to delete the key and then recreate it in T-SQL. The ALTER TABLE statement can only be used to drop or add a primary key to the table, not to alter the key itself.

Also, when adding the key, remember that the target column must have no duplicate data, nor can it accept NULL values. While NULL values are hardly duplicates, SQL Server doesn't see it that way, because it cannot reference a unique value if the value is technically missing.

The code to add a primary key constraint to the table is as follows:

```
ALTER TABLE [dbo].[CustDetails]
   ADD CONSTRAINT [PK_CustDetails]
   PRIMARY KEY NONCLUSTERED
     ([CustID])
```

NOTE *Chapter 10 also looks at the CREATE TABLE statement in more depth and highlights the differences between table-level definitions and column-level definitions.*

To add a primary key constraint, open the Design Table dialog box and take the following steps (remember you can also do this in a database diagram as discussed in Chapter 10):

1. Select Modify and click the Manage Indexes And Keys button on the toolbar. The Indexes/Keys dialog box opens, as illustrated in Figure 12-6.

2. Select the column name and sort order for the key.

3. Select the options to be used by SQL Server on the primary key clustering.

4. Click the Close button to commit the changes to the table.

Unique keys, or unique key constraints, are very similar in function to primary keys, but the difference is that the unique key can be used to generate a nonclustered index and can live in a table that already has a primary key installed on another column. The unique key can be created in T-SQL and interactively (or the SMO object model).

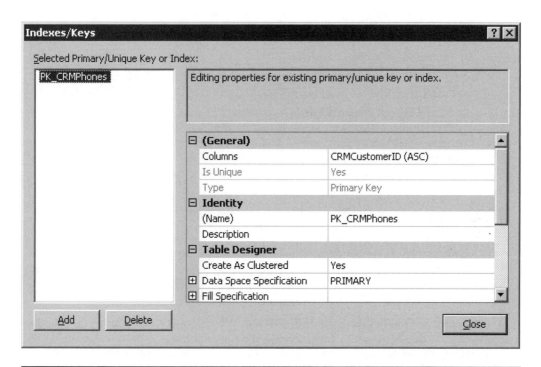

Figure 12-6   Adding primary key constraints

The Constraints Syntax

This section has been provided to help you better understanding the CONSTRAINTS section in the CREATE TABLE or ALTER TABLE statements and explains all the constraint options. The constraints as documented for CREATE TABLE or ALTER TABLE are as follows:

- **ROWGUIDCOL**   This argument indicates that the new column can hold globally unique identifiers. It is a constraint because only one such *uniqueidentifier* column (set as such) per table can be designated as the ROWGUIDCOL column.

   The ROWGUIDCOL property, however, does not enforce uniqueness of the values stored in the column. It also does not automatically generate values for new rows inserted into the table. To generate unique values for each column, either use the NEWID function on INSERT statements or use the NEWID function as the default for the column.

- **CONSTRAINT**   This is an optional keyword indicating the beginning of a PRIMARY KEY, NOT NULL, UNIQUE, FOREIGN KEY, or CHECK constraint definition.

- **NULL | NOT NULL**   These are keywords that determine if null values are allowed in the column. NULL is not strictly a constraint but can be specified in the same manner as NOT NULL, which is a constraint.

- **PRIMARY KEY**   This is a constraint that enforces entity integrity for a given column or columns through a unique index. Only one PRIMARY KEY constraint can be created per table.

- **UNIQUE**   This is a constraint that provides entity integrity for a given column or columns through a unique index. A table can have multiple UNIQUE constraints.

- **CLUSTERED | NONCLUSTERED**   These are keywords to indicate that a clustered or nonclustered index is created for the PRIMARY KEY or UNIQUE constraint. PRIMARY KEY constraints default to CLUSTERED, and UNIQUE constraints default to NONCLUSTERED.

  You can specify CLUSTERED for only one constraint in a CREATE TABLE statement. If you specify CLUSTERED for a UNIQUE constraint and also specify a PRIMARY KEY constraint, the PRIMARY KEY defaults to NONCLUSTERED.

- **FOREIGN KEY ... REFERENCES**   These are constraints that provide referential integrity for the data in the column or columns. FOREIGN KEY constraints require that each value in the column exist in the corresponding referenced column(s) in the referenced table. FOREIGN KEY constraints can reference only columns that are PRIMARY KEY or UNIQUE constraints in the referenced table.

- **ON DELETE {CASCADE | NO ACTION}**   These arguments specify what action takes place in a row in the table created, if that row has a referential relationship and the referenced row is deleted from the parent table. The default is NO ACTION.

  If CASCADE is specified, a row is deleted from the referencing table if that row is deleted from the parent table. If NO ACTION is specified, SQL Server raises an error and the delete action on the row in the parent table is rolled back (see Chapter 16, where this constraint is further discussed).
  On the other hand, if NO ACTION is specified, SQL Server raises an error and rolls back the delete action on the Customers row if there is at least one row in the Orders table that references it.

- **ON UPDATE {CASCADE | NO ACTION}**   This argument specifies what action takes place in a row in the table created, if that row has a referential relationship and the referenced row is updated in the parent table. The default is NO ACTION.

  If CASCADE is specified, the row is updated in the referencing table if that row is updated in the parent table. If NO ACTION is specified, SQL Server raises an error and the update action on the row in the parent table is rolled back.
  If NO ACTION is specified, SQL Server raises an error and rolls back the update action on the Customers row if there is at least one row in the Orders table that references it.

- **CHECK**   This is a constraint that enforces domain integrity by limiting the possible values that can be entered into a column or columns.

- **NOT FOR REPLICATION**   This is not really a constraint but an "anti-constraint" that is important for integrity consideration. The argument is used to prevent the CHECK constraint from being enforced during the distribution process used by replication. When tables are subscribers to a replication publication, do not update the subscription table directly; instead, update the publishing table and let replication distribute the data back to the subscribing table.

A CHECK constraint can be defined on the subscription table to prevent users from modifying it. Unless the NOT FOR REPLICATION clause is added, however, the CHECK constraint also prevents the replication process from distributing modifications from the publishing table to the subscribing table. The NOT FOR REPLICATION clause means the constraint is enforced on user modifications but not on the replication process.

The NOT FOR REPLICATION CHECK constraint is applied to both the before and after images of an updated record to prevent records from being added to or deleted from the replicated range. All deletes and inserts are checked; if they fall within the replicated range, they are rejected.

When this constraint is used with an identity column, SQL Server allows the table not to have its identity column values reseeded when a replication user updates the identity column. See also Chapter 8 for more specifics regarding replication between SQL Server instances.

User-Defined and Alias Data Types

User-defined types (UDTs) and alias types in SQL Server 2005 also present a means to enforce or ensure integrity, particularly domain integrity. A user-defined type is implemented in a .NET language, through a class of an assembly that executes in the common language runtime (CLR), as discussed in Chapter 11. An alias data type is based on a SQL Server native system type.

Alias types are easier to implement because they are an abstract of already existing system types. Their integrity utility becomes apparent when you need to store the same type of data in a column in a number of tables and you need to be certain that the columns across all the tables maintain the identical data type, length, and nullability.

The syntax to create an alias type is as follows:

```
CREATE TYPE [ schema_name. ] type_name
{
    FROM base_type
    [ ( precision [ , scale ] )   ]
    [ NULL | NOT NULL ]
  | EXTERNAL NAME assembly_name [ .class_name ]
} [ ; ]
```

Here is an example of using an alias data type:

```
USE SCRATCH
GO
CREATE TYPE dbo.Telephone
    FROM nvarchar(10) NOT NULL;
```

You can now use the type "Telephone" in your application and the type will conform to the system type, length, and nullability of the underlying specification . . . and it will inherit default values and so on that you specified when creating the alias. Using Management Studio, the type will appear in your selection of Data Types when you add columns on the Modify option. Or you can use the alias type in T-SQL as follows:

```
CREATE TABLE [CRM].[Phone] (
    [Phone] [dbo].[Telephone] NULL)
```

In Review

Data integrity is probably the most important subject discussed in this book, which is the reason I devoted this chapter entirely to integrity. Configuring and managing the integrity can also consume a lot of your time and can be stressful. I recommend you fully document your integrity issues and requirements in a document akin to the integrity plan I provide in this chapter. The document can then be circulated among the business's managers for input, and it will become your working document detailing all data integrity efforts.

The subject of data integrity has also been covered in chapter 13. Chapter 10 discusses integrity and the constraints in managing databases and working with the table designer and database diagrams; and Chapter 16 provides some advanced programming instruction related to integrity.

Triggers

The next quest in meeting the optimum performance data processing requirements and the integrity and business rule compliance requirements discussed in the preceding chapter is to master the art of creating and managing stored procedures and triggers. I say it is an art because both objects in SQL Server 2005 require some creative juices on your part and quite a bit of that brain power.

Stored procedures and triggers are very closely related. They are programmed in T-SQL or in managed code with a language like C#, and both are objects that are attached to your databases. When it boils down to what you can do with either object, it pays to rather list what you cannot do, and then the rest is up to your imagination.

NOTE *The SQL-SMO object model provides objects for creation, editing, and management of triggers and stored procedures. It is, however, more important for you to master these elements in T-SQL, using a query window in Management Studio.*

While the code in a trigger can be identical in function to the code of a stored procedure, the major difference between the two is that the trigger is connected to a table or view object, while a stored procedure is exposed as a database object and has to be explicitly called, like a function, and be passed parameters. If you think of your table or view as an object, which you should be doing, then think of the trigger as an event (like OnClick) that fires when an inbound DML statement "triggers" the table or the view.

Triggers are central to ensuring integrity and business rule adherence procedurally, while stored procedures are central to providing functionality and business services and functions on a broad scale. How each object is used and created will now be covered in its respective section. Because triggers are the easier of the two constructs to grasp, and because they follow up our treatise on integrity in the preceding chapter, let's start with them first. By the way, we'll also discuss some of the new features of triggers in SQL Server 2005, and I'll point these out as we progress. From here on this chapter will deal exclusively with triggers, while Chapter 14 is devoted to stored procedures.

Triggers

The SQL Server 2005 trigger is secondary to the primary built-in mechanisms for enforcing business rules and data integrity of any application or enterprise requirement, as we discussed in the preceding chapter. A trigger, however, is a lot more than a constraint check or a rule; it packs a lot more punch.

A trigger can do a lot. For all intents and purposes, it is a stored procedure that in itself is a full-blown SQL statement or batch that can query tables, calculate, evaluate, communicate, and provide complex functionality. SQL Server relates to a trigger in the same way it relates to an inline SQL statement that comes down the TDS wire. Triggers are treated as single transactions, which means that if they create an undesirable result, they can be rolled back (see Chapter 16).

Triggers are used in the following situations:

As cascades   Triggers can be used to cascade events and changes through related tables in a database. A good example is the manual cascade deletes or updates we would program in triggers in earlier versions of SQL Server (pre-Y2K) before these wishes became de facto features in SQL Server 2000 (the prodigy parent of SQL Server 2005). In many cases, cascading triggers can be used in data integrity or business rule requirements. You should, however, only consider this if the built-in cascade features and declarative integrity functions do not supply the desired end result or don't exist. Naturally the built-in stuff is more efficient (referential integrity is a good example of a constraint effort that would be wasted in a trigger).

As checks (and then some)   Triggers can do the work of the check constraints we discussed in Chapter 12, but when you need more bang for your buck, triggers come to take the lead. A trigger, created as a super constraint, is essentially a check constraint on steroids. You can reference columns in other tables (which you can't do on a check definition). You can conjure up a result set out of a trigger and then run through the result check to analyze inserted or modified data. Triggers can also talk to your users, fire off e-mail, or wake the DBA in the middle of the night. However, while constraints are proactive "filters" so to speak, triggers are reactive processes. Even the INSTEAD OF trigger fires in reaction to the DML statement sent to SQL Server.

As rule enforcers   Like badgers to honey, the existence of a database will *invariably* tempt users to attempt contradictory data access procedures on your data. Some users may just do things that the developer or DBA did not expect, while others may attempt to access the database in ways contrary to corporate or organization rules . . . and in many cases with criminal intent. A trigger can be used to ensure that a certain action cannot be attempted on a table. For example, an attempt to retrieve all credit card numbers from a table can be blocked in a trigger. The trigger can also send out alerts and even capture connection information and perform certain auditing functions. (This chapter includes the code for a highly efficient database object auditing system.) And because you can install multiple triggers on a table, you can pretty much take care of any situation that is contrary to both business rules and change control procedures.

As an evaluation mechanism   You can use a trigger to evaluate the state of your data before and after a DML statement does its work on a table or view. If the state is not up to par or compliance, then a trigger can be used to fill in the "missing links" or take some corrective action, such as rolling back, without requiring additional user input. Here's a drastic, but entirely possible, sequence of events a trigger can initiate:

```
CREATE TRIGGER Self_Destruct
  ON SwissCashAccounts
    FOR UPDATE
    AS
      IF Update(IntentToSteal)
        EXEC DotNetMailer 'Users,' 'This server will self-destruct
        in five seconds'
    WAITFOR DELAY '00:00:05'
    EXEC vaporize_server
```

An important attribute of triggers is that they have a long reach. While checks and rules are limited to tables in the current database, a trigger can reference beyond its parent table to other tables and other databases. But all good things have their limitations.

The Nuances of Triggers

DML statements, as opposed to row or column events, fire triggers. Rows and columns are the level on which integrity constraints operate, and integrity constraints *usually* fire before triggers on actual manipulation of the data. This means you have a general rule of thumb to follow, as alluded to in the preceding chapter, that when you need a broader scope of integrity-checking, triggers are the way to go. At a more granular level, the built-in integrity constraints are what you use. The two constructs have very clearly defined "fields of coverage," so to speak. *Usually* was put in italics because there is a new trigger that fires before constraints, even before the DRI constraints.

The T-SQL statements listed here are not allowed in trigger code:

- ALTER DATABASE
- CREATE DATABASE
- DROP DATABASE
- LOAD DATABASE
- RESTORE DATABASE
- DISK INIT
- DISK RESIZE
- RECONFIGURE
- LOAD LOG
- RESTORE LOG

While you can use SELECT statements in a trigger and generate result set returns, the client connections that fire the trigger usually have no means of interpreting or working with the returned data. You should accordingly avoid returning results by avoiding open SELECT statements in trigger code. By "open" I mean that the result set is not assigned to an internal structure. In addition, you should use SET NOCOUNT at the beginning of the trigger to obviate the return of any data to the client connection. You should also refrain from using cursors in triggers, because overuse can be a drain on server resources. In any event, you should be working with rowset functionality if you need to work with multiple rows in trigger code (see the discussion of cursors in Chapter 16).

Also, keep in mind that during a TRUNCATE TABLE operation (which is a delete en masse that empties a table by deallocating the table's data pages), trigger firing is suppressed. This applies to the database owner and should not be a concern of users. And the WRITETEXT statement does not activate a trigger.

Trigger Execution Types

A valuable feature in SQL Server 2005 is the capability to determine when a trigger executes. In addition to the FOR clause (FOR INSERT, FOR UPDATE, or FOR DELETE), you can define two execution types for a trigger as follows:

AFTER   This trigger is fired only after the statement that fired it completes. This is the default for SQL Server 2005. On an UPDATE statement, for example, the trigger will be activated only *after* the UPDATE statement has completed (and the data has been modified). If the DML statement fails, the AFTER trigger is never fired. You can have multiple AFTER triggers on a table (views are not supported, by the way) and list the triggers in an order of execution (see "Managing Triggers" later in this chapter). (By-the-by, AFTER triggers are never executed if a constraint violation arises.)

INSTEAD OF   This trigger is fired instead of the actual triggering action. For example, if an UPDATE arrives on the wire and an INSTEAD OF trigger is defined, the UPDATE is never executed but the trigger statement is executed instead. By contrast with its AFTER sibling, you can define an INSTEAD OF trigger for either a table or a view. INSTEAD OF triggers can be used for many scenarios, but one of the fanciest features is the capability to update view data, which are not normally updatable. As explained in the Chapter 15, it is not a simple matter to just obtain a fresh view of data using a view that has been around for a while.

Although the INSTEAD OF triggers are fired *instead* of the DML statement sent to the server, they fire before anything else, including any constraints that may have been defined (which is a big difference between the INSTEAD OF trigger and the AFTER trigger). The triggers are also not recalled, because SQL Server checks for recursion that might develop as the result of the actions the trigger itself takes on the table. In other words, it is certainly possible to create a trigger that practically replaces exactly what the original DML had intended to do to the table or view. It thus seems logical that the trigger would cause itself to be refired, but this unintended recursion is dampened.

NOTE   *While trigger overhead is very low, a time may come when you need to squeeze every drop of bandwidth out of your application. It thus makes sense to write trigger code within a trigger, such as flow-control logic (IF, CASE), that checks if the trigger really needs to run its course. For example, an INSTEAD OF trigger might check the underlying table state before it performs anything, and exit out if it determines the entire statement is not required. Also, if the constraint can be catered to using the check constraints described in Chapter 12, go with those because they incur much less overhead than triggers for simple integrity constraints.*

The Trigger Plan

Like the integrity plan described in the preceding chapter, a *trigger plan* is another important section of your overall database definition, model, or architecture. A trigger plan should also reflect the stages of trigger deployment and provide a checklist to ensure that all factors affecting triggers and affected by triggers have been taken into consideration. You can use the flow diagram in Figure 13-1 to build your trigger plan.

Gather Business Rules and Motivation for Triggers

Identify the business rules that can be best addressed by triggers. This section of the database plan identifies business rules that will impact the database model and architecture. Sit down with the people responsible for establishing the business rules and determine how best to cater to their needs using triggers.

Identify Key Trigger Issues to Cover

Issues to be catered to by triggers must be referenced or become part of the database architecture. If you are the DBA but do not write triggers, or if you are assigning the trigger writing to SQL Server developers or third parties, then it is important to list key issues that will impact the development plan. For example, note how you plan to maintain triggers. While most trigger code is straight up and down, a need may arise for the creation of a complex trigger, and the code needs to be documented and maintained and protected like all source code. Trigger code can also be dangerous if it falls into the wrong hands. And if you decide that encrypting the code is an option, then you need to be sure the source code is stored in a backup system, in documentation, or in source files that are secured. (I personally do not like encrypting objects like triggers and stored procedures. Some DBAs encrypt to protect the system against malicious or careless individuals who may have rights in the database. This is simply poor management.)

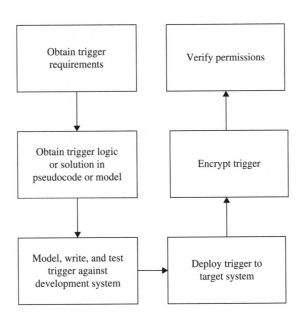

FIGURE 13-1
The trigger plan

List the Triggers and Their Objectives

In this section, list the precise objective of each trigger you need to create. As with constraints and stored procedures, an extensive system of triggers can hold a lot of trigger objects, and it will not take long for you to lose track of what triggers are installed where and for what reason. This problem is further compounded by an order of magnitude when more than one trigger is installed or defined for a table, or when you create a trigger cascade or nest.

Fully Document the Solution for Each Trigger

Once you have written a trigger or a collection of triggers, then each trigger, including the actual trigger code and the trigger's relation to other triggers, constraints, checks, and stored procs, should be fully documented. This should not only help you see the trigger trees for the trigger forest but help you pinpoint areas that could use improvement.

Most important, trigger documentation—both externally in supporting documents and internally using inline comments—can help other parties read your code. The documentation will also help you debug problems. Remember that triggers are regarded as transactions, so documenting them as such will allow you to debug and recover from problems created by rogue triggers. It is not normal to have a trigger go nuts on you and do substantial damage, but when I started out writing triggers, I once created a cascading delete that cascaded my entire database down the drain. To this day I am not sure how it happened, but it did.

In addition to documenting the solution arrived at for the trigger, it is also imperative to fully document the progress being made on the trigger or triggers under assignment. Some triggers may be extensive, and many may require the trigger writer to be supervised over several weeks or even on a permanent basis. To put it in more direct terms, you should not regard the management of a trigger or T-SQL project, in terms of managing the software creation process, as any different from a C# or Visual Basic 2005 project.

Do Cost Analysis

There are also costs attached to every trigger. As in the case of constraints, the costs are both direct, in terms of their consumption of SQL Server resources and usefulness, and indirect, in terms of the costs of programming, maintenance, documentation, and so on.

As mentioned in connection with the integrity plan, triggers are procedural and their code cannot be guaranteed by SQL Server to be ANSI-compliant or even safe. SQL Server can check code for errors, but it is not able to check trigger code for standards compliance on behalf of the trigger author or warn you that you are about to take unpaid permanent leave from your very fine DBA job.

Cost analysis of triggers should also cater to resource costs, and you should thus thoroughly test trigger code (in execution plans) and in the profiler (see Chapters 15 and 16).

Determine Error Checking Requirements

Determine a system for checking errors that materialize from trigger code. Errors can be directly caused by triggers, or they can result from the correct trigger execution with unpredictable or unintended results. Investigate the feasibility of deploying an error database, something like a bug recording system that records error messages that derive from both triggers and stored procedures. If you follow the advice dispensed in Chapter 12 and move either all or a substantial part of the processing to SQL Server, this is an essential practice.

You can also set up logging in the profiler and enable a security system to track who does what and when they did it. But the profiler does not cater to errors that occur in T-SQL code and that create problems with the database or the data.

Determine Effects in the Client Tier
Understanding the effects in the client tier or what reporting and alerting is required at the client is important. What we do in the data tier can affect the client tier, especially if the client processes have been implemented in a middle tier, especially in Web services. If you still need to maintain legacy client code, which means client-side data processing and logic, trigger implementation and especially stored procedure implementation can have unpredictable results, and these need to be considered.

Creating Triggers
Triggers, like most SQL Server objects, are created using T-SQL code, in Management Studio, and the SQL-SMO triggers collection. You can also write triggers in C# or any other .NET language and run them on the SQL Server CLR. This is covered in Chapters 11 and 14. Depending on your needs, the SQL-SMO and .NET Framework object model provides an alternative to T-SQL, and a very useful one at that. For the most part, however, the typical path to trigger creation and management is via T-SQL, so whip out Management Studio, or whatever tool you use to write and test T-SQL code, and get cracking.

Trigger Deployment
Deploying a trigger requires more than just writing the code and assigning the trigger to a table or view and then crossing your fingers that your landing gear is down. This is engineering, so you need to approach this as an engineer. The following steps, illustrated in the flow chart in Figure 13-2, document the process of trigger creation and deployment from beginning to end. Create your own deployment plan, which can act as a checklist that will take you from concept to deployment in a logical, well-controlled manner. I do trigger work for a number of clients, and thus each one has a file and trigger deployment plan for one or more triggers (and the overall trigger plan).

Step 1: Obtain trigger requirements   The requirement specs are obtained from the trigger plan. Your system may be large enough to warrant formal trigger assignment, as would large OLTP or e-commerce systems that will require several developers working on the project.

The following specification is an example of a trigger requirement on a call center application that logs the date and time and the agent connects to SQL Server on a number of tables. I could use the logging capability of the profiler, but the output is difficult to work with from the viewpoint of the call center equipment, such as the ACD scheduler that needs to have information about the CSR's open case load, and from the call center analyst who needs to export the data to decision support systems.

- **CSR Shift Log AFTER Trigger**   Record the date and time the agent (via the Web service proxy) initially logs on to SQL Server and runs Open-Shift. The Open-Shift session gets the agent oriented, reviews shift objectives, considers past shift performance, and so on. The trigger also records the Close-Shift data . . . the date and time when the agent has concluded Close-Shift and logs off the system.

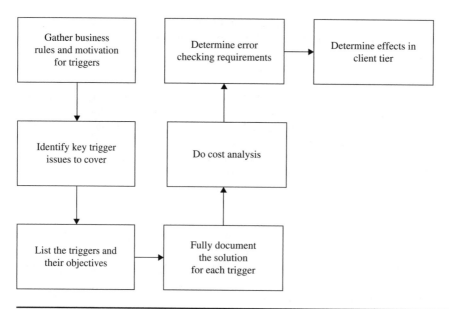

Figure 13-2   The steps to trigger deployment

The trigger can only be fired when the OpenCloseShift table is accessed, so the information records when the CSR logged on to the CRM application and when the agent logged off the CRM application. The data allows the call center manager to monitor shift duration and (not shown here) check how long agents are spending in Open-Shift and Close-Shift sessions.

- **Check Credit INSTEAD OF Trigger**   Check the credit rating of the client. If the credit rating is green, allow the CSR to take the order on account. If the credit rating is red, the CSR must advise the caller that only a money order or credit card can be accepted. The trigger can then return call center scripting (by calling a procedure) that the CSR can read back to the caller.

Step 2: Craft trigger logic or solution in pseudocode   This may be done in any custom or preferred pseudocode. The idea is to outline the trigger and sketch the scope and flow of the trigger.

In the CSR shift log specification just described, the pseudocode could be as follows:

```
Get CSR name from Windows security or login service
Function get datetime
Strip datetime into two values representing a date and the time
Write CSR name, date, and time to record
```

The check credit INSTEAD OF pseudocode could be as follows:

```
On open customer record
Query customer credit rating color
If red then restrict to cash
If green then allow to account
```

Step 3: Model, write, and test trigger against development system   Once all
pseudocode is written and you have cross-checked it with IS managers, supervisors, or
yourself, the stage is set for modeling and writing the trigger in T-SQL, testing against the
development system, checking the performance of the trigger (especially under load), and
so on. The next section goes into the actual trigger code.

Step 4: Deploy trigger to target system   This step entails installing the trigger (the job
of a DBA) to the target system if your processes have been approved by quality assurance
and your trigger testing program. You can copy objects to the production system or script
out the code for execution against the target system from Management Studio.

Step 5: Encrypt trigger   Encrypt your trigger in the development system. This is obviously not essential, but it is advisable if the systems might come under attack or cannot be
secured. One of my projects entails installing SQL Server in a number of data centers spread
throughout the United States where I cannot guarantee that the servers are off-limits or that
they are safe from access by unauthorized use of query tools.

Step 6: Verify permissions   You do not install permissions on triggers per se, but you
need to verify that users on the connections that fire the triggers have permission either to
query the table or to insert, update, or delete from it. This also applies to permissions on a
view on which INSTEAD OF triggers are installed. This stage of your trigger deployment
plan is critical. When I first started out installing triggers, I was so concerned with the actual
trigger and how impressed my clients would be that, after testing it with my super-DBA/
developer rights, I forgot to make sure the users would be able to access the tables on the
production system. SQL Server schema-level security is thus a great improvement in this area.

Creating a Trigger Using T-SQL

The principal T-SQL statement is CREATE TRIGGER, as follows (the full explanation and
usage of the arguments are documented in SQL Server Books Online):

```
CREATE TRIGGER [ schema_name . ]trigger_name
ON { table | view }
[ WITH <dml_trigger_option> [ ,...n ] ]
{ FOR | AFTER | INSTEAD OF }
{ [ INSERT ] [ , ] [ UPDATE ] [ , ] [ DELETE ] }
[ WITH APPEND ]
[ NOT FOR REPLICATION ]
AS { sql_statement  [ ; ] [ ,...n ] | EXTERNAL NAME <method specifier [ ; ] > }


<dml_trigger_option> ::=
    [ ENCRYPTION ]
    [ EXECUTE AS Clause ]


<method_specifier> ::=
    assembly_name.class_name.method_name


CREATE TRIGGER trigger_name
ON { ALL SERVER | DATABASE }
[ WITH <ddl_trigger_option> [ ,...n ] ]
{ FOR | AFTER } { event_type | event_group } [ ,...n ]
AS { sql_statement  [ ; ] [ ,...n ] | EXTERNAL NAME < method specifier >  [ ; ] }
```

```
<ddl_trigger_option> ::=
    [ ENCRYPTION ]
    [ EXECUTE AS Clause ]


<method_specifier> ::=
    assembly_name.class_name.method_name
```

You need to provide each trigger with a name and define it for a particular table or view in a database. You also have the option of encrypting the trigger so that no one (not even you, ever) can look at the original code. Triggers are secured with permissions (see Chapter 6) so that only you, the trigger creator, or the schema, can alter or drop the trigger.

After you have specified which table or view is to be the "beneficiary" of the trigger, you need to define the trigger as an AFTER or INSTEAD OF trigger. This specification may seem a little late in the syntax because you cannot define an AFTER trigger for a view.

Another important argument, NOT FOR REPLICATION, has serious implications in distributed database scenarios. This argument specifies that the trigger should not be executed when replication is the cause of table manipulation (see the chapter that covers replication, Chapter 8).

Following the AFTER or INSTEAD OF argument, you must specify the DML event the trigger fires on. This can be either DELETE, INSERT, and UPDATE. Finally, following the AS keyword, you enter the segment of T-SQL code to be executed every time the DML statement lands on the table or view. So your basic create trigger statement will look something like the following:

```
CREATE TRIGGER myTrigger
  ON Employees
  AFTER, INSERT, UPDATE
AS RAISERROR (500289, 16, 10)
```

This same trigger code specified as an AFTER or INSTEAD OF trigger would look like this in its most basic form:

```
CREATE TRIGGER myTrigger
  ON Employees
    INSTEAD OF INSERT, UPDATE, DELETE
AS . . .
```

Creating and Testing the Trigger

To create a trigger, drill down to the table on which you want to apply the trigger. Expand the table so that the Trigger folder is exposed. Right-click the folder and select New Trigger . . . . The script for creating a trigger is loaded into a query window. (If you want to add header and revision information, you can edit the template and install new template parameters, as discussed in Chapter 11.)

Write and test your trigger here to a development system or table. When you are ready to install the trigger to a table, all you need to do is extract the script and execute the query to the production table.

To alter the trigger at any time, you can drill down to the trigger as you did to create it and either choose the Modify option or the Script Trigger As option. Both routes load the Alter Trigger code into a query window. To replace the old trigger with the new one, simply execute the query.

NOTE   *You can step through trigger code in the Visual Studio debugger.*

To create and manage triggers on views, simply repeat the process just described on the views in SSMS.

Programming the Trigger

It is a good idea, as mentioned earlier, to apply conditional or evaluation logic to your trigger and, if necessary, prevent certain operations from being run by the trigger if there is no longer a need for the trigger to complete. For example, there might not be a need to complete a trigger statement after an update, if nothing was updated.

You can use the UPDATE(*column_name*) and COLUMNS_UPDATED() statements respectively to check for the completion of updates that apply to certain columns.

You can use the IF UPDATE(*column_name*) clause in your trigger code to determine if the DML (INSERT or UPDATE) statement that fired the trigger, or an earlier one, actually made any changes to write home about. This function will return true if indeed the column was assigned a value. The IF UPDATE() trigger will look like this:

```
CREATE TRIGGER myTrigger
 ON myTable
 FOR INSERT
  AS IF UPDATE(x)
  EXEC DotNetMailer.Send 'Jshapiro', 'Column x updated'
```

Or you can use the IF COLUMNS_UPDATED() clause to check which columns in a table were updated by an INSERT or UPDATE statement. This clause makes use of an integer bitmask to specify the columns to test. And the COLUMN_UPDATED() trigger looks like this:

```
CREATE TRIGGER myTrigger
 ON myTable
 FOR INSERT
  AS IF (COLUMN_UPDATED() & 1 = 1)
  EXEC DotNetMailer.Send 'Jshapiro', 'Column x updated'
```

Unfortunately, a limitation of both of the preceding functions is that they cannot test to see if a specific value in a field has been deleted; thus, neither function will return any result on a delete statement. However, you can check for row deletion using the @@ROWCOUNT function, which returns the number of rows affected by the last query.

The function @@ROWCOUNT returns the number or rows that were deleted as @@ROWCOUNT = X. Thus you can test for rows and make flow choices based on the results (see the stored procedure example in the next section). If, for example, the row count returns 0, you could exit the trigger or take some other action. If the row count is greater than 0, you could switch to a different code segment or even use a GOTO and code in a series of GOTO labels.

The Examples

Let's now look at a trigger from an actual deployment plan in which the business owner required being alerted to unusual sales activity:

```
/*
Script Name: Something Fishy
Description: Trigger to report unusually high sales
Usage: Placed on customers.dbo.orders for canship
Return Code: N/A
Author: Jeffrey R. Shapiro
Version: 1.00
Date Created: 9/25/2005
Revision History:
*/

IF EXISTS (SELECT name FROM sysobjects
    WHERE  name = N'Fishy'
    AND type = 'TR')
         DROP TRIGGER Fishy
GO

CREATE TRIGGER Fishy
ON customers.dbo.orders
FOR UPDATE
AS
BEGIN
  DECLARE @Qty int
    SELECT @Qty = (SELECT SUM(CanShip) FROM Customers.dbo.Orders)
    IF @Qty > 10000
      BEGIN
        EXEC DotNetMailer.Send 'JeffreyS',
        'Business cannot be this good,
        there is something fishy going on'
      RETURN
      END
END
GO
```

As a second example, make use of the RAISERROR message function. As discussed in Chapter 11, the RAISERROR is similar to the message dialog facility in the Win32 API (and wrapped by the .NET Framework), which has been exposed (or wrapped) by every major language capable of producing Windows applications. If you look at RAISERROR in Chapter 10 or Books Online you will see that it can take first a message string or a message ID that can get returned to the client. You can also add as parameters severity levels and replacement parameters. The replacement parameter placeholder in the function is that old familiar %d visiting T-SQL from the C language, as demonstrated next.

In the following example the trigger code tests for the number of items scheduled for shipping, and if it is over 10,000 units, an error message or alert is committed to the Windows Server 2003 application log by using the WITH LOG option. In addition I have also added the SET NOCOUNT line, which will ensure that the trigger does not return the "n rows affected" message to the user. The trigger code will not modify any rows, but SET NOCOUNT will suppress anything that might slip in when later versions of this trigger are installed.

```
ALTER TRIGGER Fishy
ON customers.dbo.orders
FOR UPDATE
AS
BEGIN
SET NOCOUNT ON
DECLARE @Qty int
    SELECT @Qty = (SELECT SUM(CanShip) FROM Customers.dbo.Orders)
    IF @Qty > 10000
      BEGIN
        RAISERROR('Total CanShip items has exceeded %d.',18,1,@Qty)
          WITH LOG
        RETURN
      END
END

GO
SET QUOTED_IDENTIFIER OFF
GO
SET ANSI_NULLS ON
GO
```

Deferred Name Resolution

You can create triggers at design time, and you are not forced to specify a table or view that already exists. (Obviously, the trigger will not fire, because the table or view object does not yet exist.) This is called *deferred name resolution*.

First and Last Triggers

If you deploy a large collection of AFTER triggers on a specific table, you can specify which of the triggers is the first AFTER trigger and which is last AFTER trigger. This essentially allows you to create a "list" of triggers with a start and an end, and all other AFTER triggers will fall in between.

You should clearly understand, however, that the feature allows you to define a first or last attribute on a trigger *after* each DML event that fires triggers. In other words, you can specify for *TableX* that trigger *triggerA* is *first after* the FOR INSERT event, that *triggerB* is *first after* the FOR UPDATE event, and that *triggerC* is *last after* the FOR DELETE event.

Here are some nuances to the application of the first/last attributes you should be aware of:

- The first AFTER trigger cannot be the last AFTER trigger as well.
- The triggers between first and last are not executed according to any order.

- The first and last triggers must be fired by DML statements (INSERT, UPDATE, and DELETE).

- INSTEAD OF triggers are not supported by the first/last feature.

- If you alter a first or last trigger, its status as first or last is dropped.

- Replicated tables will define a first trigger automatically for any table that is an immediate or queued update subscriber. In other words, the replication trigger will be positioned as the first trigger, regardless of any other trigger attributed as a first trigger, and if you try to reassign the first manually, after configuring for update subscription, SQL Server will generate an error.

- If you use an INSTEAD OF trigger on a table, it will fire before any updates on the base table fire the AFTER triggers.

- Also, if you define an INSTEAD OF trigger on a view, and that trigger updates a base table that has AFTER triggers defined, these triggers will fire before any manipulation on the base table takes place as a result of the INSTEAD OF trigger fired at the view level.

You use the sp_settriggerorder stored procedure to specify the first and last attributes for an AFTER trigger. The options that are available are as follows:

- **First**   This makes an AFTER trigger the first trigger fired *after* a fire event.

- **Last**   This makes an AFTER trigger the last trigger fired *after* a fire event.

- **None**   This cancels the first or last attribute on a trigger. Use *None* to reset the trigger to fire in any order.

The following example demonstrates the use of the trigger positioning stored proc:

```
sp_settriggerorder @triggername = 'myTrigger', @order = 'first'
```

Trigger Recursion

SQL Server 2005 provides a feature known as *recursive invocation*. Recursion can thus be invoked on two levels, *indirect recursion* and *direct recursion*. The two types permit the following behaviors:

- **Indirect**   A statement triggers *TableA, Trigger1*, which causes an event that fires *TableB, Trigger1*. *TableB, Trigger1* then causes *TableA, Trigger1* to fire again.

- **Direct**   A statement triggers *TableA, Trigger1*, which causes an event that fires *TableA, Trigger2*. *TableA, Trigger2* then causes *TableA, Trigger1* to fire again.

The recursion types can work for or against you and can break your code. You can set direct recursion off using the sp_dboption stored procedure, but that will leave indirect recursion enabled, which you may want. To disable both recursion types, you need to use sp_configure.

Trigger Nesting

Triggers can be nested (in an arrangement also described as a trigger cascade). In other words, a trigger on *TableA* can update *TableB* that fires a trigger on *TableC* that fires a trigger on *TableD* that . . . . SQL Server will prevent a chain of triggers from forming an infinite loop, and you cannot nest to more than 32 levels.

You can also disable nested trigger execution, on a server-wide basis, using the sp_configure stored procedure. The default is that trigger nesting is allowed. Nesting and recursion are controlled by the same argument in sp_configure, so if you turn off nesting, recursion goes as well, and vice versa; this is regardless of the setting you have used in the recursion attribute set by sp_dboption, discussed in the section on recursion. Trigger nesting also terminates if any trigger executes a ROLLBACK TRANSACTION statement.

You can also manage the nesting behavior of triggers from Management Studio or from the SQL-DMO object model or using the sp_configure procedure (see Chapter 8).

Rolling Back Trigger Transactions

You will recall that earlier in this chapter I advised that SQL Server treats the code in a trigger as a transaction. This means that you can undo the statements that are enclosed in the trigger transaction code. It is important to understand that when you issue a ROLLBACK TRANS-ACTION, as demonstrated in the following code, the entire batch in the trigger is reversed out. Also, you do not necessarily need to call ROLLBACK TRANSACTION if you are relying only on SQL Server to trap an error. SQL Server automatically reverses any transaction it determines to be fatal.

```
CREATE TRIGGER VoiceMessageDelete ON Messages
FOR DELETE
 AS IF EXISTS
   (SELECT delete FROM Messages m INNER JOIN conference c
      ON m.message_no = c.message_no )
 BEGIN      RAISERROR ('Message cannot be deleted until heard by
      all conference members', 10, 1)
      ROLLBACK TRANSACTION
 END
```

Managing Triggers

Triggers are a powerful and essential attribute of any DBMS, but they can be a headache to manage, especially when you have a lot of them. For this reason, if you have a big system, you will want to architect triggers in a modeling system and provide access to trigger metadata. The following sections explain how to alter and drop triggers.

Altering Triggers

To alter a trigger in T-SQL, you need to use the ALTER TRIGGER statement. The basic statement is as follows:

```
ALTER TRIGGER trigger_name
ON . . ..
```

NOTE *Management Studio adds the alter trigger code automatically the first time you open the trigger code for editing.*

The code to apply after the ON line takes the same syntax and choice of arguments as the CREATE TRIGGER statement described earlier (see the SQL Server 2005 Books Online for the full explanation and usage of the arguments).

Dropping Triggers

Dropping a trigger in T-SQL requires the DROP TRIGGER statement followed by the trigger name. Consider, for example, the following code:

```
USE MYDB
IF EXISTS (SELECT name FROM sysobjects
    WHERE name = 'SecurityViolation' AND type = 'TR')
DROP TRIGGER SecurityViolation
```

It drops the trigger SecurityViolation from *MYDB*.

You can specify multiple triggers in a DROP TRIGGER statement by separating trigger names with commas and enclosing the list in square brackets, as here:

```
DROP TRIGGER [x, y, z].
```

You should make sure to check for trigger dependencies with the sp_depends stored procedure before dropping a trigger.

To drop a trigger interactively, simply drill down to the tables in your database and the Triggers folder. Then expand the list of triggers in the folder and right-click the trigger you wish to manage. From the context menu, you can select the trigger from the drop-down list and click Delete. You can also disable a trigger at this point.

Getting Information about Triggers

To obtain information from SQL Server about the triggers installed on a table, you should execute the system stored procedure sp_helptrigger as follows:

```
--to check triggers installed on the table Items
EXEC sp_helptrigger Items
```

The sp_helptrigger procedure returns information about the triggers on the table, the trigger owners, and the DML statements they are defined for. The full syntax of this stored procedure is as follows:

```
sp_helptrigger [ @tabname = ] 'table'
[ , [ @triggertype = ] 'type' ]
```

where the @triggertype option specifies the type of triggers you require information on. With the code

```
sp_helptrigger @tabname = 'CRMCustomer'
```

the result set returned from the procedure is listed is as follows:

trigger_name	trigger_owner	isupdate	isdelete	Isinsert	isafter	isinsteadof	Trigger_schema
CRMCustomerUpdateTrigger	dbo	1	0	0	1	0	dbo
CRMCustomerInsertCascadeTrigger	dbo	0	0	1	1	0	dbo

Final Words on Developing Triggers

The following is a short list of recommendations when using triggers:

1. Use triggers when necessary to enforce business rules and integrity not adequately handled by the built-in constraints.

2. Keep trigger code simple. If there is a lot you need to accomplish in a trigger, then consider breaking your code into more than one trigger, which is akin to how you write code in traditional programming environments.

3. Be sure to check for excessive recursion.

4. Use NOCOUNT to suppress the "n rows affected" message returned to the connection. And don't leave result sets open or unassigned. Use them only for the benefit of the trigger, such as by using SELECT to find values or to compare values in multiple tables.

5. Minimize the use of ROLLBACK TRANSACTION.

6. If your triggers begin to look like general procedural code, requiring the return of result sets to clients, and functionality beyond integrity and enforcement of business rules, then you need to switch to a stored procedure, a function, or managed code.

Now, let's look at two more complicated triggers.

Putting Triggers to Good Use

The following two examples show you what can be achieved with triggers and what they should be used for. In the first example users log on to a Web site and complete a form to register for a logon account. A process in the Web service creates a user logon ID and password and sets up credentials in the *CRMCustomer* table. The logon ID is given a GUID, the 32-bit globally unique identifier. The trigger on the *CRMCustomer* table, after the insert, captures the GUID on the calling stored procedure and then sets up rows under the same GUID, as the foreign key, in a collection of related tables, such as tables for telephone numbers and *e-mail* addresses of the same customer.

```
set ANSI_NULLS ON
set QUOTED_IDENTIFIER ON
go

ALTER TRIGGER [CRMCustomerInsertCascadeTrigger]
  ON [dbo].[CRMCustomer]
AFTER INSERT
AS
BEGIN
  DECLARE @CustomerType int
```

```
DECLARE @CallingProc varchar(128)
DECLARE @Source uniqueidentifier
SELECT @CallingProc = OBJECT_NAME( SUBSTRING
    ( p.context_info, 1, 4 ) ),
     @Source = CAST( SUBSTRING
    ( p.context_info, 5, 128 ) AS uniqueidentifier )
FROM master..sysprocesses as p
WHERE p.spid = @@SPID
PRINT @CallingProc
 INSERT INTO CRMPhones (CRMCustomerID)
 SELECT CRMCustomerID FROM inserted
 INSERT INTO CRMAddresses (CRMCustomerID)
 SELECT CRMCustomerID FROM inserted
 INSERT INTO CRMFaxes (CRMCustomerID)
 SELECT CRMCustomerID FROM inserted
 INSERT INTO CRMEmails (CRMCustomerID)
 SELECT CRMCustomerID FROM inserted
 INSERT INTO AccessPermissions (UserGUID)
 SELECT CRMCustomerID FROM inserted
 INSERT INTO SystemUsers (UserGUID, LoginID)
 SELECT CRMCustomerID, Cast(CRMCustomerID as NVarChar (50))FROM inserted
 SET @CustomerType = (SELECT CRMCustomerType FROM inserted)
 If @CustomerType = 1
 Begin
   INSERT INTO CRMProducerData (CRMCustomerID)
   SELECT CRMCustomerID FROM inserted
 End
 INSERT INTO AuditTrail (Context, TransactionType, FieldChanged, TableAffected,
   NewValue, UserGUID)
 SELECT 'CRM','Insert', 'NA', 'CRMCustomer', CRMCustomerID, @Source FROM
   inserted
 INSERT INTO AuditTrail (Context, TransactionType, FieldChanged, TableAffected,
   NewValue, UserGUID)
 SELECT 'CRM','Insert', 'NA', 'CRMPhones', CRMCustomerID, @Source FROM inserted
 INSERT INTO AuditTrail (Context, TransactionType, FieldChanged, TableAffected,
   NewValue, UserGUID)
 SELECT 'CRM','Insert', 'NA', 'CRMAddresses', CRMCustomerID, @Source FROM
   inserted
 INSERT INTO AuditTrail (Context, TransactionType, FieldChanged, TableAffected,
   NewValue, UserGUID)
 SELECT 'CRM','Insert', 'NA', 'CRMFaxes', CRMCustomerID, @Source FROM inserted
   INSERT INTO AuditTrail (Context, TransactionType, FieldChanged,
TableAffected, NewValue, UserGUID)
   SELECT 'CRM','Insert', 'NA', 'CRMEmails', CRMCustomerID, @Source FROM
Inserted
 INSERT INTO AuditTrail (Context, TransactionType, FieldChanged, TableAffected,
   NewValue, UserGUID)
 SELECT 'New Login','Insert', 'NA', 'SystemUsers', CRMCustomerID, @Source FROM
   Inserted
 INSERT INTO AuditTrail (Context, TransactionType, FieldChanged, TableAffected,
   NewValue, UserGUID)
 SELECT 'New Login','Insert', 'NA', 'AccessPermissions', CRMCustomerID, @Source
   FROM inserted
END
```

This second trigger is a simple mechanism on a voice mail system that enforces a business rule on the process of deleting messages.

```
CREATE TRIGGER VoiceMessageDelete ON Messages
FOR DELETE
 AS IF EXISTS
   (DELETE FROM Messages m INNER JOIN conference c
     ON m.message_no = c.message_no )
 BEGIN
  RAISERROR ('Message cannot be deleted until heard by all conference members', 10, 1)
  ROLLBACK TRANSACTION
 END
```

To Recap

We covered a lot of ground together in this chapter dealing with triggers. As you can see, trigger writing and management can consume substantial resources, and without proper planning, documentation, change control, archiving, source code maintenance, modeling, and so on, you can create a lot of problems for yourself or the team.

If you are new to trigger writing, the change in development style and philosophy can put a lot of strain on mental and physical resources. And the conversion of client-side, in-line SQL code to server-side triggers (and stored procedures) can be expensive in terms of both time and materials.

If you have not already done so, you should read Chapter 6 carefully, or read it again, because trigger and stored procedure deployment require you to manage permissions and security so that your users can exploit the code you have written. Also, query plans are discussed in Chapter 16, and understanding them is an essential prerequisite to writing and testing stored procedures and triggers.

PART III

Stored Procedures and Functions

Stored procedures and functions are the most important objects of an RDBMS, outside of the engines and the database tables. The stored procedures and functions of an RDBMS, and how a product like SQL Server 2005 supports them, are what make the product. How procedures and functions are stored, compiled, optimized, and executed by a DBMS is what sets a DBMS apart from its competitors. They help us meet the rules of deployment we discussed in Chapter 13.

This chapter covers both legacy stored procedures and functions written in T-SQL as well as the procs and functions you can now install as part of the .NET Framework's common language runtime (CLR) support (see Chapter 11). We have not cover trigger creation using the .NET Framework because the process for writing the code, compiling and installing the assembly and installing the trigger to SQL Server is identical for all "objects" CLR.

For the most part we will be discussing stored procedures because you will be creating and using them more. If you are unfamiliar with the concept of a stored procedure, you will find that the following list sheds some light on these critical SQL Server features:

- Stored procedures are collections of Transact-SQL statements or .NET Framework language assemblies that contain inline T-SQL, that can be referenced and executed by name from a client connection. They consist of functionality that executes remotely from the calling connection—the client—that is interested in exploiting the result of the remote execution.

- Stored procedures encapsulate repetitive tasks. Often in client applications a large number of SQL statements all do the same thing. One stored procedure that accepts variables from the client can satisfy more than one query at the client, executed concurrently or at different times. More than one client can call the same stored procedure. Variable parameters that identify columns and values can replace almost all query code at the client.

- Stored procedures share application logic and code. In this respect they have a *reuse* benefit similar to that of classes in object-oriented software. A good example of an application that can greatly benefit from stored procedures is Report Server.

- Stored procedures hide database schema and catalog details. When you query a database using client-side SQL code, you need to know specifics of the tables and columns you are querying. This exposes the schema to the client connection and the user, especially in Internet applications. The stored procedure does not allow the client to have the proverbial foot in the door. The only information the client or connection has is the procedure name to call. In this regard, stored procedures provide a layer of security because the client also needs appropriate permissions to execute the procedure.

- Stored procedures conserve network bandwidth and allow you to concentrate processing needs at the data tier, which can be appropriately scaled up or out as needed (see Chapter 9).

- Like functions, stored procedures return values and error messages. But they can also return result sets from server-side queries that can be further processed on the server before being sent to the client. The return values can be used to indicate success or failure of stored procedure functionality, and the status can be returned to the client or used to control the flow and scope of the procedure logic.

- Stored procedures are created using the CREATE PROCEDURE statement, edited or updated using the ALTER PROCEDURE statement, and executed by the client connections; they return the result to the clients. The flow chart in Figure 14-1 illustrates the life-cycle (abridged) of the stored procedure.

Database developers need intimate knowledge of the workings of stored procedures. For all intents and purposes, they are to the DBMS and its databases what classes are to languages like C# and Java. Stored procedures are not inherited, derived, or cloned, nor do they sport inherited properties, methods, and the like, but they share many other valuable attributes of object-based programming such as code isolation, reuse, and sharing (by both developers and users). You cannot build any form of effective application that relies on SQL Server, nor can you be an effective DBA, without having an intimate knowledge of how to code and manage stored procedures.

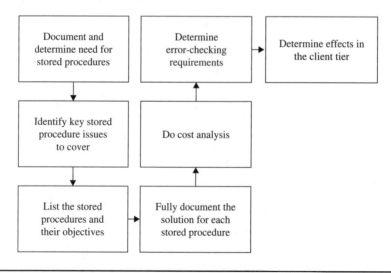

FIGURE 14-1   Requirements for stored procedures

Types of Stored Procedures

The several types of stored procedure supported by SQL Server are as follows:

- **System**   The system stored procedures are built into SQL Server and cannot be altered or tampered with short of destroying the catalog. They provide information about the database schema, object names, constraints, data types, permissions, and so on. There are several collections of system stored procedures: the catalog stored procedures, SQL Server Agent stored procedures, replication stored procedures, and so on. The system stored procedures are discussed in their respective chapters and in Appendix.

- **Local**   The local stored procedures, written by the DBA and SQL Server developer, are the focus of this chapter.

- **Temporary**   These provide the same or similar functionality as the local stored procedures discussed in this chapter, but as explained further a little later in this chapter, they only exist for the life of the connection.

- **Remote**   These stored procedures exist in remote servers and can be referenced by an originating server. These stored procedures are used in distributed applications.

- **Extended**   The extended stored procedures are similar in function to the local stored procedures but can reference functionality external to SQL Server, such as calling routines and functions in remote libraries and processes compiled, for example, in DLLs or object storehouses. For the most part extended stored procedures will be replaced by .NET Framework stored procedures.

How Stored Procedures Are Processed by SQL Server

Stored procedures are processed in two stages. In the first stage the procedure is first parsed by the SQL Server database engine (see Chapter 2) upon creation, after which two things happen. SQL Server stores the definition of the procedure, name and code, in the catalog. It also pushes the code through the Query Optimizer, as discussed in Chapter 4, and determines the best execution plan for the code.

Next the code is compiled and placed in the procedure cache. The only time the plan is flushed from the cache is when an explicit recompile is called by the client connection or the plan no longer exists in the cache, which means it had aged and had to be expelled. The cache can also be flushed via the DBCC freeproccache command discussed in Chapter 10.

In the second stage the query plan is retrieved when the stored procedure's name is referenced in code. The procedure code is then executed in the context of each connection that called the procedure. Any result sets or return values are returned to each connection.

The Nuances of Stored Procedures

Stored procedure code can vary from the most simple of DML statements to the most complex queries using flow-control, joins, calculations, and so on. However, the following nuances are important to keep in mind:

- Stored procedure names, like triggers, are stored in *sysobjects* and the code is stored in *syscomments*. To inspect the stored procedure code, execute sp_helptext in the parent database of the stored procedure. More on sp_helptext later.

- To check which objects are referenced by a stored procedure, execute sp_depends.

- The words PROCEDURE and PROC can be used interchangeably, and SQL Server recognizes both. The statements CREATE PROC, DROP PROC, and ALTER PROC are thus also valid.

- The following CREATE statements cannot be used in a stored procedure: CREATE DEFAULT, CREATE PROCEDURE, CREATE TRIGGER, CREATE RULE, CREATE VIEW.

- You can create any other database object from a stored procedure and even reference it in the stored procedure, as long as you create it before you reference it. You can even reference temporary tables in a stored procedure.

- The maximum size of a stored procedure is 128 MB.

- The number of local variables in a stored procedure is limited by available memory.

- The maximum number of parameters in a stored procedure is 1,024.

- You cannot use remote stored procedures in remote transaction scenarios. If you execute a remote stored procedure, the transaction on the remote instance cannot be rolled back.

- Stored procedures can spawn stored procedures that can access any object created by the parent stored procedure. However, if you create a local temporary table, it only exists for the stored procedure that created it. If you exit the stored procedure, the temporary table is lost.

The Stored Procedure Plan

Your stored procedure plan is almost identical in objective and scope to the trigger plan discussed in chapter 13. It should play as big a part, if not bigger, in the overall database architecture and modeling. If you have not gone over the trigger plan suggestions made earlier, or if you do not use a formal plan for the production of stored procedures, now is the time to adopt this practice. You can use the flow diagram in Figure 14-2 as a starting point to build your stored procedure plan. The steps in the plan are explained in the next sections.

FIGURE 14-2
Modeling the
stored procedure

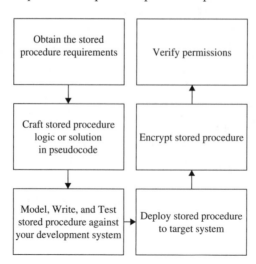

Document and Determine Need for Stored Procedures

We have looked at some of the reasons to use stored procedures earlier and at length in Chapter 10. This is the section of your plan (especially if you are motivated to move away from a desktop solution like Microsoft Access) to list and discuss the needs and reasons.

Identify Key Stored Procedure Issues to Cover

The issues to be catered to by stored procedures, or the solutions to be obtained using stored procedures, must be referenced or become part of the database architecture. (In the trigger plan, I also listed a number of issues you should cover here, so go back and apply the points there to the stored procedure plan.)

One important area to address is the development tools you use to create and debug stored procedures. You can use query windows in Management Studio, which you probably will do to write, edit, debug, and performance-test your code as described in this chapter. A few third-party SQL Integrated Development Environments (IDEs) on the market are specifically suited to SQL Server. They are worthy tools for the DBA or SQL Server developer who writes a lot of stored procedures, and perhaps some very complex ones as well. The serious developer who needs to fully step through code will use Visual Studio.

The following list provides an example of some stored procedure issues to consider in the stored procedure plan:

- Who will develop and maintain the code?
- Will we use encryption?
- What factors determine recompilation?
- How do we handle error messages and track bugs raised by the code?
- How will we monitor and assess performance and service level?
- When would we need to use an extended stored procedure, and who will create it?
- What development tools and debugging environment should we use?

List the Stored Procedures and Their Objectives

In this section, list the precise objective of each procedure you need to create. If you are converting legacy in-line SQL statements still buried in your client applications, a good way to start is to go through all the client procedures and copy the SQL statements from them. Paste each statement into a document, noting exactly where in the client code the statement is buried, and mark the statement for replacement by the stored procedure. Doing it this way can help you identify SQL statements in your code that are the same or similar and could thus make use of one stored procedure, or a variation of one or more.

In many cases, you will find that one stored procedure just needs new parameters and can be used to satisfy a number of areas in the client code. This exercise is rewarding because the code in the client application can drop dramatically. For example, a few dozen one-line EXEC PROC statements can reduce the number of code lines by several thousand.

Fully Document the Solution for Each Stored Procedure

This section is as important for stored procedures as triggers. If you have not read the trigger plan earlier and you intend to prepare a stored procedure plan, you should read the trigger plan first.

Do Cost Analysis

Stored procedures assume all the data processing overhead that was once dispersed among the clients, so a complex procedure that consumes a certain amount of processing overhead compounds the overhead for every connection associated with a procedure currently executing in the server. If you have not yet mastered the art of profiling your stored procedures and analyzing your queries, you should spend some time with the Profiler, as discussed in Chapter 18 before embarking on an extensive stored procedure development effort.

Another cost of stored procedures is the indirect cost of adopting a new style and philosophy of programming. To obtain the data from your client that you send to the stored procedure, you will likely have to change the way your client does business with the user. Bound controls, for example, are history in many cases (you don't have them on the Internet), and so you might have to add code in some places where data-bound controls have been excised. The following Java code is a good example of how you would code the assignment of data in place of a data-bound control, especially in middle-tier solutions:

```
String ProcParam1 = "Jeffrey";
String ProcParam2 = "Shapiro";
-or
String ProcParam1 = FNText.Text;
String ProcParam2 = LNText.Text;
```

NOTE *I cannot think of a better word than excise to describe getting rid of data-bound controls in a client application. Honestly, they were good in the early days of Delphi and VB, when the database engine squatted on your local PC like a warthog trapped in mud. With SQL Server solutions, they truly are a thing of the past. Since I have been working exclusively with SQL Server, I have removed all of my data-bound controls from my applications.*

Determine Error Checking Requirements

See the trigger plan discussed earlier for this section of the stored procedure plan. Error handling in stored procedures is also a lot more involved due to the code's inclination to say something to the client. I have thus discussed error handling in stored procedures in more detail later in this chapter.

Determine Effects in the Client Tier

One of the positive effects of getting rid of SQL code in the client tier is that you'll end up with clients that look a lot thinner than usual. Your code will also be cleaner and easier to document in the client. However, the downside is that the process of converting to a client/server system and adopting stored procedures can be long and involved. For example, you might make extensive use of ADO.NET visual controls that need to have their dataset methods changed from SQL to stored procedure calls, and so on. I have simply dumped data-bound grids and the like and chosen to work only at the object level in ADO.NET, pulling back a result set from a stored procedure and then looping the data up into a dataset.

To me, creating a stored procedure to replace a data-bound ADO grid is like guzzling a Bud on a hot August afternoon on Miami Beach. You'll likely have to spend a morning to code a complex procedure that returns the same data as the data-bound grid. But once you have tested the procedure in QA or whatever tool you use, seeing the data appear in a simple grid in the client is a wonderful feeling, knowing that all the client had to do was issue a single line of code to call the proc.

Creating Stored Procedures

Many companies employ SQL Server developers full time or as consultants to do nothing else but code stored procedures. No matter whether you are the IT Manager or a DBA in charge of a mob of "proc-programmers" or a one-person show responsible for everything, the stored procedure deployment plan is one of the most important plans discussed in this book.

Stored Procedure Deployment

The following steps, illustrated in the flow chart in Figure 14-3, document the process of stored procedure creation and deployment from beginning to end. Create your own deployment plan, which will be your checklist that will take you from concept to deployment in a logical, well-controlled manner.

Step 1: Obtain the stored procedure requirements   The requirement specs are obtained from the stored procedure plan as discussed earlier.

The following specification is an example of a stored procedure requirement on an order-taking system that debits stock items from the inventory or warehouse table and credits them to the customer's account.

Step 2: Craft stored procedure logic or solution in pseudocode   You should work on this section with the idea of sketching the scope, functionality, and final result of the procedure.

In the preceding example, the pseudocode could be as follows:

```
Declare variables of type Int
```

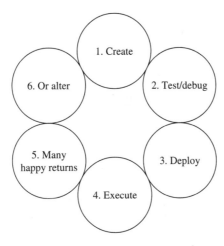

FIGURE 14-3
Executing the
stored procedure

1. Create
2. Test/debug
3. Deploy
4. Execute
5. Many happy returns
6. Or alter

Step 3: Model, write, and test the stored procedure against your development system This work is done in Management Studio or the IDE of your choice (see Chapter 4). Before you begin code, however, stored procedures should be defined in a modeling language, which would aim to capture procedure-related metadata.

Step 4: Deploy the stored procedure to the target system Deployment of the stored procedure entails executing the CREATE PROCEDURE statement against the target system.

Step 5: Encrypt the stored procedure The same motivation used to justify trigger encryption applies here. Just as with triggers, this step is done inside the CREATE PROCEDURE statement. You must not encrypt your trigger in the development system unless you have a separate and secure version of the source code elsewhere. The WITH ENCRYPTION clause in the CREATE PROCEDURE statement is like a loaded Uzi with the safety off. One slip and off goes your foot. Be sure that you are connected to the target product system to install and encrypt the procedure. More on encryption later in this chapter.

Step 6: Verify permissions Permission verification is the last step you take before allowing users to obtain service from your stored procedure. Unlike with triggers, users must have direct permission to execute a stored procedure. This can be done in T-SQL code as explained in Chapter 5.

However, the permissions issue does not stop with the right to call EXEC. You also need to verify that users on the connection that call the proc—either to query the table or to insert, update, or delete from it—have these DML permissions as well.

Creating a Stored Procedure Using T-SQL

You can use any of several methods to create stored procedures; there are a few tools floating around. The principal method, of course, is to use the T-SQL statements CREATE PROC or CREATE PROCEDURE. You can also use the SQL-SMO object model to create, alter, and manage stored procedures.

To code and test stored procedures in T-SQL, you will use a query window in Management Studio. The stored procedure's CREATE and ALTER templates are useful and will save you some coding time. The following syntax represents the CREATE PROC statement (the full explanation and usage of the arguments are documented in SQL Server Books Online):

```
CREATE { PROC | PROCEDURE } [schema_name.] procedure_name [ ; number ]
    [ { @parameter [ type_schema_name. ] data_type }
        [ VARYING ] [ = default ] [ [ OUT [ PUT ]
    ] [ ,...n ]
[ WITH <procedure_option> [ ,...n ]
[ FOR REPLICATION ]
AS { <sql_statement> [;] [ ...n ] | <method_specifier> }
;]
<procedure_option> ::=
    [ ENCRYPTION ]
    [ RECOMPILE ]
    [ EXECUTE_AS_Clause ]
```

```
<sql_statement> ::=
{ [ BEGIN ] statements [ END ] }
<method_specifier> ::=
```

AS *T-SQL statements* [...n]

A stored procedure must be named. It is a good idea to name a stored procedure with a prefix (such as the acronym of a process or module, as in jrs_storedproc). However, you should not name your stored procedures using the sp_ prefix, because those are typically reserved for system, built-in, and user-defined stored procedures.

You can create one or more parameters in a stored procedure. The client in the execution statement that calls the stored procedure must supply the values for the parameters. If a stored procedure expecting a parameter value does not receive it, the stored procedure will fail and return an error. It is thus especially important when you code stored procedures that you handle all parameter errors properly. You can code flow-control statements, return codes, and the like, as long as errors raised in the stored procedure are properly handled.

Ownership Referencing Inside Stored Procedures

Object names get resolved when a stored procedure is executed. If you reference object names inside a stored procedure and do not reference the object by ownership (name qualification), the ownership defaults to the owner of the stored procedure, and the stored procedure is thus restricted to the stored procedure owner. In other words, only the owner gets to execute the procedure.

Also, objects referenced by DBCC, ALTER TABLE, CREATE TABLE, DROP TABLE, TRUNCATE TABLE, CREATE INDEX, DROP INDEX, and UPDATE STATISTICS must also be qualified with the object owner's name so that users can execute the stored procedure. If you create a stored procedure and do not reference any table objects in the stored procedure with qualified names, then access to the tables, during execution of the stored procedure, is restricted to the owner of the stored procedure (see how permissions affect this in Chapters 5).

Encryption

As discussed in the trigger section and in the stored procedure deployment plan, you can hide the code of your stored procedure using encryption (by using the WITH ENCRYPTION clause) as you do when you create triggers. However, once the procedure is encrypted, there is no way to decrypt it; not even the SA account or an Administrator can do so. Encrypting the code is a good idea if the code you have defined in the stored procedure exposes highly sensitive data, as long as you keep a copy of the unencrypted code that only you can access. Although it has never happened to me, I did hear of someone who spent a month writing the mother of all procedures and then encrypted the code on the development system by mistake, before he made a copy of the final source.

Encryption is also useful for a turnkey product that ships with the SQL Server engine as the data store. Your product will then be in the hands of third parties, and you'll have no means of preventing them from checking out, tampering with, and even stealing the data store code. Encryption prevents all that. In fact if the product, such as a voice mail system, cannot operate without the data store, an encrypted stored procedure might obviate the need for one of those clumsy "dongles" you shove onto the parallel port to control access to the system, or prevent it from being pirated.

Grouping

You can create a group of stored procedures, each one having the same name to identify them as part of a group, by assigning each stored procedure in the group an identification number. Grouping the procedures like this allows you to maintain collections of stored procedures that pertain to a particular function or purpose. For example, I have a group of stored procedures that are all part of the accounts payable database, as follows:

```
accpay;1
accpay;2
accpay;3
accpay;4...
```

Creating each member in the group is easy: Just specify the number of the individual procedure in your CREATE PROC code. Caveat? You cannot delete an individual. When you are done with the group, the statement DROP PROCEDURE destroys the whole group.

Creating, Testing, and Debugging a Stored Procedure

The steps you take to opening a CREATE PROCEDURE template or an ALTER PROCEDURE template are almost identical to what I described for triggers earlier, so forgive me if I don't repeat those steps here. Let's instead go directly to debugging the stored procedure, which means you need to open Visual Studio 2005.

Once the proc has been written and your syntax is clear of errors, the procedure code is ready to be observed in the debugger. As you step through the code, you can see parameters change and statements executed without affecting underlying table data.

Connect to the server holding your stored procedures. Drill down to the Programmability folder and expand the list of procedures. Double-click the proc or select OPEN from the context menus so that the procedure code window opens in Visual Studio. You can then set break points in the window as you would any .NET code.

1. Right-click the procedure and select Step Into Stored Procedure from the context menus. Select Debug from the context menu; the Run Procedure dialog box loads to allow you to enter parameter values to test with. This is demonstrated in Figure 14-4. (Notice the check box Auto Roll Back; enable this to roll back all changes made to the data while debugging a stored procedure).

2. Step into the code and watch the execution of each statement in the transaction. Two tables are operated on in this procedure, and both operations must complete or nothing must complete. So the code I am stepping through is enclosed in a transaction that I can roll back if I detect a failure anywhere in the transaction. (The full code of this stored procedure is listed later in this chapter, in the section "The Example.") This illustrates that the initial queries have run and the local variables (see the parameters now for @Amt and @Debit) have been changed accordingly.

FIGURE 14-4
Debugging a stored
procedure

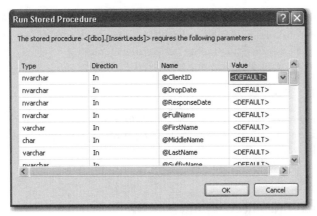

Type	Direction	Name	Value
nvarchar	In	@ClientID	<DEFAULT>
nvarchar	In	@DropDate	<DEFAULT>
nvarchar	In	@ResponseDate	<DEFAULT>
nvarchar	In	@FullName	<DEFAULT>
varchar	In	@FirstName	<DEFAULT>
char	In	@MiddleName	<DEFAULT>
varchar	In	@LastName	<DEFAULT>
nvarchar	In	@SuffixName	<DEFAULT>

3. If I keep stepping through the code, as soon as I update either of the tables in this
   procedure the appropriate triggers will fire. We have left the procedure and entered
   the trigger code after the DML statement has been executed in the transaction. I can
   now step into the trigger. Notice the trigger (fishy) is now in the call stack. Depending
   on what the trigger is looking for, or to do, it might or might not cause the
   remainder of the procedure to execute in the debugger. Naturally, if you want to
   step through the proc without the intervention of the trigger, just drop the trigger
   from the table and reinstall it later.

If you change stored procedure (or trigger) code, you must execute the ALTER query to
install the latest version of the procedure to the database. You are not editing the installed
procedure when you run Edit or script out the procedure code, so failing to re-execute after
changing the code will not help you, and you'll be as confused as an apple in a peach tree
when the bug you just squished returns to the debugger. Think of the Execute Query as the
build or compile button on your traditional IDE.

It is also a good idea to save the query out to a text file or version control system as
often as possible, because if you lose power or your system crashes before you have a
chance to re-execute the ALTER query, the source code will be lost.

Calling Stored Procedures

One of the major differences between a trigger and a stored procedure is that a stored procedure needs to be explicitly called. You cannot call a trigger. A stored procedure can be called
from a number of places, such as client applications, autoexecution, other stored procedures
and triggers, and tools like QA and EM. A stored procedure is executed using one of the
following methods.

Specifying the Name of the Stored Procedure in the Statement

For example, the code sp_who and nothing else in the statement will execute the stored
procedure by that name. There is one caveat to just naming the procedure in the procedure.
The name must be the first line of code in your statement or batch . . . even if a billion lines
of code follow it. If you stick a statement above the procedure name, the code will break.

Using the Clause Exec or Execute in Front of the Stored Procedure Name

The name is then followed by the rest of the stored procedure code. As long as you prefix the procedure with Exec or Execute, the code will execute.

The following statement is thus the preferred method:

```
EXEC | EXECUTE sp_who
```

You can execute a stored procedure, as described here, that is grouped with a collection of stored procedures by specifying the procedure number assigned to the member procedure as follows:

```
EXECUTE accpay_proc;4
```

Calling a Stored Procedure Within INSERT

You can call a stored procedure in an INSERT statement, a topic that is further discussed in Chapter 20. What happens is that the result set returned from the stored procedure is inserted into the reference table. The following code provides an example of an INSERT . . . EXEC.

```
INSERT INTO customers
EXEC employee_customer
```

Sending Data to Stored Procedures

As an application developer or a DBA proficient in T-SQL, you need to know how to write software that can pass data (parameters) to stored procedures. Stored procedure writers, on the other hand have to know how to code stored procedures to efficiently receive and process the data received from the clients. The architecture is very similar to that of functions, procedures, and methods that receive and return values. Stored procedures can also return values, and we will discuss how and what in the next section.

When a client calls a stored procedure (using one of the methods described in the earlier section), it can pass values to the procedure through parameters. These values are then used in the stored procedure to achieve the desired result. I mentioned earlier that you can write stored procedures that can contain as many as 1,024 parameters. To expand further, each parameter can be named, associated with a data type, given a direction, and even assigned a default value (even NULL).

You can pass parameters by name and by position. The following example demonstrates passing parameters by name:

```
EXEC js_newid @id1='A-1A', @id2='A-1B'
```

This is the more robust form of coding stored procedures because it means you can use the named parameters in a stored procedure without defining the order in which the parameters were received. The following code will get hairy if you start going wild on parameters:

```
EXEC js_newid 'A-1A', 'A-1B', 'A-1C', 'A-1D'
```

Default Values in Stored Procedures

When you execute stored procedures that are expecting parameters, SQL Server will report an error if none is received in your connection. If your connection might not transmit a parameter, you could code default values in the stored procedure, or even use NULL. SQL Server will then make use of the default values or place NULL into the statement's parameter placeholder instead of returning an error.

In keeping with our discussion of NULL values in the last chapter, your first choice should be to provide a default value in the parameter that makes the most sense and will enhance rather than break your code. For example, the following procedure will use your parameter values, or a default parameter:

```
EXEC js_getdiscount @discount=0, @coupon=1
```

The following example takes NULL when and if the circumstances can live with it:

```
EXEC js_getdiscount @discount=0, @coupon=NULL
```

The following code is a simple order-adding stored procedure demonstrating the use of parameters:

```
USE rainbow
  DECLARE @returncode int
  DECLARE @CustID char(8)
  DECLARE @AgentID char(6)
  DECLARE @Item char(50)
  DECLARE @Price money, @Discount real, @Quantity int
INSERT [Orders] (CustID, AgentID, Item, Quantity, Price, Discount)
  VALUES (@CustID, @AgentID,  @Item, @Quantity, @Price, @Discount)
```

This stored procedure is kept simple to demonstrate the use of parameters. Notice that you can also group parameter declarations behind one DECLARE. The following list provides some parameter tips:

- Use default values in your parameters in preference to NULL. Use the NULL value when it makes sense.

- Write code that checks for inconsistent or missing values early in your stored procedure code.

- Use easy-to-remember names that make it easier to pass the value by name rather than position.

Receiving Data from Stored Procedures

A stored procedure would not be as marvelous a tool if it were unable to return data to you. SQL Server can return data to you in any supported data type, such as characters, strings, dates, images, user-defined data types, and even tabular data and cursors from SELECT statements.

You need to identify data intended for output with the OUTPUT keyword, which also has a short form OUT. This specifies the data intended for return to the client. The following stored procedure code returns a single integer value:

```
CREATE PROC js_getatotal
  @OrderNum
  @atotal int OUTPUT
AS
 SELECT @atotal = total
 FROM items
WHERE OrderNum = @OrderNum
```

Returning Result Sets

Returning result sets to clients from stored procedures is simply a matter of coding a SELECT statement into the stored procedure. The tabulated or multirow data is returned automatically. If you need to perform complex SELECT routines (such as SELECT INTO) in your stored procedure, you can also enclose the SELECT statement into conditional or flow-control logic to prevent any result set from being returned to the client. The following code demonstrates a simple stored procedure that returns a result set to the client:

```
CREATE PROCEDURE getcustomers_pastdue @past int=14
AS
   SELECT CustID, CustName, Tel1
   FROM Customers WHERE pastdue = @past
```

Stored Procedure Nesting

You can also nest stored procedures like triggers. SQL Server 2005 supports up to 32 levels of stored procedures. If you exceed this level in a nest, the entire procedure cascade might collapse, depending on your code. You can check the nest level in any stored procedure by calling the @@NESTLEVEL function. This function returns the current nest level of the stored procedure the function was called from.

Despite the nest limit of 32, you can also spawn as many stored procedures as you want from within the nest chain or cascade. The called procedure does not increment the nest level counter as long as it completes without spawning another stored procedure.

Rolling Back Stored Procedures

You can execute a ROLLBACK command in a stored procedure; however, the rollback works differently from the ROLLBACK discussed in the trigger section earlier on. In the case of a stored procedure rollback, if the rollback is in a member of a stored procedure chain or nest, only the outermost transaction will be rolled back. The execution of the remaining stored procedures in the nest continues.

Temporary Stored Procedures

You can also set stored procedures to be temporary, which means that once a client disconnects the stored procedure is dropped. Temporary stored procedures are stored in the *tempdb database*. However, heavy use of temporary stored procedures is not a recommended practice on SQL Server 2005 databases. The support exists for backward compatibility with version 6.5 databases. The older architecture had a more primitive prepare-compile-execute architecture.

Warming Up SQL Server

As discussed in Chapter 2, stored procedures are compiled and cached only at their first call by an application. You can help increase performance and ready a server for certain forms of access and functions when a server starts up, before users access it, by automatically executing certain stored procedures. This means that when users connect and use a stored procedure, it will already be in the stored procedure cache.

Automatically executing stored procedures on startup is also highly useful for certain management applications or functionality that a server needs to have soon after startup. I call this warming up SQL Server. You should take note of a few nuances and rules before you consider using this "warm-up" capability. These nuances are as follows:

- The creator or owner of an autoexecuted stored procedure can only be the system administrator or a member of the sysadmin fixed server role.

- The stored procedure must be a background process and cannot take any input parameters.

Each autoexecuted, or startup, stored procedure makes a connection to the DBMS. You can have as many autoexecuted stored procedures as you like, but if each one consumes a connection, this could be a significant drain on resources. If the stored procedures do not need to be executed concurrently, you can nest them. Thus, you could create a single stored procedure that calls a list of stored procedures synchronously. The cascade of stored procedures only consumes one connection, the one incurred by the autoexecuting stored procedure.

By cascading or nesting stored procedures, you could thus call user-defined stored procedures and even pass parameters into them. This can be useful for an application that requires certain information and objects to be available to users when the databases come back online.

In one of my call centers, if I need to restart or "IPL" a server for any reason, or we suffer a server or host crash, an autoexecuted stored procedure sends a message to database users when the server is ready and they can reconnect. This saves the help desk from having to call or e-mail users that the server is back up and can be accessed again.

If you have a problem and you ever need to delay the autoexecuting of stored procedures, you can start the instance of SQL Server 2005 with the –f flag. This will start the server in a minimal configuration (like Safe mode on Windows Server 2003) and allow you to debug the problem. You can also specify trace flag 4022 as a startup parameter, which forces the startup to bypass autoexecution.

To create a startup or autoexecuted stored procedure, you need to be logged in as a member of the sysadmin role and you must create the procedure in the *master* database.

You can also use sp_procoption to designate an existing stored procedure as a startup stored procedure, to reset the startup option on a stored procedure, or to view a list of all stored procedures that execute on startup.

Managing Stored Procedures

Stored procedure code and objects are the most complex to manage in SQL Server. On a large system, it does not take long to lose count of the number of stored procedures written and deployed on the system. The following sections explain how to alter and drop stored procedures using either T-SQL or Visual Studio or Management Studio.

Altering Stored Procedures

To alter a stored procedure in T-SQL, you need to use the ALTER PROCEDURE statement. The basic statement is as follows:

```
ALTER PROCEDURE proc_name
ON . . .
```

The code to apply after the ON line takes the same syntax and choice of arguments as the CREATE PROC statement described earlier (see the SQL Server 2005 Books Online for the full explanation and usage of the arguments).

To alter a stored procedure in Management Studio, follow the steps described earlier for creating a stored procedure in Management Studio and edit the stored procedure accordingly. Altering a stored procedure in Management Studio is demonstrated shortly.

Dropping Stored Procedures

Dropping a stored procedure in T-SQL requires the DROP PROCEDURE statement followed by the procedure name. For example, the code

```
USE Stores
IF EXISTS (SELECT name FROM sysobjects
    WHERE name = 'DebitStores')
DROP PROCEDURE DebitStores
```

drops the stored procedure DebitStores from the *Stores* database.

You should make sure to check for stored procedure dependencies with the sp_depends stored procedure before dropping the stored procedure.

To drop a stored procedure interactively in Management Studio, simply drill down to the database and select the Stored Procedures node from the console tree. Select the stored procedure, right-click, and select Delete.

Getting Information about Stored Procedures

To obtain information from SQL Server about the stored procedures attached to the database, you should execute the system stored procedure sp_helptext. This system stored procedure returns the code for database objects like stored procedures, rules, and defaults. It queries the code in *syscomments* as mentioned earlier. Call sp_helptext as follows:

```
sp_helptext [ @objname = ] 'name'
```

and the example would look like this:

```
--to check the code of a stored procedure
EXEC sp_helptext @objname = storedprocname
```

This obviously will not work on encrypted stored procedures.

The Example

Let's now look at the debit/credit example we documented in the stored procedure deployment plan discussed earlier.

```
CREATE PROC

/*
Script Name: jrs_CRDR
Description: Credit/Debit for Items/Orders
Usage: For stock picking
Return Code: -1 to -10
Author: Jeffrey R. Shapiro
Version: 1.1
Date Created: 9/25/2005
Revision History:

*/
SET QUOTED_IDENTIFIER ON
GO
SET ANSI_NULLS ON
GO

/****** Object:  Stored Procedure dbo.jrs_CRDR  Script Date: 9/25/2005
11:34:35 PM ******/

ALTER PROCEDURE dbo.jrs_CRDR

@Credit int=0, --Amount to credit to order (3)
@SKU int=0,    --This is the SKU in the Items table (ItemNumber)
@IN Int=0      --This is the Order's ItemNumber (OrderItem)

AS
BEGIN TRANSACTION
  DECLARE @Amt int, @Debit int        --Value for current number of
  Items in stock
  SET @Amt = 0 /*assignment not necessary but nice to see how it changes
  in the debugger*/

--First get the stock level for the sku and see if we can debit
SELECT @Amt = (SELECT Quantity FROM Customers.dbo.Items
    WHERE ItemNumber = @SKU)
  IF @Amt IS NULL
  BEGIN
   ROLLBACK TRANSACTION
   RAISERROR
```

```
       ('Bad SKU. Please call stock controller about %d', 16, 1, @SKU)
     RETURN(-4)
   END

   IF @Amt < @Credit
   BEGIN
     ROLLBACK TRANSACTION
     RAISERROR
       ('Low stock level, %d. Please call stock controller', 16, 1, @Amt)
     RETURN(-5)
     END

 --Get values for debit/credit
SELECT  @Debit = (@Amt - @Credit)
--Next debit from stock (trigger on Items stock levels)
UPDATE Customers.dbo.Items Set Quantity = (@Debit)
   WHERE ItemNumber = @SKU                          --at this sku

  --check if debit items failed
  IF @@ROWCOUNT = 0
  BEGIN
   ROLLBACK TRANSACTION
   RETURN(-6)
  END

--Now credit customer order
    UPDATE Customers.dbo.ORDERS Set CanShip = (@Credit)     --credit
    orders
       WHERE OrderItem = @IN                    --at this item number

--check if credit customer order failed
  IF @@ROWCOUNT = 0
  BEGIN
   ROLLBACK TRANSACTION
   RETURN(-7)
  END

--check if any errors from

  IF @@ERROR <> 0
  BEGIN
   ROLLBACK TRANSACTION
   RETURN(-8)
  END

COMMIT
  PRINT 'Item posted'

GO
SET QUOTED_IDENTIFIER OFF
GO
SET ANSI_NULLS ON
GO
```

   In the preceding code I used PRINT to report that the item posted okay (thanks to the commit that only gets called if the transaction is kosher). But I coded in various return codes that would get returned on an error. These could be suppressed and confined to the stored procedure or returned as an output value to the client. In other words you can loop through return codes in the procedure and send a related message to the user, or just send the return code to the client and let logic on the client decide how to proceed. I prefer to keep the error codes local to the procedure, which means I can change, at any time, what I tell the client about the errors or what course of action to take.

User Defined Functions in T-SQL

The CREATE FUNCTION statement creates a user-defined function (UDF) in T-SQL that can return a value. You can use these functions just like the system functions and you can call them in your queries just like stored procedures using the EXECUTE statement. Here is a simple example that returns the abbreviation for the name of a month, returned from passing in an ordinal value representing the number of the month in a year:

```
CREATE FUNCTION [dbo].[GETMONBYSHORTNAME] (@MONNUMBER VARCHAR(2))
  RETURNS VARCHAR(3) AS
BEGIN
  declare
    @fData varchar(2),
    @val1 varchar(100),
    @returnval varchar(3)

    select @fData = @MONNUMBER
    SELECT
      @val1 = CASE @fData
      WHEN '01' THEN 'JAN'
      WHEN '02' THEN 'FEB'
      WHEN '03' THEN 'MAR'
      WHEN '04' THEN 'APR'
      WHEN '05' THEN 'MAY'
      WHEN '06' THEN 'JUN'
      WHEN '07' THEN 'JUL'
      WHEN '08' THEN 'AUG'
      WHEN '09' THEN 'SEP'
      WHEN '10' THEN 'OCT'
      WHEN '11' THEN 'NOV'
      WHEN '12' THEN 'DEC'
    END
    begin
      select @returnval = @val1
    end
    return @returnval
end
```

   User ALTER FUNCTION to change this function. UDFs in C# or VB that run on the CLR are more exciting. We discuss these next.

PART III

Procedures and Functions on the CLR

Creating stored procedures out of a .NET Framework language to run on the CLR is just as easy to do. If you are not familiar with the .NET Framework read Chapter 11, which introduced the support for the .NET Framework in SQL Server 2005 and kicked off the discussion with examples creating data types and aggregates in C#. The examples provided here are written in C#, but you can use any .NET language for your stored procedures.

The first thing you have to do before you can execute anything on the SQL Server CLR is enable it (the scope is server-wide). To enable the CLR execute the following T-SQL code in Management Studio.

```
sp_configure 'clr enabled', 1
GO
RECONFIGURE
GO
```

Now you can use Visual Studio to create your code. Create a solution for creating class libraries, and set up a new project specifically for stored procedures. Call the class StoredProcedures or something similar. In the class that is created, you will need the following directives:

```
using System;
using System.Data;
using System.Data.Sql;
using System.Data.SqlTypes;
using Microsoft.SqlServer.Server;
```

Now add the definition for a partial class (if Visual Studio has not already done so).

```
public partial class StoredProcedures
{
    [Microsoft.SqlServer.Server.SqlProcedure]
    public static void GetCurrentDate()
    {
        //Put your code here
    }
};
```

Now add some code.

```
[Microsoft.SqlServer.Server.SqlProcedure]
    public static void GetCurrentDate()
    {
        SqlPipe p = SqlContext.Pipe;
        p.Send(System.DateTime.Today.ToString());
    }
```

The stored procedure class is now ready and must be installed to SQL Server. This can be done as follows in T-SQL using Management Studio:

```
CREATE ASSEMBLY [StoredProcedures] FROM 'C:\Documents and Settings\shapj015\My
    Documents\Visual Studio
2005\Projects\StoredProcedures\StoredProcedures\bin\Debug\StoredProcedures.dll'
WITH PERMISSION_SET = SAFE;
GO
```

This code installs your assembly to SQL server. Once the assembly has been installed (you can see it under the assemblies folder in your specific database), you can add the stored procedure into SQL Server as follows:

```
CREATE PROCEDURE [dbo].[GetCurrentDate]
AS EXTERNAL NAME [StoredProcedures].[StoredProcedures].[GetCurrentDate];
GO
```

The above stored procedure simply returns the current date (of course the built-in function GetDate() does that as well but we needed a simple example). Now let's get a little more sophisticated and create a stored procedure that takes a parameter. Note the use of the SqlPipe construct, which is used to return data to the client that called the stored procedure.

```
[Microsoft.SqlServer.Server.SqlProcedure]
public static void GetFormattedDate(int Option)
{
    string s = System.DateTime.Today.ToString();
    SqlPipe p = SqlContext.Pipe;
    switch (Option)
    {
        case 1:
            s = s.Remove(10);
            p.Send(s);
            break;
        case 2:
            //other options
        default:
            break;
    }
}
```

To install this parameter-driven procedure, you need to specify the parameter in T-SQL as follows:

```
CREATE PROCEDURE [dbo].[GetFormattedDate]
(
    @Option int
)
AS EXTERNAL NAME [StoredProcedures].[StoredProcedures].[GetFormattedDate];
GO
```

You can call either procedure now as follows:

```
exec GetCurrentDate
exec GetFormattedDate 1
```

Let's now look at CLR-based UDFs. The GetFormattedDate stored procedure is actually a better candidate for a CLR function than it is as a stored procedure. So let's reimplement it accordingly.

```
[SqlFunction(DataAccess = DataAccessKind.Read)]
public static SqlString GetFormattedDate(int Option)
{
    string s = System.DateTime.Today.ToString();
    switch (Option)
    {
        case 1:
            s = s.Remove(10);
            break;
        case 2:
            //other options
        default:
            break;
    } return s;
}
```

Creating the assembly and installing it to SQL Server is the same process as described earlier for stored procedures (see also Chapter 11). The T-SQL code for installing the function is a little different.

```
CREATE FUNCTION [dbo].[GetFormattedDate] (@option int)
RETURNS [nvarchar](10) WITH EXECUTE AS CALLER
AS
EXTERNAL NAME
 [Functions].[Functions].[GetFormattedDate]
```

Remember, always make sure you specify the exact path to the function when installing the function; that is, the namespace, class and method, or you will get an error that the function cannot be found.

To Recap

We covered a lot of ground together in this chapter dealing with triggers and stored procedures. As you can see, trigger and stored procedure writing and management can consume substantial resources, and without proper planning, documentation, change control, archiving, source code maintenance, modeling, and so on, you can create a lot of problems for yourself or the team.

If you are new to trigger and stored procedure writing, the change in development style and philosophy can put a lot of strain on mental and physical resources. And the conversion of client-side, inline SQL code to server-side triggers and stored procedures can be expensive in terms of both time and materials.

PART IV

Working with SQL Server 2005

Working with Operational Data

All good things come in threes. You have the three amigos, the three stooges, the three musketeers, and so on. SQL has its famous trio, too: INSERT, DELETE, and UPDATE. I often remark to my clients that you cannot expect a database management system to work for you if you do not insert data into the system. Without these three members of SQL's *data manipulation language* (aka *data modification* language), DML, there is no way to get data into your database, to modify records, or to delete them.

The SELECT statement I discussed in the previous chapter is also considered a member of the SQL's data "DMLition" team, but we were able to chew on SELECT, and its new collateral features, because we already have data to work with in the old *pubs, northwind* or *AdventureWorks* demo databases, which you can download from Microsoft or upgrade from SQL Server 2000. However, the three statements I will explore in this chapter often need a fourth member of the posse, in the form of SELECT, to hit on some heavyweight data crunching problems, and I will discuss this as well.

Understanding the DML three is essential before you tackle Extract Transform and Load projects, online analytical processing (OLAP), or any online transaction processing (OLTP). In this chapter, I will go over all three statements in detail, discussing the basics of their usage in T-SQL and some new and advanced features for the accomplished DBAs and developers.

INSERT

The INSERT statement is straightforward. In its most basic form, it looks like this:

```
INSERT Orders VALUES (value)
```

The target table follows the INSERT keyword, and in the preceding example that table is *Orders*. After the table, you need to add the VALUES keyword (case doesn't matter), which is then followed by a list of values. In the preceding example, there is only one value, but if the table you were to insert into had several columns, you would need to provide a list of values separated by commas for each column you had a value for. If you didn't have values for each column, that column would have to accept default values or allow NULL values. Consider the following example and imagine only two columns to keep it simple for now:

```
INSERT Orders VALUES (5, 'Cat Food')
```

The VALUES list, which is enclosed in the parentheses (required), represents each column in the table starting with the first. Here, the value 5 of type integer is inserted into column 1 (or zero if you are looking at it from a zero-based result set), while the second value, of a character type, is placed into the second column.

So now go back to your imagination and add a few more columns and imagine you want to install a value into the "Amount" and "Description" columns and that both columns are somewhere in the middle of a multicolumn table. Your INSERT code will now look like this:

```
INSERT Orders (column 2, column 4) VALUES (5, 'Cat Food')
```

The integer value of 5 is inserted into column 2, while the character (description) value of "Cat Food" is inserted into column 4. You can also identify the columns by name like this:

```
INSERT Orders (Amount, Description) VALUES (5, 'Cat Food')
```

Supplying the column names is essential if you specify columns that are not in order, and possibly even in the wrong sequence. The following code demonstrates switching the order of the columns in the INSERT statement:

```
INSERT Orders (Description, Amount ) VALUES ('Cat Food', 5)
```

Is this easy enough for you? Sit tight, we are still at T minus 10 and counting . . . . Before going further, let's look over the cryptic syntax comprising the INSERT (I have added a cut line to suggest that the hint section is optional and you will probably not use the hints for 99.9 percent of your insert operations; after all, hints are only for very accomplished developers):

```
[ WITH <common_table_expression> [ ,...n ] ]
INSERT
    [ TOP ( expression ) [ PERCENT ] ]
    [ INTO]
    { <object> | rowset_function_limited
      [ WITH ( <Table_Hint_Limited> [ ...n ] ) ]
    }
{
    [ ( column_list ) ]
    [ <OUTPUT Clause> ]
    { VALUES ( { DEFAULT | NULL | expression } [ ,...n ] )
    | derived_table
    | execute_statement
    }
}
    | DEFAULT VALUES
[; ]
<object> ::=
{
    [ server_name . database_name . schema_name .
      | database_name .[ schema_name ] .
      | schema_name .
    ]
        table_or_view_name
}
```

So where did the INTO keyword spring from? I delayed mentioning it because the INTO is optional and belongs to the ANSI SQL specification. If you want to keep your code as standard as possible, you can include the INTO keyword, but it makes no difference to the SQL parser in SQL Server.

I have already discussed the table name, but as the syntax notes, you can add the optional *hint* directive to coerce SQL Server to optimize in a user-defined way.

The T-SQL syntax demonstrates that you can also insert into views and the table data type and the new common table expression (CTE) using the WITH directive. You can also just as simply insert into temporary tables designated as temporary by the # (pound or hash) sign. For example, the following code:

```
INSERT #Orders1 (Amount, Description) VALUES (5, 'Cat Food')
```

inserts the data into a temporary table created earlier. Or your recipe might need a temporary table to be created on the fly, using DDL and DML in the middle of a stored procedure perhaps, to cause a result set to persist for the duration of the connection:

```
CREATE TABLE #Orders1
(Amount int DEFAULT 0, Description varchar(50), Notes varchar(max) NULL)
INSERT #Orders1 (Amount, Description, Notes) VALUES (5, 'Cat Food', NULL)
```

I have touched a little here on the idea that you will often need to work with default and NULL values. You will also find yourself working with identity column values and columns in which SQL Server automatically adds the value, such as columns of the timestamp data type. We will deal with default, auto, and NULL values in a moment.

The *view_name* argument implies that you can insert data into a view, and you would insert rows into a view just as you would insert rows into a table or a temporary table. The new table data type, however, presents an interesting new addition to the row receptacles now supported by T-SQL.

The bullet list that follows here lists the various forms in which INSERT can be used:

- INSERT with NULL, default, and system-supplied values
- INSERT with @@Identity
- Using INSTEAD OF triggers on INSERT actions
- Using OPENROWSET and BULK to bulk-load data
- Inserting data that is not in the same order as the table columns
- Inserting data with fewer values than columns
- Inserting data into a table with an identity column
- Inserting data into a uniqueidentifier column by using NEWID()
- Inserting data into a table through a view
- Inserting data using the SELECT and EXECUTE options
- Inserting data by using the TOP clause
- Using OUTPUT with an INSERT statement
- Using WITH common table expression with an INSERT statement
- Using OUTPUT with identity and computed columns

PART IV

INSERT with NULL, Default, and System-Supplied Values

When you need to work with tables that have more columns than you are providing values with your INSERT statement, you need to either provide default values for the unspecified columns or allow the unspecified columns to accept NULL.

If your solution requires you to keep NULL out of the tables, you will have to use default values. These values must correspond to the data type accepted by the column or they must be convertible by SQL Server; or you'll need to explicitly convert them using CAST or CONVERT (see Chapter 16). You can also create default objects that have a value property and supply the object and owner name as the default's parameter.

If you do not specify the default, the insert may still succeed as long as the column accepts NULL. If the column is defined to refuse NULL, the insert will fail. In this example inserting in the temporary table we created earlier, the insert installs a default value of zero for the number of cans of cat food:

```
INSERT #Orders1 (Amount, Description, Notes) VALUES (DEFAULT, 'Cat Food',
NULL)
```

You must remember that INSERT means that you are inserting a new row into the table (actually a new row is appended) and providing data for the column values incorporated by your new row. So constraints and triggers will fire accordingly for the table, and any relationships between the target for the insert and other tables (primary and candidate keys) need to be taken into account (more about that shortly).

There are two additional circumstances in which SQL Server will automatically install values into columns. These circumstances are as follows:

- The table includes an identity column. SQL Server will automatically install the appropriate value.

- The column takes a timestamp value. SQL Server installs the timestamp automatically.

Interestingly, however, you can override the identity column value and explicitly provide a value for the identity column as long as you first invoke the IDENTITY_INSERT option. This is done using a SET statement, as follows:

```
SET IDENTITY_INSERT #Orders1 ON
INSERT #Orders1 (ItemNumber, Amount, Description, Notes) VALUES (1234,
DEFAULT, 'Cat Food', NULL)
SET IDENTITY_INSERT #Orders1 OFF
```

Don't forget to turn the IDENTITY_INSERT to OFF after the inserts complete or the next time you run the same statement, SQL Server will pop back an error telling you that IDENTITY_INSERT is already set to ON.

CAUTION *If you explicitly force a user-defined value into the identity column, you need to be sure that you are not going to violate integrity.*

INSERT and @@IDENTITY

A useful function is @@IDENTITY, which you can call after an INSERT, SELECT INTO, or BULK INSERT (discussed shortly), or after a bulk copy operation. This function returns the last identity value generated by an insert operation, as described earlier.

The identity value is not generated if the statement failed and tables were not affected, in which case @@IDENTITY returns NULL. The value returned is always the value supplied to the last insertion, and therefore, when you insert multiple rows, @@IDENTITY always returns the last identity value generated.

The @@IDENTITY value is generated by the system for your operation (as the identity provided to the last insert). Even if your statement causes one or more triggers to perform insert operations that generate identity values, calling @@IDENTITY immediately after the statement will return the last identity value generated by the last trigger. You can then use the value as needed by the application. In the following example, I simply select the identity value and use it as an item number:

```
INSERT ITEMS (Item)
  VALUES ('Calamari')
  SELECT @@IDENTITY AS 'New Menu Item'
```

SCOPE_IDENTITY() returns the value only within the current scope, while @@IDENTITY is not limited to a specific scope. IDENT_CURRENT() is not connected to any scope or session; it returns the identity value of a table name that you must pass as an argument of the function. Consider the following table:

Identity Function	What Identity It Returns
@@IDENTITY	Last identity on your connection
SCOPE_IDENTITY()	Value of current scope
IDENTITY_CURRENT(T)	The last value for table *T*

TIP *You can quickly spot the built-in functions that come in SQL Server, because they are not prefixed with the double ampersand (@@).*

To see this working, knock up the following code and run it in a query window against a demo or lab database:

```
CREATE TABLE T1 (ItemID Int IDENTITY)
CREATE TABLE T2 (ItemID Int IDENTITY)
GO
CREATE TRIGGER Trig1 ON T1 FOR INSERT
 AS
   BEGIN
    INSERT T2 DEFAULT VALUES
    END
GO
INSERT T1 DEFAULT VALUES
SELECT @@IDENTITY
```

```
SELECT SCOPE_IDENTITY()
SELECT IDENT_CURRENT('T1')
SELECT IDENT_CURRENT('T2')
```

Using NEWID()

If you need to provide a row with an unique identifier, NEWID() will do the trick. Simply call the function and assign the returned GUID to a variable of type unique identifier as follows:

```
DECLARE @MYID uniqueidentifier
 SET @MYID = NEWID()
 SELECT @MYID
```

INSERT with SELECT

Did I not tell you that SELECT will meet up with us here? SELECT can be used in the INSERT statement for a number of useful functions. The primary reason you would toss a SELECT into the INSERT statement is to gather data from one table and insert it into another. That can be easily achieved with the following statement (I have added cut lines to emphasize the inclusion of SELECT:

```
CREATE TABLE #Orders1
 (OrderItem int, CustID varchar(20))
--8< ----add the insert/select in here ----------------
      INSERT #Orders1
      SELECT OrderItem, CustID FROM Orders
--8< -------------------------------------------
SELECT * From #Orders1
```

The INSERT . . . SELECT code between the cut lines specifies to SQL Server to insert into temporary table #Orders1 the result set from the ensuing SELECT statement. The SELECT statements can be as complex as you need them to be to return the desired result set for insertion into your table or table variable. It can even be the result of a JOIN from hell.

NOTE *INSERT . . . SELECT is very similar to SELECT INTO discussed in the preceding chapter.*

You can also use the SELECT in your INSERT statement to return the result set of the last insertion or a specific selection of rows. For example, on an order entry system it is useful to insert a new order into the Orders table and then pull a result set using SELECT back to the client in the same connection.

The second SELECT in the preceding code does exactly that. The result set of the first SELECT is not returned to the client, because it gets inserted into the #Orders1 table. The second SELECT returns a result set to the client. You can obviously include a sophisticated search condition to return an updated result set that was narrowed down to the rows of interest to the client. The preceding code works for the temporary table because it persists for the connection. If you ended your session from SQL Server, you would not be able to SELECT from the same temporary table because SQL Server would have purged it from *tempdb*.

It goes without saying that you can also include the TOP optional clause in the SELECT statement

```
CREATE TABLE #Orders1
  (OrderItem int, CustID varchar(20))
GO
    INSERT #Orders1
    SELECT TOP 10 OrderItem, CustID FROM Orders
GO
SELECT * From #Orders1
```

but you might need the extra garnish like ORDER BY to achieve the desired result set.

INSERT with EXECUTE

INSERT . . . EXECUTE works like INSERT . . . SELECT. EXECUTE fires a stored procedure, function, or SQL statement that will return a result set for insertion into the target table or table variable. In many respects, very little different is happening between the two INSERT extensions. The result set that returns for the insertion is ultimately derived from a SELECT, no matter that it is buried inside a stored procedure, an extended stored procedure, a function, or the primary code.

The syntax is also straightforward, as follows:

```
INSERT [ INTO]
{ table_name WITH ( < table_hint_limited > [ ...n ] )
| view_name
| rowset_function_limited
}
  execute_statement
```

Your EXECUTE statement can either call the procedure or provide an inline SQL statement. For example, the little statement

```
INSERT NewItems (Items)
EXEC ('SELECT * FROM OldItems')
```

copies all of the rows in *OldItems* and inserts them into *NewItems*. If you use a complete SQL statement as demonstrated earlier, remember to enclose the statement between single quotes (many of us forget that). You do not need the quotes when executing a proc or function, as follows:

```
INSERT CurrentAgents (Agent)
EXEC sp_getagents
```

NOTE   *The system stored procedure sp_executesql may be used instead of EXECUTE (and temporary stored procedures) to make code easier to read and improve query performance (See "Parameterized Queries" later in this chapter).*

INSERT WITH DEFAULT VALUES

Inserting with default values is the easiest of the INSERT statements because you do not need to specify columns or values, relying on SQL Server to install defaults as defined for the column or as set up in the default objects. Here's the syntax:

```
INSERT [INTO]
{ table_name WITH ( < table_hint_limited > [ ...n ] )
| view_name
| rowset_function_limited
}
DEFAULT VALUES
```

Naturally, running this query against a table that does not yet have defaults established will either cause it to fail or install NULLs if the columns are set to accept them. You probably also noticed that no column list is required here. The INSERT will fail with an error even if you supply every column in the target table.

Keeping Tabs on Errors

The ability to report errors in the middle of your INSERT statements is useful, especially when you run a batch of INSERT statements. The following code checks for an error and switches out of the INSERT batch to an error handler, VB style:

```
INSERT BoundToFail (PK_Column) Values ('DuplicateValue')
IF (@@ERROR <> 0) GOTO MAKEITBETTER

MAKEITBETTER:
  EXEC DoSomethingPlease
```

As a matter of interest, a batch of several INSERTS are isolated from each other with respect to errors. When an INSERT in a batch fails, the remaining INSERTs will continue unless you trap the error and stop the remainder of the batch from executing.

This error isolation between INSERT statements is useful for inserting bulk data into a table where data is drawn from several sources in which duplicate records might exist. Inserting addresses for a mailing list company or managing e-mail addresses from a Web site are good examples of where duplicate records are bound to exist. You can thus build a loop that contains an INSERT that installs data into a table without first checking for duplicate rows. A unique key constraint, even a primary key on your new table, causes the duplicate insertions to error out, which will cause the INSERT to discard the row, but the loop continues inserting until all source data is exhausted. I have done stuff like this often (even with string lists in Delphi, VB, or Java), using exceptions to achieve a tacit result.

TIP *The TRY...CATCH construct is recommended for new code supported by SQL Server 2005.*

BULK INSERT

I can guarantee that, as a SQL Server DBA or SQL Server developer, you will have your chance to insert what seems to be a bazillion records into a table. Typical scenarios I hinted at earlier include bulk-inserting mailing lists and e-mail addresses culled from Web sites, moving operational data into analytical data stores, and so on (the latter is becoming less of an issue thanks to SQL Server's new support for Internet applications. I also predict that bulk insert and bulk copy operations will catch fire as DBAs rush to get data out of their inferior DBMS products into SQL Server 2005. The BULK INSERT statement is a T-SQL front end to the command-line bulk copy program, *bcp.exe*.

NOTE *SQL Server Integration Services (SSIS) can be used to import and export data. SSIS is discussed briefly in Chapter 7.*

But there will be many other occasions you will need to use the BULK INSERT over a command line utility. My data center work in large Fortune 500 companies would often include receiving banking transactions from several banks the companies used. The data represented, for example, direct deposit information, and records listing which checks had cleared the bank accounts.

I would typically download each day humongous text files containing tens of thousands of lines of information from as many as ten major banks. This information comes as delimited text files, and the data has to be inserted into the database so that the financial analysts can keep tabs on the company's financial health . . . thanks to that persistent bug that plagues our existence on this earth-bound plane—affectionately known as cash flow.

The BULK INSERT is ideal for such data loading. You might run your script in a query window in Management Studio, build a GUI front end, or create a service, as I did to automatically download and insert the data every day. The syntax of your T-SQL looks like this:

BULK INSERT

```
[ database_name . [ schema_name ] . | schema_name . ] [ table_name | view_name ]
   FROM 'data_file'
  [ WITH
 (
[ [ , ] BATCHSIZE = batch_size ]
[ [ , ] CHECK_CONSTRAINTS ]
[ [ , ] CODEPAGE = { 'ACP' | 'OEM' | 'RAW' | 'code_page' } ]
[ [ , ] DATAFILETYPE =
   { 'char' | 'native'| 'widechar' | 'widenative' } ]
[ [ , ] FIELDTERMINATOR = 'field_terminator' ]
[ [ , ] FIRSTROW  =first_row ]
[ [ , ] FIRE_TRIGGERS ]
[ [ , ] FORMATFILE = 'format_file_path' ]
[ [ , ] KEEPIDENTITY ]
[ [ , ] KEEPNULLS ]
[ [ , ] KILOBYTES_PER_BATCH =kilobytes_per_batch ]
[ [ , ] LASTROW = last_row ]
[ [ , ] MAXERRORS = max_errors ]
[ [ , ] ORDER ( { column [ ASC | DESC ] } [ ,...n ] ) ]
[ [ , ] ROWS_PER_BATCH = rows_per_batch ]
[ [ , ] ROWTERMINATOR = 'row_terminator' ]
[ [ , ] TABLOCK ]
[ [ , ] ERRORFILE = 'file_name' ]
  )]
```

The arguments required are all documented in Books Online, but the text is as sterile as moon rock. You will find further hands-on information here on several important arguments.

Target Databases and Tables

The first arguments before the FROM specify the *database name* and *owner* in the dot notation qualifier style of *object.owner*—also known as a fully qualified table name (FQTN). Then you need to specify the target table for the data. If you leave out the database details, the current database is assumed. You need to make sure the current database is going to accommodate the insert, or it will fail. If you do not specify the owner, and the login executing the script is not the owner, SQL Server will cancel the operation.

Source of Data

The *FROM* clause specifies the source data file. This is the text file containing the data you wish to load into the database. This file can reside anywhere on your network. Obviously if it is local to the computer on which your script will run, performance will be much better because data transfer across the bus is faster by an order of magnitude over a 100/1000Mbit network being shared by everyone in the company. If the files you are going to work with are huge, you might not have any choice but to source them on the local drive. Some of my bulk inserts take place across the network, however, and they are usually small files that transfer a few thousand rows every day. This should thus be a daily chore so that data does not pile up on the network and become impossible to work with.

The location of the database server is also important. Obviously you are back to square one if you locate the data on the same server as the script and the server is located out on the network. Better to run everything on one machine, or at least from separate drives (see Chapter 6). If you absolutely have no choice but to process the raw data from a network location, then the source file needs to be specified using the UNC path or a drive mapping.

BATCH SIZE

The *BATCHSIZE* parameter is an important variable. This number specifies the number of rows inserted by each execution of the BULK INSERT statement. Well, let me tell you that the batch size you choose depends on a number of factors. For starters, the size of the data file needs to be taken into consideration. The network latency and both network and local host bandwidth discussed earlier also need to be taken into account. These factors consume resources, and if you do not work out specifically how much resources are consumed by the processing of the rows, you are likely to run out of resources and cause the bulk insert to fail, especially if server resources are already borderline.

The bad news is that when you fail in the middle of a bulk insert, the entire batch is lost because SQL Server sees the disconnection in the middle and rolls back the entire batch. So it would be crazy to try to load a bazillion rows in one iteration of the BULK INSERT statement unless you are sure your data is highly refined and you have gobs of RAM and fast hard disks. If you need to insert half a million rows, specify the batch size to be a small number that's chosen in relation to the resources and the environment. Memory is released after each batch is processed, so if you loop through the BULK INSERT script at a hundred or so rows at a time, you will be sure that, if the process crashes or fails for some reason, you have only lost the current batch. Believe me, there is nothing worse than reaching row 999,999 in the Godzilla of bulk inserts only to blow the whole caboodle away on the last record.

After each batch of rows is installed, you can test for errors and rows inserted and so forth. You should also code a routine that checks the last row that was committed to the database, and you'll need some means of identifying where in the raw data file the bulk insert should begin. If you have 900,000 rows processed and the next 1,000 rows fail, it does not make sense to reprocess the whole file all over again, and force SQL Server to manage duplicates again, and so on.

The *BATCHSIZE* argument is directly related to the *ROWS_PER_BATCH* argument that can also optionally be passed in the script. This argument applies if you do not specify the *BATCHSIZE*. But I prefer to specify the former with a parameter because *ROWS_PER_BATCH* causes SQL Server to try to eat the entire data file in one sitting (and available resources come into play again). If you do not specify either, SQL Server makes its own optimization choices, but it still has no control over disasters like a network crash, which would still cause loss of the last batch to be processed.

FIELDTERMINATOR

The *FIELDTERMINATOR* argument is essential to SQL Server so that it knows how to find and separate out the fields or columns in your data. If you do not specify the terminator, SQL Server will look for tabs, which are the default. As you know, there are several characters you can use to separate out the fields. The most common are commas, quotes, semicolons, and tabs. What you specify here depends on the source data file. If you have control over the process that created the source file (such as SSIS or another system that outputs the data for you), then you could simply specify tabs and leave the argument to the SQL Server default. Often you have no choice, but it helps to ask the gurus in control of the output (with me it was the batch processing people at the banks) to give you the terminator of your choice, not that it makes any difference to SQL Server what you throw at it.

CAUTION *Do not forget to enclose the terminator values between single quote marks.*

```
BULK INSERT Reconciliation.dbo
   FROM '\\SERV04\FTP\ACCPAY.TXT'
   WITH
   (
     FIELDTERMINATOR = ';',
     ROWTERMINATOR = ';\n'
   )
```

FIRSTROW/LASTROW

The *FIRSTROW* parameter is useful but only if you are keeping track of the contents of your file. You can easily create a counter in a front-end program or in T-SQL to keep track of the row number last processed by SQL Server, at the end of each successful batch, in the source data file. Then if you have to stop the process and restart it at a later time, you start the batch from the last row installed to the database. The LASTROW argument tells SQL Server the row number to stop at. After the row number specified, the processing terminates. The default is 0 if you omit the parameter, in which case SQL Server will run until there are no more rows left in the batch.

```
BULK INSERT Reconciliation.dbo
  FROM '\\SERV04\FTP\ACCPAY.TXT'
  WITH
  (
    FIRSTROW = 9875,
    FIELDTERMINATOR = ';',
    ROWTERMINATOR = ';\n',
    LASTROW = 20000
  )
```

MAXERRORS

The *MAXERRORS* parameter is important too, especially if you use the bulk insert with unique constraints or with a primary key index on the table. If you omit the parameter, SQL Server assumes the default, which is 10 errors. After the MAXERRORS value has been reached, SQL Server terminates the processing. So if you are importing two million e-mail names and addresses and 100,000 of them are duplicates, SQL Server will continue until it has seen 100,000 errors. On the flip side of the coin, you may not be prepared to tolerate waiting around for the processing to finish if you have errors and the maximum error limit is set too high. Set it at 1 if you want the batch processing to end after the first hiccup.

```
BULK INSERT Reconciliation.dbo
  FROM '\\SERV04\FTP\ACCPAY.TXT'
  WITH
  (
    FIRSTROW = 9875,
    FIELDTERMINATOR = ';',
    ROWTERMINATOR = ';\n',
    LASTROW = 20000,
    MAXERRORS = 100
  )
```

ORDER

Another important argument is *ORDER* because BULK INSERT goes easier if your data, as it is sucked out of the source file, is explicitly ordered before the inserting begins. To use it, you must have a clustered index on the target table. SQL Server ignores the order if there is no clustered index and assumes that the data in the source files is unordered on any specific column (no matter what you specify). The insert performance is greatly improved if you use a clustered index on the columns you provide in the *column_list*. The clustered index must exist in the same order as the columns listed in *column_list*. If you intend to set multiple bulk insert processes against the table, it is better to drop the indexes and use the TABLOCK argument discussed next.

TABLOCK

Including the *TABLOCK* argument causes a special bulk insert table-level lock to be acquired by several clients on a target table with each client holding a lock for the duration of the their respective bulk insert operations, which happen concurrently. This lock obviates lock contention, but the lock in itself greatly improves insert performance. This argument is useful only if you have no indexes installed on the table, or you would have to remove them. It would be a good idea to use it if you do not have a clustered index to take advantage of the *ORDER* clause.

As demonstrated in Chapter 3, SQL Server is able to allocate separate threads and fibers to parallel processes, which makes it one of the few products that can facilitate multiple clients without having to downgrade or share resources among the connections. This means that you can launch multiple bulk insert operations, with each BULK INSERT process performing at the same level as its peer, as close to true parallelism as you will get on one CPU. But if you omit the argument, the insert degrades to a point where you might as well run single BULK INSERT statements sequentially.

FORMATFILE

The *FORMATFILE* argument specifies the name and path of the format file generated with the BCP utility. A format file is used in situations in which the number of columns in the source file is different than that of the target table, the columns are in different orders, column delimiters vary, a combination of several factors. The BCP utility can also specify additional information in the format file.

BULK INSERT and Transactions

You can encase BULK INSERT operations inside transactions as discussed later in this chapter. However, using the BULK INSERT in a transaction with the BATCHSIZE argument will cause the rollback of all batches caught in a transaction that fails to commit.

BULK INSERT, Triggers, and Constraints

The foundation of BULK INSERT and BCP, the bulk copy API, can be commanded to force SQL Server to either fire or suppress triggers on your target table. By default, bulk copy or bulk insert operations ignore triggers. Pass the FIRETRIGGERS argument, *fire_triggers*, if your solution calls for you to fire the triggers.

If you fired triggers, the insert operations will be fully logged. The triggers are also fired once for each batch in the operation instead of once for each row insert (the trigger fires for each BULK INSERT statement that references the table).

```
BULK INSERT Reconciliation.dbo
   FROM '\\SERV04\FTP\ACCPAY.TXT'
   WITH
   (
     FIRSTROW = 9875,
     FIELDTERMINATOR = ';',
     ROWTERMINATOR = ';\n',
     LASTROW = 20000,
     FIRE_TRIGGERS
   )
```

Remember to change the recovery model of the database to Bulk-Logged Recovery. This recovery model (discussed in depth in Chapter 8) offers protection against media failure with the best performance and minimal log space usage for bulk insert or bulk copy operations. The actual inserts are minimally logged.

INSERT and the Table Variable

I introduced the table data type in Chapter 10 but think it a good idea to show it in action here with the INSERT statement. The variable is created just as you create any variable, with the *DECLARE @variable* statement. You do not create the table variable as you do a regular or temporary table using the CREATE TABLE statement discussed in Chapter 10. The code

```
DECLARE @MyTableVar table (column1 varchar(30))
  INSERT Into @MyTableVar SELECT Item From Items
  Select * FROM @MyTableVar
```

creates the table variable named MyTableVar and gives it a column named *column1* of type varchar(30). Next the INSERT comes along and inserts all the rows from the *Items* tables, restricted to the *Item* column, grabbed by the subordinate SELECT statement. You can then do as you want with the table type, using it as if it were a regular table.

The table is faster than a temporary table, and it makes more sense to use it instead of one when you need to store intermediate results. Often a T-SQL statement, stored procedure, or trigger requires you to store several result sets for evaluation during the process. In the past, these had to be installed as temporary tables to the *tempdb*, and thus their creation and maintenance were cumbersome and a drain on resources. For example, if you used temporary tables in a stored procedure, you would have to delete the tables before or after (or both) executing the procedure.

UPDATE

The UPDATE statement can be a little more complex than INSERT or DELETE because you need to find the rows that will become the target of the updates, and then specify the columns to be updated. There will also be times when you specify a FROM clause, updating data residing in more than one table. Another key clause of the UPDATE statement is the SET clause, which specifies the columns that are the target for the updates and the values to be used. A simple UPDATE statement might look like this:

```
UPDATE Orders SET ShipPostalCode = '33428' WHERE CustID = 'VINET'
```

The entire syntax for the UPDATE, however, is as follows:

```
[ WITH <common_table_expression> [...n] ]
UPDATE
    [ TOP ( expression ) [ PERCENT ] ]
    { <object> | rowset_function_limited
    [ WITH ( <Table_Hint_Limited> [ ...n ] ) ]
    }
    SET
        { column_name = { expression | DEFAULT | NULL }
          | { udt_column_name.{ { property_name = expression
                               | field_name = expression }
                  | method_name ( argument [ ,...n ] )
                }
            }
```

```
        | column_name { .WRITE ( expression , @Offset , @Length ) }
        | @variable = expression
        | @variable = column = expression [ ,...n ]
    } [ ,...n ]


[ <OUTPUT Clause> ]
[ FROM{ <table_source> } [ ,...n ] ]
[ WHERE { <search_condition>
        | { [ CURRENT OF
              { { [ GLOBAL ] cursor_name }
                | cursor_variable_name
              }
            ]
          }
        }
]
[ OPTION ( <query_hint> [ ,...n ] ) ]
[ ; ]


<object> ::=
{
    [ server_name . database_name . schema_name .
    | database_name .[ schema_name ] .
    | schema_name .
    ]
        table_or_view_name}
```

The UPDATE arguments are explained in BOL in the same fashion as INSERT. But some further investigation on several clauses and arguments is warranted here. The bullet list that follows here lists the various forms in which UPDATE can be used.

- UPDATE with information from another table
- UPDATE with the TOP clause
- UPDATE with the OUTPUT clause
- UPDATE with the WITH *common_table_expression* clause
- UPDATE with the .WRITE clause to modify data in an nvarchar(max) column
- UPDATE with .WRITE to add and remove data in an nvarchar(max) column
- UPDATE with OPENROWSET to modify a varchar(max) or varbinary(max) column

Targets of the UPDATE

You can update values in all base tables, derivatives, cursor result sets, and views, as well as in the table variable and the rowset functions, as long as only one target is specified in the UPDATE. The rowset functions can be either the OPENQUERY or OPENROWSET functions. You can also use the UPDATE in user-defined functions (UDFs) only if the set being updated is an instance of the table variable. And the various shades of target table types are not treated any differently by the UPDATE. Reference them as if the variable or function was nothing more than an actual base table.

Column Names

The *column_name* argument specifies the value at the column field to be updated. The column name must be in the target table specified in the UPDATE. You can qualify each column with the table name in the standard qualifying dot notation. For example, the code

```
UPDATE [Orders] SET
[Orders].CustomerID = 'VITEN' WHERE [Orders].CustomerID = 'VINET'
```

changes five rows in the *northwind.orders* table. The where clause specifies which rows meet the update criterion. In this case, all rows that have "VITEN" as the CustomerID qualify for the update, and VITEN is changed to VINET.

The SET Value

In the preceding example, the SET value is 'VITEN' (after the =), which can be a string, or a number, or some scalar value. However, the value to be updated by SET can also be derived from an expression that can be calculated or a value returned from a SELECT statement, or the return of a function. Consider the following code, which is valid:

```
UPDATE Orders SET ShippedDate = GetDate()
  WHERE CustomerID = 'VINET'
```

All records meeting the search criterion of CustomerID = 'VINET' are updated to reflect the ship date of the date and time the statement is executed. In this example, I have simply used a standard T-SQL function to return a value for the SET clause. The next example provides the result of a calculation as the new SET value:

```
UPDATE Products SET
UnitPrice = UnitPrice * 10/100 + UnitPrice
  WHERE ProductName = 'Chai'
```

In this code, I raised the price of Chai by 10 percent. The functions or expression you use in the SET clause can thus be as complex as you need them to be; the ultimate objective is that the expression boils down to a single value. Of course the value should be of the same type required by the column, or the value should be converted automatically or explicitly, unless the column type is of sql_variant and your value is not an image or text.

The following SET expression is a little more complex, but it illustrates what you can do to arrive at the value you need for the column data. Let's imagine that a Northwind customer with two branches needed to be recorded in the *Orders* table under one CustomerID assigned to the phone number (503) 555-7555. We can change the CustomerID with the following code:

```
UPDATE Orders SET
 CustomerID = (SELECT TOP 1 CustomerID
 FROM Customers WHERE Phone = '(503) 555-7555')
 WHERE CustomerID = 'VINET'
```

Notice that the SELECT clause is between parentheses—the statement fails without the brackets. Also notice how we do not need to qualify the column names in the entire statement, because the SELECT clause is unambiguous by virtue of the FROM line.

We can also provide the result of a calculation or complex search expression in the final WHERE clause of the UPDATE statement.

Conditional Updates

Using CASE expressions in UPDATE statements can result in some fancy conditional code, especially if used in stored procedures. The following code updates several prices in Northwind's product table:

```
UPDATE Products SET
UnitPrice =
  (CASE SupplierID
    WHEN '4' THEN UnitPrice * 5/100 + UnitPrice
    WHEN '7' THEN UnitPrice * 30/100 + UnitPrice
    WHEN '23' THEN UnitPrice - UnitPrice * 10/100
    END )
```

DELETE

DELETE removes rows from a table. A simple DELETE statement looks like this:

```
DELETE Products WHERE SupplierID = '7'
```

It knocks supplier 7 from our Products table because the company raised its prices by 30 percent. The full syntax of the DELETE is as follows:

```
[ WITH <common_table_expression> [ ,...n ] ]
DELETE
    [ TOP ( expression ) [ PERCENT ] ]
    [ FROM ]
    { <object> | rowset_function_limited
      [ WITH ( <table_hint_limited> [ ...n ] ) ]
    }
    [ <OUTPUT Clause> ]
    [ FROM <table_source> [ ,...n ] ]
    [ WHERE { <search_condition>
            | { [ CURRENT OF
                    { { [ GLOBAL ] cursor_name }
                        | cursor_variable_name
                    }
                ]
              }
            }
    ]


    [ OPTION ( <Query Hint> [ ,...n ] ) ]
[; ]
```

```
<object> ::={

    [ server_name.database_name.schema_name.
      | database_name. [ schema_name ] .
      | schema_name.    ]
        table_or_view_name


}
```

As demonstrated by the syntax, you will always need to provide a source table or result set variable from which to delete a row or series of rows; however, the FROM is optional and represents the old ANSI SQL-92 standard syntax. (You use DROP if the object of the delete is the entire table.) You also do not delete columns in the DELETE statement, only rows or a range of rows that meet a certain criterion, such as where all customers are past due by five years. Of course, if you omit the WHERE clause, you could end up with an empty table, which (in a certain way) does what TRUNCATE does (discussed shortly).

TIP *Use the system function @@ROWCOUNT in all DML statements if you need to return to the client the number of rows that were affected by any of the INSERT, UPDATE, and DELETE statements, or if it is required as a parameter in a procedure.*

While the syntax says you can delete rows in a view, the delete goes down to the actual base table. But if the view is derived from two or more base tables, you would not be able to delete via the view, because there is no way to reference more than one table in the DELETE (from VIEW) statement.

The bullet list that follows here lists the various forms in which DELETE can be used:

- DELETE with no WHERE clause
- DELETE on a set of rows
- DELETE on the current row of a cursor
- DELETE based on a subquery and using the Transact-SQL extension
- DELETE with the TOP clause
- DELETE with the OUTPUT clause
- OUTPUT with *from_table_name* in a DELETE statement

TRUNCATE TABLE

I mentioned TRUNCATE TABLE earlier, but you should know that while both statements can be used to remove all the rows from a table, there are some important differences. TRUNCATE TABLE, for starters, is much faster than DELETE because TRUNCATE TABLE completely deallocates the data pages and any indexes attached to the table. DELETE removes the rows one at a time and maintains the data page even at the instant it is devoid of all rows. Also, every row removal in the DELETE statement is fully logged (and thus recoverable after each row delete transaction), while TRUNCATE TABLE cannot log each row as being removed from the deallocation of the data pages, because the rows are not actually deleted; the data page is just unhinged. However, the transaction logs the TRUNCATE TABLE's resulting page removal, which also means much less log space is used.

TIP *You can recover from a TRUNCATE if it is enclosed inside transactions.*

Here is an example of the TRUNCATE in action:

```
TRUNCATE TABLE Products
```

Very complex, isn't it? So complex is it that often you can forget to include the keyword TABLE. Running "TRUNCATE Products" will not work.

While TRUNCATE TABLE provides a handy table row eradicator, there are two places you cannot take it:

- It cannot be used on tables referenced by foreign keys.
- It cannot be used on tables that are required in replication scenarios.

DML, Integrity, and Constraints

What sets the SELECT statement, covered in the preceding chapter, apart from the INSERT, UPDATE, and DELETE statements is that the latter three result in changes being made to tables. Rows are inserted or appended with INSERT, values are changed with UPDATE, and rows are removed with DELETE. Each action will cause any triggers or check and integrity constraints defined on the target tables and columns to trap your code, and it is thus important to take this into account. For example, if an INSTEAD OF trigger is defined on a DELETE statement when your DELETE statement hits the table, the code in the trigger will run instead. The code might still delete the row, but based on a condition that can be checked at trigger run time, not on something the client process would know about.

The integrity constraints and how they work is adequately covered in Chapter 12, and triggers in Chapter 13; however, a number of aspects and new features must be discussed in this chapter, especially the new cascade operations.

Cascading Referential Integrity

Cascading referential integrity (CRI) applies to the DELETE and UPDATE statements only because they cause changes to existing rows. The CRI constraints let you define the course of action SQL Server should take when your statement hits tables on which foreign keys depend.

For example, let's say you want to delete a customer from the *Customers* table. What then should happen to that customer's records that still exist in the *Orders* table? The rows in the *Orders* table would then be separated from any rows in the *Customers* table, and thus, depending on your solution, they may no longer be accessible.

When you create a table using T-SQL DDL as discussed in Chapter 10, you can specify the action to take upon a DELETE or an UPDATE statement hitting the table. There are two courses of action that can take place for either operation:

- CASCADE or take no action on Delete ([ON DELETE { CASCADE | NO ACTION }])
- CASCADE or take no action on Update ([ON UPDATE { CASCADE | NO ACTION }])

The NO ACTION condition is the default if you incur a referential integrity condition but do not specify anything. If you do specify the cascade operation, SQL Server will cascade the DELETE or UPDATE operations to the related rows in the foreign tables. For example, a cascading delete will result in all the orders relating to the deleted customer being removed as well from the *Orders* table. This new feature is an incredible time saver as far as referential integrity is concerned, and I use it all the time now. It certainly saves you a ton of time having to code manual cascade operations that have you doing queries against foreign tables and then deleting the related rows.

There can also be multiple cascading actions that can take place if triggers and collateral constraints fire as a result of the cascade. For example, deleting a row from *T1* can cascade to delete a row from *T2*. A cascading delete defined on *T2* can thus cause a cascading delete on table *T3*, much like the domino effect.

A cascading tree or nest structure will begin to emerge, and this is okay as long as the cascade does not become circular and reference a row in a table that has already been axed or updated.

Permissions

SQL Server security will refuse permission to users to execute any of the DML statements (INSERT, DELETE, UPDATE, and SELECT) on a table or view, so you have to explicitly enable the access. Members of the sysadmin fixed server roles, the db_owner user, and the db_datawriter fixed database roles automatically have permission. Members of sysadmin, db_owner, and db_securityadmin can permit other users to run these statements (see Chapter 5).

Parameterized Queries

Use parameterized queries wherever you can. They help SQL Server reuse execution plans so that user queries execute faster after the first compile. Parameterized queries can significantly cut CPU cycles, improving overall throughput. For example, the following code suggests "slower" and "faster" options for a simple UPDATE:

```
--slower
UPDATE Customers.dbo.Orders SET
Orders.Customer = 'Shapiro' WHERE [Orders].CustomerID = 'A346'
--faster
UPDATE Customers.dbo.Orders SET
Orders.Customer = ? WHERE [Orders].CustomerID = ?
```

The second statement will obviously not run. The idea is that if SQL Server can simply store the entire second statement in an execution plan and then simply insert the parameters you send, it will not have to process an execution plan for the entire statement every time you transmit the query. If a number of separate queries have the same "shape," then one plan can be used for all queries that share that shape.

First, you can also use a special system stored procedure that lets you create and pass an entire T-SQL statement as a parameter. The system proc is sp_executesql (see Appendix); it can be used in standard T-SQL scripts and in trigger and stored procedure code. Consider the following code:

```
DECLARE @SQL1 NVARCHAR(750)
DECLARE @P1 NVARCHAR(10)
DECLARE @P2 NVARCHAR(500)


SET @SQL1 = N'UPDATE Customers.dbo.Orders SET
Orders.Customer = @P2 WHERE [Orders].CustomerID = @P1'
SET @P1 = 'A346'
SET @P2 = 'Shapiro'
EXEC sp_executesql @SQL1, @P1, @p2
```

You can take this now a step further and not only used simple stored procedures (see Chapter 14) for all queries, but use the sp_executesql stored procedure inside a stored procedure, as follows:

```
USE [Modelize]


SET ANSI_NULLS ON
GO
SET QUOTED_IDENTIFIER ON
GO


CREATE    PROCEDURE [dbo].[CopyLeadToLDTable]
  @leadTable nvarchar(10),
  @OperatorA int,
  @ClientIDA int,
  @LeadSourceA int,
  @LeadStatusA int,
  @SrcnotesA varchar(250),
  @ClientAgeA int,
  @FlagNewRecA int,
  @LocationIDA int,
  @SalesIDA int,
  @MailOnlyA bit,
  @FencoCIDA int,
  @JobIDA int

AS
```

```
DECLARE @InsertString NVARCHAR(500)
DECLARE @OrderMonth INT


-- Build the INSERT statement.


SET @InsertString = 'INSERT INTO ' + @leadTable + '(operid, clientid, lsource,
lstatus, srcnotes, clientage, newrecflag, locid, salesid, mailonly, FencoCID,
JobID)' + ' VALUES (@OperatorB, @ClientIDB, @LeadSourceB, @LeadStatusB, @SrcnotesB,
@ClientAgeB, @FlagNewRecB, @LocationIDB, @SalesIDB, @MailOnlyB, @FencoCIDB,
@JobIDB)'

EXEC sp_executesql @InsertString, N'@OperatorB int, @ClientIDB int, @LeadSourceB
int, @LeadStatusB int, @SrcnotesB varchar(250), @ClientAgeB int, @FlagNewRecB int,
@LocationIDB int, @SalesIDB int, @MailOnlyB bit, @FencoCIDB int, @JobIDB int',
@OperatorA, @ClientIDA, @LeadSourceA, @LeadStatusA, @SrcnotesA, @ClientAgeA,
@FlagNewRecA, @LocationIDA,
@SalesIDA, @MailOnlyA, @FencoCIDA, @JobIDA
```

Putting all queries into stored procedures helps get code visible to the optimizer in advance of production calls. This does not mean that you need to rush out and convert everything to stored procedures (see Chapter 18, which discussed the Database Tuning Advisor and delves further into this subject).

You can also use the "recompile" hint, but be aware that it is better suited for long queries where the cost of compilation can be justified.

Getting Bold

This chapter covers the legendary, yet powerful, DML statements INSERT, UPDATE, and DELETE, and it introduces some powerful new features that come with SQL Server 2005. We also investigated some advanced stuff including coding conditional logic into the DML statements, using INSERT and EXECUTE together, and so on. For the most part the functionality we explored in this chapter puts data into the database and changes it. Let's now look at getting data out.

Working with Tabular Data

I begin this chapter with an abstract discussion of the SQL Server table, its attributes and elements, and then move on to dissecting the SELECT statement, before hitting view and other query facilities. The coverage of the SQL Server SELECT statement is exhaustive here, covering the new features, such as support for XML data. Our discussion of the SELECT will first focus on fundamentals and the structure of its syntax, before delving into techniques and strategies, with advanced features like its COMPUTE BY clause, ROLLUPs, and CUBEs.

I also discuss the concept of *data conservation* in a client/server relational database management system (RDBMS). Notice again the phrase *data conservation*. I use this term to stress "wise use of data" and further elaborate on the concepts I discussed in Chapter 12.

"Conservation" is an interesting term. A discipline of ecology, it means the wise use of a resource and not "protectionism" or "exploitation." I would like to apply this concept of wise use to data and retrieval methods appropriate for the fat server model—the primary paradigm of data management using SQL Server (and other DBMS server systems).

But before we can explore this further and test the validity of the concepts, let's discuss the basics.

The SQL Server Table

Let me start with some recap: By now you certainly know that the table in SQL Server is the primary unit of storage. SQL Server tables are created and maintained in databases, and we described how both databases and tables get created back in Chapter 6. The database, thus, is nothing more than a container, albeit a container with numerous features that allow us to manage the data in the table and control access to it.

NOTE *A database is a SQL Server object; it has no reference in relational theory, or in the SQL ANSI standard.*

A SQL Server table is made up of columns and rows. Rows, known as *tuples* in a table, represent the complete "record" of data *within the table*. The relational model, however, allows the record to spread over several tables, but taken collectively all the interrelated rows of data combine to make the record. Often, it makes sense for us to break large tables into many smaller ones, to infuse some modularity in the structure of our data, which makes it easier to work with. For example, in a simple order-entry and order-management database, we would typically create a table for the customer's details and a table for the *customer* orders and so on.

Out of a collection of customers and each customer's orders, we are able to manipulate and farm our data (conservation again) to produce documents representing orders, statements, invoices, picklists, packing labels, mailing labels, and so forth. And with analysis services and functions, we can "milk" the data for information to assist us in business decision–making. For each document or assemblage of data, however, we still need only work two or three primary tables of operational data, at the minimum. We would create a table for customer details (company name, telephone number, contact, and so on), one for shipping information (physical addresses as opposed to billing addresses), and one for order details.

It is quite possible and often desirable to add columns to the general customer details table. My rules for this are to first investigate the attributes and the domains of the data you are storing. If new data you are adding to the table only represent one column, it would not make any sense to create a separate table for it. For example, if your business rules require payment only through credit cards and you need no more than a few columns to store credit card numbers, expiration, and name on the card, by all means attach a few more columns to the customer details table.

SQL Server tables can hold 1,024 columns. Your model might work well with a few large tables with many columns, and it might work better (or worse) if the model called for many smaller tables. For example, if the business decided to accept several forms of payments, from cash to credit (charge and account), then it would make sense to provide tables that specialize in the storage of this information. For the most part your database lets you know when its tables should be split up.

NOTE *The tables, data, and query strategies discussed in this chapter revolve around operational data (OLTP) and not analytical data (OLAP), the latter being beyond the scope of this book.*

The more tables you have, the more complex the model. There is also more of a chance of redundant data occurring in the database. Whether this is a poor, bad, or unconscionable thing depends on which relational guru you worship. We have guidelines for this dilemma, thanks to Codd, known as *normalization*. Called the Rules of Normalization, I prefer to see them as guidelines; others treat them like the Talmud. In fact, the nature of the RDBMS is such that unless you are flexible and adopt relational theory as a guideline, as opposed to gospel, you are destined to founder. SQL Server solutions may in fact contain undernormalized data, overnormalized data, and what at times may even appear to be denormalized data. It all depends on your application and what you are trying to achieve. A customer order-entry system, an accounts payable/accounts receivable system, and a database supporting the switching matrix of an automatic call distributor may bear no resemblance to one another.

However, the SQL Server database model requires us to be data conservationists. We need to thus strive to prevent, as far as possible, the repetition of data in our database. Otherwise, we will have to deal with unnecessary bottlenecks, slow queries, misleading query results, and so forth. On the other hand, we should not be so limiting that the database becomes impossible to access easily.

Table Concepts

It is often difficult to change our concept of a table, the abstract impression of it, as being something that looks like a spreadsheet. This is obviously due in large part to the GUI presentation of data in gridlike structures. For ISAM databases, data is almost always presented to the user in grids. What's worse, users are allowed to edit and update data within the grid, which doesn't sit well with SQL Server solutions (and we'll deal with why shortly).

While it is permissible in some cases to let this go with users, often the so-called data-bound grid does more harm than good for the database designers and modeling people. In fact, I have even met people who cannot see beyond the grid, and so severe is their habit, they prefer to store their data in spreadsheets and never go near relational databases. When you cannot see your data for the cells, you are severely hampering your ability to model and build effective SQL Server solutions that query well. In other words, you are unable to see the entire *record* in the database, only seeing part of it in a cell.

For example, many years ago when I made the transition from Paradox and Access databases to SQL Server, one of the first habits I found hard to kick was the autoincrement feature, and I believe this is true for a lot of Access users still today. While autoincrement, which added a new number automatically to each new "row" of data, helped ensure unique records, it also perpetuated the fixation on cells, which had to exist in a precise range where no row numbers could be missing. The identity property of a column in a SQL Server table offers the same functionality; you should use it with care and avoid fixation on an exact sequence of numbers that remind you of a spreadsheet.

In the late 1990s, I experimented with several of my database contracts, dropping grids from the entire client application and only working with hierarchical data trees, lists, and a variety of string objects. I refused (and still do as far as possible) to "bind" a grid to a SQL Server table. Not only did I find it far easier to create super-thin clients, but also I found my users beginning to work with data far more sophisticatedly. I had gotten them to see beyond the grid, to the data on a much broader scale, as part of a system with depth and perspective. Today, of course, the disconnected data set relegates much of my past pet peeves to the dust of time.

While it is impossible to dismiss columns and column names as being the fabric of SQL Server tables, you should strive to view your data in terms of the domains that make up a complete record in the database. Each row or tuple is made up of one or more (seldom one) domains, and for each of the record's domains you need to provide a value. In some cases, you might not know the value (the NULL issue again), but we will delve into that little problem later. (Domains are discussed in depth in Chapter 12.)

A customer record, for example, is made up of several domains: first names, last names, street numbers, street addresses, cities, postal codes, and so on. If one row's collection of domain values is repeated in another row in the same table, we violate the rules of uniqueness. And if the row is repeated in the same table, or another table, but is unique only by virtue of a row identifier, or an identity value, then we violate rules of data redundancy (and our wise use mission goes out the window).

We strive to ensure that no two records can be identical (at least one domain value in the record makes the record unique); there are several means to ensure this. We might get away with a "clone" of a record by giving the record an instance or column identifier. You could create a record number, a customer number, a part number, and so on.

In other words, our records are nothing more than collections of domains, or, in OO terms, objects with collections of properties. In order for us to search for single records or a group of records in a table, the table needs to be ordered according to a sequence of domains. In other words, we would say that a customer number would be domain 1, called CustomerNumbers, and that CustomerName could be called domain 2. It does not matter where in the table the domains are positioned, 1 or 76, or what they are labeled, as long as each record maintains the domain order—and the data type each domain stores. In other words, the *city* domain (in the fourth column) for record A cannot also be the *state* domain (also column 4), because that would make our data impossible and nonsensical to work with.

NOTE   *In pure object systems, this situation can be very different; in some cases, the domains may not be stored in columns. Similar to the contents of the living cell, the records as objects do not maintain properties in any order, and the property needs only to be referenced in some way.*

Thus our queries are built according to the following language: "Find me records in which the customer's *city* domain is Miami, or the customer's *order number* domain contains the values of '12-08-45-A1.'" By concentrating on the value of the data in the domain as opposed to a collection of cells, you'll have a better feel for your data when it comes to modeling and building queries.

Data-bound controls in the client tier create many problems for SQL Server solutions. To begin with, they have the habit of establishing connections to the server and maintaining them with no rhythm or reason. But mostly the controls tend to perpetuate the cell habit, encouraging you to fixate on the cells as opposed to the values. If you are moving from Access (with MDB files) to SQL Server, you should try to kick the data-bound control habit. In today's highly distributed data processing environment, the buzz word is "scalability," and nothing can trash scalability more than binding client controls to database objects.

By referencing columns according to their position in a table (thinking left to right), we can ensure that SQL Server places our values in the correct domains. Domain integrity and type constraints can of course be used to ensure that correct values get stored in the domains. But knowing the position of a column is not essential (and is outdated) because we reference the column by name, no matter where it is in the table. In other words, our insert languages would sound like "place this value into the column for the cities domain, whose record number is X."

In this regard, it is quite clear that the table is a server-side object, not something that can be instantiated or re-created in the client. In other words, it exists only within a database schema and has no foundation anywhere other than in the database.

Perhaps one of the most dangerous operators in the SQL language is the * (star, or asterisk), which means all or any. So if we say " SELECT * from the CUSTOMERS table," we are asking SQL Server to send us all the rows and all domain values (every column). This really does wonders for the network and the health of our client and user. But what is worse is that it leads to the notion that the table is being reproduced outside the database, and this is a dangerous perception.

When we query SQL Server, no matter what object the data is drawn from in the database (table, view, table variable, table expression, cursor, and so on), we are served with a replica of the data in the database, which we display at the client in grids, trees, lists, or individual text fields. Our queries thus need to be highly efficient so that only the most valid data the client needs is sent across the network, not as a table, but in tabulated form nonetheless (represented by tabular data streams or XML), so that the client can present the data in the correct fields or containers. Can you imagine what it would be like if we sat down for dinner in a crowded restaurant and asked the kitchen to send us every meal, just because we were not sure what we felt like eating?

The query at the worst should return no more than twenty rows if the client does not know the exact row it needs, but the query should always strive to send as few rows as possible. Figure 16-1 illustrates what I consider a safety zone for sending a collection of rows to the client.

Figure 16-1 demonstrates what I earlier called data ecology or data farming, which means querying only for just enough records to satisfy the client and balance the number of round trips to the server. The best scenario, as indicated in the figure, is one row, and possibly even one value. The less known about a value being searched on, the more rows get returned to the client. And conversely, the more you know about the row, the fewer the number of rows that need to be returned. If you know the exact value that makes the row unique, SQL Server will send you that row and no other.

The row or rows of data returned by SQL server is known as a result set. You can call it anything you like in the client development or external environment (recordset, resultset, rowset, dataset and so on), but from SQL Server it is the result of a query, no matter how simple or how complex. Your queries should also be written in such a way that the result returned contains not only as few records as possible, but only the exact columns needed. If you need to display all the values of a row, so be it.

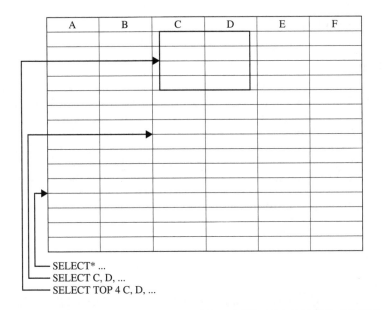

FIGURE 16-1   Narrowing down the SELECT to conserve network, server, and client resources

Sometimes you need just a domain value at the client for some reason that the client does not need to know about. Understand, however, that you are not being much of a conservationist if you write software that updates 20 fields in a record when only one needs to be updated. In other words, why send packets containing 20 values back to SQL Server when you need only send a packet to update one value. Not only do you consume more network bandwidth, but you also consume more processing bandwidth on the server.

If you ask SQL Server for the customer 100 row so that you can update the postal code, does it not make more sense to only receive the customer number, optionally the name to keep the software user sure he or she has the right record, and the postal code? You can then transmit only this field back to the server instead of directly inserting numerous values into the table using an inline SQL statement, or better still just pass a single value to a stored procedure's parameter. You could pass the values to a stored procedure to determine the most efficient means of updating the code field, leaving everything else intact, without having to transmit the search logic to find the record. We'll get back to this later.

Let's recap before we move on:

- A table is a unit of storage, maintained in a SQL Server database.

- A table has no reference outside the database: The table exists as a database object; it cannot be transferred out of SQL Server; only its data can, but as a copy in a result set.

- The data is transmitted (copied) from a table as a tabulated datagram, which is called a result set. The result set is transmitted to the client; it is formatted by the TDS protocol or within an XML text stream.

- Client components (such as OLE DB and ADO.NET) know how to read the tabulated data from the protocol stack and how to present it in the client.

- Data that is not changed is discarded; data that must be changed is returned to the server as an update.

Table Derivatives

The table object is not the only tabulated data structure you can query in SQL Server. It is quite possible, desirable, and often essential to query the subsets and other derivatives of the base tables for various operations. We already discussed how it makes sense to divvy up a database into several tables, and as such it is possible to draw data from multiple tables and also query the subsets of the base tables. These subsets are still, however, stored and maintained on the server. Some may be temporary, others permanent.

We can query the following subsets and derivative tables from the SQL Server base tables:

- On-the-fly result sets (the results of queries and subqueries, unions, intersections, joins, and so on)

- Views

- Partitions

- Cursors

- Table derivates such as temporary tables, table variables, and the common table expression (CTE)

On-the-Fly Result Sets

These are result sets, the results of SELECT statements and subqueries, that return volatile subsets of data derived from base tables. I call them "on-the-fly" because the result set, unless specifically stored in a new table or view, is not persistent. It is created within the workings of a complete SELECT statement. In other words, as soon as it is derived from the base table, it is transmitted to the client or used in a subquery and then discarded.

The only vestige of the cause of the result set remains in the form of the SELECT statement stored in the query plan cache. But no subset resulting from the query remains after it has been returned to the client. I will call these "result sets" from here on.

It is possible, however, within a stored procedure, to draw a result set from a base table and prevent the data from being returned to the client automatically, which is the opposite of what SQL Server is inclined to do. Using flow control programming and assignment, you can then derive additional result sets from the earlier result sets (nested results sets) and control exactly which data gets returned to the client, if any. Still, upon termination of the procedure and achievement of the objective or termination through error, the result set is discarded.

Despite the volatility of the result set, a result set can explicitly be saved to a new table, in the midst of SELECT execution, by using SELECT INTO, which creates a table on the fly. I talk about SELECT INTO later in this chapter.

These nonpersistent result sets are created with the T-SQL SELECT statement and its support for ANSI or SQL-92/2003 style structure, as well as some legacy SELECT syntax, which has been kept around for old time's sake.

Views and cursors can be queried in exactly the same fashion as tables, table derivatives, subsets, and result sets. There are several methods of catching fish; the most popular is the fishing pole (or rod). The SELECT is our fishing pole, and we first have to learn how to fish with it, before we can cast in the ponds of tables, views, cursors, and so on.

SELECT

The SELECT statement is the Swiss Army fishing pole of the SQL language. You will use it all the time in T-SQL and to build solid SQL Server solutions. The neat thing about this pole is that the entire fishing tackle tool box is wrapped up in its reel. With it you can strip, pare, screw, saw, hammer, combine, pick, scrape, dig, cut, and otherwise expose your data. For all intents and purposes, without the SELECT statement there is no such thing as a SQL query.

You can be as creative as a honey badger trying to expose a beehive, but you can also get stung. As with any programming language, the longer and more often you scratch and claw at it, the better you will become. At first sight, a complex SELECT statement can seem impossible to decipher, but once broken down into its constituent parts, it becomes as exposed as the bones of a boiled carp.

The anatomy of the SELECT statement is bound by the order of the clauses. The optional clauses can be added or omitted to serve your purpose, but when used, they must be placed in the appropriate order. The abridged T-SQL SELECT, which is also used to infuse views, is as follows:

```
SELECT (select_list)
   INTO (new_table)
FROM (table_source)
```

```
WHERE (search_condition)
GROUP BY (group_by_expression)
HAVING (search_condition)
ORDER BY (order_expression) [ ASC | DESC ]
```

I prefer not to kick off by expanding every section in one behemoth of a SELECT syntax. I believe that if you are new at SQL queries, it makes more sense to look at the bare-bones SELECT and move up from there. After you have mastered basic selects, you can start using the optional constructions and add fat where you need to.

If you are not familiar with the T-SQL SELECT statement, the following treatise takes you through the statement line by line, clause by clause, argument for argument. And if you are versed only in SQL-92, bear in mind that several new elements have been added, such as XML support.

SELECT 101

The SELECT keyword in the preceding code listing is marked in bold because it is the only part of the T-SQL SELECT statement that is required. All other clauses and arguments are optional. SELECT does not need a FROM clause when you are only specifying constants, variables, and arithmetic expressions in the select list. As soon as you specify column names, you need FROM, which is discussed later in this chapter. The simplest T-SQL select statement might be something as follows:

```
SELECT 'Hello Universe'
```

As I am sure you have guessed, this statement does not need any table-based data to complete successfully. It simply returns "Hello Universe" as a single value in a one-row result set. Move from characters to integers and you can perform simple arithmetic after the SELECT, which also just puts the result into a result set, albeit just one value like this:

```
SELECT 1
```

The words that come immediately after the SELECT statement in the query (in the preceding example, it's the number "1") are known as the *select list*. The select list contains the values or column names or domain names in a table you are querying. You can list as many values as you might need, but you must make sure the values are separated by the correct operators.

The rules of precedence also apply to the SELECT statement. For example, the SELECT statements

```
SELECT 5-3/(8+9)
SELECT 5-3/8+9
```

return different results thanks to rules of precedence (which are discussed in Chapter 10). When you use divergent data types in the SELECT, obviously type rules apply. You certainly will obtain an error if you try something like dividing "cat" by "dog."

You can have a SELECT statement that queries SQL Server as a system and is not "aimed" at any tables per se. For example, the line

```
SELECT @@SERVERNAME
```

returns the name of the server you are connected to as a result set of one record (see Appendix for many functions and constructions that return result set data from SQL Server's system tables). But the statement

```
SELECT @@SERVERNAME+@@SERVICENAME
```

returns servernameservicename as a single value, or MCSQL00MSSQLSERVER, which is the server I am using for this little demo. In order to retrieve each value as a column, the items in the select list must be separated correctly by the comma. Thus the statement

```
SELECT @@SERVERNAME,  @@SERVICENAME
```

is returned as follows:

(No column name)	(No column name)
MCSQL00	MSSQLSERVER

To add column names to the result set, the statement should look like this:

```
SELECT 'SERVER NAME' = @@SERVERNAME, 'SERVICE NAME' = @@SERVICENAME
```

which will return the following result set:

SERVER NAME	SERVICE NAME
MCSQL00	MSSQLSERVER

And you can use square brackets instead of the single quotes to designate the column names, which is often preferable if you need the single quotes for various concatenations. In other words, the statement

```
SELECT [SERVER NAME] = @@SERVERNAME, [SERVICE NAME] = @@SERVICENAME
```

returns the identical result set. The square brackets are also essential for identifying actual column names that are the combination of several words. For example, the column name *total fences jumped by the counting sheep* will cause SQL Server to blow a fuse unless it is enclosed in square brackets; thus,

```
SELECT [Total fences jumped by the counting sheep] = 196
```

You would need a psych consult if you named columns like in the preceding example, which is extreme for illustration. Column names should be easy to reference in your queries.

You can also use T-SQL functions in the select list to massage the data. For example, you can trim spaces from the left and right of character data and even manipulate the character strings. You can concatenate and do snazzy stuff, like adding commas between values and so forth. Here's another take on the preceding query before we move on to the harder stuff: The statement

```
SELECT [Server and Service Name] = @@SERVERNAME + ', ' + @@SERVICENAME
```

will give you the following in return:

Server and Service Name
MCSQL00, MSSQLSERVER

Many Happy Returns

Just when you thought there was nothing between you and the select list just described, we come across three "qualifying" arguments that let you determine just how many rows of data satisfying the query should be returned in the result set. But these elements are essential tools used to fulfill those "wise use" goals we spoke about earlier. The arguments are listed in the following syntax in bold:

```
SELECT [ ALL | DISTINCT ]
[ TOP n [ PERCENT ] [ WITH TIES ] ]
 . . . select_list
FROM . . . table source
```

They must also be placed immediately after the SELECT keyword and before any item in the select list, including the * (star), which specifies all columns. The rows are returned in arbitrary order, as they were entered into the table, unless you specify a particular order.

ALL

The ALL (SELECT ALL) argument is the default and can be omitted. It specifies that all rows that satisfy the query criteria must be returned in the result set, even duplicate rows (integrity rules aside) and NULLs.

DISTINCT

The DISTINCT (SELECT DISTINCT) argument specifies that only unique rows can appear in the result set. In T-SQL, the NULL values are considered equal with respect to DISTINCT (see Chapter 10 for various discussions of NULL usage in T-SQL). NULL is never equal because an unknown or missing value can never be compared to another unknown or missing value. However, for the purposes of DISTINCT, the NULL values are returned. In other words, if you have two rows of all NULL data, only one will be returned.

TOP

In SQL Server 2000, the TOP argument (SELECT TOP) replaced the now passé SET ROWCOUNT command used in the days prior to version 7.0. The syntax for TOP is as follows:

```
[

    TOP (expression) [PERCENT]
    [ WITH TIES ]
]
```

In a SELECT statement it forces the query to return only the first n rows that satisfy the query, in the order they were inserted into the table. The placeholder n must be an integer between 0 and 4294967295. For example, the query

```
SELECT TOP 2 Agent_Name FROM Agents
```

will return A1 and A2 from the table. Be careful not to forget the name of the column you are querying, or use the * condition, because it is easy to think you can just query the table as SELECT TOP 2 FROM Agents. You can also specify more than the actual number of rows in the table; SQL Server will return all available rows less than the value of n instead of returning an error.

If you follow the TOP argument with the PERCENT option keyword, the number represented by placeholder n becomes a percentage value instead of an integer. In other words, the query

```
SELECT TOP 50 PERCENT Agent_Name FROM Agents
```

will return 50 percent of the rows in the table (the TOP 50 percent, that is). As I am sure you have figured out, the PERCENT option is useful if you do not know how many records will be returned in the result set. Still, asking for the TOP 2 percent might be asking for more rows than you care to return to the client. With terabyte and exabyte databases fast becoming standard issue on the Internet, returning the TOP one percent might be enough rows to turn the network resources into something resembling mango compote. (Use the @@ROWCOUNT function to check the actual number of rows returned, and if there are too many rows you can suggest a more sensible percent value to the user).

And what about rules for PERCENT? The percent value must be between 0 and 100; anything above will error out.

The TOP can also be suffixed with the WITH TIES option. This option forces the query to return additional rows with the same value in ORDER BY columns appearing as the last of the TOP n (PERCENT) rows. As an essential rule, the WITH TIES qualifier can only be specified if your query specifies the ORDER BY clause. If this sounds confusing, have a look at the result set of the following SELECT TOP:

```
SELECT TOP 5 Agent_Name FROM Agents
```

The query returns the following result set:

Agent_Name
A1
A2
A3
A4
A5

Now suppose the sixth row was also "A5" and you specified WITH TIES followed by ORDER BY on Agent_NAME like this:

```
SELECT TOP 5 WITH TIES Agent_Name FROM Agents ORDER BY Agent_Name
```

PART IV

The result set would now be as follows for a TOP 5 query:

Agent_Name
A1
A2
A3
A4
A5
A5

Since the sixth row was also A5, WITH TIES brings it with. If you selected without the WITH TIES option TOP would honor the parameter of "5" and return only the five rows shown here.

If you have reason to use TOP accompanied by WITH TIES, it is important to understand that these arguments act on the data returned in the result sets and have nothing to do with what lies below in the base table. Also, WITH TIES only works if the query is capped with the ORDER BY clause on the pertinent column and any rows that tie at the end of the result set.

If you need to, you can also tag ASC or DESC onto the end of the query to specify returning the TOP items in ascending order or descending order. The results will be very different because the column is sorted ASC or DESC on the base table and not on the final result of the query.

You can also specify DISTINCT with TOP to drop any duplicate rows in the result set.

TOP Expression as a Variable

The TOP *expression* indicated in the syntax described earlier can be declared as an expression in T-SQL supporting SQL Server 2005. To a declare a TOP variable the syntax is as follows:

```
DECLARE @MyTopVar INT
SET @MyTopVar = 25
SELECT TOP (@MyTopVar) UserID FROM CRM.Users
```

The TOP clause with variable expressions can also be used in INSERT, UPDATE and DELETE statements.

Understanding the Select List

As mentioned earlier, items specified in the select list, separated by commas, represent the columns from which data is selected for the result set. If we look at the syntax of the select list, we see that it can be simple, as demonstrated previously, or complex enough to give you a hernia.

```
{ *
| { table_name | view_name | table_alias }.*
| { column_name | expression | IDENTITYCOL | ROWGUIDCOL }
[ [ AS ] column_alias ]
| column_alias = expression
} [ ,...n ]
```

The first * (star) operator forces the query to select all of the columns for extraction to the result set. The * should rarely be used, if ever, in SQL Server thin-client solutions. Large result sets do not sit well in browsers and devices where memory is scarce. Some exceptions might fly if the table, or a view above it, only holds a few rows and few columns, such as my *Agents* table shown earlier. The * scope can work for result sets held at the server, but make sure not to force it up against a table with many columns. And if you specify more than one table in the FROM clause, the * can end up returning more data than you care to deal with.

On the other hand, one big round trip to the server might be better than two dozen if the client can handle a thousand rows. It all depends on the solution you need. You thus need to balance "data ecology" with "network ecology."

Unless you specify an order (using GROUP BY) that you want to see in the result set, the columns are returned in the order in which they exist in the table or view. I will get back to the ORDER BY option later, but you should be aware that it applies to how the results are sorted, not how the columns are ordered in the result set.

The syntax *table_name | view_name | table_alias*.* means that you can prefix columns with the names of the tables or view, or their aliases. This practice is suggested to avoid ambiguity, especially when dealing with more than one table that has the same column names. For example, the statement SELECT Orders.CustomerID FROM Orders is the same thing as SELECT CustomerID FROM Orders. It also helps the SQL Server optimizer. (See Chapter 16 on the subject of identifiers.)

The * attached to the table name not only limits the scope of the * to the specified table or view, but it has the same result as SELECT * demonstrated earlier. The *column_name* placeholder is the name of a column to return in the result set, as mentioned earlier. However, the *column name* or *names* placeholder can also be a constant, a function, or any combination of column names and functions connected by operators and subqueries, or both.

IDENTITYCOL returns the identity column values to the result set. (See Chapter 2 and Chapter 15 for more information on IDENTITY columns.) If more than one table in the FROM clause has a column with the IDENTITY property, IDENTITYCOL must be qualified with the specific table name, such as T1.IDENTITYCOL.

The ROWGUIDCOL returns the values of the global unique identifier column. As in the IDENTITY column, if more than one table in the FROM clause has a ROWGUIDCOL property, the ROWGUIDCOL must be qualified with the specific table name, such as T1.ROWGUIDCOL.

The placeholder *column_alias* refers to an alternative name that you can use in the place of the actual column name returned in the result set. The ability to alias is useful and lets you return a more suitable column name in the result set than the actual column name in the base table. Often the base table column names are not suitable for a result set and display at the client. For example, the column name Cust_Lname is hardly a visually pleasing column name. To provide an alias for this clumsy column name, you need to precede the alias with the AS directive. For example, the statement

```
SELECT Cust_Lname AS 'Last Name'
FROM Customers
```

will return the following result set:

Last Name
Smith
Smit
Smitz

You can also use the alias to specify column names returned in the result sets of expressions. For example, the statement querying the *Qty* column in the *order details* table

```
SELECT SUM(Qty) AS 'Fruit Cakes' FROM [order details] WHERE productID = 5
```

will return the following result set:

Fruit Cakes
298

You can also use the alias feature in an ORDER BY clause. Also, if the query expression is part of a DECLARE CURSOR statement, the column alias cannot be used in the FOR UPDATE clause. By the way, using the equal sign (=) as follows also works:

```
SELECT 'Fruit Cakes' = SUM(Qty) FROM [order details] WHERE productID = 5
```

However, you might find your code easier to read using AS.

SELECT . . . INTO

The INTO clause of the T-SQL SELECT statement creates a new table to hold the result set data. The syntax is as follows:

```
[ INTO new_table ]
```

The *new_table* placeholder specifies the name of a new table to be created. The new table is composed of the columns and rows in the result set. It does not contain any of the attributes of the base table. For example, if you used an alias for the names of result set columns, then these aliases carry to the new table.

The INTO functionality creates the new table based on the expressions in the select list. This alone determines the format of the new table, and each new column has the same name, data type, and value as the corresponding expression in the select list.

There are, however, some provisions. If you include a computed column in the select list, the corresponding column in the new table does not inherit the computed column attribute, and the values in the new column are the values that were computed at the time SELECT . . . INTO was executed.

If you are moving up from earlier versions of SQL Server, you'll remember that you had to enable the *select into/bulkcopy* option. In SQL Server 2005, however, the select into/ bulkcopy option has no bearing on whether you can create a table with SELECT INTO; it only has a bearing on whether you can create a permanent table. The amount of logging for certain bulk operations, including SELECT INTO, depends on the recovery model in effect for the database (see Chapter 7).

You can choose to execute the system stored procedure sp_dboption to turn on the select into/bulkcopy option before executing the SELECT statement; however, you should be aware of the following behavior:

- If the select into/bulkcopy option is enabled for the database in which the table is to be created, a permanent table is created. The table name must be unique in the database and must conform to the rules for identifiers as a fully qualified table name.

- If the select into/bulkcopy is not enabled for the database where the table is to be created, you will not be able to create a permanent table using SELECT . . . INTO. The tables you will create have to be local or global temporary tables that must begin with a number sign (#).

Permissions, of course, apply, which means you can only execute a SELECT statement with the INTO clause if you have the CREATE TABLE permission in the target database. SELECT . . . INTO cannot be used with the COMPUTE clause or inside an explicit transaction.

FROM

Earlier I introduced you to the FROM clause, which specifies the tables from which to retrieve the rows that satisfy the SELECT query. As discussed earlier, the FROM clause is not required when the select list contains only constants, variables, and arithmetic expressions. In other words, as soon as you specify column names, you are implicating tables, and the SELECT does not know which tables unless you list them in the FROM clause. But FROM is a lot more than a subordinate clause that specifies tables name, as we will soon discover.

The FROM clause requires a source, or more specifically a table source. The table source can be tables, views, derived tables, the results of joins, and rowset functions. The base syntax for the table source is as follows:

```
table_name [ [ AS ] table_alias ] [ WITH ( < table_hint > [ ,...n ] ) ]
| view_name [ [ AS ] table_alias ]
| rowset_function [ [ AS ] table_alias ]
| derived_table [ AS ] table_alias [ ( column_alias [ ,...n ] ) ]
| joined_table
```

The *table_name* placeholder specifies to the FROM clause the name of a table or view, or a table derived from the rowset function. Using the AS directive, you can also come up with an alias to specify as the optional alias name of the table. You can also alias the name of a view. The following example specifies an alias for the base table:

```
SELECT Customers FROM Cust AS "Customers" . . .
```

At first sight, the alias for a table name specified in the FROM clause seems redundant. It is in fact redundant in simple expressions, but it will make sense when you need to do more with the table than just searching it, as you will soon discover.

The FROM keyword is needed whenever you are referencing tables, views, derived tables, joined tables, and table variables in a SELECT statement. (See Chapter 2 for a primer on tables and views in SQL Server 2005. Creating them in T-SQL or interactively is covered in Chapter 10.) In this section, we will only use FROM to specify base tables as follows:

```
SELECT * FROM table_name
```

In the preceding example, the statement makes use of the * (star) operator, which instructs the query to return all rows and columns from the table. You can also specify more than one table in the query as follows:

```
SELECT * FROM table_name1, table_name2, table_name3
```

T-SQL lets you specify up to 256 source tables after the FROM clause. If a table or view exists in another database, other than the one you are attached to, or even another server, you must provide a fully qualified table name (FQTN) *database.owner.object_name* after the FROM keyword.

CAUTION *The fully qualified table name does not guarantee you can still connect and run the query, because permissions apply. (See Chapter 5.)*

As an example, the statement

```
SELECT * FROM Agents
```

returns the following result set from a two-column table, which represents all rows and all columns:

Agent Name	Agent Nickname
A1	Captain
A2	Gish
A3	Kimlet
A4	Frog
A5	Lofty
A6	Hota

Using Derived Tables for the Table Source

Derived tables are virtual tables that you can construct on the fly using subqueries in the FROM clause. You can then use the derived table as a table source to query against. The following statement suggests a simple subquery that produces a derived table:

```
SELECT 'Fruit Cake Sales' = SUM(Qty) from (select Qty FROM [order
details] where productID = 5 ) Orders
```

The result is identical for this query as in the earlier statement for fruit cake sales; however, after the subquery has executed, a derived table is created called *Orders* (an alias), which becomes the de facto table source. This is a very useful feature because you can create a derived table from several different base tables or from some construction that does not use a base table at all. Derived tables can also be concocted in WHERE clauses as a means of providing keys for search conditions and other useful stuff. And speaking of searches . . . .

The Search Is On

While you know that you can SELECT records from a table without searching for a specific record, the SELECT statement would be more than limiting without the ability to search for single rows or a small collection that meets some criteria. The search for rows in the table, or in multiple tables, is provided by a chunk of code within the SELECT statement known as the *search condition*.

The search condition makes use of comparison operators and relationship predicates to look for matching records with which to satisfy the query. The syntax looks a little arcane but is really pretty simple to grasp. The T-SQL official search condition syntax looks like this:

```
{ [ NOT ] < predicate > | ( < search_condition > ) }
[ { AND | OR } [ NOT ] { < predicate > | ( < search_condition > ) } ]
} [ ,...n ]

< predicate > ::=
{ expression { = | < > | ! = | > | > = | ! > | < | < = | ! < } expression|
string_expression [ NOT ] LIKE string_expression
[ ESCAPE 'escape_character' ]
| expression [ NOT ] BETWEEN expression AND expression
| expression IS [ NOT ] NULL
| CONTAINS
( { column | * } , '< contains_search_condition >' )
| FREETEXT ( { column | * } , 'freetext_string' )
| expression [ NOT ] IN ( subquery | expression [ ,...n ] )
| expression { = | < > | ! = | > | > = | ! > | < | < = | ! < }
{ ALL | SOME | ANY} ( subquery )
| EXISTS ( subquery )
}
```

The search condition is used in several places in the SELECT statement. It is also used in the UPDATE and DELETE statements, where it specifies the rows to be updated and the rows to be deleted, respectively.

You can pretty much build a search condition that tests scores of possibilities using as many predicates and operators as you need. In addition, operators like NOT can be used to negate Boolean expressions specified by the predicate. And you can use AND to combine two conditions that must both test for TRUE to be included in the result set. OR is also here for the search posse, allowing you to combine two conditions, which will test for true if at least one of the conditions is true.

The order of precedence for the logical operators is NOT (highest), followed by AND, followed by OR. The order of evaluation at the same precedence level is from left to right. The Parentheses can be used to override this order in a search condition, as discussed earlier in the chapter.

The < *predicate* > placeholder represents an expression that returns TRUE, FALSE, or UNKNOWN. It can test on a column name, a constant, a function, a variable, a scalar subquery, or any combination of column names, constants, and functions connected by the operators or subqueries. You can also build an expression that contains an entire CASE function. The following operators can be used in the search condition:

- The = (equal) operator tests for equality between two expressions.
- The <> (not equal) operator tests the condition of two expressions for *not* being equal to each other.
- The != is the ANSI not-equal operator that works the same as the T-SQL operator.
- The > (greater than) operator tests the condition of one expression being greater than the other.
- The >= (greater than or equal to) operator tests the condition of one expression being greater than or equal to the other expression.
- The !> (not greater than) operator tests the condition of one expression not being greater than the other expression.
- The < (less than) operator tests the condition of one expression being less than the other.
- The <= (less than or equal to) operator tests the condition of one expression being less than or equal to the other expression.
- The !< (not less than) operator tests the condition of one expression not being less than the other expression.

The [NOT] LIKE expression indicates that the subsequent character string is to be used with the pattern matching.

The ESCAPE *escape_character* expression lets you search for the exact string that also includes a wildcard character (not functioning in the capacity of a wildcard character) to be searched for.

The *escape_character* you denote replaces the usual wildcard character. To denote this, you need to place the new wildcard character in front of the old wildcard character. For example, the statement

```
select * from items where item like 'Tz_square' ESCAPE 'z'
```

lets you search for all rows that contain the column value "T_square" where "z" replaces the underscore as the wildcard. The key to remember here is that you are searching for the exact string, not a pattern match on several characters. So if you just search on "T_s" the search will fail.

The NOT BETWEEN lets you specify an inclusive range of values between one point and another. Use AND to separate the beginning and ending values.

IS NOT NULL lets you specify a search for nulls or for values that are not null, depending on the keywords used. An expression with a bitwise or arithmetic operator evaluates to NULL if any of the operands is NULL.

The CONTAINS keyword lets you search for columns containing character-based data for precise or "fuzzy" (which means less precise) matches to single words and phrases, the proximity of words within a certain distance of one another, and weighted matches. CONTAINS can only be used with SELECT statements.

The FREETEXT keyword provides a simple form of natural language query by searching columns containing character-based data for values that match the meaning rather than the exact words in the predicate. FREETEXT can only be used with SELECT statements.

The NOT IN keywords let you specify the search for an expression, based on the expression's inclusion in or exclusion from a list. The search expression can be a constant or a column name, and the list can be a set of constants or a subquery, which is the usual approach. The list of values must be enclosed in parentheses.

The *subquery* clause can be considered a restricted SELECT statement and is similar to the <query_expresssion> in the SELECT statement. You cannot use the ORDER BY clause, the COMPUTE clause, or the INTO keyword in these subqueries.

The ALL keyword is used with a comparison operator and a subquery. It will return TRUE for <predicate> if all values retrieved for the subquery satisfy the comparison operation, or FALSE if not all values satisfy the comparison or if the subquery returns no rows to the outer statement.

The SOME | ANY keywords are used with a comparison operator and a subquery. They will return TRUE for the predicate if any value retrieved for the subquery satisfies the comparison operation, or FALSE if no values in the subquery satisfy the comparison or if the subquery returns no rows to the outer statement. Otherwise, the expression is unknown.

EXISTS is used with a subquery to test for the existence of rows returned by the subquery.

WHERE

The WHERE keyword specifies to the SELECT a search condition to be used to filter the rows returned in the result set. It is also used, as described earlier, to specify the legacy and outmoded outer join as indicated by the following syntax as follows:

```
[ WHERE < search_condition > | < old_outer_join > ]
column_name { * = | = * } column_name
```

The < *search_condition* > placeholder refers to the search condition statement, which can be a simple equality check or can be a lot more complex, using a combination of one or more predicates and the logical operators AND, OR, and NOT.

NOTE *The search condition syntax also applies to the other DML statements, such as DELETE and UPDATE.*

The < *old_outer_join* > placeholder specifies an outer join using the legacy syntax and the WHERE clause. The *= operator specifies a left outer join, and the =* operator specifies a right outer join. It is possible to specify outer joins by using join operators in the FROM clause or by using the nonstandard *= and =* operators in the WHERE clause.

You can use both the old and new in your SELECT statement. The more modern syntax goes in the FROM clause, and the older syntax goes in the WHERE clause. The two methods, however, cannot both be used in the same statement.

GROUP BY

The GROUP BY takes the result set and chops it up into groups. Each group can thus have its own aggregate values, which is useful for ad hoc reporting, as you will soon see. The syntax of this clause is as follows:

```
[ GROUP BY [ ALL ] group_by_expression [ ,...n ]
[ WITH { CUBE | ROLLUP } ]
]
```

Let's go over the arguments and then look at some examples.

GROUP BY Arguments

The GROUP BY ALL directive tells SQL Server to generate all possible groups and result sets. It even returns groups that do not have any rows meeting the search condition that you specified in the WHERE clause. When ALL is specified, null values are returned for the summary columns of groups that do not meet the search condition.

The *group_by_expression* placeholder offers an expression that you can use to obtain a particular grouping. It can also be used as a grouping column in which the *group_by_expression* can be a column or a nonaggregate expression that references a column. However, T-SQL does not allow you to use a column alias defined in the select list to specify a grouping column.

NOTE   *Columns of type varchar(max), nvarchar(max), or varbinary(max) cannot be used in group_by_expression.*

When you have GROUP BY clauses that do not contain a CUBE or ROLLUP, the number of *group_by_expression* items is restricted to the GROUP BY column sizes, the aggregated columns, and the aggregate values involved in the query. This is an architecture limitation that originates from the storage limits on the intermediate worktables that hold the intermediate query results. In addition, you cannot use more than ten grouping expressions when specifying CUBE or ROLLUP, which now follow.

WITH CUBE

The WITH CUBE argument lets you direct SQL Server to introduce summary rows to the result set, in addition to rows provided by the GROUP BY clause. This clause essentially results in a data explosion that returns a multidimensional cube.

ROLLUP

The ROLLUP argument also specifies that in addition to rows provided by the GROUP BY clause, summary rows must be introduced into the result set. The groups, however, are summarized in a hierarchical order, from the lowest level in the group to the highest. The group hierarchy is determined by the order in which the grouping columns are specified. Changing the order of the grouping columns can affect the number of rows produced in the result set.

Distinct aggregates such as AVG(DISTINCT *column_name*), COUNT(DISTINCT *column_name*), and SUM(DISTINCT *column_name*) are not supported as part of CUBE or ROLLUP queries.

When GROUP BY is specified in a query, either each column in any nonaggregate expression in the select list should be included in the GROUP BY list, or the GROUP BY expression must match exactly the select list expression.

If aggregate functions are included in the select list, the GROUP BY calculates a summary value for each group. However, if the ORDER BY clause is not specified, groups returned using the GROUP BY clause are not in any particular order. You should thus make it a habit to always use the ORDER BY clause to specify a particular ordering of returned data.

NOTE *GROUP BY ALL is not supported in queries that access remote tables if there is also a WHERE clause in the query.*

The following is a simple GROUP BY query, which you can later expand with more advanced capabilities such as joins:

```
SELECT Item, Quantity, Category FROM Items
```

returns the following result set:

Item	Quantity	Category
Cabbage	3199	Veggie
Plums	15	Fruit
Squash	98	Veggie
Apes	3434	Animals
Peaches	23423	Fruit
Monkeys	342	Animals

But if you add the GROUP BY

```
GROUP BY Category, Item, Quantity
```

the result set is grouped as follows on Category:

Item	Quantity	Category
Apes	3434	Animals
Monkeys	342	Animals
Peaches	23423	Fruit
Plums	15	Fruit
Cabbage	3199	Veggie
Squash	98	Veggie

HAVING

The HAVING keyword specifies a search condition for a particular group or aggregate. HAVING is usually used with the GROUP BY clause to limit the rows returned by the query. When GROUP BY is not used, HAVING behaves like a WHERE clause, which is why I gave it its own section. The HAVING syntax is as follows:

```
[HAVING < search_condition >]
Arguments < search_condition >
```

The search condition here specifies the search condition for the group or the aggregate to meet. When HAVING is used with GROUP BY ALL, the HAVING clause overrides ALL.

NOTE *Columns of type varchar(max), nvarchar(max), or varbinary(max) cannot be used in a HAVING clause. Also, the HAVING clause in the SELECT statement does not affect the way the CUBE operator groups the result set and returns summary aggregate rows.*

Getting back to our simple example, if we now add a HAVING clause as follows:

```
SELECT Item, Quantity, Category FROM Items
  HAVING Category LIKE 'Animals'
```

the following result set is returned:

Item	Quantity	Category
Apes	3434	Animals
Monkeys	342	Animals

ORDER BY

You can use the ORDER BY clause to specify a sort order for a result set. Limitations are that you cannot use the ORDER BY clause in views, inline functions, derived tables, and subqueries, unless TOP is also specified. The ORDER BY syntax is as follows:

```
[ ORDER BY { order_by_expression [ ASC | DESC ] } [ ,...n] ]
```

The *order_by_expression* placeholder specifies the column on which to sort. The sort column can be specified as a name or column alias (which can be qualified by the table or view name); an expression; or a nonnegative integer representing the position of the name, alias, or expression in the select list. Multiple sort columns can be specified. The sequence of the sort columns in the ORDER BY clause defines the organization of the sorted result set.

The ORDER BY clause can include items not appearing in the select list. However, if SELECT DISTINCT is specified, or if the SELECT statement contains a UNION operator, the sort columns must appear in the select list. Furthermore, when the SELECT statement includes a UNION operator, the column names or column aliases must be those specified in the first select list.

NOTE *You cannot use columns of type varchar(max), nvarchar(max), or varbinary(max) in an ORDER BY clause.*

The ASC and DESC (ascending, descending) arguments are used as follows:

- **ASC**   The ASC argument directs the SELECT that the values in the specified column be sorted in ascending order, from lowest value to highest value.
- **DESC**   The DESC argument directs that the values in the specified column be sorted in descending order, from highest value to lowest value. NULL values are treated as the lowest possible values.

There is no limit to the number of items in the ORDER BY clause (...*n*). However, there is a limit of 8,060 bytes for the row size of intermediate worktables needed for sort operations. This limits the total size of columns specified in an ORDER BY clause.

In our short example, if we now add the ORDER BY as follows:

```
SELECT Item, Quantity, Category FROM Items
  HAVING Category LIKE 'Animals'
  ORDER BY Quantity
```

the following result set is returned ordered on the Quantity column with ASC as the default:

Item	Quantity	Category
Monkeys	342	Animals
Apes	3434	Animals

COMPUTE

The COMPUTE keyword directs SQL Server to generate totals that appear as additional summary columns at the end of result sets. When you use the COMPUTE with BY, the clause forces control-breaks and subtotals in the result set. You can also specify COMPUTE BY and COMPUTE in the same query. The syntax for the COMPUTE is as follows:

```
[COMPUTE
{{ AVG | COUNT | MAX | MIN | STDEV | STDEVP
|VAR | VARP | SUM }
( expression ) } [ ,...n ]
[ BY expression [ ,...n ] ]
]
```

The following list of COMPUTE arguments specifies the aggregation to be performed:

- **AVG**   Average of the values in the numeric expression
- **COUNT**   Number of selected rows
- **MAX**   Highest value in the expression
- **MIN**   Lowest value in the expression

- **STDEV**   Statistical standard deviation for all values in the expression
- **STDEVP**   Statistical standard deviation for the population for all values in the expression
- **SUM**   Total of the values in the numeric expression
- **VAR**   Statistical variance for all values in the expression
- **VARP**   Statistical variance for the population for all values in the expression

Rules to consider when using the COMPUTE arguments:

- You cannot use the DISTINCT keyword with row aggregate functions when they are specified with the COMPUTE clause.

- When adding or averaging integer data, SQL Server will treat the result as an int value. This behavior persists, even if the data type of the column was set to smallint or tinyint. For more information about the return types of added or average data, see the BOL references to SUM and AVG.

- When you use a SELECT statement that includes a COMPUTE clause, the order of columns in the select list overrides the order of the aggregate functions in the COMPUTE clause. This order requirement is important for ODBC and DB-Library application programmers to remember, so that aggregate function results are placed in the correct place.

- The COMPUTE cannot be used in a SELECT INTO statement. COMPUTE statements generate tables, and their summary results do not get stored in the database. If you do use the COMPUTE in the SELECT INTO, SQL SERVER will ignore the COMPUTE results and they will not be installed in the new table.

- The COMPUTE clause cannot be used in a SELECT statement that is part of a DECLARE CURSOR statement.

The *expression* placeholder specifies a variable, such as the name of a column, on which the calculation is performed. The expression must appear in the select list and must be specified exactly the same as one of the expressions in the select list. As you can see from the syntax, you place the expression after the COMPUTE argument. A column alias specified in the select list obviously cannot be used within the COMPUTE expression.

Using BY

The BY expression is used to generate control-breaks and subtotals in the result set. Listing multiple expressions after BY breaks a group into subgroups and applies the aggregate function at each level of grouping. If you use the keywords COMPUTE BY, you must also use an ORDER BY clause. The expressions must be identical to or a subset of those listed after ORDER BY, and they must be in the same sequence. For example, if the ORDER BY clause is

```
ORDER BY s, l, t
```

then the COMPUTE clause can be any (or all) of these:

```
COMPUTE BY s, l, t
COMPUTE BY s, l
COMPUTE BY s
```

NOTE *The aforementioned aggregation and computer facilities of the SELECT statement are useful for ad hoc reporting and the like. If you need to present substantial statistical analysis or create extensive or repetitive financial results, these queries can be a drain on the resources of a standard OLTP database. Rather, take your reporting to the logical level and report against the data warehouse using OLAP facilities.*

FOR

The FOR clause is used to specify either the BROWSE or the unrelated XML option. The FOR syntax is as follows:

```
[ FOR { BROWSE | XML { RAW | AUTO | EXPLICIT }
[ , XMLDATA ]
[ , ELEMENTS ]
[ , BINARY BASE64 ]
}
]
```

See Chapter 17 for the complete lowdown on the XML support in SQL Server 2005.

BROWSE

The BROWSE argument specifies that updates are possible while viewing data in a DB-Library browse-mode cursor. A table can be browsed in an application if the table includes a time-stamped column (defined with the timestamp data type), the table has a unique index, and the FOR BROWSE option is at the end of the SELECT statement(s) sent to SQL Server. You also cannot use the FOR BROWSE option in SELECT statements that are joined by the UNION operator.

FOR XML

FOR XML specifies that the results of a query are to be returned as an XML document. One of these XML modes must be specified: RAW, AUTO, EXPLICIT. XML support in SQL Server 2005 is discussed in depth in Chapter 17.

RAW

The RAW mode takes the query result and transforms each row in the result set into an XML element with a generic identifier <row /> as the element tag (see Chapter 17).

AUTO

The AUTO mode returns query results in a simple, nested XML tree. Each table in the FROM clause for which at least one column is listed in the SELECT clause is represented as an XML element. The columns listed in the SELECT clause are mapped to the appropriate element attributes.

EXPLICIT

The EXPLICIT mode specifies that the shape of the resulting XML tree is defined explicitly. Using this mode, queries must be written in a particular way so that additional information about the desired nesting is specified explicitly.

XML Parameters

The following XML parameters specify the type of data returned in the XML result set:

- **XMLDATA**   A parameter that returns the schema but does not add the root element to the result. If XMLDATA is specified, it is appended to the document (see Chapter 17).

- **ELEMENTS**   Specifies that the columns are returned as subelements. Otherwise, they are mapped to XML attributes.

- **BINARY BASE64**   Specifies that the query returns the binary data in binary base 64–encoded format. In retrieving binary data using RAW and EXPLICIT mode, this option must be specified. This is the default in AUTO mode.

Joins

As I discussed in the opening to this chapter, it is rare, especially with SQL Server, to encase all of your columns in one table. Such a scenario certainly means denormalized data and poor performance; you would rarely escape serious data redundancy and duplication. When you have more than one table and you need to combine data from the collection into a result set, this is known as a *join*. For some reason, joins strike fear into the hearts of new converts to client/server databases and SQL Server. But we can throw this animal into the same fish stew that boiled down SELECT.

The definition of a *join* is as follows: "A join is the result set that is the product of two or more tables." A join can be a simple referencing of two or more tables as illustrated, using a copy of the Northwind database (*Orders* cut to 20 rows), in the following statement:

```
SELECT Customers.CompanyName AS 'Customer', Orders.OrderID AS 'Order Numbers'
FROM Customers, Orders WHERE Customers.CustomerID = Orders.CustomerID
```

The result set is as follows:

Customer	Order Numbers
Berglunds snabbköp	10278
Berglunds snabbköp	10280
Chop-suey Chinese	10254
Frankenversand	10267
Frankenversand	10791
Gourmet Lanchonetes	10790
GROSELLA-Restaurante	10268
Hanari Carnes	10250
Hanari Carnes	10253
Lehmanns Marktstand	10279

LILA-Supermercado	10283
Richter Supermarkt	10255
Romero y tomillo	10281
Romero y tomillo	10282
Suprêmes délices	10252
Toms Spezialitäten	10249
Victuailles en stock	10251
Vins et alcools Chevalier	10248
Wellington Importadora	10256
Wolski Zajazd	10792

The statement that produced the preceding result set is a legacy inner join statement, which is still supported in SQL Server 2005 (and I don't see "Sequelists" parting with it for some time). The ANSI/ISO SQL-92 version supported in SQL Server 2005 looks like this:

```
SELECT Customers.CompanyName AS 'Customer', Orders.OrderID AS 'Order Numbers'
FROM Customers JOIN Orders ON (Customers.CustomerID = Orders.CustomerID)
```

The result set is identical, but notice the addition of the JOIN and ON keywords and the absence of the WHERE keyword used in the legacy code. Incidentally, if you look at the query plans for both queries, you will see that they are identical in every way. The old method was more limiting because it trapped the "join" in a WHERE clause and produced ambiguities in complex operations.

The JOIN keyword specifies that the tables to the left and right of it should be joined. Additional tables can then be joined to the result set to produce an additional result set. The ON < search_condition > specifies the search condition on which the join is based. The condition can specify any predicate, although columns and comparison operators are often used as demonstrated earlier.

However, when the condition specifies columns, the columns do not have to have the same name or same data type. If the data types are not identical, they must be either compatible or types that SQL Server 2005 can implicitly convert. If the data types cannot be implicitly converted, the condition must explicitly convert the data type using the CAST or CONVERT functions.

Let's look at the syntax that uses joins as a table source in the SELECT:

```
| joined_table = < table_source > < join_type > < table_source > ON < search_condition >
| < table_source > CROSS JOIN < table_source >
| < joined_table >
```

Types of Joins

In the preceding syntax, the <*join_type*> placeholder (SQL-92 compliant) can represent a simple join as described earlier or a more complex left, right, or full inner or outer join. This might become more clear to you if you study the table source syntax for joins as follows:

```
[ INNER | { { LEFT | RIGHT | FULL } [ OUTER ] } ]
[ < join_hint > ]
```

The *INNER* join is the default join type if the type is NOT specified in your query. The keyword INNER specifies to the query that all rows that have matching values specified in the search condition *(Customers.CustomerID = Orders.CustomerID)* are returned. All unmatched rows from both tables are ignored (which was our first example where the *orders* table contained only 20 rows).

The *LEFT OUTER* join specifies to the query that all rows from the table to the left of the join type declaration that do not meet the specified condition are included in the result set in addition to all rows returned by the inner join. Output columns from the left table are set to NULL. The LEFT [OUTER] of our first INNER example now looks like this after I abridged it from 95 to 20 rows:

```
SELECT Customers.CompanyName AS 'Customer', Orders.OrderID AS 'Order Numbers'
FROM Customers LEFT OUTER JOIN Orders ON (Customers.CustomerID = Orders.CustomerID)
```

Customers	Order Numbers
Alfreds Futterkiste	NULL
Ana Trujillo Emparedados y helados	NULL
Antonio Moreno Taquería	NULL
Around the Horn	NULL
Berglunds snabbköp	10278
Berglunds snabbköp	10280
Blauer See Delikatessen	NULL
Blondesddsl père et fils	NULL
Bólido Comidas preparadas	NULL
Bon app'	NULL
Bottom-Dollar Markets	NULL
B's Beverages	NULL
Cactus Comidas para llevar	NULL
Centro comercial Moctezuma	NULL
Chop-suey Chinese	10254
Comércio Mineiro	NULL
Consolidated Holdings	NULL
Drachenblut Delikatessen	NULL
Du monde entire	NULL
Eastern Connection	NULL

If we now tag an ORDER BY on the end of the query, we can see the 20 records returned in the default INNER join shown earlier. The following table has been abridged from 95 records for paper conservation:

```
SELECT Customers.CompanyName AS 'Customer',
  Orders.OrderID AS 'Order Numbers'
```

```
 FROM Customers LEFT OUTER JOIN Orders ON (Customers.CustomerID = Orders
.CustomerID) ORDER BY 2 DESC
```

Customers	Order Numbers
Wolski Zajazd	10792
Frankenversand	10791
Gourmet Lanchonetes	10790
LILA-Supermercado	10283
Romero y tomillo	10282
Romero y tomillo	10281
Berglunds snabbköp	10280
Lehmanns Marktstand	10279
Berglunds snabbköp	10278
GROSELLA-Restaurante	10268
Frankenversand	10267
Wellington Importadora	10256
Richter Supermarkt	10255
Chop-suey Chinese	10254
Hanari Carnes	10253
Suprêmes délices	10252
Victuailles en stock	10251
Hanari Carnes	10250
Toms Spezialitäten	10249
Vins et alcools Chevalier	10248
Die Wandernde Kuh	NULL
Wartian Herkku	NULL
White Clover Markets	NULL
Wilman Kala	NULL
Tortuga Restaurante	NULL

The *RIGHT OUTER* join specifies to the query that all rows from the table to the right of the join type declaration that do not meet the specified condition are included in the result set in addition to all rows returned by the inner join. Output columns from the right table are set to NULL. The RIGHT OUTER looks like this:

```
SELECT Customers.CompanyName AS 'Customer', Orders.OrderID AS 'Order
Numbers' FROM Customers RIGHT OUTER JOIN Orders ON (Customers.CustomerID
= Orders.CustomerID)
```

It returns the following result set, where all rows in the right table (consisting of 20 rows) were returned (in my example all 20 records met the search condition).

Customers	Order Numbers
Vins et alcools Chevalier	10248
Toms Spezialitäten	10249
Hanari Carnes	10250
Victuailles en stock	10251
Suprêmes délices	10252
Hanari Carnes	10253
Chop-suey Chinese	10254
Richter Supermarkt	10255
Wellington Importadora	10256
Frankenversand	10267
GROSELLA-Restaurante	10268
Berglunds snabbköp	10278
Lehmanns Marktstand	10279
Berglunds snabbköp	10280
Romero y tomillo	10281
Romero y tomillo	10282
LILA-Supermercado	10283
Gourmet Lanchonetes	10790
Frankenversand	10791
Wolski Zajazd	10792

NOTE *Your results may differ because I cut the number of rows from my Northwind tables for illustration.*

The *FULL OUTER* join specifies to the query that, if a row from either the left or right table does not match the selection criteria, the row be included in the result set, and any output columns that correspond to the other table be set to NULL. This is in addition to all rows usually returned by the inner join. The statement for the FULL OUTER JOIN looks like this:

```
SELECT Customers.CompanyName AS 'Customer',
  Orders.OrderID AS 'Order Numbers'
  FROM Customers FULL OUTER JOIN Orders ON (Customers.CustomerID = Orders.CustomerID)
```

I am sure by now you can figure out what the result set looks like.

The *CROSS JOIN* specifies to the query to return the cross-product (the Cartesian product) of two tables. This join returns the same rows as if the tables to be joined were simply listed in the FROM clause and no WHERE clause was specified. For example, both of the following queries return a result set that is a cross-join of all the rows in *Customers* and *Orders*:

```
SELECT ColA, ColB FROM Customers, Orders
SELECT ColA, ColB FROM Customers CROSS JOIN Orders
```

As you can tell, joining tables can be very useful for producing test data.

Join Hint

In the preceding join syntax, the placeholder < *join_hint* > specifies a join hint or execution algorithm to be followed by SQL Server. If the join hint is specified, INNER, LEFT, RIGHT, or FULL must also be explicitly specified.

Union

The UNION operator is much like a marriage between two people, even two companies: The union can be consummated, but that does not mean the parties are compatible. So it is with the UNION operator that can be used to combine the results of two or more queries into a single result set. The coupling results in the containment in the final result set of all the rows belonging to all the parties to the union.

While the UNION appears easy enough, it has a few sneaky rules that could scuttle the marriage:

- The number and the order of the columns in all source result sets must be identical.
- The data types in each corresponding column must be compatible. If they are different, it must be possible for SQL Server to implicitly convert them, and if not, then you will need to convert them using the CAST() or CONVERT() function before you can attempt the UNION. If you don't, SQL Server will error out.
- If you combine columns that are assignment compatible, but of different types and thus implicitly converted by SQL Server, the resulting column is the data type of the column that was higher in the order of precedence.
- If you combine columns of fixed-length char, then the result of the UNION will produce a column that will be the length of the longer of the original columns.
- If you combine columns of fixed-length binary, the result of the UNION will produce a column that will be the length of the longer of the original columns.
- If you combine columns of variable-length char (varchar), then the result of the UNION will produce a column that will be the variable length of the longest character string of the original columns.
- If you combine columns of variable-length binary (varbinary), the result of the UNION will produce a column that will be the variable length of the longest binary string of the original columns.

PART IV

- If you combine columns of different yet convertible data types, the result of the UNION will produce a column data type equal to the maximum precision of the two columns. In other words, if the source column of table *A* is of type integer and the source column of table *B* is of type float, then the data type of the UNION result will be float because float is more precise than integer.

- If the source columns specify NOT NULL, then the result of the UNION will also be NOT NULL.

- Unless explicitly provided, column names in the final result set are inherited from the first query.

The syntax for the UNION is as follows:

```
{ < query specification > | ( < query expression > ) }
UNION [ ALL ]
< query specification | ( < query expression > )
[ UNION [ ALL ] < query specification | ( < query expression > )
[ ...n ] ]
```

UNION Arguments

According to Microsoft's documentation, the placeholder *< query_specification >* | (*< query_expression >*) represents the query specification or query expression that returns the data to be combined with the data from another query specification or query expression. As mentioned earlier, the definitions of the columns that are part of a UNION do not have to be identical, but they must be compatible through implicit conversion.

The UNION argument is the keyword that specifies that multiple result sets are to be combined and returned as a single result set.

The ALL used as in UNION ALL incorporates all rows into the results, including duplicates. If it is not specified, duplicate rows are removed. If you can deal with duplicates and your result set is large, you may think about foregoing ALL because it will force SQL Server to sort and evaluate the data in order to remove the duplicates. The UNION ALL thus costs a lot more than just UNION, as demonstrated in the two query plans.

Views, and Then Some

We have discussed views in several places in this book, starting back in Chapter 2, and it is fitting to discuss them further here on the heels of the SELECT statement and other useful SQL facilities like UNIONs and JOINs. But let's recap before we look at some of the advanced attributes of view technology in SQL Server 2005. A *view* is a way of looking at an underlying table through a filter. Over the years many database books, SQL Server Books Online included, have referred to a view as a virtual table. But this is simplistic, because a view is really a specialized query that computes to create a filter over the table, thereby hiding tables, schema, and thus data not specified in the query, from direct access. A view is like a pair of sunglasses. You are not seeing a copy of the world through the lenses; you are seeing the same world but with the ultraviolet and gamma rays filtered out.

A view looks like a table, feels like a table, and works like a table with a few exceptions coming up for discussion. You build a view with a SELECT query that is processed against the underlying table. The following CREATE VIEW statement creates a simple view of the *Items* tables, resulting in the *Items2* table:

```
CREATE VIEW Items2
  AS
   Select Item, Category FROM Items
```

The view Items2 is created in the database and can now be worked just like a table. So the statement

```
SELECT * From Items2
```

returns the following view:

Item	Category
Cabbage	Veggie
Plums	Fruit
Squash	Veggie
Apes	Animals
Peaches	Fruit
Monkeys	Animals

The data for this table is still derived from the *Items* table. But the view Items2 filters out the *Quantity* column.

You can also think of a view as a stored query; in fact, this is probably the best explanation, and one that would be appreciated by Access converts, who no doubt still remember how to create "stored queries," built using SQL and stored in an Access database.

Views have been in use for many years. Their primary function has been to hide tables and provide a measure of security and distance from the underlying tables. You can use views to do the work of complex queries, even to prepare the data for stored procedures, by creating joins, UNION queries, select queries, and so on. Views can also contain aggregations and other complex functionality that returns precise result sets that can then be further queried against.

They continue to do all these things and more. But of late they have begun to play a much more auspicious role in SQL Server, as a partitioning facility. While it was possible to partition views across databases in a single instance and across multiple servers, partitioned views were not updatable prior to SQL Server 2000, so they had limited use.

Indexed Views

Indexed views allow you to store the actual view data along with the view definition in the database (as opposed to just the SELECT query). Indexed views are useful for providing faster access to view data.

We discussed indexed views, schema binding, and so on earlier, so let's go directly to creating the index on a view. For a change, let's create the view in Management Studio:

1. Drill down to the database, to the Views node into which you need to install the indexed view. Right-click New and select New View. The New View panel loads, as illustrated in Figure 16-2

2. Create the view using the tools in Management Studio, as shown, or create it using your own T-SQL code. Check the syntax and create the view after all checks out.

3. To create an index, first create the view and then expand that view in Management Studio. Select the Indexes folder. At the Indexes folder you can right-click and select New Index. The New Index dialog box, illustrated in Figure 16-3, loads. Create the index and click Close. You are finished.

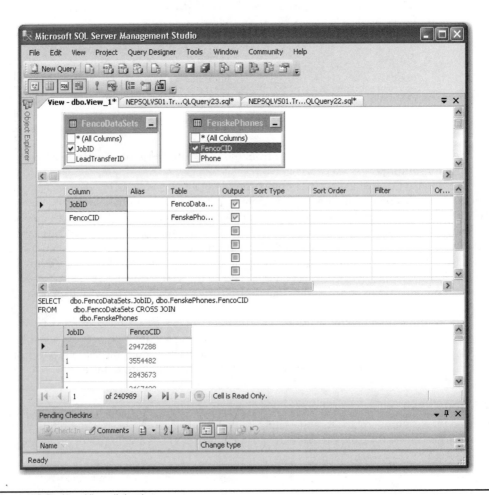

Figure 16-2   New View dialog box

FIGURE 16-3   The New Index dialog box

4. You can also create the index in code. The CREATE VIEW code is as follows:

```
CREATE VIEW dbo.NOOVIEW
WITH SCHEMABINDING
AS
    SELECT OrderItem, CanShip
    FROM dbo.Orders
```

Notice that the view is created WITH SCHEMABINDING, which will prevent the source table from being altered (at the schema level). To alter the underlying table (such as by adding a column), you would first have to destroy the view and index.

Updatable Partitioned Views

Updatable partitioned views can be used to partition data across multiple databases. They can also be used to partition data across databases on multiple servers, thus providing horizontal scalability of the highest magnitude. Partitioning tables, linking servers in federations, and building distributed partitioned views are really very easy as long as you stick to the rules and follow logic. Here's a checklist with a couple of tips:

- Build your federation in a single domain, or across transitive trusts. Intradomain federations are much more complex to set up from a security standpoint.

- Use Windows Authentication to keep the security provisioning simple. If you have a complex security setup, you might have to go down to nontrusted access using a remote login.

- Optimize the member tables so that each federation member is working as well as it can. Also balance the resources (it does not make sense to partition the tables and put one part on a small server and the other part on a large server).

- Make sure you can properly access all the linked servers from Management Studio before you start building the partitions.

- Use unique identifiers and fully qualified table names to build the views.

When views are partitioned across databases in the same instance, they are known as *local partitioned views*. When they are partitioned across multiple server instances, they are called *federations*.

The route to federated partitioned views (after linking the servers) is to first divide a table into a number of smaller tables. These so-called member tables, which contain a portion of the rows from the main table, are then installed on multiple servers—each member table in a new host database on a member of the federation. The configuration looks like this for the example I am going to show here:

- Old configuration: *Table1* = 4,000,000 rows on Server1

- New configuration: *Table1a* on Server1 = first two million rows from *Table1*; *Table1b* on Server2 = second two million rows from *Table1*

Let's say we want to partition a view across two servers using a large order table that is being constantly updated from the Internet. One server is struggling and, as discussed in Chapter 13, has reached its scale-up limit. The business is also at a point where it cannot afford the downtime to further boost the initial cluster-pair. So the answer is to add another server cluster while the primary cluster is still getting hits and then, for a small amount of downtime, partition that data across the two servers, thereby reducing the load on the primary cluster-pair. The order of business is as follows:

1. **Link the Servers** Before we can create the partitioned view over the servers, we first have to link them. To link the servers, we have to call the system stored procedure sp_addlinkedserver to add the servers to each other's respective catalogs. You can also use Management Studio, but there is more clutter in the dialog boxes to distract you. If you are setting up inside a single domain, you only need a few parameters. The details go into the sysservers table. Important: The linking is bidirectional, or two-way. Each server must configure linked servers pointing to the remote server. The code looks like this:

```
EXEC sp_addlinkedserver
     @server='FED_1',
     @srvproduct='',
     @provider='SQLOLEDB',
     @datasrc='MCDC10\MCDCSQL01'
GO
--FED_2 is the local node (default instance)
EXEC sp_addlinkedserver
     @server='FED_2',
     @srvproduct='',
     @provider='SQLOLEDB',
     @datasrc='MCSQL00'
GO
```

2. **Create member tables** The first step, after making a full backup, is to split the primary 4,000,000-row table into two smaller tables, one containing a range of rows, say 1 through 2,000,000, and the other containing the range of rows 2,000,001 through 4,000,000. There are number of ways you can do this, such as copying the database to the other server, restoring to the new server, or using SQL Server Integration Services (SSIS). The primary node is called MCSQL00, while the secondary is called MCSQL01.

3. **Create the Partitioned View** Before this step can be achieved, you must first link the servers and place the member tables on each respective member of the new federation. A primary key must be placed in each member table so that the view can be updated.

Create the Partitioned View

A view is now created that combines the two tables and makes them look like one again to the hungry Web browsers out on the shopping-mad Internet. Before the views can be created, however, there are several rules you have to follow, and these can be a bit tricky. See Books Online for the list of rules; you'll find them by searching for the topic "Creating a Partitioned View."

The T-SQL code to create the partitioned view is as follows:

```
--the view on FED_1
CREATE VIEW OrdersP
AS
  SELECT * FROM Orders1_2M
    UNION ALL
    SELECT * FROM FED_2.Customers.dbo.Orders2_4M
```

and for FED_2:

```
--the view on FED_2
CREATE VIEW OrdersP
AS
  SELECT * FROM Orders2_4M
    UNION ALL
    SELECT * FROM FED_1.Customers.dbo.Orders1_2M
```

Once the view OrdersP has been created, clients can continue to access the view without needing to know which server it resides on. In other words, the query

```
UPDATE OrdersP SET CanShip = '10' WHERE OrderItem = '246'
```

updates the table on the primary node. On the other hand, the query

```
UPDATE OrdersP SET CanShip = '53' WHERE OrderItem = '3469872'
```

updates the table on the secondary node, unbeknownst to the client. The distributed, updatable, partitioned view is now able to balance hits against the data across two server clusters. To check if the update succeeded, we can just query the partitioned view as follows:

```
SELECT OrderItem, CanShip FROM OrdersP WHERE OrderItem = '3469872'
```

and the result set will be:

OrderItem	CanShip
3469872	53

TIP *Remember to provide a primary key on all source tables to the view, so that the view can be updated.*

Part of the effort to partition the data is discussed in terms of linking servers, in Chapter 12, with respect to data transformation, which discusses scale-out concepts in more depth. Now to a new friend . . . .

The Common Table Expression

Result sets on the tabulated data stream, even XML streams, are not referenceable within a T-SQL statement, direct or on the back end in a stored procedure or a trigger. As soon as a SELECT pulls the rows and columns, the data travels to the client, where it can be accessed, but you no longer have access to the data at the server. You can, as shown earlier, use temporary and derived tables and cursors to access "in-process" result sets, but these constructs are very heavy and not simple to construct and operate for small queries that return only a small number of rows.

The common table expression (CTE), introduced in SQL Server 2005, is basically a temporary result set that you create and access within the execution context of a SELECT, INSERT, UPDATE, or DELETE statement. You can also create and use it as part of the CREATE VIEW statement and use it in cases you would typically use a view. The CTE can also be created in user-defined code, such as functions, stored procedures, or triggers. The CTE lasts only for the duration of a query and is also destroyed quickly and automatically by SQL Server. The main difference between a CTE and temporary or derived tables is that a CTE can reference itself recursively. You can also reference it multiple times in the same query.

CTEs are very flexible. You can create a CTE for one part of a statement and then use the CTEs as "components" to put together complex queries, all of which can be the means of generating a final complex result set that is returned to the client. The example here shows the use of multiple CTEs to generate a result set that was impossible to achieve in a simple query on a collection of underlying tables that were very badly designed to begin with.

Structure of a CTE

A CTE is created with syntax that is similar to Visual Basic. First you name the CTE using a WITH statement. Then you add an optional column list, and a query defining the result set within the CTE. Once you define the CTE, you can access it as you would any table or view in a SELECT, INSERT, UPDATE, or DELETE statement.

Here is the basic syntax structure for the CTE:

```
WITH expression_name [ ( column_name [,...n] ) ]
  AS
( CTE_query_definition );
```

The list of column names is optional only if distinct names for all resulting columns are supplied in the query definition.

The statement to run the CTE is

```
SELECT *
FROM cte_name
```

The following example shows the components of the CTE structure: expression name, column list, and query. The CTE expression Sales_CTE has three columns (*SalesPersonID*, *NumberOfOrders*, and *MaxDate*) and is defined as the total number of sales orders and the most recent sales order date in the *SalesOrderHeader* table for each salesperson. When the statement is executed, the CTE is referenced two times: one time to return the selected columns for the salesperson, and again to retrieve similar details for the salesperson's manager. The data for both the salesperson and the manager are returned in a single row.

```
USE MODELIZE
WITH Sales_CTE (SalesPersonID, NumberOfOrders, MaxDate)
  AS
  (
    SELECT SalesPersonID, COUNT(*), MAX(OrderDate)
    FROM Sales.SalesOrderHeader
    GROUP BY SalesPersonID
);


SELECT E.EmployeeID, OS.NumberOfOrders, OS.MaxDate, E.ManagerID,
OM.NumberOfOrders, OM.MaxDate FROM HumanResources.Employee AS E


    JOIN Sales_CTE AS OS ON E.EmployeeID = OS.SalesPersonID
    LEFT OUTER JOIN Sales_CTE AS OM
    ON E.ManagerID = OM.SalesPersonID
ORDER BY E.EmployeeID
GO
```

The following code shows multiple CTEs used in a single complex query for use in a sales related report on a database so horrendously designed that intelligent query is extremely difficult:

```
Use MODELIZE
go
declare @sDate datetime
declare @eDate datetime
set @sDate = '06/01/06'
set @eDate = '06/13/06';

with CTE(SalesID) as
(
    select con1.salesid
    from mcontracts_1 as con1
    where con1.crdate between CONVERT(DATETIME, @sDate, 102) AND CONVERT(DATETIME,
    eDate + '23:59:59', 102)
    group by con1.salesid
),


CTE1(SalesID, [PIF W/T]) as
(
    select con1.salesid, count(*)
    from mcontracts_1 as con1 left outer join mtransd_1 as tran1 on con1.connum =
    tran1.actref where con1.crdate between CONVERT(DATETIME, @sDate, 102) AND
    CONVERT(DATETIME, @eDate + '23:59:59', 102) and
    tran1.pifflag = 1 and tran1.pmtdpflag = 1 and con1.travflag = 1 and
    tran1.trvflag = 1
    group by con1.salesid
),
CTE2(SalesID, [$499 W/T]) as
(
    select con1.salesid, count(*)
    from mcontracts_1 as con1
    where con1.crdate between CONVERT(DATETIME, @sDate, 102) AND CONVERT(DATETIME,
    eDate + '23:59:59', 102) and
    con1.pifflag = 0 and con1.travflag = 1 and con1.odownp >= '499'
    group by con1.salesid
),


CTE3(SalesID, [$299 W/T]) as
(
    select con1.salesid, count(*)
    from mcontracts_1 as con1
    where con1.crdate between CONVERT(DATETIME, @sDate, 102) AND
CONVERT(DATETIME,
    @eDate + '23:59:59', 102) and con1.pifflag = 0 and con1.travflag = 1 and
    con1.odownp >= '299' and con1.odownp < '499'
    group by con1.salesid
),


CTE4(SalesID, [PIF]) as
(
```

```
    select con1.salesid, count(*)
    from mcontracts_1 as con1 left outer join mtransd_1 as tran1 on con1.connum =
    tran1.actref
    where con1.crdate between CONVERT(DATETIME, @sDate, 102) AND CONVERT(DATETIME,
    eDate + '23:59:59', 102) and
    tran1.pifflag = 1 and tran1.pmtdpflag = 1 and con1.travflag = 0
    group by con1.salesid
),


CTE5(SalesID, [$499]) as
(
    select con1.salesid, count(*)
    from mcontracts_1 as con1
    where con1.crdate between CONVERT(DATETIME, @sDate, 102) AND CONVERT(DATETIME,
    eDate + '23:59:59', 102) and
    con1.pifflag = 0 and con1.travflag = 0 and con1.odownp >= '499'
    group by con1.salesid
),


CTE6(SalesID, [$299]) as
(
    select con1.salesid, count(*)
    from mcontracts_1 as con1
    where con1.crdate between CONVERT(DATETIME, @sDate, 102) AND CONVERT(DATETIME,
    @eDate + '23:59:59', 102) and con1.pifflag = 0 and con1.travflag = 0 and
    con1.odownp >= '299' and on1.odownp < '499'
    group by con1.salesid
)
--NOW Query it


SELECT CTE.SalesID, sm.smfirstnam + ' ' + sm.smlastnam, isnull(CTE1.[PIF W/T],0)
    AS [PIF W/T], isnull(CTE2.[$499 W/T],0)
    AS [$499 W/T], isnull(CTE3.[$299 W/T],0)
    AS [$299 W/T], isnull(CTE4.[PIF],0)
    AS [PIF], isnull(CTE5.[$499],0)
    AS [$499], isnull(CTE6.[$299],0)
    AS [$299], isnull(CTE1.[PIF W/T],0)
      + isnull(CTE2.[$499 W/T],0)
      + isnull(CTE3.[$299 W/T],0)
      + isnull(CTE4.[PIF],0)
      + isnull(CTE5.[$499],0)
      + isnull(CTE6.[$299],0)
AS Total from CTE full outer join CTE1 on CTE.SalesID = CTE1.SalesID full
    outer join CTE2 on CTE.SalesID = CTE2.SalesID full outer join CTE3 on
    CTE.SalesID = CTE3.SalesID full outer join CTE4 on CTE.SalesID = CTE4.SalesID
    full outer join CTE5 on CTE.SalesID = CTE5.SalesID full outer join CTE6 on
    CTE.SalesID = CTE6.SalesID left outer join msmandb as sm on CTE.SalesID =
    sm.salesid
ORDER BY CTE.SalesID, sm.smfirstnam + ' ' + sm.smlastnam
```

While the above code demonstrates what is possible with the CTE, it would be better
that the database this code was used against be redesigned from the ground up.

In Review

This chapter provides an in-depth discussion of the mainstay of the SQL language, SELECT, and its Transact-SQL "additives." We looked at how SELECT queries can be used to join rows from more than one table using join constructions and view definitions.

The new support for indexed views was also discussed, as was Microsoft's scale-out strategy for distributed partitioned views, which are built across linked servers that are combined to provide a load-balanced, single, federated access to data.

While this chapter concentrates primarily on query (returning result sets), the next chapter looks at the data manipulation language (DML).

Working with Transactional Data

As powerful as SQL Server 2005 is, most applications work just fine with its default values, and often there is no need to override or assume control of its innermost data-processing functionality. But there are also many times that applications are required to have specialized and critical control over sophisticated, yet still standards-compliant, RDBMS features: locking, transactions, and so on.

No doubt many of you will require such access to functionality and control from the get-go, especially if you are supporting applications and solutions that are not run-of-the-mill. While e-commerce applications, .NET applications, transaction processing, and other distributed solutions are no longer exceptional situations (thanks to the Internet), they still represent areas in database programming that are fairly new-age stuff, especially for desktop or PC solution developers who have finally decided that they need to be liberated. This chapter uncovers what you need to know to tame SQL Server's innermost data processing services.

We will also use this chapter to talk about cursors, functions, and a number of advanced programming concepts.

Locking

SQL Server, like all DBMSs, supports locking and implicitly and automatically manages it for you for the most part. You can create applications that work with SQL Server and never have to worry about locking data. But, in many respects, that's like driving a motor car and thinking you don't need to know what goes on in the engine—until you break down in the middle of Alligator Alley without a fan belt or a fuel line and Skeeter and his tow truck are 100 miles away.

Why Do We Need Locking

SQL Server 2005 is a multiuser database management system. Today you can have one person accessing data, and tomorrow you can have one million people all accessing the data concurrently. Some of those people may only need to read the data, and if they are allowed to, then they can all share the data or the document. But what if more than one person has a contribution to make; what if more than one person needs to modify the record? What if one user decides to modify a record you are working with and another comes along with information that requires the record to be deleted? Now you have a problem akin to two buyers fighting over an item at a garage sale, each pulling on the item until it breaks in half. When more than one person accesses a record for modification, the record or row may break—in database lingo, the data can no longer be guaranteed to be reliable. Data integrity is violated, and the data is no longer trustworthy.

I love that old saying that "there is nothing more constant than change." Change is happening all the time. But change often needs to be managed, or the transition from one state to the next may become corrupt and the outcome of the change sequence compromised. In high-end multiuser systems the concurrency problem is highly exacerbated.

My first encounter with locking in computer systems takes me back 20 years to when I was a junior reporter working for a daily newspaper. We had this huge computer system called the Atex system, and I would type my news stories into it. Once the article was finished, I would enter the send command and off it would go to the news desk. After that, I no longer had write access to the news story. I could read the story, and every time I accessed it I would see that it was being edited or updated and so on. If I tried to change something, the system would tell me that I no longer had write access to the file because it was being updated by the copy editor. The only way I could get write access was to be part of the copy editor group.

One day I managed to hack into the system (I made a friend in the computer room) and reprogrammed my access (so started my sojourn into computer systems and software development). I was then able to get write permission to the file in the copyediting stage, even before the chief copy editor had finished with the file. So I would go in and change my byline from "By Daily Mail Reporter" to "By Jeffrey Shapiro." When the chief copy editor found out, he had me "sentenced" to spend six months as a junior subeditor, and my shift started at midnight.

Today you can experience the same thing in your average word processor. It is possible to lock the document so that someone else can read it but not update it. And you can even control the access (read or write) to the file.

In SQL Server databases you cannot afford to be working with data that suddenly becomes updated under your nose. If you receive a message like "the record you are reading no longer exists in the database," then you know that the record was not locked and someone deleted it (or a serious lock or access violation has occurred). The following list explores four specific problems that occur in weak locking situations:

- **Lost update**   The lost update occurs when two or more users open a record or document at the same time. One updates the record and moves on. But a second or even a third user updates the record before the original user has finished with it. When the first user finally updates the record, the update made before lost. Getting back to my copyediting experience: I would change my byline before the copy editor was finished, only to find later that he overwrote my update with the copy still sitting in his terminal's session and my change was lost.

- **Uncommitted dependency**   The uncommitted dependency occurs when you allow a record to be read or accessed while another user is still working with it. In database jargon, we say that the user or session is able to obtain a *dirty read* on the data. This means that the later session can read the data and make some decision concerning it. To speed up data processing in certain situations, it might make sense to allow a dirty read. For example, when building computer telephony systems, a dirty read was a necessity on certain records because the overhead of locking was intolerable. For example, if the user was currently setting up his or her telephone extension and locked the record, it would have been unacceptable for an inbound caller to have to wait on the phone until the user was done.

In that situation, the dirty read was acceptable, but it would not be on a financial analysis system in which a session had critical information required to be updated to a record. A lock would be required to prevent the dirty read so that no new sessions could make decisions on the data until the update was complete. If you were about to issue an urgent sell order, you would not want other sessions to keep buying the shares in the time it takes to click the Commit button that updates the record.

- **Nonrepeatable read**   The nonrepeatable read is a situation a session finds itself in when it performs multiple reads on data for a specific purpose; only each time it reads the data before its processing is finished, the original variables it depends on for its analysis have changed. This is also known as an *inconsistent analysis problem*. In data centers, often reports and processing can be so complex that the analysis or processing takes hours, even the whole night or a weekend. The processor needs to lock the data from updates so that no variables can be changed before it has completed its task.

- **Expropriated data**   Expropriated data, often termed *phantom data* or *phantom reads*, can cause severe integrity problems for databases, even system crashes and failure. If locking is not enforced and access to a record is not denied for the most critical of applications, it is likely in a multiuser environment that a record you have opened in your application is moved or deleted before you are done with it. Now you have data that you can no longer save because you are in edit mode and the data you need to update no longer exists or has been moved to another location. I call this "expropriated data" because you cannot update or delete a record that no longer exists. This is one of the first issues I had to deal with when developing voice mail systems. A caller would try to leave a message for a user whom the administrator had already deleted from the system.

In situations where these problems cannot be tolerated, you have to turn to locking. And if the level of automated or default locking applied by SQL Server is insufficient or does not meet the solution requirements, you need to manually manage the locking process. Let's now turn to SQL Server's locking features.

Isolation

Even though more than one transaction is executing in SQL Server at any given time, the transactions execute in complete ignorance of each other; the primary benefit being performance. This transaction "traffic" is desirable because the very purpose of a client/ server database management system is to allow more than one user to have access to the database at the same time. But the isolation has a downside. It means that two or more transactions without knowledge of each other can collide when they are after the same data. A real-world analogy often amused me and my fellow New York University students in

Isolation Level	Dirty Read	Nonrepeatable Read	Phantom Read
Read Uncommitted	Possible	Possible	Possible
Read Committed	No	Possible	Possible
Read Repeatable	No	No	Possible
Serialized	No	No	No

TABLE 17-1   Isolation Levels

Washington Square Park. People would throw a chunk of bread into a crowd of pigeons and have a laugh on the ones that collided. When two pigeons grab the same piece of food, one of them, usually the weaker, will have to yield. If neither yields, you have a deadlock.

So data integrity is assured by the ability of the DBMS to isolate transactions from each other, and the level of that isolation, in order to prevent the collisions. This is referred to as the *transaction isolation level.* The only way to absolutely guarantee that data being used by one transaction cannot be interfered with by another transaction is to give only one transaction access to the data. Then when that transaction is done with the data, the next transaction in line gets its chance. This is known as *serialization.* However, if all transactions were simply made to wait in a long line, then a transaction that only needed to read data would have to wait unnecessarily for the transactions ahead of it to complete. This would adversely affect the concurrency of data access and result in a slow system exhibiting poor performance.

It is thus possible to relax the serialization of transactions by adjusting the isolation level of the transactions—depending on the nature of the transactions using the data. An isolation scale is thus available that permits for a lower isolation level with higher data integrity risk on the one end of the scale and a higher isolation level with lower data integrity risk on the other end.

SQL Server follows the isolation level recommendations specified by the SQL-92 standard. These are defined in Table 17-1.

What is demonstrated in the table is that a transaction given a serialized isolation level is assured that no other transaction is reading or accessing the data. Lesser isolation levels relax the serialization of the transactions; transaction performance is increased, but data integrity is at more risk.

SQL Server 2005 Lock Management

A *lock* is an object that obtains information about the dependency that any process might have on data. Locks are managed by the lock manager, which is responsible for setting and releasing locks, the order of priority of the locks, and so on. The lock manager controls how sessions access data that is locked. It doesn't just prevent access; it assesses how to manage access in such a way that the data is not compromised by the session that "owns" the lock.

SQL Server 2005 automatically locks data that is being accessed by multiple users. It also automatically decides when data gets locked, who gets the benefit of the lock, the duration of the lock, and so on. SQL Server employs dynamic locking architecture, which means that the DBA does not have to manage the locking thresholds of transaction, and the developer can concentrate on making good query code without having to worry about locking. We will return to dynamic locking later in this chapter.

All locks are issued to connections on a first-come, first-served basis. The locking architecture is pessimistic by default. In terms of locking, "pessimistic" means that SQL Server assumes that the data is subject to concurrent access and could thus be compromised. The manager manages the locks on a *transaction* basis and on a *session* basis. You cannot, for example, obtain a lock in one session, even as one user, and then try to access the data from another session (connection). For example, you cannot execute a stored procedure in one connection that obtains a lock on the row and then execute another stored procedure, even another instance of the same procedure, in another session in the hope that the two sessions can access the data. This is only permitted through a bound connection, as is discussed later.

Lock Granularity

Locks can be placed at many different levels in your database. SQL Server can obtain a lock on a single row at the one end of the "granularity scale" and on the entire database at the other end of the scale. The various levels of granularity are, from lowest level to highest level, *row, page, key* or *key-range, index, table,* and *database.* Table 17-2 illustrates the actual objects that are protected from clashing interests.

The lock manager manages the level at which locks are acquired; the user or administrator is not required to perform any specific manual configuration unless an exceptional situation calls for it. Likewise, an application does not need to specify the granularity for a session. If a table is very small and there is only one session attached to it, the manager may place a table lock on behalf of the session. However, on a very large table that has many sessions attached to it, the manager will automatically lock rows and not tables. And depending on the isolation level, SQL Server may resort to a key-range lock.

A key-range lock locks index rows and the ranges between the index rows. SQL Server uses a key-range lock to solve the phantom read concurrency problem. The lock also supports serialization of transactions. The lock is used to prevent phantom insertions and deletes inside a range of records accessed by the transaction. If you want more detail of how the key-range lock works, consult Books Online. SQL Server pretty much handles the key-range lock for you automatically as part of its end-to-end lock management technology.

Object Name	Object Description
RID	Row identifier
Key	A row lock within an index, which can protect a key or key range in serializable transactions
Page	The 8KB data or index page
Extent	The eight data or index pages that make up an extent
Table	All data pages and indexes that make up a table
Database	The entire database and its objects

TABLE 17-2   Lock Granularity

Lock Mode

The manager also ensures that sessions respect the locks, and that a lock at one level is respected by locks at other levels. The respect that locks have for each other depends on the lock mode. For example, if a session has a shared-mode lock on a row, no other session can attempt to acquire an exclusive lock on the same row. The various modes are *shared, update, exclusive, intent, schema,* and *bulk update.* Table 17-3 describes the benefit of each lock mode.

Shared Locks

A *shared lock (S)* is issued to allow transactions to read data concurrently. For example, multiple concurrent SELECT statements can all read the same data concurrently. However, the data cannot be updated by any transaction for the duration of shared locks on the object. (See "Lock Duration" later in this chapter for information peculiar to each type of lock.)

Update Locks

A common form of deadlock occurs in a database when more than one transaction has acquired a shared lock. When a transaction (T1) is ready to change data it has just read using a shared lock, it attempts to convert the shared lock to an exclusive lock. But if another transaction (T2) has a shared lock and the same idea, it must wait for T1 to release its shared lock. However, T1 sees the shared lock of T2 and also has to wait for T2 to release its shared lock. The two locks wait indefinitely until a time-out or the DBA decides to throw the server out the window (if it is not SQL Server).

To avoid such a problem, SQL Server supports the concept of an *update lock (U).* Only one transaction can acquire an update lock, which means that even if another transaction tries to convert from a shared lock, it cannot. When the update lock is ready to modify the object, it converts to an exclusive lock. The update lock is akin to a shared lock with a red flag.

Exclusive Locks

Exclusive locks (X) get *exclusive* access the object, and no other transaction can gain access to the same object.

Lock Mode	Benefit
Shared	Used for operations that do not change data (read only). Can be acquired by multiple sessions.
Update	Used for operations that do not change data. Can be acquired with a shared lock in place.
Exclusive	Used for operations that insert, delete, *and* update data. The lock has exclusive use of the object.
Intent (intent shared, intent exclusive, intent and shared with intent exclusive)	Used to establish a lock at one level in the hierarchy with intent to move to another level.
Schema (schema stability)	Used for operations dependent on schema stability.
Bulk Update	Used for bulk copy with TABLOCK specified.

TABLE 17-3   Lock Modes

Intent Lock

The best way to explain an *intent lock* is with an analogy from physical reality. When you walk into a supermarket and to the deli counter, you will often have to pull a tag with a number out of a machine. Everyone holding a number is able to maintain a serving position without having to stand in line, but it gives them the right to step forward for service when their number is called. By holding the tag and the number, they signify an intent to be served. An intent lock is similar in that instead of standing in line to place a lock on an object, a transaction can place an intent lock on an object higher up on the hierarchy when it actually needs to lock an object lower down. It is actually reserving its position for the service of a more stringent lock. Intent locks are placed on table objects. They improve performance because this is the only place the lock manager checks them.

There are three types of intent locks in SQL Server 2005:

- **Intent Shared (IS)**   This lock indicates the intention to read resources lower down in the hierarchy (shared locks are placed higher up).

- **Intent Exclusive (IX)**   This lock indicates the intention to lock exclusive (for updates or changes) resources lower down in the hierarchy (exclusive locks are placed higher up).

- **Shared with Intent Exclusive (SIX)**   A shared lock with intent exclusive allows other intent locks to be placed on the table while one transaction is holding the option to lock exclusive an object lower down the hierarchy.

Schema Lock

A *schema lock (Sch-M)* is acquired by a transaction that issues DML statements on a table, such as column adding, changing, or dropping. This lock prevents access to the schema until the transaction has completed the schema update.

A second type of schema lock is called the *schema stability lock (Sch-S),* which is used to prevent any operation from making changes to the schema while a query is in process. For lengthy statements that make several trips to the table or take a long time to compute, a schema lock is essential. The last thing you want to happen while executing the query of the millennium is for a DBA to make changes to the very table you are working on.

Bulk Update Lock

The *bulk update lock (BU)* is used when you need to perform a bulk copy or bulk insert and the TABLOCK is specified or the "table lock on bulk load" option is set using the sp_tableoption stored procedure.

Lock Duration

The manager holds locks in place for an amount of time needed to ensure the protection of the data. The duration is known as the *lock duration.* SQL Server supports several lock duration scenarios.

The transaction isolation level (discussed later in this chapter) governs shared lock duration. If the default isolation level of READ COMMITTED is specified, then the shared lock is held as long as it takes to read the page. The lock is released when the read completes. If upon opening the transaction the HOLD LOCK hint is issued or the transaction isolation level is set to REPEATABLE READ or SERIALIZABLE, the locks are held until the end of the transaction or after COMMIT TRANSACTION is issued.

Cursors, which are coming up after the discussion on transactions, can fetch one row or block of rows at a time and may acquire shared-mode scroll locks to protect the fetching of additional data. Scroll locks are held until the next fetching of rows or the closing of the cursor. If HOLDLOCK is specified for the cursor, the scroll locks are held until the end of the transaction.

Locks acquired as exclusive are held until the transaction has completed.

Lock Blocks

No connection can acquire a lock if the lock it is trying to acquire conflicts with another lock already in place. This problem is known as *lock blocking*. For example, if a session attempts to acquire a table lock on a row that has an exclusive row lock established, the session attempting the lock is blocked. The block persists until either the in-place lock is released or a certain amount of time for the former connection has passed. Time-outs are not normally set for locks, but this may become necessary to prevent an indefinite wait caused by a transaction that has not completed by a certain amount of time.

Lock Compatibility

You cannot place a lock on an object if it is not compatible with any other locks that are already in place on the objects. If a shared lock is placed on an object, only other shared locks or update locks can also be acquired. If an exclusive lock is placed on an object, then no lock of any other kind can be placed on the same object. But exclusive locks cannot acquire a lock on a resource until a transaction that owns a shared lock has been released. The matrix in Table 17-4 illustrates the compatibility of each lock type.

Note that an IX lock can be placed on the table that already has another IX lock on it. This is permitted because the IX signals intent to update one or more rows, but not all of them. However, if one IX lock wants to jump the gun, so to speak, and update the same rows as another IX lock, it is blocked.

The schema locks do not feature in the matrix illustrated in Table 17-4, because they are compatible with all the lock modes. However, the schema modification lock cannot be used on a table if a schema stability lock is in place and vice versa.

RM/GM	IS	S	U	IX	SIX	X
IS	Yes	Yes	Yes	Yes	Yes	No
S	Yes	Yes	Yes	No	No	No
U	Yes	Yes	No	No	No	No
IX	Yes	No	No	No	No	No
SIX	Yes	No	No	No	No	No
X	No	No	No	No	No	No

TABLE 17-4   Lock Compatibility Matrix. Key: IS = Intent Shared, S = Shared, U = Update, IX = Intent Exclusive, SIX = Shared with Intent Exclusive, X = Exclusive

The bulk update lock is only compatible with the schema stability lock and other bulk update locks.

Lock Escalation

SQL Server automatically escalates fine-grain locks into coarse-grain locks as it needs to. This helps reduce system overhead: the finer the lock granularity, the harder SQL Server works. A key range or row, for example, requires more resources than a page lock or a table lock

SQL Server escalates row locks and page locks into table locks when a transaction exceeds an escalation threshold. In other words, when the number of locks held by the transaction exceeds its threshold, SQL Server will attempt to change the intent lock on the table to a stronger lock—an IX to an X. If it succeeds, it can release the row or key-range locks.

These lock escalation thresholds are handled automatically by SQL Server, and you cannot configure their usage or reference them in T-SQL code.

Obtaining Information about Locks

You can obtain and read information about locks by executing the system stored procedure sp_lock in your code (see Appendix). A result set returning a mass of information is obtained. The result set, fully documented in Books Online, returns information about lock modes, locked objects, type status, and so forth.

Examining the information about the locking activity undertaken by SQL Server can tell you a lot about your code and the optimization of queries (especially what goes into your stored procedures and triggers). SQL Server employs a dynamic locking algorithm which determines the most cost-effective locks. These decisions are made on the fly by the optimizer that considers, inter alia, the characteristics of the schema and the nature of the query. The sp_lock stored procedure will give you information about the lock activity SQL Server has been undertaking. Getting lock information can also help you troubleshoot deadlocks, as discussed shortly. The dynamic locking eases the administrative burden of SQL Server so you do not need to be adjusting lock escalation thresholds. This automation also means SQL Server works faster because it makes lock decisions on the fly and decides which locks are appropriate for the query at hand and the nature of the transaction.

Deadlocks

A deadlock occurs when a transaction cannot complete because another process has a lock on a resource it needs. The other process also cannot complete because the former process has a lock on a resource the latter needs. For example, Transaction A (TA) has a lock on the credit table but requires a lock on the debit table before the transaction can complete; it first updates the credit table and then needs to update the debit table. Transaction B (TB) is working in the reverse and has a lock on the debit table, exactly where TA wants a lock. A tug of war ensues, and you now have a deadlock because TA cannot complete (commit) nor can TB; each has a lock on the resource the other requires. SQL Server will have to decide which transaction yields.

While SQL Server makes use of many resources, such as threads, to prevent deadlocks, a deadlock is still entirely possible. SQL Server thus employs a sophisticated lock monitor thread that is devoted to deadlock detection and resolving. The lock monitor handles deadlocks as follows:

1. It is alerted to a thread that has been waiting for a resource for a specified amount of time. The lock monitor identifies all threads queued to the resource in the event that it needs to take further action.

2. If the scenario persists, the lock monitor begins to determine where the deadlock exists and initiates what is termed an "eager deadlock search." The eager deadlock search is a process whereby the lock monitor thread traces the thread activity to the point the deadlock occurred.

3. SQL Server then chooses a deadlock victim. This is usually the thread that is the least expensive to kill (in terms of resources).

When the deadlock victim is chosen, SQL Server rolls back its transaction and sends error message 1205 back to the application in the open session that led to the deadlock in the first place. The application will get the following message:

```
Your transaction (process ID #52)was deadlocked on {lock | communication
buffer | thread} resources with another process and has been chosen as
the deadlock victim. Rerun your transaction.
```

This information is also placed in the error log, and thus an application does not have to store the error message, just be aware of it. You should code an error handler in the client application to deal with the error message because it means that the transaction just initiated did not complete. So you might have to ask the user to repeat the exercise or the application might have to take some special covert steps. Pushing the message up to the GUI usually serves no purpose because the user of your application will have no idea what it means. Just the words, "deadlock," "victim," and "Rerun your transaction" are enough to cause a heart attack.

The message is returned to the client as soon as the lock monitor "shoots" the deadlock victim, so you wait about a 100 milliseconds for the deadlock mess to be cleaned up. Resubmitting immediately could end up repeating the deadlock.

You can take certain steps to minimize deadlocks because there is always a chance a deadlock will occur. Consider the following:

- *Acquire your resources late and release them early.* Don't code transactions that lock objects early, and then keep them locked while you perform the mother of all subqueries. Intelligent code should keep the object locked for the time it is needed and then immediately release it. Ensure your code accesses and releases the objects in the same order.

- *Avoid asking for user input in a transaction.* Gather up the data from the user before you start the transaction and avoid asking for data from the user in the middle of a transaction. If there is one thing you cannot control, it is the user. What would happen in the middle of a transaction when you need user input and he or she has fallen asleep, switched to eBay to place a bid, or decided to leap off the roof?

- *Keep transactions short and code them in a single batch.* The longer and more complex the transaction, the higher the chance of a deadlock, because the resources are locked for longer. Keeping transactions short also means you can code them in a single small batch. Minimizing round trips means you can complete the transaction quickly and avoid deadlocks.

- *Use bound connections.* This allows two or more connections opened by the same application to cooperate and not block each other. So any locks acquired by the secondary connections are held as if they were acquired by the primary connection.

- *Use a low isolation level in your transactions.* First decide if the transaction can run at a low isolation level. For example, if you use "read committed" for the isolation level, the transaction is allowed to read data previously read but not modified by another transaction without waiting for the other transaction to complete. Read committed maintains the lock for less time than a higher isolation level such as serializable, which means less of a chance for lock contention. (Working with the isolation levels is discussed further in the section "Transaction Processing" of this chapter.)

NOTE   *A block is a mechanism by which one process prevents another from obtaining access—a lock—to a resource. A block prevents a deadlock and should not be confused with one.*

Working with the Lock Time-Out Setting

SQL Server permits you to change the LOCK_TIMEOUT setting in your application. If your application is blocked from a resource and has waited longer than the LOCK_TIMEOUT setting, SQL Server will send it a message to the effect that the LOCK_TIMEOUT exceeded the time it was set for. This is message 1222 or "Lock request time-out period exceeded."

This situation needs to be explicitly handled by your application with the same diligence described in the deadlock event. Rather than automatically rolling back your transaction as SQL Server does after selecting a deadlock victim, it cancels the statement that was waiting on the resource. You need to then make a determination of what to do next, such as resubmitting the statement or rolling back the entire transaction.

To check the lock time-out, execute the @@LOCK_TIMEOUT function.

Locking Hints

You can specify locking hints to SQL Server in your code within your SELECT and DML statements. Although you can use the hints to influence SQL Server, it is recommended you leave the locking process entirely to SQL Server because the hints override the current transaction isolation level for the current session. Unless you know exactly what you are doing and why you are doing it, hints can have a negative impact on concurrency and cause problems for you.

In the same fashion you can customize locking for an index if you have a very special reason to do so. In most cases you would be better off leaving SQL Server to make the determinations for you.

Transaction Processing

As discussed back in Part I and earlier in this chapter, the essence of a client/server DBMS is its capability to provide access to multiple users concurrently. This is achieved through establishing a session to the server and then in that session sending a series of commands to the server; possibly receiving back a result set, single values, or status information. When you connect to the server, the execution of your code at the server takes place inside a construct known in DBMS parlance as a *transaction.*

A transaction is considered a single unit of work by the DBMS. No matter what you do in the code, nested stored procedures, triggers, constraints, cascading deletes or updates, and so on, the transaction is still regarded as a single unit of work.

I know then that you would probably agree—especially if you are a DBA or a software developer—that our lives could also be considered transactions, single units of work. When you take all the activities and, logically, look at them as one unit, a life, you can see a single transaction, with each activity in it connected to the next. Life is one workload from the day we begin to the day we are committed. It is often said that when you die, time stands still and your entire life is replayed for you. We will not be able to confirm that until it happens to one of us, and we do not really know who controls our transaction logs. But DBMS transactions too have the capability to roll back. This capability to completely undo a transaction, before it too is committed, is called the *transaction rollback.*

The inherent rollback of a transaction thus makes it not only a logical unit of work but also a logical unit of recovery, because everything that is done within the scope of the transaction is undone. The rollback ensures that, if at any point in the middle of transaction something goes wrong, the DBMS can undo the work that has preceded the processing up the point of the rollback. This makes the transaction an all-or-nothing event. Either everything in the transaction happens, or nothing happens. This is often referred to as the *atomicity* of the transaction.

If a DBMS were to allow certain statements in the transaction to carry on, and the changes they caused to persist, that would lead to suspect data, or data that cannot be considered to be in a consistent or reliable state. Even if everything that was done in the transaction up to the rollback state was copacetic, we still cannot allow only parts of a transaction to complete. It is almost impossible, and taxing on a system, to obtain up-to-the-nanosecond checks that data is "safe," because at any time in the transaction a system can fail.

The transaction management architecture in SQL Server, however, provides the next best thing to the nanosecond safety check. As long as the data persists in the write-ahead transaction log, the transaction will be committed to the database. But if the data is not in any usable form, the server will roll back the transaction to the state before the transaction began. Starting all over, so to speak, as if the transaction had not even started. This mechanism ensures the *consistency* of the data.

SQL Server employs a sophisticated transaction manager monitor that ensures an *atomicity* or "all-or-nothing" rule and a data *consistency* rule. The transaction's start is signaled by the BEGIN TRANSACTION statement, which tells the transaction processor (TP) that work has begun. Transaction failure is signaled explicitly by the ROLLBACK statement, or automatically if the TP itself detects a failure. If the transaction completes successfully, the TP is given the "thumbs-up" with the COMMIT statement and the data is committed to the database. At this point, even if the system crashes, the updates or inserts to the database survive. This is known as the *durability* rule for a DBMS.

NOTE *If you are wondering if the COMMIT can be undone, it can. You can use the transaction log to rebuild the database to the point of a disaster that was still logically sound according to the TP. For example, if you delete a bunch of data in a human error (like truncating the wrong table), transaction log recovery will heal that (see Chapter 8).*

You will recall from the discussion of locking that transactions are isolated from each other (see the section "Isolation" earlier in this chapter). Following this, we can say that transactions have four important properties, which have become fondly known as the ACID properties or laws—*atomicity, consistency, isolation,* and *durability.* A transaction must adhere to the laws or it is considered to have failed the "ACID test."

Types of Transactions

If you are new to SQL Server development, you will probably now be wondering how in previous chapters, and in any code you were writing in T-SQL or with an object model like ADO.NET, you were able to get away with not writing transactions. Well, the truth is that you have been writing transactions, or at least that's how SQL Server sees it. SQL Server considers everything executed against it a transaction. Any code you send to the server that is not part of a user-defined transaction is automatically placed into an autocommit transaction. In other words, SQL Server automatically handles the transaction management for you. If your code executes properly, SQL Server automatically commits any data changed or inserted; if not, it rolls back and you get an error.

Three types of transaction are supported by SQL Server: *explicit, implicit,* and *autocommit.* Let's look at the autocommit first because it is the easiest to work with. You don't have to do any transaction management.

Autocommit Transactions

The *autocommit* transaction is the default transaction mode of SQL Server. No matter what statement is issued to SQL Server, changes are committed if the transaction completes properly or rolled back if it encounters an error. The autocommit transaction is also the default of any statement transmitted to the server from ADO.NET, ADO, OLE DB, ODBC, or the old legacy DB-Library.

However, in autocommit mode, SQL Server takes the batch of SQL statements and processes each one as a separate transaction. For example, in the following code SQL Server encounters a syntax error and is unable to formulate an execution plan for the entire batch, so the entire batch is aborted and rolled back:

```
CREATE TABLE TestTable (Col1 INT PRIMARY KEY, Col2 VARCHAR(10)
   INSERT TestTable VALUES (1, 'apples')
   INSERT TestTable BALUES (2, 'bananas')
    SELECT * FROM TestTable
```

The query at the end fails and no result is returned because the optimizer was unable to compile the batch on the second INSERT because of the syntax problem. In the next example, the first statement is committed even though there is an error in the batch. It does this because in autocommit mode every statement is considered a separate transaction:

```
CREATE TABLE TestTable (Col1 INT PRIMARY KEY, Col2 VARCHAR(10)
   INSERT TestTable VALUES (1, 'apples')
   INSERT TestTable VALUES (1, 'bananas')
    SELECT * From TestTable
```

Autocommit mode compiles the batch because the error in the primary key (1) is only trapped at the constraint check after the query has been compiled and optimized (this is known as *delayed name resolution*). There is no syntax error, and if you run the preceding code in Management Studio, it will tell you that the code checks out. If we run this code, perform the SELECT, and then examine the table, we see in the second batch that the first INSERT is committed but not the second.

Running this code in Management Studio returns the following error, which indicates that one row was committed:

```
(1 row(s) affected)
Server: Msg 2627, Level 14, State 1, Line 1
Violation of PRIMARY KEY constraint 'PK__test_table__5EBF139D'. Cannot
insert duplicate key in object 'test_table'.
The statement has been terminated.
(1 row(s) affected)
```

Now this behavior may seem contrary to what we have just learned about transactions and the atomicity rule. But if you examine the results, is it not clear that the database is still in a *durable* state, even after the error? It is; this is not the issue. What if the first statement and the second statement *are* both required by your application or code? Consider the following code for a voice message system:

```
UPDATE Extensions SET PrimaryExt = '555-1212'
INSERT NewExtension (VoiceMailExt) VALUES ('5551212')
```

If the phone extension numbers are required to be in 3 + 4 notation separated by a dash and we install a check constraint on the columns to catch the mask error, then in autocommit mode the NewExtension will never receive a call that is not answered on the primary extension. The problem with this is that only a portion of the query code will result in data being committed to the database when the entire batch should have done so. This would clearly be an error by the voice mail system because it would risk leaving an extension without message-taking capability. This is a simple example, but it illustrates the point that in autocommit mode you might have only part of your data committed to the table, leaving the application, as opposed to the data, in an inconsistent state. The way to ensure that all the values or none get installed is with an explicit transaction.

Explicit Transactions

To use an *explicit transaction,* you (and not SQL Server) explicitly define the beginning and end of the transaction. In T-SQL or with DB-Library, you use the following statements:

- **BEGIN TRANSACTION**   This statement marks the starting point of your transaction.

NOTE *SQL Server supports the abbreviated TRAN in place of TRANSACTION.*

- **COMMIT TRANSACTION; COMMIT WORK**   These statements are used to signal to the transaction manager that the transaction completed successfully and the data insertions or modifications should be committed to the database.

- **ROLLBACK TRANSACTION; ROLLBACK WORK**   These statements signal to the transaction manager that the transaction failed and the work should be rolled back; completely undone, get ready to start over.

Using our simple example demonstrated earlier, we ensure that either the entire batch is "kosher" or it all goes into the trash can. The following code rolls back everything between BEGIN TRANSACTION and ROLLBACK TRANSACTION:

```
BEGIN TRANSACTION
  INSERT Extensions (PrimaryExt) VALUES ('555-1212')
  INSERT Extensions (VoiceMailExt) VALUES ('5551212')
ROLLBACK TRANSACTION
```

NOTE *SQL Server returns to autocommit mode automatically after an explicit or implicit transaction completes.*

Implicit Transactions

A third mode for transactions is called *implicit mode.* To operate in implicit mode, you do not need to delineate a transaction with the BEGIN TRANSACTION statement, but you need to specifically place the session into implicit mode with the SET IMPLICIT_TRANSACTIONS ON statement. But you need to signal the end of each transaction with the ROLLBACK TRANSACTION or COMMIT TRANSACTION statement.

Using the implicit mode allows you to issue a long batch of statements, enclosing collections of statements in implicit transactions. When you are done in the implicit mode, you need to issue the SET IMPLICIT_TRANSACTIONS OFF statement.

SQL Server also automatically starts a transaction every time it encounters one of the statements in Table 17-5 while in implicit mode.

Transactions and SQL Server Development

The database APIs, such as ODBC, ADO, ADO.NET and OLE DB, each contain functions or methods that allow you to manage transactions from the client application. Consult each API or object model for the peculiarities of the function or method call. Naturally, you cannot mix and match the API calls; you cannot begin a transaction in ODBC and end it with a call to the ADO API.

TABLE 17-5 Statements That Require Transactions in Implicit Mode	ALTER TABLE	REVOKE
	CREATE	OPEN
	DELETE	INSERT
	DROP	TRUNCATE
	FETCH	UPDATE
	GRANT	SELECT

The ACID rules no doubt extend to the client connection and the client. If a client is in the middle of an extensive transaction and then gets squashed by a steamroller, the transaction manager detects the failure and rolls back the transaction. Thus in mission-critical applications, with unreliable network connections, it makes sense not to use the default autocommit transaction mode.

An extensive update or insert to, say, a bank account, over the Internet or even filling in a form, requires you to prevent a situation in which only part of the data is committed to the database. Often it happens that as a browser fills in a form on the Internet, the user loses the connection and has to start all over. Then when the user tries to reissue the user ID that was available before, he or she gets the message that the user ID is taken—case of the partly committed form.

Distributed Transactions

In Chapters 1 and 3, I mentioned that SQL Server actually supports a form of transaction management that is not necessarily local to the server on which a session is established. This form of transaction is known as the *distributed transaction* (DT). Instead of processing on just the local server, the transaction is able to span multiple servers that engage in the distributed processing as resource managers, while to the originating session it appears that the transaction is executing locally. The transaction manager on each server coordinates the transaction processing according to standards of operation defined by either the Microsoft Distributed Transaction Coordinator (MS DTC) or the X/Open Specification for Distributed Transaction Processing.

Distributed transactions are mainly used to update multiple instances of SQL Server (and any other DBMS that supports either of the DT protocols just mentioned). This is how it works:

At the originating server, the session or client manages the transaction exactly as it does a regular transaction. However, when it comes time to either roll back or commit, a coordination effort is required between all the participating servers to ensure that either all or none of the servers can commit or roll back successfully. In a distributed transaction, some of the servers in the "mob" might be on the ends of unreliable network connections (like the Internet) and may be at risk of being lost in the middle of a transaction.

A coordination effort is required to ensure that all servers were able to run the transactions through to their logical conclusions. The coordination is carried out by what is known as a two-phase commit process (2PC), encompassing a prepare phase and a commit phase. The phases operate as follows:

1. **Prepare phase**   When the transaction manager receives a commit request, it sends a prepare command to all the resource managers involved in the distributed transaction scenario. Each participant then goes about ensuring that it has what it takes to ensure the durability of the transaction. For example, all transaction logs are flushed to disk. As each member succeeds or fails in the prepare phase, it updates the transaction coordinator or manager with a success or failure flag.

2. **Commit phase**   If the transaction coordinator receives the okay from all servers, it sends out commit commands to the participants. The resource managers on each server complete their respective commits and notify the transaction coordinator of

success or failure. If any resource manager reports a failure to prepare, or does not respond after the commit, the coordinator sends a rollback message to the other servers.

There are two options to managing distributed transactions. You can go through a database API, or you can use T-SQL, the preferred method for SQL Server developers. Going through T-SQL enlists the services of the Microsoft Distributed Transaction Coordinator (MS DTC), so there is really not much work that you have to do, and issuing a distributed transaction is not much more work than issuing a local transaction.

The transaction originates either from a stored procedure called by a client application, or a statement executed against the server, or in a script executed either from a command line application or from one of the GUI interfaces that can transmit a T-SQL batch to the server.

There are a number of ways to start a distributed transaction in T-SQL:

- **Explicit**   You can start an explicit distributed transaction using the BEGIN DISTRIBUTED TRANSACTION statement.

- **Distributed Query**   While in a local transaction, you can execute a distributed query against a linked server.

- **REMOTE_PROC_TRANSACTIONS**   If this statement is issued ON and the local transaction calls a remote stored procedure, the local transaction is automatically promoted to a distributed transaction. If REMOTE_PROC_TRANSACTIONS is off, calls to the remote stored procedures execute outside of the scope of the local transaction. A rollback in the local transaction does not affect the remote transaction, and vice versa. Similarly, the transaction processing of the remote transaction is unaffected by the local transaction processing. They commit their work independent of each other.

NOTE   *The REMOTE_PROC_TRANSACTIONS statement is issued if you plan to make remote stored procedure calls to the remote server defined with sp_addserver. See Chapter 14 for more information on stored procedures.*

Working with Cursors

Throughout this book I have told you that data is returned to clients as a result set—the set of rows resulting from a query. At the client the result set is looped through by a client process, which populates a grid or a collection of fields. Sharp queries allow us to return a single row of data that is used to populate the fields, but often we are not sure exactly which row is required and thus we send back as small a result set as possible and allow the user to make the final choice.

There are situations that you may find yourself in, in which it is impossible to work with a result set returned to the client. Online or Internet applications are a good example, in which a result set cannot be returned to the client for further processing. A browser has no functionality to accommodate a long stream of rows coming up the wire (although XML is beginning to make this a reality). Still, if a result set will disappear into a black hole when returned to the client, you need a facility to work with the result set on the server. In other words, instead of holding the result set at the client, the result set is stored on the server, where the client can work with it one row at a time. This is the essence of a cursor.

You could consider a cursor to be an extension to result set architecture because it enables the following capabilities:

- You can retrieve one row or a block of rows from the result set on the server.
- You can take aim at a specific row on the result set, a feature called row positioning.
- You can modify data at the current position in the result set.

A cursor also allows you to set different levels of visibility to changes made by other users to the underlying data of the result set. And you can access the data from scripts, stored procedures, and triggers.

There are two methods for requesting a cursor on a result set:

- You can use T-SQL, which is compliant with SQL-92 cursor syntax.
- You can use an API or Object Model that supports using cursors. (APIs include DB-Library, OLE DB, and ODBC. And the ADO.NET Object Model supports cursor functionality.)

CAUTION *Never mix cursor request methods in your application. If you are going native (such as ODBC) stick to the native API. If you use an ADO.NET object, then use the ADO.NET model only.*

SQL Server cursors have to be explicitly called. If you do not use a cursor call, SQL Server defaults to returning the result set to the client.

Types of Cursors

SQL Server provides support for three types of cursors:

- **T-SQL Cursors**   These are created using the DECLARE CURSOR syntax and are used mainly in T-SQL scripts, stored procedures, and triggers. These cursors are instantiated on the server by T-SQL statements transmitted by the client. The DECLARE CURSOR syntax is also often used in stored procedures, T-SQL batches, and triggers. Using cursors in triggers is tricky, however, and badly written or very long and involved "cursorized" triggers can bring a SQL Server instance to dead stop.

- **API Cursors**   These cursors are also server-based and are instantiated by API calls from the likes of OLE DB, ODBC, and DB-Library.

- **Client Cursors**   These cursors are implemented on the client though either API or Object Model features. While the result set is still supported at the server, the result set rows are cached in a client facility. So the rows that are modified are the rows that are cached at the client.

You should know that many seasoned SQL Server developers eschew cursors unless they are really needed. The reason for this is simple: performance. The result set is maintained on the server, and so SQL Server has to commit resources to the cursor. When a result set is sent to the client, SQL Server is done with the query and moves on to something else.

Cursors also have limitations that might not help you. For example, they do not support all T-SQL statements, and you cannot use statements that generate multiple result sets—so that means you are limited to one SELECT statement in a cursor-creating batch. Statements that contain the keywords COMPUTE, COMPUTE BY, FOR BROWSE, or INTO are SQL *non grata* for cursors.

Why is a cursor less efficient than a default result set? The answer is this: When you query SQL Server for data, a default result set is created by a batch of code, in one connection, sent to the server from a client or from a stored procedure. But with cursors every time you need data, you have to send out a FETCH statement from the client to the server, and every FETCH is parsed and compiled into an execution plan.

Getting back to the data conservation philosophy expounded in this book, you should rather code tight queries that aim to return the exact data needed by the client. If the result set is small, or you use new modern technologies such as XML (see Chapter 16 and later in this chapter), you might be able to avoid a cursor and gain not only in the performance arena, but also in the feature and complexity arenas.

If you need to use a cursor, do this: Favor server cursors and add more resources to the server if you need to because client cursors cache the entire result set on the client and that's not very efficient. Remember, think "thinner is better" for the client. On the Internet or a widely distributed application you never really know what resources the client has, and asking a client to cache a cursor is like firing a torpedo that has delayed detonation technology.

Server cursors also by their nature support more features. For example, a server cursor can directly support positioned operations such as update and delete statements. Client cursors make updates and deletes a lot more difficult to manage and are more complex to code. Server cursors also allow your application to open concurrent cursor connections and support multiple active statements to those cursors.

T-SQL Cursors

I could write an entire book on using cursors and demonstrate them in the various APIs and object models, but since this is a SQL Server reference, let's stick to T-SQL cursors.

Where can you use a T-SQL cursor? As mentioned earlier, they are best used in standard SQL scripts, from stored procedures, and in triggers. I am not in favor of using them in triggers. Triggers should be used for enforcing business rules and not iterating through cursors. Sure, there will be times when you need to work with a collection of rows in a cursor, but most of the time you can do the job with the standard default result set held on the server, which gives you cursor benefits (server-held result sets) without the overhead. If your solution calls for a trigger-created cursor, try to find a way around it, and as a last resort, keep the trigger-cursor code small.

NOTE *A T-SQL cursor does not support the fetching of a block of rows, but I do not see this as a big drawback.*

The following steps take you through generating a T-SQL cursor:

1. First, you need to declare T-SQL variables that will hold the data returned by the cursor. You will need to declare one variable for each result set column. The variables should be large enough to hold the values. You should also use data types that can be implicitly converted from the data type of the column.

2. Next, you need to associate the cursor with a SELECT statement. This is done using the DECLARE CURSOR statement. The statement also defines the characteristics of the cursor. It gives the cursor its name and properties, such as whether the cursor is read only or forward scrolling.

3. The OPEN statement is then used to run the SELECT statement into the cursor.

4. FETCH INTO then gets individual rows and puts the data into the variables you created. You can also use other statements to work with variables.

5. When you are done with the cursor, get rid of it using the CLOSE statement. By closing the cursor, you free up resources and drop locks and the result set. But the same cursor can still be resurrected by reissuing the OPEN statement. This also means that the name you gave the cursor is still in circulation and cannot be used in another DECLARE CURSOR statement.

6. Finally, you use the DEALLOCATE statement to completely destroy the cursor, its name, and its properties. The name becomes available again, and you cannot resurrect a deallocated cursor.

The T-SQL cursor syntax is as follows (SQL-92 and T-SQL extensions):

```
---SQL-92 Syntax

DECLARE cursor_name [ INSENSITIVE ] [ SCROLL ] CURSOR
FOR select_statement
[ FOR { READ ONLY | UPDATE [ OF column_name [ ,...n ] ] } ]

---Transact-SQL Extended Syntax

DECLARE cursor_name CURSOR
[ LOCAL | GLOBAL ]
[ FORWARD_ONLY | SCROLL ]
[ STATIC | KEYSET | DYNAMIC | FAST_FORWARD ]
[ READ_ONLY | SCROLL_LOCKS | OPTIMISTIC ]
[ TYPE_WARNING ]
FOR select_statement
[ FOR UPDATE [ OF column_name [ ,...n ] ] ]
```

Consult SQL Server Books Online for the complete explanation of the arguments. The following code is an example of a simple DECLARE CURSOR statement in action:

```
DECLARE CustomerCursor CURSOR
  FOR SELECT * FROM CustDetails
```

Next, you open the cursor thus

```
OPEN CustomerCursor
```

and then fetch the first record as follows:

```
FETCH NEXT FROM CustomerCursor
```

Each time that you issue the FETCH NEXT statement, you advance one row in the cursor. In the preceding example the FETCH NEXT is the only FETCH you can use because the SCROLL option was not specified. In other words, the cursor rolls forward only (remember the DAO forward-scrolling snapshot recordset). The more complex the cursor and the more options you enable on it, the more resources required to operate the cursor and the less efficient it will be. The complete FETCH SYNTAX is as follows:

```
FETCH
[ [ NEXT | PRIOR | FIRST | LAST
| ABSOLUTE { n | @nvar }
| RELATIVE { n | @nvar }
]
FROM
]
{ { [ GLOBAL ] cursor_name } | @cursor_variable_name }
[ INTO @variable_name [ ,...n ] ]
```

Monitoring a T-SQL Cursor

As if I needed to tell you, SQL Server comes equipped with an assortment of system stored procedures and functions you can use to monitor and track cursors. (See Appendix for the cursor stored procedures and functions.) To get a list of cursors that are visible to your connection, you can execute the sp_cursor_list stored procedure. Then you can use the several described cursor stored procedures to determine the characteristics of the cursor. The @@FETCH_STATUS returns the status of the last fetch.

Each fetch positions the cursor on the row whose data was just returned to you. The cursor does not advance a row after the data is returned but rather fetches the data of the row in front of it and then moves forward. The fetched row is thus called the current row, and you can then execute an UPDATE or DELETE on the current row.

Of course what we have discussed on cursors is just enough to tickle your taste buds, and the subject warrants a few chapters of its own. See my book's sister reference *SQL Server 2005 Developer's Guide*, by Michael Otey and Denielle Otey (McGraw-Hill/Osborne, 2005), for more client "how to" stuff.

SQL Server 2005 XML

It came out of nowhere. Suddenly there was XML, and now everyone is labeling this language as the "Lingua Franca of the World Wide Web." But there is lot more to XML than a stale cliché. While there are a lot of good books on XML and tons of material on the Internet, this brief introduction investigates XML in the context of its value to SQL Server 2005 and to you, the SQL Server developer or DBA or both.

If you are new to XML, this section will give you the heads-up, and what you need to know before you go out and grab a six-pack of XML tomes (see also Chapter 10, which describes the XML data type in SQL Server 2005). After introducing XML we will briefly cover several important XML constructs supported by SQL Server 2005.

So what exactly is XML? Well, in short, XML is simply data formatted in a certain way. The Microsoft XML SDK defines XML as "a meta-markup language that provides a format for describing structured data." And actually, this is precisely the case. XML is simply a way of formatting data so that it is "self-describing and easy to transform."

XML had its beginnings years ago, circa 1986, as the Standardized General Markup Language (SGML) came to be a standard for marking up data in a way that would facilitate easy transformation and description of information. The goal of the SGML architects was to define a way in which any type of data could be transferred and processed by any type of application, written in any programming language, and processed automatically. This means that there would be no need to write special conversion programs, protocols, and so on, just to handle someone else's data.

The problem from the beginning was that SGML was very complex. I guess everyone was afraid of it. Anything too complex will never be totally accepted. So in comes XML, a subset of SGML. XML retains all the "good points" of SGML, and it is simpler to use. As a result of creating a simpler version of SGML, a broader developer target was reached. Along with an easier-to-use SGML, the Web is everywhere, and XML was streamlined for Web delivery, hence the XML buzz.

As of October 2000, the W3C recommendation for XML version 1.0 Second Edition was published by the XML Core Working Group. (These guys are responsible for maintaining and reporting on updates, errata, and new submissions on XML.) Currently, they are working with the XML Syntax, XML Fragment, and XML Information Set Working Groups. To be up-to-date on the latest XML recommendations and updates, keep an eye on http://www.w3.org and http://www.xml.org.

So why is XML important to me? Well, for starters, common data formats sure make life easier. In the early '90s, I worked for a large data processing firm in Michigan. The whole purpose of my existence was to write COBOL programs that converted data from one format to another. We had our defined format, but all of the companies that sent us their data had their own formats. So I would receive a magnetic tape from a bank or brokerage firm, print out a dump of the first 20 records, and start figuring out how I was going to get it into our format for printing. This was a real pain in the neck. No matter how hard we tried, we could never get all of our customers to stick to a common format. As I look back, if we had everyone sending the data in XML, my life would have been much easier. The bottom line is a common way of describing the data. If Customer X would send me their data, a schema, and some processing instructions, I could write a one-stop application that reads the XML and outputs it to my format without reinventing the wheel every time I received new data. That is the beauty of XML: data that describes itself.

SQL Server and the XML Love Affair

One of the main questions that's probably on your mind is, why do I need XML if I have T-SQL? Are they two separate languages that SQL Server supports, or are they like the doubles partners of a tennis match—where they each have their respective strengths and weaknesses that combine to make it game, set, and match? This section explains how the two languages coexist and how XML caters to the shortcomings of traditional methods of storing, manipulating, and analyzing data.

T-SQL Versus XML or T-SQL and XML

Does XML replace T-SQL, and if not, how are the two technologies used together or interchangeably? The answer to the first question is straight and easy: No, XML does not replace T-SQL. In order for us to send and receive data to and from SQL Server, we need to use T-SQL in the same manner that we use T-SQL to retrieve ADO.NET datasets right now. Because XML is primarily the way our data is defined, T-SQL is still the language of choice to talk to SQL Server. No two ways about it. We will explore the many ways that T-SQL and XML can be used together to produce robust SQL-XML solutions, and I think you will see that XML alone cannot really do anything all by itself. XML needs help in formatting, data retrieval, and data manipulation.

So you might ask, why do I need to use XML if it cannot do everything all by itself? Well, in the past, we still had all of these problems with different data formats, poor data description, and the need to continuously worry about what our client was sending us. As we have stressed before, XML solves this problem by being self-describing. Self-describing data makes life easier: no more custom applications to convert every single type of data format we receive. Furthermore, XML is highly optimized for electronic transmission.

Marshaling large ADO recordsets across the wire caused poor application performance and network bottlenecks. With XML, the data is streamlined for transmission over media such as the Internet, in XML constructs such as ADO.NET datasets. In conjunction with the server-side processing of SQL Server, and with the combination of T-SQL, XML, and other client-side programming languages such as Visual Basic 2005, JScript, C++ (.NET), and C#, we have all the tools for creating the most robust solution that we possible can. We are, however, leaving out a very important point. Imagine this: Oracle, DB2, and SQL Server *all* supporting XML natively. The conversion and incompatibility problems between *all* database servers will go to hog heaven. No more driver problems, or language differences between PL-SQL and T-SQL. All data can move happily from any client to any server in XML documents. What a relief that would be—no more compatibility issues. It's definitely something to look forward to.

What Is an XML Document?

Before we go any further, let's take a look at exactly what an XML document is. These details are important to understand once we start getting XML from SQL Server 2005. Though SQL does the formatting for us, we need to understand what we are getting out of the server before we can start manipulating it.

An XML document is made up of *tags* and *elements*. You might say that HTML does the same thing, and you would be correct. The difference is XML is data; HTML is how to format the data. HTML and XML work together to make our data look good. In HTML, we are given a specific number of tags we can use, which will instruct the browser how to format the output. In XML, we can generate our own tags that actually define the meaning of the data we are sending. So I may have a <company> tag that contains my company name. If I were to do this in HTML, the browser would ignore the invalid tags and continue processing.

Here, we can see how HTML describes how to display data:

```
<Table>
 <TR>
  <TD>Company</TD><TD>Microsoft</TD>
   </TR>
     <TR>
         <TD>Address</TD><TD>One Microsoft Way</TD>
     </TR>
     <TR>
     <TD>City</TD><TD>Redmond</TD>
     </TR>
     <TR>
         <TD>State</TD><TD>Washington</TD>
     </TR>
</Table>
```

Now here is XML, defining the actual meaning of data:

```
<Customer>
    <businessdetails>
      <companyname>Microsoft</companyname>
       <address>One Microsoft Way</address>
        <city>Redmond</city>
        <state>Washington</state>
      </businessdetails>
</Customer>
```

So let's go over the contents of an XML document. Understanding the contents will allow you to write well-formed XML documents. Being well-formed is very important. Remember, as with anything else, garbage in, garbage out. If we do not format our XML correctly, our processing application or browser will not know what to do with it.

Elements of an XML Document

The following are the essential elements of the XML document:

- Prolog
- Comments
- Elements
- Root
- Child element
- Empty element
- Attributes

Prolog

The prolog contains the metadata that describes the document, such as processing instructions, telling the XML parser how to interpret the XML document, including style sheet information, encoding details, or version information. The very first line of an XML document should contain the processing instruction. The tag definition for the processing instruction is "<?" for the open tag and "?>" for the close tag.

```
<?xml version="1.0"?>
```

If I wanted to include a reference to a style sheet, I would do the following:

```
<?xml-stylesheet type="text/xsl" href="URL for XSL Stylesheet"?>
```

Comments

In an XML document, *comments* can be inserted between individual elements of the documents. Comments are defined with the start tag (<--) and the end tag (-->). In an XML document, the comments will be "grayed out" when displayed in the browser.

```
<?xml version="1.0"?>
<Customer>
    <-- Customer details are contained below-->
      <company>
          <name>Microsoft</name>
             <businessaddress>
                      <-- this is the address-->
                      <address>One Microsoft Way</address>
                      <city>Redmond</city>
                      <--this is the state-->
                      <state>Washington</state>
                </businessaddress>
      </company>
</Customer>
```

Comments can span multiple lines, so make sure you include the "-->" end tag, or else you may be excluding information that shouldn't be excluded. It is very similar to the way comments are handled in SQL Server. Without your ending the comment, everything becomes a comment (as in all programming languages).

Elements

Elements are the basis of XML documents. Without elements, there is no XML document. XML elements are made up of *start tags* and *end tags,* just like HTML. The difference is that in XML, the *start tag* and *end tag* define the data within the tags, not how to format the data, as is the case in HTML. Herein lies the power of XML. We can create our own elements as we need to; we are not boxed into a strict set of rules governing how our data gets described.

There are still some rules regarding XML elements, which is basically the definition of the "well-formed" XML document:

- The root node is a single, unique element, containing all other elements.
- Open/close tags must match.
- Elements are case sensitive.

- Correct nesting—child elements must be contained within parent elements.
- Attributes are enclosed in either single or double quotes.
- Attributes cannot be repeated within an element.

The *root node* is the very first element in your XML document. It is the single, unique element that describes the rest of the document data. In the preceding example, the root element is <customer>, and at the end of the document, we close out the document with the </customer> end tag. If we fail to include the end tag, the document errors out and is not parsed. Within the <customer> root node, we can have multiple elements and child elements.

Now that we've defined the root node, we can start describing our data. Referring to the preceding example again, the next element is <company>. The <company> element contains child elements that further describe the data. This "parent" element contains "child elements" that are actually describing the <customer> details. Since each <company> could have many addresses, such as mailing, shipping, or headquarters, we can *nest* elements such as <businessaddress> to describe a particular address. That is the "X" in XML. Our document is *extensible*.

The rules still apply, though; we need to make sure that each element has the open and close portion of the element. Without these, the document becomes invalid. Notice also the nesting; the elements do not overlap. An example of poorly nested elements would be

```
<name>
     <customer>
     </name>
     </customer>
```

The <customer> element overlaps the closing </name> element. The correct nesting would look like this:

```
<name>
   <customer>
   Some Data in the middle
   </customer>
</name>
```

An empty element is an element that does *not* contain any data or child elements. Empty elements can be defined in two ways:

```
<companyname></companyname>
```

or the shorthand way:

```
<companyname/>
```

I do not like the shorthand way; it throws me for a loop when I see it. It reminds me of not declaring your variables in a Visual Basic program. So do everyone a favor and avoid them if you can, if only to make your XML easier to read.

Attributes

Attributes are another way to provide further details about an element. The only rules to follow are these:

- Attributes can be specified only once; the order is not important.
- Attributes must be defined in the start tag of an element.
- Attribute values must be enclosed in either single or double quotes.

```
<state region='Northwest'>WA</state>
```

The attribute "region" further describes the State element. In an attribute, white space is ignored, so another acceptable version of the preceding element is

```
<state
     region = 'Northwest'>
     WA
</state>
```

SQL Server 2005 does all the correct formatting for us, so we will always get a valid XML document back from a query. When you start to delve further into XML, you will find a couple of useful tools available on the MSDN Web site. The XML Tree Viewer and the XML Validator will both assist you in debugging your XML. They can be downloaded at http://msdn.microsoft.com as can XML Notepad, a useful utility for writing and editing XML files.

XQuery

The XML data type introduced in Chapter 10, is supported with a method to retrieve all or part of an XML document. The is made possible by the support of T-SQL for a subset of the XQuery language specifically to query the xml data type.

XQuery is a new adventure in XML that is based on the existing XPath query language. It has better support for iteration, sorting, and the construction of the XML. XQuery operates on the XQuery data model. To query an XML instance stored in a variable or column of xml type, you use the xml Data Type Methods. For example, you can declare a variable of xml type and query it by using the query() method of the xml data type. Have a look at the following code:

```
DECLARE @X XML
set @X = '<MyTable><Field1>One</Field1></MyTable>'
select @X.query('/MyTable')
```

produces

```
<MyTable>
  <Field1>One</Field1>
</MyTable>
```

or

```
DECLARE @X XML
set @X = '<MyTable><Field1>One</Field1></MyTable>'
select @X.query('/MyTable/Field1')
```

produces

```
<Field1>One</Field1>
```

and

```
DECLARE @X XML
set @X = '<MyTable><Field1>One</Field1></MyTable>'
select @X.query('/MyTable/Field1 [1]')
```

produces

```
<Field1>One</Field1>
```

The method is also useful when working with ADO.NET datasets. For example the following dataset XML can be assigned to the variable as follows:

```
DECLARE @X XML
set @X =
'<NewDataSet>
  <Table>
    <ClientID>12145</ClientID>
    <ContactID>124201</ContactID>
    <DropDate>2006-05-02T02:00:00-04:00</DropDate>
    <ResponseDate>2006-05-22T11:02:34.837-04:00</ResponseDate>
    <ResponseTypeID>1</ResponseTypeID>
    <FullName>Ms Janet Roach</FullName>
    <FirstName>Janet</FirstName>
    <LastName>Roach</LastName>
    <Address>Under the sink</Address>
    <City>Filthy Lake</City>
    <State>FL</State>
    <ZipCode>Y21962</ZipCode>
    <Phone>555XXX2222</Phone>
    <LocationID>25</LocationID>
    <LeadSourceID>0</LeadSourceID>
    <SourceCode>0506_flor_a</SourceCode>
    <DoNotCall>false</DoNotCall>
    <DoNotMail>false</DoNotMail>
    <DoNotContact>false</DoNotContact>
    <Deceased>false</Deceased>
    <Email1>janetcroach@holeinthewall.damp</Email1>
    <WebCCComments>stopbotheringme</WebCCComments>
  </Table>
</NewDataSet>'
```

And it can be queried thus:

```
select @X.query('/NewDataSet/Table/DoNotMail')
```

to return

```
<DoNotMail>false</DoNotMail>
```

XQuery is now the staple query language for all things XML and SQL Server as we will see in the next sections.

Understanding the FOR XML Clause in T-SQL

As discussed, it is very easy to get XML from SQL Server. But we must understand the different methods of retrieving data, and what exactly the output will look like. Let's start with the FOR XML clause of the SELECT statement, which looks like this:

```
Select fields from table FOR XML mode
[,XMLDATA] [,ELEMENTS] [,BINARY BASE64]
```

The AUTO mode of the FOR XML statement tells SQL Server that you want field names as attributes, not as elements.

Mode can be any one of the following: RAW, AUTO, or EXPLICIT. RAW transforms each row from the query result into an XML element with a generic identifier row as the element tag. So the following XML document:

```
<?xml version="1.0" encoding="utf-8" ?>
- <MyCustomers>
      <row CompanyName="Alfreds Futterkiste" ContactName="Maria Anders" />
      <row CompanyName="Ana Trujillo Emparedados y helados"
      ContactName="Ana Trujillo" />
  </MyCustomers>
```

is returned from the following statement:

```
http://localhost/xdesk?sql=select top 2 CompanyName, ContactName
from customers for XML Raw&root=MyCustomers
```

AUTO returns the XML results as a nested XML tree. Each table in the FROM clause for which at least one column is listed in the SELECT clause is represented as an XML element. Each of the columns listed in the SELECT clause is mapped to the element's attributes.

```
  <?xml version="1.0" encoding="utf-8" ?>
- <MyCustomers>
  <customers CompanyName="Alfreds Futterkiste" ContactName="Maria
Anders" />
  <customers CompanyName="Ana Trujillo Emparedados y helados"
      ContactName="Ana Trujillo" />
  </MyCustomers>
```

PART IV

The preceding XML document is returned from the following query:

```
http://localhost/xdesk?sql=select top 2 CompanyName, ContactName from
customers for XML Auto&root=MyCustomers
```

EXPLICIT You can EXPLICITly define the shape of the XML tree. This requires queries to be written in a certain way, so that the additional information you wish to supply is made part of the XML document.

Optional parameters are XMLDATA, ELEMENTS, and BINARY BASE64.

XMLDATA Returns the XML schema with the result set. The root element is not added to the result set; the schema is appended to the document.

ELEMENTS Columns are returned as subelements. The default is mapping columns to XML attributes.

```
<?xml version="1.0" encoding="utf-8" ?>
- <MyCustomers>
- <customers>
   <CompanyName>Alfreds Futterkiste</CompanyName>
   <ContactName>Maria Anders</ContactName>
   </customers>
- <customers>
   <CompanyName>Ana Trujillo Emparedados y helados</CompanyName>
   <ContactName>Ana Trujillo</ContactName>
   </customers>
   </MyCustomers>
```

The preceding document is returned from this query (notice the [,ELEMENTS] parameter specified after the FOR XML AUTO):

```
http://localhost/xdesk?sql=select top 2 CompanyName,
ContactName from customers for XML Auto, ELEMENTS&root=MyCustomers
```

BINARY BASE64 Binary data from the query is returned in base64-encoded format. This must be specified when retrieving binary data using RAW and EXPLICIT mode. This is the default in AUTO mode.

FOR XML Type Mode

When FOR XML was introduced in SQL Server 2000, its result was directly returned to the client in text form. Now that SQL Server 2005 supports the xml data type, you can optionally request that the result of a FOR XML query be returned as a variable in the xml data type. This is achieved by simply specifying the TYPE directive in the FOR XML query. This means that you can process the result of a FOR XML query on the server and then specify an XQuery against it, or assign the result to an xml type variable, or write Nested FOR XML queries in your backend code.

The following code demonstrates the use of FOR XML query with TYPE directive.

```
SELECT FirstName, LastName, Email1
FROM CRM.Customer
ORDER BY LastName
FOR XML AUTO, TYPE
```

And returns something like

```
<Customer FirstName="Jeff" LastName="Shapiro" Email1 ="jshapiro@codetimes.com"/>
```

With the FOR XML clause specifying the TYPE directive, the XML is returned as xml type and is assigned to a variable. You can also use the FOR XML query results in INSERT, UPDATE, and DELETE statements The following code illustrates the FOR XML returning returns an instance of xml type, and in turn the INSERT statement inserts this XML into a table:

```
CREATE TABLE Table1(Col1 int, XmlCol xml)
go
INSERT INTO Table1
VALUES(1, '<Root><ItemID="1" /></Root>')
go


CREATE TABLE Table2(XmlCol xml)
go


INSERT INTO Table2(XmlCol)
SELECT (SELECT XmlCol.query('/Root')
FROM Table1 FOR XML AUTO,TYPE)
go
```

PATH Mode

The new PATH mode makes it easier to combine elements and attributes as a simpler way to introduce additional nesting when you need to represent complex properties. In other words, the PATH mode provides a simpler alternative to the more complex EXPLICIT mode queries.

By specifying PATH mode, column names or column aliases are treated as XPath expressions. These expressions in turn are used to map values to XML. Here is a list of conditions for mapping columns in a rowset:

- Columns without a name
- Columns with a name
- Columns with a name specified as a wildcard character (*)
- Columns with the name of an XPath Node Test
- Column names with the path specified as data()
- Columns that contain a NULL value by default
- Columns without a name

Here is an example:

```
SELECT 2+1
FOR XML PATH
```

Generates the following output:

```
<row>3</row>
```

Getting XML Data Through HTTP

So we have seen the syntax of the FOR XML clauses and its variations. But there is more to retrieving XML data from SQL Server than just typing in a query from a URL. Let's look at some other methods of getting XML back to the client.

First, we will look at *template files* as a means of retrieving data. A *template* is a predefined file that resides in your virtual directory on a Web site. Since most queries tend to get complex, and normally we need a better format back from SQL instead of raw XML data, we can define templates that further enhance our XML experience.

With templates, we can apply XSL formatting to our XML document, and we can define long queries, pass parameters easily to queries, and declare XML namespaces. Another great reason to employ templates is security. When we start putting schema information in URLs, we are opening ourselves to allowing users to see data we might not really want them to see, such as the specifics of our queries. And if we consider removing URL query processing from the virtual root, we are letting the XML SQL Server XML ISAPI process the files and return the XML document, further improving security.

So let's build a couple templates and see how they work out for us. For starters, we need to specify the template name in an IIS virtual root. We set up these virtual directories when we configure IIS.

Now, open up XML Notepad and type in the following:

```
<ROOT xmlns:sql="urn:schemas-microsoft-com:xml-sql">
  <sql:query>
    SELECT top 2 ContactName, CompanyName
    FROM   Customers Where ContactName Like 'J%'
    FOR XML AUTO
  </sql:query>
</ROOT>
```

This is a template in its most simple form. You can isolate the T-SQL very easily. We are asking for the ContactName and CompanyName for Customers whose names begin with "J." Save this document as *xdesk1.xml* in the *C:\Inetpub\your_web_app* directory. Now from the browser, type the following into the URL: http://localhost/your_web_app/template/xdesk1.xml

The result should look like this:

```
- <ROOT xmlns:sql="urn:schemas-microsoft-com:xml-sql">
  <Customers ContactName="Janine Labrune" CompanyName="Du monde entier"/>
  <Customers ContactName="José Pedro Freyre"
   CompanyName="Godos Cocina Típica" />
  </ROOT>
```

How cool is that? We define a query, save it as a file, and just reference the virtual template directory and the template name from the browser—we are off to the races. From this small sample, the power of the template should become clearer to you.

Now we need to get a little more complex. Let's run through a few scenarios that we might run into in real life. Most likely, our T-SQL resides in stored procedures on the server, and we normally do not do a "Select *"; we pass parameters to limit our result set to get useful data. So how can we do that? You got it: *templates.*

But let's hold on for a second and examine the syntax of a template file. Understanding the syntax of the template will ensure success as we move forward.

```
<ROOT xmlns:sql="urn:schemas-microsoft-com:xml-sql"
      sql:xsl='XSL FileName' >
  <sql:header>
    <sql:param>..</sql:param>
    <sql:param>..</sql:param>...n
  </sql:header>
  <sql:query>
    sql statement(s)
  </sql:query>
  <sql:xpath-query mapping-schema="SchemaFileName.xml">
    XPath query
  </sql:xpath-query>
</ROOT>
```

Here are the specifics:

```
<ROOT>
```

Required for a well-formed XML document. Since the template file follows the rules of a well-formed document, this is required.

```
<sql:header>
```

This tag is used to hold any header values. In the current implementation, only the <sql:param> element can be specified in this tag. The <sql:header> tag acts as a containing tag, allowing you to define multiple parameters. With all the parameter definitions in one place, processing the parameter definitions is more efficient.

```
<sql:param>
```

This element is used to define a parameter that is passed to the query inside the template. Each <param> element defines one parameter. Multiple <param> elements can be specified in the <sql:header> tag.

```
<sql:query>
```

This element is used to specify SQL queries. You can specify multiple <sql:query> elements in a template.

```
<sql:xpath-query>
```

This element is used to specify an XPath query. Because the XPath query is executed against the annotated XML-Data Reduced (XDR) schema, the schema filename must be specified using the mapping-schema attribute.

`sql:xsl`

This attribute is used to specify an XSL style sheet that will be applied to the resulting XML document. A relative or absolute path can be specified for the location of the style sheet, similar to the way you would reference a hyperlink or image in a Web page.

`mapping-schema`

This attribute is used to identify the annotated XDR schema. This attribute is specified only if you are executing an XPath query in the template. The XPath query is executed against the annotated XDR schema. Just as when referencing a style sheet, a relative or absolute path can be specified here.

XML Updategrams and OpenXML: Data Manipulation Through XML

How can we insert, update, and delete data through XML? Microsoft has released the concept of updategrams that allow us to manipulate XML on the client and pass it back to the server so that it will update the SQL Server database, in a complete XML solution. We also have the ability to insert data with the OpenXML clause. While we have covered different methods of data retrieval, in reality, once we get data, we normally change it, and those changes must be stored in a database. Our updategrams and OpenXML give us the ability to do so with SQL Server 2005.

OpenXML

OpenXML is a T-SQL keyword that provides a result set, which we can equate to a table or a view, over an XML document that is retained in memory. OpenXML allows us access to XML data as if it were a relational recordset by providing a tabular, relational view of the internal representation of an XML document.

OpenXML can be used in SELECT and SELECT INTO statements wherever a table, a view, or OPENROWSET can appear as the source of the query. The syntax for OpenXML is as follows:

```
OpenXML(idoc int [in],rowpattern nvarchar[in],[flags byte[in]])
[WITH (SchemaDeclaration | TableName)]
```

Here is a description of the syntax.

idoc

The *idoc* is the document handle of the internal representation of an XML document. Calling sp_xml_preparedocument creates this internal representation of the XML document.

rowpattern

The *rowpattern* refers to the XPath pattern used to identify the nodes to be processed as rows. These are the rows passed from the document handle received in the *idoc* parameter.

flags

The *flags* indicates the mapping that should be used between the XML data and the recordset, and how the spill-over column should be filled. *Flags* is an optional parameter.

SchemaDeclaration

The *SchemaDeclaration* is the schema definition in the form following this pattern:

```
ColName ColType [ColPattern | MetaProperty] [, ColName ColType
[ColPattern | MetaProperty] ...]
```

ColName   *Colname* is the column name in the rowset.

ColType   *ColType* represents the SQL data type of the column. If the column types differ from the underlying XML data type of the attribute, type coercion occurs. If the column is of type timestamp, the present value in the XML document is disregarded when selecting from an OpenXML recordset, and the autofill values are returned.

ColPattern   The *ColPattern* is an optional XPath pattern that describes how the XML nodes should be mapped to columns. If the ColPattern is not specified, the default mapping (attribute-centric or element-centric mapping as specified by flags) takes place. The XPath pattern specified as ColPattern is used to specify the special nature of the mapping (in case of attribute-centric and element-centric mapping) that overwrites or enhances the default mapping indicated by flags. The general XPath pattern specified as *ColPattern* also supports the metaproperties.

MetaProperty   *MetaProperty* is one of the metaproperties provided by OpenXML. If the metaproperty is specified, the column contains information provided by the metaproperty. The metaproperties allow you to extract information such as relative position and namespace information about XML nodes, which provides more information than is visible in the textual representation.

TableName

If a table with the desired schema already exists and no column patterns are required, the table name can be given instead of *SchemaDeclaration*.

To write queries against an XML document using OpenXML, you must first call sp_xml_preparedocument, which parses the XML document and returns a handle to the parsed document that is ready for consumption. The parsed document is a tree representation of various nodes (elements, attributes, text, comment, and so on) in the XML document. The document handle is passed to OpenXML, which then provides a recordset view of the document based on the parameters passed to it.

The internal representation of an XML document must be removed from memory by calling the sp_xml_removedocument system stored procedure to free the memory.

So those are the gory details on the specifics of OpenXML. It all looks good on paper, but what does it all mean? Here is a brief summary, and then we will do a living, breathing example of OpenXML.

Basically, OpenXML allows us to leverage our existing relational model and use that with XML. I can send XML data to the server, execute a stored procedure that inserts or selects data, and then return XML back to the client.

To read BOL is a little weird because the samples have the XML embedded within the stored procedure. It would have been nice to see an example of an XML document being passed as a parameter. So that is exactly what we will do. Let's create a page that adds new Knowledgebase entries in a support help desk application. We will do that with OpenXML. Here is the stored procedure that we need to create:

```
CREATE PROC sp_ins_KB @kb ntext
AS
    DECLARE @hDoc int
    EXEC sp_xml_preparedocument @hDoc OUTPUT, @kb
    INSERT INTO KnowledgeBase
      SELECT *
      FROM OpenXML(@hDoc, '/KnowledgeBase')
            WITH KnowledgeBase
    EXEC sp_xml_removedocument @hDoc
GO
```

This code is pretty simple. All we are doing is passing the XML as the @kb parameter; executing the sp_xml_preparedocument system stored procedure, which will give us a handle to the XML document; and then calling the INSERT INTO T-SQL against the XML document. So whatever we pass as an XML document will be inserted into the Knowledgebase table. The cool thing is that the XML document can contain multiple records to insert, so we can add many records with a single OpenXML call. An important note: Since we are creating an internal representation of the XML document, we need to run the system stored procedure sp_xml_removedocument to remove the document from memory. Just another example of good housekeeping.

Now we open up our handy Notepad and create a template called *insertKB.xml* in our XDesk virtual template directory that will accept this XML document as a parameter from an HTML page. Here is what the code should look like:

```
<root xmlns:sql='urn:schemas-microsoft-com:xml-sql'>
<sql:header>
<sql:param name="jason"><KnowledgeBase/></sql:param>
</sql:header>
<sql:query>exec sp_ins_KB @jason
</sql:query>
</root>
```

We are accepting the "Jason" parameter from the HTML form. Notice the <sql:param> elements. We used this same technique earlier to pass parameters to our template for the stored procedure. So the template syntax for accepting parameters is exactly the same here. The next element, the <sql:query> element, is also the same as we described earlier in the chapter. We are simply executing a stored procedure and passing it the parameter that we took in from the <sql:param> element.

Last, we create an HTML page that accepts some user input and then actually calls the template file. Here is a sample HTML file that will accomplish just this:

```
<html>
<META name=VI60_defaultClientScript content=JavaScript>
<body>
  <form action="http://localhost/xDesk/template/InsertKB.xml"
```

```
         method="post">
    <input type="hidden" id="kb" name="jason">
    <input type="hidden" name="contenttype" value="text/xml">
    <br>
            Q#:<input id=kbid value="Q19878" ><br>
        Title: <input id=title value="Linux-Crash" ><br>
        Description: <input id=details value="Reinstall" ><br>
        <input type=submitonclick="UpdateKB(kb,kbid,title,details)"
                    value="Update Knowledgebase"><br><br>
<script>
    function UpdateKB(kb, kbid, title, details)
     {
      kb.value = '<KnowledgeBase
      KBID="' + kbid.value +
      '" Title="' + title.value +
      '" Details="' + details.value + '"/>';
     }
</script>
</form>
</body>
</html>
```

This HTML page has a few input boxes that allow the user to enter in an Article Number, a Title, and a Description for the Knowledgebase article. On the Submit action, we execute the UpdateKB script, which builds the XML document, and then the FORM action takes over and calls our InsertKB template, which inserts the XML document into the database.

Basically, we are building an XML document and passing the XML document to a template; the template in turn passes the XML document to the stored procedure, which uses OpenXML to read the XML and insert the data into the SQL Server table.

Keep in mind that, in our example, we have assumed that the schema of the table (field names) is the same as the elements that we have sent over in the XML document. This works fine in a perfect world. There may be times when you need to match elements from the XML elements to field names in the database. With OpenXML, this is no problem at all. Consider the following WITH clause in the OpenXML statement:

```
SELECT *
FROM OpenXML (@idoc, '//Customers')
      WITH (CustomerID  varchar(10)    'CustomerID',
            Zipcode     datetime       'Zip',
            StateCode   varchar(10)    '@STATE',
            Address     varchar(30)    '@MailAddress')
```

In the preceding example, we have elements being passed by the XML document that do not match the field names in the database. In order to correctly match up the elements to the fields, we are using a *schemadeclaration* that will map the fields correctly according to the *rowpattern* specified in the OpenXML statement. So this is another example of the great flexibility that OpenXML gives us in tailoring our inserts to the database.

UpdateGrams

Updategrams consist of "blocks" of XML that describe which parts of our data we want to change. The XML data is enclosed in the < sync> element. Within this element, there are

<before> and <after> elements indicating the blocks of XML that represent XML data before the changes and after the changes. SQL Server will receive this as a T-SQL update, insert, or delete query, depending on what XML the <before> and <after> blocks consist of.

For example, the XML contained within the <before> may contain a primary key element with the actual primary key data value. The <after> element will contain XML elements that contain the updated values for the matching element/field value pairs. OLE DB, running in the middle tier through *xmlisapi.dll,* then creates the correct T-SQL update statement that will update the database with the correct data values.

The syntax for the updategram is as follows:

```
<ROOT xmlns:updg="urn:schemas-microsoft-com:xml-updategram">
 <updg:sync>
    <updg:before>
          <TABLENAME [updg:id="value"] col="value" col="value"...../>
    </updg:before>
    <updg:after>
          <TABLENAME [updg:id="value"] [updg:at-identity="value"]
          col="value" col="value"...../>
    </updg:after>
 </updg:sync>
</ROOT>
```

Let's do a simple Update, Insert, and Delete updategram to demonstrate how we can use this feature in real life. We will use the *Customers* table from the Northwind database.

Example 1: Update
We will use Notepad to create a template file that we will execute from a URL.

```
<ROOT xmlns:updg="urn:schemas-microsoft-com:xml-updategram">
<updg:sync >
<updg:before>
     <Incidents IncidentID="1001" />
</updg:before>
<updg:after>
     <Incidents DateResolved="7-29-2000" />
</updg:after>
</updg:sync>
</ROOT>
```

Save this file as *UpdateIncidents.xml* in the XDesk template virtual root, and type the following in the browser to execute our updategram:

http://localhost/XDesk/template/UpdateIncidents.xml

What we have done is to pass the IncidentID field as the initial element value that we are searching for in the Incidents table in the <before> block. In the <after> block, we pass the element attribute value DateResolved to instruct the updategram to update this field in the database. Even though we are passing only a single field to update, we can pass as many attributes or elements as we need in the <after> block to update fields in the database.

Example 2: Insert

In the Update updategram, we passed data in both the <before> and <after> blocks. In order to insert new values into the database, we do *not* include any elements or attributes in the <before> block. Here is an example of inserting a new record into the Incidents table:

```
<ROOT xmlns:updg="urn:schemas-microsoft-com:xml-updategram">
<updg:sync>
<updg:before>
</updg:before>
<updg:after>
      <Incidents CustomerID="ALFKI" OperatingSystem="Linux" />
</updg:after>
</updg:sync>
</ROOT>
```

How easy was that? All we do is pass attribute values and the table name, and the data is inserted into the table when we run this template from the URL. What is even more cool is that to insert multiple records, we simply add as many <Incidents> elements with attributes as we like. Here is a code snippet of an <after> block that will insert several records into the *Incidents* table:

```
<updg:after>
<Incidents CustomerID="ALFKI" OperatingSystem="Linux" />
<Incidents CustomerID="ISLAT" OperatingSystem="Linux"
Description="Unstable" />
<Incidents CustomerID="HSEN" OperatingSystem="Unix"
Keywords="Crash,Burn" />
</updg:after>
```

So now all of a sudden, I can insert multiple records without all the typing involved in the OpenXML statement. I think this is really cool. Another point that needs to be made is that I am using attributes instead of elements in many of the template examples. This just saves some typing on my part. Either attributes or elements will work fine in any sample.

Example 3: Delete

We have done an Insert and an Update, so Delete is next. I am so amazed at how easy this is so far. There is really nothing to it. I know that you probably can already imagine how we are going to create the Delete template, but we'll go ahead and type it in anyway:

```
<ROOT xmlns:updg="urn:schemas-microsoft-com:xml-updategram">
<updg:sync >
<updg:before>
      <Incidents IncidentID="10014" />
</updg:before>
</updg:sync>
</ROOT>
```

Notice there is no <after> block. Since we do want any after data, SQL Server looks at this as a delete. The actual T-SQL that is generated by the middle tier is

```
DELETE FROM Incidents WHERE IncidentID = 10014
```

Remember, all template processing occurs in the middle tiers, so the actual XML processing occurs in the ISAPI DLLs, which send SQL Server the T-SQL to process.

I know by now you are probably thinking that you will most likely need to pass the update, insert, or delete values as parameters. Well, the good news is you can. Since the updategrams are run though templates, we know that templates can take parameters. If you recall the <header> element, which took the <param> value in the previous templates, we were accepting parameters. We use the same syntax for passing parameters to updategram templates. So to pass, for example, an IncidentID to delete from the Incidents table, we would need to create the following template (I will save this as DeleteGram.xml in the XDesk virtual template root):

```
<ROOT xmlns:updg="urn:schemas-microsoft-com:xml-updategram">
<updg:header>
            <updg:param name="IncidentID"/>
</updg:header>
      <updg:sync >
            <updg:before>
                   <Incidents   IncidentID="$IncidentID" />
            </updg:before>
      </updg:sync>
</updg:sync>
</ROOT>
```

Now from the URL, I will type the following:

```
http://localhost/XDesk/template/DeleteGram.xml?IncidentID=1043
```

Finito. So we have actually created something useful that we can use in real life. How can we pass the value from an HTML page? Just copy the same code we used on the KnowledgeBase page. Modify the "Form Action=" tag to reference the *DeleteGram.xml* file, and change the OnClick code to pass the ID value that you are entering into the input box. It does not get much easier than this.

If you wish to pass the Update or Insert parameter, no problem. Simply change the parameters that the template accepts and you have a full-fledged data entry middle tier. In summation,

- If you specify only <after> data, you are doing an Insert statement.
- If you specify only <before> data, you are doing a Delete statement.
- If you specify both <before> and <after>, you are doing an Update statement.

The X-Files

Simple Object Access Protocol (SOAP) Primer

The *Star Trek* Universal Translator is not as far off as the twenty-third century after all. Since we made first contact with other species, we immediately realized the need to understand their languages. This was by no means an easy task, but thank God we first made progress in the twenty-first century with the advent of the Simple Object Access Protocol (SOAP), which opened the way for the advances that led to the invention of a tool that will help all species understand each other. The Universal Translator. The only good thing about First Contact was that it was with the Vulcans, who just happened to speak English too. But imagine if First Contact was made with the Klingons, or even my Alyssa and Jessica, my one- and two-year-old nieces. We would be sitting across the table just looking at each other, wondering what all that gibberish was about.

This is why SOAP is so important. SOAP is a messaging protocol based on XML for transmitting data across the internet. The current submission of the SOAP standard to the W3C is supported by the following companies: Ariba, Inc., Commerce One, Inc., Compaq Computer Corporation, DevelopMentor, Inc., Hewlett-Packard Company, IBM, IONA Technologies, Lotus Development Corporation, Microsoft Corporation, SAP AG, and UserLand Software, Inc. I would say that is a pretty impressive list, which also means that we have a support base for the future. It is not going to be a fly-by-night technology!

Currently, there are many languages: Visual Basic, C, C++, Java, CGI, COBOL, C#, and so on. Most likely, all of these languages have some pretty clever code that developers would love to use and show other developers. But we can't share, because we don't understand the other language. My Visual Basic component does not know how to process CGI instructions. With SOAP, we have an opportunity to write objects in such a way that they can be accessed from any language from any platform. How, you ask? XML-SOAP is an XML-based proposal (submitted to the W3C), which allows developers to package objects in a plain XML format so that they can be understood by any type of object that can understand XML.

So what is the deal with SOAP, and why did they really create it? Initially, the idea was to create a way for distributed applications to communicate over HTTP through corporate firewalls. This idea has grown, creating a whole new way of writing applications that are platform neutral on both the client and the server. Hence the Microsoft term "Web Service." Web Services are everywhere.

Finally, there is a platform-neutral way of accessing objects and using them in our applications. For example, DCOM is a great technology, but in order for it to work, the platform is Microsoft, or more exactly a Win32 platform. ASP.NET is great too, but what if my component is running on a non-IIS server? How can I expose methods to other applications? Rewrite? Not anymore. With SOAP, we can *package* our components so that they can be called by anything from anywhere. Another important point is the client side. It seems nowadays everyone is writing applications that are browser based. Do we really need to rewrite our C++ or VB apps to take advantage of the new components we have written for the Web? No, because we can use SOAP from a fat client too.

When I first heard of SOAP, I thought to myself "Another way to write stuff, now I have more to learn, I need more sleep, there are not enough hours in the day to keep track of all this new technology." Well, once that thought was complete, I decided to investigate further. It really wasn't that bad. I can leverage my existing knowledge of XML with this new technology and do some pretty cool stuff.

Let's look at the basic syntax of a SOAP message:

```
<SOAP-ENV:Envelope
    xmlns:SOAP-ENV=http://schemas.xmlsoap.org/soap/envelope/

    SOAP-ENV:encodingStyle=
```

```
"http://schemas.xmlsoap.org/soap/encoding/">

<SOAP-ENV:Header>

  <t:XDeskTrans

    xmlns:t="some-URI"

  SOAP-ENV:mustUnderstand="1">1

  </t:XDeskTrans>

</SOAP-ENV:Header>

<SOAP-ENV:Body>

  <m:GetOpenIncident

    xmlns:m="Some-URI">

      <IncidentID>1001</IncidentID>

  </m:GetOpenIncident>

</SOAP-ENV:Body>

</SOAP-ENV:Envelope>
```

SOAP Message
A SOAP message consists of a SOAP envelope, a SOAP header, and a SOAP body.

SOAP Envelope
The SOAP envelope is a mandatory element in the SOAP message. This is the top element representing the message and optional attributes, which must be qualified by valid namespaces. In the preceding example, we include a reference to a namespace that will understand this message grammar and a namespace that describes the encoding of this message.

SOAP Header
The header is an optional element in the SOAP message and is always the first child element after the SOAP Envelope element. The SOAP header normally defines how a recipient of the SOAP message should process the message.

SOAP Body
The SOAP body is actually the guts of what we need to execute our method calls and to pass any variables to the server that out method call may need. In our example, we are passing the GetOpenIncident method with the IncidentID attribute containing our variable of "1001". This will instruct the server we are executing this to return the open incidents for the customer who has the ID of 1001.

Now that we have a brief explanation of what a SOAP message is and what all the good parts are, you are probably wondering what this means to you. Well, not much unless you have a tool that can help you use your existing COM components and start using this new SOAP way of executing methods and moving data. Here is where the SOAP Toolkit from Microsoft comes into play.

SOAP Toolkit

Microsoft realized the need to start getting developers moving in the SOAP direction, so until all the new server products come out that natively support SOAP, or Web services, we need to leverage our existing applications and knowledge to implement SOAP solutions now. The SOAP Toolkit is a download from MSDN that helps you move in the right direction. If you haven't downloaded it yet, grab it and install it on your development machine. With the SOAP Toolkit, you have a simple wizard that takes existing COM or .NET components you have written and creates all the files necessary to execute SOAP method calls—it does all the dirty work for you.

Here is how it works: Tell the SOAP Wizard which COM component you want to execute method calls against. The toolkit then creates an XML file containing the SDL, or Service Description Language, which is unique to your method calls in the component that describes the methods I am publishing. During the wizard process, a couple things happen: First, a listener file is created, either as an ASP page or an ISAPI application. This file "listens" for incoming SOAP calls on your server. The wizard also creates an Active Server Page that has is actually a wrapper function for your COM component. The cool thing about the ASP is that you can add any custom business logic that you desire, it just gives you the code needed to call the methods. Sounds easy, right? Well, there is one more thing we forgot to talk about, and that is ROPE.

SQL Server 2005 SOAP Endpoints for Web Services

SOAP endpoints are a new XML feature now supported in SQL Server 2005. They essentially allow a Web service consuming client, as described earlier, to access SQL Server objects, such as stored procedures and functions, using either CLR-based objects or traditional T-SQL functionality.

The following example creates an endpoint called my_endpoint, with the following method: NumberAsMonth, based on the CLR function we discussed in Chapter 14.

```
CREATE ENDPOINT my_endpoint
STATE = STARTED
AS HTTP(
    PATH = '/sql',
    AUTHENTICATION = (INTEGRATED ),
    PORTS = ( CLEAR ),
    SITE = 'SERVER'
    )
FOR SOAP (
    WEBMETHOD 'NumberAsMonth' (name='master.sys.NumberAsMonth'),
    WSDL = DEFAULT,
    SCHEMA = STANDARD,
```

```
    DATABASE = 'master',
    NAMESPACE = 'http://tempUri.org/'
    );
GO
```

A client can now consume the end point as it would any Web service, by simply referencing the Web service and the exposed method in its code.

In Review

This chapter examines some of SQL Server's advanced features. We investigated its locking capability and examined how SQL Server excels for concurrent access and transaction processing. We also discussed how for the most part programming against SQL Server does not require you to explicitly manage locks, isolation levels and transactions or result sets. For advanced functionality and powerful control, however, you can take over the locking, isolation levels and transaction mechanisms from the DBMS.

We also touched on cursors. These are server-maintained result sets that can be accessed by clients one row at a time. There are several types of cursors, but the SQL Server cursor is the most convenient to work with, and while the subject of cursors is still very complex, creating and working with a cursor is not rocket science.

We also covered a little SQL Server XML support (well a little more than a little). There, is so much to this area that there will be many articles, books, arguments, and so on written on the topic.

Monitoring SQL Server

A number of monitoring tools come standard with the operating system platform for SQL Server, namely Windows Server 2003 and later. Despite the services of these operating systems, SQL Server comes equipped with its own set of tools for monitoring events in the DBMS.

At any point in the lifetime of a SQL Server system, no matter the application and the data needs, there will be a need to monitor and report on what's going on inside SQL Server. The type of monitoring and performance tools you will use depend on what you are looking for. If the server is not responding well, then you will need to use a tool tailored to performance analysis and monitoring. On the other hand, you may have applications that are reporting errors, or users who report losing connections, data, or worse. In the latter case you will need to use tools that can trace connections to the server and can monitor what is coming across the client connections, what may be returned, and what code is being executed at any given time.

Table 18-1 lists the choice of monitoring tools you have at your disposal. You will also monitor your server reactively, to troubleshoot problems that have appeared on the system, or proactively, to ensure the server is performing to required operations and performance metrics. Proactive analysis means taking periodic snapshots of performance and comparing the results against established baselines. If you see that performance is degrading to the point that you are seeing signs of bottlenecks, or spikes in processor use or disk use against your base line, then it's time to react and look further into the causes. If you do nothing, your server will be harder to fix when something awful happens.

To monitor any component of SQL Server effectively, follow these steps:

- Determine your monitoring goals.
- Select the appropriate tool.
- Identify components to monitor.
- Select metrics for those components.
- Monitor the server.
- Analyze the data.

Event or Activity	SQL Server Profiler	System Monitor	Activity Monitor	T-SQL	Error logs
Trend analysis	Yes	Yes			
Replaying captured events	Yes				
Ad hoc monitoring	Yes		Yes	Yes	Yes
General alerts		Yes			
Graphical interface	Yes	Yes	Yes		Yes
Using within a custom application	Yes*			Yes	

TABLE 18-1   Options for Monitoring SQL Server *Using SQL Server Profiler Stored Procedures

These steps are discussed in turn in the text that follows.

- Determine Your Monitoring Goals

To monitor SQL Server effectively, you should clearly identify your reason for monitoring. Reasons can include the following:

- Establish a baseline for performance.
- Identify performance changes over time.
- Diagnose specific performance problems.
- Identify components or processes to optimize.
- Compare the effect of different client applications on performance.
- Audit user activity.
- Test a server under different loads.
- Test database architecture.
- Test maintenance schedules.
- Test backup and restore plans.
- Determining when to modify your hardware configuration.
- Select the Appropriate Tool

Windows provides the following tools for monitoring applications that are running on a server:

- System Monitor: With this tool you can collect and view real-time data about activities such as memory, disk, and processor usage.
- Performance logs and alerts.
- Task Manager.

We will discuss these tools later in this chapter. SQL Server provides the following tools for monitoring components of SQL Server:

- SQL Trace
- SQL Server Profiler
- SQL Server Management Studio Activity Monitor
- SQL Server Management Studio Graphical Showplan
- Stored procedures
- Database Console Commands (DBCC)
- Built-in functions
- Trace flags

The SQL Server Profiler

The Profiler is a graphical user interface to SQL Trace for monitoring an instance of the SQL Server Database Engine or Analysis Services. SQL Profiler enables you to monitor server and database activity (for example, number of deadlocks, fatal errors, traces of stored procedures and Transact-SQL statements, or login activity). You can capture SQL Profiler data to a SQL Server table or a file for later analysis, and you can replay the events captured on SQL Server, step by step, to see exactly what happened. SQL Profiler tracks engine process events, such as the start of a batch or a transaction.

System Monitor

The System Monitor lets you monitor server performance and activity using collections of predefined objects and counters—or user-defined counters—to monitor events. The System Monitor collects process counts as opposed to the data about the events (for example, memory usage, number of active transactions, number of blocked locks, or CPU activity). The monitor allows you to set thresholds on specific counters to generate alerts that notify operators as described earlier. System Monitor primarily tracks resource usage, such as the number of buffer manager page requests in use.

The System Monitor works only on Windows 2000 and Windows Server 2003. It can also be used to remotely or locally monitor an instance of SQL Server installed on another server.

The Activity Monitor Window in SQL Server Management Studio

The Current Activity window in Management Studio graphically displays information about the processes running currently on an instance of SQL Server. It displays information about blocked processes, locks, and user activity. The Current Activity folder is useful for ad hoc assessment of current activity.

Error Logs

The error logs contain additional information about events in SQL Server. They contain information about errors that go beyond what is available anywhere else. You can use the information in the error log to troubleshoot SQL Server–related problems. Each error has an error ID you can use for research or to address a technical support team at Microsoft.

The Windows application event log contains all the events occurring on the system as a whole. However, it also picks up events generated by SQL Server, SQL Server Agent, and full-text search. As demonstrated in Chapter 10, you can code a T-SQL error handler using RAISERROR with the WITH LOG option to place an error message and other parameters into the error log.

sp_who

The sp_who stored procedure reports snapshot information about current SQL Server users and processes. It also includes the currently executing statement and whether the statement is blocked. This facility provides an alternative, through T-SQL code, to viewing user activity in the current activity window in Management Studio.

sp_lock and sys.dm_tran_locks

The sp_lock stored procedure (legacy) and the sys.dm_tran_locks view reports snapshot information about locks, including the object ID, index ID, type of lock, and the type of resource to which the lock applies. These facilities provide an alternative, through T-SQL code, to viewing user activity in the current activity window in Management Studio.

sp_spaceused

The sp_spaceused stored procedure displays an estimate of the current amount of disk space used by a table (or a whole database). This facility provides an alternative, through T-SQL code, to viewing user activity in the current activity window in Management Studio.

sp_monitor

The sp_monitor stored procedure displays statistics. It includes the CPU usage, I/O usage, and the amount of time idle since sp_monitor was last executed.

DBCC Statements

DBCC statements enable you to check performance statistics and the logical and physical consistency of a database. They also allow you to troubleshoot database problems. The DBCC statements are discussed later in Appendix.

Built-in Functions

You also have built-in functions that display snapshot statistics about SQL Server activity since the server was started. These statistics are stored in predefined SQL Server counters. You have, for example, @@CPU_BUSY, which contains the amount of time the CPU has been executing SQL Server code. Then there is @@CONNECTIONS, which contains the number of SQL Server connections or attempted connections; and @@PACKET_ERRORS, which contains the number of network packets occurring on SQL Server connections.

SQL Profiler Stored Procedures and Functions

The SQL Profiler uses stored procedures and functions to gather SQL Profiler statistics.

Trace Flags

Trace flags can display information about a specific activity within the server. They are also used to diagnose problems or performance issues (for example, deadlock chains).

Simple Network Management Protocol (SNMP)

The old favorite Simple Network Management Protocol (SNMP) is a member of the maintenance team offering network management services. With SNMP, you can monitor an instance of SQL Server across different platforms. With SQL Server and the Microsoft SQL Server Management Information Base (MSSQL-MIB), an SNMP application can monitor the status of SQL Server installations. The SNMP services lets you monitor performance information, access databases, and view server and database configuration parameters.

SQL Profiler or System Monitor

The main difference between these two monitoring tools—SQL Profiler and System Monitor—is that the SQL Profiler monitors engine events, while System Monitor monitors resource usage associated with server processes. In other words, SQL Profiler can be used to monitor deadlock events, including the users and objects involved in the deadlock (see Chapter 17). System Monitor, on the hand, can be used to monitor the total number of deadlocks occurring in a database or on a specific object.

Windows 2000 Server and Windows Server 2003 platforms also provide the following monitoring tools:

- **Task Manager**   This tool provides a synopsis of the processes and applications running on the system. It is useful for quick analysis, or to kill a process.
- **Network Monitor Agent**   This tool helps monitor network traffic.

The System Monitor is a tool that can be used to monitor resource usage on a computer running Microsoft Windows 2000 Server or Windows Server 2003. It lets you set up charts that present resource usage data in graphical form. The Windows System Monitor provides access to many different counters, each of which measures some resource on the computer.

The Windows System Monitor is also extensible. In other words, server applications can add their own performance counters that System Monitor can access. SQL Server 2005 adds counters to Windows System Monitor to track items such as

- SQL Server I/O
- SQL Server memory usage
- SQL Server user connections
- SQL Server locking
- Replication activity

The monitoring and performance tools on the OS include the following:

- System Monitor
- Task Manager
- Event Viewer

- Quality of Service
- Windows Management Interface
- SNMP

Monitoring the SQL Server Platform

The first step in monitoring the platform is to identify the components to monitor. For example, if you are using SQL Server Profiler to trace a server, you can define the trace to collect data about specific events. You can also exclude events that do not apply to your situation.

Next, select Metrics for Monitored Components. After identifying the components to monitor, determine the metrics for components you monitor. For example, after selecting the events to include in a trace, you can choose to include only specific data about the events. Limiting the trace to data that is relevant to the trace minimizes the system resources required to perform the tracing.

Next you will run the monitoring tool that you have configured to gather data. For example, after a trace is defined, you can run the trace to gather data about events raised in the server.

Finally you will analyze the data. After the trace has finished, analyze the data to see if you have achieved your monitoring goal. If you have not, modify the components or metrics that you used to monitor the server.

The following outlines the process for capturing event data and putting it to use.

Apply Filters to Limit the Event Data Collected   Limiting the event data allows the system to focus on the events pertinent to the monitoring scenario. For example, if you want to monitor slow queries, you can use a filter to monitor only those queries issued by the application that take more than 30 seconds to run against a particular database.

Monitor (Capture) Events   As soon as it is enabled, active monitoring captures data from the specified application, instance of SQL Server, or operating system. For example, when disk activity is monitored using System Monitor, monitoring captures event data such as disk reads and writes and displays it to the screen.

Save Captured Event Data   Saving captured event data lets you analyze it later or even replay it using SQL Server Profiler. Captured event data is saved to a file that can be loaded back into the tool that originally created it for analysis. SQL Server Profiler permits event data to be saved to a SQL Server table. Saving captured event data is important when you are creating a performance baseline. The performance baseline data is saved and used when comparing recently captured event data to determine whether performance is optimal. For more information, see the section on SQL Server Profiler later in this chapter.

Create Trace Templates That Contain the Settings Specified to Capture the Events   Trace templates include specifications about the events themselves, event data, and filters that are used to capture data. These templates can be used to monitor a specific set of events later without redefining the events, event data, and filters. For example, if you want to frequently monitor the number of deadlocks and the users involved in those deadlocks, you can create a template defining those events, event data, and event filters; save the template; and reapply the filter the next time that you want to monitor deadlocks. SQL Server Profiler uses trace templates for this purpose.

Analyze Captured Event Data   To be analyzed, the captured, saved event data is loaded into the application that captured the data. For example, a captured trace from SQL Server Profiler can be reloaded into SQL Server Profiler for viewing and analysis.

Analyzing event data involves determining what is occurring and why. This information lets you make changes that can improve performance, such as adding more memory, changing indexes, correcting coding problems with Transact-SQL statements or stored procedures, and so on, depending on the type of analysis performed. For example, you can use the Database Engine Tuning Advisor to analyze a captured trace from SQL Server Profiler and make index recommendations based on the results.

Replay Captured Event Data   Event replay lets you establish a test copy of the database environment from which the data was captured and repeat the captured events as they occurred originally on the real system. This capability is only available in SQL Server Profiler. You can replay them at the same speed as they originally occurred, as fast as possible (to stress the system), or more likely, one step at a time (to analyze the system after each event has occurred). By analyzing the exact events in a test environment, you can prevent harm to the production system.

Getting Ready to Monitor SQL Server

I am not going to provide an exhaustive exposé into the service-level management tools that ship with the OS or how to use each and every feature. Such an advanced level of analysis would take several hundred pages and is thus beyond the scope of this book. Performance monitoring is also one of the services and support infrastructures that ships with Windows Server 2003 but takes some effort to get to know and master. However, the information that follows will be sufficient to get you started.

Windows Server 2003 monitors or analyzes the bandwidth used by storage, memory, networks, and processing resources. The data analysis is not done on these actual devices. In other words, you do not monitor memory itself, or disk usage itself, such as how often a disk accesses data, but rather how your software components and functionality use these resources. In other words, monitoring does not present a useful service if you just report that 56MB of RAM were used between x time and y time. The investigations need to go further and uncover what processes used the RAM at a certain time and why so much was used.

Let's say a system runs out of memory. Then would it not be possible that an application is stealing the RAM somewhere? In other words, the application or process or server has a bug that is leaking memory like a ship with a hold below the water line. When we refer to a memory leak, it means that a process has used the memory and has not released it after it is done processing. Software developers should watch their applications on servers and be sure they release all memory they use.

But what if you are losing memory and you do not know which application is responsible? Not too long ago, I found myself running Windows NT mail servers on the Internet supporting high-end mail applications that would simply run out of RAM. After extensive system monitoring, I found out that the leak was in the latest release of the

Winsock libraries. At about the same time I discovered the leak, another company in Europe found it too. A patch was soon released by Microsoft. What transpired was that the library functions were not closing the sockets fast enough and the Winsock libraries could not cope with the traffic.

The number of software components, services, and threads of functionality in Windows Server 2003 are so numerous that it is very difficult, if not impossible, to monitor the tens of thousands of instances of storage, memory, network, or processor usage. But the tools you have on the platform are some of the richest in the server operating systems business.

To achieve such detailed and varied analysis, Windows Server 2003 comes equipped with built-in software objects that are associated with these services and applications. They are able to collect data in these critical areas. So when you collect data, you will focus your data collection on these software components. When you perform data collection, the system will collect the data from the targeted object managers in each respective monitoring location or facility.

There are two methods of data collection that are supported. First you can access Registry functions for performance data, which is a legacy method that is still used. You would use function calls in your code to call performance counter DLLs in the operating system. The second is the new way introduced on the Windows 2000 platform that supports collecting data through the Windows Management Instrumentation (WMI).

Under the WMI, the operating system installs a new technology for recovering data. These are known as managed object files (MOFs). These MOFs either correspond to or are associated with resources in a system. The objects that are the subject of performance monitoring are too numerous to list here, but they can be looked up in the OS' Performance Counters Reference. You can find the reference in the Windows Server 2003 operations guides. They also include the operating system's base services, which include the services that report on RAM, paging file functionality, physical disk usage, and so on. You can also monitor the operating system's advanced services—Active Directory, Active Server Pages, the FTP service, DNS, WINS, and so on.

But to understand the scope and usage of these objects, it first behooves us to understand some performance data and analysis terms.

Performance Monitoring

There are three essential concepts you need to grasp before a complete understanding of performance monitoring is achieved. These concepts are *throughput, queues,* and *response time.* Only after you fully understand these terms can you broaden your scope of analysis and perform calculations to report transfer rate, access time, latency, tolerance, thresholds bottlenecks, and so on . . . and be sure SQL Server is performing at optimum efficiency.

What Is Rate and Throughput?

Throughput is the amount of work done in a unit of time. An example I like to use is drawn from observing my son. If he is able to construct 100 pieces of Legos or K'nex per hour, I can say that his assemblage rate is 100 pieces per hour, assessed over a period of *x* hours, as long as the rate remains constant and he gets enough chocolate milk. However, if the rate of assemblage varies, through fatigue, lack of cheese slices, lack of milk, and so forth, I can calculate the throughput.

The throughput will increase as the number of components increases, or the available resources are reduced. In a computer system, or any system for that matter, the slowest point in the system sets the throughput for the system as a whole, which is why you often hear people use the cliché "the chain is only as strong as its weakest link." We might be able to make references to millions of instruction per second, but that would be meaningless if a critical resource, such as memory, was not available to hold the instruction information, or worse, someone switched off the power.

What Is a Queue?

If I give my son too many K'nex to assemble or reduce the available time he has to perform the calculations and build the model, the number of pieces will begin to pile up. This happens too in software and IS terms, where the number of threads can back up, one behind the other, forming a *queue*. A typical scenario is the line at the bank or the supermarket that forms because there are more people waiting for service than there are tellers or cashiers. When a queue develops, we say that a bottleneck has occurred. Looking for bottlenecks in the system is the essence of monitoring for performance and troubleshooting or problem detection. If there are no bottlenecks, the system might be considered healthy; on the other hand, a bottleneck might soon start to develop.

Queues can also form if requests for resources are not evenly spread over the unit of time. If my son assembles 45 K'nex, at the rate of one K'nex per minute, he will get through every piece in 45 minutes. But if he does nothing for 30 minutes and then suddenly gets inspired, a bottleneck will occur in the final 15 minutes because there are more pieces than can be processed in the remaining time. On computer systems, when queues and bottlenecks develop, systems become unresponsive. No matter how good SQL Server 2005 may be as a DBMS, if queues develop, due for example to a denial of service attack on the server, additional requests for processor or disk resources will be stalled. When requesting services are not satisfied, the system begins to break down. To be alerted of this possibility, you need to reference the response time of a system.

What Is Response Time?

When we talk about *response time,* we talk about the measure of how much time is required to complete a task. Response time will increase as the load increases. A system that has insufficient memory or processing capability will process a huge database sort or a complex join a lot slower than a better-endowed system, with faster hard disks, CPUs, and memory. If response time is not satisfactory, we will have to either work with less data or increase the resources . . . which can be achieved by scale-up of the server and its resources (as by adding more CPUs) or scale-out, which means adding more servers. Scale-up and scale-out are fully discussed in Chapter 9.

How do we measure response time? Easy. You just divide the queue length by the throughput. Response time, queues, and throughput are reported and calculated by the Windows Server 2003 reporting tools, so the work is done for you.

How the Performance Objects Work

Windows Server 2003's performance monitoring objects are endowed with certain functionality known as *performance counters.* These so-called counters perform the actual analysis for you. For example, the hard-disk object is able to calculate transfer rate averages, while a processor-associated object is able to calculate processor time averages.

To gain access to the data or to start the data collection, you would first have to instantiate the performance object. The base performance object you need is stored in the operating system, but you first need to make a copy of one to work with. This is done by calling a create function from a user interface or some other process. As soon as the object is created, its methods, or functions, are called to begin the data collection process and store the data in properties, or they stream the data out to disk, in files or RAM. You can then get at the data to assess the data and present it in some meaningful way.

The objects can be instantiated, or created, at least once. This means that, depending on the object, your analysis software can create at least one copy of the performance object and analyze the counter information it generates. There are also other performance objects that can be instantiated more than once. Windows allows you to instantiate an object for a local computer's services, or you can create an object that operates on a remote computer.

Two methods of data collection and reporting are made possible using performance objects. First, the objects can sample the data. In other words, data is collected periodically rather than when a particular event occurs. This is a good idea because all forms of data collection place a burden on resources and you don't want to be taxing a system when the number of connections it is serving begins to skyrocket. So sampled data has the advantage of being a period-driven load, but it carries the disadvantage that the values may be inaccurate when certain activity falls outside the sampling period.

The other method of data collection is called *event tracing*. Event tracing, new to the Windows platform, enables us to collect data as and when certain events occur. And as there is no sampling window, you can correlate resource usage against events. As an example you can "watch" an application consume memory when it executes a certain function and monitor when and if it releases that memory when the function completes.

But there is a downside to too much of a good thing. Event tracing can consume more resources than sampling. You would thus only want to perform event tracing for short periods where the objective of the trace is to troubleshoot, and not just to monitor per se.

Counters report their data in one of two ways: instantaneous counting or average counting. An *instantaneous counter* displays the data as it happens; you could call it a snapshot. In other words, the counter does not compute the data it receives; it just reports it. On the other hand, *average counting* computes the data for you. For example, it is able to compute bits per second, or pages per second, and so forth. There are other counters you can use that are better able to report percentages, difference, and so on.

Platform Monitoring Tools

As mentioned earlier, Windows ships with two primary monitoring tools that can be used to monitor a SQL Server platform—the Performance Console and Task Manager. Task Manager provides an instant view of systems activity such as memory usage, processor activity and process activity, and resource consumption. It is also very helpful when you need immediate detection of a system problems. On the other hand, Performance Console is used to provide performance analysis and information that can be used for troubleshooting and bottleneck analysis. Performance Console is the tool you would use to establish regular monitoring regimens and continuous server health analysis.

Performance Console comes equipped with two important tools: System Monitor and Performance Logs and Alerts. We will talk about them some more a little later in this chapter. The first tool to whip out, because of its immediacy and as a troubleshooting-cum-information utility, is Task Manager.

Task Manager

The Task Manager is useful for providing quick access to information on applications and services that are currently running on a server. This tool provides information such as processor usage in percentage terms, memory usage, task priority, response, and some statistics about memory and processor performance.

The Task Manager is thus very useful for quick system status check. It is usually started up in response to slow response times, lockups or errors, or messages pointing to lack of systems resources and so forth.

Task Manager, illustrated in Figure 18-1, is started in any of several ways:

- Right-click in the taskbar (right-bottom area where the time is usually displayed) and select Task Manager from the context menu.

- Select CTRL+SHIFT and press the esc key.

- Select CTRL+ALT and press the DELETE key. The Windows Security dialog box loads. Click Task Manager.

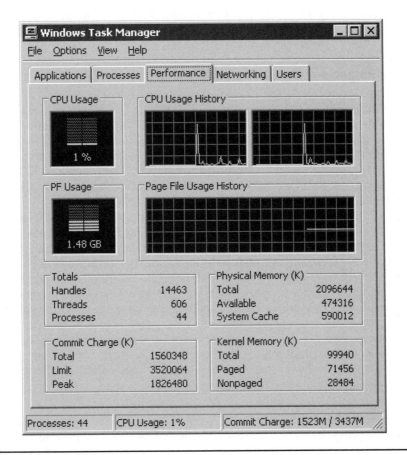

FIGURE 18-1 Task Manager

When the Task Manager loads, you will notice that the dialog box it comes in has three tabs: Applications, Processes, and Performance. There are a number of ways you can display the Task Manager:

- When the Task Manager is running, a CPU gauge icon displaying CPU information is placed into the taskbar on the right-bottom of the screen. If you drag your mouse cursor over this area, you will obtain a pop-up of current accurate CPU usage.

- You can also keep the Task Manager button off the taskbar if you use it a lot. This is done by selecting the Options menu and then checking the Hide When Minimized option. The CPU icon next to the system time remains in place.

- Keep the Manager visible all the time by selecting Always on Top from the Options menu.

- Press CTRL+TAB to switch between the tabs.

- Sort the columns in ascending or descending order by clicking the column heads.

- Columns can also be resized.

You can control the rate of refresh or update from the View | Update Speed menu. You can also pause the update to preserve resources and click Refresh Now to update the display at any time.

Monitoring Processes

The Processes page is the most useful on the Task Manager; it provides a list of running processes on the system and it measures their performance in simple data terms. These include CPU percent used, the CPU Time allocated to a resource, and memory usage.

A number of additional performance or process measures can be added to or removed from the list on the Processes page. Go to the View menu and click the Select Columns option. This will show the Select Columns dialog box, which will allow you to add or subtract Process measures to the Processes list. By the way, a description of each Process Counter is available in Windows Online Help.

You can also terminate a process by selecting the process in the list and then clicking the End Process button. Some processes, however, are protected, but you can terminate them using the kill or remote kill utilities that are included in the operating system (see the Windows Server 2003 operations guides for more information on kill and rkill).

The Performance page allows you to graph the percentage of processor time in kernel mode. To show this, select the view menu and check the Show Kernel Times option. The Kernel Times is the measure of time that applications and services are using operating system services.

If your server sports multiple processors, you can select CPU History on the View menu and graph each processor in a single graph pane or in separate graph panes. The Application page also lists all running applications. It lets you to terminate an application that has become unresponsive. Task Manager thus makes it easy to determine what is in trouble or the cause of trouble on your server.

The Performance Console

The Performance Console comes equipped with the System Monitor, which I will discuss first, and Performance Logs and Alerts. Performance Monitor—often referred to as "perfmon"—is

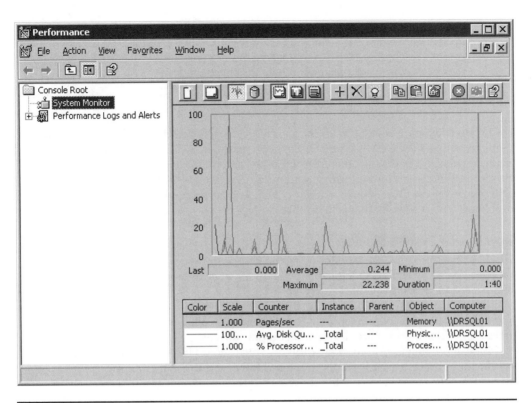

Figure 18-2 System Monitor

usually found on the Administrative Tools menu as Performance. You can also load it like all MMC snap-ins from the Run console, Task Manager, or the command line as *perfmon.msc*. When perfmon starts, it loads a blank System Monitor graph into the console tree, as shown in Figure 18-2.

System Monitor

The System Monitor allows you to analyze system data and research performance and bottlenecks. The utility, which is also hosted in the MMC, allows you to create graphs, histograms (bar charts), and textual reports of performance counter data. The system monitor is ideal for short-term viewing of data and for diagnostics. It includes the following features:

- System Monitor is hosted in MMC, so it is portable. The snap-in can be aimed at any server and remotely monitor the processing on that computer.

- It also provides a toolbar that can be used to copy and paste counters, purge or clear counters, add counters, and so forth.

- It allows you a wide berth on how counter values are displayed. For example, you can change the line style and width to suit your viewing needs. You can change the color of the lines for clarity or to make it easier to read. You can also change the color of the chart and then manipulate the chart window as you deem fit.

- You can use the legends to indicate selected counters and associated data such as the name of the computer, the objects, and object instances.

By the way, the System Monitor is an ActiveX control named *sysmon.ocx*. This means that you can load the OCX into any OLE-compliant application, such as Microsoft Word or Visio, or even an HTML page on a Web site. The OCX is also useful in applications that can be specifically created for performance monitoring and analysis. You can load several into a browser and point them at your "stable" of SQL Server machines. This would enable you to at a glance detect a server that is in trouble.

How to Use System Monitor

First, you can configure the monitor using the toolbar or the shortcut menu. The shortcut menu is loaded by right-clicking in the blank-graph area and selecting the appropriate option. The toolbar is available by default.

With the toolbar, you can configure the type of display you want to view by clicking the View Chart, View Histogram, or View Report button. In other words, the same information can be viewed in either chart, histogram, or report format.

There are differences in the view formats which should be noted. The histograms and charts can be used to view multiple counters. However, each counter only displays a single value. You would use these to track current activity, viewing the graphs as they change. The report is better suited to multiple values.

To obtain a real-time data source, click the View Current Activity button. You can also select the View Log Data button. This option lets you to obtain data from a completed set of running logs.

You first have to select the counters. The counters buttons in the middle of the toolbar includes Add, Delete, and New Counter Set. The last button mentioned resets the display and allows you to select new counters. When you click the Add Counters button, the dialog box illustrated in Figure 18-3 loads.

The Add Counters Dialog Box

This dialog box lets you select the server to monitor, and lets you select performance objects and counters. You should also take notice of the Explain button. This is a useful feature that lets you learn more about the individual counters you select with a single click.

You can also update the display with the Clear Display option. And you can freeze the display with the Freeze Display button, which suspends data collection. Click the Update Data button to resume collection.

When you click the Highlight button, you can select chart or histogram data. This serves the purpose of highlighting the line or bar for a selected counter that is positioned against a white or black background. Noticed that the display can also be exported. It is possible to save it to the Clipboard. Conversely, you can also import the display into another console.

The Properties button gives you access to settings that control fonts, colors, and so forth. Clicking it loads the System Monitor Properties dialog box, as shown in Figure 18-4.

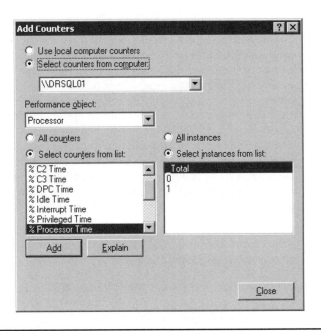

FIGURE 18-3   Add Counters

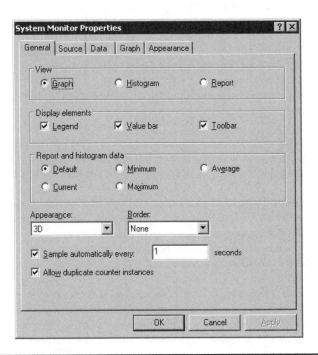

FIGURE 18-4   System Monitor Properties

There are also several ways you can save data from the monitor. You have the option of the Clipboard, and you can add the control, as discussed earlier, to a host application. You can also easily preserve the look and feel of the display by saving it as an HTML file. If you right-click in the pane you are presented the option of saving the display as an HTML file.

You can also import the log file in comma-separated (CSV) or tab-separated (TSV) format and then import the data into a spreadsheet, a SQL Server table, or a report program such as Crystal Reports. Naturally once the data is in a SQL Server database, you can report against it or use it for analysis.

The Add Counters dialog box lets you select all counters and instances to monitor, or specific counters and instances from the list. Understand, however, that the more you monitor, the more system resources you will use. If you use a large number of monitors and counters, consider redirecting the data to log files and then reading the log file data in the display. It makes more sense to work with fewer counters and instances.

TIP   *It is possible to run two instances of System Monitor (in two Performance consoles). This may make it easier to compare data from different sources.*

If you have a look at the Instances list box, the first value, _Total, allows you sum all the instance values and report them in the display. And the lines in the display can be matched with their respective counters. You just have to select them.

The SQL Server Objects

SQL Server comes equipped with objects and counters that can be used by System Monitor to monitor activity in computers running an instance of SQL Server. The *object* is any Windows or SQL Server resource, such as a SQL Server lock or Windows process. Each object contains one or more counters that determine various aspects of the objects to monitor. For example, the *SQL Server Locks* object contains counters called Number of Deadlocks/sec or Lock Timeouts/sec.

Some objects have several instances if multiple resources of a given type exist on the computer. For example, the *Processor* object type will have multiple instances if a system has multiple processors. And the *Databases* object type has one instance for each database in operation on a single instance of SQL Server. Some object types, such as the *Memory Manager* object, have only one instance. If an object type has multiple instances, you can add counters to track statistics for each instance. You may also make a case for monitoring all instances at once.

The performance condition alerts are only available for the first 99 databases. Thus any databases you create after the first 99 will not be included in the sysperfinfo system table in SQL Server. If you use the *sp_add_alert* stored procedure, you will get an error.

When you add counters to the chart, or remove them, and then save the chart settings, you can specify which of the SQL Server objects and counters are monitored when System Monitor is started up.

Table 18-2 provides a list of SQL Server objects and their respective counters.

You can configure System Monitor to display statistics from any SQL Server counter. You can also set a threshold value for any SQL Server counter and then generate an alert when a counter exceeds a threshold. Tie that into the Agent service and you have a system that can make your life as a DBA a lot easier to live.

SQL Server Object	Counter
Buffer Manager	Buffer Cache Hit Ratio
General Statistics	User Connections
Memory Manager	Total Server Memory (KB)
SQL Statistics	SQL Compilations/sec
Buffer Manager	Page Reads/sec
Buffer Manager	Page Writes/sec

TABLE 18-2   Server Objects and Counters

The SQL Server statistics are displayed only when an instance of SQL Server is running. So if you stop the instance of SQL Server, the display of statistics stops. When you start the instance again, then the statistics reporting resumes. The SQL Server objects are listed in Table 18-3.

SQL Server Object	Description
Access Methods	This object searches through and measures allocation of SQL Server database objects. It can also handle the number of index searches or number of pages that are allocated to indexes and data.
Backup Device	This object provides information about backup devices used by backup and restore facility. With it you can monitor the throughput of the backup device, which is key to maintaining a high-end OLTP system.
Buffer Manager	This object provides information about the memory buffers used by an instance of SQL Server, such as free memory and the buffer cache hit ratio.
Cache Manager	This object provides information about the SQL Server cache which is used to store objects such as stored procedures, triggers, and query plans.
Databases	This object provides information about a SQL Server database, such as the amount of free log space available or the number of active transactions in the database. There can be multiple instances of this object, but only up to 99.
General Statistics	This object provides information about general server-wide activity, such as the number of users who are connected to an instance of SQL Server.
Latches	This object provides information about the latches on internal resources, such as database pages, that are used by SQL Server.

TABLE 18-3   Objects and What They Are Used For

SQL Server Object	Description
Locks	This object provides information about the individual lock requests made by SQL Server, such as lock time-outs and deadlocks. There can also be multiple instances of this object.
Memory Manager	This object provides information about SQL Server memory usage, such as the total number of lock structures currently allocated.
Replication Agents	Provides information about the SQL Server replication agents currently running.
Replication Dist	This object measures the number of commands and transactions read from the distribution database and delivered to the Subscriber databases by the Distribution Agent.
Replication Logreader	This object measures the number of commands and transactions read from the published databases and delivered to the distribution database by the Log Reader Agent.
Replication Merge	This object provides information about SQL Server merge replication, such as errors generated or the number of replicated rows that are merged from the Subscriber to the Publisher (see Chapter 10).
Replication Snapshot	This object provides information about SQL Server snapshot replication, such as the number of rows that are bulk-copied from the publishing database.
SQL Statistics	This object provides information about aspects of SQL queries, such as the number of batches of T-SQL statements received by SQL Server.
User settable object	This object performs custom monitoring. Each counter can be a custom stored procedure or any T-SQL statement that returns a value to be monitored. This is a very valuable resource that can be used to monitor the resources consumed by a complex query.

TABLE 18-3   Objects and What They Are Used For (*Continued*)

Monitoring with Transact-SQL Statements

SQL Server provides several T-SQL statements and system stored procedures that allow you to perform ad hoc monitoring of an instance of SQL Server. You can use these resources when you need to gather, at a glance, information about server performance and activity. You can obtain information, in the form of result sets, of the following:

- Current locks
- Current user activity
- Last command batch submitted by a user
- Data space used by a table or database
- Space used by a transaction log

- Oldest active transaction (including replicated transactions) in the database
- Performance information relating to I/O, memory, and network throughput
- Procedure cache usage
- General statistics about SQL Server activity and usage, such as the amount of time the CPU has been performing SQL Server operations or the amount of time SQL Server has spent performing I/O operations.

Most of this information, however, can also be monitored in SQL Server Management Studio, using the SQL-SMO, or System Monitor as earlier discussed.

Performance Logs and Alerts

Performance Monitor includes two types of performance-related logs: counter logs and trace logs. These logs are useful when you want to perform advanced performance analysis and include record keeping that can be done over a period of time. There is also an alerting mechanism built in. The Performance Logs and Alerts tree is shown in Figure 18-5. You can find the tool in the Performance console snap-in, and it is thus started as described earlier.

The *counter logs* record sampled data about hardware resources and system services based on the performance objects. They also work with counters in the same manner as

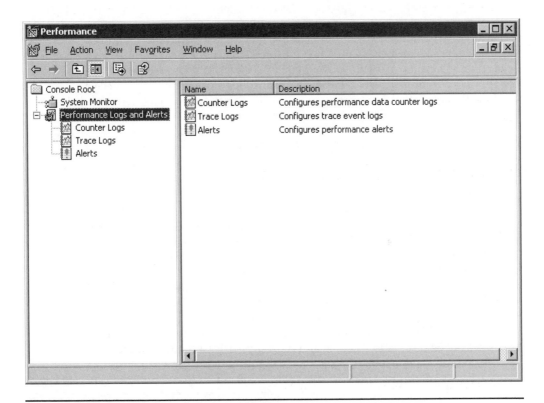

Figure 18-5 Performance Console Logs and Alerts

does the System Monitor. The Performance Logs and Alert Service obtains the data from the operating system as soon as the update interval has elapsed.

The *trace logs* collect the event traces. Trace logs let you measure performance associated with events related to memory, storage file I/O, and so on. As soon as the event occurs, the data is transmitted to the logs. The data is measured continuously from the start of an event to the end of an event. This is different from the sampling that is performed by the system monitor.

The Performance Logs data is obtained by the default Windows kernel trace provider. You can analyze the data using a data-parsing tool, or store it in a SQL Server database for later analysis.

With the alerting function you can define a counter value that will trigger an alert that can send a network message, execute a program, or start a log. This is useful for maintaining a close watch on systems, and when it is coupled with the SQL Server Agent, you can conjure up a sophisticated reporting and alerting storm. You can, for example, monitor unusual activity that does not occur consistently and define an alert to let you know when the event has been triggered. Security-related events are good candidates for the alert service. When you are trying to catch a hacker, there is no better time than when he or she is in the act, trying to break into your accounts database.

You can also configure the alert service to notify you when a particular resource drops below or exceeds certain values or thresholds or baselines that you have established. Counter logs, for example, can also be viewed in System Monitor, and the counter log data can be saved to CSV format and viewed in a spreadsheet, through report software, or in a special SQL Server database that can hold the data for later analysis. You can configure the logs as circular, which means that when the log file reaches a predetermined size, it will be overwritten. The logs can be linear, and you can collect data for predefined lengths of time. The logs can also be stopped and restarted according to parameters you specify.

As with the System Monitor, you can save files to various formats, such as HTML, or import the entire control OCX into an OLE container.

Using Logs and Alerts with SQL Server 2005

You can get started using Logs and Alerts by right-clicking the Details pane and select the New Log Settings option. You will first be asked to name the log or alert before you can define any of its properties.

Before you can start using Logs and Alerts, you need to check that you have Full Control access to the following subkey: HKEY_CURRENT_MACHINE\SYSTEM\ CurrentControl-Set\Services\SysmonLog\Log_Queries. This key provides access to administrators by default, but access can also be bestowed on a user in the usual fashion through group membership. To do this, open the registry editor (Regedit) and access the Security menu in. In addition in order to run or configure the service, you will need the right to start or configure services on the server. Administrators also have this right by default. It can also be given through security group membership and group policy.

When you choose the Properties option, the Counter Log Properties or Trace Log Properties dialog box loads. The Log and Alert properties are now configured as discussed here. To configure alerts, you first need to configure counters for the alerts, the sample interval, and the alert threshold. The next step requires you to configure an action to take when the event occurs. These can include running a program, sending a message, triggering a counter log, or writing to the event log. You can also configured Alert startup by providing the Start and Stop parameters.

In order to configure counter logs, set the counter log counters and provide a sample interval. To write to log files, provide a file type, size, and path, as well as any automatic naming parameters that might be needed. The counter logs should be defined as either CSV files or TSV files, text files, binary linear, or binary circular files.

The counter logs can also be scheduled to start automatically. However, you cannot configure the service to automatically restart if a log file is configured to stop manually. This also applies to Trace Logs.

Getting to Know Your Servers

It goes without saying, and any good DBA will back me up, that to maintain service level and keep servers and databases available, you need to become familiar with each server, the applications and services running on that server, and the resources they need and use. I am not saying that you have to strike up an intimate relationship with a database server, but it is insufficient to just maintain a subjective feel for how a server is "supposed" to operate. All the monitoring and diagnostics we have covered in this chapter will enable you to quickly reverse a bad situation—the shutting down of mission-critical applications, server attacks, system failures, and so on. System monitoring is thus a critical job that you need to be continuously engaged in.

The first task at hand is to generate data, because otherwise you basically have nothing to compare against. Only after a considerable amount of data has been collected will you have the data with which to make comparisons. Data collection should take place over several weeks, possibly even months, and then, after assessing that data, you will be able to establish baselines against which to base future observations and decision making. This is an important step for any new project involving the operation of SQL Server, especially SQL Server machines engaged in replication in widely distributed data centers.

A new database underpinning a Web application is a good example of a system that needs to be gathering data from the moment it is launched. Unless you have the data for your baseline, how can you say that the system is running "normally?" You first have to determine the baseline before you can make judgment calls. What's considered normal for some machines may be aggressive for others. Other machines may sit idle for most of their lives, and that could be because they are not getting traffic or are endowed with resources that would drive a battleship.

NOTE: *If a server is starting to become unstable, collecting data and setting alerts like crazy might exacerbate the problem. Your first option will be to try and stabilize the system; only then should you set up monitoring and alerts to determine the cause of the instability in the future. In the event of an unresponsive system, you might have to run Task Manager and attempt to end the tasks, applications, and processes that are causing the problems. Fortunately, such events are unlikely to be associated with SQL Server.*

With a baseline in hand, you will quickly be alerted to performance that is out of the ordinary. For example, if you notice that at night the database server's responsiveness begins to diminish suddenly, you may find that the server has received a query that is consuming considerable processing bandwidth . . . the result of a bug or a trigger that has 2,000 lines of cursor code in it. A memory counter would be the object that alerts you when this is taking place.

Your information should also reflect various points in system performance. You should note what constitutes "normal" on a server. For example, at a client we noticed that an Analysis Server was low on RAM and had begun to page out to disk excessively. When we asked the MIS about this, he advised it was "normal" for this time of the day because of replication services that fire. So we moved the drill-downs to a later part of the day and later moved the services to a new server.

It is thus important to note periods of low use, average use, and high or peak use. Systems that provide real-time communications are a good example of servers that should be monitored continuously for this type of information.

TIP *Make baseline performance information available within an arm's reach of your server. This can be in the form of clipboards or journals into which you can paste data. This will allow other system operators to look up a server and determine what might be considered normal.*

Do not expect to obtain any instant insight into system performance either, because the baselines you develop will establish typical values to expect when your system is not experiencing problems.

Monitoring for Bottlenecks

When your system's performance deviates from the baselines you have established, as discussed earlier, bottlenecks occur. So it behooves you to have guidelines. Table 18-4 suggests thresholds for a minimum set of system counters.

The values presented in the table are recommended values for a minimum performance monitoring set. Some of these options may vary and still be satisfactory for SQL Server. The following list of notes provides some additional guidance:

- Depending on what your server is doing (a high-end OLTP system, or an OLAP server) a threshold of 15 percent may be too low. You can also ensure that the disk quota threshold is never suddenly exceeded (you might have to manage the quota manually because most SQL Server databases are installed on standard disks (as opposed to dynamic disks) because they rely on hardware RAID technology that is not compatible with dynamic disk architecture). While not all processes can be blocked from using disk space, it is still a good idea to configure alerts to raise the alarm when this threshold is exceeded.

- The value given for Disk Time in the table is the length of the usage period. In other words, the disk should not be used more than 90 percent of the time. You need to check this value, however, against the advice of the manufacturer. Disks that exceed this may not last too long. I have seen disks easily overheat and crash and burn when the threshold scaled to 100 percent and pegged there for a considerable length of time. This is an important factor to watch in a high-end OLTP system.

Resource	Object	Counter	Threshold
Disk(1)	LogicalDisk	% Free Space	15%
Disk(2)	LogicalDisk	% Disk Time	80%
Disk(3)	PhysicalDisk	Disk Reads/Sec or Disk Writes/Sec	Check manufacturer's specifications
Disk(4)	PhysicalDisk	Current Disk Queue Length	Number of spindles plus 2
Memory(5)	Memory	Available Bytes	4 MB, but best not to drop below 16 MB
Memory(6)	Memory	Pages/Sec	20 per second
Network(7)	Network Segment	% Net Utilization	30%
Paging File(8)	Paging File	% Usage	70% +
Processor (9)	Processor	% Processor Time	85%
Processor(10)	Processor	Interrupts/Sec	1,500 per second
Server (11)	Server	Bytes Total/Sec	N/A
Server(12)	Server	Work Item Shortages	3
Server(13)	Server work queues	Queue Length	4
Multiple Processors(14)	System	Processor Queue Length	2

TABLE 18-4   Thresholds for a Minimum Set of System Counters

- The transfer rate information of your disk is usually printed on the disk or provided in a booklet that ships with the product. You should program alerts if the monitor reports that your rates are exceeding this. If the services are hammering away your disks, you should upgrade to faster technology, such as Ultra-Wide SCSI. Favor 15,000 RPM disks over the lower 10,000 RPM technology. I know the former are more expensive, but it may be worth it.

- The number of spindles is a snapshot evaluation. You should thus observe this value over several intervals. You can also use the Average Disk Queue Length for analysis.

- If free memory drops below 4 MB, the paging activity will begin to increase and system will become sluggish. If the condition continues, you get that familiar message that often popped up on servers advising you that system resources are getting low.

- If the server's memory use increases, you need to keep an eye on this threshold, lest the server exceed baselines and run out of memory.

- This threshold varies according to the type of network you are running. In the case of your typical Ethernet network, the threshold will be around 30 percent.

- Before you try to use this counter, make sure you should fully understand how paging works. The reason I say this is that the threshold varies according to the nature of the hardware and the number of instances you have running on the server, so understanding how all the factors influence paging is an important prerequisite.

- Processor Time can be easily observed in the Task Manager, and any level of processor use at the 85 percent or higher mark should make you nervous. You should first try and use Task Manager to identify the process that is using up your CPU's bandwidth. If it is a critical function in SQL Server, you might need to add another processor or upgrade to a faster CPU. When SQL Server is idle, the System Idle Process uses the CPU most of the time.

- This processor counter can be used to raise the alarm to possible hardware problems. If you notice that this counter increases dramatically without a corresponding increase in server activity, it points to a piece of hardware that is responsible for the flood in interrupts. The problem hardware might be a disk controller card or interface, a network interface card, or something less obvious.

- You can sum the total (Bytes Total/sec) for all servers with this counter. And if the value is equal to the maximum transfer rate for the network, you may have some network topology problems to sort out.

- Don't let Bytes Total/sec value exceed 3. If it does, you may have to change parameters in the Registry. Advanced information on WorkItems is beyond the scope of this book, but you can look up the information on WorkItems in the Microsoft Knowledge Base, which has a complete discussion of the Work Item Shortages counter.

- The server work queue is another snapshot counter that may signal a processor bottleneck. Keep a watch on this counter over several intervals.

- Another snapshot counter, the processor queue length, should monitored over several intervals. If you notice a value higher than 2 over several intervals, you should start an investigation.

Identifying Bottlenecks

Bottlenecks will arise as sure as the sun sets in the West when excessive demand is placed on a system's resources. Bottlenecks are present in every system, albeit to varying degrees. Even the human body can only take so much before the soul is squeezed out of it. When you monitor SQL Server for bottlenecks, you gain the ability to determine whether changes can be made to a limiting component with the objective of getting it to perform at an optimal level.

There are several reasons that bottlenecks occur:

- The server has insufficient resources. You are thus required to add additional or upgraded components.

- You have resources of the same type that do not share workloads evenly. A good example is a collection of hard disks in which one is being monopolized.

- Your have malfunctioning resources.

- Resources are incorrectly configured.

Analyzing Bottlenecks on SQL Server

When you analyze event data, you will often discover that low numbers can be just as meaningful as high numbers. If you find that a number is lower than you expected, it may point to a problem in another area. For example,

- There might be another component that is preventing the load from reaching the component in question.

- Network congestion may be preventing client requests from reaching the server. It is also possible that your network connection is down and the server is still because no one is connected to it.

- A bottleneck somewhere in or on the network may be preventing client computers from accessing the server as frequently as they usually do. On the other hand, the Internet might have finally shut down.

- You may also have not configured the performance monitoring tools correctly. For example, if you have not turned on the disk counters, or you are looking at the wrong instance, the wrong counters, or the wrong computer, event data numbers may appear inexplicably low and even nonexistent. I guess you might need a counter for Murphy's law, all things considered.

So when a low number indicates that the system is performing better than expected, you should not become nonchalant. Table 18-5 lists five key areas to monitor when tracking server performance and identifying bottlenecks.

Bottleneck Candidate	Effects on the Server
Memory usage	Insufficient memory allocated or available to SQL Server will degrade performance. Data must be read from the disk continually rather than residing in the data cache. Windows NT 4.0 and Windows 2000 perform excessive paging by swapping data to and from the disk as the pages are needed.
CPU processor utilization	A constantly high CPU rate may indicate the need for a CPU upgrade or the addition of multiple processors. You need to be sure of what the cause is. Adding another CPU might require you to fork out another $20,000 in licensing.
Disk I/O performance	A slow disk I/O (disk reads and writes) will cause transaction throughput to degrade. The higher the RPM the better the performance.
User connections	An improperly configured number of users can cause the system to run slowly. It can also limit the amount of memory that would otherwise have been made available to SQL Server.
Blocking locks	A process may be forcing another process to wait, thereby slowing down or stopping the blocking process.

TABLE 18-5   Tracking SQL Server Performance

Performance Monitoring Overhead

There are several techniques you can use to ensure that performance-monitoring overhead is kept to a minimum on any database server you are monitoring.

The System Monitor application can be demanding on resources. It may be better for you to use logs than to display graphs. You can then import the data into report programs and databases for later analysis. Save the logs to storage that is not being monitored, or to a hard disk that is not the object of some form of analysis. Also make sure the logs are not growing too big. If you are restricted from setting a quota or an alert on the disk space, make sure to keep your eye on the disks.

Do not overdo it on the number of counters you are using at the same time. Some counters are costly on performance and can actually increase overhead, which will be counterproductive. It is also tough to monitor many things at once. Factor in what each counter consumes in overhead. This information is available in the Windows Server 2000 support CDs.

Tight collection intervals can also be costly, and you can over-monitor if you get too eager. Microsoft recommends that you leave a ten-minute interval between data collection periods.

Keep monitoring during peak usage periods to obtain the best assessment of resource usage. And at the same time, take care not to impact available resources. Naturally it makes no sense to monitor a system that is idle, and that is something you should only do if you need to know what the server looks like when it is not under load.

You should also monitoring remotely. Remote monitoring allows for a centralized data collection. You can also collect data from several servers and save the data to the local machine or a local database server. However, network bandwidth increases as you collect more data and you collect it more often. So consider keeping the number of servers in a monitored group to no more than between 10 and 15. To increase network bandwidth, consider saving the remote data to log files on the remote servers and then either copying the data to the local computer or database or viewing it remotely.

Finally, I guess there is also a case for being too cautious. As I said earlier, monitoring is in itself resource intensive. As long as you frequently gather data and analyze, it you'll be okay.

DBCC

T-SQL provides DBCC statements that act as Database Console Commands for SQL Server 2005. These statements check the physical and logical consistency of a database. The DBCC statements can fix detected problems. They are grouped into the categories listed in Table 18-6.

The DBCC statements take input parameters and return values. All DBCC statement parameters can accept both Unicode and DBCS (double-byte character set) literals. Many DBCC commands can produce output in tabular form using the WITH TABLERESULTS option. This information can be loaded into a table for further use. The DBCC commands are fully covered in the Books Online, and based on the vastness of the documentation, it would be redundant to cover them in this book. As a shortcut, however, Appendix provides a brief explanation of each command.

Statement Category	Process
Maintenance statements	Maintenance tasks on a database, index, or filegroup.
Miscellaneous statements	Miscellaneous tasks such as enabling row-level locking or removing a dynamic-link library (DLL) from memory.
Status statements	Status checks.
Validation statements	Validation operations on a database, table, index, catalog, filegroup, system tables, or allocation of database pages.

TABLE 18-6   The DBCC Statement Categories

In Review

This chapter is devoted to the monitoring tools for SQL Server. I devoted most of this chapter to performance monitoring because it is such a critical area and not adequately covered in Books Online or in other volumes. Many a DBA forgets that the maintenance of the platform and its resources are critical to the health of any server service or DBMS.

Often a server will be upgraded for no reason because bottlenecks were detected but not identified. Throwing in another CPU or two does not always solve the problem, and in many cases does not warrant the stress of the upgrade.

T-SQL Reference

T his appendix provides brief explanations of the T-SQL constructions such as functions, general commands, and system stored procedures. It essentially summarizes T-SQL reference information, providing a quick look-up facility. The full text and usage code are available in Books Online. These commands can be used in your application, in Query Analyzer, Enterprise Manager, and from the command-line utilities such as ISQL and OSQL. They represent the bulk of the most frequently used facilities provided by T-SQL. Many more procedures are available, such as the extended stored procedures, but they are less frequently used and can be referenced in SQL Server Books Online. The full explanation and usage of arguments and parameters is accessible from SQL Server Books Online.

T-SQL Construct	Usage, Usage Tips, Suggestions, and References
+ (Add)	Adds two numbers. This addition arithmetic operator can also add a number, in days, to a date.
+ (Positive)	A unary operator that returns the positive value of a numeric expression.
+ (String Concatenation)	An operator in a string expression that concatenates two or more character or binary strings or columns, or else a combination of strings and column names into one expression.
– (Negative)	A unary operator that returns the negative value of a numeric expression.
– (Subtract)	The arithmetic operator subtracts two numbers and can also subtract a number of days from a date.
* (Multiply)	The arithmetic multiplication operator multiplies two expressions.
/ (Divide)	The arithmetic division operator divides one number by another.
% (Modulo)	Provides the remainder of one number divided by another.
% (Wildcard—Character(s) to Match)	Matches any string of zero or more characters and can be used as either a prefix or a suffix.

T-SQL Construct	Usage, Usage Tips, Suggestions, and References
& (Bitwise AND)	Performs the bitwise logical AND operation between two integer values.
| (Bitwise OR)	Performs the bitwise logical OR operation between two given integer values as translated to binary expressions within Transact-SQL statements.
^ (Bitwise Exclusive OR)	Performs the bitwise exclusive OR operation between two given integer values as translated to binary expressions within Transact-SQL statements.
~ (Bitwise NOT)	Performs a bitwise logical NOT operation for one given integer value as translated to binary expressions within Transact-SQL statements.
= (Equal)	A comparison operator that compares two expressions for equality. When you compare nonnull expressions, the result is TRUE if both operands are equal; otherwise, the result is FALSE. If either or both operands are NULL and SET ANSI_NULLS is set to ON, the result is NULL. If SET ANSI_NULLS is set to OFF, the result is FALSE if one of the operands is NULL, and TRUE if both operands are NULL.
> (Greater Than)	A comparison operator that compares two expressions to determine if the left value is the *greater* value. When you compare nonnull expressions, the result is TRUE if the left operand has a higher value than the right operand; otherwise, the result is FALSE. If either or both operands are NULL and SET ANSI_NULLS is set to ON, the result is NULL. If SET ANSI_NULLS is set to OFF, the result is FALSE if one of the operands is NULL, and TRUE if both operands are NULL.
< (Less Than)	A comparison operator that compares two expressions to determine if the left value is the *lesser* value. When you compare nonnull expressions, the result is TRUE if the left operand has a lower value than the right operand; otherwise, the result is FALSE. If either or both operands are NULL and SET ANSI_NULLS is set to ON, the result is NULL. If SET ANSI_NULLS is set to OFF, the result is FALSE if one of the operands is NULL, and TRUE if both operands are NULL.
>= (Greater Than or Equal To)	A comparison operator that compares two expressions to determine if the left value is *greater than or equal to* the right value. When you compare nonnull expressions, the result is TRUE if the left operand has a higher or equal value than the right operand; otherwise, the result is FALSE. If either or both operands are NULL and SET ANSI_NULLS is set to ON, the result is NULL. If SET ANSI_NULLS is set to OFF, the result is FALSE if one of the operands is NULL, and TRUE if both operands are NULL.

T-SQL Construct	Usage, Usage Tips, Suggestions, and References
<= (Less Than or Equal To)	A comparison operator that compares two expressions to determine if the left value is *less than or equal to* the right value. When you compare nonnull expressions, the result is TRUE if the left operand has a lower or equal value than the right operand; otherwise, the result is FALSE. If either or both operands are NULL and SET ANSI_NULLS is set to ON, the result is NULL. If SET ANSI_NULLS is set to OFF, the result is FALSE if one of the operands is NULL, and TRUE if both operands are NULL.
<> (Not Equal To)	A comparison operator that compares two expressions to determine if the left value is *not equal to* the right value. When you compare nonnull expressions, the result is TRUE if the left operand is not equal to the right operand; otherwise, the result is FALSE. If either or both operands are NULL and SET ANSI_NULLS is set to ON, the result is NULL. If SET ANSI_NULLS is set to OFF, the result is FALSE if one of the operands is NULL, and TRUE if both operands are NULL.
!< (Not Less Than)	A comparison operator that compares two expressions to determine if the left value is *not less than* greater value. When you compare nonnull expressions, the result is TRUE if the left operand does not have a lower value than the right operand; otherwise, the result is FALSE. If either or both operands are NULL and SET ANSI_NULLS is set to ON, the result is NULL. If SET ANSI_NULLS is set to OFF, the result is FALSE if one of the operands is NULL, and TRUE if both operands are NULL.
!= (Not Equal To)	A comparison operator that compares two expressions to determine if the left value is *not equal to* the right value. Functions the same as the Not Equal To (<>) comparison operator.
!> (Not Greater Than)	A comparison operator that compares two expressions to determine if the left value is *not greater than* the right value. When you compare nonnull expressions, the result is TRUE if the left operand does not have a higher value than the right operand; otherwise, the result is FALSE. If either or both operands are NULL and SET ANSI_NULLS is set to ON, the result is NULL. If SET ANSI_NULLS is set to OFF, the result is FALSE if one of the operands is NULL, and TRUE if both operands are NULL.
- - (Comment)	Indicates user-provided text that is not evaluated by SQL Server. Comments can be inserted on a separate line, nested (- - only) at the end of a Transact-SQL command line, or within a Transact-SQL statement. Two hyphens (- -) is the SQL-92 ((or later)) standard indicator for comments.

T-SQL Construct	Usage, Usage Tips, Suggestions, and References
/*...*/ (Comment)	Indicates user-provided text that is not evaluated by SQL Server. The text between the /* and */ commenting characters is ignored by SQL Server.
[ ] (Wildcard - Character(s) to Match)	The wildcard characters are used to match any single character within the specified range or set that is specified inside the square brackets.
[^] (Wildcard - Character(s) Not to Match)	The wildcard characters are used *not* to match any single character within the specified range or set that is specified inside the square brackets.
_ (Wildcard - Match One Character)	The underscore can be used to match any single character, and can be used as either a prefix or a suffix. The underscore can also be replaced by another wildcard if it exists in the values you are scanning, for example jeff_shapiro@sql2ktcr.book.
$PARTITION	This construct returns the partition number into which a set of partitioning column values would be mapped for any specified partition function.
@@CONNECTIONS	This function returns the number of connections, or attempted connections, that have occurred since SQL Server was last started.
@@CPU_BUSY	This function returns the time in milliseconds—based on the resolution of the system timer—that the CPU has spent working since SQL Server was last started.
@@CURSOR_ROWS	This function returns the number of qualifying rows currently in the last cursor opened on your connection. To improve performance, SQL Server can populate large keysets and static cursors asynchronously. @@CURSOR_ROWS can be called to determine that the number of the rows that qualify for a cursor are retrieved at the time @@CURSOR_ROWS is called.
@@DATEFIRST	This function returns the current value of the SET DATEFIRST parameter, which indicates the specified first day of each week: 1 for Monday, 2 for Wednesday, and so on through 7 for Sunday.
@@DBTS	This function returns the value of the current timestamp data type for the current database. This timestamp is guaranteed to be unique in the database.
@@ERROR	This function returns the error number for the last Transact-SQL statement you executed.
@@FETCH_STATUS	This function returns the status of the last cursor FETCH statement issued against any cursor currently opened by the connection.
@@IDENTITY	This function returns the last inserted identity value.

T-SQL Construct	Usage, Usage Tips, Suggestions, and References
@@IDLE	This function returns the time in milliseconds (based on the resolution of the system timer) that SQL Server has been idle since it was last started.
@@IO_BUSY	This function returns the time in milliseconds (based on the resolution of the system timer) that SQL Server has spent performing input and output operations since it was last started.
@@LANGID	This function returns the local language identifier (ID) of the language currently in use.
@@LANGUAGE	This function returns the name of the language currently in use.
@@LOCK_TIMEOUT	This function returns the current lock time-out setting, in milliseconds, for the current session.
@@MAX_CONNECTIONS	This function returns the maximum number of simultaneous user connections allowed on a SQL Server. The number returned is not necessarily the number currently configured.
@@MAX_PRECISION	This function returns the precision level used by decimal and numeric data types as currently set in the server.
@@NESTLEVEL	This function returns the nesting level of the current stored procedure execution (initially 0).
@@OPTIONS	This function returns information about current SET options.
@@PACK_RECEIVED	This function returns the number of input packets read from the network by SQL Server since last started.
@@PACK_SENT	This function returns the number of output packets written to the network by SQL Server since last started.
@@PACKET_ERRORS	This function returns the number of network packet errors that have occurred on SQL Server connections since SQL Server was last started.
@@PROCID	This function returns the stored procedure identifier (ID) of the current procedure.
@@REMSERVER	This function returns the name of the remote SQL Server database server as it appears in the login record.
@@ROWCOUNT	This function returns the number of rows affected by the last statement.
@@SERVERNAME	This function returns the name of the local server running SQL Server.
@@SERVICENAME	This function returns the name of the Registry key under which SQL Server is running. @@SERVICENAME returns MSSQLServer if the current instance is the default instance. The function also returns the instance name if the current instance is a named instance.

T-SQL Construct	Usage, Usage Tips, Suggestions, and References
@@SPID	This function returns the server process identifier (ID) of the current user process.
@@TEXTSIZE	This function returns the current value of the TEXTSIZE option of the SET statement, which specifies the maximum length, in bytes, of text or image data that a SELECT statement returns.
@@TIMETICKS	This function returns the number of microseconds per tick.
@@TOTAL_ERRORS	This function returns the number of disk read/write errors encountered by SQL Server since it was last started.
@@TOTAL_READ	This function returns the number of disk reads (not cache reads) by SQL Server since it was last started.
@@TOTAL_WRITE	This function returns the number of disk writes by SQL Server since it was last started.
@@TRANCOUNT	This function returns the number of active transactions for the current connection.
@@VERSION	This function returns the date, version, and processor type for the current installation of SQL Server 2005.
ABS	This function returns the absolute, positive value of the given numeric expression.
ACOS	This function returns the angle, in radians, whose cosine is the given float expression; also called arccosine.
ALL	This compares a scalar value with a single-column set of values.
ALTER APPLICATION ROLE	This changes the name, password, or default schema of an application role.
ALTER ASSEMBLY	This changes a .NET assembly by modifying the SQL Server catalog properties of an assembly.
ALTER ASYMMETRIC KEY	This changes the properties of an asymmetric key.
ALTER AUTHORIZATION	Changes ownership.
ALTER CERTIFICATE	Changes the properties of a certificate.
ALTER CREDENTIAL	Changes the properties of a credential.
ALTER DATABASE	Adds or removes files and filegroups from a database. Can also be used to modify the attributes of files and filegroups, such as changing the name or size of a file. ALTER DATABASE provides the capability to change the database name, the filegroup names, and the logical names of data files and log files.
ALTER ENDPOINT	Enables modifying an existing endpoint by adding a new method to an existing endpoint; or by modifying or dropping an existing method from the endpoint; or by changing the properties of an endpoint.
ALTER FULLTEXT CATALOG	Changes the properties of a fulltext catalog.
ALTER FULLTEXT INDEX	Changes properties of a fulltext index.

T-SQL Construct	Usage, Usage Tips, Suggestions, and References
ALTER FUNCTION	Alters an existing user-defined function, which was first created by executing the CREATE FUNCTION statement. It does not change permissions or any dependent functions, stored procedures, or triggers. For more information about the parameters used in the ALTER FUNCTION statement, also see the CREATE FUNCTION statement.
ALTER INDEX	Used for modifying an index in a view or table, either XML or relational.
ALTER LOGIN	Lets you changes the properties of a login.
ALTER MASTER KEY	Changes the properties of a master key.
ALTER MESSAGE TYPE	Changes the properties of message type.
ALTER PARTITION FUNCTION	Alters a partition function by splitting or merging its boundary values.
ALTER PARTITION SCHEME	Alters the properties of a partition scheme.
ALTER PROCEDURE	Alters a previously created procedure, which is created by executing the CREATE PROCEDURE statement. It does not change permissions or affect any dependent stored procedures or triggers. For more information about the parameters used in the ALTER PROCEDURE statement, see the CREATE PROCEDURE statement.
ALTER QUEUE	Alters the properties of a queue.
ALTER REMOTE SERVICE BINDING	This changes the user associated with a remote service binding. You can also change the anonymous authentication setting for the binding.
ALTER ROLE	This lets you change the name of the role.
ALTER ROUTE	Alters route information.
ALTER SCHEMA	Transfers the schema information between objects.
ALTER SERVICE	Lets you change the service.
ALTER SERVICE MASTER KEY	Changes the service master key for SQL Server.
ALTER SYMMETRIC KEY	Lets you change the properties of a symmetric key.
ALTER TABLE	This statement modifies a table definition by altering, adding, or dropping columns and constraints. It is also used to disable or enable constraints and triggers.
ALTER TRIGGER	This statement alters the definition of a trigger created previously by the CREATE TRIGGER statement. For more information about the parameters used in the ALTER TRIGGER statement, see also CREATE TRIGGER.
ALTER USER	Renames the user or changes its default schema.

PART IV

T-SQL Construct	Usage, Usage Tips, Suggestions, and References
ALTER VIEW	Allows you to alter a previously created view (created by executing CREATE VIEW), including indexed views, without affecting dependent stored procedures or triggers and without changing permissions. For more information about the parameters used in the ALTER VIEW statement, see also CREATE VIEW.
ALTER XML SCHEMA COLLECTION	Adds new schema components to an existing XML schema collection.
AND	Used to combine two Boolean expressions and returns TRUE when both expressions are TRUE. When more than one logical operator is used in a statement, AND operators are evaluated first. You can change the order of evaluation by using parentheses.
ANY	Used to compare a scalar value with a single-column set of values. For more information, see also SOME|ANY.
APPLOCK_MODE	This returns the lock mode owned by the lock owner on a particular application resource. It is an application lock function, which operates on the current database to which it is scoped.
APPLOCK_TEST	Returns information for the application of the APPLOCK-MODE.
APP_NAME	Used to return the application name for the current session, if set by the application.
ASCII	This command will return the ASCII code value of the leftmost character of a character expression.
ASIN	Will return the angle, in radians, whose sine is the given float expression. It is also called arcsine.
ASSEMBLY PROPERTY	Returns assembly information.
ASYMKEY_ID	Returns the key information.
ATAN	Will return the angle in radians whose tangent is the given float expression. It is also called arctangent.
ATN2	Will returns the angle, in radians, whose tangent is between the two given float expressions. It is also called arctangent.
AVG	Used to return the average of the values in a group. The Null values are ignored.
BACKUP	This statement backs up an entire database or transaction log, or one or more files or filegroups. For more information about database backup and restore operations see Chapter 7.
BACKUP KEYS	Used to export keys.
BEGIN...END	A block that encloses a series of Transact-SQL statements so that a group of Transact-SQL statements can be executed. BEGIN and END are control-of-flow language keywords, similar to standard procedures in languages like Pascal.

T-SQL Construct	Usage, Usage Tips, Suggestions, and References
BEGIN COVERSATION TIMER	Starts a timer for the service broker.
BEGIN DIALOG CONVERSATION	Starts the interservice dialog.
BEGIN DISTRIBUTED TRANSACTION	This clause specifies the start of the T-SQL distributed transaction managed by Microsoft Distributed Transaction Coordinator (MS DTC).
BEGIN TRANSACTION	This clause marks the starting point of an explicit, local transaction. BEGIN TRANSACTION increments @@TRANCOUNT by 1.
BETWEEN	This clause specifies a range to test.
binary and varbinary	Binary data types of either fixed-length (binary) or variable-length (varbinary).
BINARY_CHECKSUM	This command returns the binary checksum value computed over a row of a table or over a list of expressions. BINARY_CHECKSUM can be used to detect changes to a row of a table.
bit	Integer data type 1, 0, or NULL.
BREAK	Use this command to exit the innermost WHILE loop. Any statements following the END keyword are ignored. BREAK is often, but not always, activated by an IF test.
BULK INSERT	Used to copy data into a database table or view in a user-specified format. It is frequently used for the initial load of data warehouse tables.
CASE	Used in flow-control segments, this evaluates a list of conditions and returns one of multiple possible result expressions.
CAST and CONVERT	Explicitly converts an expression of one data type to another. CAST and CONVERT provide similar functionality.
CATCH (TRY...CATCH)	The CATCH block of a T-SQL exception handler (see also TRY).
CEILING	This returns the smallest integer greater than, or equal to, the given numeric expression.
CertProperty	Gets you the value of a certificate property.
char and varchar	Fixed-length (char) or variable-length (varchar) character data types.
CHAR	This function converts an int ASCII code to a character.
CHARINDEX	This function returns the starting position of the specified expression in a character string.
CHECKPOINT	Forces all dirty pages for the current database to be written to disk. Dirty pages are data or log pages modified after being entered into the buffer cache, but for which the modifications have not yet been written to disk.

T-SQL Construct	Usage, Usage Tips, Suggestions, and References
CHECKSUM	This function returns the checksum value computed over a row of a table, or over a list of expressions. CHECKSUM is intended for use in building hash indices.
CHECKSUM_AGG	This function returns the checksum of the values in a group. Null values are ignored.
CLOSE	Closes an open cursor by releasing the current result set and freeing any cursor locks held on the rows on which the cursor is positioned. The CLOSE leaves the data structures accessible for reopening, but fetches and positioned updates are not allowed until the cursor is reopened. CLOSE must be issued on an open cursor; it is not allowed on cursors that have only been declared or are already closed.
CLOSE KEYS	Used to close keys in open sessions.
COALESCE	This function returns the first nonnull expression among its arguments.
COLLATE	A clause that can be applied to a database definition or a column definition to define the collation, or to a character string expression to apply a collation cast. *Windows Collation Name* specifies the Windows collation name in the COLLATE clause. The Windows collation name is composed of the collation designator and the comparison styles. *SQL Collation Name* is a single string that specifies the collation name for a SQL collation.
COLLATIONPROPERTY	This function returns the property of a given collation.
COL_LENGTH	This function returns the defined length of a column.
COL_NAME	This function returns the name of a database column given the corresponding table identification number and column identification number.
COLUMNPROPERTY	This function returns information about a column or procedure parameter.
COMMIT TRANSACTION	Marks the end of a successful implicit or user-defined transaction. If @@TRANCOUNT is 1, COMMIT TRANSACTION makes all data modifications performed since the start of the transaction a permanent part of the database, frees the resources held by the connection, and decrements @@TRANCOUNT to 0. If @@TRANCOUNT is greater than 1, COMMIT TRANSACTION decrements @@TRANCOUNT only by 1.
COMMIT WORK	Marks the end of a transaction.
COMPUTE	Use this call to generate a total as an additional summary column at the end of the result set. You can use this with BY, and the COMPUTE clause will generate control-breaks and subtotals in the result set. You can specify COMPUTE BY and COMPUTE in the same query.

T-SQL Construct	Usage, Usage Tips, Suggestions, and References
Constants	A constant, also known as a literal or a scalar value, is a symbol that represents a specific data value. The format of a constant depends on the data type of the value it represents.
CONTAINS	Is a predicate used to search columns containing character-based data types for precise or fuzzy (less precise) matches to single words and phrases, the proximity of words within a certain distance of one another, or weighted matches. CONTAINS can search for words and phrases, prefixes, words near other words, and so on.
CONTAINSTABLE	This function returns a table of zero, one, or more rows for those columns containing character-based data types for precise or fuzzy (less precise) matches to single words and phrases, matches according to the proximity of words within a certain distance of one another, or weighted matches. CONTAINSTABLE can be referenced in the FROM clause of a SELECT statement as if it were a regular table name.
CONTINUE	Restarts a WHILE loop. Any statements after the CONTINUE keyword are ignored. CONTINUE is often, but not always, activated by an IF test. For more information, see also WHILE.
CONTEXT_INFO	Use this to returns the context_info value that was set for the current session or batch.
CONVERT	See CAST and CONVERT earlier.
COS	A mathematical function that returns the trigonometric cosine of the given angle (in radians) in the given expression.
COT	A mathematical function that returns the trigonometric cotangent of the specified angle (in radians) in the given float expression.
COUNT	This function returns the number of items in a group.
COUNT_BIG	This function returns the number of items in a group. COUNT_BIG works like the COUNT function. The only difference between them is their return values: COUNT_BIG always returns a bigint data type value. COUNT always returns an int data type value.
CREATE AGGREGATE	Creates a user-defined (.NET Framework) aggregate function whose implementation is defined in a class. See also CREATE ASSEMBLY later.
CREATE APPLICATION ROLE	Adds and application role.
CREATE ASSEMBLY	Used to bind an assembly to the SQL Server .NET Framework Common Language Runtime (CLR) engine.
CREATE ASYMMETRIC KEY	Creates an asymmetric key.
CREATE CERTIFICATE	Creates a certificate.
CREATE CONTRACT	Used for service broker message definitions.

PART IV

T-SQL Construct	Usage, Usage Tips, Suggestions, and References
CREATE CREDENTIAL	Creates a credential.
CREATE DATABASE	Creates a new database and the files used to store the database, or attaches a database from the files of a previously created database.
CREATE DEFAULT	Creates an object called a *default*. When bound to a column or a user-defined data type, a default specifies a value to be inserted into the column to which the object is bound (or into all columns, in the case of a user-defined data type) when no value is explicitly supplied during an insert. Defaults, a backward compatibility feature, perform some of the same functions as default definitions created using the DEFAULT keyword of ALTER or CREATE TABLE statements. Default definitions are the preferred, standard way to restrict column data because the definition is stored with the table and automatically dropped when the table is dropped. A default is beneficial, however, when the default is used multiple times for multiple columns.
CREATE ENDPOINT	Creates an ENDPOINT and defines its properties for Web service clients.
CREATE EVENT NOTIFICATION	Creates an object that sends information pertaining to a database or server to service broker service.
CREATE FULLTEXT CATALOG	Creates a FULLTEXT service and all its properties.
CREATE FULLTEXT INDEX	Creates the FULLTEXT INDEX for the catalog.
CREATE FUNCTION	Creates a user-defined function, which is a saved Transact-SQL routine that returns a value. User-defined functions cannot be used to perform a set of actions that modify the global database state. User-defined functions, like system functions, can be invoked from a query. They also can be executed through an EXECUTE statement like stored procedures.
CREATE INDEX	Creates an index on a given table or view.
CREATE LOGIN	Creates a SQL Sever login and its associated components, such as password and password policy.
CREATE MASTER KEY	Creates the database master key.
CREATE MESSAGE TYPE	Creates a new message type that defines the name of a message and the validation that the Service Broker performs on messages with that name. Both sides of a conversation define the same message types.
CREATE PARTITION FUNCTION	Creates a function in the current database that maps the rows of a table or index into partitions based on the values of a specified column.
CREATE PARTITION SCHEME	Creates a scheme in the current database that maps the partitions of a partitioned table or index to filegroups.

T-SQL Construct	Usage, Usage Tips, Suggestions, and References
CREATE PROCEDURE	Creates a stored procedure, which is a saved collection of Transact-SQL statements that can take and return user-supplied parameters.
CREATE QUEUE	Creates a new queue in a database for the messages that get sent to a service. The Service Broker places the message on the queue associated with the service.
CREATE REMOTE SERVICE BINDING	Creates a binding that defines the security credentials used to initiate a conversation with a remote service.
CREATE ROLE	Creates a new database role in the current database.
CREATE ROUTE	Adds a new route to the routing table for the current database.
CREATE RULE	Creates an object called a rule. When bound to a column or a user-defined data type, a rule specifies the acceptable values that can be inserted into that column. Rules, a backward compatibility feature, perform some of the same functions as check constraints. CHECK constraints, created using the CHECK keyword of ALTER or CREATE TABLE, are the preferred, standard way to restrict the values in a column (multiple constraints can be defined on one or multiple columns). A column or user-defined data type can have only one rule bound to it. However, a column can have both a rule and one or more check constraints associated with it. When this is true, all restrictions are evaluated.
CREATE SCHEMA	Creates a schema that can be thought of as a conceptual object containing definitions of tables, views, and permissions.
CREATE SERVICE	Creates a new service in the Service Broker.
CREATE STATISTICS	Creates a histogram and associated density groups (collections) over the supplied column or set of columns.
CREATE SYMMETRIC KEY	Creates a symmetric key.
CREATE SYNONYM	Create a synonym.
CREATE TABLE	Creates a new table.
CREATE TRIGGER	Creates a trigger, which is a special kind of stored procedure that executes automatically when a user attempts the specified data-modification statement on the specified table. SQL Server allows the creation of multiple triggers for any given INSERT, UPDATE, or DELETE statement.
CREATE TYPE	Creates a user-defined (.NET Framework) data type whose implementation is defined in a class. See also CREATE ASSEMBLY earlier.
CREATE USER	Creates a user and its associated properties such as password and account policy.

PART IV

T-SQL Construct	Usage, Usage Tips, Suggestions, and References
CREATE VIEW	Creates a virtual table that represents the data in one or more tables in an alternative way. Views are used as security mechanisms by granting permissions for a view but not on the underlying (base) tables.
CREATE XML SCHEMA COLLECTION	Imports an XML SCHEMA collection into a database.
CURRENT_REQUEST_ID	Returns the request ID of the current session.
CURRENT_TIMESTAMP	This function returns the current date and time. This function is equivalent to GETDATE().
CURRENT_USER	This function returns the current user. This function is equivalent to USER_NAME().
cursor	A data type for variables or stored procedure OUTPUT parameters that contain a reference to a cursor. Any variables created with the cursor data type are nullable.
CURSOR_STATUS	A scalar function that allows the caller of a stored procedure to determine whether or not the procedure has returned a cursor and result set for a given parameter.
Cursors	SQL Server statements produce a complete result set, but there are times when the results are best processed one row at a time. Opening a cursor on a result set allows processing the result set one row at a time. SQL Server version 7.0 also introduces assigning a cursor to a variable or parameter with a cursor data type.
DATABASEPROPERTY	This function returns the named database property value for the given database and property name.
DATABASEPROPERTYEX	This function returns the current setting of the specified database option or property for the specified database.
DATALENGTH	This function returns the number of bytes used to represent any expression.
DATEADD	This function returns a new datetime value based on adding an interval to the specified date.
DATEDIFF	This function returns the number of date and time boundaries crossed between two specified dates.
DATENAME	This function returns a character string representing the specified date part of the specified date.
DATEPART	This function returns an integer representing the specified date part of the specified date.
datetime and smalldatetime	Date and time data types for representing date and time of day.
DAY	This function returns an integer representing the day date part of the specified date.
DB_ID	This function returns the database identification (ID) number.

T-SQL Construct	Usage, Usage Tips, Suggestions, and References
DB_NAME	This function returns the database name.
DBCC	The Transact-SQL programming language provides DBCC statements that act as Database Console Commands for SQL Server 2005. These statements check the physical and logical consistency of a database. Many DBCC statements can fix detected problems.
DBCC CHECKALLOC	Checks the consistency of disk space allocation structures for a specified database.
DBCC CHECKCATALOG	Checks for consistency in and between system tables in the specified database.
DBCC CHECKCONSTRAINTS	Checks the integrity of a specified constraint or all constraints on a specified table.
DBCC CHECKDB	Checks the allocation and structural integrity of all the objects in the specified database.
DBCC CHECKFILEGROUP	Checks the allocation and structural integrity of all tables (in the current database) in the specified filegroup.
DBCC CHECKIDENT	Checks the current identity value for the specified table and, if needed, corrects the identity value.
DBCC CHECKTABLE	Checks the integrity of the data, index, text, ntext, and image pages for the specified table or indexed view.
DBCC CLEANTABLE	Reclaims space for dropped variable-length columns and text columns.
DBCC CONCURRENCYVIOLATION	Displays statistics on how many times more than five batches were executed concurrently on SQL Server 2005 Express Engine. Also controls whether these statistics are also recorded in the SQL Server error log.
DBCC DBREINDEX	Rebuilds one or more indexes for a table in the specified database.
DBCC DBREPAIR (switch around)	Drops a damaged database.
DBCC dllname (FREE)	Unloads the specified extended stored procedure dynamic-link library (DLL) from memory.
DBCC DROPCLEANBUFFERS	Removes all clean buffers from the buffer pool.
DBCC FREEPROCCACHE	Removes all elements from the procedure cache.
DBCC FREEE SESSIONCACHE	Flushes the distributed query connection cache used by distributed queries against an instance of SQL Server.
DBCC FREESYSTEMCACHE	Releases all unused cache entries from all caches.
DBCC HELP	This function returns syntax information for the specified DBCC statement.
DBCC INDEXDEFRAG	Defragments clustered and secondary indexes of the specified table or view.

PART IV

T-SQL Construct	Usage, Usage Tips, Suggestions, and References
DBCC INPUTBUFFER	Displays the last statement sent from a client to SQL Server.
DBCC OPENTRAN	Displays information about the oldest active transaction and the oldest distributed and nondistributed replicated transactions, if any, within the specified database. Results are displayed only if there is an active transaction or if the database contains replication information. An informational message is displayed if there are no active transactions.
DBCC OUTPUTBUFFER	This function returns the current output buffer in hexadecimal and ASCII format for the specified system process ID (SPID).
DBCC PINTABLE (DEPRACTED)	Marks a table to be pinned, which means SQL Server does not flush the pages for the table from memory.
DBCC PROCCACHE	Displays information in a table format about the procedure cache.
DBCC SHOWCONTIG (SWITCH)	Displays fragmentation information for the data and indexes of the specified table.
DBCC SHOW_STATISTICS	Displays the current distribution statistics for the specified target on the specified table.
DBCC SHRINKDATABASE	Shrinks the size of the data files in the specified database.
DBCC SHRINKFILE	Shrinks the size of the specified data file or log file for the related database.
DBCC SQLPERF	Provides statistics about the use of transaction-log space in all databases.
DBCC TRACEOFF	Disables the specified trace flag(s).
DBCC TRACEON	Turns on (enables) the specified trace flag.
DBCC TRACESTATUS	Displays the status of trace flags.
DBCC UNPINTABLE	Marks a table as unpinned. After a table is marked as unpinned, the table pages in the buffer cache can be flushed.
DBCC UPDATEUSAGE	Reports and corrects inaccuracies in the sysindexes table, which may result in incorrect space usage reports by the sp_spaceused system stored procedure.
DBCC USEROPTIONS	This function returns the SET options active (set) for the current connection.
DEALLOCATE	Removes a cursor reference. When the last cursor reference is deallocated, the data structures making up the cursor are released by SQL Server.
decimal and numeric	Numeric data types with fixed precision and scale.

T-SQL Construct	Usage, Usage Tips, Suggestions, and References
DECLARE @ *local_variable*	Variables are declared in the body of a batch or procedure with the DECLARE statement and are assigned values with either a SET or SELECT statement. Cursor variables can be declared with this statement and used with other cursor-related statements. After declaration, all variables are initialized as NULL.
DECLARE CURSOR	Defines the attributes of a Transact-SQL server cursor, such as its scrolling behavior and the query used to build the result set on which the cursor operates. DECLARE CURSOR accepts both a syntax based on the SQL-92 ((or later)) standard and a syntax using a set of Transact-SQL extensions.
DecryptBy...	Commands used to decrypt using keys, certificates and passwords.
DEGREES	Given an angle in radians, returns the corresponding angle in degrees.
DELETE	Removes rows from a table.
DENSE_RANK	Returns the rank of rows within the partition of a result set.
DENY	Creates an entry in the security system that denies a permission from a security account in the current database and prevents the security account from inheriting the permission through its group or role memberships.
DIFFERENCE	This function returns the difference between the SOUNDEX values of two character expressions as an integer.
DISABLE TRIGGER	Disables a trigger such that it will not fire.
DROP AGGREGATE	Drops the aggregate from a database.
DROP APPLICATION	Drops the application.
DROP ASSEMBLY	Drops an assembly.
DROP ASYMMETRIC KEY	Drops an asymmetric key.
DROP CERTIFICATE	Drops a certificate.
DROP CONTRACT	Drops a contract.
DROP CREDENTIAL	Drops a credential.
DROP DATABASE	Removes one or more databases from SQL Server. Removing a database deletes the database and the disk files used by the database.
DROP DEFAULT	Removes one or more user-defined defaults from the current database.
DROP ENDPOINT	Removes the endpoint from the system.
DROP EVENT NOTIFICATION	Removes an even notification.
DROP FULLTEXT CATALOG	Removes a fulltext catalog.
DROP FULLTEXT INDEX	Removes a fulltext index associated with a catalog.

T-SQL Construct	Usage, Usage Tips, Suggestions, and References
DROP FUNCTION	Removes one or more user-defined functions from the current database. User-defined functions are created using CREATE FUNCTION and modified using ALTER FUNCTION.
DROP INDEX	Removes one or more indexes from the current database.
DROP LOGIN	Removes the login.
DROP MASTER KEY	Removes the master key.
DROP MESSAGE TYPE	Removes the message type.
DROP PARTITION FUNCTION	Removes the partition function from the database.
DROP PARTITIION SCHEME	Removes the partition scheme from the database.
DROP PROCEDURE	Removes one or more stored procedures or procedure groups from the current database.
DROP QUEUE	Removes a queue.
DROP REMOTE SERVICE BINDING	Removes the remote service binding.
DROP ROLE	Removes a role from the database.
DROP ROUTE	Removes a route from the service broker.
DROP RULE	Removes one or more user-defined rules from the current database.
DROP SCHEMA	Removes the schemas associated with a database.
DROP SERVICE	Removes a service on the server.
DROP SIGNATURE	Removes a signature.
DROP STATISTICS	Drops statistics for multiple collections within the specified tables (in the current database).
DROP SYMMETRIC KEY	Removes the symmetric key.
DROPY SYNONYM	Removes a synonym.
DROP TABLE	Removes a table definition and all data, indexes, triggers, constraints, and permission specifications for that table. Any view or stored procedure that references the dropped table must be explicitly dropped by using the DROP VIEW or DROP PROCEDURE statement.
DROP TRIGGER	Removes one or more triggers from the current database.
DROP TYPE	Removes a user defined data type.
DROP USER	Removes a user from a database.
DROP VIEW	Removes one or more views from the current database. DROP VIEW can be executed against indexed views.
DROP XML SCHEMA	Removes a XML schema from the database.

T-SQL Construct	Usage, Usage Tips, Suggestions, and References
DUMP	Makes a backup copy of a database (DUMP DATABASE) or makes a copy of the transaction log (DUMP TRANSACTION) in a form that can be read into SQL Server using the BACKUP or LOAD statements.
ELSE (IF...ELSE)	Imposes conditions on the execution of a Transact-SQL statement. The Transact-SQL statement *(sql_statement)* following the *Boolean_expression* is executed if the *Boolean_expression* evaluates to TRUE. The optional ELSE keyword is an alternate Transact-SQL statement that is executed when *Boolean_expression* evaluates to FALSE or NULL.
ENABLE TRIGGER	Makes a trigger active so that it will fire when the table or database is accessed.
ENCRYPTBY	Used to encrypt using keys, certificates and passwords.
END (BEGIN...END)	Encloses a series of Transact-SQL statements that will execute as a group. BEGIN...END blocks can be nested.
END CONVERSATION	End the current conversation on the database.
ERROR	Several ERROR commands let you work with SQL Server error messages.
EVENT DATA	The message data in the error.
EXCEPT and INTERSECT	Returns distinct values by comparing the results of two queries.
EXECUTE, EXECUTE AS	Executes a scalar-valued, user-defined function, a system procedure, a user-defined stored procedure, or an extended stored procedure. Also supports the execution of a character string within a Transact-SQL batch.
EXISTS	Specifies a subquery to test for the existence of rows.
EXP	This function returns the exponential value of the given float expression.
Expressions	A combination of symbols and operators that SQL Server evaluates to obtain a single data value. Simple expressions can be a single constant, variable, column, or scalar function. Operators can be used to join two or more simple expressions into a complex expression.
FETCH	Retrieves a specific row from a Transact-SQL server cursor.
FILE_ID	This function returns the file identification (ID) number for the given logical filename in the current database.
FILE_IDEX	Returns the file identification (ID) number for the specified logical file name of the data, log, or full-text file in the current database.
FILE_NAME	This function returns the logical filename for the given file identification (ID) number.

T-SQL Construct	Usage, Usage Tips, Suggestions, and References
FILEGROUP_ID	This function returns the filegroup identification (ID) number for the given filegroup name.
FILEGROUP_NAME	This function returns the filegroup name for the given filegroup identification (ID) number.
FILEGROUPPROPERTY	This function returns the specified filegroup property value when given a filegroup and property name.
FILEPROPERTY	This function returns the specified filename property value when given a filename and property name.
float and real	Approximate number data types for use with floating-point numeric data. Floating-point data is approximate; not all values in the data type range can be precisely represented.
FLOOR	This function returns the largest integer less than or equal to the given numeric expression.
fn_get_sql	Returns the text of the SQL statement for the specified SQL handle.
fn_helpcollations	This function returns a list of all the collations supported by SQL Server 2005.
fn_listextendedproperty	This function returns extended property values of database objects.
fn_my_permissions	Returns a list of the permissions effectively granted to the principal on a securable.
fn_servershareddrives	This function returns the names of shared drives used by the clustered server.
fn_trace_geteventinfo	This function returns information about the events traced.
fn_trace_getfilterinfo	This function returns information about the filters applied to a specified trace.
fn_trace_getinfo	This function returns information about a specified trace or existing traces.
fn_trace_gettable	This function returns trace file information in a table format.
fn_virtualfilestats	This function returns I/O statistics for database files, including log files.
fn_virtualservernodes	This function returns the list of nodes on which the virtual server can run. Such information is useful in fail-over clustering environments.
FOR (XML)	FOR clause is used to specify either the BROWSE or the XML option. BROWSE and XML are unrelated options.

T-SQL Construct	Usage, Usage Tips, Suggestions, and References
FORMATMESSAGE	Constructs a message from an existing message in sysmessages. The functionality of FORMATMESSAGE resembles that of the RAISERROR statement; however, RAISERROR prints the message immediately, and FORMATMESSAGE returns the edited message for further processing.
FREETEXT	Is a predicate used to search columns containing character-based data types for values that match the meaning and not the exact wording of the words in the search condition. When FREETEXT is used, the full-text query engine internally "word-breaks" the *freetext_string* into a number of search terms and assigns each term a weight and then finds the matches.
FREETEXTTABLE	This function returns a table of zero, one, or more rows for those columns containing character-based data types for values that match the meaning, but not the exact wording, of the text in the specified *freetext_string*. FREETEXTTABLE can be referenced in the FROM clause of a SELECT statement like a regular table name.
FROM	Specifies the tables, views, derived tables, and joined tables used in DELETE, SELECT, and UPDATE statements.
FULLTEXTCATALOGPROPERTY	This function returns information about full-text catalog properties.
FULLTEXTSERVICEPROPERTY	This function returns information about full-text service-level properties.
GET CONVERSATION GROUP	Returns the conversation group identifier for the next message to be received, and locks the conversation group for the conversation that contains the message.
GET TRANSMISSION_STATUS	Returns the status for the last transmission for one side of a conversation.
GETANSINULL	This function returns the default nullability for the database for this session.
GETDATE	This function returns the current system date and time in the SQL Server standard internal format for datetime values.
GETUTCDATE	This function returns the datetime value representing the current UTC time (Universal Time Coordinate or Greenwich Mean Time). The current UTC time is derived from the current local time and the time zone setting in the operating system of the computer on which SQL Server is running.
GO	Signals the end of a batch of Transact-SQL statements to the SQL Server utilities.

T-SQL Construct	Usage, Usage Tips, Suggestions, and References
GOTO	Alters the flow of execution to a label. The Transact-SQL statement(s) following GOTO are skipped, and processing continues at the label. GOTO statements and labels can be used anywhere within a procedure, batch, or statement block. GOTO statements can be nested.
GRANT	Creates an entry in the security system that allows a user in the current database to work with data in the current database or execute specific Transact-SQL statements.
GROUP BY	Divides a table into groups. Groups can consist of column names or results or computed columns. For more information, see SELECT.
GROUPING	Is an aggregate function that causes an additional column to be output with a value of 1 when the row is added by either the CUBE or ROLLUP operator, or 0 when the row is not the result of CUBE or ROLLUP.
HAS_DBACCESS	This function returns information about whether the user has access to the specified database.
Has_Perms_By_Name	Evaluates the effective permission of the current user on a securable.
HashBytes	Gets the MD2, MD4, MD5, SHA, or SHA1 hash of its input.
HAVING	Specifies a search condition for a group or an aggregate. HAVING can be used only with the SELECT statement. It is usually used in a GROUP BY clause. When GROUP BY is not used, HAVING behaves like a WHERE clause. For more information, see SELECT.
Hints	Hints are the options you can specify to SQL Server 2005's query processor on SELECT, INSERT, UPDATE, or DELETE statements to override any execution plan the query optimizer might select for a query.
HOST_ID	This function returns the workstation identification number.
HOST_NAME	This function returns the workstation name.
IDENT_CURRENT	This function returns the last identity value generated for a specified table in any session and any scope.
IDENT_INCR	This function returns the increment value (returned as numeric(@@MAXPRECISION,0)) specified during the creation of an identity column in a table or view that has an identity column.
IDENT_SEED	This function returns the seed value (returned as numeric (@@MAXPRECISION,0)) specified during the creation of an identity column in a table or a view that has an identity column.

T-SQL Construct	Usage, Usage Tips, Suggestions, and References
IDENTITY (Property)	Creates an identity column in a table. This property is used with the CREATE TABLE and ALTER TABLE Transact-SQL statements.
IDENTITY (Function)	Is used only in a SELECT statement with an INTO *table* clause to insert an identity column into a new table.
IF...ELSE	Imposes conditions on the execution of a Transact-SQL statement. The Transact-SQL statement following an IF keyword and its condition is executed if the condition is satisfied (when the Boolean expression returns TRUE). The optional ELSE keyword introduces an alternate Transact-SQL statement that is executed when the IF condition is not satisfied (when the Boolean expression returns FALSE).
Image	Information pertaining to the "image" datatype.
IN	Determines if a given value matches any value in a subquery or a list.
INDEXKEY_PROPERTY	This function returns information about the index key.
INDEXPROPERTY	This function returns the named index property value given a table identification number, index name, and property name.
INDEX_COL	This function returns the indexed column name.
INSERT	Adds a new row to a table or a view.
int, bigint, smallint, and tinyint	Exact number data types that use integer data.
INTO	Creates a new table in the SELECT statement to hold the data.
IS_MEMBER	Indicates whether the current user is a member of the specified Windows NT group or SQL Server role.
IS_SRVROLEMEMBER	Indicates whether the current user login is a member of the specified server role.
ISDATE	Determines whether an input expression is a valid date.
IS [NOT] NULL	Determines whether or not a given expression is NULL.
ISNULL	Replaces NULL with the specified replacement value.
ISNUMERIC	Determines whether an expression is a valid numeric type.
Key_GUID	Returns the GUID of a symmetric key.
Key_ID	Return the ID of a symmetric key.
KILL	Terminates a user process according to the system process ID (SPID) or unit of work (UOW). If the specified SPID or UOW has a lot of work to undo, the KILL command may take some time to complete, particularly when it involves rolling back a long transaction.
KILL QUERY NOTIFICATION SUBSCRIPTION	Removes query notification subscriptions from the instance. This statement can remove a specific subscription or all subscriptions.

T-SQL Construct	Usage, Usage Tips, Suggestions, and References
KILL STATS JOB	Kills the asynchronous statistics update job.
LEFT	This function returns the part of a character string starting at a specified number of characters from the left.
LEN	This function returns the number of characters, rather than the number of bytes, of the given string expression, excluding trailing blanks.
LIKE	Determines whether or not a given character string matches a specified pattern. A pattern can include regular characters and wildcard characters. During pattern matching, regular characters must exactly match the characters specified in the character string. Wildcard characters, however, can be matched with arbitrary fragments of the character string. Using wildcard characters makes the LIKE operator more flexible than using the = and != string comparison operators. If any of the arguments are not of the character string data type, SQL Server 2005 converts them to the character string data type, if possible.
LOAD	Loads a backup copy of one of the following: Database, Transaction Log, Load Header Only. This statement is available for backward compatibility with earlier versions of SQL Server.
LOG	This function returns the natural logarithm of the given float expression.
LOG10	This function returns the base-10 logarithm of the given float expression.
LOWER	This function returns a character expression after converting uppercase character data to lowercase.
LTRIM	This function returns a character expression after removing leading blanks.
MAX	This function returns the maximum value in the expression.
MIN	This function returns the minimum value in the expression.
money and smallmoney	Monetary data types for representing monetary or currency values.
MONTH	This function returns an integer that represents the month part of a specified date.
MOVE COVERSATION	Moves the conversation to another group.
NCHAR	This function returns the Unicode character with the given integer code, as defined by the Unicode standard.
nchar and nvarchar	Character data types that are either fixed-length (nchar) or variable-length (nvarchar) Unicode data and use the UNICODE UCS-2 character set.
NEWID	Creates a unique value of type uniqueidentifier.

T-SQL Construct	Usage, Usage Tips, Suggestions, and References
NEWSEQUENTIALID	Creates a GUID that is greater than any GUID previously generated by this function on a specified computer.
NOT	Negates a Boolean input.
ntext, text, and image	Fixed- and variable-length data types for storing large non-Unicode and Unicode character and binary data. Unicode data uses the UNICODE UCS-2 character set.
NULLIF	This function returns a null value if the two specified expressions are equivalent.
numeric	For more information about the numeric data type, see DECIMAL and NUMERIC.
OBJECT_DEFINITION	Returns the Transact-SQL source text of the definition of a specified object.
OBJECT_ID	This function returns the database object identification number.
OBJECT_NAME	This function returns the database object name.
OBJECTPROPERTY	This function returns information about objects in the current database.
OBJECTPROPERTYEX	Returns information about schema-scoped objects in the current database. For a list of these objects, see sys.objects (Transact-SQL). OBJECTPROPERTYEX cannot be used for objects that are not schema-scoped, such as data definition language (DDL) triggers and event notifications.
OPEN	Opens a Transact-SQL server cursor and populates the cursor by executing the Transact-SQL statement specified on the DECLARE CURSOR or SET *cursor_variable* statement.
OPEN MASTERKEY, SYMMETRICKEY	Opens and/or decrypts the keys of the current database.
OPENDATASOURCE	Provides ad hoc connection information as part of a four-part object name without using a linked server name.
OPENQUERY	Executes the specified pass-through query on the given linked server, which is an OLE DB data source. The OPENQUERY function can be referenced in the FROM clause of a query as though it is a table name. The OPENQUERY function can also be referenced as the target table of an INSERT, UPDATE, or DELETE statement, subject to the capabilities of the OLE DB provider. Although the query may return multiple result sets, OPENQUERY returns only the first one.
OPENXML	OPENXML provides a rowset view over an XML document. Because OPENXML is a rowset provider, OPENXML can be used in Transact-SQL statements in which rowset providers such as a table, view, or the OPENROWSET function can appear.

T-SQL Construct	Usage, Usage Tips, Suggestions, and References
OPENROWSET (SWITCH)	Includes all connection information necessary to access remote data from an OLE DB data source. This method is an alternative to accessing tables in a linked server and is a one-time, ad hoc method of connecting and accessing remote data using OLE DB. The OPENROWSET function can be referenced in the FROM clause of a query as though it is a table name. The OPENROWSET function can also be referenced as the target table of an INSERT, UPDATE, or DELETE statement, subject to the capabilities of the OLE DB provider. Although the query may return multiple result sets, OPENROWSET returns only the first one.
OPTION	
OR	Combines two conditions. When more than one logical operator is used in a statement, OR operators are evaluated after AND operators. However, you can change the order of evaluation by using parentheses.
ORDER BY	Specifies the sort order used on columns returned in a SELECT statement. For more information, see SELECT.
ORIGINAL_LOGIN	Returns the name of the login that connected to the instance of SQL Server.
OUTPUT	Returns information from, or expressions based on, each row affected by an INSERT, UPDATE, or DELETE statement. These results can be returned to the processing application for use in such things as confirmation messages, archiving, and other such application requirements. Alternatively, results can be inserted into a table or table variable.
OVER	Determines the partitioning and ordering of the rowset before the associated window function is applied.
PARSENAME	This function returns the specified part of an object name. Parts of an object that can be retrieved are the object name, owner name, database name, and server name.
PATINDEX	This function returns the starting position of the first occurrence of a pattern in a specified expression, or zeros if the pattern is not found, on all valid text and character data types.
PERMISSIONS	This function returns a value containing a bitmap that indicates the statement, object, or column permissions for the current user.
PI	This function returns the constant value of PI.
POWER	This function returns the value of the given expression to the specified power.

T-SQL Construct	Usage, Usage Tips, Suggestions, and References
Predicate	Is an expression that evaluates to TRUE, FALSE, or UNKNOWN. Predicates are used in the search condition of WHERE clauses and HAVING clauses, and the join conditions of FROM clauses.
PRINT	This function returns a user-defined message to the client.
PUBLISHINGSERVERNAME	Returns the name of the originating Publisher for a published database participating in a database mirroring session.
QUOTENAME	This function returns a Unicode string with the delimiters added to make the input string a valid SQL Server 2005 delimited identifier.
RADIANS	This function returns radians when a numeric expression, in degrees, is entered.
RAISERROR	This function returns a user-defined error message and sets a system flag to record that an error has occurred. Using RAISERROR, the client can either retrieve an entry from the sysmessages table or build a message dynamically with user-specified severity and state information. After the message is defined, it is sent back to the client as a server error message.
RAND	This function returns a random float value from 0 through 1.
RANK	Returns the rank of each row within the partition of a result set. The rank of a row is one plus the number of ranks that come before the row in question.
READTEXT	Reads text, ntext, or image values from a text, ntext, or image column, starting from a specified offset and reading the specified number of bytes.
real	For more information about the real data type, see *float* and *real*.
RECEIVE	Retrieves one or more messages from a queue. Depending on the retention setting for the queue, either removes the message from the queue or updates the status of the message in the queue.
RECONFIGURE	Updates the currently configured (the config_value column in the sp_configure result set) value of a configuration option changed with the sp_configure system stored procedure. Because some configuration options require a server stop and restart to update the currently running value, RECONFIGURE does not always update the currently running value (the run_value column in the sp_configure result set) for a changed configuration value.
REPLACE	Replaces all occurrences of the second given string expression in the first string expression with a third expression.

T-SQL Construct	Usage, Usage Tips, Suggestions, and References
REPLICATE	Repeats a character expression for a specified number of times.
RESTORE	Restores backups taken using the BACKUP command. For more information about database backup and restore operations see Chapter 7.
RESTORE FILELISTONLY	This function returns a result set with a list of the database and log files contained in the backup set.
RESTORE HEADERONLY	Retrieves all the backup header information for all backup sets on a particular backup device. The result from executing RESTORE HEADERONLY is a result set.
RESTORE LABELONLY	This function returns a result set containing information about the backup media identified by the given backup device.
RESTORE MASTER OR SERVICE MASTER KEY	Restores the master or service keys of a database.
RESTORE REWINDONLY	Rewinds and closes specified tape devices that were left open by BACKUP or RESTORE statements executed with the NOREWIND option. This command is supported only for tape devices.
RESTORE VERIFYONLY	Verifies the backup but does not restore the backup. Checks to see that the backup set is complete and that all volumes are readable. However, RESTORE VERIFYONLY does not attempt to verify the structure of the data contained in the backup volumes. If the backup is valid, SQL Server 2005 returns the message: "The backup set is valid."
RETURN	RETURN is an unconditional exit from a query or procedure that is immediate and complete and can be used at any point to exit from a procedure, batch, or statement block. Statements following RETURN are not executed.
REVERSE	This function returns the reverse of a character expression.
REVOKE	Removes a previously granted or denied permission from a user in the current database.
RIGHT	This function returns the part of a character string starting a specified number of *integer_expression* characters from the right.
ROLLBACK TRANSACTION	Rolls back an explicit or implicit transaction to the beginning of the transaction, or to a savepoint inside a transaction.
ROLLBACK WORK	Rolls back a user-specified transaction to the beginning of a transaction.
ROUND	This function returns a numeric expression, rounded to the specified length or precision.

T-SQL Construct	Usage, Usage Tips, Suggestions, and References
ROWCOUNT_BIG	This function returns the number of rows affected by the last statement executed. This function operates like @@ROWCOUNT, except that the return type of ROWCOUNT_BIG is bigint.
ROWNUMBER	
RTRIM	This function returns a character string after truncating all trailing blanks.
SAVE TRANSACTION	Sets a savepoint within a transaction.
SCHEMA_ID	Returns the ID of a schema.
SCHEMA_NAME	Returns the name of a schema.
SCOPE_IDENTITY	This function returns the last IDENTITY value inserted into an IDENTITY column in the same scope. A scope is a module—a stored procedure, trigger, function, or batch. Thus, two statements are in the same scope if they are in the same stored procedure, function, or batch.
Search Condition	Is a combination of one or more predicates using the logical operators AND, OR, and NOT.
SELECT @*local_variable*	Specifies that the given local variable (created using DECLARE @*local_variable*) should be set to the specified expression.
SELECT	Retrieves rows from the database and allows the selection of one or many rows or columns from one or many tables. The full syntax of the SELECT statement is complex, and it is fully documented in Books Online.
SEND	Sends a message, using an existing conversation.
SERVERPROPERTY	This function returns property information about the server instance.
SESSION_USER	Is a niladic function that allows a system-supplied value for the current session's username to be inserted into a table when no default value is specified. Also allows the username to be used in queries, error messages, and so on.
SESSIONPROPERTY	This function returns the SET options settings of a session.
SET @*local_variable*	Sets the specified local variable, previously created with the DECLARE @*local_variable* statement, to the given value.
SET	The Transact-SQL programming language provides several SET statements that alter the current session handling of specific information.
SETUSER	Allows a member of the sysadmin fixed server role or db_owner fixed database role to impersonate another user (deprecated).
SHUTDOWN	Stops SQL Server.

T-SQL Construct	Usage, Usage Tips, Suggestions, and References
SIGN	Returns the positive (+1), zero (0), or negative (-1) sign of the specified expression.
SET ANSI_DEFAULTS	Controls a group of SQL Server 2005 settings that collectively specify some SQL-92 ((or later)) standard behaviors.
SET ANSI_NULL_DFLT_OFF	Alters the session's behavior to override default nullability of new columns when the ANSI null default option for the database is true. For more information about setting the value for ANSI null default, see also sp_dboption.
SET ANSI_NULL_DFLT_ON	Alters the session's behavior to override default nullability of new columns when the ANSI null default option for the database is false. For more information about setting the value for ANSI null default, see also sp_dboption.
SET ANSI_NULLS	Specifies SQL-92 ((or later)) compliant behavior of the Equal (=) and Not Equal to (<>) comparison operators when used with null values.
SET ANSI_PADDING	Controls the way the column stores values shorter than the defined size of the column, and the way the column stores values that have trailing blanks in char, varchar, binary, and varbinary data.
SET ANSI_WARNINGS	Specifies SQL-92 (or later) and later standard behavior for several error conditions.
SET ARITHABORT	Terminates a query when an overflow or divide-by-zero error occurs during query execution.
SET ARITHIGNORE	Controls whether error messages are returned from overflow or divide-by-zero errors during a query.
SET CONCAT_NULL_YIELDS_NULL	Controls whether or not concatenation results are treated as null or empty string values.
SET CONTEXT_INFO	Associates up to 128 bytes of binary information with the current session or connection.
SET CURSOR_CLOSE_ ON_COMMIT	Controls whether or not a cursor is closed when a transaction is committed.
SET DATEFIRST	Sets the first day of the week to a number from 1–7.
SET DATEFORMAT	Sets the order of the date parts (month/day/year) for entering datetime or smalldatetime data.
SET DEADLOCK_PRIORITY	Controls the way the session reacts when in a deadlock situation. Deadlock situations arise when two processes have data locked, and each process cannot release its lock until other processes have released theirs.
SET DISABLE_DEF_CNST_CHK	Specified interim deferred violation checking; was used for efficiency purposes in SQL Server version 6.x.

T-SQL Construct	Usage, Usage Tips, Suggestions, and References
SET FIPS_FLAGGER	Specifies checking for compliance with the FIPS 127-2 standard, which is based on the SQL-92 (or later) standard.
SET FMTONLY	This function returns only metadata to the client.
SET FORCEPLAN	Makes the SQL Server 2005 query optimizer process a join in the same order as tables appear in the FROM clause of a SELECT statement only.
SET IDENTITY_INSERT	Allows explicit values to be inserted into the identity column of a table.
SET IMPLICIT_TRANSACTIONS	Sets implicit transaction mode for the connection.
SET LANGUAGE	Specifies the language environment for the session. The session language determines the datetime formats and system messages.
SET LOCK_TIMEOUT	Specifies the number of milliseconds a statement waits for a lock to be released.
SET NOCOUNT	Stops the message indicating the number of rows affected by a Transact-SQL statement from being returned as part of the results.
SET NOEXEC	Compiles each query but does not execute it.
SET NUMERIC_ROUNDABORT	Specifies the level of error reporting generated when rounding in an expression causes a loss of precision.
SET OFFSETS	This function returns the offset (position relative to the start of a statement) of specified keywords in Transact-SQL statements to DB-Library applications.
SET PARSEONLY	Checks the syntax of each Transact-SQL statement and returns any error messages without compiling or executing the statement.
SET QUERY_GOVERNOR_COST_LIMIT	Overrides the currently configured value for the current connection.
SET QUOTED_IDENTIFIER	Causes SQL Server 2005 to follow the SQL-92 (or later) rules regarding quotation mark delimiting identifiers and literal strings. Identifiers delimited by double quotation marks either can be Transact-SQL reserved keywords or can contain characters not usually allowed by the Transact-SQL syntax rules for identifiers.
SET REMOTE_PROC_TRANSACTIONS	Specifies that when a local transaction is active, executing a remote stored procedure starts a Transact-SQL distributed transaction managed by the Microsoft Distributed Transaction Manager (MS DTC).
SET ROWCOUNT	Causes SQL Server 2005 to stop processing the query after the specified number of rows are returned.

T-SQL Construct	Usage, Usage Tips, Suggestions, and References
SET SHOWPLAN_ALL	Causes SQL Server 2005 not to execute Transact-SQL statements. Instead, SQL Server returns detailed information about how the statements are executed and provides estimates of the resource requirements for the statements.
SET SHOWPLAN_XML	Causes SQL Server not to execute Transact-SQL statements. Instead, SQL Server returns detailed information about how the statements are going to be executed in the form of a well-defined XML document.
SET STATISTICS IO	Causes SQL Server 2005 to display information regarding the amount of disk activity generated by Transact-SQL statements.
SET STATISTICS PROFILE	Displays the profile information for a statement. STATISTICS PROFILE works for ad hoc queries, views, triggers, and stored procedures.
SET STATISTICS TIME	Displays the number of milliseconds required to parse, compile, and execute each statement.
SET TEXTSIZE	Specifies the size of text and ntext data returned with a SELECT statement.
SET TRANSACTION ISOLATION LEVEL	Controls the default transaction locking behavior for all SQL Server 2005 SELECT statements issued by a connection.
SET XACT_ABORT	Specifies whether SQL Server 2005 automatically rolls back the current transaction if a Transact-SQL statement raises a run-time error.
SETUSER	Allows a member of the sysadmin fixed server role or db_owner fixed database role to impersonate another user.
SHUTDOWN	Immediately stops operation of SQL Server 2005.
SIGN	This function returns the positive (+1), zero (0), or negative (−1) sign of the given expression.
SignByAsymKey	Signs a clear text message with an asymmetric key.
SignByCert	Signs a clear text message with a certificate.
SIN	This function returns the trigonometric sine of the given angle (in radians) in an approximate numeric (float) expression.
smalldatetime	For information about the smalldatetime data type, see datetime and small datetime.
smallint	For information about the smallint data type, see int.
smallmoney	For information about the smallmoney data type, see money and small money.
SOME | ANY	Compares a scalar value with a single-column set of values.
SOUNDEX	This function returns a four-character (SOUNDEX) code to evaluate the similarity of two strings.

T-SQL Construct	Usage, Usage Tips, Suggestions, and References
SPACE	This function returns a string of repeated spaces.
sql_variant	A data type that stores values of various SQL Server–supported data types, except text, ntext, image, timestamp, and sql_variant.
SQL_VARIANT_PROPERTY	This function returns the base data type and other information about a sql_variant value.
SQUARE	This function returns the square of the given expression.
SQRT	This function returns the square root of the given expression.
STATS_DATE	This function returns the date that the statistics for the specified index were last updated.
STDEV	This function returns the statistical standard deviation of all values in the given expression.
STDEVP	This function returns the statistical standard deviation for the population for all values in the given expression.
STR	This function returns character data converted from numeric data.
STUFF	Deletes a specified length of characters and inserts another set of characters at a specified starting point.
SUBSTRING	This function returns part of a character, binary, text, or image expression. For more information about the valid SQL Server 2005 data types that can be used with this function, see Books Online.
SUM	This function returns the sum of all the values, or only the DISTINCT values, in the expression. SUM can be used with numeric columns only. Null values are ignored.
SUSER_ID	This function returns the user's login identification number.
SUSER_NAME	This function returns the user's login identification name.
SUSER_SID	This function returns the security identification number (SID) for the user's login name.
SUSER_SNAME	This function returns the login identification name from a user's security identification number (SID).
System Stored Procedures	Usage, Usage Tips, Suggestions, and References.
sp_add_alert	This procedure creates an alert.
sp_addalias	This procedure maps a login to a user in a database. sp_addalias is provided for backward compatibility. SQL Server version 7.0 provides roles and the ability to grant permissions to roles as an alternative to using aliases.
sp_addapprole	This procedure adds a special type of role in the current database used for application security.

PART IV

T-SQL Construct	Usage, Usage Tips, Suggestions, and References
sp_add_data_file_recover_suspect_db	This procedure adds a data file to a filegroup when recovery cannot complete on a database due to an insufficient space (1105) error on the filegroup. After the file is added, this stored procedure turns off the suspect setting and completes the recovery of the database. The parameters are the same as those for ALTER DATABASE ADD FILE.
sp_addextendedproc	This procedure registers the name of a new extended stored procedure to SQL Server.
sp_addextendedproperty	This procedure adds a new extended property to a database object. If the property already exists, the procedure fails.
sp_addgroup	This procedure creates a group in the current database. sp_addgroup is included for backward compatibility. SQL Server version 7.0 uses roles instead of groups. Use sp_addrole to add a role.
sp_add_category	This procedure adds the specified category of jobs, alerts, or operators to the server.
sp_add_job	This procedure adds a new job executed by the SQLServerAgent service.
sp_add_jobschedule	This procedure creates a schedule for a job.
sp_add_jobserver	This procedure targets the specified job at the specified server.
sp_add_jobstep	This procedure adds a step (operation) to a job.
sp_addlinkedserver	This procedure creates a linked server, which allows access to distributed, heterogeneous queries against OLE DB data sources. After creating a linked server with sp_addlinkedserver, this server can then execute distributed queries. If the linked server is defined as SQL Server, remote stored procedures can be executed.
sp_addlinkedsrvlogin	This procedure creates or updates a mapping between logins on the local instance of SQL Server and remote logins on the linked server.
sp_add_log_file_recover_suspect_db	This procedure adds a log file to a filegroup when recovery cannot complete on a database due to an insufficient log space error (error number 9002). After the file is added, this stored procedure turns off the suspect setting and completes the recovery of the database. The parameters are the same as those for ALTER DATABASE ADD LOG FILE. See "Troubleshooting Recovery" in Books Online.
sp_addlogin	This procedure creates a new SQL Server login that allows a user to connect to an instance of SQL Server using SQL Server Authentication.
sp_add_log_shipping_database	This procedure specifies that a database on the primary server is being log shipped.

T-SQL Construct	Usage, Usage Tips, Suggestions, and References
sp_add_log_shipping_plan	This procedure creates a new log shipping plan and inserts a row in the log_shipping_plans table.
sp_add_log_shipping_plan_database	This procedure adds a new database to an existing log shipping plan.
sp_add_log_shipping_primary	This procedure adds a new primary server to the log_shipping_primaries table.
sp_add_log_shipping_secondary	This procedure adds a secondary server to the log_shipping_ secondaries table.
sp_add_maintenance_plan	This procedure adds a maintenance plan and returns the plan ID.
sp_add_maintenance_plan_db	This procedure associates a database with a maintenance plan.
sp_add_maintenance_plan_job	This procedure associates a maintenance plan with an existing job.
sp_addmessage	This procedure adds a new error message to the sysmessages table.
sp_add_notification	Sets up a notification for an alert.
sp_add_operator	This procedure creates an operator (notification recipient) for use with alerts and jobs.
sp_addremotelogin	This procedure adds a new remote login ID on the local server, allowing remote servers to connect and execute remote procedure calls.
sp_addrole	This procedure creates a new SQL Server role in the current database.
sp_addrolemember	This procedure adds a security account as a member of an existing SQL Server database role in the current database.
sp_addserver	This procedure defines a remote server or the name of the local SQL server. sp_addserver is provided for backward compatibility. Use sp_addlinkedserver.
sp_addsrvrolemember	This procedure adds a login as a member of a fixed server role.
sp_addtask	This procedure creates a scheduled task.
sp_addtype	This procedure creates a user-defined data type.
sp_add_targetservergroup	This procedure adds the specified server group.
sp_addumpdevice	This procedure adds a backup device to SQL Server.
sp_add_targetsvrgrp_member	This procedure adds the specified target server to the specified target server group.
sp_adduser	This procedure adds a security account for a new user in the current database. This procedure is included for backward compatibility. Use sp_grantdbaccess.
sp_altermessage	This procedure alters the state of a sysmessages error.

T-SQL Construct	Usage, Usage Tips, Suggestions, and References
sp_apply_job_to_targets	This procedure applies a job to one or more target servers or to the target servers belonging to one or more target server groups.
sp_approlepassword	This procedure changes the password of an application role in the current database.
sp_attach_db	This procedure attaches a database to a server.
sp_attach_single_file_db	This procedure attaches a database having only one data file to the current server.
sp_autostats	This procedure displays or changes the automatic UPDATE STATISTICS setting for a specific index and statistics, or for all indexes and statistics for a given table or indexed view in the current database.
sp_bindefault	This procedure binds a default to a column or to a user-defined data type.
sp_bindrule	This procedure binds a rule to a column or to a user-defined data type.
sp_bindsession	This procedure binds or unbinds a connection to other transactions in the same instance of Microsoft SQL Server 2005. A bound connection allows two or more connections to participate in the same transaction and share the transaction until a ROLLBACK TRANSACTION or COMMIT TRANSACTION is issued.
sp_can_tlog_be_applied	This procedure verifies that a transaction log can be applied to a database.
sp_catalogs	This procedure returns the list of catalogs in the specified linked server, which is equivalent to databases in SQL Server.
sp_certify_removable	This procedure verifies that a database is configured properly for distribution on removable media and reports any problems to the user.
sp_change_monitor_role	This procedure performs a role change on the log shipping monitor, setting the current secondary database to be a primary database.
sp_change_primary_role	This procedure removes the primary database from a log shipping plan.
sp_change_secondary_role	This procedure converts the secondary database of a log shipping plan into a primary database.
sp_change_users_login	This procedure changes the relationship between a SQL Server login and a SQL Server user in the current database.
sp_changedbowner	This procedure changes the owner of the current database.

T-SQL Construct	Usage, Usage Tips, Suggestions, and References
sp_changegroup	This procedure changes the role membership for the security account of a user in the current database. This procedure is provided for backward compatibility. SQL Server version 7.0 uses roles instead of groups. Use sp_addrolemember instead.
sp_changeobjectowner	This procedure changes the owner of an object in the current database.
sp_column_privileges	This procedure returns column privilege information for a single table in the current environment.
sp_column_privileges_ex	This procedure returns column privileges for the specified table on the specified linked server.
sp_columns	This procedure returns column information for the specified tables or views that can be queried in the current environment.
sp_columns_ex	This function returns the column information, one row per column, for the given linked server table(s). The sp_columns_ex returns column information only for the given column if *column* is specified.
sp_configure	This procedure displays or changes global configuration settings for the current server.
sp_create_log_shipping_monitor_account	This procedure creates the log_shipping_monitor_probe login on the monitor server, and assigns update permissions to the msdb.dbo.log_shipping_primaries and msdb.dbo.log_shipping_secondaries tables.
sp_create_removable	This procedure creates a removable media database. It essentially creates three or more files (one for the system catalog tables, one for the transaction log, and one or more for the data tables) and places the database on those files.
sp_createstats	This procedure creates single-column statistics for all eligible columns for all user tables in the current database. The new statistic has the same name as the column on which it is created. The computed columns and columns of the ntext, text, or image data types cannot be specified as statistics columns. Columns already having statistics are not touched; for example, the first column of an index or a column with explicitly created statistics. The CREATE STATISTICS statement is executed for each column that satisfies the above restrictions. The option FULLSCAN is executed if fullscan is specified.
sp_cursor_list	This procedure reports the attributes of server cursors currently open for the connection.

PART IV

T-SQL Construct	Usage, Usage Tips, Suggestions, and References
sp_cycle_errorlog	This procedure closes the current error log file and cycles the error log extension numbers just like a server restart. The new error log contains version and copyright information and a line indicating that the new log has been created.
sp_databases	This procedure lists databases that reside in an instance of SQL Server, or the databases that are accessible through a database gateway.
sp_datatype_info	This procedure returns information about the data types supported by the current environment.
sp_dbcmptlevel	This procedure sets certain database behaviors to be compatible with the specified earlier version of SQL Server (versions 8, 7, and so on).
sp_dbfixedrolepermission	This procedure displays the permissions for each fixed database role.
sp_dboption	This procedure displays or changes database options. sp_dboption should not be used on either the master or tempdb databases. sp_dboption is supported for backward compatibility. You should use ALTER DATABASE to set database options.
sp_dbremove	Removes a database and all files associated with that database. This procedure is included for backward compatibility, and you should use the procedure sp_detach_db to "unhinge" a database from SQL Server.
sp_defaultdb	This procedure changes the default database for a login.
sp_defaultlanguage	This procedure changes the default language of a login.
sp_define_log_shipping_monitor	This procedure sets up the log shipping monitor account on the monitor server.
sp_delete_alert	This procedure removes an alert.
sp_delete_backuphistory	This procedure deletes the entries in the backup and restore history tables for backup sets older than oldest_date. Because additional rows are added to the backup and restore history tables when a backup or restore operation is performed, sp_delete_backuphistory can be used to reduce the size of the history tables in the msdb database.
sp_delete_category	This procedure removes the specified category of jobs, alerts, or operators from the current server.
sp_delete_job	This procedure deletes a job.
sp_delete_jobschedule	This procedure removes a schedule from a job.
sp_delete_jobserver	This procedure removes the specified target server.
sp_delete_jobstep	This procedure removes a job step from a job.

T-SQL Construct	Usage, Usage Tips, Suggestions, and References
sp_delete_log_shipping_database	This procedure deletes a database from the log_shipping_ databases table on the primary server.
sp_delete_log_shipping_plan	This procedure deletes a log shipping plan.
sp_delete_log_shipping_plan_ database	This procedure removes a database from a log shipping plan.
sp_delete_log_shipping_primary	This procedure deletes the primary server from the log_shipping_primaries table.
sp_delete_log_shipping_secondary	This procedure removes a secondary server from log_shipping_secondaries table.
sp_delete_maintenance_plan	This procedure deletes the specified maintenance plan.
sp_delete_maintenance_plan_db	This procedure disassociates the specified maintenance plan from the specified database.
sp_delete_maintenance_plan_job	This procedure disassociates the specified maintenance plan from the specified job.
sp_delete_notification	This procedure removes all notifications sent to a particular operator in response to an alert.
sp_delete_operator	This procedure removes an operator.
sp_delete_targetserver	This procedure removes the specified server from the list of available target servers.
sp_delete_targetservergroup	This procedure deletes the specified target server group.
sp_delete_targetsvrgrp_member	This procedure removes a target server from a target server group.
sp_denylogin	This procedure prevents a Microsoft Windows NT user or group from connecting to Microsoft SQL Server.
sp_depends	This procedure displays information about database object dependencies (for example, the views and procedures that depend on a table or view, and the tables and views that are depended on by the view or procedure). It also references objects outside the current database that are not reported.
sp_describe_cursor	This procedure reports the attributes of a server cursor.
sp_describe_cursor_columns	This procedure reports the attributes of the columns in the result set of a server cursor.
sp_describe_cursor_tables	This procedure reports the base tables referenced by a server cursor.
sp_detach_dbsp_dropalias	This procedure detaches a database from a server and, optionally, runs UPDATE STATISTICS on all tables before detaching. It also removes an alias to a user in the current database from a login. The procedure sp_dropalias is provided for backward compatibility only. You should use roles and the sp_droprolemember stored procedure instead of aliases.

T-SQL Construct	Usage, Usage Tips, Suggestions, and References
sp_dropapprole	This procedure removes an application role from the current database.
sp_dropdevice	This procedure drops a database device or backup device from SQL Server, deleting the entry from master.dbo.sysdevices.
sp_dropextendedproc	This procedure drops an extended stored procedure.
sp_dropextendedproperty	This procedure drops an existing extended property.
sp_dropgroup	This procedure removes a role from the current database. The procedure sp_dropgroup is provided for backward compatibility. In SQL Server version 7.0, groups are implemented as roles.
sp_droplinkedsrvlogin	This procedure removes an existing mapping between a login on the local server running SQL Server and a login on the linked server.
sp_droplogin	This procedure removes a SQL Server login, preventing access to SQL Server using that login name.
sp_dropmessage	This procedure drops a specified error message from the sysmessages system table.
sp_dropremotelogin	This procedure removes a remote login mapped to a local login used to execute remote stored procedures against the local server running SQL Server.
sp_droprole	This procedure removes a SQL Server role from the current database.
sp_droprolemember	This procedure removes a security account from a SQL Server role in the current database.
sp_dropserver	This procedure removes a server from the list of known remote and linked servers on the local SQL Server.
sp_dropsrvrolemember	This procedure removes a SQL Server login or a Microsoft Windows NT user or group from a fixed server role.
sp_droptask	This procedure is provided for backward compatibility only. For information about the Microsoft SQL Server version 7.0 replacement procedures see Books Online.
sp_droptype	This procedure deletes a user-defined data type from systypes.
sp_dropuser	This procedure removes a SQL Server user or Microsoft Windows NT user from the current database. sp_dropuser is provided for backward compatibility. Use sp_revokedbaccess to remove a user.
sp_dropwebtask	This procedure deletes a previously defined Web task.
sp_enumcodepages	This procedure returns a list of the code pages and character sets supported by sp_makewebtask.

T-SQL Construct	Usage, Usage Tips, Suggestions, and References
sp_executesql	This procedure executes a T-SQL statement or batch that can be reused many times, or that has been built dynamically. The T-SQL statement or batch can contain embedded parameters.
sp_fkeys	This procedure returns logical foreign key information for the current environment. This procedure shows foreign key relationships including disabled foreign keys.
sp_foreignkeys	This procedure returns the foreign keys that reference primary keys on the table in the linked server.
sp_fulltext_catalog	This procedure creates and drops a full-text catalog, and starts and stops the indexing action for a catalog. Multiple full-text catalogs can be created for each database.
sp_fulltext_column	This procedure specifies whether or not a particular column of a table participates in full-text indexing.
sp_fulltext_database	This procedure initializes full-text indexing or removes all full-text catalogs from the current database.
sp_fulltext_service	This procedure changes Search Service (Full-text Search) properties.
sp_fulltext_table	This procedure marks or unmarks a table for full-text indexing.
sp_getapplock	This procedure places a lock on an application resource.
sp_getbindtoken	This procedure returns a unique identifier for the transaction. This unique identifier is referred to as a bind token. sp_getbindtoken returns a string representation to be used to share transactions between clients.
sp_get_log_shipping_monitor_info	This procedure returns status information about a "Log Shipping Pair." A log shipping pair is a set of primary server–primary database and secondary server–secondary database.
sp_grantdbaccess	This procedure adds a security account in the current database for a SQL Server login or Windows NT user or group, and enables it to be granted permissions to perform activities in the database.
sp_grantlogin	This procedure allows a Windows user or group account to connect to Microsoft SQL Server using Windows Authentication. See Chapter 5.
sp_help	This procedure reports information about a database object (any object listed in the sysobjects table), a user-defined data type, or a data type supplied by SQL Server.
sp_help_alert	This procedure reports information about the alerts defined for the server.
sp_help_category	This procedure provides information about the specified classes of jobs, alerts, or operators.

PART IV

T-SQL Construct	Usage, Usage Tips, Suggestions, and References
sp_helpconstraint	This procedure returns a list of all constraint types, their user-defined or system-supplied name, the columns on which they have been defined, and the expression that defines the constraint (for DEFAULT and CHECK constraints only).
sp_helpdb	This procedure reports information about a specified database or all databases.
sp_helpdbfixedrole	This procedure returns a list of the fixed database roles.
sp_helpdevice	This procedure reports information about SQL Server database files. sp_helpdevice is used for backward compatibility with earlier versions of SQL Server that used the term "device" for a database file.
sp_help_downloadlist	This procedure lists all rows in the sysdownloadlist system table for the supplied job, or all rows if no job is specified.
sp_helpextendedproc	This procedure displays the currently defined extended stored procedures and the name of the dynamic-link library to which the procedure (or function) belongs.
sp_helpfile	This procedure returns the physical names and attributes of files associated with the current database. Use this stored procedure to determine the names of files to attach to or detach from the server.
sp_helpfilegroup	This procedure returns the names and attributes of filegroups associated with the current database.
sp_help_fulltext_catalogs	This procedure returns the ID, name, root directory, status, and number of full-text indexed tables for the specified full-text catalog.
sp_help_fulltext_catalogs_cursor	This procedure makes use of a cursor to return the ID, name, root directory, status, and number of full-text indexed tables for the specified full-text catalog.
sp_help_fulltext_columns	This procedure returns the columns designated for full-text indexing.
sp_help_fulltext_columns_cursor	This procedure makes use of a cursor to return the columns designated for full-text indexing.
sp_help_fulltext_tables	This procedure returns a list of tables that are registered for full-text indexing.
sp_help_fulltext_tables_cursor	This procedure makes use of a cursor to return a list of tables that are registered for full-text indexing.
sp_helpgroup	This procedure reports information about a role, or all roles, in the current database. This procedure is included for backward compatibility with version 7.0 and can be executed against a version 7.0 database.
sp_helphistory	This procedure is provided for backward compatibility.

T-SQL Construct	Usage, Usage Tips, Suggestions, and References
sp_help_job	This procedure returns information about jobs that are used by SQLServerAgent service to perform automated activities in SQL Server.
sp_help_jobhistory	This procedure provides information about the jobs for servers in the multiserver administration domain.
sp_help_jobschedule	This procedure returns information about the scheduling of jobs used by SQL Server Enterprise Manager to perform automated activities.
sp_help_jobserver	This procedure returns information about the server for a given job.
sp_help_jobstep	This procedure returns information for the steps in a job used by SQLServerAgent service to perform automated activities.
sp_helpindex	This procedure reports information about the indexes on a table or view.
sp_helplanguage	This procedure reports information about a particular alternate language or about all languages.
sp_helplinkedsrvlogin	This procedure provides information about login mappings defined against a specific linked server used for distributed queries and remote stored procedures.
sp_helplogins	This procedure provides information about logins and the associated users in each database.
sp_help_maintenance_plan	This procedure returns information about the specified maintenance plan. If a plan is not specified, this stored procedure returns information about all maintenance plans.
sp_help_notification	This procedure reports a list of alerts for a given operator or a list of operators for a given alert.
sp_helpntgroup	This procedure reports information about Microsoft Windows NT groups with accounts in the current database.
sp_help_operator	This procedure reports information about the operators defined for the server.
sp_helpremotelogin	This procedure reports information about remote logins for a particular remote server, or for all remote servers, defined on the local server.
sp_helprole	This procedure returns information about the roles in the current database.
sp_helprolemember	This procedure returns information about the members of a role in the current database.
sp_helpprotect	This procedure returns a report with information about user permissions for an object, or statement permissions, in the current database.

T-SQL Construct	Usage, Usage Tips, Suggestions, and References
sp_helpserver	This procedure reports information about a particular remote or replication server, or about all servers of both types. Provides the server name; the server's network name; the server's replication status; the server's identification number; collation name; and time-out values for connecting to, or queries against, linked servers.
sp_helpsort	This procedure displays the SQL Server sort order and character set.
sp_helpsrvrole	This procedure returns a list of the SQL Server fixed server roles.
sp_helpsrvrolemember	This procedure returns information about the members of a SQL Server fixed server role.
sp_helpstats	This procedure returns statistics information about columns and indexes on the specified table.
sp_help_targetserver	This procedure lists all target servers.
sp_help_targetservergroup	This procedure lists all target servers in the specified group. If no group is specified, SQL Server returns information about all target server groups.
sp_helptask	This procedure is provided for backward compatibility only.
sp_helptext	This procedure prints the text of a rule, a default, or an unencrypted stored procedure, trigger, or view.
sp_helptrigger	This procedure returns the type or types of triggers defined on the specified table for the current database.
sp_helpuser	This procedure reports information about SQL Server users, Windows NT users, and database roles in the current database.
sp_indexes	This procedure returns index information for the specified remote table.
sp_indexoption	This procedure sets option values for user-defined indexes.
sp_invalidate_textptr	This procedure makes the specified in-row text pointer, or all in-row text pointers, in the transaction invalid. sp_invalidate_textptr can be used only on in-row text pointers, which are from tables with the "text in row" option enabled.
sp_linkedservers	This procedure returns the list of linked servers defined in the local server.
sp_lock	This procedure reports information about locks.
sp_makewebtask	This procedure creates a task that produces an HTML document containing data returned by executed queries.
sp_manage_jobs_by_login	This procedure deletes or reassigns jobs that belong to the specified login.
sp_monitor	This procedure displays statistics about SQL Server.

T-SQL Construct	Usage, Usage Tips, Suggestions, and References
sp_MShasdbaccess	This procedure lists the name and owner of all the databases to which the user has access.
sp_msx_defect	This procedure removes the current server from multiserver operations.
sp_msx_enlist	This procedure adds the current server to the list of target servers available for multiserver operations. Only a SQL Server version 7.0 database server running on Windows NT can be enlisted.
sp_OACreate	This procedure creates an instance of the OLE object on an instance of SQL Server.
sp_OADestroy	This procedure destroys a created OLE object.
sp_OAGetErrorInfo	This procedure obtains OLE Automation error information.
sp_OAGetProperty	This procedure gets a property value of an OLE object.
sp_OAMethod	This procedure calls a method of an OLE object.
sp_OASetProperty	This procedure sets a property of an OLE object to a new value.
sp_OAStop	This procedure stops the server-wide OLE Automation stored procedure execution environment.
sp_password	This procedure adds or changes a password for a SQL Server login.
sp_pkeys	This procedure returns primary key information for a single table in the current environment.
sp_primarykeys	This procedure returns the primary key columns, one row per key column, for the specified remote table.
sp_post_msx_operation	This procedure inserts operations (rows) into the sysdownloadlist system table for target servers to download and execute.
sp_processmail	This procedure uses extended stored procedures (xp_findnextmsg, xp_readmail, and xp_deletemail) to process incoming mail messages (expected to be only a single query) from the inbox for SQL Server. It uses the xp_sendmail extended stored procedure to return the result set to the message sender.
sp_procoption	This procedure sets procedure options.
sp_purgehistory	This procedure is provided for backward compatibility only.
sp_purge_jobhistory	This procedure removes the history records for a job.
sp_reassigntask	This procedure is provided for backward compatibility only.
sp_recompile	This procedure forces stored procedures and triggers to be recompiled the next time they are run.

PART IV

T-SQL Construct	Usage, Usage Tips, Suggestions, and References
sp_refreshview	This procedure refreshes the metadata for the specified view. Persistent metadata for a view can become outdated because of changes to the underlying objects upon which the view depends.
sp_releaseapplock	This procedure releases a lock on an application resource.
sp_remoteoption	This procedure displays or changes options for a remote login defined on the local server running SQL Server.
sp_remove_job_from_targets	This procedure removes the specified job from the given target servers or target server groups.
sp_remove_log_shipping_monitor	This procedure deletes the log shipping monitor information from the log_shipping_monitor table.
sp_rename	This procedure changes the name of a user-created object (for example, table, column, or user-defined data type) in the current database.
sp_renamedb	This procedure changes the name of a database.
sp_resetstatus	This procedure resets the status of a suspect database.
sp_resolve_logins	This procedure resolves logins on the new primary server against logins from the former primary server.
sp_resync_targetserver	This procedure resynchronizes all multiserver jobs in the specified target server.
sp_revokedbaccess	This procedure removes a security account from the current database.
sp_revokelogin	This procedure removes the login entries from SQL Server for a Windows NT user or group created with sp_grantlogin or sp_denylogin.
sp_runwebtask	This procedure executes a previously defined Web job and generates the HTML document. The task to run is identified by the output file name, by the procedure name, or by both parameters.
sp_server_info	This procedure returns a list of attribute names and matching values for SQL Server, the database gateway, or the underlying data source.
sp_serveroption	This procedure sets server options for remote servers and linked servers.
sp_setapprole	This procedure activates the permissions associated with an application role in the current database.
sp_setnetname	This procedure sets the network names in sysservers to their actual network computer names for remote instances of SQL Server. This procedure can be used to enable execution of remote stored procedure calls to computers that have network names containing invalid SQL Server identifiers.

T-SQL Construct	Usage, Usage Tips, Suggestions, and References
sp_settriggerorder	This procedure specifies which AFTER triggers associated with a table will be fired first or last. The AFTER triggers that will be fired between the first and last triggers will be executed in undefined order.
sp_spaceused	This procedure displays the number of rows, disk space reserved, and disk space used by a table in the current database, or displays the disk space reserved and used by the entire database.
sp_special_columns	This procedure returns the optimal set of columns that uniquely identify a row in the table. Also returns columns automatically updated when any value in the row is updated by a transaction.
sp_sproc_columns	This procedure returns column information for a single stored procedure or user-defined function in the current environment.
sp_srvrolepermission	This procedure returns the permissions applied to a fixed server role.
sp_start_job	This procedure instructs SQL Server Agent to execute a job immediately.
sp_statistics	This procedure returns a list of all indexes and statistics on a specified table or indexed view.
sp_stop_job	This procedure instructs SQLServerAgent to stop the execution of a job.
sp_stored_procedures	This procedure returns a list of stored procedures in the current environment.
sp_tableoption	This procedure sets option values for user-defined tables. sp_tableoption may be used to turn on the text in row feature on tables with text, ntext, or image columns.
sp_table_privileges	This procedure returns a list of table permissions (such as INSERT, DELETE, UPDATE, SELECT, REFERENCES) for the specified table(s).
sp_table_privileges_ex	This procedure returns privileged information about the specified table from the specified linked server.
sp_tables	This procedure returns a list of objects that can be queried in the current environment (any object that can appear in a FROM clause).
sp_tables_ex	This procedure returns table information about the tables from the specified linked server.
sp_trace_create	This procedure creates a trace definition. The new trace will be in a stopped state.
sp_trace_generateevent	This procedure creates a user-defined event.

PART IV

T-SQL Construct	Usage, Usage Tips, Suggestions, and References
sp_trace_setevent	This procedure adds or removes an event or event column to a trace. sp_trace_setevent may be executed only on existing traces that are stopped (*status* is 0). SQL Server 2005 will return an error if this stored procedure is executed on a trace that does not exist or whose *status* is not 0.
sp_trace_setfilter	This procedure applies a filter to a trace. sp_trace_setfilter may be executed only on existing traces that are stopped (*status* is 0). SQL Server 2005 will return an error if this stored procedure is executed on a trace that does not exist or whose *status* is not 0.
sp_trace_setstatus	This procedure modifies the current state of the specified trace.
sp_unbindefault	This procedure unbinds (removes) a default from a column or from a user-defined data type in the current database.
sp_unbindrule	This procedure unbinds a rule from a column or a user-defined data type in the current database.
sp_update_alert	This procedure updates the settings of an existing alert.
sp_update_category	This procedure changes the name of a category.
sp_updateextendedproperty	This procedure updates the value of an existing extended property.
sp_update_job	This procedure changes the attributes of a job.
sp_update_jobschedule	This procedure changes the schedule settings for the specified job.
sp_update_jobstep	This procedure changes the setting for a step in a job that is used to perform automated activities.
sp_update_log_shipping_monitor_info	This procedure updates the monitoring information about a log shipping pair.
sp_update_log_shipping_plan	This procedure updates information about an existing log shipping plan.
sp_update_log_shipping_plan_database	This procedure updates an existing database that is part of a log shipping plan.
sp_update_notification	This procedure updates the notification method of an alert notification.
sp_update_operator	This procedure updates information about an operator (notification recipient) for use with alerts and jobs.
sp_updatestats	This procedure runs UPDATE STATISTICS against all user-defined tables in the current database.
sp_update_targetservergroup	This procedure changes the name of the specified target server group.
sp_updatetask	This procedure is provided for backward compatibility only.

T-SQL Construct	Usage, Usage Tips, Suggestions, and References
sp_validname	This procedure checks for valid SQL Server identifier names. All nonbinary and nonzero data, including Unicode data that can be stored by using the nchar, nvarchar, or ntext data types, are accepted as valid characters for identifier names.
sp_validatelogins	This procedure reports information about orphaned Windows NT users and groups that no longer exist in the Windows NT environment but still have entries in the Microsoft SQL Server system tables.
sp_who	This procedure provides information about current SQL Server users and processes. The information returned can be filtered to return only those processes that are not idle.
sp_xml_preparedocument	Reads the Extensible Markup Language (XML) text provided as input, then parses the text using the MSXML parser (*Msxml2.dll*), and provides the parsed document in a state ready for consumption. This parsed document is a tree representation of the various nodes (elements, attributes, text, comments, and so on) in the XML document.
sp_xml_removedocument	This procedure removes the internal representation of the XML document specified by the document handle and invalidates the document handle.
SYSTEM_USER	This statement allows a system-supplied value for the current system username to be inserted into a table when no default value is specified.
table	The *table* is a special data type that can be used to store a result set f(or later) processing. Its primary use is for temporary storage of a set of rows, which are to be returned as the result set of a table-valued function.
TAN	TAN returns the tangent of the input expression.
text	Text provides information about the text data type, see ntext, text, and image.
TEXTPTR	This function returns the text-pointer value that corresponds to a text, ntext, or image column in varbinary format. The retrieved text pointer value can be used in READTEXT, WRITETEXT, and UPDATE statements.
TEXTVALID	This is a text, ntext, or image function that checks whether a given text pointer is valid.
timestamp	This is a data type that exposes automatically generated binary numbers that are guaranteed to be unique within a database. Timestamp is used typically as a mechanism for version-stamping table rows. The storage size is 8 bytes.
tinyint	See int, bigint, small int and tinyint.

PART IV

T-SQL Construct	Usage, Usage Tips, Suggestions, and References
TOP	Used to specifies that only the first set of rows specified in the variable will be returned from a query result. The set of rows can be either a number or a percent of the rows. The TOP expression can be used in SELECT, INSERT, UPDATE, and DELETE statements.
Trace Flags	The trace flags are used to temporarily set specific server characteristics or to switch off a particular behavior. For example, if trace flag 3205 is set when SQL Server starts, hardware compression for tape drivers is disabled. Trace flags are often used to diagnose performance issues or to debug stored procedures or complex computer systems.
Transactions	A transaction is a single unit of work. If a transaction is successful, all the data modifications made during the transaction are committed and become a permanent part of the database. If a transaction encounters errors and must be canceled or rolled back, all the data modifications are erased.
TRIGGER_NESTLEVEL	This function returns the number of triggers executed for the UPDATE, INSERT, or DELETE statement that fired the trigger. TRIGGER_NESTLEVEL is used in triggers to determine the current level of nesting.
TRUNCATE TABLE	This directive removes all rows from a table without logging the individual row deletes.
TRY	See CATCH.
TYPE_ID	Returns the ID of a type.
TYPE_NAME	Returns the unqualified name of the type.
TYPEPROPERTY	The function returns information about a data type.
UNICODE	This function returns the integer value, as defined by the Unicode standard, for the first character of the input expression.
UNION	This clauses combines the results of two or more queries into a single result set consisting of all the rows belonging to all queries in the union. For more information, see chapters Chapters 15-17.
uniqueidentifier	The globally unique identifier (GUID).
UPDATE, UPDATE()	Changes existing data in a table.
UPDATE STATISTICS	This statement caused an update of information about the distribution of key values for one or more statistics groups (collections) in the specified table or indexed view. To create statistics on columns, see also CREATE STATISTICS.
UPDATETEXT	This statement updates an existing text, ntext, or image field. Use UPDATETEXT to change only a portion of a text, ntext, or image column in place. Use WRITETEXT to update and replace an entire text, ntext, or image field.

T-SQL Construct	Usage, Usage Tips, Suggestions, and References
UPPER	This function returns a character expression with lowercase character data converted to uppercase.
USE	This directive changes the database context to the specified database.
USER	USER allows a system-supplied value for the current user's database username to be inserted into a table when no default value is specified.
USER_ID	This function returns a user's database identification number.
USER_NAME	This function returns a user database username from a given identification number.
VAR	VAR returns the statistical variance of all values in the given expression.
varbinary	For information about the varbinary data type, see binary and varbinary.
varchar	For information about the varchar data type, see char and varchar.
VARP	This function returns the statistical variance for the population for all values in the given expression.
VerifySignedByCert, VerifySignedByAsmKey	Tests whether digitally signed data has been changed since it was signed.
WAITFOR	Specifies a time, time interval, or event that triggers the execution of a statement block, stored procedure, or transaction.
WHERE	This statement specifies the condition for the rows returned by a query.
WHILE	This is a flow control statement that sets a condition for the repeated execution of an SQL statement or statement block. The statements are executed repeatedly as long as the specified condition is true. The execution of statements in the WHILE loop can be controlled from inside the loop with the BREAK and CONTINUE keywords.
WITH (Common Table Expression)	The common table expression (CTE) specifies a temporary named result set that can be used in a query within the execution scope of a SELECT, INSERT, A CTE can include references to itself; a recursive common table expression.
WITH XMLNAMESPACES	Declares a XML namespace.
WRITETEXT	This statement permits nonlogged, interactive updating of an existing text, ntext, or image column. This statement completely overwrites any existing data in the column it affects. WRITETEXT cannot be used on text, ntext, and image columns in views.

PART IV

T-SQL Construct	Usage, Usage Tips, Suggestions, and References
XACT_STATE	A scalar function that reports the transaction state of a session, indicating if the session has an active transaction, and if it is capable of being committed.
xml	The xml data type
xml_schema_namespace	This construct reconstructs all the schemas or a specific schema in the specified XML schema collection, and then returns an xml data type instance.
YEAR	This function returns an integer that represents the year part of a specified date.

Index